501

MUST-VISIT NATURAL WONDERS

501

MUST-VISIT NATURAL WONDERS

Bounty
Books

Publisher: Polly Manguel

Project Editor: Emma Beare

Publishing Assistant: Jo Archer

Designer: Ron Callow/Design 23

Picture Researchers: Jenny Faithfull, Suzy Cooper, James Stringer

Production Manager: Neil Randles

Production Assistant: Pauline LeNavenec

This edition first published in Great Britain in 2007 by
Bounty Books, a division of Octopus Publishing Group Ltd
2-4 Heron Quays, London E14 4JP

An Hachette Livre UK Company

A CIP catalogue record is available from the British Library

ISBN: 978-0-753715-91-8

Printed and bound in China

Please note that the seasons given in this book relate to the relevant hemisphere. Be sure to check that you visit at the correct time.

Contents

Introduction

There really is no limit to the number of natural wonders on our planet Earth. While this book gives you the opportunity to read and learn about 501 of the most spectacular examples, there are an infinite number of natural wonders all around us. Whether it is the trees that grow in our woods, fields and parks, the plants (and weeds!) that thrive in our gardens and hedgerows, the ants' nests, the spiders' webs or the amazingly varied landscape of our countryside – virtually anywhere you look there is something 'naturally wonderful'.

Yet if it's the spectacular natural wonders you're after – and who isn't? – this is the book for you. Here you will find described the cave where 20 million bats roost, the remote Indian Ocean island that is home to 100, 000 Giant Tortoises as well as the world's most active volcano, the longest cave system and the lake that is so deep that it would take all the world's rivers more than a year to refill it. Mountain ranges, deserts, gorges, rivers, glaciers, marshes, cliffs, waterfalls, coral reefs, tropical rainforests – there is a wealth of wonders here to exhaust even the most intrepid of armchair travellers.

While quite a few, such as Mount Everest, the Rock of Gibraltar and the Great Rift Valley, are world famous, even more are unfamiliar to most of us. Apart from locals or avid geographers, how many have even heard of Hungary's Hortobágy National Park or Japan's Shirakami-Sanchi Forest or the hauntingly beautiful Wrangel Island within the Arctic Circle? At the same time there are natural wonders here that we do know about, indeed probably some that we live quite close to and yet we still haven't seen them!

There is no doubt that many of the world's natural wonders are under threat – from desertification, pollution, the pressure from increasing human population or the effects of global warming. Only a rash or very optimistic individual would predict that all the 501 must-visit natural wonders in this book will still be there in the year 2100. In a hundred years will you still be able to enjoy the sight of polar bears in Churchill? Will there be enough fish in Lake Victoria to feed the millions living on and near its shores? Will loggerhead turtles still be nesting on the Greek isle of Zakynthos? Will Lake Chad exist at all? The challenges that many natural wonders face in the future are very considerable – and nearly all of them are caused by man's existence on this planet. One can only hope that we are able to alter our behaviour in time.

Whilst one often reads nowadays about the harmful effects of global tourism, the result of tourists' visits to many natural wonders is generally a positive one. Many of the world's wildlife parks only exist because of the income they derive from tourism. There are many instances where tourists' interest in a natural wonder makes the local population realize its importance and its value to them. Frequently too, these locals can gain an income – as guides or guards, or by providing accommodation, food or numerous services to tourists. Many of the world's natural wonders, especially those in poorer countries, will only be preserved if there is a benefit to the 'host' countries. This can of course be in the form of grants or gifts from the richer countries but the advantage of tourism, in this tough capitalist world, is that there is a benefit to both parties.

Despite the remoteness and inaccessibility of some of these natural wonders, if you have the determination it is possible to visit virtually all of them. To obtain the most benefit from the experience you should read as much as you can about your natural wonder, be aware of the potential problems, make a careful, realistic plan for the journey, ensure you take appropriate clothing and equipment etc.... and enough money. Don't expect comfortable beds, fine restaurants and an ATM on every corner.

Some places are scorchingly hot, some are freezing cold, some very high, at some you will be surrounded by mosquitoes, and at others you may be pursued by bears. Whether you choose to go to Denali in Alaska or the Tsingy of Bemaraha in Madagascar or the Scottish Highlands, make sure you go prepared.

So which of these 501 natural wonders are you going to visit first?

AMERICAS AND THE CARIBBEAN

Niagara Falls

WHAT IS IT?
The world's most famous waterfall.
HOW TO GET THERE:
By road or rail from Toronto.
WHEN TO GO:
Late spring to early autumn.
NEAREST TOWN:
Niagara Falls, Ontario 4 km (2.5 mi)
DON'T MISS:
A boat trip to the base of the falls.
YOU SHOULD KNOW:
Wet-weather gear is a must.

Although they are not the highest or broadest falls in the world, Niagara are the best known. Lying across the border between Canada and the United States, they were formed towards the end of the last ice age, when the glaciers of the Laurentide ice sheet retreated creating the Great Lakes. Water flowing from Lake Erie to Lake Ontario carved a gorge past the Niagara escarpment and over the millennia since, it has eroded the shale below the hard dolomitic rock at the top. The falls are currently retreating at a rate of about 1 m (3 ft) a year.

On the American side of the border, the Niagara falls carry about 10 per cent of the flow, while on the Canadian side the Horseshoe falls carry far more. The water flows at the astonishing rate of 56.3 kph (35 mph).

The local tribespeople call the falls 'onguiaahra', a 'thundering noise', which may seem like an understatement when you are faced with the sheer noise of almost 185,000 cubic m (6,600,00 cubic ft) of water roaring into the gorge every minute.

The *Maid of the Mist* takes visitors up the gorge to the base of the Horseshoe falls for a truly dramatic, and wet, experience and photogenic views as the sun creates rainbows in the mists.

Niagara Falls

Hoodoo Mountain

On the northern edge of the Iskut River in remote north western British Columbia rises the commanding, flat-topped volcano, Hoodoo Mountain. Few people are aware of the fact that both British Columbia and the Yukon are home to large regions of volcanic activity, and are situated within the volatile Pacific Ring of Fire.

Hoodoo Mountain rises to the west of the Stikine volcanic belt, and is considered to be an active volcano that could erupt again. Its flat top has an ice cap that is some 3-4 km (2-2.5 mi) in diameter. The fact that it is flat suggests that it was formed beneath glacial ice, its earliest eruptions occurring some 100,000 years ago. Most of the volcanic deposits found here are lava flows, although there are also some pyroclastic rocks that prove it has also had one or more periods of explosive activity. The most recent lava flows seem to have originated from under the ice cap.

Two valley glaciers flank the volcano: Twin Glacier to the northeast and Hoodoo Glacier to the northwest. Only the southern slope, which reaches down to the Iskut River floodplain, is free of ice. There is considerable mining activity for wollastonite and gold within 15 km (9 mi) of its southern flank, and this could be endangered should there be more lava flows in the near future. If the volcano should erupt through its ice cap or onto the surrounding glaciers, flooding of both the Iskut and Stikine rivers could cause many problems, including damage to the salmon fishery situated on the latter.

WHAT IS IT?
An active volcano.
HOW TO GET THERE:
By privately chartered helicopter from Stewart, or try to arrange a lift with a mining operation.
WHEN TO GO:
July to September.
NEAREST TOWN:
Stewart 100 km (63 mi)
YOU SHOULD KNOW:
Hoodoo Mountain is one of 10 Canadian volcanoes with recent seismic activity. No tourist infrastructure exists here.

Hoodoo Mountain

Caribou silhouetted against the evening sky as they travel near the headwaters of the Thelon River.

Caribou Migration

There are over 2.4 million caribou (*Rangifer tarandus*) in Canada and they are found from British Columbia in the west, to Newfoundland in the east, and from the U.S. border in the south, to Ellesmere Island, north of the Arctic Circle. Half of these are barren-ground caribou, most of which live in eight large migratory herds that move from the tundra in the far north to the sparsely treed coniferous forests to the south. These summer and winter ranges can be as far as five hundred miles apart and this migration is one of the greatest wildlife spectacles on earth.

In spring the caribou set off north to the open tundra where they can feed well on various broad-leafed plants and grasses. These are the calving grounds and the newborns grow rapidly thanks to their mothers' super-rich milk. In four weeks they are weaned, and growing strong enough to travel south. Whilst the calves are very young, caribou live in small groups headed by an older female, but soon the males join them, ready for the autumn rut. Finally they set out, in their thousands, to travel the same route back to the edges of the boreal forests that provide some shelter from the bitter cold. During winter, caribou mainly feed on lichen, and both sexes have antlers that are used as shovels to clear the snow from their food.

The migration itself is fraught with danger. They have many predators – wolves, black and grizzly bears, lynx, coyotes and golden eagles. Caribou travel great distances, sometimes as much as 80 km (50 mi) per day, and they must cross wild, icy rivers, through blizzards and snowdrifts whilst trying to protect themselves and their young.

HOW TO GET THERE:
Several tour companies take groups by light plane to tent base camps on the migration routes.
WHEN TO GO:
August to mid-September.
NEAREST TOWN:
Yellowknife, Northwest Territories would be one good starting point.
YOU SHOULD KNOW:
Global warming will have a detrimental impact on caribou herds.

Yoho National Park

Yoho National Park is the smallest of four national parks that together make up the Canadian Rocky Mountain Parks World Heritage Site. Located in south-eastern British Columbia on the western slopes of the Rocky Mountains, the park is a breath-taking region of snowy peaks – 28 of which are over 3,000 m (9,900 ft), glacial lakes, waterfalls, wild rivers and deep, dark forest.

In 1909 Charles Walcott of the Smithsonian Institution, discovered a unique deposit of Cambrian era fossils here. Approximately 120 soft-bodied marine species from 515 million years ago have been found, perfectly preserved from the time when warm, shallow seas washed over land that has long since been uplifted to a major mountain range. These simple life forms took on bizarre shapes, and the fossils found in the Burgess Shale have provided scientists with a mass of new information about the evolutionary process itself. There are only two other known sites of these fossils in existence.

These craggy mountains were a nightmare for the builders of the Canadian Pacific rail line, but resulted in two remarkable spiral tunnels, which climb up inside the mountain towards Kicking Horse Pass. The mighty river of the same name is responsible for having gouged out a natural bridge through solid rock, and water erosion has also formed hoodoos – boulders balanced on pillars of glacial debris. Glacial melt produces the amazing colour that gave Emerald Lake its name, the Takakkaw Falls is the third highest waterfall in the country and all these features are quite accessible either by car or by hiking some of the 400 km (250 mi) of very well maintained trails.

WHAT IS IT?
One of only three known sites of Cambrian fossils.
HOW TO GET THERE:
By road.
WHEN TO GO:
All year round, but July to October for guided hikes to the fossil beds.
NEAREST TOWN:
Field, in the centre of the Park; Lake Louise 27 km (17 mi)
DON'T MISS:
Lake O'Hara.
YOU SHOULD KNOW:
An entry fee is payable.

Emerald Lake and the Canadian Rockies

13

The Great Lakes

WHAT IS IT?
Five lakes making up the largest body of fresh water on Earth.
HOW TO GET THERE:
By road from Chicago, Detroit or Toronto.
WHEN TO GO:
Summer, but take mosquito repellent.
NEAREST TOWN:
There are numerous cities and towns situated on the shores of the lakes.

North America's five Great Lakes – Erie, Huron, Michigan, Ontario and Superior – lie on the Canadian/US border and were carved out of the landscape by great glaciers during the last Ice Age, then filled with meltwater as the glaciers retreated.

These interconnected lakes make up the largest body of fresh water on the Earth, with a volume of 22,812 cu km (5,473 cu mi) and a total area of 151,681 sq km (94,250 sq mi), with their main outlet to the Atlantic being via the St Lawrence River. This link with the ocean led to their exploitation, particularly on the US side, for heavy industry but the successive advents of rail, road and air freight mean that they are far quieter than in their heyday. Away from the major cities, such as Detroit, Chicago, Buffalo and Montreal there are quiet bays and peaceful countryside with stunning landscapes to explore.

Concerted efforts are being made to preserve the wilderness areas, particularly in the various national parks that surround the lake shores, where it is possible to lose yourself for days. Wildlife that can be seen in the quieter areas includes peregrines and bald eagles, but to see black bears, elk, grey wolves and, if extremely lucky, the Canada lynx, visitors should head for the really remote wilderness. The lakes themselves can also be explored by canoe or kayak.

These lakes are so large that in places it is impossible to see the lake shores and this size also affects the area's climate. In summer, heat is absorbed by the water, so cooling the surrounding area; in autumn, the heat is slowly lost, delaying the winter cold; and in winter, dry air from the west absorbs moisture from the lakes and when it reaches colder land to the east and cools rapidly is no longer able to hold on to the moisture and drops it as heavy snow falls.

Whether you are visiting to watch wildlife, explore the landscapes or to take in the scenery from the lakes, the scale and beauty of this wild area will leave you in awe.

View from the space shuttle Atlantis of an icy Lake Superior in late March. Lakes Michigan and Huron can also be seen.

Kluane Lake in winter

Mount Logan and Kluane National Park

Kluane National Park is situated in the south-western corner of the Yukon, and together with Tatshenshini-Alsek, Wrangell-St Elias and Glacier Bay Parks, was inscribed as a UNESCO World Heritage Site in 1979. It is famous as the site of Canada's highest peak, and North America's second highest after Mount McKinley, Mount Logan which stands at 5950m (19,521 ft). High mountains and mighty glaciers cover 80% of the park's territory, some 22,000 sq km (8,490 sq mi). Mount Logan is part of the St Elias Mountains and it is still growing taller due to tectonic activity. Reputedly, it has the largest circumference of any mountain on the planet.

A glaciated plateau covers the top of the Logan massif, and Mount Logan is the highest of the twelve other peaks that rise from it. Ridges lead up to the plateau from every direction, but in order to climb here a license must be applied for at least three months in advance. The upper part of the mountain can be hit by severe snowstorms at any time of year because of its proximity to the Gulf of Alaska. Mount Logan is famously cold – in 1991 a temperature of -77.5 °C was recorded.

Kluane National Park is much more than Mount Logan, however. It teems with flora and fauna. Some 150 species of birds live here, including rock ptarmigan, peregrine falcons and golden eagles. Grizzly bears, caribou, snowshoe hares and the world's largest population of Dall sheep thrive in a variety of habitats, ranging from ancient coastal and valley forests to alpine tundra and meadows swathed in colourful wildflowers.

WHAT IS IT?
Part of the first bi-national entry on the World Heritage list: Wrangell-St Elias and Glacier Bay are both in Alaska.

HOW TO GET THERE:
By air to Whitehorse, then by road to Haines Junction. Mount Logan is accessed by ski-equipped aircraft or helicopters.

WHEN TO GO:
Mid-June to August.

NEAREST TOWN:
Haines Junction is at the park boundary.

YOU SHOULD KNOW:
The Park is managed in co-operation with the Champagne and Aishihik First Nations, as it has always been part of their traditional territory.

The Prince of Miguasha, a fossil of the extinct lobe-finned fish Eusthenopteron foordi, *is one of the most studied fossils in the history of evolution. The strong spine and bony even-numbered fin structure is a precursor to the emergence of tetrapods, linking this fish to the conquest of land as vertebrates passed from the water onto the beach.*

Miguasha National Park

Miguasha National Park is situated on the Gaspé Peninsula in the eastern Canadian province of Quebec. The peninsula is separated from the rest of the province by the St. Lawrence River, which forms its northern boundary.

Today the area supports aspen, birch and fir forests, but 370 million years ago the now austere southern coast of the peninsula was a tropical estuary, and a vast array of fish swam in the warm, tidal waters. Some of these were armour plated, some had spines, and others (*Eusthenopteron foordi*) had lungs and lobe-like fins that enabled them to take a major evolutionary leap. These fish crawled from the water and evolved into tetrapods, the original four legged, air breathing land animals.

Miguasha National Park contains the world's greatest number of fossils from the Devonion Period, and was designated a UNESCO World Heritage Site in 1999 in recognition of this. The fossil beds were discovered in 1842 and thousands of fossils were sent to universities and museums around the world, including the British Museum in London. The coastal cliffs are made of ancient grey rock formed from layers of sandstone and silt. They hold the fossils of ancient species of flora and fauna, including one of the oldest flowering species on earth. However, Miguasha is most famous for its 21 species of fish fossil.

The Natural History Museum in the park has an excellent collection of fossils and there is a fascinating cliff-top trail with fabulous views over the Restigouche Estuary, and steps leading to the beach. This is a major piece of the world's heritage and so far over 5,000 fossils have been identified, categorized and catalogued on computer from this single site.

WHAT IS IT?
A chance to see and learn about a unique part of our evolution.
HOW TO GET THERE:
By road.
WHEN TO GO:
The park is open all year.
NEAREST TOWN:
Carleton 20 km (12.5 mi) or Campbellton, New Brunswick.
YOU SHOULD KNOW:
A small entry fee is payable.

Grizzly Bears, Cariboo Chilcotin

The Cariboo Chilcotin coast is situated in British Columbia's central region, some 240 km (150 mi) north of Vancouver. It stretches from the Pacific Ocean in the west, to the Cariboo Mountains in the east, and encompasses three of British Columbia's national parks. Two major rivers cut through the area – the clear Chilcotin and the muddy Fraser, and countless other river systems and lakes contribute to the wild beauty here.

The western side of the coastal range is the drier side. Here, the Fraser Plateau was formed millions of years ago by an ice sheet that smoothed and flattened it, and the two rivers to the east and west gouged out the steep sided valleys through which they flow. This is grizzly bear country. Grizzlies (*Ursus arctos*) are omnivores, eating plants and roots, newborn deer, elk, caribou and, in full summer, vast quantities of the salmon which swim upstream to spawn.

A fully-grown male bear can reach 2.8 m (9 ft) in length, 1.5 m (5 ft) at shoulder height and can weigh up to 800 kg (1,750 lb). They have shaggy, brown to black fur, usually grizzled on the shoulders and back. They live alone for the most part, but will congregate at a good food source, such as the salmon runs, when each adult will eat up to a ton of fish over a six-week period. It is essential for bears to fatten themselves up so that they can survive their winter hibernation. Bears mate in the late spring and give birth to between one and four tiny hairless cubs in mid-winter. Nourished by their mother's milk, by the time spring comes again and there are new leaves and buds to eat, mother and cubs emerge into the sunshine once more.

WHAT IS IT?
A beautiful, wilderness area where you can not only pursue all types of outdoor activity such as hiking, canoeing and white water rafting, but also go grizzly bear watching.
HOW TO GET THERE:
Fly or drive from Vancouver.
NEAREST TOWN:
Quesnel or Prince George.
DON'T MISS:
Watching grizzlies fish for salmon from mid-July to late August.

A grizzly bear

The Bay of Fundy

WHAT IS IT?
A bay in south-eastern Canada with spectacular tides and landscape and wonderful wildlife.
HOW TO GET THERE:
By air to Halifax or Saint John, then by road or rail.
WHEN TO GO:
Summer.
DON'T MISS:
A boat trip on one of the tidal bores.

The bay in south-eastern Canada is famous for its extraordinary tidal range. Spring tides, a couple of days after the new moon, can reach as much as 16 m (53 ft) in Minas Basin, as 100 billion tonnes of water surge towards the head of the bay and beyond into the rivers, causing phenomena such as the tidal bore at Truro in Nova Scotia and the Reversing Falls in the St John River in New Brunswick.

The waters are also very fast moving, as the tide travels 280 km (174 mi) in about six hours, and the currents swirl around the islands and underwater mountains, causing areas of turbulence, small waterspouts and small whirlpools, but if conditions are right, the feature called 'Old Sow' near the New Brunswick shore of Passamaquoddy Bay can form a single large whirlpool within an area of churning water as much as 76 m (250 ft) across. The feature gets its name from the moaning sounds that the rough waters make.

The erosion caused by this mass of water being sucked in and out of the bay for thousands of years has formed a spectacular landscape of cliffs, sea stacks such as the Flower Pot Rocks, and sea caves, in places revealing fossils that have lain here for hundreds of millions of years.

The area is vital for wildlife: on land the saltmarsh and mudflats provide breeding and feeding areas for waders, and there are also abundant puffins and terns during the breeding season. The nutrient-rich waters of the bay support billions of plankton and krill, which form the basis of a complex food chain, with crustaceans, seabirds and fish (including basking and mako sharks), seals, porpoises and Atlantic white-sided, bottlenose, saddle-back and striped dolphins. But it is the big cetaceans for which the Bay of Fundy is most famous. Among frequent visitors here are finback, minke and sei whales, while blue and humpback whales and orca are spotted less often. However, it is the terrifyingly rare and endangered northern right whales that come here in summer that make the Bay of Fundy such a special place for wildlife-watching.

Low tide at Advocate Harbour on the shores of the Bay of Fundy which has the world's highest tidal range.

The Laurentians

The Laurentian Mountains are an outstandingly beautiful range in Quebec. This area of mountain and lakeland scenery was first colonized in the late nineteenth century and has been a popular attraction for outdoor enthusiasts for more than sixty years. These ancient mountains, ground down by glaciers, wind and water over millions of years, average between 300 and 520 m (984 and 1,706 ft) in height, with the highest being Mont Tremblant at 968 m (3,175 ft). The village and resort of the same name are at the centre of the winter skiing area.

This land had long been a fruitful area for Amerindians to hunt wildlife and gather food and it is still rich in wildlife. Birdwatchers, in particular, are spoiled for choice by the range of birds here in the summer: it is best known as a haven for great northern divers, known locally as loons, whose eerie laughing and wailing are a constant background noise on the lakes in summer.

The sugar maples that add red to the yellows, browns and golds of autumn in late September are tapped in spring, and in summer the area is popular for hiking, horse-riding, cycling, fishing, rafting and kayaking. The landscape is spectacular, and worth a visit at any time of year, whether it is blanketed in deep snow, just flushed with the greens of spring leaves or filled with birdsong in summer.

WHAT IS IT?
A beautiful mountain range in Quebec.
HOW TO GET THERE:
By road from Montreal or Quebec city.
WHEN TO GO:
December to April for skiing, late spring and summer for birdwatching, late September for the autumn colours.
NEAREST TOWN:
L'Annonciation 15 km (9 mi)
DON'T MISS:
The Tremblant 'Symphony of Colours' festival in September.
YOU SHOULD KNOW:
Flies and mosquitoes can be a persistent nuisance in May and June.

The Laurentian Mountains in autumn

Orca whales

Orcas in Western Canada

Orcas, (*Orcinus orca*) commonly known as killer whales, are one of the world's best-known marine mammals. They are, in fact, members of the dolphin family, and are the world's fastest swimming sea mammals. Growing up to 9 m (29 ft 6 in) in length and weighing up to 10 tons, orcas are immediately recognizable by their black and white markings and their high, up to 1.8 m (6 ft) triangular, dorsal fin.

One of the best places in the world to see orcas is off the coast of British Columbia, where a population known as the Southern Residents live. Their range stretches from Puget Sound, across the United States border, north to about halfway up Vancouver Island. These resident orcas feed solely on fish, largely salmon, unlike transient and offshore orcas that also eat marine mammals such as seal. A second population, the Northern Residents, inhabit the waters of northern British Columbia, but are not as well known.

The Southern Residents support a whale watching industry that is worth more than the salmon fishery business throughout the whole of British Columbia. However, these orcas are under threat. Between 1993 and 2003 their population fell by 20% and there are now fewer than 80 individuals. The orcas are an indicator species that show the state of the marine environment, and unhappily, scientific studies show that these are some of the world's most contaminated marine mammals. Not only that, but as the salmon stocks decline so does their food supply, and they also face constantly increasing boat traffic and noise pollution. Both Canada and the United States are currently attempting to reach a legal agreement regarding a joint approach to dealing with this problem and agreeing a recovery plan.

HOW TO GET THERE:
By boat, kayak or canoe, or from the shore.
WHEN TO GO:
May to November.
NEAREST TOWNS:
Vancouver, Victoria, and Tofino.
YOU SHOULD KNOW:
Orcas live in matriarchal units – a mother with one or two young. These units socialize in larger groups known as pods.

Gros Morne National Park

The island of Newfoundland is the easternmost part of Canada and, situated on its rugged west coast, is Gros Morne National Park – part of the Long Range Mountains that stretch the whole length of that side of the island. The mountains here are the weathered remains of a range formed some thousand million years ago, making them 20 times older than the Rocky Mountains of western Canada. The range resulted from a continental collision and during the last 3 million years, 30 periods of glaciation have occurred. As the ice came and went, the peaks wore down to the rounded summits that we see today.

Gros Morne National Park is an area of extraordinary natural beauty. It was declared a UNESCO World Heritage Site in 1987 not only for its visual impact but also because its topography reveals the major stages of the evolutionary history of the planet. Possibly its most spectacular feature is Western Brook Pond, a 30 km (19 mi) long fjord-like structure formed by the same glacial action that produced Norway's fjords. Western Brook Pond, however, was later cut off from the ocean, and is filled with pure, fresh, dark-blue water that cascades from the plateau above it. Pissing Mare Falls, the highest falls in eastern North America, flow into it.

Another unique feature, known as the Tablelands, is a 600 m (1,950 ft) high plateau made of rock from the earth's mantle that was forced to the surface hundreds of millions of years ago. It is a mysterious and barren area, hardly able to support plant life. Elsewhere the park has a wide variety of habitat from coastal lowlands to wooded mountains, supporting 14 species of land mammal, including black bear, lynx, caribou and arctic hare.

HOW TO GET THERE:
By a combination of plane, ferry, car or bus.
WHEN TO GO:
Any time, weather permitting, but from May to October an entry fee is payable.
NEAREST TOWN:
Deer Lake 32 km (20 mi) from the park entrance or Rocky Harbour, in the Park itself.
DON'T MISS:
The rhododendrons in spring and the autumn colours.
YOU SHOULD KNOW:
Fascinating boat trips are available – enjoy the stunning coastline and, if you are very lucky, spot a whale.

Western Brook Pond and Fjord

The Rocky Mountains

The Rocky Mountains form part of an almost continuous chain of mountains that stretch from Alaska down practically the entire length of the west coast of the Americas. The Canadian Rockies encompass a vast area that includes five national parks. Four of these, Banff, Jaspar, Yoho and Kootenay not only interlock with each other but also with three British Columbia provincial parks. Altogether these parks were declared a UNESCO World Heritage Site in 1984.

The Canadian Rockies are both older than and geologically different from the American Rockies. They are largely formed of sedimentary rock that has been severely glaciated, resulting in sharp, craggy-peaked mountains separated by broad valleys created by glaciers. The highest is the impressive Mount Robson, which stands at 3,954 m (12,972 ft).

The backbone of the Canadian Rockies is the Continental Divide, which runs the length of the range and separates Alberta from British Columbia. The scenery is utterly spectacular on both sides of the mountains, although the parks of Banff and Jaspar are the best known. Roads run parallel on both sides of the range, and there are four routes that cross over it. The most spectacular of these runs through Glacier National Park, with its awe-inspiring glacial peaks and vivid, turquoise alpine lakes.

The Rockies provide the opportunity to explore one of the most beautiful wilderness areas imaginable. Here you can hike, climb and horse ride to your heart's content. The more adventurous can heli-hike through fabulous landscapes swathed in wild flowers during spring or heli-ski in winter. Helicopters fly visitors up to lodge resorts, and then ferry them to high mountain peaks for several different ski runs per day, each on virgin snow.

Winter at Boom Lake in the Canadian Rockies

Georgian Bay Islands National Park

Some of the many small islands of Georgian Bay

Georgian Bay Islands National Park stretches along the eastern shoreline of the bay, and is made up of 59 small islands and shoals. Within a 30,000 island archipelago, it is part of the world's largest group of freshwater islands and lies on the edge of the Canadian Shield. Known for the extraordinary variety of flora and fauna existing within an unusually small area, this beautiful region of fabulous vistas and crystal clear waters is perfect for kayaking and canoeing, camping and hiking.

Beausoleil Island, the largest in the park, is formed from hard Shield rock that supports plant species such as juniper, red oak and white pine, twisted and buffeted by the wind. Scraped clean by the retreat of ancient glaciers, the barren rocks are lichen covered and speckled with small bogs and ponds, enabling 33 species of amphibian and reptile to live here – more than in any other part of the country. This ruggedly beautiful landscape has always attracted artists, particularly Canada's well-known Group of Seven.

Southern Beausoleil is covered in mixed coniferous and hardwood forest. The soil, developed on limestone, is completely different from that of the north. In summer, colourful wildflowers abound. Come autumn, the forests are aflame with reds and yellows as the leaves put on their magnificent display. Many rare species of fauna live here, for example, the tiny, cobalt blue ring-necked snake, and the sole Canadian lizard, the five-line skink. This is one of the only places where you might see the threatened eastern Missasauga rattlesnake.

HOW TO GET THERE:
The park can only be reached by boat.
WHEN TO GO:
All year round.
NEAREST TOWNS:
Shuttles and water taxis run from Honey Harbour or Port Severn on the mainland.
DON'T MISS:
Hiking the Cambrian trail on northern Beausoleil Island.

Before midnight near the Arctic Circle at Echo Bay on Great Bear Lake in the North West Territories

Great Bear Lake

Canada's Northwest Territories cover almost one third of the country – an area of approximately 3 million sq km (1.88 million sq mi), with half of it lying north of the Arctic Circle. Great Bear Lake, the largest lake in the country, straddles the Arctic Circle, on the edge of the Canadian Shield. Visited by traders from the North West Company circa 1800, a trading post was subsequently set up, and in 1825 a British explorer began building a town on the southwest shore, now know as Deline, which is still inhabited. In the 1930s radium was discovered at the eastern side of the lake, and numerous mines, all long exhausted, were sited there.

Great Bear Lake drains to the west, where the Great Bear River flows down into Canada's longest river, the Mackenzie, which itself finally empties into the Beaufort Sea. The lake is about 320 km (200 mi) long and its width varies from 40-177 km (25-110 mi). Its shoreline is 2,719 km (1,690 mi) around. Formed from pre-glacial valleys reshaped by ice during the Pleistocene age, and changed again when the ice melted, the lake has five 'arms' and contains numerous little islands.

Great Bear Lake, which is frozen for eight months of the year, remains extraordinarily clear to a depth of about 31 m (100 ft). It is, of course, a freshwater lake, and its pristine waters teem with fish. Probably the world's biggest Lake Trout and Grayling can be fished here, though hunting regulations, which also apply to anglers, ensure the conservation of the rich natural resources. The shoreline shelters a variety of wildlife, including elk and pine martens, as well as the grizzly bears from which it took its name.

WHAT IS IT?
The largest lake in Canada and the eighth largest in the world.
HOW TO GET THERE:
By charter plane from Norman Wells. A landing strip serves all the camps on the lake. It is possible to canoe down the Great Bear River from Tulita.
WHEN TO GO:
June, July and August.
NEAREST TOWN:
Tulita 128 km (80 mi)
YOU SHOULD KNOW:
The temperature on the lake can reach -57°C (-70°F) in winter.

Dinosaur Provincial Park

Approximately 75 million years ago this region was a sub-tropical wilderness consisting of dense forest and lush vegetation covering a coastal plain. Rivers ran east into a shallow, inland sea, producing a habitat perfect for numerous creatures, including sharks, crocodiles, marsupials and, of course, dinosaurs. This habitat was also perfect for the preservation of their fossilized skeletons.

Situated in southern Alberta, Dinosaur Provincial Park is located in the valley of the Red Deer River, amidst the province's spectacular badlands. Not only is the scenery extraordinary, but also it contains some of the most important dinosaur fossil beds ever to have been found. Five trails meander through the park, enabling visitors to see the three separate habitats it encompasses. Gently rolling prairie grassland suddenly becomes eerie sandstone badlands, haunted by extraordinarily beautiful pinnacles and buttes carved by wind and water.

Listed as a Natural World Heritage Site in 1979, the next 12 years produced a collection of over 23,000 fossils, including 300 dinosaur skeletons from almost 40 distinct species.

In 1987, a field station of the Royal Tyrell Museum of Palaeontology was opened within the park to support the on-going, long-term research and monitoring programmes that are in progress here. A visitor centre provides a wealth of fascinating information not only regarding the fossils but also about the park and its complex eco-system. This supports a wide variety of birds and mammals. Over 150 species of bird have been recorded here, including golden eagles, prairie falcons and ferruginous hawks. Pronghorn antelope and white-tailed deer populate the prairie grassland and waterfowl can be seen in the cottonwood groves. At dusk the park echoes with the haunting sounds of coyotes and nighthawks.

WHAT IS IT?
A natural World Heritage Site.
HOW TO GET THERE:
Two hours drive east from Calgary.
WHEN TO GO:
Open all year except for weekends and holidays from October to May.
NEAREST TOWN:
Brooks 48 km (30 mi)
DON'T MISS:
The Badlands Bus Tour and the guided Centrosaurus Bone Bed Hike.
YOU SHOULD KNOW:
The park covers an area of 7,493 hectares (18,500 acres), including the largest badlands in Canada.

Fossilized dinosaur bones lie at Dinosaur Provincial Park, near Brooks, Alberta. Hundreds of dinosaur fossils and skeletons have been discovered amongst the rocks here.

Nahanni National Park

This pristine wilderness park was one of the very first places in the world to be listed as a UNESCO World Heritage Site in 1978. This reflects its remarkably beautiful and unusual nature. Nahanni's key feature is the wild and wonderful South Nahanni River that, uniquely amongst mountainous rivers, was formed when the region was still a wide, flat plain. As the mountains rose upwards the river gouged four steep canyons to maintain its original winding course.

The South Nahanni River originates from the Selwyn Mountains and flows 540 km (340 mi) through the Mackenzie Mountains and into the Liard River. About 300 km (190 mi) of the river's length runs through the national park, dropping in elevation from 825 m to 350 m (2,681 ft to 1,137 ft) above sea level. The spectacular, vertical plunge of Virginia Falls is responsible for 90 m (292 ft) of this drop – double that of the far more famous Niagara Falls.

There are a number of unique features along the river and different types of habitat producing a rich diversity of flora. For example, there is an area of rare orchids near the falls. Nahanni is home to wolves, black and grizzly bears, caribou, Dall's sheep and mountain goats. These animals either migrate to a kinder environment during winter, or they hibernate.

The four dramatic canyons are up to 1,200 m (3,900 ft) deep, but as you travel downstream you will come across Rabbitkettle Hotsprings, where there are two vast terraced mounds of tufa, some 27 m (88 ft) high and 70 m (228 ft) in diameter, the largest in Canada. There are cave systems and lakes and wild, white water that attract up to 1,000 adventurous visitors each year to kayak or canoe different sections of the river according to their skill.

The Nahanni River in the Northwest Territories

Wood Buffalo National Park

Red samphire surrounds salt crystallized on mud flats in the salt plains in Wood Buffalo National Park.

Wood Buffalo National Park was established in 1922. It is located on the boundary between Alberta and the Northwest Territories, and was designated a UNESCO World Heritage Site in 1983. It was created specifically to protect North America's largest free-roaming bison herd, some 2,500 animals, but it also contains the only natural nesting grounds of the critically endangered whooping crane.

Wood Buffalo is Canada's largest national park, a boreal forest zone covering 44,807 sq km (17,300 sq mi). Within its boundaries there are fire-scarred forested uplands, a glacially eroded plateau, a major freshwater delta formed by three major rivers, salt plains and some of the best examples of karst topography in North America. It also contains the largest undisturbed grass and sedge meadows in North America, making ideal bison country.

The park has the longest tradition of native subsistence use in the country. It has been inhabited since the glaciers retreated, most recently by nomadic Micasew-Cree First Nation groups, some of whom still fish, hunt and trap here. The climate is one of long, cold winters and short, warm summers, and it is only frost-free in June, July and August.

There are 47 species of mammal here, including caribou, arctic fox, black bear, moose, beaver and muskrat, and 227 bird species have been recorded, including peregrine falcon, bald eagles, great grey and snowy owls. The bison are self-regulating and it is one of the few places left in the world where a genuine predator-versus-prey relationship exists between wolves and bison. The whooping cranes number some 140 individuals, of which there are 40 breeding pairs. The careful management and protection of these birds within the park, and the protection of their winter grounds in Texas, may have saved them from extinction.

WHAT IS IT?
Home to the largest herd of bison in North America, and the only nesting grounds of the whooping crane.
HOW TO GET THERE:
By plane from Edmonton to Fort Smith, then by plane or by road.
NEAREST TOWN:
Hay River, adjacent to the park or Fort Smith in the NWT, 280 km (175mi)
YOU SHOULD KNOW:
There are 36 campsites in the park, but only one is accessible by road. Park offices are located in Fort Smith and Fort Chipewyan.

Polar Bears and Churchill

WHAT IS IT?
The polar bear capital of the world.
HOW TO GET THERE:
By plane or train from Winnipeg.
WHEN TO GO:
October and November.
DON'T MISS:
A trip in a tundra buggy to see the bears in their natural habitat.
YOU SHOULD KNOW:
If you visit during summer you can see the only remaining healthy population of Beluga whales, which migrate here at this time.

Churchill is found on the western shore of Hudson Bay, in northern Manitoba. Each autumn thousands of visitors flock here, anxious to view the polar bears (*Ursus maritimus*) for which the town is internationally known. During the season you can expect to see up to 20 bears a day. However come the end of November both the polar bears and the visitors depart, leaving the 900 full time residents to their bitter winter.

This is a polar bear migration route. As they return from their summer on land, they congregate near Churchill waiting for the ice to form at sea so they can begin their annual seal hunt. In Churchill itself, bears are drawn to the municipal rubbish dumps. They are aggressive, dangerous animals, but troublesome bears are captured and transported to a safer – for everyone – location.

Adult male polar bears are the world's largest terrestrial carnivore. Their apparently off-white fur is made of long, light, hollow, pigment-free hairs, specially adapted to maximize heat retention. Their huge feet, furred underneath to protect their pads from frostbite, spread their weight thus enabling them to walk on ice that would not hold a human.

Tragically, polar bears are seriously threatened by global warming. There are some 25,000 animals in the world, 60% of which live in Canada. The number of western Hudson Bay bears has dropped by 22% since the 1980s because the Arctic ice pack is rapidly shrinking. The bears need a frozen platform from which to hunt their most important food – seal. As the Arctic warms, the bears find it harder to reach solid ice, and while some starve, others drown during their attempt to swim there.

The Grand Canyon

The Grand Canyon, cut into layer after layer of the colourful sedimentary rocks of the Colorado Plateau by the Colorado River and its tributaries, is one of the world's most spectacular landmarks. It lies within northern Arizona's Grand Canyon National Park, which was designated in 1919. The first westerner to see it was Garcia Lopez de Cardenas in 1540.

The youngest rocks, at the top, were laid down by an inland sea some 260 million years ago and a journey down into the canyon peels away millions of years of geological history as the different layers of rock – red-stained limestones, sandstones, shales and mudstones, down to twisted granites and schists and the river bed, which was laid down more than 1.7 billion years ago – are revealed.

It is not just the sense of our planet's past that is awe-inspiring; it is the sheer size of the canyon, which some 1.5 km (1 mi) deep and has views that stretch across more than 16 km (10 mi), a scale different to imagine until you are confronted with the reality of it. The rocks are coloured and stained gold, orange and crimson, and the river's waters are red with the sediment it carries down to the sea.

The southern rim is more popular because it is easier to reach, but a new Skywalk has been opened on the northern rim. Hiking trails and mule rides allow access to the canyon walls, while plane and helicopter trips operate from Las Vegas and Phoenix and the adventurous can travel downriver by raft or boat.

WHAT IS IT?
A 322-km (200-mi) chasm in the Earth's surface.
HOW TO GET THERE:
Highway 64 or rail from Williams.
WHEN TO GO:
The south rim is open all year, but is busy in summer. The north rim is shut from mid-October to mid-May. The lower reaches of the canyon are extremely hot in summer.
NEAREST TOWN:
Williams 95 km (60 mi)
DON'T MISS:
A mule ride into the canyon.
YOU SHOULD KNOW:
The Skywalk viewing platform is over a side canyon off the north side of the river, and is accessible only by a shuttle bus trip from Grand Canyon West or as part of a tour package.

The Grand Canyon from Toroweap Point

Horseshoe crabs coming ashore at Delaware Bay.

Horseshoe Crabs, Delaware Bay

At the mouth of the Delaware River, with New Jersey to the north east and Delaware to the west and south, lies Delaware Bay. This is the largest spawning area in the world of the Horseshoe crab (*Limulus polyphemus*), an ancient creature more closely related to spiders and scorpions than to crabs. Sometimes referred to as 'living fossils' they evolved some 500 million years ago, and have changed very little during the last 350 million years.

Horseshoe crabs look forbidding, growing up to 50 cm (20 in) in length, and covered with hard, curved shells. The fearsome tail, far from being a weapon, is used partly as a rudder and partly to right itself if it is accidentally flipped over. They have a dozen legs, mainly clawed, and gills allowing them to breathe both underwater and, for brief periods, on land.

Horseshoe crabs are extremely valuable in medical research. Most of what is known about human eye function, and malfunction, is as a result of studying their large, compound eyes. They also possess a brilliant immune system that traps bacteria in a clot of gel-like substance. Blood samples are taken for testing intravenous drugs and for finding remedies for diseases that have become immune to antibiotics. All intravenous drugs used in hospitals have had a Horseshoe crab test, and the crabs themselves are left unharmed.

The crabs' eggs are essential to migratory shorebirds, in particular the Red Knot, which fly north from Brazil to the Arctic each spring. As they arrive at Delaware Bay, they are at their lowest weight, and recent studies have shown their numbers have halved. This is due to a decline in the crabs, which fishermen use as bait, but major efforts are now being made to protect these miraculous creatures.

HOW TO GET THERE:
By road.
WHEN TO GO:
April to October.
NEAREST TOWN:
Dover, Delaware's capital,
13 km (8 mi)
DON'T MISS:
New Castle; Lewes; Delaware's beaches.

Bluegrass Country, Kentucky

Kentucky's Bluegrass Country is located in the north central part of the state. It is a highly attractive area of rolling hills, green, green grass, elegant, antebellum mansions, picturesque villages, miles of stone and wooden fencing and horses galore. It is also peppered with historic Bourbon distilleries, including that of the famous Jim Beam. The limestone soil is extremely fertile here, rich with calcium and other minerals. The grass (*pratensis Poa*) is not actually blue, but in spring it produces purple-blue buds which, seen from a distance, lends a blue hue to the pastoral scenery. The Kentucky River with its associated karst topography runs through the region, which contains the best agricultural land in the state.

The Bluegrass region was first settled in the 1770s by wealthy families whose slaves helped create large estates, reminiscent of those in England – even the countryside looked somewhat similar. Today, farms in the area are losing land to developers, and it has been placed on the worldwide list of 100 most endangered sites of the World Monuments Fund.

Lexington is the self-styled 'horse capital of the world', and indeed there are more thoroughbred breeding farms in the area than in any other part of the world. The calcium-rich bluegrass is good for the horses' bones, and horses provide Kentucky with a multi-million dollar industry. The Kentucky Derby, held annually at Louisville, is the USA's premier horserace.

The Bourbon Trail was invented by the local distillers, and provides fascinating information about both the history and production of the whiskey. Here you will find the oldest distillery in the country, Maker's Mark, as well as various small, specialised distilleries, producing brands unheard of in other parts of the USA.

WHAT IS IT?
A peaceful, verdant region with more than 500 horse farms.
HOW TO GET THERE:
Fly to Lexington and hire a car, or drive.
WHEN TO GO:
Any time of year, but don't forget Derby Day is held on the first Saturday in May.
NEAREST TOWN:
Towns and villages abound. The state capital is Frankfort.
DON'T MISS:
The Shaker village of Pleasant Hill, the Covered Bridges, Cedar Creek Lake.
YOU SHOULD KNOW:
Bluegrass music was named after Bill Monroe's band, The Blue Grass Boys, and not after this specific region. Bill Monroe, the 'father' of bluegrass came from western Kentucky.

An aerial view of farmland in Kentucky's Bluegrass region

Bracken Cave Bat Roost, San Antonio, Texas

WHAT IS IT?
Home to the largest known bat colony in the world.
HOW TO GET THERE:
By road from San Antonio.
WHEN TO GO:
May to September.
NEAREST TOWN:
San Antonio 32 km (20 mi)
DON'T MISS:
The emergence of the colony at dusk.
YOU SHOULD KNOW:
Bracken Cave is only open to BCI members, and only on certain nights at present. However, there will be a viewing platform and other viewing areas in due course.

Ever since the end of the last ice age, some 10,000 years ago, Bracken Cave has been a home to bats. Today, during the summer months, an enormous colony of Mexican Free-Tailed bats (*Tadarida brasiliensis*) breed and rear their young here. These bats are widely distributed across the southern states of the USA, through Central America and most of western South America as far south as central Chile. Most of them, however, live in Mexico and Texas.

Since 1992, Bat Conservation International (BCI) has been doing its best to buy up land around Bracken Cave in order to form a protection zone for the colony. Thanks to local landowners and various foundations, BCI has managed to acquire 280 hectares (692 acres) around the cave, upon which they intend to build an international centre for the study of bats.

Bracken Cave contains the largest known concentration of mammals in the world. Each spring over 20 million Mexican Free-Tailed bats arrive from Mexico to breed, giving birth to one baby each, and leaving again in the late autumn. They eat airborne insects – by the ton! This colony eats about 15,000 tons of insects each summer. These high-speed bats fly as high as 3,000 m (10,000 ft) in order to catch the corn earworm moths, also migratory, which fly that high to catch the winds that will carry them north. The caterpillars of this moth wreak havoc on corn and cotton crops.

The sight of 20 million bats emerging from this cave at dusk is truly one of nature's most awesome wonders. Like a genie from a bottle they begin to appear, a thin wisp of smoke that rapidly turns into a mighty plume, millions of wings twisting upwards like a tornado in reverse.

Mexican Freetail Bats near Bracken Cave

Glacier Bay National Park and Preserve

Grand Pacific Glacier and Tarr Inlet

Situated on the Gulf of Alaska in the south eastern part of the country, Glacier Bay National Park and Preserve are an icy wonderland of snowy mountains and dazzling glaciers. It was designated a National Monument in 1925, and added to the UNESCO World Heritage Site as part of a vast trans-border park system that includes Canada's Tatshenshini-Alsek and Kluane National Parks.

The park covers 13,053 sq km (8,160 sq mi) and includes much of Mount Fairweather and the American section of the Alsek River as well as Glacier Bay itself. In 1794, Captain George Vancouver discovered Icy Strait, situated at the southern end of the bay. All he could find was an enormous glacier, but by 1879 John Muir, the naturalist, found that the glacier had retreated roughly 80 km (50 mi) leaving Glacier Bay in its wake.

Today the National Park is formed from the largest group of high peaks on the continent, the largest ice fields outside the polar caps and 16 huge, tidewater glaciers. These last are still retreating by almost 460 m (1,500 ft) every year, and vast icebergs sheer off and plunge, crashing into the water. Probably the best-known glacier is the magnificent Muir Glacier. Rising 81 m (265 ft) above the water, it is almost 3 km (2 mi) wide.

Vegetation in the Park ranges from alpine tundra through coastal forest to temperate rainforest, and black and grizzly bears, mountain goats, moose, deer and wolves and Dall sheep can be seen here. Humpback whales and orcas can be seen, as can sea lions and sea otters, and there is a wide variety of birds. The Alsek River is swift and glacial, it rushes and tumbles to the sea and attracts experienced kayakers and rafters.

WHAT IS IT?
A chance to see the most impressive glaciers outside the polar caps.
HOW TO GET THERE:
By plane from Juneau, Anchorage or Seattle, or by boat. No roads lead there.
WHEN TO GO:
June to October
NEAREST TOWN:
Juneau 80 km (50 mi)
YOU SHOULD KNOW:
You can stay in the small community of Gustavus that is adjacent to the park.

Petrified Forest, Arizona

WHAT IS IT?
Probably the world's largest and most colourful collection of petrified wood.
HOW TO GET THERE:
By car.
WHEN TO GO:
All year round, except Christmas Day.
NEAREST TOWN:
Holbrook 19 km (12 mi)
DON'T MISS:
The Painted Desert.
YOU SHOULD KNOW:
An entry fee is payable.

In 1906, President Theodore Roosevelt named the Petrified Forest a National Monument, and archaeology shows that there has been a human presence here for over 2,000 years. This region was a trade route through to the Pacific coast, and has been used by everyone, from ancient Indians to the visitors of today. In the 1850s a surveyor for the transcontinental railroad brought back tales of 'trees turned to stone', and soon afterwards ranchers and farmers arrived, who mined the petrified wood for semi-precious stones.

The Petrified Forest contains the remains of 225 million-year-old forests that were home to dinosaurs, giant fish-eating amphibians, and large reptiles, some of whose fossilized remains have been discovered here too. This was once a floodplain, and the forests were washed into it and covered with volcanic ash and silt, slowing their decay. Silica bearing water gradually seeped through and encased the trees, eventually crystallizing them into quartz. The region later flooded and sank, and during its next uplift, the trees cracked into giant logs. Even today erosion continues to break the logs and expose more beneath the surface of the ground. In some places 92m (300 ft) of fossil bearing material remains to be exposed.

Scientists continue to study all aspects of this extraordinary area. The Rainbow Forest Museum has a fantastic collection of fossils, including dinosaurs, from the Triassic era, and throughout the area there are wonderful examples of rock art, carved by early inhabitants, depicting birds, reptiles, animals and the human form.

Petrified logs

34

Denali (Mt McKinley)

Denali, more generally known as Mt. McKinley, is a majestic, towering, snow and ice-clad mountain, flanked by five large glaciers. It is situated in the centre of the Alaska Mountain Range and utterly dominates Denali National Park of which it is the centrepiece. In the local Athabascan language, Denali means 'the High One' and today, despite the continuing controversy regarding the name, many people call the National Park 'Denali' and the mountain 'Mt. McKinley'.

The Alaska Range was formed some 65 million years ago when two tectonic plates moved against each other, thrusting up rock from the earth's core through North America's largest crustal break, the Denali Fault. According to geologists, Mt. McKinley is still rising to this day.

This is the highest peak in North America, rising to 6,194 m (20,320 ft), and it has a larger bulk and rise than that of Mount Everest. More than 50% of the mountain is covered with snow and ice, and it is a magnet for mountaineers. Technically it is not too difficult to climb, but conditions on the mountain are the worst in the world. Apart from the extreme cold (which can reach -71°C (-95°F) in winter) and ferocious winds exacerbated by its proximity to the jet stream, climbers face a severe risk of altitude sickness due to the high latitude. This is a dangerous mountain to climb, some 50% of attempts fail to reach the summit, and about 100 climbers have lost their lives here.

WHAT IS IT?
The highest peak in North America.
HOW TO GET THERE:
By road to the National Park or plane to the Kahiltna Glacier.
WHEN TO GO:
April, May and June are the best climbing months.
NEAREST TOWN:
Talkeetna 120 km (75 mi); Anchorage 209 km (130 mi)
YOU SHOULD KNOW:
The first successful climb was made in 1913.

Lenticular clouds shrouding the peaks of Mount McKinley

Aerial view of islands in the Everglades

The Florida Everglades

The Everglades National Park, in southern Florida, is the largest protected wilderness in the south-eastern United States and was designated by President Truman in 1947 in order to protect it from land reclamation for agriculture. This stunning green marshy landscape, with wide blue skies, is also a UNESCO World Heritage Site because of the importance of the habitat and animals it shelters. It is formed by the slow movement of fresh water southwards from the Orlando Kissimmee River system via the massive Lake Okeechobee. The park protects one-fifth of the original extent of the Everglades, of which about a half remains.

The wildlife in this lush, green landscape is justifiably famous: seemingly innumerable alligators and much rarer American crocodiles sun themselves on river banks or skulk beneath the water waiting for prey; the estuaries are full of such birds as egrets, spoonbills, wood storks and herons; while the endangered manatee may be seen around the coast and in estuaries.

Although they contain both cypress and mangrove swamps, the Everglades are technically a very slow-moving river, known locally as the river of grass: this subtropical land also has broad swathes of sawgrass and internationally important areas of rock pineland.

The main road through the park runs from Florida City on the east coast to Flamingo on the Gulf of Mexico and is known as 'Alligator Alley' because of the hundreds of these prehistoric animals that can be seen from the road.

Short-distance walking trails, long-distance hiking routes, canoes and air boat tours allow visitors to explore this beautiful and threatened landscape.

WHAT IS IT?
The largest protected wilderness area in the south-eastern US.
HOW TO GET THERE:
On State Road 9336 (Alligator Alley) from Florida City.
WHEN TO GO:
December to April is mild, relatively dry and mosquito-free.
NEAREST TOWN:
Florida City 15 km (9 mi)
DON'T MISS:
An exhilarating airboat ride.
YOU SHOULD KNOW:
The park headquarters is at the Ernest F. Coe Visitor Center and there are visitor centres at Everglades City, Flamingo and Shark Valley.

The Smoky Mountains

One of the most popular recreation areas of the eastern United States, the Smoky Mountains lie on the border between Tennessee and North Carolina. They are part of the Appalachians, the range that runs north-east/south-west from Maine to Georgia. Like the Blue Ridge Mountains in Virginia and the Blue Mountains of New South Wales in Australia, they get their name from the bluish haze, given off by trees, that hovers over them in summer.

In summer, this beautiful area is a haven for hikers and walkers, and has some of the most stunning scenery and challenging ground to be found on the entire length of the 3,500-km (2,174-mi) Appalachian National Scenic Trail, the AT. At 2,030 m (6,643 ft) Clingmans Dome is the highest point on the AT, but the less adventurous can get to within 91 m (300 ft) of the summit by car to appreciate the magnificent views.

The park is noted for the wealth of its wildflowers, including spectacular meadow flowers, orchids, rhododendrons and azaleas and in autumn it nearly rivals the leaf colours of New England. Its most famous inhabitants are black bears.

Other popular activities in the park are white-water rafting and tubing in summer and skiing during the brief winter season.

WHAT IS IT?
One of the most popular national parks in the US.
HOW TO GET THERE:
By road from Atlanta or Charlotte
WHEN TO GO:
Any time of year.
NEAREST TOWN:
Gatlinburg
DON'T MISS:
The view from Clingmans Dome.

Fog in the Smoky Mountains

Crater Lake, Oregon

HOW TO GET THERE:
By road.
WHEN TO GO:
The National Park is open throughout the year. At its best from May to November, park facilities close during winter, but visitors can cross-country ski, snowshoe hike, and see the lake depending on the weather.
NEAREST TOWN:
Ashland 128 km (80 mi)
DON'T MISS:
The Shakespeare Festival in Ashland.
YOU SHOULD KNOW:
An entry fee is payable during the summer months.

Some 7,700 years ago a large volcano in what is now known as the Cascade Range, produced an enormous, spectacular eruption, 42 times more powerful than the 1980 eruption of Mount St. Helens. The uppermost 1,538 m (5,000 ft) of the volcano collapsed to form a caldera that was subsequently sealed by lava flows and is now known as Crater Lake.

Named Mount Mazama by the local Native American Klamath people, this geological event is an important part of their oral history. Their account tells of a battle between the chiefs of the World Beneath and the World Above resulting in the destruction of Mount Mazama. The Klamath people considered the lake and its surroundings to be sacred, with the result that it remained undiscovered by white explorers until 1853.

In 1902 Theodore Roosevelt designated the lake area a National Park, largely due to the efforts of William Steel, who dedicated most of his life to its conservation. Steel was also responsible for the establishment of the wonderful, 53 km (33 mi) long Rim Drive which, during the summer months, affords visitors spectacular views from many different vantage points around the lake. A small, volcanic island named Wizard Island rises from the water. It too has a crater on the summit, but this, though filled with snow during winter, remains dry during summer.

The lake lies high up, at over 1,846 m (6,000 ft), and is the deepest in the United States. It is also the deepest lake in the world above sea level. Remarkably, it has no inlets or outlets and the exceedingly pure water comes from melted snow and rain. The lake is 8 km (5 mi) in diameter and is surrounded by high rock walls. It is known for its extraordinary, deep blue colour and is an utterly magnificent, awe-inspiring sight.

Sunrise over Crater Lake

Chesapeake Bay

Chesapeake Bay was formed 10,000 years ago and is the largest estuary on the continent. Almost 320 km (200 mi) long, it stretches from southern Virginia to northern Maryland and is a shallow, tidal area where salt and fresh water come together. Historically renowned for its rich supply of seafood, particularly clams, crabs and oysters, it still yields a larger harvest of seafood than any other estuary in the country.

The shoreline of Chesapeake Bay covers almost 19,000 km (12,000 mi) – a glorious region of channels, waterways, farmland, historic towns, marinas and picturesque harbours. Roughly 16 million people live in the region and the population continues to increase, meaning more houses, more roads and more usage of water and power. Sadly the health of the Bay itself is suffering as a result.

During the 1970s algae blooms formed, caused by run-off from farm and industrial waste often originating from far up-stream, and much of the marine vegetation died out. This in turn damaged the marine habitat, killing large numbers of fish and, in particular, seriously damaging the oysters. Oysters filter water, and with their decline came a further decline in the water quality of the Bay. There are important restoration and conservation programmes attempting to resolve the problems, so far with only limited success.

Despite these difficulties, Chesapeake Bay is still a wonderful region to visit and supports thousands of species of plants and animals, including a third of all the migratory waterfowl that spend the winter on the Atlantic coast. Find a tranquil haven in which to anchor, and enjoy silence broken only by birdcalls, eat crabs at a lively waterfront restaurant or search for fossilized sharks teeth at the foot of Calvert Cliffs - there is something here to appeal to everyone.

WHAT IS IT?
The largest estuary on the continent.
HOW TO GET THERE:
Chesapeake Bay touches Maryland, Virginia and Delaware and is easily accessed from all of them.
WHEN TO GO:
April to November is probably the best time, with soft and hard shell crabs available from June to October.
NEAREST TOWN:
There are towns situated along the shoreline of Chesapeake Bay, as well as cities such as Baltimore and nearby Washington D.C.
DON'T MISS:
Annapolis, the 'Sailing capital of the World'.

The San Andreas Fault, seen from above as it bisects the Carrizo Plain in San Luis Obispo County. Note the difference in terrain on either side of the fault line, a result of the fault's lateral movement over the centuries.

San Andreas Fault, Carrizo Plain, California

The legendary San Andreas Fault is at least 16 km (10 mi) deep and runs for some 1,280 km (800 mi) through western and southern California. The fault is caused by the meeting and shifting of the Pacific and the North American Plates and forms the boundary between the two. Earthquakes occur along this boundary. These plates move past one another very slowly, but not continuously. Thus years will pass when they simply push against each other, but when the build-up of pressure breaks open the fault the plates will lurch several metres. The shock waves produced by this movement are what we call earthquakes.

The San Andreas Fault is quite visible as a linear trough, particularly from the air, though on the ground it can be clearly seen on the Carrizo Plain. Here on this long, arid, treeless plain, geological research has been conducted since 1908, two years after the devastating San Francisco earthquake. Studies have shown that large earthquakes have occurred in this region roughly every 150 years for the past 1,500 years, making it a potential danger area – the last large quake in the central section of the fault was in 1857. Although it is impossible to prevent earthquakes, structures can be built to withstand them. Intelligent design and a good advance warning system may prevent great destruction when, inevitably, the next large earthquake occurs.

Here on Carrizo Plain, streams can be seen turning sharply north as they cross the fault line, and small, undrained, salt-laden ponds containing brine shrimp also feature. In the centre of the plain lies Soda Lake, which forms each winter and provides habitat for migratory birds. Having no outlet, the lake evaporates during summer, and the salts that are left are blown skyward in great white columns.

WHAT IS IT?
One of the longest, most geologically active faults in the world.
HOW TO GET THERE:
There are hundreds of cities, towns and villages near the San Andreas Fault – Palmdale, for example, is located directly upon it.
WHEN TO GO:
All year round.
DON'T MISS:
San Francisco.
YOU SHOULD KNOW:
The almost mythical status of the fault has resulted in numerous films, songs and video games.

Cadillac Mountain, Acadia National Park, Maine

Acadia National Park, off Maine's Atlantic coast, comprises Mount Desert Island, parts of three smaller, neighbouring islands, and some of the mainland's Schoodic Peninsula. Mount Desert Island contains seventeen mountains, including the famous Cadillac Mountain.

Cadillac Mountain is formed of pink granite, and covered with pitch pine and spruce forests. Its summit, between October 7th and March 6th of every year, is thought to be the first place in the USA to receive the sun's rays. From here, on a clear day, it is possible to see both Nova Scotia, lying over 160 km (100 mi) to the east and, at a similar distance to the north, Maine's highest peak, Mount Katahdin. Views over the park itself are utterly delightful, and can be explored in greater detail by following the glorious 43 km (27 mi) long, one-way Park Loop Road.

The park is unique in that it exists largely thanks to private citizens who, realizing the dangers of over development, helped to create it. President Woodrow Wilson designated it a National Monument in 1916, and in 1929 it was named Acadia. It remains a tribute to John D. Rockefeller Jr., who not only donated about a third of the land but was also responsible for designing more than 80 km (50 mi) of carriage trails through the park, as well as seventeen granite bridges and two gate lodges.

The park contains a mass of wildlife – 40 types of mammal, marine life including seals and off-shore whales and over 300 species of birds, almost half of them breeding pairs, including peregrine falcons. These magnificent raptors are endangered but several pairs of chicks have been successfully raised here during the past fifteen years.

WHAT IS IT?
The only national park in New England.
HOW TO GET THERE:
A causeway links Mount Desert Island to the mainland.
WHEN TO GO:
Open all year, but the best weather is in July and August.
NEAREST TOWN:
There are three towns on Mount Desert Island itself, Bar Harbor, Southwest Harbor and Northeast Harbor.
DON'T MISS:
Sunrise from the summit of Cadillac Mountain.
YOU SHOULD KNOW:
At 471 m (1,532ft) high, Cadillac Mountain is the highest peak on the eastern seaboard.

Autumn on Cadillac Mountain

The Black Hills, South Dakota

WHAT IS IT?
A beautiful region of national parks, waterfalls, wildlife and recreation.
HOW TO GET THERE:
By road from Dakota, Wyoming and Nebraska.
WHEN TO GO:
All year round.
NEAREST TOWN:
There are towns all over the area. The major hub is Rapid City to the east.
DON'T MISS:
The Badlands and Yellowstone National Park.
YOU SHOULD KNOW:
These ancient granite mountains were formed some 60 million years ago and are the USA's oldest mountains.

The Black Hills of South Dakota are named for the dark, Ponderosa pines that cover them. The area covers some 12,800 sq km (8,000 sq mi) and has been aptly described as 'an island of trees in a sea of grass'. The Hills are dotted with lush mountain meadows and the southern edge is covered with a dry pine savannah due to the rain shadow of the higher elevations. In fact these are mountains rather than hills, with elevations of up to 2,154 m (7,000 ft).

This legendary region contains a wealth of treasures, including one of the USA's most popular tourist attractions, Mount Rushmore. This high, granite cliff is carved with the 18.5 m (60 ft) faces of four of the country's most influential presidents. Just north of Custer, a similar carving is in progress. The memorial to Crazy Horse, the inspirational Sioux warrior who defeated General Custer, was begun in 1939. This may take centuries to finish, but will eventually be 173 m (563 ft) high and 197 m (641 ft) long, making it the largest monument on earth.

Custer State Park, at the heart of the Black Hills, is a stunning area and is home to many species of wildlife, including bison. Drive the amazing Needles Highway that twists and turns through tunnels and around extraordinary rock formations. Needles Eye, a narrow rock spire standing almost 12.3 m (40 ft) high, can be found near the exit of one tunnel.

There are fascinating towns and cities in this region too, including Rapid City, Keystone, Custer, Hot Springs and Deadwood. These names bring to mind images of outlaws and gold mining, cowboys and Indians, and indeed the Lakota Nation is still in dispute over the ownership of the Hills – the treaty confirming their ownership was broken in the 1870s when gold and silver were discovered in the region.

Prairie meets the Black Hills in Wind Cave National Park

Cave of the Winds, Colorado

Situated on the eastern slopes of the Rocky Mountains in the Pikes Peak region of Colorado, the Cave of the Winds is a vast, underground, limestone cave network. Still being explored and mapped, it is currently recognized as the fourth longest cave in the world, with the most complex boxwork of any known cave. So far over 195 km (121 mi) of passages have been mapped, largely by volunteers.

Serious exploration of the caves began in the 1890s, and the first official survey began in 1902. However the big breakthrough did not occur until the 1960s, with the discovery of a new passageway that was named the Spillway. This led to the realization that there was an enormous labyrinthine area to the west, and indeed most of the new discoveries made during the subsequent years have been thanks to the Spillway.

The original caves and sinkholes were formed some 320 million years ago, but the major cave development occurred some 40-50 million years ago, after the uplift of the hills. The caves are full of extraordinary formations including diverse and beautiful mineral formations: helectite bushes, sawtooth flowstone, gypsum lustre and rare crystalline speleotherms. As suggested by its name, air flows through the cave system. A revolving door has been installed at the Walk-in Entrance, but prior to that, the highest recorded measurement of airflow at the entrance was 120 kph (75 mph).

There are a number of guided tours that lead you through this maze of rooms and passageways. Some, such as the Lantern Tour and the Explorer's Trip are more adventurous than others. Whatever your choice, you can't fail to be awed and impressed by this extraordinary underground world.

Inside the Cave of the Winds

WHAT IS IT?
A vast system of limestone caves.
HOW TO GET THERE:
By road.
WHEN TO GO:
Open to the public every day.
NEAREST TOWN:
Colorado Springs 16 km (10 mi).
DON'T MISS:
Pikes Peak; the Garden of the Gods Park.

White lines of sedimentary strata run through a red sandstone formation called the Eye.

The Painted Desert

The Painted Desert is an area of multi-coloured badlands that curves south east from the Grand Canyon to the Petrified Forest National Park. It is roughly 256 km (160 mi) in length, and between 16 km (10 mi) and 64 km (40 mi) wide. Part of the Chinle Formation, these hills are formed from layers of sediments of sandstone and mudstone deposited on what was once a huge flood plain.

This high plateau is an arid region, with little vegetation, and it has been – and continues to be – heavily eroded by wind and water: the flat-topped mesas and buttes we see today will eventually be just another part of the rolling hills. Deep gullies have been carved through the hills, the tops of which have been softened and rounded as the soil is washed away, but it is this same erosion that enables us to see the fantastic banded colours that have given the region its name. These are the result of the different mineral content of the sediments, and the rate at which they were laid down. When the process is slow, oxides of aluminium and iron become highly concentrated, turning the soil orange, red and pink. When it occurs quickly, a lack of oxygen creates blues, lavenders and greys. Seen at sunset, the colours positively glow.

Much of the Painted Desert is within the Navajo Nation, and archaeological work has shown that humans have been here for about 2,000 years, although when Spanish explorers found it in 1540, it was uninhabited. Today the inhabitants of the Navajo towns of Cameron and Tuba City sometimes find their neighbourhoods covered in bright red dust that has blown in from the desert, and they use red desert clay for pottery making.

WHAT IS IT?
An area of colourful badlands within the Petrified Forest National Park.
HOW TO GET THERE:
By road.
WHEN TO GO:
All year round, except Christmas Day.
NEAREST TOWN:
Holbrook 64 km (40 mi)
DON'T MISS:
Painted Desert Inn National Historic Landmark.
YOU SHOULD KNOW:
An entry fee is payable. The park is closed at night.

The Catskill Mountains, NY

Situated north west of New York City, the Catskill Mountains are actually a mature dissected plateau region of the Appalachian Mountains. This is an area of some 9,600 sq km (6,000 sq mi) to the west of the Hudson River, and is made up of heavily wooded, rolling terrain studded with gorges and rivers, waterfalls and lakes which supply New York with water. Many of the peaks reach an elevation of 923 m (3,000 ft) and the highest, Slide Mountain, is a little over 1,230 m (4,000 ft). The glaciers of successive ice ages rounded the mountain peaks and widened the valleys, and today the many rivers and streams continue the process of erosion.

During the 1800s the area was quite rapidly developed as a centre for lumber, and bluestone and flagstone was excavated from the mountains. The first railway line was opened in 1828, adding to the speed of development. This is turn led to one of the earliest conservation movements, and from 1885 legislation was enacted to protect and preserve the area.

This region has attracted holiday makers from the city for over 100 years, and it contains resorts, attractive riverside towns and villages and outdoor recreation centres. There are endless recreational opportunities here, available at all times of year, including fly fishing in Beaverkill River, possibly the most famous trout river in the country, and many fashionable, arty towns such as Woodstock and Kingston to explore.

Here, too, is the Catskill Park and Forest Preserve, 285,000 hectares (700,000 acres) of scenic parkland and forest, part of which is designated 'forever wild'. Catskill Park is a mixture of publicly and privately owned land – two thirds is privately owned, but the state is constantly acquiring land that is added to the Forest Preserve, which will continue to be explored and enjoyed by all-comers for all time.

WHAT IS IT?
A beautiful getaway area within easy reach of New York City.
HOW TO GET THERE:
By road.
WHEN TO GO:
Throughout the year.
NEAREST TOWN:
New York City 160 km (100 mi)
YOU SHOULD KNOW:
The Catskills are well known for the Jewish 'Borscht Belt' resorts, where famous comics such as Mel Brooks first came to public attention.

Hudson River

Sun breaking through the Redwood canopy

The Giant Redwoods of California

Giant Redwood trees, or Sequoias, are the largest trees in the world, and possibly the largest living organisms on the planet. Members of the yew family, there are three distinct species: Giant redwood, Coastal redwood and Dawn redwood. The first two types are to be found in California, and the last is native to China.

Sequoias only grow in the Sierra Nevada Mountains, and are a breath-taking sight. Humboldt Redwood State Park contains the last virgin redwood groves in the world, and is both a World Heritage Site and part of an International Biosphere reserve. These trees are up to 3,000 years old, and grow to a height of over 91 m (300 ft) reaching up through the mist and fog of California's coastal climate to tower over the surrounding forest of firs and pines. The largest tree of all is named General Sherman, and in 2002 it was measured at 112.6 m (369 ft 6 in).

Sequoias are not only tall, they are also broad: the trunk of Shrine Drive Through Tree can indeed be driven through, and Tharp's Log is a cabin built in one, fallen, hollowed out tree. Roads wind up into the Giant Forest where a new museum provides information about the trees and the efforts being made to protect them. The grandeur of these remarkable trees is truly one of nature's wonders. The lofty tranquillity of these groves gives the visitor a feeling of awe in the knowledge that the Sequoias will still be standing here long after we have gone.

WHAT IS IT?
The home of the world's largest trees.
HOW TO GET THERE:
By road.
WHEN TO GO:
Open all year.
NEAREST TOWN:
Visalia 78 km (49 mi)
DON'T MISS:
Kings Canyon National Park.
YOU SHOULD KNOW:
An entrance fee is payable.

Mauna Loa and Kilauea, Hawaii

The Hawaiian Islands are some of the most isolated islands on earth. They lie 2,000 miles from the nearest continental landmass, and were formed by volcanic activity beneath the seabed. Mauna Loa and Kilauea are the Big Island's (Hawaii itself) southernmost volcanoes and together they form the Hawaii Volcanoes National Park.

The Big Island is both the youngest and largest of the group, and has five volcanoes on it. Mauna Loa and Kilauea are both very volatile, active volcanoes, about 600,000 years old, and both are constantly monitored. Kilauea was thought to be a satellite vent of Mauna Loa, but they have been shown to have two separate magma chambers. Since 1984 they have been showing considerable seismic activity. Mauna Loa erupted at that time, since when the volcano has been inflating, and the caldera walls moving further apart. This is due to magma moving into a reservoir beneath the summit. Kilauea has been erupting for decades, sending lava flows down its sides from the summit and two other rift zones. Together these volcanoes have ensured that the Big Island continues to grow, year by year.

Mauna Loa is the world's largest shield volcano. At almost 100 km (62 mi) long and 50 km (31 mi) wide it covers roughly half of the Big Island. It has gentle slopes and very liquid lava and its gasses are able to escape without plumes of ash and cinders. Earthquakes open fissures from which streams of lava known as 'curtains of fire' spew forth, but most flows move at about walking pace and only rarely is anyone harmed. However, as the island becomes more developed, property is more likely to suffer damage. Driving through this extraordinary, unpredictable landscape with its steaming craters and lava flows is an unforgettable experience.

WHAT IS IT?
Two active volcanoes on the island of Hawaii.
HOW TO GET THERE:
By air to Honolulu, then by road.
WHEN TO GO:
March to November.
NEAREST TOWN:
Volcano is right at the entrance to the National Park.
DON'T MISS:
Crater Rim Drive, Chain of Craters Road.

Pahoehoe lava flows from an erupting Kilauea

Cape Cod

WHAT IS IT?
New England's favourite summer holiday area.
HOW TO GET THERE:
By plane, train, ferry or car.
WHEN TO GO:
High summer for beach holidays, spring and autumn for quieter times.
NEAREST TOWN:
There are towns all over the peninsula, from Wood's Hole in the south to Provincetown at the northern tip.
DON'T MISS:
The islands of Martha's Vineyard and Nantucket.
YOU SHOULD KNOW:
This is a haunt of the rich and famous and staying here can be seriously expensive.

The easternmost part of Massachusetts is the peninsula known as Cape Cod. Shaped like an arm flexing its muscles, it reaches 96 km (60 mi) into the ocean. Attached to the mainland at the 'shoulder', the opening of the Cape Cod Canal in 1914 turned the peninsula into an island accessed by bridges.

Around 18,000 years ago the Laurentide ice sheet was in retreat, and as it melted, so sea levels rose. Finally the sea was sufficiently high to start eroding the glacial deposits left on the peninsula, some of which were washed to the peninsula's northern tip, others to the south, where they formed islands. Cape Cod's Atlantic facing shore is still being reshaped by the tides and the winds – indeed a proposed wind farm, known as Cape Wind and intended to provide some 80% the Cape's electricity, has just received state environmental approval.

Cape Cod has a population of about 230,000, but every summer thousands of visitors flock here from New England and further afield to enjoy the pleasant climate, beautiful beaches and delicious seafood. The nearby islands have attracted America's wealthiest and most aristocratic families for over 100 years. In 1961, John F. Kennedy was instrumental in getting federal protection for 64 km (40 mi) of open beach and rippling sand dunes as well as 17,000 hectares (43,000 acres) of Outer Cape land, which is known as Cape Cod National Seashore. No doubt this area would otherwise have been heavily developed by now.

The National Seashore contains many habitats and eco-systems including marine, estuarine, forest, heathland and sandplain grassland. Many of these are uncommon and are home to increasingly rare species. There is a National Marine Sanctuary to the north where whale watchers can see finback, humpback and sei whales.

A red rowing boat sits in lush grasses on a salt marsh on Great Island at Cape Cod National Seashore.

The Badlands

Prairie grass at Badlands National Park

South-west South Dakota's Badlands National Park is an area rich in human history and palaeontology. Its banded rocks, a mixture of sand, silt and clay and volcanic ash, were laid down one on top of the other in the Oligocene Period, which lasted from 35.4 to 23.3 million years ago and the fossils uncovered in them reveal the evolution of North America's unique fauna in such mammals as three-toed horses, sabretooth cats, pigs, elephant-like creatures, rhinoceroses and camels the size of dogs. The area was a vast floodplain and the fossils are the remains of animals caught in floods and quickly buried in sedimentary rocks.

Over hundreds of thousands of years, the White River carved out a course in the soft rocks, at an average of 2.5 cm (1 in) a year, although at times erosion occurs much more rapidly. The Wall, the sheer cliff that marks the river's course, is continually moving northwards, exposing the harder, older rocks underneath, and leaving an eerie, beautiful land of isolated buttes, ridges, pinnacles and spires behind, particularly in the wind-sculpted forms of the Sage Creek Wilderness Area.

This area was used as summer hunting grounds by native Americans for some 11,000 years, and eventually saw some of the most bitter struggles between native Americans and settlers, culminating in the 1890 Sioux Ghost Dances and the massacre of the Lakota at Wounded Knee on 29 December.

The Badlands are an area of stunning, if desolate, beauty that must be seen.

WHAT IS IT?
A startling landscape of desolate beauty.
HOW TO GET THERE:
By road from Sioux Falls.
WHEN TO GO:
Spring or autumn.
NEAREST TOWN:
Scenic 5 km (3 mi).
DON'T MISS:
Highway 240 'Badlands Loop Road'.
YOU SHOULD KNOW:
The site of the Wounded Knee massacre is 72 km (45 mi) to the south.

A fishing guide paddles his canoe across a still pond in the Adirondack State Park.

Adirondack State Park

Situated in north eastern New York State lies a vast region of 2.5 million hectares (6.1 million acres): the Adirondack State Park. This is the largest park in the USA, covering an area of about the same size as Vermont. First considered in 1870, it was finally established in 1882 by the New York State Legislature. The park is a combination of publicly and privately owned land. The publicly owned portion, about 43%, is constitutionally bound to remain 'forever wild'.

To the north east rise the Adirondack Mountains, part of the Canadian Shield. These are relatively young mountains, formed by intense upward displacement of the earth's crust, but the rock from which they are formed, anorthosite, is some of the oldest on earth. There are 42 peaks reaching over 1,230 m (4,000 ft), 11 with alpine summits, and people come here from all over the world to enjoy downhill and cross-country skiing, dog-sledding and other winter sports.

The majority of the public land is forested with both hard and softwoods such as Scots and red pine, spruce, maple, birch and black cherry. 200,000 acres of this old growth forest has never been logged. The western and southern Adirondacks are made up of gentle hills, streams, lakes and ponds. Black bears, bobcats, coyotes and white tailed deer are amongst the mammals that live here, along with trout and land-locked salmon populations in the lakes and streams. Efforts are being made to re-introduce fauna that was lost in the past – American beaver, lynx, moose and osprey for example. There are 3,200 km (2,000 mi) of hiking trails and 2,400 km (1,500 mi) of rivers, so it comes as no surprise that some 7-10 million visitors come here annually.

HOW TO GET THERE:
More than 40 roads enter the park and there is also the Adirondack regional airport.
WHEN TO GO:
All year round.
NEAREST TOWN:
There are 105 towns and villages within the park's boundaries.
DON'T MISS:
Mount Marcy; Algonquin Peak; Lake Placid.
YOU SHOULD KNOW:
There is no entrance gate and no admission fee, although fees apply at state camp grounds.130,000 people live and work within the private lands. Some of the great American families built summer 'camps' here, a few of which are now luxury hotels.

Carlsbad Caverns National Park

Carlsbad Caverns, in the Chihuahuan Desert, was first designated a National Monument in 1923. It became a National Park in 1930 and a World Heritage Site in 1995. It was established to protect and preserve over 100 known caves that include the deepest limestone cave in the United States.

The caves are the remains of a fossil reef in an inland sea that covered the region some 250 million years ago. When this evaporated the reef was buried under mineral salts and gypsum. Millions of years later the reef began to re-appear as the area uplifted and corrosive gasses from enormous oil and gas deposits beneath the reef began to dissolve the limestone and form the huge caverns that we can see today.

Pre-historic Native Americans sheltered in Carlsbad Cavern more than 1,000 years ago, leaving fascinating pictograms on the walls near the entrance. However the caves are renowned for their fantastic stalactites, stalagmites and rare formations of calcite and aragonite. Jim White, a cowboy, found the caves in 1898. He explored and named many of the rooms and significant formations such as the Big Room, which at 3.3 hectares (8.2 acres) is the largest chamber in the complex, and the Queen's Chamber, the most beautiful room of all.

Exploration of this cave system is on going. In 1966 a park ranger found the second largest chamber here, with an amazing collection of 'soda straw' stalactites, and named it the Guadalupe Room. The Lechuguilla Cave was found in 1986 and, mapped to a depth of 489 m (1,590 ft), it is the deepest cave in the country.

The Chinese Theater in Carlsbad Caverns

WHAT IS IT?
An extraordinary cave complex in the Guadalupe Mountains of New Mexico.
HOW TO GET THERE:
By road from Carlsbad, New Mexico or El Paso, Texas.
WHEN TO GO:
The Park is open throughout the year; the busiest months are June, July and August.
NEAREST TOWN:
Carlsbad 37 km (23 mi)
DON'T MISS:
The King's Palace; the Hall of the White Giant; the Green Lake Room.
YOU SHOULD KNOW:
Carlsbad Cavern is the summer home of a large and well-known colony of Mexican Free-Tailed bats.

Sunrise over St. Mary Lake

Glacier National Park, Montana

This magnificent region of pristine wilderness is located in the north west of Montana. It is dominated by mountains and valleys shaped by vast glaciers during the last ice age. Today the last few glaciers are in retreat, with only 27 remaining, and it is thought that they will all be gone by 2030 if global warming continues unabated.

There are no large cities anywhere nearby, and few roads, but in 1921 construction began on the Going to the Sun Road, a staggering feat of engineering that took eleven years to complete. This is one of the most beautiful drives in North America – 80.5 km (52 mi) from east to west, it crosses the Continental Divide at Logan Pass, in the northern Rocky Mountains.

The Park contains over 1,120 km (700 mi) of hiking trails, almost 1,600 km (1,000 mi) of rivers and streams and 2,000 lakes, of which 130 are named, including the stunning glacial St. Mary Lake and Lake McDonald. The park is largely covered with coniferous forest, with deciduous trees such as aspen and cottonwood at lower elevations. Altogether, 1,132 plant species have been identified here. The remoteness of the area makes it rich in wildlife, including two threatened species: Grizzly bear and Canadian lynx. Other large mammals such as wolverine, cougar, big horn sheep, elk, moose and deer live here too – altogether 62 species of mammal have been documented.

This is a marvellous place to get away from it all. There are beautifully sited, historic lodges in which to relax after a hard day's hiking. Sit back and enjoy spectacular views in perfect peace, and you might get to see Harlequin ducks and Great Blue herons on the lake beneath you, and Golden eagles and Peregrine falcons riding the thermals high in the sky above.

WHAT IS IT?
A World Heritage Site made up of 485,000 hectares (1.2 million acres) of pristine wilderness.
HOW TO GET THERE:
By plane, train or road.
WHEN TO GO:
June to September.
NEAREST TOWN:
West Glacier and East Glacier are both on the edges of the Park, or Kalispell 40 km (25 mi)
DON'T MISS:
Going to the Sun Road.
YOU SHOULD KNOW:
Hunting is illegal, but regulated fishing is permitted. Snowmobiling is illegal, but cross-country skiing is permitted at lower elevations.

Death Valley

Situated in south-eastern California, Death Valley is a region of extremes. Even though its name suggests a barren, desolate place, over 1,000 plant species and many animals live here, having adapted successfully to the harsh environment. Sunk between two mountain ranges, most of the valley lies below sea level, and the area known as Badwater Basin is the lowest place in North America.

The area has been formed over millions of years and was once covered in a warm, shallow sea. The oldest rocks here are about 1.7 billion years old and the mountains that border the valley show an incredibly complex geological history. This is the hottest, driest place in the country, yet there are snow capped, forested mountains here as well as sand dunes, stone desert, and water carved canyons.

Very little rain falls here, but when it does the desert suddenly blooms with a million wildflowers. Some species have roots that spread out in every direction just below the surface. Others have roots that go down and down, and yet more have stems and leaves that hold their precious water tight, losing virtually nothing by evaporation. At night the temperature drops rapidly – during winter it dips below freezing. However, day temperatures in the summer months are regularly around 50°C (120°F) so be prepared.

Many of the animals living here are small, nocturnal mammals. Larger species such as mountain lion, coyotes and desert bighorn live at higher, cooler altitudes where more water and vegetation are available. The valley is also home to rattlesnakes, scorpions and black widow spiders. This is an unforgiving, inhospitable place, but it is also remarkably beautiful in its way, and there are various popular spots such as Zabriskie Point and Dante's View, where visitors come to watch the sun rise or set over this unique landscape.

WHAT IS IT?
The hottest, driest and lowest National Park in the USA
HOW TO GET THERE:
By road – there is no public transport.
WHEN TO GO:
November to May is the best time.
NEAREST TOWN:
Pahrump 102 km (64 mi)
DON'T MISS:
Artist's Palette; Marble Canyon; Scotty's Castle.
YOU SHOULD KNOW:
The hottest temperature ever recorded in the USA was 56.7 °C (134 °F) on July 10th 1913 in Death Valley.

A dry lake bed in the valley

Meteor Crater, Arizona

HOW TO GET THERE:
By road.
WHEN TO GO:
October to May.
NEAREST TOWN:
Winslow 32 km (20 mi)
DON'T MISS:
Flagstaff; Sedona.
YOU SHOULD KNOW:
The crater is still owned and run by the Barringer family. An entry fee is payable. Visitors may not enter the crater itself.

Meteor Crater is a huge, almost circular hole in the arid Arizona desert. It is 1,200 m (4,100 ft) in diameter and 173 m (570 ft) deep, and has a rim of rocks and boulders rising some 45 m (150 ft) above the surrounding area. Although there are other, larger meteorite craters in the world, the studies made of this one provided the first proof of meteoritic impact upon the earth's surface.

Estimated to be some 50,000 years old, the meteorite, formed of nickel iron, was about 50 m (165 ft) across. It hit the ground at about 12.8 km (8 mi) per second, and roughly half its bulk was vapourized as it ploughed through our atmosphere before impact. Even so, it will have produced an incredible explosion, in the region of 150 times the force of the atomic bombs at Hiroshima and Nagasaki.

Daniel Moreau Barringer, a mining engineer, originally suggested that this was a meteorite crater in 1903. Prior to this it had been thought to be the result of volcanic activity. Barringer's company bought the crater and found that it had been caused by a violent impact. His conclusions were met with disbelief from the scientific community so he decided to prove them by digging up the remains of the meteorite, not knowing that it had disintegrated when it hit. He spent 26 years drilling for metallic iron without success, and in 1929 he died, his hypothesis still unproven. It was not until 1960 that Eugene M. Shoemaker found two forms of silica in the crater that can only be created through an impact event, and was able to conclusively confirm Barringer's theory.

Saint Francois Mountains, Missouri

WHAT IS IT?
A relatively small area of ancient mountains containing famous Missouri landmarks.
HOW TO GET THERE:
By road.
WHEN TO GO:
June to September.
NEAREST TOWN:
There are several small towns in the area such as Arcadia, Ironton and Pilot Knob. The slightly larger Farmington is 24 km (15 mi) from these.
DON'T MISS:
St. Louis.
YOU SHOULD KNOW:
Part of the famous Ozark Trail winds through the Saint Francois Mountains.

The Saint Francois Mountains were formed by violent volcanic activity over 1.4 billion years ago. These low, rounded mountains rise over the Ozark Plateau, and contain some of the oldest visible igneous rock in the country. They are thought to have been the only area in the mid-west that was never submerged by ancient seas, and the fossilized remains of reefs can still be seen at the base of the mountains.

This is the centre of the Missouri mining area, and it also contains a great number of marvellous natural features, such as the Devil's Honeycomb, an area of igneous rhyolite that has formed unusual geometric honeycomb shapes, as well as rare flora and fauna. Here, too, is Tam Sauk Mountain, at 540 m (1,772 ft), the highest point in Missouri, and easy to reach via a paved trail. Missouri's highest waterfall, Mina Sauk Falls, falls in cascades, the main one dropping almost 32 m (105 ft).

Johnson's Shut-ins is a natural water park. Formed as the Black River carved its way through fractures within black and pink volcanic rocks, it is an area of deep waterholes, waterslides, whirlpools and cascades that attract so many visitors during summer that only a limited number of cars is allowed entry to the State Park at any one time.

Another place of interest here is Elephant Rocks State Park, an area of granite that at one time was quarried to supply much of the building and facing stone in St. Louis. The Elephant Rocks are actually huge, pink granite boulders that have been worn down to shapes that roughly resemble elephants. The largest of these is hundreds of feet long, and forms a platform from which the surrounding area can be viewed.

The unusual rock formations of the Saint Francois Mountains

Yosemite National Park

Yosemite, high in California's Sierra Nevada, is a startlingly beautiful place, with iconic mountains and rock formations, stunning waterfalls, lush alpine meadows and forests filled with awe-inspiring trees. Features such as Half Dome and El Capitan are hauntingly familiar even to those who have never been here, because of the photographer Ansel Adams, who made documenting this valley his life's work. Yosemite is one of the oldest national parks in the US, having been designated in 1890.

This is a rock climber's paradise: the smooth face of Half Dome and the jagged granite of El Capitan provide even the most experienced with a challenge. But Yosemite is not just for the active, the views from along, and across, the valley floor are amazing. The three cascades of Yosemite Falls, one of the highest waterfalls in the world, drop a total of 740 m (2,425 ft) and in May, when the runoff is at its peak, the noise is overwhelming.

One of the most popular areas of the valley for walkers is Mariposa Grove, where hundreds of giant sequoias reach high into the sky, making visitors feel very small indeed. The Tuolumne Meadows are worth a hike, especially in late spring and early summer when they are filled with typical alpine plants. The surrounding scenery, however, is stunning at any time of the year.

Perhaps the best overview of the area can be obtained in summer from Glacier Point, about an hour's drive away from the main valley.

As well as rock-climbing, there is something to do all year, from skiing and snowboarding to fishing, hiking, rafting, horse-riding, birdwatching, stargazing at overnight camps and cycling. There is also an abundance of wildlife, including black bears and deer, bobcats, yellow-bellied marmots, Sierra Nevada bighorn sheep, coyotes, white-tailed hare, mountain beavers, grey foxes, martens and golden-mantled ground squirrels. Birds include spotted owls, Steller's jays, rosy finches, great grey owls, white-headed woodpeckers and northern goshawks.

Whether you go to Yosemite for adventure or to simply gaze in awe at the magnificent landscape, Yosemite is a true must-see.

WHAT IS IT?
One of the world's most magnificent landscapes.
HOW TO GET THERE:
By road from San Francisco or Fresno.
WHEN TO GO:
The park is open all year, although some approaches are shut during winter. The waterfalls are at their best in May.
NEAREST TOWN:
Mariposa 70 km (43 mi)
YOU SHOULD KNOW:
The black bears are effective scavengers: all food must be kept secure and covered so they cannot smell it.

El Capitan and the Yosemite Valley

Great Salt Lake playa

Great Salt Lake, Utah

The Great Salt Lake covers an area about 120 km (75 mi) long and 56 km (35 mi) wide, with an average depth of about 9 m (30 ft). The largest salt lake in the Western Hemisphere, it is the remains of the great Lake Bonneville, which covered most of western Utah, and receded after the end of the Ice Age. Ancient terraces carved by wave action can be seen as dark lines high up on the surrounding hills.

Water from rivers and streams empties into the lake, bringing dissolved salt and other minerals with it, and as there is no outlet, constant evaporation concentrates the salt and leaves it there. Great Salt Lake is three to five times more saline than the ocean, and no fish inhabit it. However, several types of algae live in the lake, and brine shrimp that feed on algae thrive here. Since the 1970s their eggs are sold mainly to South America and the Far East as food for fish and shellfish farms. Other commercial operations extract salts and potassium sulphate from the lake.

Antelope Island, a State Park, is one of several islands in Great Salt Lake. It is popular for its clean white sand beaches, and for the fact that the warm water is so salty that it is impossible not to float. Wildlife is plentiful on Antelope Island. Elk, antelope, bobcat and coyote can often be seen, but it is bird life for which the area is known. There are several bird management areas and sanctuaries both around the shores and on some of the smaller islands. The lake is ringed with wetlands providing habitat for millions of migratory shorebirds and waterfowl and brine shrimp and brine flies provide their main source of food.

WHAT IS IT?
The largest saltwater lake in the Western Hemisphere.
HOW TO GET THERE:
By road.
WHEN TO GO:
June to September.
NEAREST TOWN:
Salt Lake City 26 km (16 mi)
DON'T MISS:
The Bonneville Salt Flats.

Devils Tower, Wyoming

Devils Tower is a remarkable, monolithic rock formation that rises from the top of a forested area near the Belle Fourche River, in the wilderness of north eastern Wyoming. As the hill is some 182 m (600 ft) and Devils Tower is 263 m (867 ft), the whole eerie structure can be seen from 160 km (100 mi) away.

Formed by the intrusion of igneous material 50 million years ago, Devils Tower is a good example of columnar and horizontal fracturing. This occurred when the green grey igneous rock cooled, causing the cracking that formed these multi-sided (often hexagonal) columns. The flat top was probably produced by molten rock meeting a layer of hard rock, forcing it to spread out.

Originally Devils Tower would have been beneath overlying sedimentary rock, and it is erosion that has worn away surrounding sandstone, allowing the Tower to rise above the surrounding area. Rain and snow are still eroding the rocks at the base of the Tower, but the Tower itself is also being eroded, as can be seen in the broken columns, boulders and smaller rocks lying at its base.

Devils Tower is sacred to several Native American peoples, including the Lakota Sioux, and in their legend the monolith was formed when three Sioux girls were attacked by a giant bear. The Great Spirit made the rock upon which they were standing rise up, out of the bear's reach and, in frustration, it clawed the rock, leaving the deep scoring that we see today. Every June visitors are requested to refrain from climbing the Tower, in order that sacred ceremonies can be performed around the base.

HOW TO GET THERE:
By road.
WHEN TO GO:
May to October is the best time.
NEAREST TOWN:
Hulett 16km (10 mi).
DON'T MISS:
Yellowstone National Park.
YOU SHOULD KNOW:
In 1906 President Theodore Roosevelt declared Devils Tower the first National Monument. In 1978 Stephen Spielberg used it in *Close Encounters of the Third Kind*.

Alabaster Caverns, Oklahoma

WHAT IS IT?
A state park containing the world's largest gypsum cave open to the public.
HOW TO GET THERE:
By road.
WHEN TO GO:
The park is open all year round.
NEAREST TOWN:
Freedom 10 km (6 mi)
DON'T MISS:
The Cedar Canyon Trail.
YOU SHOULD KNOW:
An entry fee is payable. The cavern is not recommended for those with mobility, heart, and respiratory or claustrophobic conditions.

The Alabaster Caverns are the centrepiece of the Alabaster Caverns State Park. The main cave is 1.2 km (3/4 mi) long, and is the largest natural gypsum cave open to the public in the world. The first known exploration of the caverns was made in 1898, although the area itself had previously been lived in. In 1928 Charles Grass bought the land and, 25 years later, sold it to the State of Oklahoma for $34,000.

The underground cavern system was formed some 200 million years ago, when this area was an inland sea. Today a perennial stream flows through it, fed via several lateral tunnels as well as seepage from the roof. Geological evidence shows that this stream was once a mighty river that totally filled the cavern and you can see weird and wonderful water-sculpted gypsum formations here.

Gypsum caves tend to be large, and as you make your way through the entrance in the rock cliff, you find yourself in the first of a series of huge, beautifully lit rooms, 60 m (195 ft) in diameter and 23 m (75 ft) high. The walls are covered in 50 cm (1 ft 8 in) thick selenite crystals, (the crystallized form of gypsum) a glass-like mineral, but many of the formations here are made of alabaster. Several types of alabaster are found here, including white, pink and the extremely rare black. There are only two other veins of black alabaster in the world, one in Italy and the other in China.

The caverns are home to five species of bat, some of which are solitary and some live in colonies. The roosting sites provide shelter during the day, and a place to hibernate for those that do not migrate in winter.

Alabaster Caverns

Mount Whitney, California

Standing at 4,417 m (14,491 ft), Mount Whitney is not only the highest point in California but also the highest mountain in the United States, outside Alaska. Located in the northern Mohave Desert, the western slope is actually in Sequoia National Park, and the two faces, west and east, are utterly different from one another. Ironically, the lowest point in the United States, Badwater Basin in Death Valley, is less than 160 km (100 mi) from here.

This mountain is one of the most frequently climbed peaks in the country, having something to offer everyone. The east face consists of almost sheer, granite cliffs that plunge down to the Owens Valley, and provides a variety of climbs, from the East Face route and the Mountaineer's route, to world-class big wall rock climbing. The west slope is much easier, the most popular route being the Mount Whitney Trail. This is a 35 km (22 mi) trail, with camp sites along the way.

Black bears are fairly common here, and backpackers must carry a bear-resistant canister with them, which can be rented from the Visitors Centre. They are also advised to travel in large groups at night, with bright lights and loud whistles to warn off the bears. Most people take between two and four days to complete the hike. During summer the daytime temperatures can be hot, but at night they can drop below freezing at any time. In spring, ice axes and crampons may be necessary but by July the trail should be snow-free.

WHAT IS IT?
The highest mountain in the contiguous United States.
HOW TO GET THERE:
By road.
WHEN TO GO:
Best from June to September.
NEAREST TOWN:
Lone Pine 21 km (13 mi)
YOU SHOULD KNOW:
Between May and October everyone must obtain a permit, and daily numbers are restricted. Apply early, or hope for a cancellation.

Mount Whitney in Sequoia National Park

Glorious colours reflected in a lake

Autumn colours of New England

Every autumn, a vast area of the north-eastern coastal United States – from Maryland to Vermont, turns vibrant shades of red, golden, russet, purple, yellow, orange, crimson and scarlet as the days shorten and temperatures begin to drop. This is a beautiful landscape at any time of year, but the changing colours of the leaves make this time of year a special time to visit.

The leaves change colour as part of deciduous trees' preparation for winter. They do not need the leaves while they are dormant, so they cease the production of chlorophyll, the substance that photosynthesizes sunlight, water and chemicals to create energy and colours the leaves green. The dominant green of the leaves fades and the colours of other chemicals become visible. This prosaic explanation of the process belies the magical effect that it creates.

Each species of tree has different chemicals in its leaves, so they all turn different colours and the mixed woodlands become a spectacular patchwork of vivid hues: bronze hickories rub shoulders with scarlet maples, purplish red dogwoods stand side by side with golden-yellow birch and crimson sourwood provides a brilliant contrast to russet oak in what seems like nature's last glorious fling of the year.

The most reliable time to observe this spectacle is early October, but exactly when the change takes place in any area is dependent on the weather, so 'tree peepers' need to be prepared to travel. A telephone service keeps people updated about the best locations.

WHAT IS IT?
One of nature's most colourful spectacles
HOW TO GET THERE:
By road from anywhere in the US eastern seaboard.
WHEN TO GO:
Early October is the most reliable time.

Jewel Cave, South Dakota

Jewel Cave was formed when stagnant, acid-rich water dissolved the existing limestone and enlarged the cracks that had appeared some 60 million years ago when the Black Hills were uplifted. When the water drained away, the speleothems (cave formations) began to grow, mainly formed from calcite, though in the drier parts the formations are made of gypsum.

In 1900, Frank and Albert Michaud passed through the Black Hills on their way home from the Alaskan gold rush. They had reached Hell Canyon when they heard a strange noise and discovered it was the sound of cold air forcing its way from a small hole in the hillside. Returning later to this spot, they dynamited their way in, and found an amazing series of low caves that sparkled with jewel-like calcite crystals.

During the next ten years, the Michauds tried unsuccessfully to turn the cave into a tourist attraction. In 1908, news of their find reached President Roosevelt, who declared it a National Monument. The family later sold its claim to the government. By 1939 various programmes had made the cave much more accessible, and a cabin and campground had been established. Thus far, only half a mile of cave had been discovered, but a Ranger was available to conduct cave tours. By 1961 the known length of the cave had grown to 24 km (15 mi), and since then over 208 km (130 mi) have been mapped, apparently a fraction of the site.

Jewel Cave is now the third longest cave in the world. It is beautifully decorated with gleaming calcite crystal spars, stalactites, stalagmites, flowstone and frostwork. It even has a very rare hydromagnesite balloon, a substance formed by magnesium that has been inflated by gas from an unknown source.

WHAT IS IT?
The third longest cave in the world.
HOW TO GET THERE:
By road.
WHEN TO GO:
All year round.
NEAREST TOWN:
Custer 21 km (13 mi)
DON'T MISS:
Custer State Park.

Beautiful jewel-like calcite crystals

Mammoth Cave, Kentucky

WHAT IS IT?
The world's largest known cave system set in a beautiful national park.
HOW TO GET THERE:
By road.
WHEN TO GO:
Open all year, but best from May to September.
NEAREST TOWN:
Cave City 8 km (5 mi).
DON'T MISS:
Frozen Niagara; Echo River.
YOU SHOULD KNOW:
The caves are chilly so bring a jacket.

Mammoth Cave National Park is situated in the Green River Valley, a lovely area of limestone cliffs and hills draped with hardwood forest. Established in 1941 to protect the vast labyrinthine cave system that lies beneath those hills, it was designated a World Heritage Site in 1981, and in 1990, an International Biosphere Reserve. As long as 12,000 years ago these caves were used by Ancient Indians, and archaeologists have found evidence that the region continued to be used and hunted by Native Americans until the first white settlers forced them off the land.

This is the world's longest cave system. Unique geological circumstances have combined since the Ice Age to form a cave system of multiple levels. The Green River Valley deepened and as the water sank it found different flow paths through layers of limestone. Vertical shafts were also formed, at a later stage, due to water flowing from the edge of the harder, sandstone caprock into the limestone beneath. These shafts intersect with the passageways, forming a complex, interconnected system with a few large passages and many smaller ones.

Apart from the marvellous, multi-hued speleothems, including those made of sulphate which look like gold or white flowers growing from the walls, more than 200 species of animal live in Mammoth Cave, from surface animals that have either fallen in accidentally or those that have found their way in to hibernate, there are 42 species of troglobites, animals that have adapted to a life of darkness. The waters here are home to eyeless fish and cave shrimp and there are flatworms, cave beetles and more that spend their entire life cycle here. Food is provided by the animals that come and go from the caves, such as rats, bats and crickets.

Stalactites in Mammoth Cave

Ancient Bristlecone Pine Forest, California

Bristlecone pines are a small group of pine trees, one species of which, *Pinus longaeva*, contains the oldest living organism known to man. Nicknamed Methuselah, this tree is about 4,700 years old, and is still growing. It stands, with many only marginally younger companions, in California's Ancient Bristlecone Pine Forest, itself an area of the Inyo National Forest in the White Mountains.

The great age of these trees was discovered by Edmund Schulman who found that certain species of trees living in stressful conditions in the upper forest zones showed sensitive records of drought in their growth rings. In 1953, following a rumour of ancient trees in the area, he visited the White Mountains and found these ancient trees, several 3,000 to 4,000 years old, growing in seemingly impossible locations at 3,048 - 3,354 m (10,000 - 11,000 ft). In 1957 Methuselah itself was found to be 4,723 years old.

The White Mountains are formed of quartzitic sandstone and granite bedrock with outcrops of dolomite. In the rain shadow of the Sierras, these mountains receive less than 12 in (30 cm) of precipitation annually, mainly as snow. The climate here is cold, dry and windy, and the soil quality is poor. The trees themselves are stunted and distorted with large areas of deadwood and thin strips of living bark.

There are two groves of ancient Bristlecone pine, the Schulman Grove and the Patriarch Grove, home to the largest Bristlecone pine in the world after which the grove is named. This is a remote area, near the tree line, and is a favourite location for film and photography, having the most spectacular, panoramic views of the Sierras and the Nevada basin.

Bristlecone Pine

HOW TO GET THERE:
By road.
WHEN TO GO:
Mid May to November, depending on snowfall.
NEAREST TOWN:
Bishop 55 km (34 mi)
DON'T MISS:
Wild flowers in August; Sierra View Overlook.
YOU SHOULD KNOW:
A small fee is payable. The site of Methuselah is not made public in order to protect the tree from vandalism.

Alaska Peninsula National Wildlife Refuge

HOW TO GET THERE:
Fly from Anchorage to King Salmon.
WHEN TO GO:
It is accessible all year round.
NEAREST TOWN:
King Salmon is within the complex of National Parks on the Alaska Peninsula. The Refuge can be accessed by small aircraft or boat only. The Visitor Center in King Salmon will assist you with air charter information and/or guides.
YOU SHOULD KNOW:
Summer temperatures vary from 0 ºC to 27 ºC (32 ºF to 80 ºF). The Bristol Bay lowlands average 50 cm (20 in) rain per annum, with up to 406 cm (160 in) on the Pacific side. Most rain and fog occurs between July and October.

The Alaska Peninsula National Wildlife Refuge was established in 1980 in order to conserve the on-shore and off-shore wildlife, to provide for the continued subsistence of the various Alaska Native Peoples who inhabit the area, and to ensure water quality. This is a magnificent landscape of high mountain peaks, wide valleys, rolling tundra, glacial lakes, and a rugged Pacific coastline of cliffs, fjords and sandy beaches.

The Alaska Peninsula NWR also contains active volcanoes, including Mount Veniaminoff. This volcano is huge – its base has a 48 km (30 mi) diameter and the summit crater is 32 km (20 mi) in circumference – and it last erupted between 1993 and 1995. It not only has the largest crater glacier in the country but also is the only known glacier in America with an active volcanic vent in its centre.

The area supports a large number of species: brown bear, the roughly 7,000 strong Northern Alaska Peninsula reindeer herd, wolf, wolverine, fox and beaver. There are moose here too – first seen at the beginning of the last century, they are now abundant. Fish teem both in the lakes and rivers and the sea – five species of Pacific salmon for example. Off-shore there are sea otters, seals, sea lions and migratory grey whales, and there are more than 200 species of bird, including raptors, game birds, seabirds, shore birds and freshwater birds such as duck, geese and swans.

This region has sustained humans for 10,500 years. Originally they seem to have been nomadic reindeer hunters, but soon they moved toward the coast and began hunting fish and sea mammals as well. Today the area's resources are gathered and used by the First Nation and Inuit peoples who live here.

Lava flow from Mount Veniaminoff

Diamond Head Crater, Oahu

If you visit Waikiki, on the Hawaiian Island of Oahu, you will instantly become aware of Diamond Head, the island's best-known landmark and probably the best-known volcanic crater in the world. With a height of 230 m (760 ft) and diameter of 1,060 m (3,500 ft), Diamond Head dominates the city. From its summit, spectacular 360-degree views can be enjoyed.

Formed over 200,000 years ago, the volcano is thought to have been extinct for about 150,000 years. Ancient Hawaiians named it Laeahi, meaning 'Brow of the Tuna', after the shape of the rim, seen in silhouette. When, in the 1880s, British sailors saw it from afar, they could see calcite crystals in the lava rock twinkling and shining in the sun. Thinking them to be diamonds, and imagining they would make their fortunes, the sailors gave it the name we know today.

Diamond Head crater has been used militarily since the turn of the last century. During World Wars I and II it was heavily fortified and a four level underground command post was constructed within the crater walls. A switchback trail, classified as 'easy to moderate' ascends the inside slope of the crater until it reaches a series of steep steps and tunnels that bring you out on to the summit with its stupendous views of the island. Stepping out into the sunshine, the ground still sparkles, and one can only feel sympathy for those poor disappointed sailors.

WHAT IS IT?
An extinct volcanic crater whose iconic silhouette represents the Hawaiian Islands.
HOW TO GET THERE?
Bus or car from Waikiki.
WHEN TO GO:
All year round.
NEAREST TOWN:
Waikiki is just beneath it.
DON'T MISS:
Honolulu; Hanauma Bay; Pearl Harbor.

Diamond Head Crater and Honolulu

*The Blue Ridge Mountains
in autumn*

The Blue Ridge Mountains, Virginia

The Blue Ridge Mountains form the eastern rampart of the Appalachians, running from Pennsylvania to Georgia. They are made of ancient granite dating from some 1.2 billion years ago and lava flows of up to 28 m (90 ft) deep from 570 million years ago. The sedimentary rocks of sandstone and quartzite were formed later. At one time these mountains were probably as high as the Rockies, but they have been rounded and eroded over time. Today their top elevation is just over 1,231 m (4,000ft).

The Blue Ridge Parkway, known as America's Favourite Drive, twists and turns for 750 km (469 mi) from the Great Smoky Mountains National Park in the south to Shenandoah National Park to the north. The landscape is stunning: endless vistas of forested mountains, valleys speckled with old farmsteads, wildflower-rich meadows, and a wonderful variety of wildlife. The blue morning mists that rise from the forests give the Blue Ridge its name.

The Parkway was a public works project initiative – in 1933 there were almost 14 million unemployed people in the country, and President Roosevelt created a Civilian Conservation Corps to employ 500,000 young men. The Blue Ridge Parkway was an enormously difficult road to build, and it took some 50 years to complete.

People have lived here for at least 10,000 years. Iroquois and Shawnee hunted and fished in the foothills, but were displaced in the early 1600s when the English began to settle Virginia. By the 1800s the lowlands were being farmed and as good land became scarce people moved up into the mountains, where life was harsh and settlements scarce. Gradually they developed a culture of their own – indeed some of the Appalachian people inhabiting the most remote and isolated spots speak an English dialect similar to that of the Elizabethan era.

HOW TO GET THERE:
By car from Georgia, South and North Carolina, Virginia, Washington DC, Maryland, Pennsylvania, or east across the Appalachians.
WHEN TO GO:
May to October.
NEAREST TOWN:
There will always be a town or village accessible to you, no matter which part of the mountains you are in.
DON'T MISS:
Shenandoah National Park.
YOU SHOULD KNOW:
In the 1930s Laurel and Hardy sang 'The Trail of the Lonesome Pine' in their film, *Way Out West*. The chorus begins 'In the Blue Ridge Mountains of Virginia...' The recording became a posthumous hit record in 1975.

The Finger Lakes

To the north east of New York City, on the far side of the Catskill Mountains, lies the region known as Finger Lakes. This was the heart of the Iroquois homeland, and legend has it that, as a reward for their courage in battle, the Great Spirit brought part of paradise down to earth, the lakes being formed by the impression of his fingers. Geologically, the lakes were pre-glacial stream valleys. The deposits left behind when the glaciers retreated dammed these valleys, and the lakes, parallel to each other and orientated from north to south, were born.

Historic cities and towns such as Ithaca and Auburn can be found at the head and toe of most of the lakes. The southern ends of the lakes are particularly attractive, with steep hills and many lovely waterfalls. Honeoye Lake, the shallowest, is the favourite for water-based recreation. The longest and largest lakes, Cayuga and Seneca are both extremely deep, the latter reaching down to 188 m (618 ft). As the population expands and new properties are built, water quality has become a priority, and efforts are being made to control pollution.

This is a fertile, beautiful region of rolling farmland and vineyards intersected by eleven lakes that drain north to Lake Ontario. Quaker, Amish and Mennonite families settled here during the 19th and 20th centuries, and dairy farms are common, as well as arable farms growing wheat, oats barley and soya beans. The region is probably best known for its vineyards, the first of which was planted in the 1860s. Today the number is approaching 100, and the white wines produced here are known throughout the country.

WHAT IS IT?
A delightful region of 19th century towns, bucolic countryside and eleven gorgeous lakes.
HOW TO GET THERE:
By road.
WHEN TO GO:
All year round, but between May and October to make the most of the lakes.
NEAREST TOWN:
There are towns and villages around every lake.
DON'T MISS:
The Museum of Glass at Corning; the Harriet Tubman Home at Auburn; Cornell University at Ithaca.

Canandaigua Lake in the Finger Lakes region of New York State

Yellowstone National Park

During the first half of the nineteenth century, reports from hunters and mountain men of an area of the Rocky Mountains with mud pools, geysers, petrified forests and hot springs were dismissed as myths. However, after expeditions in 1869 and 1870 confirmed the tales, moves were quickly made to preserve this beautiful, otherworldly landscape and the area was designated as Yellowstone National Park, the first national park in the world, in 1872.

The geothermal features are the result of water passing through extremely hot rock underground, which is still cooling down from a volcanic eruption thousands of years ago. In the 1960s and 1970s, it gradually became apparent that the main feature of the park is a series of three giant volcanic calderas – craters formed when a massive volcano erupted and blew out so much material that the surface above collapsed. These three eruptions occurred 2.1 million years ago, 1.3 million years ago and 640,000 years ago. The most recent of these created a caldera roughly 85 km (52 mi) by 45 km (28 mi) and nearly 1 km (3,300 ft) deep and blanketed most of North America in a deep layer of volcanic ash. It was the result of the eruption of a 'supervolcano' over a mantle plume (or hot spot), where material from the Earth's mantle gradually rises to its surface and pools until a cataclysmic explosion occurs. Smaller lava flows and steam eruptions occur every few thousand years and there are frequent small earthquakes and at times parts of the ground rise or fall over a period of years, which may be the result of the movement of magma or the build-up and gradual release of pressure below ground.

As well as the geothermal features, such as Old Faithful geyser, Yellowstone has spectacular pristine landscapes and wildlife, including several thousand bison, as well as elk, grizzly bear, moose, mule deer, black bear, puma, wolverine and re-introduced wolf. The seriously threatened lynx may also be present in very small numbers.

WHAT IS IT?
The first national park in the world, centred on the caldera of an active volcano.
HOW TO GET THERE:
By air to Bozeman, Montana then by road via Gardiner, the only entrance gateway open all year.
WHEN TO GO:
April to November.
NEAREST TOWN:
Bozeman, Montana 77 km (47 mi)
DON'T MISS:
Old Faithful Geyser, Grand Prismatic Springs, mudpots such as Fountain Paint Pot, and Mammoth Hot Springs' travertine terraces.
YOU SHOULD KNOW:
The bears in Yellowstone are dangerous. Do not approach them and obey trail closure signs.

LEFT: The Gardiner River meanders through the park.
RIGHT: A Bison ignores 'Old Faithful' as it lets off steam.

Monument Valley

Monument Valley is not, strictly speaking, a valley at all, but a series of spectacular rock formations sculpted out of the Colorado Plateau through the actions of rivers over millions of years. The shale, sandstone and siltstone formations, rising 300 m (1,000 ft) up from the desert floor in layers of browns, reds and greys are among the most iconic sights of America's wild west and have appeared in countless films. Among the best known features are the East Mitten and West Mitten buttes, the North Window, John Ford's viewpoint, the Thumb, the Totem Pole, the Three Sisters and the Ear of Wind arch.

The valley lies within the Navajo Nation Reservation in south-east Utah and is sacred to them. The most scenic areas are in the Monument Valley Navajo Tribal Park. Although much of the valley can be seen from the Valley Drive, a 27-km (17-mi) road, it is best experienced by guided tour, hike or horseback trail, especially as some areas such as Mystery

Valley are accessible only with a Navajo guide. The Navajo have lived here for centuries, but the ancient cliff dwellings of their predecessors, the Anasazi, and age-old petroglyphs can also be seen.

This colourful, desolate landscape leaves most visitors awestruck at its scale and beauty.

HOW TO GET THERE:
On Highway 163
WHEN TO GO:
April to November
NEAREST TOWN:
Bluff, Utah 105 km (65 mi)
DON'T MISS:
A guided tour to the hidden areas.
YOU SHOULD KNOW:
Rock climbing is strictly forbidden

Olympic National Park

WHAT IS IT?
A national park containing three distinct ecosystems.
HOW TO GET THERE:
By bus or ferry to Port Angeles, then by car and on foot.
WHEN TO GO:
July to September.
NEAREST TOWN:
Port Angeles, on the northern edge of the Park.

The Olympic Peninsula protrudes into the Pacific Ocean at the far north western tip of Washington State, just to the south of Vancouver Island. Almost all of it is designated wilderness and Olympic National Park covers 373,347 hectares (922,561 acres), having become an International Biosphere Reserve in 1976 and a World Heritage Site in 1981.

The Park naturally divides into three areas: the Pacific coastline, temperate rainforest and the Olympic Mountains that separate the peninsula from the land to the south. This isolation has resulted in many endemic flora and fauna, such as the Olympic marmot, as well as endangered species such as the Northern Spotted owl and Marbled Murrelet. The mountains are topped with ancient glaciers, with the 2,428 m (7,965 ft) peak of Mount Olympus dominating the western half.

The temperate rainforest is in the west of the park, which receives more rain than anywhere else in the country, with the exception of Kauai in Hawaii. This is an amazing area of old growth forest, dense with Sitka spruce, western hemlock, Douglas fir, cedar, maple, alder and black cottonwood, producing habitat for many different creatures.

The coastal area is wild and wonderful, with some sandy beaches often covered with logs and other flotsam and others covered with great lumps of rock. There are arches and sea stacks, tide pools full of shells and other marine life, and birds such as Oyster catchers and Bald eagles. There are still a few Native American communities living in this marvellous wilderness, and several roads enter the park, though none penetrate far, leaving the interior only accessible by trail.

A stream flows through moss covered rocks.

Mohave Desert

The Mohave Desert region is one of the country's most popular tourist areas. It contains four national parks: Death Valley, Grand Canyon, Joshua Tree and Zion, all of which are extremely beautiful. Here too are oases, sand dunes for off-road recreation and the lure of easy money in Las Vegas. There are many other cities and towns in the desert, and several major highways cross the area. There are also ghost towns to visit, the best known being Calico, an old silver mining area.

The Mohave Desert is the smallest and most arid of North America's deserts, covering some 35,000 sq km (22,000 sq mi) of land, including much of southern California, and parts of Arizona, Nevada and Utah. Sandwiched between the Great Basin Desert to the north and the Sonoran Desert to the south, the Mohave has average elevations of between 909 m – 1,818 m (3,000 ft – 6,000 ft). It also contains the lowest spot in the country, in Death Valley.

As a result of the surrounding mountains the desert is in a rainshadow, receiving an average of less than 15 cm (6 in) of rain annually. However, it contains a large variety of habitats, flora and fauna, including some 200 plant species endemic to the Mohave. Over 2,500 species survive here, of which more than 100 are considered to be at risk. The best-known plant here, indeed the symbol of this desert, is the Joshua tree, a type of yucca. So called by Mormons, who saw the gnarled branches as the arms of Joshua, pointing the way to the Promised Land, Joshua Trees only live at higher elevations, and indeed, they only live here.

HOW TO GET THERE:
By road.
WHEN TO GO:
Spring and Autumn are the best times.
NEAREST TOWN:
There are towns and cities all over the region. The nearest town to the Joshua Tree National Park is Twentynine Palms, a three-hour drive from Los Angeles.
DON'T MISS:
The four national parks; Las Vegas.

Joshua Trees in late afternoon

Cascade Range

The Cascade Range stretches for some 1,120 km (700 mi) from southern British Columbia to Northern California, about 160 - 240 km (100 - 150 mi) inland. They are part of the Pacific Rim of Fire, and the section known as the High Cascades contains vast, snow-capped volcanoes including Mount Rainier, the highest peak at 4,434 m (14,410 ft), and Mount St. Helens, the most notorious. The latter produced a major eruption in 1980, blowing up the northern part of the mountain, wiping out forests, and showering the northwest of the country with ash. The volcano continues to have minor eruptions, the last of which was in 2006. It became a National Volcanic Monument after 1980 in order to preserve the area and to enable scientists to study its recovery.

The volcanoes stand alone in magnificent isolation, separated from each other by vast plateaux, but there are also many non-volcanic mountains in the range. Their sharp, rocky peaks seldom exceed 3,077 m (10,000 ft) but they receive extremely heavy snow and, together with many glaciers, provide excellent climbing. Thick forests of Douglas fir and red alder cover the wetter, western slopes. The eastern side is much drier, reflected by forests of larch and ponderosa pine. There are roads and trails to all the most popular peaks, and routes to the summits of all the volcanoes.

The Cascades include many national monuments, forests and wilderness areas as well as four national parks. The Oregon region in particular is a famous tourism area, containing Mount Hood, the Columbia River Gorge and Crater Lake. Several million visitors come here each year during summer to hike, canoe, camp and climb and during winter to enjoy excellent skiing on the many slopes.

WHAT IS IT?
A mountain range extending through California, Washington, Oregon and southern British Columbia.
HOW TO GET THERE:
By road.
WHEN TO GO:
The Cascade Range has wonderful recreational facilities and can be visited throughout the year.
DON'T MISS:
Lava Beds National Monument in California, Snoqualmie Falls in Washington.
YOU SHOULD KNOW:
There are fascinating visitor centres at Mount St. Helens enabling the public to see for themselves the devastated mountain and its recovery.

The eruption of Mount St. Helens on May 18, 1980, seen from Yale Lake.

Saguaro National Park

WHAT IS IT?
A bizarrely beautiful national park.
HOW TO GET THERE:
By road.
WHEN TO GO:
Open all year round, but March and April to see the flowers.
NEAREST TOWN:
Tucson 24-27 km (15-17 mi)
DON'T MISS:
Biosphere 2.
YOU SHOULD KNOW:
Over a third of Arizona belongs to the Native American Navajo, Hopi and Apache peoples.

The Saguaro cactus (*Carnegiea gigantea*) is the state symbol of Arizona, and a universally recognizable symbol of the American south-west. First named a National Monument in 1933, Saguaro was given National Park status in 1994 to protect great tracts of land covered with these giant, multi-armed cacti.

The Saguaro is an exceedingly slow-growing plant, specially adapted to its desert environment. Seedlings often grow beneath the protective cover of a 'nurse' tree such as Mesquite, and the young plant only achieves growth of 2.5 - 3 cm (1 - 1.5 in) during its first eight years. Large white flowers appear down the sides of the plant when it is about 35, and this occurs every spring until eventually the flowers will also grow on the ends of the branches. These, however, do not appear until the saguaro is at least 50 years old.

Saguaros are pleated in order that the plants can expand to ingest vast amounts of water when it rains. As the water is used, the pleats contract. These plants live for up to 200 years and can grow to 15 m (50 ft). Because of the high water content, they can weigh between 6 – 8 tons. Their blossoms provide nectar for bees, long-nosed bats, moths and doves, and the sweet fruits that follow provide food for coyotes, foxes, rodents, ants and birds.

Saguaro National Park is divided between the Rincon Mountain district, east of the city of Tucson, and the Tucson Mountain district to the west. Both conserve sections of the Sonoran Desert to which the Saguaro cactus is endemic, and the park provides over 205 km (128 mi) of trails to enable visitors to enjoy not only the Saguaros but the numerous other varieties of cactus that are native to the area.

In winter the saguaros, chollas and prickly pear cacti populate the desert in Saguaro National Park, Arizona.

Mount Rainier National Park

Established in March 1889, Mount Rainer was the fifth National Park to be formed in the USA, and it encompasses the whole of the mountain within its boundaries. It is, in fact, an episodically active volcano, rising suddenly from the surrounding landscape to a height of 4,392 m (14,410 ft) to loom over both Puget Sound and a population of over 2.5 million people living in the Seattle Tacoma metropolitan area.

Mount Rainer with a wildflower meadow in the foreground

Mount Rainier is notable for the glaciers that radiate from its summit, of which 26 are named. Together with the snow and ice fields, it forms the greatest single-peak glacial system in the contiguous USA, with Carbon Glacier the largest by volume and Emmons Glacier the largest by area. One of the most accessible glaciers is Nisqually, which has advanced and retreated several times during the past 45 years, providing important indications of climatic change. The splendid, 149 km (93 mi) long Wonderland Trail that encircles the mountain gives hikers superb views of the summit and the glaciers.

The lower areas of the park are covered with old growth forests of cedar, fir and pine, which gradually give way to glorious sub-Alpine wildflower meadows, valleys and waterfalls before reaching the snowline. The area is rich with mammals such as Columbian black-tailed deer, elk and black bear, as well as numerous species of birds, though invertebrates are the most successful creatures here, inhabiting all areas right up to the summit, Columbia Crest.

Over two million visitors come to this much-loved park each year, for hiking and climbing, camping and cross-country skiing. Numerous (around 600) campsites and lodges enable visitors to explore some of the 480 km (300 mi) of trails at their leisure, and Paradise Valley, on the south slope of the mountain, is the most visited destination and should not be missed.

WHAT IS IT?
A national park containing the majestic volcano, Mount Rainer.
HOW TO GET THERE:
By car, or on a day trip by coach from Seattle.
WHEN TO GO:
The park is open year round, but July and August have the best of the weather.
NEAREST TOWN:
Ashford, at the Nisqually entrance to the Park.
DON'T MISS:
Sunrise, the Ohanapecosh River, Longmire.
YOU SHOULD KNOW:
Mount Rainier receives a huge amount of rain and snow each year – even in high summer, so go prepared.

Islands of the Sea of Cortez

WHAT IS IT?
A chain of island reserves, protecting
varies, pristine habitats.
HOW TO GET THERE:
By air to La Paz or San Carlos, then
by boat.
WHEN TO GO:
October to March.
NEAREST TOWN:
Kino
DON'T MISS:
Blue and Finback whales in the Canal
de las Bellenas (Whale Channel) off
Isla Angel de Guardia.
YOU SHOULD KNOW:
Different rules apply to different
islands - check in advance. A small
charge may be payable for visitors'
permits.

From the Colorado River delta in the north, to the tip of the Baja California peninsula, the emerald waters of the Sea of Cortez are studded by a chain of over 240 islands, great and small. Their natural beauty is enhanced by extraordinary diversities of terrain, habitat, and even microclimate, from temperate wetlands to mountainous desert to tropical abundance. Each has evolved in unique symbiosis with its surrounding marine ecology – a relationship so fruitful that Jacques Cousteau called the Sea of Cortez "the aquarium of the world".

Isla de Tiburon, due west of Hermosillo on the mainland, is the largest. It's an Eden for birdwatching, fishing, diving and walking; a truly pristine example of the high chaparral of mountain desert, with rare flora and fauna as unusual as they are beautiful; and its beaches are a cornucopia for shell lovers. The island used to be home to the Seri Indians – and since you have to get your visitor's permit from Kino, the very traditional Mexican township on the mainland, it's well worth the 27 km (17 mi) detour north to Punta Chueca, the rustic fishing village where the remaining 1,000 Seri people still live in a time warp. (Be warned – the Seri do not like to be photographed.)

Boats anchored at Isla San Francisco

Isla Espiritu Sancto, off the coast of La Paz at the south of the peninsula, is a sub-tropical jewel, and typical of so many of the islands. It lies on the migration route of millions of birds, and of thousands of whales who come to Baja California to breed in the warm, shallow water. It's the best place on earth to watch whales super-close, along with 39 per cent of the world's total of marine mammal species, and a third of the world's cetacean species.

Inevitably, the islands are magnets for tourists seeking subtropical R&R; but they are now protected, along with the surrounding seas, by World Heritage status. Their eco-marvels will continue to be there to be enjoyed.

Popocatepetl

Its name is the Aztec word for 'smoking mountain', and
Popocatepetl is one of Mexico's most active volcanoes. For the last
600 years, its eruptions have been relatively mild, with columns of
ash rising only a few km above the summit. But its position, 45 km
(28 mi) from Puebla and 70 km (44 mi) from the heart of Mexico
City, and its height of 5,465 m (17,760 ft), mean that its activities
are a constant threat to some 40 million people living within its
potential range. As recently as 2000 it roared back into life, melting
snow into mudslides and hurling red-hot rocks down the nearest
valleys.

Popocatepetl is a particularly lovely volcano, with impressive
green slopes marching steeply to the ring of snow and ice encircling
the smoking crater. Almost symmetrical from every angle, it is as
much an icon of modern Mexico as it was for the Aztecs and the
colonial Spanish. The latter left their mark on the mountain: 14 well-
preserved monasteries built by the early Franciscan, Dominican and
Augustinian missionaries. They are among Mexico's best examples of
colonial architecture, and provide a welcome destination and
resting-place for visitors to the volcano.

WHAT IS IT?
An active volcano, the second
highest in North America.
HOW TO GET THERE:
By road from Puebla.
WHEN TO GO:
Year round.
NEAREST TOWN:
Puebla 40 km (25 mi)
DON'T MISS:
The colonial monasteries.
YOU SHOULD KNOW:
In Aztec mythology, Popocateptl was
a fierce warrior.

Sian Ka'an Biosphere

The Sian Ka'an Biosphere Reserve is a 526,000 hectare (1.3 million acre) park on the eastern side of the Yucatan peninsular in the State of Quintana Roo. Set aside to preserve tropical forests, mangroves, savannas, cenotes (sink holes), coral reefs, and more than 25 Mayan ruins, some of it is prohibited to any kind of human access to protect its authentic pristine environment. But the majority of this huge area is a playground for some of the world's most exotic eco-tourism.

The reserve is both threatened by, and dependent on the tourist facilities between Cancun and Tulum on its northern boundary. Other than camping, it offers almost nowhere for people to stay except for a few specialist fishing lodges catering to its world-class saltwater flats fishing opportunities. Anglers can pursue bonefish, permit, barracuda and other species among the mangroves; most other visitors should take advantage of the sensitively guided tours that start from tourist centres, and visit the very best of Sian Ka'an.

Guides will take you by boat round 'islands' of mangroves full of nesting birds, where roseate spoonbills, ibis and tri-coloured heron are common. Less so (but trust to luck) are jabiru, jaguars, deer, peccaries, manatees and spider monkeys. Then, heading inland where the salt of the lagoon turns into the fresh water of a coastal spring, blooming orchids and bromeliads cling to the mangrove trellis – and the guide passes out life jackets for you to float downstream in the cool spring water.

Of course you can drive yourself around the reserve, stopping off to snorkel the reefs or dive in a cenote. It's free to enter – but the roads will crack all but the sturdiest axle, and finding fuel beyond Tulum is a matter of chance.

Sian Ka'an Biosphere Reserve

Cueva de la Boca bat roost

Mexican free-tailed bats

Situated close to Monterrey in the north east, Cueva de la Boca is one of Mexico's most important bat caves, and the first to be bought solely in the interests of conservation. Its size and one-time population of 20 million bats, along with its proximity to the US border, has ensured its status as a tourist attraction. The same factors very nearly caused its destruction. Conservationists recently discovered that the bat populations of Cueva de la Boca and another nine of the major publicly accessible caves in northern Mexico had dropped by 90 per cent; la Boca had only 600,000 left. Hikers anxious to explore the cave were inadvertently suffocating the bats and their pups with smoke from the makeshift torches they made from rags and plastic bottles. Happily, just two years after its purchase, the number of residents had risen to 2 million.

There's a mighty sigh of beating wings and the twilight briefly darkens as the colony leaves the cave each evening. Emerging in a single burst, their presence in the skies shows up on Doppler radar. Pug-nosed, with a wrinkly lower lip and long, loose tail, these are Mexican free-tailed bats, just one of 140 species found in Mexico. They are of special ecological importance because of one characteristic: their favourite food is the corn earworm, a vicious moth that devours corn crops as it migrates and lays eggs all the way from Texas to the Canadian border. The bats of la Boca travel more than 96 km (60 mi) from their cave every night, eating around 15 tons of bugs before they return. They are the perfect pest control, discriminating their targets without damage to the rest of nature.

The success of the Cueva de la Boca project is now a model for the eco-tourism development of a further 120 bat caves along the Mexico-US border.

WHAT IS IT?
A 'maternity cave' of Mexican free-tailed bats.
HOW TO GET THERE:
By road from Monterrey.
WHEN TO GO:
April to November.
NEAREST TOWN:
Monterrey 23 km (14 mi)
DON'T MISS:
6.00 pm – bats leave on time.
YOU SHOULD KNOW:
Bring a proper flashlight, if at all.

El Vizcaíno Biosphere Reserve

WHAT IS IT?
Mexico's biggest Biosphere Reserve.
HOW TO GET THERE:
By air or boat to San Ignacio.
WHEN TO GO:
October to April
NEAREST TOWNS:
Santa Rosalia (Sea of Cortez) and
Guerrero Negro (Pacific).
DON'T MISS:
Cochimi cave paintings
YOU SHOULD KNOW:
There may be small charges for
visitor permits.

This is Mexico's biggest and most dramatic reserve. It straddles the centre of the Baja California peninsula between the Pacific Ocean and the Sea of Cortez, and includes 450 km (281 mi) of coast in its total of 25,000 sq km (15,625 sq mi). But apart from the 5 km (3 mi) deep littoral zone, animals and plants of El Vizcaíno have had to adapt to extreme desert conditions of little rain and intense winds, defining characteristics of an ecosystem which has produced thousands of endemic species unknown anywhere else on earth.

Trekking the Sierra San Francisco in the reserve's heart, you'll see the pronghorn antelope, desert bighorn sheep, mule deer and coyote among dozens of sub-species. They roam an ancient landscape of as much cultural as natural significance: you can see proof of human ability to live in harmony with nature in the caves that pepper the Sierra. Over 200 contain the elaborate cave-art of the Cochimi, nomads who lived here 11,000 years ago. It is their legacy, as much as the fauna and 469 species of flora, that the Reserve exists to protect from the threats of encroaching agriculture and illegal hunting.

But Vizcaíno's greatest treasure is its whale sanctuaries. The bays of San Ignacio and Ojo de Liebre on the Pacific coast lie at the southernmost point of one of the longest known migrations. Grey whales travel over 8,000 km (5,000 mi) from the Arctic Circle to breed in the protection of their warm, shallow lagoons. Now, some 900 calves are born each year within the reserve, and with the threat of extinction lifted by the reserve's existence, the grey whale population has been restored to more than 27,000. Knowing they are safe, the whales tolerate boats and divers nearby. Nowhere else can you get so close – and besides the enormous grey whale, you can see the humpback, fin, sei and blue whales, all of which frolic in Vizcaíno's gulf and Pacific waters.

A Cardon cactus in the Vizcaíno Desert

Cenotes & the underground rivers of the Yucatan

Behind the beach playgrounds of its Caribbean coast lies Yucatan's most magical secret. The whole peninsula is like a giant Swiss cheese made of limestone. Hollowed out by millennia of tropical rainstorms, the porous rock has allowed an entire river system to evolve in its underground heart. About 560 km (350 mi) of criss-crossing waterways have been mapped between Playa del Carmen and Tulum – just 10 per cent of the total.

These underground rivers can be long. One twists and turns for 153 km (96 mi) through halls of stalactites and stalagmites as big as jumbo jets and fissures only wide enough for a single diver. In a straight line, the same river covers just 10 km (6 mi). Gigantic meanders like these are the reason why fresh water is distributed so well across the peninsula; why the jungle is so lush, and why the Mayan empire was able to flourish in the region. Then, as now, the underground rivers were accessible via surface sinkwells, or 'cenotes'. They look like sunlit pools dotted randomly in the dense green, and many have steep walls as if a hole had been punched through the limestone. The Mayans believed the cenotes to be gateways to 'the Other World', and in one way they were right: each cenote connects to the only source of fresh water to be found.

Descending into a cenote can be like being suspended inside a jewel. Emerald shafts from the holes in the cavern roof cut through the crystal water, itself a shimmer of rainbow fish darting between tree roots and languid trailing foliage. Slightly deeper, where the freshwater meets the seawater at the halocline, the water seems oily and colours divide into a swirling kaleidoscope. Visibility clears as you emerge into full seawater, but the eerie beauty is intensified by the faint green glow now far above. Real magic.

Stalactites hang from the cave roof of the eerie Cenote X-Keken at Dzitnup.

WHAT IS IT?
A unique regional freshwater system.
HOW TO GET THERE:
From Merida/Chichén Itzá (west) or Playa del Carmen (east).
WHEN TO GO:
November to May.
NEAREST TOWN:
Cancun, Valladolid and Chichén Itzá are good regional bases.
DON'T MISS:
Swimming in the fresh water of a cenote.
YOU SHOULD KNOW:
Open Water diving qualification is necessary for cavern (cenote) diving. Full cave diving (defined as 'beyond sunlight') requires specialist training.

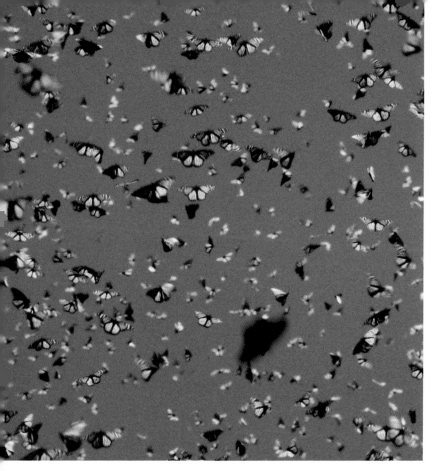

Monarch butterflies in flight

Monarch Butterfly Sanctuaries

Each November, as the North American summer ends, hundreds of millions of Monarch butterflies stream south en masse to the mountains of Michoacan, west of Mexico City. They fill the sky with a blizzard of orange and black, and settle in such dense clusters that trees sag beneath their weight. Their destination is the group of Oyamel fir forests where, at around 3,040 m (10,000 ft), they depend on a unique micro-climate to overwinter. But the area is notorious for its poverty, and the surviving forests remain under relentless threat from legal and illegal logging. Only gradually are the local co-operatives coming to understand that eco-tourism can provide them with a viable alternative income, and to support the three main Bio-Reserves of El Rosario, El Capulin, and Piedra Herrada

The awesome spectacle of up to 250 million Monarchs is not necessarily a wilderness adventure. The butterflies share the small pueblos and mountain villages with the farmers, schoolchildren and storekeepers who live in the forests, as well as eco-tourists. They settle everywhere, on corn-cribs, prams and street signs – even on the twin cathedrals of Angangueo, the town whose steep valley and winding cobblestone lanes mark the centre of Monarch country. But you'll see them at their most dazzlingly prolific within the official sanctuaries. At El Rosario they carpet the forest floor in search of water, and you must step gingerly to avoid them. A sign enjoins you to *Guarda Silencio*: the same sign you see in Mexican churches. And it's true that the butterfly groves inspire holy awe. Sometimes, local guides feel this so strongly that they put logs across the forest trails to discourage too many visitors from exploring the groves' heart. No matter – everywhere inside the sanctuaries you will encounter rivers of butterflies streaming around you, and even stand inside their kaleidoscope of flashing brilliance.

WHAT IS IT?
The region is an Eco-Sanctuary of international importance.
HOW TO GET THERE:
By car/bus from Mexico City (4hrs) W to Zitacuaro, then N to Angangueo; then by local taxi with a guide, or a tough hike N to El Rosario.
WHEN TO GO:
November to April.
NEAREST TOWN:
Angangueo 6 km (4 mi)
DON'T MISS:
The classic Mexican countryside and the colonial town of Valle de Bravo.
YOU SHOULD KNOW:
Take good walking shoes or boots, however you get there.

Paricutin

Paricutin is a volcano in the state of Michoacan. It is merely the youngest of more than 1,400 volcanic vents in Mexico, but it is unique because every phase of its formation was witnessed from the start.

In 1943, it erupted suddenly in a cornfield, showering ash and stones on the farmer ploughing it. In a year it grew to a height of 336 m (1,100 ft), burying the villages of Paricutin and San Juan Parangaricutiro. The eruptions continued with diminishing violence over eight years, spreading layers of lava over 25 sq km (16 sq mi), and raising the summit to 424 m (1,390 ft); until in 1952, after a six month display of renewed, explosive glory, they stopped for ever. Luckily, Paricutin is a monogenetic volcano, which means it will never erupt again.

The stain of the lava flow stands proud on the tranquil, fertile land. From Angahuan, the 16th century town that sits on the lip of the mountains overlooking Paracutin, a winding trail leads down the valley. Lush vegetation yields to the deep black, glittering, metallic ash. From the fluid waves of volcanic rock engulfing it, the walls and belltower of the church of San Juan Parangaricutiro emerge in silent witness to other, buried ruins. Beyond, a steady 5 km (3 mi) climb brings you to the desolate cinders of the summit. The view is majestic.

WHAT IS IT?
A monogenetic volcano.
HOW TO GET THERE:
By road from Morelia via Uruapan and Angahuan.
WHEN TO GO:
Year round.
NEAREST TOWN:
Angahuan 6 km (4 mi)
DON'T MISS:
The 'plateresco' architecture (a mix of Spanish, Arab and native Mexican styles) of Angahuan.
YOU SHOULD KNOW:
When you rent a horse, make sure it's for the full return journey.

Paricutin is a black cone volcano that erupted on Feb. 24, 1943. Two Tarascan villages were totally buried in lava. The volcano is now dormant.

Bathers at the sacred waters

Semuc Champey

Semuc Champey means "sacred water" in Mayan and it lives up to its name. It is quite unlike anything you have ever seen, in an idyllic mountain setting of tropical forest, full of wildlife, with radiantly coloured butterflies, hummingbirds and kingfishers darting around.

You make your way through the forest along the River Cahabon to meet an extraordinary sight - a series of small ponds and pools, 1-4 m (3-13 ft) deep, fed by the waterfalls and streams that run down the mountainsides. They are a scintillating range of colours, varying in intensity from pale turquoise to deep emerald and violet. Then you realise that the river is running below you and that these pools are set in the dented surface of a natural limestone bridge that crosses the Cahabon River. It is an almost unbelievable sight and it is impossible not to be awestruck by its strange overwhelming beauty.

The torrential river beneath you spins wildly down, with a deafening noise as it is forcibly sucked into a limestone tunnel, only to re-emerge 350 m (1,150 ft) further on, where water from the top of the bridge cascades down in waterfalls to join it.

It is a difficult spot to reach so it is worth spending one or two nights camping here. There are remarkably few tourists and you can spend your time swimming, diving from the mountainside into the pools and watching the abundant wildlife – 90 species of bird alone. It is well worth making the journey, for it is arguably the most beautiful sight in the whole of Guatemala.

WHAT IS IT?
A unique limestone formation.
HOW TO GET THERE:
By road, 7 hours from Guatemala City and 3 hours from Coban.
WHEN TO GO:
Less hot and humid in the dry season, November to April
NEAREST TOWN:
Lanquin 11 km (7 mi)
DON'T MISS:
The caves of Lanquin, with navigable streams, wildlife and pre-Hispanic artefacts.
YOU SHOULD KNOW:
It is best to hire a guide to take you through the sometimes precipitous, heavily forested terrain. Tourists have died falling into the river and then being dragged down into the tunnel under the bridge.

The Blue Mountains

The Blue Mountains are aptly named. They are enveloped in a permanent mist that, from a distance, suffuses them with a blue tint. They are renowned for their varied topography, biodiversity and staggering views, as well as the world's finest coffee, which is cultivated on the lower slopes.

The mountains rise from foothills at the north-eastern edge of the capital city of Kingston in a steeply inclined escarpment over 2,000 m (7,000 ft) high that sweeps along eastern Jamaica for 48 km (28 mi). On a clear day, you can see Cuba from Blue Mountain Peak, the highest point in Jamaica at 2,256 m (7,402 ft). The heavily forested, rugged hinterland, 20 km (12 mi) deep, is scored with rapidly flowing rivers, streams and waterfalls, which cascade down into luxuriantly vegetated valleys causing frequent floods and landslides. More than 760 cm (300 in) of rain a year falls here, providing water for almost half Jamaica's population. The terrain is so wild that parts of it are still uncharted.

In the eighteenth century, the Maroons, fugitive slaves, set up their headquarters in the heart of this inaccessible mountainous jungle. They were so successful in waging guerrilla war against the British that eventually they were granted land rights. Today, their descendants, Rastafarian country farmers, conceal their ganja (marijuana) fields here.

There are more than 500 flowering plant species in the mountains, including the extraordinary Jamaica bamboo, *Chusquea abietifolia*, which flowers only once every 33 years, (it is next due to flower in 2017). Over 200 species of resident and migrant bird thrive here, including hummingbirds (known locally as the "doctor bird"), and it is the home of the world's second largest butterfly, *Papilo homerus*.

In 1992 the Blue Mountain and John Crow National Park – with a total area of 780 sq km (255 sq mi) – was established to protect the remaining forest and watershed.

WHAT IS IT?
Mountainous rainforest.
HOW TO GET THERE:
International airport, Montego Bay or Kingston then bus from Kingston.
WHEN TO GO:
Dry season: December to April. It is unwise to hike in rainy season because of risk of landslides and floods.
NEAREST TOWN:
Kingston (less than an hour's drive).
DON'T MISS:
The numerous pools and waterfalls on northern slopes.
YOU SHOULD KNOW:
It is not safe to hike on your own. Always use a guide in order to avoid getting into trouble by stumbling into illegal ganja fields or losing your way.

Palms are part of the lush vegetation in the Blue Mountains.

The Blue Lagoon near Port Antonio

Blue Lagoon

WHAT IS IT?
A beautiful, quiet swimming hole in spectacular surroundings.
HOW TO GET THERE:
Along the A3 coast road from Port Antonio.
WHEN TO GO:
The climate is warm throughout the year, but the hurricane season runs from May to November.
NEAREST TOWN:
Port Antonio 11 km (7 mi)
DON'T MISS:
The nearby Frenchman's Cove and Somerset Falls.
YOU SHOULD KNOW:
There is a dive shop that rents out scuba gear and kayaks.

Just outside Port Antonio, in the east of Jamaica, lies the beautiful swimming hole known as the Blue Lagoon. Almost surrounded by lush, tropical greenery and steep cliffs, and separated from the Caribbean Sea by only a narrow strip of land, it is thought to be the crater of an extinct volcanic cone, which now happens to be more or less at sea-level. Its blue and green, mineral-rich waters come from springs fed from higher up in the slopes of the Blue Mountain. In places the sides are steep, while in others the slope is shallow enough to allow you to walk into the lagoon.

At their greatest depth, the waters are 56 m (185 ft) deep, and in places swimmers may feel warm or cold currents of water as they emerge from the springs: the warmer water is thought to have passed through rocks deep under the surface that are still warm from the last time the volcano erupted. Cooler currents may have passed through rock nearer the surface. In places, where the water is shallow, it can be seen bubbling out of the ground.

Away from the hustle and bustle that characterizes other Jamaican attractions like Kingston, this secluded spot is a must for any visit to the island.

The Soufrière Hills

The Soufrière Hills are a series of lava domes, rising to 915 m (3,000 ft), in the southern half of the island of Montserrat. This "Emerald Isle of the Caribbean" – named after the 17th Century Irish indentured workers who settled there – is one of the few places in the world where you can witness a live volcano at work. A grey steaming plume of gas dramatically overshadows Montserrat's breathtaking scenery of tropical forest, sheer cliff-faces and sandy coves. At night, the gases emitted from the volcano's cone glow an eerie red in the darkness.

The volcano was thought to be dormant until, in 1995, it suddenly started to erupt. The town of Plymouth, Montserrat's capital, was enveloped in a thick ash cloud, so dense that it blacked out all daylight for a full quarter of an hour. The authorities, not wanting to take any chances, ordered the evacuation of the whole of south Montserrat, displacing about 12,000 people. Eventually, in 1997, a massive flow of lava and boulders swept down from the volcano, set the town on fire and buried it 12 m (40 ft) deep. A further eruption later that year killed 23 people. Two thirds of the island is off-limits and all the remaining inhabitants have moved to the area in the north.

Scientists at the Montserrat Volcano Observatory constantly monitor the Soufrière Hills and as recently as 8 January 2007 an evacuation order was issued for the slopes of the volcano. There is a 34 sq km (11 sq mi) "safe zone" from where you can see the apocalyptic scene at Plymouth. Among the remains, a church tower and the roofs of houses poke through the layer of volcanic debris, which suffocated the town - an extraordinary sight, reminiscent of Pompeii.

WHAT IS IT?
An active volcano.
HOW TO GET THERE:
Scheduled air services or ferry from Antigua.
WHEN TO GO:
December to June (to avoid the rainy, hurricane season).
NEAREST TOWN:
None. Destroyed in volcanic eruption.
DON'T MISS:
The Oriole Walkway.
YOU SHOULD KNOW:
Montserrat is the only country in the world apart from Ireland where St Patrick's Day is a public holiday.

Montserrat Volcano in 1997

Basse-Terre

WHAT IS IT?
Volcano and rainforest.
HOW TO GET THERE:
Fly to Pointe à Pitre, Grand-Terre.
WHEN TO GO:
January to June to avoid tropical storms and hurricanes.
NEAREST TOWN:
Basse-Terre
DON'T MISS:
Jacques Cousteau Marine Reserve on the Pigeon Islands; Sainte Marie de Capesterre and the Hindu temple.

Basse-Terre is a sub-tropical volcanically active island, widely recognized as one of the most spectacular rainforests in the West Indies. It is the larger of the two main islands of Guadeloupe, separated from Grande-Terre only by a narrow sea channel, the Rivière Salée. It is 848 sq km (372 sq mi) in area with 180 km (112 mi) of coastline and is covered in dense sub-tropical forest of 170 sq km (56 sq mi) with over 300 km (185 mi) of paths running through it.

The island has been shaped by 4 million years of volcanic activity, leading to the formation of La Soufrière, the tallest mountain in the Lesser Antilles 4813 ft (1467 m), about 250,000 years ago. La Soufrière is still an active volcano today. The stark silhouette of its truncated cone dominates the island. From a distance, the jagged rock formations make it look as though its peak has been roughly hacked off. Close up, the bare blackened volcano top is dotted with sulphurous vents and naturally heated mineral bathing springs. Then the rainforest, full of flowers all year round, including orchids, bougainvillea, alamanda, hibiscus and lilies, and teeming with rivers and waterfalls, plunges steeply down to beaches of red or black sand. There are over 3,000 tree and plant species and thousands of colourful birds and butterflies. At higher altitudes there are wild pineapple trees, mosses and lichens.

La Soufrière has erupted six times in the last 350 years, most recently in 1976-7 when 26 explosions took place over a period of eight months and the island was evacuated. Werner Herzog made a film, *La Soufrière*, about three remaining peasants who refused to abandon their homes on the slopes of the volcano. He described the experience as "an inevitable catastrophe that didn't take place".

La Cascade aux Ecrevisses (Crayfish Waterfall) in the National Park of the Basse Terre region.

Hell

Ironshore rock formations at Hell

Located near West Bay, in Grand Cayman, Hell is an extraordinary field of ancient black rock, around 1.5 million years old and about half the size of a football pitch. Although it looks volcanic, it is in fact what is known as "ironshore" – a spiky, porous combination of dolomite and limestone. This is a common enough rock, both on the Caymans and elsewhere, but it is extremely rare to find it in such a dramatic form.

The stone is naturally white but has become gradually discoloured by acid-secreting algae, which have darkened and eroded the surface of the rock to form blackened, craggy shapes with sharp jagged edges. At first sight, the field gives the impression of the charred remains of a huge fire. This "hellfire" appearance is one of the possible explanations for the site's name. Another is that a visiting dignitary, on being shown around this strange place, exclaimed: "This is what hell must look like"; and the name stuck.

Hell is a major tourist attraction. There are so many visitors that they have had to be banned from walking around in the rock field itself and are restricted to viewing it from two large purpose-built platforms. There is a small community near the field and in 1962 a district post office was opened to accommodate innumerable requests from tourists that they should be able to send cards from the site, postmarked "Hell".

WHAT IS IT?
Rock formation.
HOW TO GET THERE:
Scheduled flights to Owen Roberts International Airport, Grand Cayman.
WHEN TO GO:
All year. March and April are the driest months.
NEAREST TOWN:
West Bay
DON'T MISS:
Cayman Turtle Farm.

93

Seven Mile Beach

WHAT IS IT?
Coral-sand beach.
HOW TO GET THERE:
Scheduled flights to Owen Roberts
International Airport.
WHEN TO GO:
All year but the drier months of
December to April are high season
NEAREST TOWN:
George Town
DON'T MISS:
Snorkelling in Stingray City.
YOU SHOULD KNOW:
The area around the beach was
severely damaged by Hurricane Ivan
in September 2004. The
infrastructure has now been more or
less fully repaired, but you may still
see some traces of the devastation.

Seven Mile Beach is a crescent of immaculate coral-sand beach running along the western shore of Grand Cayman, the largest of the three Cayman Islands. The beach is world-renowned for its translucent aquamarine water, huge expanse of fine white sand, glorious sunsets, scented air from the Australian pines that grow in the hinterland and an ideal average winter temperature of 27°C (81°F). Not surprisingly, it recently received an award for being the "Caribbean's Best Beach".

Although a consequence of its outstanding natural beauty is that it has become the most developed part of the island, this has its advantages in that there is something here to suit all tastes in the way of bars, restaurants, hotels and entertainment. There are extremely strict environmental laws to prevent the beach from being ruined by building development and it is so spacious that it feels remarkably uncrowded.

Seven Mile belies its name, being in fact only 5.5 miles (9 km) long and becoming progressively smaller due to constant erosion by the sea. However, it feels endless as you walk along this outstandingly beautiful stretch of shore, especially in the evenings when you can watch an amazing orange sun going down over the sparkling ocean, reflecting its colours in the darkening water. The whole beach is public property and you can walk its entire length unhindered. It has a completely relaxed atmosphere with few restrictions on behaviour; only nudity is forbidden. The unpolluted clear sea is superb for both swimming and snorkelling with many off-shore reefs to explore, teeming with radiant tropical fish among the corals. Seven Mile is the epitome of the ideal beach holiday.

Seven Mile Beach

Mount Pelée

Mount Pelée ("Bald Mountain") is an active volcano on the island of Martinique, 24 km (15 mi) northwest of the capital, Fort-De-France. It is part of the curved volcano chain of the Lesser Antilles that stretches 700 km (530 mi) from Puerto Rico to Venezuela. Mount Pelée towers over the island at a height of 1,397 m (4,583 ft) and its ravined slopes sustain a magnificent tropical rainforest.

Analysis of deposits has shown that more than 30 major eruptions have taken place in the past 5,000 years, making it one of the world's most dangerous volcanoes. The original Carib inhabitants of the island called it "Fire Mountain" (accurately, as it turned out) but it was renamed by French settlers, who were struck by its barren cone, composed of hardened volcanic ash and lava, which stood out in such contrast to the luxuriant vegetation and flowers covering the rest of the island.

The residents of Martinique lived in their tropical paradise for over 200 years unperturbed by odd minor eruptions. Nobody foresaw the terrible tragedy of 8 May 1902 when suddenly, after weeks of rumbling, a cloud of superheated gas, ash and rock shot down the mountainside at 160 kph (100 mph). It literally vapourized the colonial city of Saint Pierre, killing around 30,000 people in less than two minutes. There were only two known survivors, one of them a local villain who had been imprisoned and was protected by the thick walls of his cell. Saint Pierre, "The Paris of the Caribbean", never regained its former status as the cultural and commercial capital of the French West Indies.

Today an apparently docile Mount Pelée stands quietly over the town of Saint Pierre and the beautiful Martinique countryside. However, it could re-awaken at any time and is under constant watch by volcanologists.

View of Mount Pelée.

WHAT IS IT?
An active volcano.
HOW TO GET THERE:
Fly to Lamentin International Airport, 10 minutes drive from Fort-de-France, or ferries and catamarans from St Lucia, Guadeloupe and Dominica.
WHEN TO GO:
Warm sunny weather all year. April is the driest month, September the wettest.
NEAREST TOWN:
Morne Rouge
DON'T MISS:
The Musée Vulcanologique and the ruins of the old theatre in Saint Pierre
YOU SHOULD KNOW:
Martinique was the birthplace of the Empress Josephine, Napoleon's wife.

Tobago Cays

WHAT IS IT?
Coral reef islands
HOW TO GET THERE:
Access by boat only. Powerboat from
Union Island.
WHEN TO GO:
December to May to avoid the
hurricane season.
NEAREST TOWN:
Clifton Harbour on Union Island
10 km (6 mi)
YOU SHOULD KNOW:
In the film *Pirates of the Caribbean*
Johnny Depp was marooned on one
of the beaches of the Tobago Cays.

Not to be confused with the island of Tobago, this cluster of five uninhabited islets in the Grenadines is straight out of Robinson Crusoe. The Tobago Cays are a 24-hectare (58 acres) desert island haven of palm trees, pure white sandy beaches and secret rocky coves, set in crystal-clear shallow water. All except one of the islands are enclosed within a huge Horseshoe Reef, about 3 km (2 mi) in diameter. They are renowned as a unique beauty spot and, despite their relative inaccessibility, have become the most popular anchorage of the Grenadines attracting around 70,000 visitors a year with some of the finest snorkelling and diving in the world.

On the seaward side of Horseshoe Reef, the deep ocean water is a dazzling emerald green, while the colours of the shallows (less than 4 m [13 ft] deep) it harbours are simply spectacular – enchanting shades of blues and aquamarines sparkle with shoals of iridescent coloured fish. The 18 m (60 ft) reef wall, glowing with sponges and corals and teeming with a myriad of sea creatures, is a hunting ground for barracuda, shark, and turtles.

The Tobago Cays have had a troubled history. From the seventeenth century onwards they passed through several families of private owners until eventually in 1999, after some fifteen years of negotiations, they were wrested from the hands of speculators and bought by the government to become the National Marine Park of St Vincent & the Grenadines. The mission of the park is to "protect, conserve and improve the natural resources of the Tobago Cays and to be a natural heritage for the children of St Vincent & the Grenadines, and for the children of the world".

Aerial view of the Tobago Cays group of islands near Union Island in St. Vincent and the Grenadines.

Mustique

The island of Mustique

This privately owned tropical island, the "Gem of the Caribbean", is renowned as a playground for the privileged. It is less well known that Mustique is a protected nature reserve and offshore conservation area of incredible beauty.

The 5 km (3 mi) long, 2 km (1¼ mi) wide island in the north of the Grenadines, was once used to cultivate sugar but was abandoned in the nineteenth century and allowed to revert to its natural state. The rolling hills, with panoramic views, are criss-crossed with nature trails. From a height of 150 m (495 ft) you descend through forested valleys to immaculate white coral-sand beaches and limpid turquoise water. The many sheltered coves around the island were once favourite hiding places for pirates and are a natural habitat for frogs, lizards, iguanas and crabs. The whole island is a profusion of flora and fauna. Even the island's airstrip is in a forest of bougainvillea and palm trees, with terns, herons, sandpipers, and frigate birds flying overhead. There are over 50 indigenous bird species including the Mangrove Cuckoo and Tropical Kingbird.

Mustique was once owned by Lord Glenconner, who famously gave a ten-acre plot of land to HRH Princess Margaret as a wedding present in 1960. Today the island is owned by the Mustique Company Ltd, a consortium of island homeowners set up specifically to protect the island from the ravages of property development. There are fewer than 100 villas, most of them available for rent, and only two hotels. Around 500 people live permanently on the island and, even at peak season, the island population is never more than about 1,300. A perfect balance has been struck, so that the island is habitable at the same time as retaining all its natural tranquil beauty.

WHAT IS IT?
A tropical island.
HOW TO GET THERE:
Daily direct scheduled flights from Barbados. Air shuttle and ferry service to and from St Vincent.
WHEN TO GO:
All year but January to May is peak tourist season.
NEAREST TOWN:
Kingstown on the island of St Vincent. 24 km (15mi)
DON'T MISS:
The wreck of The Antilles, a French liner that ran aground on the northern coast in 1971.
YOU SHOULD KNOW:
Mick Jagger, Kate Moss and Bill Gates are among the many celebrities who frequent the island.

97

Water flows over Concord Falls on Grenada's west coast in Saint John Parish.

Grenada's Waterfalls

WHAT IS IT?
Waterfalls in a volcanic landscape.
HOW TO GET THERE:
International flights to Point Salines Airport, about 5 km (3 mi) from St George's, the capital of Grenada. Regular local flights, cargo boats and catamarans several times a day between Grenada and Carriacou.
WHEN TO GO:
Year round balmy temperature, lowest between November and February. Rainy, hurricane season June to November. Driest months January to April.
NEAREST TOWN:
St George's.
DON'T MISS:
A day or two exploring St George's, Grenada's picturesque capital city, with its steep winding streets and colonial pastel-painted architecture. It is one of the prettiest places in the Caribbean. Visit Fort George for brilliant views over the whole area and try to spend a Saturday morning at the market.
YOU SHOULD KNOW:
The Grenadians are a serious and conservative people. It is disrespectful to them to dress inappropriately by wandering around town wearing beach gear, as they are busy working.

It is not the height or the grandeur of Grenada's waterfalls that make them so special. It is quite simply that they are nature at her best – idyllically beautiful spots in the rainforest, with pools of clear mountain water to swim and dive in, all set in a rugged environment of mountain slopes that sweep steeply down, through wild backwoods, plantations of sweetly-scented spice trees and carpets of wild lilies, to deserted coral beaches.

There are more than a dozen waterfalls scattered over this 34 km (21 mi) long "Isle of Spice" – each magnificent in its own way. The Royal Mount Carmel falls, which are the highest, cascade vertically down 21 m (70 ft), and have won an eco-tourism award. On the other side of the island are the three dramatic Concord Falls, with a crystal clear pool 6 m (20 ft) deep. Then there are the Seven Sisters, reached by trekking through a plantation of cocoa, nutmeg and banana trees into virgin rainforest. After about an hour, hot, tired and sweaty, you stumble upon the group of seven waterfalls. The water tumbles down terraces into limpid green pools where you can swim, examine the pond life, have a natural Jacuzzi, or just sit on the rocks, watched by gaudy-coloured birds and butterflies and even some of the island monkeys – imported from Africa 300 years ago. Nearby, if you explore the forest a bit further, is the hidden Honeymoon Falls – a secret gem.

There is a special kind of silence to be found in the rainforest, and then an indescribable thrill when you first hear the sound of a waterfall, followed by the irresistible urge to plunge into the clear forest pools and watch the mesmerizing torrent of water as it endlessly splashes down over the rocks – as close to paradise as it gets.

Shark Watching in the Bahamas

The Bahamas is one of the few places in the world that still provides a benign habitat for sharks. The sparklingly clean waters of The Bahama Banks are trenched with chasms plunging 4,000 m (13,000 ft) deep. This combination of precipitous drops and calm shallows, coral reefs and sandy shores, warmed by the Gulf Stream currents, creates a fabulous fish metropolis – and a superbly well-stocked snack bar for the sharks to gorge on. Meanwhile, the coastal inlets, mangrove swamps and lagoons are perfect breeding grounds, providing a safe nursery environment for newborn sharks to thrive in.

More than 40 species of shark can be found here, the Caribbean Reef shark (*Carcharhinus perezi*) being the most common. These 2-3 m (6.5-10 ft) long sharks hover around the reefs and can move at lightning speed with incredible agility. The sight of a dozen or so miraculously appearing, seemingly out of nowhere, may well be the most exhilarating underwater experience of your life.

Sharks, despite their reputation as "killing machines", are wary of humans and will not usually attack unless provoked. However, the growing popularity of shark watching is beginning to affect their natural behaviour. They have started to congregate around the dive areas, waiting for food. It does not take much imagination to see the potential for a feeding frenzy – when the sharks react to over-stimulation by attacking everything, including each other.

The tourist interest has proved a mixed blessing. It has raised awareness of the need for conservation. However, it inevitably leads to coastal development and pollution. The sharks are part of a delicate eco-system. There is a very real danger in the Bahamas that human interference will unbalance the marine environment as well as the coastal mangrove swamps, which are vital for the continued survival of the shark.

WHAT IS IT?
Marine habitat. Group of 700 islands and 2,500 cays surrounded by tropical waters.

HOW TO GET THERE:
International airports of Nassau and Freeport with connecting flights from major US cities.

WHEN TO GO:
November to April. The wet season lasts from May to October.

NEAREST TOWNS:
New Providence: Cable Beach; Nassau: Paradise Island; Grand Bahama: Freeport and Lucaya.

YOU SHOULD KNOW:
Sharks bite fewer people per year than New Yorkers, according to public health records. More than 73 million sharks are killed every year for their fins. A single live shark is worth as much as $200,000 in tourism revenue over its lifetime. Sharks are essential to preserve the ecological balance. Studies have shown that where sharks are a key species, if stocks are depleted the food chain is unbalanced and the reef is destroyed.

Tiger Shark (Galeocerda cuvier), *Northern Bahamas*

Exuma Cays

WHAT IS IT?
A coral island archipelago.
HOW TO GET THERE:
Fly from US or Nassau, or ferry from Nassau to Georgetown.
WHEN TO GO:
December to May, to avoid the hurricane season.
NEAREST TOWN:
Georgetown.
DON'T MISS:
Iguanas on Allen's Cay – one of the few places you can still see these prehistoric-looking but harmless creatures.
Thunderball Cave on Staniel Cay – this beautiful grotto was a location in the film *Thunderball*.

The Exuma Cays are a 150 km (90 mi) long chain of more than 360 cays and islands. Starting at Beacon Cay, 40 km (25mi) southeast of Nassau, they stretch southwards to the two main islands of the archipelago, Great Exuma and Little Exuma.

They are bounded on the west by the shallow waters and treacherous shifting sands of The Great Bahama Bank and on the east by the deep emerald green water of Exuma Sound, an undersea chasm whose sheer reef wall plummets hundreds of metres, with huge caverns and tunnels sheltering fish of all sorts and sizes. The Cays can only be explored by boat, which gives them a wonderful aura of remoteness and isolation even though they are only hours from civilization. They are sparsely populated, mainly by conch fishermen; the only sizeable settlement is Georgetown, on Great Exuma.

The Cays vary enormously in both size and terrain. Some are barely more than barren sandy chunks of reef; others are islands of densely vegetated rolling hills, with caves and grottos. Narrow channels of translucent aquamarine water, teeming with corals and tropical fish, run between them. The water visibility (25-45 m [80-145 ft]) and abundant marine life make them an outstanding place for diving and underwater photography.

The Exuma Cays Land and Sea Park, a no-fishing conservation area of 456 sq km (176 sq mi), contains 50,000 marine species. The Park is also a vital refuge for several rare iguana species, sea turtles, marine birds and an indigenous hutia. The Bahamas National Trust established the Park in 1959 with its headquarters on Warderick Wells Cay, 105 km (65 mi) southeast of Nassau. It is the oldest marine conservation park in the world.

The Caribbean Sea surf on a beach on the Bahamas' Exuma Cays

Pillory Beach, Grand Turk

The turquoise waters of Pillory Beach.

History has it that Christopher Columbus landed on Pillory Beach during his first Atlantic trip of 1492. Today, amazingly, the beach is still a completely unspoilt stretch of clean white sand bordering on a translucent turquoise sea.

Pillory Beach runs along the western shore of the island of Grand Turk, the administrative capital of the Turks and Caicos. Only eight of this group of 40 relatively undeveloped Caribbean islands are inhabited. They are encircled by the third largest coral reef system in the world, 100 km (65 mi) across and over 300 km (200 mi) long.

Some of the most impressive walls of coral in the Caribbean are to be found here, and the Turks and Caicos are well deserving of their reputation as superb diving territory. But Pillory Beach is considered by many to be the best spot of all. One of the world's greatest wall dives, the "Grand Canyon of the Caribbean" is a mere 300 m (1,000 ft) offshore and there are 15 dive sites within a ten-minute swim.

From the shallow waters of the beach, the reef shelf suddenly plunges 2,000 m (7,000 ft) into the Columbus Trench, a huge undersea passage that separates the Turks from the Caicos. The walls of this chasm are punctured with water chutes, caverns, ledges and tunnels, and the passage itself is crowded with a glorious assortment of brilliantly coloured marine life meandering through delicately tinted coral gardens. Apart from diving, sailing, snorkelling and deep-sea fishing, Pillory Beach is an idyllic place in which to unwind and watch for dolphins, or even an occasional humpbacked whale.

WHAT IS IT?
A coral reef.
HOW TO GET THERE:
Direct international flights to Providenciales (Turks and Caicos). Daily flights from there to Grand Turk.
NEAREST TOWN:
Cockburn Town 2 km (1¼ mi).
WHEN TO GO:
January to April, if you want to see the migration of the entire herd of 2,500 humpback whales. High season is December to June.
DON'T MISS:
The rare black coral garden.
YOU SHOULD KNOW:
The beach is part of a conservation area, the Columbus Landfall National Marine Park.

Pico Turquino

WHAT IS IT?
Mountainous tropical forest:
ecologically and historically significant.
HOW TO GET THERE:
Fly to Santiago de Cuba. Bus via
Bayamo to Buey Arriba (about 3 hours).
WHEN TO GO:
Not advisable in June to October
when weather conditions can be very
adverse.
NEAREST TOWN:
Bartolomé Masó, 35 km (22 mi)
DON'T MISS:
Marea del Portillo Beach; the islet of
Cayo Blanco; Las Yaguas waterfall.
YOU SHOULD KNOW:
Badly storm damaged by Hurricane
Emily in 2005. Tours through the park
must be with a guide.

*Palm trees dominate the
landscape near Turquino
mountain in Cuba's Sierra
Maestra mountain range.*

At 1,974 m (6475 ft) Pico Turquino is the highest peak in Cuba. It towers over the western edge of The Pico Turquino National Park, an isolated area of some 170 sq km (66 sq mi) in the Sierra Maestra.

This wildly rugged and remote mountain chain runs along the south coast of Cuba for 140 km (87 mi), only a little way inland from the sea, near the charming secluded beach resort of Marea del Portillo. Some of the most pristine mountain scenery in the entire Caribbean is here – rivers, forests, peaks and valleys of overwhelming beauty.

The area was virtually inaccessible until a road was built twenty years ago, and only a few indigenous subsistence farmers live here, as they always have done, in close harmony with nature. A huge variety of endemic plant life flourishes in the park as well as around 600 species of fauna, including unusual butterflies, more than 60 species of bird, and 30 different kinds of reptile.

Pico Turquino is just as important historically as it is ecologically. On the climb to its summit, you can visit La Comandancia de la Plata – the headquarters of the revolutionary movement, where Fidel Castro and his followers based themselves

in 1956. This National Monument is in an extraordinarily beautiful spot, deep in the forest, with nearby streams and springs of water. The cleverly concealed wooden structures of La Comandancia, which can only be reached on foot, are completely integrated into the surrounding landscape.

The Pico Turquino National Park is a fascinating place for anyone – whether you enjoy mountain trekking or bird watching, or are interested in ecology, history and culture, or simply love nature.

Desembarco del Granma National Park

Desembarco del Granma National Park is a land and sea conservation area of more than 325 sq km (125 sq mi), 64 sq km (25 sq mi) of it underwater. Here, on the southwest tip of Cuba, where Castro landed his forces to start the Revolution, are the spectacular Escalera de los Gigantes (Giants' Stair) – the largest and best-preserved marine limestone terrace system in the world.

Vertical cliffs descend dramatically, from a height of 360 m (1,180 ft) to a depth of 180 m (590 ft) under the sea, in a series of twenty steps – eight of them on land, twelve in the water. The steps are carpeted in lush vegetation both above and below the waterline. The deep-sea currents ensure that the water is immaculately clean, which makes for superb diving among the myriads of brightly coloured fish that inhabit the pristine coralline reefs and underwater caverns.

The rolling forested hills and ancient caves of the Park are equally unspoilt – a profusion of ferns and orchids grow in a practically virgin forest that teems with butterflies and birds. More than 500 plant species thrive here, around 60% of which are endemic. The Park is also a habitat for 13 mammal, 110 bird and 44 reptile species, including the Cuban Iguana (*Cyclura nubila nubile*), once widespread throughout the island but today almost vanished. There are also rare amphibians and molluscs living on the terraces. Fewer than 1,000 people live in the Park, most of them in the village of Cabo Cruz.

The Park contains numerous archaeological sites. You can explore miles of cave shafts full of remains of the ancient Taínu Indian culture, including ceremonial caves. The Park was designated a World Heritage Site in 1999 on the basis of its "outstanding universal value" and global significance, both ecologically and geomorphologically.

WHAT IS IT?
A karst marine and land terrace system.
HOW TO GET THERE:
Fly to Manzanillo or Santiago de Cuba then bus to Niquero.
WHEN TO GO:
Dry season: November to April. September/October is the hurricane season.
NEAREST TOWN:
Niquero 15 km ((10 mi) from Los Colorados.
DON'T MISS:
The hole of Morlotte, 77 m (253 ft) deep and 52 m (171 ft) wide, and The Fustete Cave, 5 km (3 mi) of galleries and rare plants.
YOU SHOULD KNOW:
You can follow the 22 km (14 mi) route between the mangrove swamps of Los Colorados, near Cabo Cruz, and the sugar cane plantations of Alegria de Pio that Fidel Castro and his band of 79 revolutionaries took when they disembarked from their yacht, Granma, on 2 December 1956.

Trafalgar Falls, two spectacular cascades that tumble 27 m (90 ft) from the lip of a gorge, in the Roseau Valley on the edge of Morne Trois Pitons National Park, a UNESCO World Heritage Site in southern Dominica.

Morne Trois Pitons National Park

The island of Dominica has the wildest and most diverse scenery of the entire Caribbean. In particular, the Morne Trois Pitons National Park, in the south of the island, has a truly astounding, uniquely varied landscape. The dramatic volcanic terrain of precipitous ridges and deeply-inclined valleys is blanketed in a vibrant jungle of mature, montane and elfin rainforest and is pitted with craters, fumaroles, hot water springs, waterfalls, lakes and the world's second largest "boiling lake" – all in an area of less than 7 sq km (3 sq mi).

Morne Trois Pitons, the "mountain of three peaks", is a relatively young 1,342 m (4,402 ft) high volcanic pile only 8 km (5 mi) from the sea. An eruption in the 1880s left the Valley of Desolation in its wake – a deeply cratered, starkly barren landscape of sulphurous vents, mud pots and hot springs, in striking contrast to the verdant rainforest surrounding it. Then there is the Boiling Lake, a 63 m (207 ft) wide flooded fumarole at an altitude of 760 m (2,500 ft). It is a truly spooky place. The lake emits low menacing growls and is veiled in a mist of volcanic vapour through which you can catch glimpses of the belching grey water spewing out bubbles. Higher up still, at 870 m (2,850 ft), is the Boeri Lake, a tranquil freshwater lake reminiscent of the Scottish Highlands.

The Park is a haven for wildlife including indigenous bats and lizards, innumerable butterflies and small mammals. At least half of Dominica's 175 bird species are to be found here, including two of the world's most endangered parrots, the Imperial and Red-Necked Amazons, known locally as the Sisserou and Jaco. In 1997, Morne Trois Pitons Park was recognized as a World Heritage Site for its outstanding scientific interest and scenic value.

WHAT IS IT?
Actively volcanic rainforest.
HOW TO GET THERE:
There are no international flights to Roseau, the capital of Dominica. Fly from nearby Caribbean islands to Canefield Airport near Roseau. A catamaran ferry service connects Roseau with Pointe-à-Pitre on Guadeloupe, Fort-de-France on Martinique, and Castries on St Lucia.
WHEN TO GO:
Tropical climate with temperatures above 20°C (68°F) most of the time. Best between February and May. Avoid the hurricane season July to November.
NEAREST TOWN:
Laudat, a 20-minute drive from Roseau.
DON'T MISS:
The Trafalgar Falls and The Emerald Pool.
YOU SHOULD KNOW:
Don't attempt to go to Boiling Lake or the top of Trois Pitons without a guide – the trails are difficult and can be dangerous.

Hummingbirds, Trinidad

The native Carib Indians called Trinidad the "The Land of the Hummingbirds". There is no better place to observe these tiny, feisty creatures. And, once you start watching them, it is impossible not to succumb to their charm. Their names alone – Blue-tailed Emerald, Ruby-Topaz, Black-throated Mango, Purple Honeycreeper, Golden-headed Manakin, and Blue-chinned Sapphire – are irresistible. As you watch them darting around like living jewels, you cannot help being captivated.

Hummingbirds can fly incredibly fast, up to 40 kph (25 mph), and in any direction – sideways, backwards and even upside-down – as well as hover in mid air, their wings humming with a beat of up to 80 times a second. They live on a diet of insects and flower nectar and have such fast metabolisms that they have to consume two to three times their weight in food every day. Each species' long pointed bill is specifically designed to penetrate deep into the throat of their favourite flower, so that they can drain the last drop of nectar.

Their intense iridescent colours are illusory. Really they are a dull green or brown; the selective refraction of light by a particular species' feathers tricks us into seeing them in paint box neon shades. Despite their fragile appearance, they are tough enough to survive in climates ranging from the Arizona desert to above the snow line in the Andes. And what they lack in size, they make up for in aggression levels – they have been known to attack birds of prey.

One of the best places to observe and photograph them is the Asa Wright Nature Centre – an 80-hectare (198 acre) nature reserve. It is not even necessary to walk anywhere – you can just sit and be seduced from the comfort of a balcony.

The white-necked jacobin is only one of many tropical bird species that live around the Asa Wright Nature Centre near Arima, Trinidad.

HOW TO GET THERE:
International flights and from other Caribbean islands to Piarco International Airport 23 km (14 mi) from Port-of-Spain.
WHEN TO GO:
Equable temperature all year. December to May are the driest months, June to August the wettest. Outside the hurricane belt so generally doesn't experience severe weather.
NEAREST TOWN:
Arima 11 km (7 mi) or Port-of-Spain 38 km (24 mi)
DON'T MISS:
Pitch Lake – an asphalt lake, one of only three in the world – in the southwest of the island.
YOU SHOULD KNOW:
Only visitors actually staying at Asa Wright Centre are allowed to wander around alone. Day-trippers are escorted in a group. Apart from buses and private taxis, you can get round the island in a maxi taxi – a minibus carrying up to 25 people with set routes and standardized fares.

Pitch Lake, Trinidad

WHAT IS IT?
An asphalt lake.
HOW TO GET THERE:
International flights, and local flights from other Caribbean islands to Piarco International Airport, 23 km (14 mi) from Port-of-Spain.
WHEN TO GO:
Equable temperature all year. December to May is the driest time, June to August the wettest. Outside the hurricane belt and generally not subject to severe weather conditions.
NEAREST TOWN:
La Brea, 88 km(55 mi) from Port-of-Spain.
YOU SHOULD KNOW:
Pitch Lake is thought to be about 75 m (245 ft) deep and is one of only three natural asphalt lakes in the world – the others being in California and Venezuela.

A perverse joke of nature can be found in southwest Trinidad. Here, in the middle of an idyllic tropical scene, where kingfishers and hummingbirds flit around the wild fruit trees and herons calmly wander among the water lilies, there is a foul stench. It comes from a travesty of a lake – 40 hectares (99 acres) of sulphurous, hissing and occasionally fire-spitting asphalt.

Nobody can really explain how it was formed. Scientists think that large oil deposits must have seeped into an area of muddy clay and somehow been compressed into an emulsion of oil, clay and water, from which the volatile parts of the oil evaporated, leaving a tarry asphalt (pitch) residue. Narrow streams of it still seep out from underground, damaging nearby roads and buildings. But it is also a valuable resource – the asphalt is mined, refined and exported.

Pitch Lake is mostly sound enough to walk on, except for a small area in the middle, "the mother of the lake", where what looks like solid surface could swallow you up. The lake is gouged with troughs, as deep as 1.5 m (5 ft), which exude sulphur and collect rainwater. People regularly bathe here, believing that the sulphur water eases their rheumatism. Many ancient artefacts and fossil remains, including a mastodon's tooth and a 4,000 year-old tree have been found in the asphalt.

The Amerindians believed the lake was punishment from the heavens. The local tribe is said to have celebrated a great victory by feasting on hummingbirds, even though they knew perfectly well that these birds were the spirits of their ancestors. The winged god was so angry that he tore open the earth and drowned the whole village. For the Indians, Pitch Lake was a symbol of emptiness. For today's inhabitants, it is money.

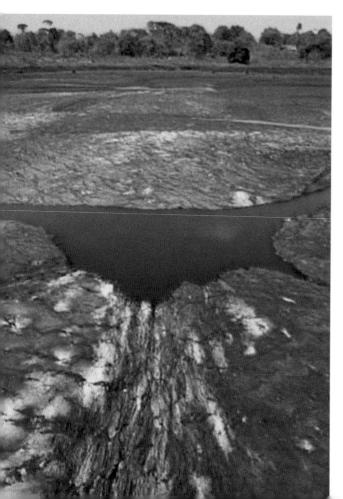

Pitch Lake

Pico Duarte

The 60 million-year-old Cordillera Central is a huge mountain range on the island of Hispaniola. The mountains rise in Haiti and cut across the border deep into the Dominican Republic. They are the highest and most beautiful mountains of the Caribbean. And Pico Duarte is the tallest peak of them all – although its exact height is a matter of continuing debate; it is usually recorded as being 3,175 m (10,414 ft) but recent measurements have reduced it to 3,087 m (10,125 ft). Still, it is an impressive size.

Pico Duarte straddles the boundary between the Armando Bermudez and José del Carmen Ramirez National Parks, a protected area of 795 sq km (306 sq mi). Pico Duarte's peak is only a few metres taller than that of her sister mountain, La Pelona. These twin peaks are separated only by a beautiful high meadow pass of tussock-grass, the Valle de Lilis, which, in the early mornings, glistens with a thin layer of frost.

The 23-km (14 mi) trek up the mountain is packed with adventure: fording clear mountain rivers and hacking your way through dense rainforest of palms, ferns, wild avocado, banana and banyan trees, full of small animals, as well as the occasional wild boar, and surrounded by exotic birds, including the Dominican Republic's emblematic Cigua Palmera (Hispaniolan Palm Crow) and the Hispaniolan Parrot. At higher levels you emerge from the rainforest to find yourself in the heady scented air of a Hispaniolan Pine wood as you approach Aguita Fria, the headwaters of the two longest rivers in the Dominican Republic – Yaque del Norte and Yaque del Sur. From here, there are breathtaking views of Quisqueya (the "mother of all lands" in Taino Indian). Many Dominicans regard the ascent of this myth-laden mountain as an essential rite of passage.

WHAT IS IT?
A mountain peak.
HOW TO GET THERE:
Santa Domingo, Santiago and Puerto Plata all have international airports. Direct flights from Europe and the Americas. Land crossing from Haiti.
WHEN TO GO:
Dominican Republic has temperatures of 28-31°C (82-88°F) all year round. In the mountains the highest temperature is 24°C (75°F) and generally fluctuates between 12°C and 21°C (53°F and 70°F). It can be very cold in the early mornings, 0°C (32°F) or below. December to March is the drier time so best for climbing.
NEAREST TOWN:
Santa Domingo (then bus to Jaracoboa – about 35 km (22 mi) from trailhead)
YOU SHOULD KNOW:
Park permits are required and you are not allowed to go without a guide. Camping is allowed but campers are asked to use pre-existing campsites and fire-rings and, of course, to clear up their litter. Even though there are huts along the standard routes, you will probably be more comfortable in your own tent.
It is a good idea to take water purifying tablets or a filter if you are going to drink the mountain water.

Established in 1956, this was the first national park in the Dominican Republic. It contains the 3,087 m (10,128 ft) tall Pico Duarte, the highest mountain in the Caribbean.

Barrier Reefs, Belize

Barrier reefs surrounding the Blue Hole

As you approach Belize from the air, you will see an unbroken line of white surf. A gigantic breakwater cleaves a 250 km (156 mi) long path through the sea, splitting the clear turquoise coastal waters from a dazzling royal blue ocean. This is the longest barrier reef in the Western Hemisphere. It is also one of the most diverse reef formations in the world. Apart from the Barrier Reef itself, there are fringing reefs along the coast and three atoll reefs, as well as sea grass beds and mangroves in the coastal wetlands, altogether creating diverse ecosystems for an abundance of wildlife.

Divers will witness a fabulous array of marine life – rainbow tinged tropical fish, sea fans, mauve and purple sponges and golden red coral gardens. Around the atolls and outside the reef, where the seabed drops sharply to depths of 3,000 m (10,000 ft), there are numerous big fish – stingrays, nurse and whale sharks, tuna, marlin – and dolphins. The most popular diving area is off the 40 km (25 mi) long Ambergris Caye, the largest of some 200 cayes that dot the coastline of Belize. The reef here is less than 2 km (1 mi) offshore and part of it is a conservation area with nesting grounds for three endangered species of sea turtle.

The Belize Reef is particularly species rich as it is one of the last places in the world with extensive areas of almost pristine reef, much of it as yet unexplored – so far around 350 fish and 65 coral species have been documented and it is expected that many more are waiting to be discovered. It is also a habitat for 200 kinds of bird, including hummingbirds, parakeets, blue herons and egrets. The reef was designated a World Heritage Site in 1996.

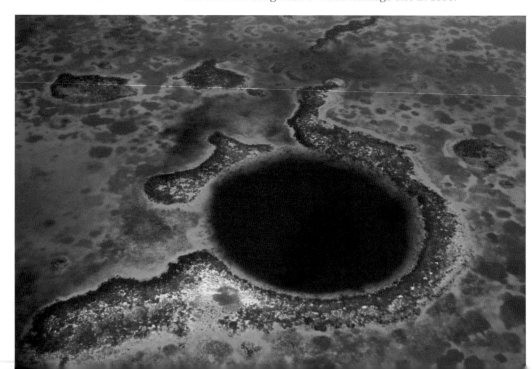

Mosquitia

The Mosquitia wilderness

The Mosquitia is a wilderness in the remote eastern corner of Honduras. Bounded by the mountains of Río Plátano to the west and Río Coco to the south, it is a vast region, about a fifth of the total area of Honduras, covering 84,000 sq km (32,000 sq mi) of incredible ecological diversity – coastal swamp, lagoons, tropical rainforest, rapids and mountain savannah.

Only the adventurous traveller should set out to explore the Mosquitia; you really are off the beaten track – there are no roads into the region – with extremely basic accommodation and food. You go everywhere by river in traditional dugout canoes or on rafts, and walk along narrow jungle trails. Every bend in the river brings some astounding new impression, and travelling here is an overwhelming sensory experience of vivid colours, strange sounds and tropical scents.

There are five separate reserves in the Mosquitia. The area around the Río Plátano, an extensive swathe of almost pristine tropical rainforest, is a World Heritage Biosphere Reserve. It was listed as endangered in 1996 in an attempt to keep intact one of the most valuable tracts of primary tropical forest left in Central America. In the basin of Río Plátano, the tropical forest looks much as it must have done at the dawn of time, yet the petroglyphs on huge boulders attest to an ancient civilization. People have inhabited this region for at least 3,000 years and there is a pervasive legend of a fabulous lost city, Ciudad Blanca.

The Mosquitia is inhabited by Amerindians and there is a serene harmony between the people, their animals and nature. However traditional methods of subsistence farming cannot satisfy population demands and the economic pressures from the outside world. The Amerindians' precious way of life is seriously endangered as their land is increasingly raided for its resources.

WHAT IS IT?
A diverse tropical wilderness with indigenous culture.
WHEN TO GO:
The temperature is a constant 25-28°C (77-82°F) but can fluctuate near the ocean. December to April and August to September are the dry seasons and the best time to visit. Hurricane season is June to November.
HOW TO GET THERE:
International flights to La Ceiba or Tegucigalpa and then connecting flight to Puerto Lempira or Palacios.
NEAREST TOWNS:
The regional capital is Puerto Lempira. You can access the Biosphere Reserve from Palacios and Brus Laguna.
DON'T MISS:
The Plaplaya turtle project, to protect the endangered giant leatherbacks, the largest species in the world reaching up to 3m (10 ft) in length and 900 kg in weight. A 3-hour walk from Plaplaya to Raistá, where there is a butterfly farm which breeds and exports rare species.
YOU SHOULD KNOW:
A film called *The Mosquito Coast* – based on a novel by Paul Theroux – starred River Phoenix and Harrison Ford. It is the story of an American family making a new life for themselves in the Honduran Mosquitia.

Cocos Island

Cocos is an uninhabited treasure island of 24 sq km (9 sq mi) in the Eastern Pacific Ocean, 550 km (344 mi) off the coast of Costa Rica. It has been described as "the most beautiful island in the world" and was the inspiration for the film *Jurassic Park*.

The island is composed of 2 million year old volcanic rock, draped in misty primeval rainforest, and scored with ravines and waterfalls. Treacherous 600 m (1,970 ft) high cliffs, whose sheer walls plunge deep underwater, are riddled with secret caves. The coastline is so precipitous that the only safe landing places are two small bays, separated by a ridge. The island was discovered in 1526, first appeared on a world map in 1542, and soon became legendary as a pirate stash for stolen gold. The treasure from the *Mary Deare* is supposed to have been buried here by Captain Thompson in 1821. Over the years at least 300 expeditions have been mounted in search of lost pirate bounty, and even now people have not given up hope of stumbling across a hoard of bullion in one of the innumerable coastal caves or jungle ravines.

Today, Cocos Island has become just as legendary for its fish – the "truck stop" of the Pacific, a Marine World Heritage Site with one of the richest concentrations of pelagic species in the world. It has a perfect marine environment – a pollution-free, no-fishing zone at a crossing point of currents and counter-currents – for every sort of fish, from tiny baitfish to huge whale sharks. Diving here is an unforgettable experience – like falling into a fish tank, full of literally hundreds of hammerhead and white-tip sharks, mantas, rays, tuna, bottlenose dolphins, green sea turtles, whale sharks and even humpback whales.

Silhouetted school of whitetip reef sharks swim off Costa Rica's Cocos Island.

WHAT IS IT?
A World Heritage Marine Park.
WHEN TO GO:
Hot and humid all year round. Diving is best between March and December.
HOW TO GET THERE:
Fly to San José, Costa Rica. Then go by pre-arranged tour boat for a ten-day trip.
YOU SHOULD KNOW:
You can only go on an organized seasonal diving trip and with the permission of the island rangers. You are not permitted to camp or sleep on the island.

La Amistad National Park

La Amistad ("Friendship") is part of a cooperative Central American conservation project to create one continuous forest corridor from Mexico to Panama – an attempt to preserve the remains of a region in which 80 per cent of natural habitats have been destroyed.

The Park has a core zone of almost 6,000 sq km (2,300 sq mi) of pristine tropical rainforest in the ancient granite Cordillera de Talamanca – a vital watershed between the Pacific and Caribbean coasts containing the highest peaks of each country: Cerro Chirripó 3,819 m (12,526 ft) in Costa Rica, and Volcan Barú 3,475 m (11,398 ft) in Panama. The 25,000-year-old virgin rainforest is home to four Amerindian tribes – more than three quarters of Costa Rica's indigenous inhabitants.

There is an incredible diversity of species here, at the junction of North and South America. Tens of thousands of different kinds of plants flourish in the various life zones, which range from sea level mangrove habitats and lowland rainforest to montane forest and sub-alpine ecosystems. There is an area of virgin oak woodland containing seven species of oak (*Quercus*) and there are around 400 bird species and 260 sorts of reptile and amphibian. It is a habitat for Baird's tapirs, coatis, and howler, spider and capuchin monkeys as well as being one of the last refuges of the Central American wildcats – ocelot, tiger cat, jaguar and puma.

The Costa Rican side of the park is relatively inaccessible and only partially explored. There are no paved roads so you must travel on foot or horse. It is much easier to explore the park from the Panama side, but whichever route you choose, it is an amazing place for forest adventure, mountain hikes, riding, fishing and bird watching in multivarious environments of outstanding natural beauty.

WHAT IS IT?
A diverse tropical wilderness.
HOW TO GET THERE:
There are several routes.
From Costa Rica: Bus from San José to San Vito.
Or drive from San José to San Isidro el General 153 km [92 mi]
From Panama: Fly or drive to David, then an hour's drive to Cerro Punta and another 5km (3 mi) to Las Nubes (Amistad Administrative Centre).
Or fly to Changuinola then an hour's drive to El Silencio and boat trip to Bocas del Toro (Amistad Administrative Centre).
WHEN TO GO:
Caribbean side: hot and wet all year.
Pacific side: dry season, December to April. The temperature varies according to altitude.
NEAREST TOWN:
Costa Rica: San Isidro el General 25 km (15 mi); Panama: Cerro Punta 5 km (3 mi)
YOU SHOULD KNOW:
Much of the park has never been explored and it would be foolish to go very far without a guide. The park has entrance stations (puestos) where you pay a fee and pick up a map. Camping is allowed at Estacion Altimira and at Estacion Las Tablas but there is no lodging anywhere in the park. Much of the area is 2,000 m (6,560 ft) above sea level so be prepared for altitude.

La Amistad National Park

Darién National Park

WHAT IS IT?
A diverse tropical wilderness with indigenous culture.

HOW TO GET THERE:
Fly to Tocumen International Airport, Panama City. (This is the only airport that maintains international security). By land: direct buses from San José (Costa Rica) to Panama City. Fly (or by road and boat via Yaviza) to El Réal de Santa Maria 325 km (203 mi) from Panama City).

WHEN TO GO:
Anytime. Tropical climate with temperature changing according to altitude not season. Two seasons: verano (dry season) December to April, invierno (rainy season) May to December.

NEAREST TOWN:
El Réal de Santa Maria (about 30 minutes by boat from Yaviza) houses the administrative headquarters of the park.

DON'T MISS:
The Cana area in the middle of the park. The overgrown remains of the famous Esperitú Santo Gold Mines are here – one of the ten most important places in the world for bird watching.

YOU SHOULD KNOW:
You need permission to enter the park and can lodge there at one of the ranger stations. You should check embassy advice as to whether the region is safe. The security situation changes frequently.

As you drive south from Panama City, the road comes to an abrupt halt 100 km (60 mi) from the Colombian border. You have reached the Darién Gap – a hiccup in the Pan-American Highway, the only missing bit in the 25,000 km (16,000 mi) of road that connects Alaska with Argentina. This impenetrable rainforest frontier is one of the most beautiful yet dangerous regions in the world – a haven for renegades, guerrillas, adventurers and drug traffickers.

Darién National Park, a UNESCO Biosphere Reserve, is a vast 5,800 sq km (2,240 sq mi) expanse of wilderness stretching the length of Panama's border. It is the largest tract of undeveloped land in Central America, encompassing diverse terrain. It rises from the rocky beaches of the Pacific, through lowland and upland rainforest crisscrossed with rivers, and rugged mountains wreathed in cloud forest, to culminate at Cerro Tacarcuna, a 1,845 m (6,050 ft) high peak only a few kilometres from the Caribbean.

The Park's strategic geographical position, bridging North and South America, makes it a melting pot for plants and wildlife of both continents. There are 2,500 plant species here as well as countless birds, animals, and river fish. The indigenous mammals include peccaries, tapirs, and the forest fox (*Marmosops invictus*) as well as pumas, jaguars, and ocelots. Among the 533 bird species is the harpy eagle, the most powerful bird of prey in the world.

Amerindian tribes – the Emberà warrior society, Wounaan artisans, who decorate their bodies with intricate black-ink geometrical designs, and Kuna fishermen – still live here, preserving their ancient culture in harmony with their environment. Darién is one of their last remaining enclaves. And as long as the road remains unbuilt, the Darién rainforest has a chance of staying unspoilt.

Trees in the clouds in Darién National Park

El Yunque

The Caribbean National Forest is the oldest nature reserve in the Western Hemisphere and is renowned for its primeval atmosphere and remarkable biodiversity.

Known as El Yunque, after the most important mountain in the Sierra de Luquillo, south east of San Juan, it is a relatively small subtropical rain forest, covering an area of 1,125 sq km (434 sq mi). The land was originally given protected status by King Alfonso XII of Spain in 1876, his aim being to prevent his enemies taking wood from the forest for building boats. Today it is administered by the US Forest Service as part of the US National Forest System.

El Yunque is composed of four distinct vegetation types according to altitude: tabonuco, palo colorado, palma sierra and finally, at heights above 750 m (2,460 ft), the extraordinary dwarf or "cloud forest" in which distorted trees, twisted into strange shapes by the wind, are shrouded in permanent mist.

A wide variety of plants thrive in the warm, wet environment. It rains almost every day, sometimes several times; in a year, the equivalent of 100 billion gallons of water flows down the mountainsides in cascading rivers and waterfalls. This abundance of water creates a benign habitat for over 240 tree and plant species, 26 of which are unique. There are 50 species of native orchid as well as tree vines, mosses, lichens, giant ferns and epiphytes. Rare wildlife includes the distinctive blue, green and red Puerto Rican parrot (*Amazonia vittata*), one of the ten most endangered species in the world, as well as the endangered Puerto Rican boa constrictor. The forest is also home to 13 species of *coqui* or tree frog, known for its distinctive sound, together with bats, lizards and 50 bird species.

Bromeliads in the rainforest

WHAT IS IT?
A subtropical rainforest.
HOW TO GET THERE:
Scheduled international flights to San Juan.
WHEN TO GO:
All year. High season: December to April. Hurricane season: May to November (especially intense August to October).
NEAREST TOWN:
San Juan 40 km (25 mi)
DON'T MISS:
El Portal Rainforest Centre, Luquillo Beach.

Roraima

WHAT IS IT?
A table mountain (tepui).
HOW TO GET THERE:
There are no flights direct from Caracas. Fly to Ciudad Bolivar and then fly to Santa Elena de Uairén, or go by road across Gran Sabana from Puerto Ordaz.
WHEN TO GO:
Climbing is easier in the dry season between December and April. However, the weather is always changeable and, if you are intending to visit Angel Falls as well, the waterfall is far more spectacular in the rainy months of June to October.
NEAREST TOWN:
Santa Elena de Uairén (2 hours from Paraitepui, where you start your climb).
DON'T MISS:
The endemic black toad that lives here, which curls itself up into a ball when you approach.

A trip to Roraima, the highest of the extraordinary Venezuelan table mountains or tepuis, is a truly memorable experience. You will find yourself transported to a surreal primeval world full of rare endemic species, in which all sense of time and scale is distorted. Roraima's ancient Precambrian sandstone rock towers 2,810 m (9,220 ft) high, rising abruptly out of the jungle at the furthest tip of Canaima National Park, marking the point where the boundaries of Venezuela, Brazil and Guyana meet. It is part of a World Heritage site, treasured not only for its breathtaking scenery but its unique plant and animal life.

A trek up Roraima starts in a long stretch of savanna meadowland alive with brightly coloured birds by day, and hundreds of fireflies flashing at night. You ford one or two rivers and then make your way up through jungle-covered misty slopes, full of hummingbirds and flowers, always under the awe-inspiring shadow of Roraima's sheer walls. Finally, you reach a spectacular 400 m (1,312 ft) cliff of quartzite and find yourself in a cloud forest of ferns and prehistoric looking vegetation. You really could be on another planet. This is a world of strange valleys, the ground under your feet carpeted in quartz crystals, gorges with fissures tens of metres deep, swirling mists which suddenly clear to reveal incredible views, bizarre rock amphitheatres clothed with strange lichens and mosses, apparently stark rock outcrops suddenly revealing amazing lush meadows, bathing pools with fairy gardens of strange flora and fauna, caverns, rivers and waterfalls.

Tributaries to three of the continent's greatest rivers – the Orinoco, Amazon and Essequibo – rise in this unbelievable place. According to Pemón Indian legend, Roraima is the "mother of all waters", and the home of the goddess Kuín, "the grandmother of all men".

An aerial view shows Roraima Mountain at Canaima National Park. World Heritage Canaima National Park, in southeastern Venezuela, is one of the ancient geological formations with tepuis, flat-topped mountains, that inspired Conan Doyle to write The Lost World.

Angel Falls

Salto Ángel, on the Rio Churun, is the world's highest waterfall, 16 times the height of Niagara. It is the most famous feature in the 30,000 sq km (11,580 sq mi) Canaima National Park, in the Gran Sabana of south east Venezuela. The waterfall plummets 979 m (3,211 ft) from the top of Auyan tepui (Roaring Mountain) freefalling 807 m (2,648 ft) into the impenetrable jungle of the Cañon del Diablo (Devil's Canyon) below.

Canaima National Park is in an extraordinary savanna region of huge primeval, sandstone tepuis (flat-topped mountains or mesas) formed billions of years ago, crossed by broad rivers with their sides swathed in rainforest. The top of Auyan tepui is an intricate maze of jagged sandstone, weathered into weird rock formations that are inundated with holes and caves. Giant monoliths of rock lie across each other at crazed gravity-defying angles, and below, in the Cañon del Diablo, is a dense rainforest full of wildlife, including monkeys, pumas, giant anteaters, and porcupines.

There are no land trails through the forest; to reach Angel Falls, you must take a canoe upriver, negotiating rocks and rapids, and then hike for an hour up the mountain to a rocky outcrop. From here, you get a magnificent view of Río Churun taking off from the mountain top, straight over a precipice in an incredible cascade of water as it crashes down into the canyon in a swirling mist of spray.

Angel Falls gets its name from an American adventurer – Jimmy Angel – who crash-landed his plane here in 1937. Before his discovery of the falls, the local inhabitants, the Pemón Indians, called them Kerapukai-meru, "Fall of the Deepest Place". They believed that evil soul-stealing spirits lurked in the mysterious water vapour mists that swirl around the top of the tepui.

Angel Falls, the world's highest uninterrupted falls, descends through the clouds, dropping 979 m (3,212 ft) from a high cliff in Venezela's Canaima National Park.

WHAT IS IT?
Plunge Waterfall
HOW TO GET THERE:
Fly to Caracas or Ciudad Bolivar. Daily flights via Puerto Ordaz to Canaima. From here go by plane or boat.
WHEN TO GO:
Best in the wet season, June to October. In the dry season the river level can become low, reducing the waterfall to a dribble.
NEAREST TOWN:
Canaima. 50 km (31 mi)
DON'T MISS:

*A Manta Ray (*Manta birostris*), swimming with a school of fish, off Malpelo Island.*

Isla de Malpelo

WHAT IS IT?
A marine ecosystem
HOW TO GET THERE:
International flight to Bogota and connecting flight to Buenaventura. 8-day tours are run from Buenaventura.
WHEN TO GO:
Maritime wet tropical climate with average temperature of 28ºC (82ºF) all year. December to May: northern winds bring calm cold water and clear skies. May to November: the Equatorial Counter-Current brings rain and warmer water rich in plankton.
YOU SHOULD KNOW:
You must have an open water diving pass and should be a relaxed drift diver in the presence of sharks. You can only go on an escorted tour and must obtain a permit from the Colombian Ministry for Ecology.

The Isla de Malpelo is a 350-hectare lump of sheer basalt rock that sticks incongruously out of the Pacific Ocean like some giant prehistoric monolith. It is the highest peak of a "hot spot" in the oceanic crust, a 240 km (150 mi) long undersea volcanic ridge, 500 km (314 mi) off Colombia's Pacific coast. Malpelo is tall enough, at 376 m (1,233 ft), to create its own weather system and in the mornings, however clear the sky, it is often mysteriously wreathed in cloud.

The weather's constant battering has eroded Malpelo into its dramatic shape. Precipitous cliffs, peaking some 376 m (1234 ft) above sea level, their vertical sides pitted with caves, plunge straight into the sea. The island looks like barren rock but, in fact, it is covered in algae, lichen and mosses, with a few scraggy shrubs and ferns. It is an important breeding ground for a huge bird colony of around 25,000 Masked Boobies.

The unpolluted waters of Malpelo and its surrounding rocks are amazingly clear, with visibility to 50 m (160 ft). Drift-diving here is one of the most memorable experiences you are ever likely to have. Powerful warm and cold ocean currents interact to create a unique habitat for a huge variety of marine life at all levels of the food chain. Here is the largest shark population in the world – schools of 500 hammerheads and hundreds of silkies are a common sight – as well as innumerable other large fish, 17 sorts of marine mammal, and a newly discovered deepwater shark – the Short-nosed Ragged-toothed Shark.

A small garrison of the Colombian army is stationed on Malpelo to guard an 8,575 sq km (3,310 sq mi) area of the ocean – a World Heritage Site and the largest no-fishing zone in the Eastern Tropical Pacific.

Sangay National Park

Sangay is over 5,000 sq km (1,930 sq mi) of contrasts and extremes – valleys and mountains; volcanoes and lagoons; forest and plains. This remote wilderness ranges in altitude from its low-lying Amazon Basin valleys, only 600 m (1,970 ft) above sea level, to towering snow-capped volcano peaks of over 5,000 m (16,400 ft). Here you will find the entire spectrum of ecosystems. At least nine life zones have been identified, from sub-arctic to tropical lowland forest. Sangay is extraordinary in that it sustains an incredible biodiversity (of at least 3,000 different species) at the same time as a high proportion of endemism (species unique to the area).

It is an area of outstanding natural beauty with 324 lagoons set in a rugged volcanic landscape, with three of the country's highest peaks – the snow-capped volcanoes of El Altar (inactive), Tungurahua, and Sangay itself 5,230m (17,154 ft) are surrounded by glacial valleys leading into the Amazonian lowlands.

Sangay is one of the world's most active volcanoes, continuously steaming and every so often angrily vomiting out glowing coals and hot rocks from its mouth.

The remoteness of this dramatic wilderness has enabled the survival of several endangered indigenous mammals – 28 kinds of large mammals have been documented so far, and there are probably more waiting to be discovered. These include the Andean fox, red howler monkey, and South American tapir as well as ocelots, pumas and porcupines. There are probably around 500 species of birds including the Andean condor and a giant hummingbird. A peculiar event takes place in the Lagoons of Osogoche and Atillo – every so often, for no known reason, hundreds of birds are attracted to the water and hurl themselves in to drown.

WHAT IS IT?
World Heritage Site Diverse Ecosystems
HOW TO GET THERE:
Fly to Quito. Road to Baños 120 km (75 mi) south of Quito.
WHEN TO GO:
The climate is variable with significant local differences. No well-defined wet or dry season – May to August tends to be wetter and October to January drier. Temperature varies dramatically from 24°C to 0°C (75°F to 32°F) and below according to altitude.
NEAREST TOWN:
Baños 70 km (44 mi). Best route into the park is via Riobamba to Aloa.
DON'T MISS:
The Pailón, near Palora – not actually in the park but very near by. Recommended for its scenic beauty and animals.
YOU SHOULD KNOW:
UNESCO has placed the park on its endangered list because of the attempted unplanned construction of a road through it. It is threatened by logging, over-grazing, poaching and uncontrolled tourism. Tungurahua has recently begun erupting again causing evacuation of nearby villages. News should be monitored before attempting to go there.

Lava flows from the Tungurahua volcano in Sangay National Park in central Ecuador.

Galápagos Islands

WHAT IS IT?
A stunning volcanic archipelago and one of the world's most important sites for conservation.
HOW TO GET THERE:
By air from Quito or Guayaquil
WHEN TO GO:
Any time of year.
NEAREST TOWN:
Guayalquil 1,000 km (620 mi)
DON'T MISS:
The colonies of nesting birds
YOU SHOULD KNOW:
Visitors to the islands must be accompanied by an accredited guide.

Ecuador's Galápagos Islands, a small archipelago straddling the Equator 965 km (600 mi) west of South America, are best known for being the site where Charles Darwin made the observations of the indigenous fauna that led him to develop his theory of evolution through natural selection. The group contains 13 main islands, 6 isles and 107 smaller rocks and islets, all of which are volcanic in origin.

On land, the land iguana and giant tortoises can be seen, and birds that nest here include masked, blue- and red-footed boobies, albatrosses, flightless cormorants, Galápagos flamingos, magnificent frigatebirds, Galápagos penguins and the buntings commonly called Darwin's finches. As well as an abundance of fish in the waters and among the reefs around the islands, the marine animals here include Galápagos sea lions, otters and marine iguanas.

Despite being a UNESCO World Heritage Site and marine reserve, these islands are under threat from a rapidly increasing population needing more resources, introduced species such as goats, cats and dogs and overfishing. The government of Ecuador has imposed strict controls on tourist access in order to prevent too many visitors destroying the very islands and wildlife that they come to see – a tour guide certified by the national park authority must accompany each group.

These spectacular but fragile islands, each with its own character, are a world treasure.

Green Sea Turtle (Chelonia mydas), *an endangered species, swimming underwater in the Galápagos Islands.*

Cotopaxí

The colossal snow-capped cone of the Cotopaxí volcano is an image that is etched into the Ecuadorian national psyche. It is revered as the world's highest active volcano and was once worshipped as a god by the native Andean Indians. It has a history of more than fifty eruptions in the last 300 years. The most famous was in 1877, when mudflows swept as far as the Pacific coast, 100 km (63 mi) away.

Cotopaxí rises out of a 3,800 m (12,465 ft) high grassland and forest plateau (páramo) to a peak of nearly 5,900 m (19,350 ft). Apart from being an active volcano, often spouting steam from its summit, it has one of the few equatorial glaciers in the world.

The Cotopaxi National Park is more than 330 sq km(127 sq mi) of páramo landscape that sustains over 2,000 species of flora and fauna. It has magnificently varied scenery with panoramic views and the chance to see wild horses, deer, llamas, Andean foxes, and even the rare Andean spectacled bears. The spectacular birdlife includes condors, eagles, falcons and exquisite hummingbirds.

The sub-Andean plains of the plateau are characterised by tough tussock grasses (pajonal) and hardy shrubs in which a multitude of butterflies, stick insects and grasshoppers flourish. Bright orange Chuquiragua flowers vie for your attention with brilliant yellow asteraceas and red and yellow ranunculus. Then there is humid high mountain forest around Lake Limpio Pungo, overlooked by snowy volcano peaks and home to Andean gulls, ducks, and lapwings. At even higher altitudes, of 4,400-4,700 m (14,430-15,415 ft), only lichen and moss tundra can survive. Finally, you ascend the glacier itself and arrive on top of the world at the Equator.

WHAT IS IT?
Glacier stratovolcano.
HOW TO GET THERE:
Fly to Quito, then take a train or drive 60 km (37.5 mi) south via Aloag, to Lasso.
WHEN TO GO:
The best climbing months are December and January followed by August and September.
NEAREST TOWN:
Lasso 5 km (3 mi)
YOU SHOULD KNOW:
You must spend a few days acclimatizing to the altitude. Cotopaxí is a 6-8 hour climb and although not technically difficult, it is arduous and requires some mountaineering experience.

Snow covers Ecuador's Cotopaxí volcano

Chapada dos Veadeiros

WHAT IS IT?
Tropical savanna (Cerrado)
HOW TO GET THERE:
By road from Brasilia via São Gabriel to Alto Paraiso 250 km (156mi) then along unpaved road to park entrance in the village of São Jorge.
WHEN TO GO:
All year, though the scenery is at its best between April and September.
NEAREST TOWN:
Alto Paraiso 37 km (23 mi)
DON'T MISS:
Valle da Lua (Valley of The Moon) and the Terra Ronca and São Domingos caves.
YOU SHOULD KNOW:
The luminosity of the landscape has attracted New Age acolytes. It is known as "The Capital of the Third Millennium" and is one of the ten most visited parks in Brazil.

The Chapada dos Veadeiros National Park is a spectacular 655 sq km (252 sq mi) area in the Cerrado – the vast tropical savanna region of Central Brazil. The park is a World Heritage Site of outstanding natural beauty, famous for the spectacular quality of its seasonal landscapes.

Beneath a panorama of huge changing skies, parched and yellow winter prairies are magically transformed by the summer rains into lush green meadows bursting with flowers. The high plains at 1,200 m (3,940 ft) above sea level are incised with deep rocky canyons, with some of the oldest rock formations on the planet, formed some 1.8 billion years ago. Viewed from space, the region emits a strange luminous glow due to the quantity of quartz crystals in the soil.

The Cerrado is one of the world's oldest and most diverse tropical ecosystems and is the richest savanna area on earth – with an estimated 10,000 species of plants, nearly half of which are endemic, it ranks with the Amazon in importance. Its "bushy savanna" is characterized by grassland plateaux with peculiar gnarled trees and cut by networks of thickly forested river valleys and depressions. It is a habitat for more than 900 species of birds, and around 300 mammals, including several endangered species: vultures, toucans, the giant anteater, deer, maned wolves, cerrado fox, tapirs and jaguars.

The Rio Preto flows through the park from the north west with several beautiful waterfalls and riverside forests of palm, cork, jacaranda and pepper trees. You can immerse yourself in nature as you walk, cycle, or climb through the breathtaking scenery.

The gallery forest, and a waterfall on the Preto River, Brazil.

Mouths of The Amazon & Amazon Bore

The Amazon estuary is so vast it is known as "the River Sea". It is a complex network of rivers and channels, which crisscross each other in a watery maze, merging with the estuary of the Araguari River. The river mouth is 330 km (206 mi) wide and, with water up to 90 m (295 ft) deep, is navigable for large ocean steamers all the way up to Manaus – 1500 km (940 mi) inland.

The Amazon basin drains an area of nearly 7 million sq km (2.7 million sq mi), 40 per cent of South America; a fifth of the freshwater entering the oceans of the world comes from its mouth. The outpouring of water is so vast that it dumps 3 million tons of sediment daily. Both the colour and salinity of the ocean are affected for a distance of about 320 km (200 mi) out to sea, and early explorers were amazed to find that they could drink the seawater long before they could see land.

The Amazon does not have a river delta. A belt of half-submerged islands and shallow sandbanks follows the coast for 160 km (100 mi) around the mouth, built up from the silt washed back by the Atlantic tides. Here the alarming seasonal phenomenon of the tidal bore, or *pororoca*, occurs. A wall of water, up to 4 m (13 ft) high, rolls upriver a distance of around 13 km (8 mi). As it gradually gathers a speed of up to 25 kph, it starts to emit a low growling sound which crescendos into a loud roar. This twice-daily dramatic occurrence attracts surfers from all over the world for, where a normal sea wave lasts for only about 15 seconds, a skilled surfer can ride the *pororoca* for up to 30 minutes. Surfing the *pororoca* is a particularly dangerous experience since, as the wave sweeps upstream, it rakes the river banks dragging trees, debris, snakes and alligators in its wake.

The 'Pororoca' tidal bore wave slices its way through the Amazon jungle on the Araguari river, in the Amazon basin of Brazil in the northern state of Amapa. The tidal bore phenomenon known locally as the Pororoca, *an indigenous word meaning 'Great Noise' or 'Destroyer' occurs at the tail end of the rainy season.*

WHAT IS IT?
An estuary and tidal bore.
HOW TO GET THERE:
Fly to Belém or Macapá.
WHEN TO GO:
The pororoca occurs during February and March.
NEAREST TOWN:
São Domingos do Capim.

Atol das Rocas, Brazil

Atlantic Islands (Atol das Rocas)

The remote archipelago of Fernando de Noronha and the Atol das Rocas are peaks of the South Atlantic submarine volcanic ridge sticking up above the surface of the ocean. These islands, and more than 420 sq km (160 sq mi) of the surrounding waters, are a World Heritage marine conservation site containing colonies of endangered turtles and dolphins as well as an abundance of fish and marine birds. The shelter of the islands, in unpolluted seas teeming with food, provides ideal breeding grounds for sharks, tuna, turtles and dolphins. They play a vital part in aiding the reproduction, dispersal and biodiversity of marine life through the Tropical South Atlantic.

Rocas, 100 km (60 mi) to the west of Noronha, is the only atoll in the South Atlantic. It is an almost closed coralline ring surrounding a 7.5 sq km (3 sq mi) lagoon, cut by two channels. The surface of the atoll is covered in grasses, a few palm trees, and a light house. At low tide the bare reef is transformed into a fantastic aquarium – the lagoon and tidal pools brimming with the brilliant colours of thousands of tropical fish. It is one of the most remarkable as well as remote places in the world – do not be put off by the travel obstacles in your way.

WHAT IS IT?
Marine reserve
WHEN TO GO:
Any time – mild equatorial marine climate. The island is at its most beautiful in the rainy season, February to July. Best surfing waves December to February, best diving and snorkelling rest of year.
HOW TO GET THERE:
Daily flights or boat from Natal or Recife on Brazilian mainland.
NEAREST TOWN:
Vila dos Remédios
DON'T MISS:
The Baia de Golfinhos resident dolphin community, at their liveliest in the early mornings.
YOU SHOULD KNOW:
A permit must be obtained to visit the smaller islands of Fernando de Noronha and Atol das Rocas. A maximum of 420 tourists are allowed to stay on Fernando de Noronha at any one time.

Fernando de Noronha

Declared a UNESCO World Heritage Site – along with the Atol dos Rocas - in 2001, the Fernando de Noronha archipelago is a group of 21 volcanic islands and rocks in the Atlantic Ocean just south of the Equator and some 350 km (220 mi) east of Brazil, to whom they belong. The largest island, after which the group is named, is the only inhabited one and visitor numbers are strictly limited, in order to minimize the impact of tourism on the islands' landscapes and wildlife.

Rising from the sea floor 756 m (2,480 ft below), these islands are the remnants of part of the volcanic Southern Atlantic Submarine Ridge and provide a vital stopping- and feeding-point for animals such as sharks and turtles as they migrate to and fro across the southern Atlantic.

Most of the area around these isolated islands was declared a National Marine Reserve in 1988 in order to give protection to the abundant marine wildlife and today most visitors to these islands come for the superb diving: manta rays, lemon sharks and many types of other fish including tuna and billfish can be seen in the warm waters.

From above the water, one of the main spectacles to watch is the daily gathering of hundreds of playful spinner dolphins in the Bay of Dolphins, while in season many of the wide sandy beaches are used as nesting grounds by marine turtles, especially the rare hawksbill turtle. These lush, green islands also provide a refuge for the largest concentration of tropical seabirds in the western Atlantic.

WHAT IS IT?
A beautiful archipelago of 21 islands, surrounded by amazing wildlife.
HOW TO GET THERE:
By air from Recife or Natal on the mainland or on a cruise.
WHEN TO GO:
The dry season is from September to March with the height of the tourist season in December and January.
NEAREST TOWN:
Natal 360 km (220 mi)
DON'T MISS
The spinner dolphins in the Bay of Dolphins.
YOU SHOULD KNOW:
A permit is needed to visit the other islands in the group.

Boldro's beach on Fernando de Noronha

Sugarloaf Mountain

WHAT IS IT?
Rock monolith, urban climbing area.
HOW TO GET THERE:
Fly to Rio de Janeiro
WHEN TO GO:
Easter, to experience Carnival.
NEAREST TOWN:
Rio de Janeiro.
DON'T MISS:
A trip to Corcovado, the highest of
the nearby mountains, with the
famous statue of Christ The
Redeemer.
YOU SHOULD KNOW:
The climb up the Sugarloaf is
extremely rugged and much harder
than it looks. It should not be
undertaken without pre-planning.
Getting down is even more difficult
than getting to the top.

The Sugarloaf (Pāu do Açúcar) is the icon of Rio de Janeiro. This unearthly green monolith soars straight up 396 m (1,299 ft) into the sky from the end of a peninsula, which juts into the Atlantic from Guanabara Bay.

It is said to derive its name from the fact that it is in the traditional shape of a piece of refined loaf sugar, but it is just as likely that the name actually comes from the indigenous Tamoioa Indian language Pau-nh-Acuqua, which translates as "high hill".

The mountain is the most famous of several 600 million year-old monolithic granite and quartz morros that rise straight from the edge of the sea near Rio de Janeiro. Because of its position, it was used as a landmark by sailors crossing the Atlantic to guide them in the direction of Rio.

A cable car, first built in 1912, regularly travels a 1,400 m (4,265 ft) route, connecting its peak with that of Morro da Urca. The ride is not only an incredible experience in itself but you are rewarded with staggering panoramic views of the city, mountains and Atlantic beaches as well as another half dozen of these extraordinary morros sticking up from the water's edge. It is well worth timing your expedition to coincide with sunset when the surroundings are truly magical. The intrepid climber can also trek to the top. The morros are very popular among urban climbers – together, they form one of the longest urban climbing areas in the world with more than 270 routes around them.

*Sunset over the harbour and
Sugarloaf Mountain*

Central Amazon

An aerial view of the Amazon River and rainforest

The Amazon is the largest tropical rainforest in the world, a region of unparalleled diversity, with more than 150,000 species of plants 75,000 types of tree and 2,000 birds and mammals. Much of it is still unexplored – amazingly, we know less about the rainforest than we do about the ocean depths. "The Lungs of the Planet" stretches across several nations and, in Brazil, 22,000 sq km (8,490 sq mi) has been set aside as the Jau National Park.

The usual route is by boat up the Rio Negro, whose black-coloured water is caused by decomposed organic matter and iron. It is the largest river in the world, apart from the Amazon itself. The rivers join at the Encontra Das Aguas ("Meeting of the Waters"). Here the pale waters of the Amazon and the dark ones of Rio Negro flow side by side in two distinct channels. You will pass through dark, flooded igapó, in water up to 12 m (39 ft) deep – mysterious forest where strange epiphytes cling to the trees and the fauna has evolved complex survival strategies; varsea – a floating mosaic of vegetation, where the waters contain innumerable electric fish, the endangered manatee and the river dolphin; terra firme, above the water line – where, among huge tropical trees, you can pick up the trails of wild pig, jaguars and armadillos.

As you glide along this wide, slow river, past jungle shores of tangled vines under a magnificent green 45 m (148 ft) tall canopy, you cannot help being overwhelmed by a sense of the primitive forces that have shaped evolution. You will see plants of every conceivable shape and size, flashes of brilliant iridescent colours from butterflies and birds, and hear the sometimes spine-tingling calls of birds and animals echoing across the jungle. A trip into the Amazon rainforest is a truly life-transforming experience.

WHAT IS IT?
The largest tropical rainforest in the world.
HOW TO GET THERE:
International or domestic flights to Manaus.
WHEN TO GO:
Any time – hot and rainy all year.
NEAREST TOWN:
Manaus 16 km (10 mi) from Encontra Das Aguas.
DON'T MISS:
The Black River Basin, the largest area of black water in the world, and the Carabinani Waterfalls, both in Jau National Park.
YOU SHOULD KNOW:
Amazonia produces 20 per cent of the earth's oxygen but is under serious threat. Of the 10 million or more indigenous people who once lived and worked in harmony with their surroundings, a mere 200,000 survive. Although what is lost can never be reclaimed, at least there is reason for some optimism for the remainder: from 2002-2006 the amount of protected forest has tripled and the rate of deforestation has dropped by up to 60 per cent.

Patos Lagoon

Five rivers converge at the city of Porto Alegre to form the Lagoa Dos Patos, a tidal lagoon in extreme south-eastern Brazil. It is the second largest lagoon in South America, 280 km (174 mi) long and 70 km (44 mi) wide, and is navigable even by large ships. It is separated from the Atlantic by an 8 km (5 mi) wide sandbar.

The "Lagoon of the Ducks" gets its name from some wily 16th century Jesuit colonialists, who asked the King of Spain to grant them title to start a duck-breeding colony. He soon revoked it when he discovered he had just handed over one of the largest lagoon systems in the world.

The lagoon is the remains of an ancient depression, closed off from the sea by the combined action of wind and water currents building up the sandbank. It has several islands in it, the largest being the Ilha dos Marinheiros, inhabited by people labelled "outcasts" because they scratch a living by picking over the refuse from the city of Porto Alegre at the northern end of the lagoon.

To the south of Patos is another large lagoon, the Mirim. The lagoons are connected by the Sao Gonçalo channel, on one side of which is the city of Rio Grande and the other, Pelotas. A plume of sediment flows into the sea from an opening at the extreme south end of Patos, which led explorers to believe that it was the mouth of a huge river, hence the name Rio Grande.

The land is very low lying here and there is a 250 km (125 mi) stretch of spectacular uninterrupted sand-duned coastline. The lagoon is important for its reeds and grasses, numerous fish and bird species, and sea turtles, which are found here in spring and summer.

The lagoons of Lagoa dos Patos and Lagoa Merin form a fragile intertidal ecosystem. The water quality of the lagoons is suffering from agricultural and industrial runoff, and the demands of increased population in the area.

Emas National Park

The remote Parc Nacional das Emas is a spectacular savanna plain (cerrado) of more than 1,300 sq km (500 sq mi) in central Brazil. Combined with the protected cerrado of Chapada dos Veadeiros further north, it is a UNESCO Biosphere Reserve.

The granite plateau, ranging in altitude from 400-1,000 m (1,310-3,280 ft), is a magnificent cerrado landscape – a vista of vast changing skies above rolling open-wooded grasslands. The plains are dotted with innumerable red earth termite mounds, scored with dramatic canyons and crisscrossed by rivers and clear rushing streams, with high waterfalls and black water drop pools.

The Park is part of the great dividing cerrado plateau between the Amazon and Paraná River basins and is the site of the headwaters of the Araguaia, Formosa and Taquari rivers and their tributaries, which diverge across the plains making their separate ways to the Atlantic.

This is the place for hardcore nature lovers. Large mammals – troupes of monkeys, giant anteaters, tapirs, capybaras, armadillos, wild dogs, maned wolves, foxes, herds of deer, cougars and ocelots – roam freely here on a scale comparable with the savannas of East Africa, 87 species in all. It is also a birdwatcher's paradise, with more than 350 sorts of bird, including Aplomado falcons, Burrowing owls, Yellow-faced parrots and Macaws.

The termite mounds, which sprout surreally out of the ground, can be more than 2 m (6.6 ft) high. They are used as shelter by all sorts of wildlife including the larvae of the cumpinzeiro, a luminescent beetle. At night you may be fortunate enough to witness an extraordinary ephemeral display of nature when, after the rains, the landscape is transformed by the emergence of huge numbers of these insects. They light up the mounds in a fantastic display, transforming them into Christmas trees.

WHAT IS IT?
Tropical savanna (Cerrado)
HOW TO GET THERE:
By road from Brasilia 700 km (440 mi) or Goiânia 500 km (312 mi) to Chapadao do Céu.
WHEN TO GO:
April to October, to avoid scorching heat.
NEAREST TOWN:
Chapadeu do Céu 26 km (16 mi)
YOU SHOULD KNOW:
Access is difficult so you need to be determined. There are no paved roads in the area and you require a permit to enter, obtainable from the tourist centre in Chapadao de Céu.

A dirt road runs through flat grassland

The Atlantic Forests

WHAT IS IT?
Coastal, montane and high altitude forest
HOW TO GET THERE:
Fly to Rio de Janeiro or São Paulo
WHEN TO GO:
Always warm, dependent on altitude. January to September is drier.
NEAREST TOWN:
São Paulo 100 km (63 mi)
DON'T MISS:
Visiting some of Brazil's spectacular caves, most of which are to be found in the Atlantic Forests. There are 200 in the state of São Paulo.

In terms of biodiversity the glorious Mata Atlântica is the richest in the world. Cut off from the rest of South America by the Cerrado savannas, the complex eco-system of the Atlantic Forest has evolved separately, which explains the incredibly high degree of endemism here: 40 per cent of the 20,000 plant species are unique. More than 400 tree species have been recorded in a single hectare of forest, including the very rare Brazilwood and Brazilian rosewood. Of around 260 species of mammals, 70 are endemic – there are 14 sorts of primate alone, including three critically endangered species of marmoset. Fifteen per cent of the 950 bird species are endemic, including several endangered parrots. The forest is also a habitat for hundreds of species of amphibian, reptile and freshwater fish, up to half of which are unique.

However, the forest that once stretched north to south along Brazil's coast is now less than 10 per cent of its former size, surviving only in fragmented patches. The magnificent scenery of wooded mountains, rivers, waterfalls and lakes is in startling contrast to the urban sprawl of Rio de Janeiro and São Paulo, which threatens to invade it even further. Over the past 500 years the forest has been gradually plundered for wood and cleared of trees to make way for cattle ranches, sugar and coffee plantations and, latterly, urban development. Still, there is a great deal of hope for what remains – the Brazilian environmentalist movement, an increasingly powerful lobby, has taken up its cause. It has been placed in the top five of the world's ecological "hotspots" for its diversity and endemism; 23,800 sq km (9,190 sq mi) has now been strictly protected in 224 separate areas, with 4,700 sq km (1,814 sq mi) under the auspices of UNESCO, as an irreplaceable part of the earth's heritage.

The Atlantic Forest in Rio de Janeiro

The Pantanal Wetlands

The Pantanal swamp in Brazil

The cattle ranching country of the Pantanal is the largest wetland area in the world. The diversity and abundance of vegetation and wildlife here is comparable to the Amazon and it is one of the most important eco-systems on the planet.

The Pantanal is a bowl-shaped depression covering a vast area of 250,000 sq km (96,500 sq mi) in central west Brazil, with two major river systems flowing through Río Paraguay and Río Cuiabá. In effect, the region is a massive inland delta. In the rainy season the rivers burst their banks, flooding 80 per cent of the surrounding alluvial plain, providing nourishment for the world's largest collection of aquatic plants. These form floating islands of vegetation, *camalotes*, on which animals and birds take refuge from the water.

The region is habitat for 75 mammal species, among them the maned wolf, giant anteater, and the world's largest rodent, the capybara, weighing up to 60 kg, as well as five species of howler monkey, giant otters, peccaries, tapirs, deer and the occasional jaguar. There are over 300 species of fish, and Caiman alligators loll brazenly in the grassy river banks. You will also see plenty of lizards, chameleons, land turtles, boa constrictors and anacondas. The region is a birdwatcher's paradise with more than 600 species – home to the jabiru, with its distinctive red crop white plumage, black head and dark skinny legs, along with macaws, toucans, eagles, rheas and countless water birds.

It is a matter of great concern to conservationists that such a vital ecological region is largely unprotected, privately owned land used for ranching and eco- tourism. You can stay on one of these ranches and explore the marshes of the Pantanal by canoe or on horseback to catch superb sights of the wildlife, bird watch or go fishing.

WHAT IS IT?
The world's largest freshwater wetlands.
HOW TO GET THERE:
Fly to Campo Grande or Cuiabá
WHEN TO GO:
Waters start to recede in April. Best from June to August
NEAREST TOWN:
Porto Jofre, Corumbá
YOU SHOULD KNOW:
The novel *The Testament* by John Grisham is largely set in the Pantanal.

Lake Titicaca with the Cordillera Real in the background

Lake Titicaca

High in the Altiplano between Peru and Bolivia, the limpid cobalt-blue waters of Lake Titicaca are central to Incan mythology and history: the origin of the world was here, the sun, moon and stars emerged from its waters, and powerful spirits as well as Spanish gold are in its depths.

Lake Titicaca is the highest commercially navigable lake in the world, at 3,812 m (12,503 ft). It is 176 km (110 mi) long and 50 km (31 mi) wide with water up to 281 m (922 ft) deep. More than 25 rivers and glaciers flow down from the sierras into the Altiplano to feed this huge stretch of water. The lake drains into Rio Desagaudero but most of its water simply evaporates in the fierce winds and burning sun of the Altiplano.

There are 41 islands in the lake, inhabited by Quechuan Indians who have largely preserved their traditional culture. They eke out a living from terrace farming, fishing and making ethnic garments for the tourist trade.

The extraordinary "Islas Flotantes" are a major tourist attraction. These reed islands, which need constant repairs to stop them rotting, were originally built by the Uro Indians to avoid the harassment of Spanish colonists but are now settled by Aymara Indians who have built reed houses and even a church. They float on the lake surviving from fishing and tourism.

Despite the pressures of mass tourism, Titicaca is an amazing sight. It seems to stretch forever under the huge skies of the Altiplano, the snow-capped peaks of the sierra Cordillera just visible in the distance, and an aura of the legendary Incan civilization pervading the atmosphere.

WHAT IS IT?
A high altitude tropical lake.
HOW TO GET THERE:
Fly/train/bus from Lima 1,315 km (822 mi). Train/bus from Cusco 389 km (243 mi). Fly/train from Arequipa 188 km (117 mi)
WHEN TO GO:
May to November.
NEAREST TOWN:
Puno.
DON'T MISS:
The islands of Amantaní or Taquile, for an overnight stay if possible, and the ruins on Isla del Sol.
YOU SHOULD KNOW:
The people of Lake Titicaca have preserved their culture against the odds. You should try to be sensitive to what might appear a "hard-sell" approach.

Huascarán National Park

The Cordillera Blanca is one of the highest mountain ranges in the world. It extends for 180 km (112 mi) covering the 3,400 sq km (1,310 sq mi) conservation area of Huascarán National Park. There are more than 50 glaciated peaks, fifteen of which are more than 6,000 m (20,000 ft) high. Nevado Huascarán, at 6,768 m (22,200 ft), is the highest mountain not only in Peru but also in the whole of the tropics. Here is some of the most spectacular mountain scenery you will ever see.

You will be overwhelmed with views of startlingly blue glacial lakes, dramatic gorges, torrential cascades, and sparkling icy streams, set in a vast white landscape. Numerous trails will take you though welcoming Andean communities and pre-Incan ruins. You will wander through meadows full of strange endemic plants, scramble along deep ravines lined with red-barked queñua and medicinal quísuar trees, find yourself surrounded by glaciers and be amazed by the hundreds of aquamarine and turquoise lakes and the staggering views of the sheer rock and ice walls of the northern peaks of the Cordillera Blanca.

At the foot of Nevado Huascarán are the beautiful twin lakes of the Llanganuco glacier – the intense green waters of Chinancocha (female) enclosed by queñua forest and, out in the open at the other end of the valley, the smaller translucent blue Orconcocha (male).

The north-west face of Huascarán is an almost vertical cliff from where a huge chunk of the mountain fell off in an earthquake in 1970. The entire region was devastated by the worst avalanche disaster in history: In June 1970 10 million cu m (353 million cu ft) of rock fell straight down at an estimated speed of 200 kph (125 mph) crushing the town of Yungay, instantly killing 20,000 people in the town itself and another 50,000 in the vicinity.

WHAT IS IT?
The highest mountain range in the tropics.
HOW TO GET THERE:
Seven hours by road from Lima, to Huaraz 450 km (280 mi). From Huaraz about an hour to Yungay 60 km (37 mi) or Caraz 72 km (45 mi).
WHEN TO GO:
May to September to avoid rainy season but always extremely cold at high altitude.
NEAREST TOWN:
Yungay 21 km (13 mi) from Nevado Huascarán.
DON'T MISS:
A trek to Alpamayo – "the most beautiful mountain in the world"
YOU SHOULD KNOW:
To ascend Huascarán takes 6 to 7 days.

Nevado Huascarán, the highest peak in Peru at 6,768 m (22,200ft)

Andes Cordillera

WHAT IS IT?
A mountain range.
HOW TO GET THERE:
Fly to Lima or Cuzco.
WHEN TO GO:
Year round but June to August best
because dry season in highlands.
DON'T MISS:
Nevado Huaracán, Machu Picchu,
Lake Titicaca.
YOU SHOULD KNOW:
It takes time to acclimatize to the
altitudes here so you should make
your travel plans accordingly.

The Andes Cordillera is the longest continuous mountain chain on earth and the highest outside Asia. It extends more than 7,000 km (4,000 mi), running through seven South American countries from Tierra del Fuego to Venezuela. At its widest, the range is 500 km (300 mi) across with an average height of 4,000 m (13,000 ft). The mountains are largely composed of limestone, sandstone, slate and some granite, with large amounts of lava in the volcanic regions. Frequent earthquakes attest to the dynamic nature of these awesome mountains.

The Central Andes runs down the whole length of Peru, home to some of the most spectacular mountains in the world – steep granite peaks rise above icy ridges with huge glaciers snaking down the valleys to provide some of the most magnificent landscapes you will ever come across. The Pacific coast is never more than 100 miles away making for incredibly fast short rivers – a source of energy for the whole country. To the east, the glaciers feed the headwaters of the Amazon.

The Peruvian Andes are divided into five sub-ranges: Cordilleras Blanca and Huayhuash in the north, Central, Occidental and Oriental Cordilleras. Cordillera Blanca is by far the most accessible with the highest mountain in Peru, Nevada Huaracán. The Cordillera Occidental is an actively volcanic, more remote range in extreme southwest Peru, with mountains that are significantly easier to climb. The Oriental, in the region around Cuzco, the ancient capital of the Incan empire, is composed of several small ranges and isolated massifs, including Urubamba, the location of the famous abandoned Inca city of Machu Picchu. The southernmost range of the Oriental Cordillera, extending into Bolivia, is the remote and extremely glaciated Apolobamba. Its isolation gives it a unique quality and it is well worth exploring.

The Cordillera Blanca Mountains in Peru

Andes Cloud Forests

The mysterious cloud forests of Peru occur only at altitudes of 2,000-3,500 m (6,500 – 11,500 ft) on high mountains where the annual rainfall is 50-1,000cm (20-400in). The twisted, stunted trees with epiphytes and lichens trailing eerily from their branches are shrouded in perpetual mist. This is a unique ecosystem for thousands of species, 80 per cent of which are still undocumented. There are more than 1,000 species of orchid alone, and more than 30 per cent of the 272 endemic species of Peruvian mammals, birds and frogs live here.

The epithet "Nature's water towers" applies with good reason: the forest is a vital source of pure water. The leaves of the trees and ferns draw moisture out of the clouds and drip it into the sodden peaty ground at a constant rate, contributing a regular controlled water supply to rivers lower down the mountains. The forest protects the watershed by preventing soil erosion as well as acting as a water collector. It is threatened by both climate change and man's encroachment, with potentially disastrous consequences for water supplies, quite apart from the loss of habitat for thousands of species of flora and fauna.

The huge 150,000 sq km (58,000 sq mi) World Heritage Site of Manú National Park was established to protect the remaining Peruvian cloud forest. Manú is a bird and wildlife watcher's utopia – a habitat for an incredible diversity of species. Here you will see the Andean Cock-of-the-Rock – the bright scarlet national bird of Peru, the Mountain Toucan, quetzals, hummingbirds, and a myriad of butterflies unlike any you have ever seen. Amongst many other mammals, the Park is home to spectacled bears, woolly and brown capuchin monkeys, giant otters and jaguars.

This unique, romantic and fragile world makes up a mere 2.5 per cent of the tropical rainforest but its ecological significance is immeasurable.

Cloud Forest in the Cosnipati Valley

WHAT IS IT?
A forest habitat for bird and wildlife watching
HOW TO GET THERE:
Fly to Lima then domestic flight or road to Cusco. 7 hours drive from Cusco to Paucartambo.
WHEN TO GO:
Any time but June to September is driest.
NEAREST TOWN:
Paucartambo 35 km (22 mi) from Ajunaco Pass, entrance to Manú National Park.
YOU SHOULD KNOW:
New species are being discovered all the time. The latest is a nocturnal rodent about the size of a squirrel (*Isothrix barbarabrownae*).

Noel Kempff Mercado National Park

WHAT IS IT?
A diverse wilderness, designated by UNESCO as "Natural Patrimony of Humanity".

HOW TO GET THERE:
Fly to Santa Cruz. Fly or drive 600 km (375 mi) from Santa Cruz to Flor de Oro or Los Fierros Park lodges.

WHEN TO GO:
. The ideal season is October to December.

DON'T MISS:
The awe inspiring Caparú Plateau – a Precambrian sandstone mesa (table mountain), rising straight up from the rainforest, one of the places that lays claim to being the inspiration for Sir Arthur Conan Doyle's story *The Lost World*.

YOU SHOULD KNOW:
There are very few visitors because of the park's remoteness. You approach the park from either the north or south depending upon where you have pre-arranged your stay – Flor de Oro (north) or Los Fierros (south).

This exceptional biological reserve, named after a renowned Bolivian biologist, is a truly awe-inspiring region of more than 15,000 sq km (5,790 sq mi) of remote wilderness in northeast Bolivia. It is one of the least disturbed expanses of land in the Amazon basin, and one of the most biologically diverse areas in the world. The scenery is breathtaking – extraordinary landscapes, vast rivers, and stunning waterfalls.

A visit to the Park is a fantastic eco-adventure. The sheer scale of the wilderness cerrado (the largest remaining virgin tract of this rich savanna land in the world) is staggering – broad rivers cut through the savanna, their banks lined with strangely contorted trees, and great cascades of water thunder down into the streams and creeks of the rainforest. The terrain ranges in altitude from 200-1,000 m (655-3,280 ft) and encompasses five distinct eco-systems. It is a refuge for wildlife that has largely disappeared from the rest of the Amazon. There are more than 130 species of mammal here, including rare river otters, river dolphins, spider and howler monkeys, maned wolves, giant armadillos and an endangered population of black jaguars. So far, biologists have documented around 4,000 species of flora, 110 species of orchid alone, as well as at least 620 sorts of bird and 70 kinds of reptile, some of the world's rarest insects and an incredible population of butterflies, of all colours and sizes.

The park dates back over a billion years, to the Pre-Cambrian period. Its remoteness and diversity make it an ideal laboratory for biological research into the evolution of ecosystems. Nowhere else in South America can you see such a wide variety of species and habitats with so little effort.

The rainforest in the Noel Kempff Mercado National Park

Cape Horn

The continent of South America ends at a treeless granite promontory. This is Cape Horn – the southern headland of Isla Hornos, part of the Chilean Hermite Islands of Tierra del Fuego. The most southerly of all the great capes, Cape Horn juts out into Drake Passage, the strait between South America and Antarctica, marking the dividing line between the Pacific and Atlantic Oceans.

The perilous seas of Cape Horn are a sailing legend. Gale-force winds and fearsome currents combine to stir up lashing great waves more than 20 m (65 ft) high, which, together with the threat of icebergs, make it one of the most hazardous sea routes in the world. Despite the danger, the route was in frequent use until the Panama Canal was built in 1914, particularly in the years of the California Gold Rush when adventurers considered it marginally less risky than attempting to cross the great North American prairies by land. Hundreds of ships have been wrecked here, and sailors who successfully rounded the Horn westwards were treated as a special breed – they were entitled to wear a gold ring in their left ear or nipple as a mark of their authority.

The Cape Horn archipelago is one of the most pristine island ecosystems in the world and has been designated a UNESCO Biosphere Reserve. It covers a remote area inhabited by indigenous Yagán Chileans, a nomadic fishing culture that is threatened by economic development and tourism.

There is an extensive area of untouched temperate forest, sub-polar forests and tundra all linked by an intricate system of channels, estuaries and bays. The sea is a hotspot for dolphins and whales, while the shores, with masses of rare flora, are important nesting sites for Magellan and rock hopper penguins and havens for albatrosses, condors, coscoroba swans and cormorants.

WHAT IS IT?
The southern tip of the American continent. Temperate and sub-polar forest; coastal marine systems.
HOW TO GET THERE:
Fly to Ushuaia (or from Santiago to Punta Arenas). Take boat or plane to Puerto Williams then boat to Cabo de Hornos (Cape Horn) through the Beagle Channel.
WHEN TO GO:
January to March and October to December.
NEAREST TOWN:
Puerto Williams

Cape Horn

Aguas Calientes Salt Flat and the Atacama Desert

The Atacama Desert

At its centre, the Atacama Desert is the driest place on earth – 50 times drier than California's Death Valley. The average annual rainfall is a mere 1 mm (0.004 in) a year and some parts never see any rain at all. The desert is at an altitude of over 2,000 m (6,560 ft), on a narrow plateau, only 150 km (94 mi) wide, which extends 1,000 km (625 mi) from the border with Peru into northern Chile. The rain shadow cast by the Andes on one side and the Pacific coastal mountains on the other has created an extraordinary landscape of alluvial saltpans.

Incredibly, about a million people manage to scratch a living out of the Atacama, inhabiting the few oases and the Pacific fringes of the desert where coastal mists supply just enough moisture to sustain algae, mosses and the odd cactus.

The terrain is 15 million years old and there is a wealth of remains from a Paleo-Indian civilization. Incan artifacts and mummies have been found perfectly preserved, desiccated in the sterile desert soil. The desert is the world's largest source of saltpetre, and 40 per cent of the world's lithium reserves are to be found in Salar de Atacama, a 3,000 sq km (1,160 sq mi) salt lake covered with a bizarre white crust.

The desert landscape is visually superb – a weird lunar scenery straight out of Salvador Dali, where the amazing shapes and extraordinary tones of the earth contrast with reflections from the sky in the salt lagoons. The main oasis is the village of San Pedro, from where there are views of the vast peaks of the Andes to the east, and the Salt Mountains, moulded by erosion into giant mineral sculptures, to the west.

WHAT IS IT?
A mountainous desert.
HOW TO GET THERE:
International flight to Santiago. Domestic flight to Calama 100 km (62 mi) away then a shuttle flight /road to San Pedro.
WHEN TO GO:
It is a high altitude desert climate with extreme temperature changes. Avoid September to November when winds reach up to 100 kph (62 mph).
NEAREST TOWN:
San Pedro
DON'T MISS:
Chaxa Lagoon Reserva Nacional Los Flamencos – a flamingo breeding ground.
YOU SHOULD KNOW:
There are around 170 abandoned nitrate mining centres, including Chacabuco which was made into a concentration camp under Pinochet – it is said to be surrounded by lost landmines and to be guarded by one man who lives there alone.

El Tatio Geyser Field

Situated in the Atacama Desert in the Altiplano of Northern Chile, at an altitude of 4,200 m (13,775 ft), El Tatio ("The Grandpa") is the third largest geyser field in the world. There are more than 80 active geysers, 30 of which are perpetual spouters, as well as hot springs and five mud pots.

The steaming water makes incredible hissing and whistling sounds as it is forced up all over the field through fissures in the earth – varying from delicate little puffs of steam, floating past like small clouds, to jets of water, hot enough to boil an egg in, squirting up to a metre into the air.

El Tatio is surrounded by stunning scenery – a desert plain enclosed by enormous, perfectly conical 6,000 m (19,680 ft) high volcanoes, capped in snow. As you watch El Tatio at work, you begin to get some inkling of the awesome forces that have shaped the surrounding mountains. The combined activity of the geysers, mud pots, colourful pools reflecting the light, and cinder terraces makes the field a really awe-inspiring place. If you sit quietly and look around you, you will start to notice the wildlife. There are several species of small bird as well as foxes, chinchillas, and a flamingo family, and you may even find yourself approached by friendly Andean camels.

El Tatio is best visited in the early morning when, apart from the wonderful light, for some reason the geysers are at their most active. As you wander around the field you must tread extremely carefully – the cauldron crusts are thinner than they look. More than one person has been very badly burned when apparently stable rock has suddenly given way and tipped them into a cauldron of boiling water.

WHAT IS IT?
A geyser field.
HOW TO GET THERE:
International airport Santiago, then fly to Calama and bus to San Pedro.
WHEN TO GO:
It is a high altitude desert climate with sharp temperature drops at night. Avoid September to November when there are high winds.
NEAREST TOWN:
San Pedro 82 km (51 mi)
YOU SHOULD KNOW:
Take warm clothes because it can be extremely cold.

El Tatio Geysers, San Pedro de Atacama

Desert grass alongside Lake Chungará with the snowcapped Payachatas volcanoes in the distance.

Lauca World Biosphere Reserve

Lauca is in the Altiplano – the most extensive area of high plateau in the world outside Tibet, and one of the most beautiful regions of Chile. It is a protected area of almost 3,600 sq km (1,390 sq mi) along the border with Bolivia, designated a UNESCO World Biosphere Reserve.

More than 3,000 m (9,840 ft) above sea level, the Altiplano separates the Atacama Desert from the Amazon Basin. It is homeland to a dwindling number of llama and alpaca herdsmen – the remnants of a pastoral society of Aymará Indians whose culture is rich in a tradition of music and festivals. There are many archaeological sites and geoglyphs, attesting to a civilization that goes back thousands of years.

The terrain is gashed by deep gorges with fast flowing rivers and streams, dotted with lagoons, lava outcrops, brackish marshes and sparkling saltpans, with a stunning backcloth of active and dormant volcanoes. It sustains three distinct sorts of plant life: shrubs and cacti; perennial grass, paja brava – used for thatch; llareta, a pungent cushion plant, which only grows 1 mm (0.004 in) per year, traditionally used as medicine and for fuel. Around 130 bird species, including Andean gulls and condors, and 21 kinds of mammal live here. In Salar de Surire, an extensive salt marsh, there are numerous rare plants and animals, including three species of flamingo.

One of the most beautiful places in Lauca is Lago Chungará, an emerald coloured lake formed 8,000 years ago when a major eruption caused 6 cu km (1.5 cu mi) of volcanic debris to avalanche. Whether or not Lago Chungará is the world's highest lake at 4,500 m (14,760 ft), as the locals claim, it is a spectacular place to visit for the hundreds of unusual birds and incredible views of the Payachatas volcanoes, with their perfectly symmetrical snowy-tipped cones.

WHAT IS IT?
A beautiful region of mountains and highlands.
HOW TO GET THERE:
International airports Santiago or Iquique, then domestic flight to Arica 145 km (91 mi) from park and road to Putre.
WHEN TO GO:
Anytime. Extreme high altitude desert climate with a sharp drop in temperature to below 0 ºC (32ºF) at night.
NEAREST TOWN:
Putre 12 km (7.5 mi)
DON'T MISS:
The Cotacotani lagoons, connected by channels and cascades with wonderful colours reflected from the sky.
YOU SHOULD KNOW:
Very high elevations so you must give yourself time to acclimatize in order to avoid altitude sickness.

Península Valdés

The Valdés Peninsula, on Patagonia's arid Atlantic coast, is one of the most important marine mammal habitats in the world. Colonies of southern elephant seals, fur seals, southern sea lions, penguins, dolphins and orcas congregate on and around its shore. But, above all, Valdés is famous for its right whales. The Southern Right Whale was once hunted almost to extinction but thanks to conservation efforts, up to 2,000 of them now migrate here to breed.

Valdés is a stark 3,600 sq km (1,390 sq mi) axe-shaped promontory that juts 100 km (63 mi) into the Atlantic, connected to the mainland by a 25 km (16 mi) long isthmus. It has a 400 km (250 mi) coastline of gulfs, enclosing tidal mud flats in calm, shallow bays. The seals and sea lions shelter at the bottom of the sheer cliffs, relying on the warm coastal waters for an abundant food supply.

Although, at first sight, Valdés seems completely barren, there are in fact 130 species of plant, mainly tussock-grasses – an enormous number for such a small area. Guanacos (*Lama guanicoe*) graze here, and the marshy salt flats harbour rheas, hares, grey foxes and wild cats. The peninsula is a haven for around 180 species of marine and shore birds. Apart from a colony of Magellan penguins there are cormorants, egrets, herons and kelp gulls. Orcas prowl the open seas around the peninsula. They have invented a risky do-or-die hunting method – a daring orca will hurl itself onto the beach, grab its prey and wiggle backwards into the sea to share the kill. Inevitably, one sometimes gets stranded and dies from dehydration.

The sheer numbers of marine mammals that the peninsula harbours is overwhelming and you can spend many peaceful hours watching these charming creatures playing, mating and breeding in their natural habitat.

WHAT IS IT?
A marine mammal habitat.
HOW TO GET THERE:
Fly to Trelew International Airport, 60 km (40 mi) from Puerto Madryn. Take a tour from Puerto Madryn or bus to Puerto Pirámides.
WHEN TO GO:
June to December to watch the whales. All year for seals and sea lions.
NEAREST TOWN:
Puerto Madryn 105 km (65mi)
DON'T MISS:
A trip to Punta Tombo Nature Reserve 180 km (112 mi) to the south of Puerto Madryn to see huge colonies of Magellan penguins.

A young Southern Elephant Seal emerging from the ocean.

141

Patagonia

WHAT IS IT?
A vast area of beautiful landscapes in the south of South America.
HOW TO GET THERE:
Fly to Buenos Aires then by road or take a domestic flight to Comodoro Rivadavia.
WHEN TO GO:
November - April
DON'T MISS:
Perito Moreno glacier.

The southernmost part of Argentina and Chile, Patagonia is a beautiful, untamed land of fjords, rugged mountains, enormous glaciers, windswept plateaux, petrified forests and flat grasslands.

Dominated in the west by the heights of the Andes, Patagonia is home to some of the most beautiful landscapes in the world and covers an area of over 900,000 sq km (347,000 sq mi). The main economic activities of the area have been whaling, mining, agriculture (sheep in the south, and wheat and fruit in the north) and oil, after it was discovered in 1907 near Comodoro Rivadavia.

The Northern Lakes area of Argentina's Lake District has a number of national parks in the foothills of the Andes, and a trek through these will reveal a beautiful landscape of wildflower meadows, lakes and rugged peaks. The Southern Lakes are perhaps even more spectacular, and adjoin the Los Glaciares National Park. This area has hundreds of glaciers, remnants of an ancient ice sheet, perhaps the most famous of which is Perito Moreno. This glacier, with its nose stretching 5 km (3 mi) across, periodically advances across the Lago Argentino and blocks it until the mass of water held behind this frozen dam becomes too great and it ruptures, crashing into pieces as the water surges through.

Farther south still lie the Straits of Magellan, Tierra del Fuego and Cape Horn.

The range of different habitats in Patagonia, from high volcanoes to pampa and beaches, mean that it has a huge variety of wildlife, from condors that soar effortlessly in thermals to engaging emperor penguins, rheas, hummingbirds, flamingoes, steamer ducks, upland geese and long-tailed parakeets. Mammals on land include the Brazilian fox, guanacos and cougars while in the oceans there are southern right whales, orcas and elephant seals.

This remote land offers both awe-inspiring spectacle and tranquillity for any visitor.

Guanaco (Lama guanicoe) *grazing on the pampa.*

Los Glaciares

The World heritage site of Los Glaciares National Park is a region of awe-inspiring beauty in The Southern Patagonian Ice Field – the third largest continental icecap in the world after Antarctica and Greenland. Los Glaciares extends 170 km (106 mi) along the Chilean border, more than a third of it covered in ice. It is 4,450 sq km (1,720 sq mi) of arid steppe, wondrous coloured beech forests, glacial lakes and the towering mountains of the Andean ice cap.

The ice cap is the direct source of 47 large glaciers and there are around 200 smaller unconnected ones. Glaciers normally occur at altitudes of 2,500 m (8,200 ft) or more. Here, uniquely, they are only 1,500m (4,920 ft) above sea level, so are easily accessible.

The park has two huge lakes – the 160 km (100 mi) long Lake Argentino in the south and Lake Viedma in the north – around which you can explore some of the most extreme scenery in the world.

Lake Viedma is dominated by the awesome granite spikes of the FitzRoy Massif, great jagged walls of rock towering up out of the forest. Otherwise known as Cerro Chaltén (Smoking Mountain) because of the ring of cloud round its peak, Mount FitzRoy has the reputation of being "ultimate", not because it is particularly high at 3,375 m (11,070 ft) but because of its sheer granite sides.

At one end of Lake Argentino is the incredible spectacle of continual ice-falls. It is the junction of three glaciers – The Onelli, the Upsala and Spegazzini. Together with the immense 5 km (3 mi) wide Perito Moreno glacier, they make their inexorable descent from the ice cap, eroding the mountain in their path, to disgorge colossal icebergs into the milky waters of the lake in an overwhelming display of nature's power.

WHAT IS IT?
Glaciers
HOW TO GET THERE:
Fly to El Calafate International airport or by road from Río Gallegos.
WHEN TO GO:
October to April. High season January and February.
NEAREST TOWN:
El Calafate 40km (25 mi)
DON'T MISS:
The Walichu Caves; La Leona Petrified Forest. Only one day away, on the other side of the border in Chile, is the Torres del Paine Biosphere Reserve.

Perito Moreno Glacier

Sierra Pampeanas

WHAT IS IT?
A desert palaeontological site.
WHEN TO GO:
Any time. Desert climate with extreme temperature drops at night.
HOW TO GET THERE:
International flights to San Juan then bus 250 km (156 mi) north-east to San Agustín de Valle Fértil
NEAREST TOWN:
San Agustín de Valle Fértil (80 km from Ischigualasto, 190 km (119 mi) from Talampaya)
YOU SHOULD KNOW:
Best time of day to visit –Ischigualasto in mid to late afternoon, when light and shade is at its most dramatic.

In the parched hills and pure air of Sierra Pampeanas in North West Argentina, there is a World Heritage Site that reveals the story of evolution. The unique geological formations in the Ischigualasto and Talampaya National Parks contain the most complete known fossil record of plants, dinosaurs and mammalian ancestors. The desert here is a testament to the evolution of vertebrate life on the planet and the nature of palaeo-environments in the Triassic Period (245-208 million years ago). No other place on earth has remotely comparable fossil traces.

Together, the parks cover an area of 2,753 sq km (1,063 sq mi). Ischigualasto, or Valle de la Luna, is a clay rift valley with surreal landscapes of bizarre grey-green rocks. You do not need to be interested in palaeontology to be overawed by the delicate rock formations, the petrified trees more than 40 m (130 ft) tall, and the layers of earth that have been eroded to reveal complete dinosaur skeletons from 228 million years ago. At one point the ground is covered in perfectly formed spheres of rock. In other places the intricate designs are reminiscent of a Gaudi palace.

Talampaya is a sandstone desert of rainbow coloured rock, extending over 2,150 sq km (830 sq mi) at an altitude of 1,500 m (4,920 ft). Condors, vultures and eagles perch in the

The surreal landscape of Valle de la Luna (Moon Valley)

150 m (490 ft) high walls of sheer rust coloured cliffs. The wind and rain have sculpted the rock into dramatic Gothic formations. Here are some of the most important petroglyphs in Argentina – figurative human and animal engravings as well as abstract geometrical patterns.

The sparsely populated region of Sierra Pampeanas has a unique charm, unexploited by mass tourism. The Puno Indian inhabitants continue to live traditionally in their outstandingly beautiful land of intense earth colours and desert mountain air.

144

Tierra del Fuego

Tierra del Fuego is known to its inhabitants as El fin del Mundo (the end of the world). It is a remote archipelago of islands at the tip of South America, ending at Cape Horn. The largest island is separated from the mainland by the Magellan Strait, which was the fastest and safest route between the Atlantic and Pacific Oceans until the Panama Canal was built. The island is divided between Chile and Argentina while the remaining islands of the archipelago, including Cape Horn, are mainly Chilean territory.

On the Argentine side of the main island is "the southernmost city in the world", Ushuaia, and a National Park stretching 60 km (37 mi) northwards from the Beagle Channel along the Chilean border. The Pan-American Road, running all the way from Alaska, comes to an end here, at Lapataia Bay – an exquisite, remote stretch of coast where the Beagle Channel meets the Pacific Ocean.

There are colonies of sea lions as well as penguins and thousands of other birds, including rare species such as the albatross, oystercatchers, steamer ducks and petrels.

The park is 630 sq km (243 sq mi) of superb mountain scenery, up to 2,000 m (6,560 ft) high, with isolated glacial valleys, lakes and forest. It is situated around Lake Roca whose waters flow into the turbulent River Lapataia and out into the bay. This is the only part of Patagonia where the sub-arctic forests of beech woods (lenga) and evergreen (coihue) are close to the coast. There are large flooded areas of peat bog where strange red mosses grow, fringed with rush beds, and trees whose branches sprout lichen like a beard – a haven for birds, animals and freshwater fish. Close to the shore, there are numerous traces of ancient Yámana Indian settlements and sensational views of snow-capped mountains.

WHAT IS IT?
A sub-arctic marine forest.
HOW TO GET THERE:
Fly from Buenos Aires or El Calafate to Ushuaia.
WHEN TO GO:
All year.
NEAREST TOWN:
Ushuaia 9 km (6 mi).
DON'T MISS:
Tren del Fin del Mundo (End of the World Train) to take you to the park.
YOU SHOULD KNOW:
Charles Darwin described his journey here in *The Voyage of the Beagle* and used his observations of the region as evidence for his Theory of Evolution.

The Beagle Channel, named after the ship HMS Beagle, which was involved in two hydrographic surveys of the coasts of the southern part of South America in the early 19th century.

145

Nahuel Huapí National Park

Known as the Argentine Lake District, the Nahuel Huapí is a picture postcard region of deep blue glacial lakes and snowy mountain peaks, with wooded river valleys, meadows and countless streams.

The park covers more than 7,000 sq km (2,700 sq mi) of the Andes foothills in the southwest corner of Patagonia, along the Chilean border. The highest mountain is Cerro Tronador 3,491 m (11,450 ft), which gets its name from the frequent avalanches that you can hear thundering down its slopes. Nahuel Huapí – 560 sq km (216 sq mi) – is the largest of the many breathtaking lakes. It is more than 460 m (1,500 ft) deep with jagged peninsulas and islands.

The terrain ranges in altitude from 700 to 3,000 m (2,300 to 9,840 ft), with rainfall varying from 30 cm (12 in) in the eastern grasslands to 400 cm (156 in) in the western forests. These extremes support diverse ecosystems. In the sparse vegetation of the high mountains there are condors, pumas and the endangered huemul (Andean deer). On the lower slopes, the native beech and evergreen woods are full of flowers, which during spring are a blaze of colour. The luxuriant Valdivian forest is dense jungle of ferns, orchids and liana creepers. And the unique Bosque Los Arrayanes is a wood of weird 300-year-old trees with twisted trunks and strange cinnamon bark, cold and soft to the touch, inhabited by a small Bambi-like deer called the pudú. In the east, the semi-arid plateau, scored with dramatic canyons and carpeted with yellow and orange-hued grasses, is a habitat for foxes, guanacos, and birds of prey.

The natural diversity of Nahuel Huapí makes it an outstandingly popular year round resort for everything from skiing to bird watching in an idyllic setting.

An aerial view of lakes Nahuel Huapí and Correntoso in the Seven Lakes region of Patagonia. The Nahuel Huapí National Park is Argentina's oldest national park.

WHAT IS IT?
Mountains, lakes and plateau formed by glaciation.
HOW TO GET THERE:
Fly to San Carlos de Bariloche or take the magnificent scenic route from Chile by bus and boats across the lakes.
WHEN TO GO:
All year

NEAREST TOWN:
San Carlos de Bariloche
DON'T MISS:
Valle Encantada with strange rock configurations sculpted by wind and rain.
YOU SHOULD KNOW:
This is such a popular resort that the region is in serious danger of becoming ecologically degraded, so it must be treated with utmost respect.

Aconcagua

Cerro Aconcagua is the highest mountain in the Americas, at 6,962 m (22,835 ft), and is one of the "Seven Summits" – the highest mountains in each of the seven continents. The mountain is a gargantuan mass of non-volcanic rock with glaciers in all its northern and eastern valleys. Its snowbound peak towers over the dramatic scenery of the Uspallata Pass – the border crossing between Argentina and Chile.

Edward Fitzgerald, an English mountaineer, became the first person in 1897 to scale Aconcagua. In 1985, the mummified corpse of an Incan, preserved by the cold, was discovered at an altitude of 5,300 m (17,380 ft), proving that pre-Columbian civilizations explored these heights. It is not a technically difficult mountain to climb, and for that reason, it is all too often under-estimated. Aconcagua has one of the highest death tolls for any mountain in the world. Every year people die because they fail to realize the scale of the challenge, and have not made adequate psychological and physical preparations for the arduous task ahead of them. Extreme and unpredictable weather in the form of high winds, blizzards and electrical storms as well as the effects of altitude can make it a daunting prospect and climbers are frequently beaten back by the weather or altitude sickness.

You can trek through the wild high country around the mountain, admiring the many breathtaking views, or take one of several routes up to its summit, according to your climbing experience. The starkly beautiful mountain, with desolate slopes completely bare of any vegetation, casts its gigantic shadow for miles. At the summit you are on the roof of the Americas, gazing down at the Pacific Ocean on one side and the plains of Argentina on the other.

WHAT IS IT?
The highest mountain in the Americas
HOW TO GET THERE:
Fly to Santiago (Chile) or Buenos Aires (Argentina) then Mendoza 182 km (113 mi) from Puenta del Inca
WHEN TO GO:
Mid-December to mid-March. Outside these dates the mountain is out of bounds.
NEAREST TOWN:
Puenta del Inca
YOU SHOULD KNOW:
You must obtain a permit in Mendoza. You need at least two weeks, with five days for the actual climb, to acclimatize to the high altitudes.

The wild country around Aconcagua Mountain

147

AFRICA

The Atlas Mountains

Tizin'Test Pass and Atlas Mountains

The Atlas Mountains extend through Morocco, Algeria and Tunisia in a series of separate ranges that continue for about 2,400 km (1,500 mi). Within Morocco, they are divided north to south into the Middle Atlas, High Atlas and Anti-Atlas, rising at the Atlantic coast and stretching east to Algeria. These mountains were formed millions of years ago when the tectonic plates of Europe and Africa collided, causing uplift. They effectively separate the more moderate, Mediterranean climate to the north from the drier, harsher, Saharan climate of the south.

The Middle Atlas, the most westerly of the ranges, rises to the south of Fes. Its lovely oak, cork and cedar covered mountains hold waterfalls and plateaux studded with volcanic lakes. This region is not much visited, and to explore it properly you will need a car. Travelling south you will reach Midelt, beyond which rise the dramatic peaks of the High Atlas.

Further west, the High Atlas is usually approached via Marrakech. This is the best region for trekking holidays. Innumerable trails wind through lush, summertime valleys and mountainsides dotted with small Berber villages. One of the most popular routes includes Djebel Toubkal, at 4,167 m (13,668 ft), the highest mountain in Morocco. Two dramatic passes, the Tizi n'Test and the Tizi n'Tichka have been carved through these peaks, both affording spectacular views from their narrow, hairpin bends. The High Atlas is snow covered in winter and the skiing at Oukaimeden is thought to be the best in the country.

The Anti-Atlas extends from the Atlantic northeast to Ouarzarzate. These are starkly beautiful mountains reaching a maximum height of 2,531 m (8,302 ft). A particularly scenic journey can be made from Taroudant to Tafraoute, a gorgeous small town on the slopes of the Ameln Valley, surrounded by jagged mountains and strangely shaped granite rocks.

Tassili N'Ajjer

Designated a UNESCO World Heritage Site in 1982, Tassili N'Ajjer is a massive mountain plateau extending for nearly 500 km (300 mi) across the Sahara Desert of south-eastern Algeria. The soft sandstone has been carved by the wind and sand grains that howl across the desert into fantastic landforms, with sheer cliffs and sudden, unexpected, deep chasms and more than 300 rock arches. Because of its isolation, this beautiful landscape remains relatively undisturbed.

During the last ice age, this area used to be far wetter than it is today, and the sandstone has managed to retain some of the ancient moisture, allowing the growth of sparse woodland, including the Saharan myrtle and Saharan cypress. The wildlife was also much richer thousands of years ago, as can be seen from the cave paintings that dot the area and show such animals as antelope and crocodiles, as well as cattle, indicating that there must have been land for grazing and pasture and waterholes for the crocodiles. There are also vivid depictions of the life of the people who lived here. In order to protect the rock paintings from further damage, visitors can only enter the central area with an official guide or accredited tour group.

WHAT IS IT?
A strange landscape carved out of the stone of the Sahara.
HOW TO GET THERE:
By air from Algiers to Djanet or Tam.
WHEN TO GO:
Mid-autumn or mid-spring.
NEAREST TOWN:
Djanet 10 km (6 mi)
DON'T MISS:
The amazing lunar landscape.

Rock formations at sunset at Tassili N'Ajjer

Sand dunes stretch to the horizon in the vast dune sea known as the Grand Erg Occidental.

Grand Erg Occidental

Algeria, on Africa's Mediterranean coast, possesses some of the starkest but most beautiful landscapes on earth. Dominated in the north and south by mountain ranges and plateaux, and crossed by the Sahara Desert, it also has several of the largest inland sand-dune systems in the world, including the Grand Erg Occidental and Grand Erg Oriental: the Great Western and Eastern sand seas. In lowland basins, they are thought to be the remnants of ancient shallow seas or lakes. Unlike most of the Sahara, whose ground is a mixture of stones and pebbles, the ergs are the epitome of everyone's romantic image of deserts, with seemingly endless ranks of golden, knife-edged dunes marching into the distance.

There are no oases, so no-one can settle here and there are no roads or villages. A road skirts around the southern side of the erg, affording magnificent, if distant, views of the dunes and it is possible to travel a short way into the area from the beautiful oasis towns around its edge, like El Goléa, Beni Abbès and Tarhit. Even a brief walk into this surreal landscape leaves visitors in awe of the scale of these giant natural sculptures and with a readjusted sense of their own importance.

WHAT IS IT?
The second-largest sand sea in Algeria.
HOW TO GET THERE:
By air from Algiers to Ghardia, El Goléa or Timimoun, then by road.
WHEN TO GO:
Winter is cooler, while summer can be extremely hot.
NEAREST TOWN:
El Goléa 1 km (0.5 mi)
YOU SHOULD KNOW:
Go with an organized group, who will help to arrange permits, and an authorized guide.

Hurghada's Underwater Gardens

The Red Sea coast stretches south from the Suez Canal for some 800 km (500 mi). Hurghada, until fairly recently just a small, quiet fishing village, is now an internationally known diving and snorkelling centre, and the gateway to many vibrantly coloured underwater 'gardens'. The joy of Hurghada is that there are fabulous reefs teeming with multi-coloured fish within 10 m (33 ft) of the beach, enabling everyone to enjoy this underwater world. Even if you can't swim you can take a trip in a glass-bottomed boat from which you can gaze through the brilliantly clear waters to the reefs below.

There are many well-known sites here – each with its speciality. Dolphin House is a pinnacle situated at the western tip of Sha'ab El Erg, a large reef shaped like a half moon, with a shallow inner lagoon. Covered with table corals and giant fans, and home to several families of dolphins, the maximum depth here is just 12 m (39 ft). Small Giftun, within the Giftun Island National Park, is a fantastic playground for experienced divers. Here are caves, canyons and steep walls, black corals and large fish such as white tip sharks, barracudas and whale sharks. The Aquarium is part of a network of coral gardens and with a maximum depth of 15 m (49 ft) is an excellent spot in which to learn to dive.

Altogether there are 400 types of coral to be seen, and 1,500 species of fish, as well as turtles and dolphins. The marine environment here is protected, and the small daily fee that is charged goes towards conservation initiatives, marine park rangers and other protective measures. There are over 100 dive operations in the area, and whilst coral takes many years to grow, it is extremely delicate and easily damaged.

WHAT IS IT?
A large area of fabulously beautiful reefs, perfect for snorkelling, diving and other aquatic sports.
HOW TO GET THERE:
By air to Hurghada.
WHEN TO GO:
All year round, but the water is warmest from May to October.
NEAREST TOWN:
Hurghada is on the beach.
DON'T MISS:
The Roman remains at Gabal Abu Durkan.
YOU SHOULD KNOW:
The famed wreck graveyard at Sha'ab Abu Nuhas can be visited by joining an extended 'live aboard' dive trip.

Lionfish and turkeyfish are just two of the species on show in the gardens.

Reflection of sandstone in water, Siwa Oasis

Siwa Oasis

WHAT IS IT?
A remote oasis in Egypt's Western Desert
HOW TO GET THERE:
Overland from Cairo via Mersa Matruh or by air from Cairo to the new airport in Al-Alamein
WHEN TO GO:
Spring or autumn
NEAREST TOWN:
Siwa
DON'T MISS
A swim in Fatnas Spring
YOU SHOULD KNOW:
Women should cover up and alcohol is forbidden.

This remote oasis in the Western Desert, on the edge of the Great Sand Sea, only a few miles from the Libyan border and 550 km (342 mi) west of Cairo, has provided a place of refuge for many thousands of years. It is set in a depression 82 km (52 mi) long and 9–28 km (5.5–17 mi) wide. The average depth is 18 m (60 ft) below sea level. More than 1,000 slightly saline springs bring water through the sandstone rock to the surface here, and there are three major saltwater lakes. The slightly saline water allows the area's inhabitants to grow olives and dates, and lush, dense groves of these occupy the floor of the depression. Several of the springs can be bathed in, and their mineral waters are reputed to have medicinal qualities. A favourite is the Cleopatra Bath, where the water bubbles up from the ground into a deep pool. However, bathing in the lake belonging to the Oracle, which was famously visited by Alexander the Great, is regarded as sacrilegious.

The mountains and hills that lie within the oasis have caves in which people have lived or buried their dead and these may be reached via numerous tracks that wind through the landscape, offering views over this beautiful, peaceful landscape. Although technology is beginning to make its presence felt here and tourism is growing, Siwa is in large part an unspoiled, serene refuge, where the locals' cultural heritage is respected and maintained.

The Bandiagara Escarpment

The Bandiagara Escarpment

Listed as a UNESCO World Heritage Site in 1989, the stunning Bandiagara Escarpment lies in the south of Mali, and has a flora and fauna unique in the region. Eroded from rocks that are more than 400 million years old, the escarpment separates the sandstone plateau of the same name from the plaine du Séno. The stunning cliff runs north-east to south-west for roughly 150 km (90 mi) and ranges from 100 m (330 ft) in height in the south to 500 m (1,650 ft) in the north. The region's high seasonal rainfall – an average of 600 mm (2 ft) has been recorded between June and September – escapes underground through fissures and caves and re-emerges in springs along the bottom of the escarpment that allow the local Dogon to cultivate crops here.

Fissures in the rocks, ravines known as thalwags, rock pools and the areas around the springs have a unique microclimate and support a wide range of plants missing from the surrounding region, which is too dry for most of the year or has been ravaged by fire. In turn, these support a variety of migrant and resident wildlife, including scarlet-chested sunbirds, rose-ringed parakeet, yellow-billed shrike, numerous cliff chats, Egyptian plover, grey-headed kingfisher and hooded vultures, while the bustard is a speciality of the dry areas above the escarpment. Mammals that may be seen here include porcupine and rock hyrax, as well as the jackal and pale fox, with which the Dogon have a spiritual relationship.

WHAT IS IT?
A high escarpment, rich in natural history, archaeology and culture.
HOW TO GET THERE:
By plane to Bandiagara, then by road.
WHEN TO GO:
October–February, best during November–December.
NEAREST TOWN:
Bandiagara 44 km (27 mi)
DON'T MISS:
The ancient rock art.
YOU SHOULD KNOW:
The best way to see the area is with a Dogon guide.

157

W National Park

WHAT IS IT?
A national park, famous for its abundant wildlife, covering Niger, Benin and Burkina Faso.
HOW TO GET THERE:
By road from Niamey, Niger's capital.
WHEN TO GO:
December to April (the park is closed July to November).
NEAREST TOWN:
Niamey 152 km (95 mi)
YOU SHOULD KNOW:
You will need a registered park guide and a four-wheel drive vehicle in the park.

Niger's only national park, which also extends deep into the neighbouring countries of Benin and Burkina Faso, acquired its name because of the giant W shape of the double bend in the River Niger that forms its northern border. Covering a total area of 10,000 sq km (3,860 sq mi), of which some 2,200 sq km (850 sq mi) is in Niger, it was officially designated in 1954 and, in 1996, was included on the UNESCO World Heritage list. Because of its wetlands and the rich variety of birds which they attract, the park has also been designated a Wetland of International Importance under the Ramsar Convention.

Occupying a transition zone between savannah and forest, the park is known for its many large mammals, including elephants, buffalos, antelopes, hippos, spotted hyenas, baboons and warthogs as well as the cat carnivores – lion, leopard, cheetah and serval. Numerous waterholes have been constructed throughout the park to attract wildlife. There are thought to be at least 500 different plant species present in the park along with some 350 species of resident and aquatic migratory bird.

The W Park has managed to avoid the worst of the catastrophic consequences of unchecked poaching that has been seen in other West African parks. Yet now it is subject to another potential threat: plans for phosphate mining and the construction of a hydroelectric dam on its southern border, both of which could have long term serious ecological consequences for the park's well-being.

Tall termite mounds in W National Park

Lake Chad

Fifty years ago Lake Chad was the fourth largest lake in Africa and covered an area in excess of 25,000 sq km (9,650 sq mi), mostly in the far west of Chad but also extending into the neighbouring countries of Niger, Nigeria and Cameroon. Believed to be a remnant of a former inland sea, at its largest around 4,000 BC it measured some 400,000 sq km (154,000 sq mi). Today, however, as a result of reduced rainfall and desertification combined with increased demand for the lake's water, the area of the lake has been dramatically reduced to less than 1,000 sq km (386 sq mi) and it is now entirely within the borders of Chad.

The lake, which has an average depth of only 1.5 m (5 ft) and is a mere 7 m (23 ft) at its deepest, has many islands and mudflats within it and is home to a wide variety of wildlife, including fish, crocodiles, waterfowl and shore birds. It is surrounded by swampy vegetation mostly made up of reeds and papyrus, which is used to make canoes. Some of the islands are inhabited and used as bases for fishing, though the annual fish catch from the lake is about 20 per cent of what it was 40 years ago.

The lake is a vital resource for the 10 million people living in the area, yet while there are various ambitious schemes to divert river water into the lake, it is by no means impossible that Lake Chad will have completely dried up by the end of this century.

Lake Chad from space

WHAT IS IT?
A major water resource on the southern fringe of the Sahara.
HOW TO GET THERE:
By road (four-wheel drive recommended) from N'Djamena.
WHEN TO GO:
November to March.
NEAREST TOWN:
N'Djamena 100 km (62 mi) from the lake's southern end.
DON'T MISS:
Watching boats being made from reeds.
YOU SHOULD KNOW:
The lake is known for its yield of natural soda, which contributes to keeping the lake water fresh. Don't swim or wade in the lake (due to the presence of bilharzia parasites).

Niokolo-Koba National Park

WHAT IS IT?
One of West Africa's most important wildlife reserves.
HOW TO GET THERE:
By road from Tambacounda via Kedougou and Dar Salam.
WHEN TO GO:
March to May (closed June to November).
NEAREST TOWN:
Tambacounda 140 km (90 mi)
DON'T MISS:
The chimpanzees in the area of Mount Assirik.
YOU SHOULD KNOW:
There is an entrance fee. You must travel in a vehicle as walking is not allowed in the park.

One of the largest national parks in West Africa, Niokolo-Koba National Park is situated in the south east of Senegal and is famous for its diverse wildlife. The park, which covers an area of over 9,000 sq km (3,474 sq mi), is home to over 80 different mammal species, including lions, leopards, elephants, buffalos, hippos and hyenas, as well as some 30 types of reptile and over 300 different bird species.

The landscape throughout the park is generally flat; the varied vegetation includes savannah, forests, lakes and marshes. The park is well watered as the Gambia River, along with its tributaries, the Niokolo-Koba and the Koulountou, runs though it.

Included on the UNESCO list of World Heritage Sites in 1981, the park is also an international biosphere reserve. Today many of the large mammals are under threat from poaching: the numbers of leopards and elephants – the only herds remaining in Senegal – have shown significant decreases in recent years. The park's future is further threatened by several dam schemes and a road project which are under consideration in the area. While more tourists have been visiting the park of late, the numbers are still fairly modest due to the park's relative remoteness and its distance from Dakar, the capital. Potential visitors to the park may need to be reminded that, as in many wildlife reserves, though you will almost certainly see animals such as antelope and buffalo at Niokolo-Koba, sightings of lions or elephants, for example, are by no means guaranteed.

A Senegal parrot

Waza National Park

Buffon's Kob at a waterhole in Waza National Park

Waza National Park is a vast, remote area in the far North Province of Cameroon. Situated on the edge of the Sahel, between Chad and Nigeria, these flat acacia plains lie to the south of Lake Chad's floodplain, and are only accessible from mid-November to mid-June due to summertime flooding.

The park, which is an area of about 170,000 hectares (420,000 acres), was listed as a UNESCO Biosphere Reserve in 1982. It consists of a forested area, and huge expanses of feathery grasslands and seasonal marshes, making it home both to forest and savannah animals, as well as permanent and migrating birds.

This is probably the best place in Central Africa to observe wildlife, and in late spring, when only a few waterholes remain, a constant parade of fabulous animals arrive in search of water and shade, finding moments of much needed relief from the blistering sun.

The plains are teeming with animals – giraffe, antelope, hyena, cheetah, serval, warthog, elephants and lions. A multitude of birds can be seen here, as both African and Palearctic migrants are attracted by the habitat. Some 397 species have been sighted, including raptors such as griffon vultures, eagles, goshawks and buzzards, flocks of cranes, storks and egrets, and many species of migrant ducks and waders.

Needless to say, Waza National Park suffers from poaching. Unfortunately there are very few guards, making it impossible to secure the entire area, even with extra funding given by the World Wildlife Fund and the Netherlands IUCN Committee. Visit as part of an organized tour or bring your own 4 wheel drive vehicle. Whatever way you travel, you are bound to see a wealth of marvellous creatures roaming these golden plains.

WHAT IS IT?
A vast area of plains and woods, where myriads of birds and animals can be observed.
HOW TO GET THERE:
By 4 wheel drive from Maroua.
WHEN TO GO:
Mid-November to mid-June, but April/May is the optimum time to see lions.
NEAREST TOWN:
Mokolo 160 km (100 m)
YOU SHOULD KNOW:
Visitors are obliged to take a guide with them, and may not disembark from their vehicle.

161

A young Ethiopian goatherd in the Simien Mountains National Park north of the ancient city of Gondar.

Simien National Park

The Simien National Park lies in one of the most spectacular landscapes on earth. Over millennia, the Ethiopian plateau has been eroded to created a lunar vista of flat areas and peaks separated by dramatic steep-sided gorges that run down to broad valleys and grasslands.

At 4,620 m (15,157 ft), Ras Dejen is the fourth highest peak in Africa and snow often falls in the highest areas of the park, even though it is only about 13 degrees north of the equator, and temperatures can fall below 0 °C (32 °F) at almost any time of the year.

The park's specialities include several very rare animals, including the walia ibex, which occurs only here and is the reason for the park being set up, gelada (bleeding heart) baboons, Simien fox and small numbers of Ethiopian wolves.

This breathtaking landscape is perfect for trekking: from the lower slopes where farmers grow crops and graze animals, through the alpine forests and up to the high grasslands, where spectacular plants include giant lobelia and kniphofia. Mountain tracks between villages allow for easy access to most areas.

WHAT IS IT?
A national park and UNESCO World Heritage Site with stunning landscapes.
HOW TO GET THERE:
By road from Gondar
WHEN TO GO:
September to November is best
NEAREST TOWN:
Gondar 101 km (60 mi)
YOU SHOULD KNOW:
A guide and an armed guard are mandatory.

The Danakil Depression

This geological depression, sometimes called the Afar Triangle or the Afar Depression, is situated in the north east of Ethiopia and extends into neighbouring Eritrea and Djibouti, the area that is commonly known as the Horn of Africa. It is probably the most inhospitable place on the planet and is deserving of its nickname, the "Devil's Kitchen".

Part of Africa's Great Rift Valley, it is one of the hottest areas on earth and one of the driest, with only a few inches of rain falling each year. It is also one of the lowest regions, in places more than 120 m (390 ft) below sea level. Apart from the narrow green strip along the banks of the Awash River, the landscape is a mixture of desert scrub, rocky outcrops and mountains. About 1,200 sq km (463 sq mi) of the Depression is covered in salt and salt mining is still the principal source of income for many of the nomadic Afar tribespeople who inhabit this hostile environment.

The base of the Depression is composed of basalt lava and the whole area is a great source of interest to geologists and volcanologists. Hundreds of small earthquakes shake the area every year and volcanic cones and deep cracks in the earth are common sights. There are bright yellow fields of sulphur to be seen, not to mention places where boiling water and steam come bubbling out of rocks.

Despite the almost unremitting bleakness of the area, the few intrepid travellers who make the effort to go there are always left with a deep and lasting impression of this most extraordinary landscape.

WHAT IS IT?
One of the hottest, driest, lowest and most desolate places on earth.
HOW TO GET THERE:
By road (4 wheel drive) from Mekele.
WHEN TO GO:
September to March.
NEAREST TOWN:
Mekele.
DON'T MISS:
Erta Ale, one of the world's great active volcanoes.
YOU SHOULD KNOW:
A special permit to travel required; daytime temperatures can reach 50 ºC (145 ºF).

Cattle in the Danakil Depression

Lake Tana

WHAT IS IT?
The source of the Blue Nile, one of the world's great rivers.
HOW TO GET THERE:
By road to Bahir Dar.
WHEN TO GO:
December to April.
NEAREST TOWN:
Bahir Dar, one of Ethiopia's largest towns, lies on the lakeshore.
DON'T MISS:
The Blue Nile Falls at Tis Issat, 30 km (19 mi) from Bahir Dar. A trip on the lake on one of the local boats made from papyrus reed.
YOU SHOULD KNOW:
At least 15,000 people live on the islands in Lake Tana. The lake is the unique habitat for 15 species of barbus fish.

Situated in the northern highlands of Ethiopia, Lake Tana is not only the country's largest lake; it is also the source of the Blue Nile, which flows for a distance of some 1,500 km (938 mi) to Khartoum in Sudan. There it joins the White Nile to become the famous River Nile, flowing through the entire length of Egypt until it reaches the Nile Delta and the Mediterranean. Thus Lake Tana is important both as a source of food and water, as well as hydro-electric power, for Ethiopia, and it also contributes enormously to the livelihoods of tens of millions of people in the lower Nile basin.

About 85 km (53 mi) long and 65 km (41 mi) wide and at an altitude of about 1,800 m (5,900 ft), the lake, fed by four perennial rivers and numerous seasonal streams, has an average depth of only 8 m (26 ft) which can vary by as much as 2 m (6 ft 6 in) between the wet and dry seasons. The surface area of the lake similarly varies from 3,000 to 3,500 sq km (1,160 to 1,350 sq mi) dependant on the season.

Lake Tana contains a wealth of fish – the annual catch is over 10,000 metric tons – and there is an extraordinary variety of birds along the shores of the lake itself and its islands. There are 37 islands in the lake upon which stand some 20 monasteries and churches. Some of these date as far back as the 13th century and many of them contain paintings, frescoes and various historical religious artifacts.

Men paddling reed boats on Lake Tana.

Mgahinga Gorilla National Park

Despite being the smallest of Uganda's National Parks, Mgahinga, at 33.7 sq km (13 sq mi), is still one of the most important. It adjoins both Rwanda's Volcano National Park and the Democratic Republic of Congo's Virunga National Park. The Virunga Mountains are a series of both active and extinct volcanoes that straddle the border of these three countries, three of which (all extinct) can be climbed in Mgahinga.

Mgahinga is famous for its tiny population of endangered Mountain gorillas, including one family consisting of nine animals (including two silverbacks and three adult females) that are familiarized with tracking. This family often moves across the border into Rwanda, and therefore gorilla-tracking safaris can only be confirmed a short time in advance. Groups from the neighbouring countries sometimes visit the area for a month or two.

The tropical rainforest that covers the lower slopes has been somewhat depleted for farmland, but higher up there are abundant bamboo and Alpine forests. Largely vegetarian, male Mountain gorillas weigh as much as 430 lbs and can eat up to 75 lbs of vegetation each day. Gallium vines form a large part of their diet but they also love bamboo shoots, moving down to the bamboo forests when new shoots are available. They will also climb up to sub-alpine regions in order to eat another delicacy, the soft centre of the giant Senecio tree.

Mountain gorillas are almost extinct. There are thought to be between 650 and 700 animals left in the world, shared between these three countries. One of two sub-species of gorilla, they have longer, darker hair than other gorillas, enabling them to live at higher, colder altitudes. These charming, fascinating creatures are endangered by habitat loss, poaching and disease, particularly human diseases such as colds and flu to which they have no immunity.

WHAT IS IT?
Uganda's smallest national park, home to the Mountain gorilla.
HOW TO GET THERE:
By road from Kampala, or fly to Kisoro and then go by road.
WHEN TO GO:
June, July, August or January.
NEAREST TOWN:
Kisoro 10 km (6 mi)
DON'T MISS:
The view from the top of Mount Muhavura.
YOU SHOULD KNOW:
Gorilla tracking permits are in high demand, so organise your trip and permit several months in advance.

A family group of Mountain gorillas in Mgahinga National Park

Bwindi Impenetrable National Park

WHAT IS IT?
True African jungle – one of East Africa's largest forests; home to over a third of the world's population of Mountain Gorillas.
HOW TO GET THERE:
By road from Kampala via Kabale.
WHEN TO GO:
December to February and May to August.
NEAREST TOWN:
Kabale 29 km (18 mi)
DON'T MISS:
The many spectacular birds and butterflies
YOU SHOULD KNOW:
In many places the forest is indeed impenetrable; only 12 visitor permits are issued per day.

Bwindi Impenetrable National Park is, at 331 sq km (128 sq mi), one of the largest areas of tropical rainforest in east Africa. Situated in a landscape of steep, rugged hills and deep, narrow valleys along the border with the Democratic Republic of Congo, it warrants its name. This is a prime example of the jungle of our imagination – vast trees, draped with creepers, mistletoe and orchids, struggle to reach the sunlight, while beneath them the dense undergrowth of twisting vines and ferns occasionally gives way to thickets of bamboo, swamps, marshes, rivers and grassland. Where the sun breaks through the leafy canopy, exotic and colourful plants such as heliconia add sudden splashes of colour.

The flora and fauna in Bwindi are incredibly impressive, with over 200 types of tree and 100 species of fern. At least 120 species of mammal live here, and the area is rich with primates – Colobus monkeys leap between branches, families of chimpanzees search for fruit, vervets and baboons chatter and hoot, adding a subtext to the twittering and screeching of some 350 different species of bird.

Amongst Bwindi's populations of endangered species are some 23 families of Mountain gorilla. Living at a lower altitude than those in the Virunga Mountains, it is thought that these may be a distinct sub-species, with shorter hair and longer limbs. Four of the families are used to humans and can be tracked and observed, but there are other fascinating safaris and hiking trails here too – even on the shortest stretch you are likely to see primates, duikers and both forest and grassland birds as well as some of the glorious 202 types of butterfly. Stand in the jungle and wonder at the silence as you watch the cream-banded swallowtail, which occurs only here, flutter past, then enjoy the sudden sounds of monkeys and birds exploding into action for a few minutes before stillness and tranquillity reign again.

A view of the sunrise over Uganda's forests and Bwindi region

Rwenzori Mountains National Park

A Uganda Kob (Kobus kob) *herd in front of the Ruwenzori Mountains.*

The Rwenzori National Park lies on the border between Uganda and the Democratic Republic of Congo, in the forested slopes of the Mubuku Valley. It consists of six massifs, which, unlike many of the other mountains in the Great Rift Valley, are not volcanic. The highest mountain is Mount Stanley, named after the British explorer, who was the first European to see it, in 1887. At 5,109 m (16,762 ft), it is the third highest mountain in Africa. The other five massifs are Mount Speke, Mount Baker, Mount Emin, Mount Gessi and Mount Luigi di Savoia. They are separated by deep gorges with lush vegetation, which ranges from tropical rainforest, through giant moss-covered heathers, alpine meadows and bogs, up to the snow-capped peaks. The rainforest's cushiony canopy shades ginger, tree ferns, begonias, aram lilies, balsam and hibiscus, which fill the air with heady aromas. Higher up are giant lobelias, groundsel and senecios.

Animals that visitors may see include bushbuck, forest elephants, giant forest hogs, black-and-white colobus monkeys, blue monkeys and chimpanzees, as well as massive pink and green worms. Birdlife includes purple-breasted and regal sunbirds, handsome francolins and Rwenzori turacos.

In common with Kilimanjaro and Mount Kenya, the Rwenzoris are losing their ice cover, with more than half of their glaciers disappearing in less than a century. The effect that this loss will have on the range's ecosystem is not yet known.

WHAT IS IT?
A beautiful wildlife haven and World Heritage Site.
HOW TO GET THERE:
By road or rail from Kampala to Kasese, then by road to the park.
WHEN TO GO:
July to August or December to February, when it is driest
NEAREST TOWN:
Kasese 25 km (16 mi)

167

Lake Victoria

WHAT IS IT?
The largest lake in Africa, the third largest fresh water lake in the world and source of the White Nile.
HOW TO GET THERE:
The towns of Kampala and Entebbe (Uganda), Kisumu (Kenya) and Mwanza (Tanzania) all lie on the shores of the lake.
WHEN TO GO:
June to October and December to February.
DON'T MISS:
Fishing for Nile perch (some weigh over 80 kg)
YOU SHOULD KNOW:
In the 1990s the lake was being choked by water hyacinth – this was solved by the introduction of a small South American beetle which devoured the weed.

As well as being Africa's largest lake, Lake Victoria is the largest tropical lake in the world. It covers a vast area of some 68,800 sq km (26,560 sq mi) – about the same size as Ireland. Like Africa's other two great lakes (Tanganyika and Malawi) it lies within the Great Rift Valley, yet unlike them, it is relatively shallow with an average depth of 40 m (131 ft).

The lake is situated on the great plateau between the Western and Eastern Rift Valleys at a height of 1,134 m (3,720 ft) above sea level. Most of its shoreline of 3,440 km (2,138 mi) lies within Uganda and Tanzania with a smaller part in Kenya. This is one of the most densely populated regions in Africa and the lake plays a vital part in supporting the millions of people living in the many towns and villages both on and close to its shores. Fishing, particularly for Nile perch and tilapia, provides a living for many along the lakeside; fish from Lake Victoria are exported all over the world, as well as being sold locally. There are 200 species of fish to be found in the lake, though the introduction of the Nile perch in the 1950s has led to the extinction of some further 300 species of fish that had survived there for hundreds of years. As a result, Lake Victoria could unenviably lay claim to having experienced the greatest mass extinction of vertebrates in modern times. Hippos and crocodiles were once numerous in the lake too but their numbers are now much reduced as a result of pollution and over population by humans.

There are over 3,000 islands in the lake, many of which are inhabited; the 62 islands that form the Sese archipelago are famous for their fishing both by locals and foreign tourists. The lake is also important for its transport – there are many passenger boats and cargo vessels that ply between the trading towns and villages lining the lake's shores.

Masai Mara National Reserve

Wildebeest (Connochaetes taurinus) *crossing the Mara River during their migration.*

Set in the south-west of Kenya, near the border with Tanzania, the Masai Mara National Reserve is one of the best wildlife sites in the world. Its plains and acacia scrub are home to lions and cheetahs, baboons, zebras, spotted hyenas, waterbuck, Masai, Rothschild's and common giraffes, buffalo, white rhino, Thomson's and Grant's gazelles, dik dik, Coke's hartebeest, topi, impala and Roan antelope.

Elephant herds roam the bush, while the Mara River itself provides pools and wallows for hippos and cover for leopards and crocodiles. Black rhino are increasingly rare and difficult to spot.

More than 450 species of birds have been seen here, including crowned crane, flamingo, ostrich, pelican, hornbill, marabou stork, secretary bird and thousands of vultures that stalk the migrating herbivores, hoping to profit from a lion's leftovers.

Of course, the Masai is best known as being the site of one of nature's greatest spectacles: the annual migration of 1,200,000 wildebeest, more than 350 thousand Thomson's gazelles and more than 190,000 zebra. In May and June, these animals leave the neighbouring Serengeti and head north, beginning their return journey in October, following the fresh pasture that springs up after seasonal rains.

A visit to this vast rich landscape, full of spectacular wildlife is not an experience that anyone will easily forget.

WHAT IS IT?
One of the best game reserves in the world.
HOW TO GET THERE:
There are two airfields within the reserve, but most tours arrive by road from Nairobi.
WHEN TO GO:
July to September for the migration, or any time of year for the resident wildlife.
NEAREST TOWN:
Narok 67 km (41 mi)
DON'T MISS
A balloon trip over the reserve.
YOU SHOULD KNOW
For safety, visitors must stay with their guides or Masai guards.

169

Mount Kenya

WHAT IS IT?
The second highest mountain in Africa.
HOW TO GET THERE:
By road from Nairobi
WHEN TO GO:
The dry seasons are January-March and July-October. The wet seasons are from March-June and October-December.
NEAREST TOWN:
Naro Moru 17 km (11 mi)
YOU SHOULD KNOW:
At this height, the air is thinner and altitude sickness is a possibility. Don't over exert yourself until you have adjusted.

An extinct stratovolcano of extreme beauty, Mount Kenya is the second highest mountain in Africa, at 5,119 m (17,058 ft). Despite being not far south of the equator it has for thousands of years been capped with glaciers, although these are now retreating at an alarming rate. The national park was created in 1949 and it became a UNESCO World Heritage Site in 1997.

The high peaks, above the beautiful U-shaped glacial Makinder Valley and emerald-green tarns, are a draw for climbers, but the lower slopes hold a fantastic array of wildlife in their beautiful and varied habitats.

During the dry periods, large mammals, such as eland, elephant, buffalo and zebra, move upwards to the high open moorland, and have been seen as high up as 4,000 m (13,120 ft).

Below the moorland is an area of high-altitude heath and shrubs, then a layer of upper forest with small trees and mosses, then a dense forest of bamboo followed by a montane forest with podocarpus, juniper and cedar, and finally a dry upland forest. These varied habitats support black-and-white Colobus and Sykes monkeys, baboons, bushbuck, waterbuck, bush pigs, giant forest hogs, black rhinos, leopards, genet cats and hyenas, black-fronted duiker, bongos and sunni buck. With such a range of heights and habitats, Mt Kenya is also known for its amazing variety of birds.

There are many climbing routes within the park, with huts to stay in overnight, suitable for different levels of fitness and ability. Although there are enough beautiful landscapes and amazing animals lower down, it is only by getting to the higher reaches of the mountain that you can appreciate the worth of this spectacular place.

Mount Kenya

The Great Rift Valley

The Great Rift Valley is probably the greatest natural wonder in the world. This amazing fissure in the earth's crust was formed some 30 million years ago when the shifting and separating of several tectonic plates uplifted volcanoes and caused parts of the earth's crust to sink between parallel fault lines. It runs for about 6,000 km (3,750 mi) from the Lebanon to Mozambique, and its most dramatic section divides Kenya in two.

The Western Rift is edged by some of Africa's highest mountain ranges. Mounts Kilimanjaro, Kenya, Meru and other volcanoes can also be found here, as can some of the world's deepest and largest lakes. Boiling hot springs provide evidence of the continuing volcanic activity of the region.

A series of lakes runs along the Rift Valley. Some, like Lake Naivasha are freshwater lakes, irrigating fertile orchards, vegetable crops and flowers, many of which are exported to Europe. Others, such as Lake Bogoria, are soda lakes, their waters full of sodium carbonate upon which blooms of blue-green algae form, producing a habitat for tilapia and other fish, thus drawing vast flocks of birds. Lake Nakuru lies at the narrowest point of the Rift Valley, between the Mau Escarpment and the Aberdare Mountains. Coming from Nairobi, the road climbs gently up through the highlands, arriving abruptly at the edge of the Rift. The valley is at its deepest here, dropping dramatically by some 1,800 m (5,904 ft) to the floor below and providing visitors with an awe-inspiring view.

The national parks and game reserves of the Rift Valley are home to hundreds of thousands of exotic animals that graze and hunt on the golden grasslands. There is no more extraordinary place on earth, and it is no surprise that the fossilized remains of some of humanity's earliest ancestors have been found here, providing us with essential information about our evolution.

The Eburru Mountains form part of the western wall of the Rift Valley.

WHAT IS IT?
The world's greatest geological feature.
HOW TO GET THERE:
By road from Nairobi.
WHEN TO GO:
July to September and December to February.
NEAREST TOWN:
Nairobi 60 km (37 mi)
DON'T MISS:
The Samburu Game Reserve, Naivasha National Park, Hell's Gate National Park.
YOU SHOULD KNOW:
Karen Blixen's marvellous book *Out of Africa* gives a fascinating insight into some of the colourful characters she knew during 17 years of coffee farming in the Rift Valley in the early part of the 20th century.

171

Great White Pelicans fly over feeding flamingos at Lake Nakuru.

Lake Nakuru

Less than 160 km (100 mi) from Nairobi, Kenya's capital city, Lake Nakuru is world famous for the huge number of flamingos that inhabit its shores. The extraordinary sight of the continually shifting mass of pink created by often more than a million flamingos on the lake is truly breathtaking.

The flamingos are attracted by the algae that thrive in the shallow, warm and strongly alkaline waters of the lake. Scientists estimate that the flamingos consume as much as 250,000 kg (551,200 lbs) of algae per hectare per year. In the dry season the lake's area reduces to little more than 5 sq km (2 sq mi) but the rains increase it to about 45 sq km (17 sq mi) and the flamingo population on the lake varies accordingly. Pelicans and cormorants are also common and there are thought to be over 400 resident bird species on the lake and in the surrounding park.

In recent years the flamingo population has decreased alarmingly partly as a result of intensive crop production in the surrounding area and the increased water usage in nearby Nakuru, which is Kenya's fourth largest city.

The lake and the surrounding area was designated Lake Nakuru National Park in the 1960s and later enlarged to some 190 sq km (73 sq mi) as well as being fenced off primarily to protect the populations of Rothschild giraffes, and the black and white rhinos which have been introduced to the park. It is the only fully fenced national park in Kenya.

WHAT IS IT?
Home to up to 2 million flamingos.
HOW TO GET THERE:
By air and/or road from Nairobi via Nakuru.
WHEN TO GO:
July to February.
NEAREST TOWN:
Nakuru 5 km (3 mi)
DON'T MISS:
The many fauna (especially the rhinos) and flora in Lake Nakuru National Park.
YOU SHOULD KNOW:
The best vantage point to view the flamingos is Baboon Cliff. Nakuru means 'dust' or 'dusty place' in the Maasai language.

Lake Turkana

Lake Turkana lies within a mainly arid landscape. It is fed by three rivers, but has no outflow, so water levels fluctuate during the year, creating an ever-changing landscape. Set in the eastern part of the Great Rift Valley in northern Kenya, this UNESCO World Heritage Site is a rich haven for wildlife. The surrounding land is littered with extinct volcanoes and old basalt lava flows, and one of the volcanic islands in the lake, Central Island is still active.

Europeans first discovered the lake in 1888, but it is obvious that it had been inhabited for far longer than that: the palaeontologist Richard Leakey discovered human remains here dating from some three million years ago.

Visitors today come to see the wildlife: mammals here include plains, Burchell's and Grevy's zebras, Grant's gazelles and reticulated giraffes, as well as their predators, lions and cheetahs. Like many of the Rift Valley lakes, Lake Turkana is a hotspot for migrating birds, the most spectacular of which are the flocks of pink flamingos, although wood and common sandpipers, African skimmers and white-necked cormorants may also be seen. However, Turkana's best known wildlife attraction is its 22,000 Nile crocodiles, which colonized the lake long ago when its waters were higher and they could reach it from the White Nile.

Although remote and not easy to reach, the jade-green waters of Lake Turkana and its abundant wildlife make this spectacular site a true must-see.

WHAT IS IT?
The world's largest alkaline lake.
HOW TO GET THERE:
By three-day road trip from Nairobi.
WHEN TO GO:
October–April for the birds, April–May for the crocodile hatch.
NEAREST TOWN:
Lodwar 75 km (47 mi)
YOU SHOULD KNOW
Ranger-led tours are a must: much of the wildlife is dangerous.

A volcano next to Lake Turkana

Sipi Falls on the slopes of Mount Elgon

Mount Elgon National Park

The extinct volcano of Mt Elgon, lies at the heart of the spectacular national park that bears its name. It is an area with a rich variety of wildlife, including spotted hyenas, rock hyraxes and leopards, but it is for its herd of elephants that it has, rightly, become famous.

The sparse vegetation that many herbivores in Africa eat does not give them sufficient minerals in their diet, including sodium, so they have to find sources elsewhere, such as natural salt licks, where salt has been leached from the rocks and deposited by water. These sites are sometimes found near the water holes that the animals use. However, in Mt Elgon National Park, the elephants have taken things a step further.

There are several caves here that contain deposits of salt and over many centuries the largest of them, Kitum, has been carved 200 m (660 ft) into the mountainside by the elephants so that they can exploit the salt. Each night, led by one of the herd elders, they wend their way to the cave and through its twisting passages to the salt deposit, gouging the rock surface with their tusks before licking the salt off.

It is an eerie spectacle to watch, as 100 or more of these large mammals approach the cave through the night, finding their way blindly along a route memorized by previous generations of elephants over hundreds of years.

WHAT IS IT?
A beautiful landscape with one of nature's most special wildlife watching moments.
HOW TO GET THERE:
By road via Kitale
WHEN TO GO?
June-August or December-March
NEAREST TOWN:
Mbale 24 km (15 mi)
YOU SHOULD KNOW
The caves also harbour bats.

Serengeti National Park

The Serengeti covers 60,000 sq km (23,000 sq mi) of Tanzania and Kenya, of which 14,763 sq km (5,700 sq mi) make up the former's Serengeti National Park, which was established in 1951 to protect the millions of animals that live here. Its rolling plains are covered in savanna grasses and areas of acacia trees. The three African big cats – lion, cheetah and leopard – can all be seen here, as can their prey: zebra, gazelle, wildebeest and antelope. Other mammals here include elephant, giraffe, hippopotamus, buffalo, rhino, hyena and baboon. More than 500 species of bird have been identified here.

Serengeti means 'endless plains' in Maasai, and it is the openness of the landscape here that makes wildlife viewing relatively easy and the park such a popular place for safaris.

Twice a year, the Serengeti witnesses one of the greatest spectacles in nature: the mass migration and return of millions of wildebeest, zebra and Thomson's gazelles from here to the plains of the Masai Mara to the north, in pursuit of seasonal vegetation and water. Seeing, and hearing, seemingly endless herds of animals thundering across the plains is an experience no one will ever forget. Although the exact timing depends upon when the rains arrive, the migration generally starts in April-May and the return journey is usually completed by October-November.

WHAT IS IT?
One of the best places in the world to go on safari.
HOW TO GET THERE:
By road or charter flight from Arusha or Mwanza
WHEN TO GO:
It is spectacular all year, but the migration April-June migration season is best.
NEAREST TOWN:
Arusha 335 km (210 mi)
DON'T MISS:
A balloon ride over the plains

An adult leads baby African elephants (Loxodonta africana) across the Serengeti plain.

Ngorongoro Conservation Area

Centred around the collapsed crater of an ancient volcano in the southern part of the Great Rift Valley, the Ngorongoro Conservation Area is a stunningly beautiful landscape that holds a fantastic range of wildlife. There are good populations of lion and cheetah, as well as resident wildebeest, zebra, eland, Grant's and Thomson's gazelles, mountain reedbuck, hippo, black rhino, hartebeest, elephant, spotted hyena, jackal and buffalo. Twice a year, millions of migrants pass through on their way to and from the Serengeti, following the rains that bring fresh pasture. More than 550 species of birds have been seen in the park, with the flamingos of Lake Magadi being perhaps the most special.

The huge crater formed some two million years ago when the volcano erupted violently and its magma chamber collapsed, creating the largest unbroken volcanic caldera in the world, with a maximum diameter of 22.5 km (14 mi) and a depth of 610 m (2,000 ft).

In the wider park, there are more mountains, including several active volcanoes, forests, lakes and wide plains. In the north are the Maasai sacred mountain, Oldoinya Lengai, the Olduvai Gorge where some of the earliest remains of modern man (*Homo habilis*) as well as early man (*Paranthropus boisei*) were discovered and the soda lake, Lake Natron, where thousands of pink flamingos breed on little mud mounds.

A visit to this remote park, with its awe-inspiring landscapes and plentiful wildlife, is a must-see for any wildlife lover.

WHAT IS IT?
The largest intact volcanic caldera on Earth.

HOW TO GET THERE:
By road from Kilimanjaro International Airport.

WHEN TO GO:
The wildlife is always spectacular, but is particularly special during the migration season in December and June.

NEAREST TOWN:
Arusha 190 km (120 mi)

DON'T MISS:
A guided walking safari.

Olduvai Gorge

WHAT IS IT?
Often called 'The Cradle of Mankind'.
HOW TO GET THERE:
By road (4 wheel drive) from Arusha.
WHEN TO GO:
September to February.
NEAREST TOWN:
Arusha 150 km (94 mi)
DON'T MISS:
Serengeti National Park; The ruins at Engaruka; Empakai Crater Lake; Lake Manyara.
YOU SHOULD KNOW:
You must hire an official guide. The name Olduvai originates from a European misspelling of Oldupaai, the Maasai word for the wild sisal plant that grows throughout the gorge.

One of the most significant prehistoric sites in the world, the Olduvai Gorge is located in northern Tanzania, at the border of the Ngorongoro Conservation Area and the Serengeti National Park. The steep sided gorge is about 48 km (30 mi) long and is situated on a series of fault lines, which, thanks to centuries of erosion, have yielded an unequalled treasure trove of fossilized bones, teeth, tools, flora and fauna.

The land is now semi-desert, but thousands of years ago it was covered with lush forest, fed by streams flowing into the Olduvai Lake. Successive layers of volcanic ash and stones covered the area, but exposed fossil deposits show seven distinct layers, covering a time span from about 2.1 million to 15,000 years ago.

Louis and Mary Leakey began excavations here in the1950s, and work continues to this day. The earliest discoveries showed that primitive hominids lived here in small camps, hunting for food and using stone tools made of flakes of basalt and quartz. These tools were named Oldowan as this is the first site in which they were ever found. The skeletal remains of various early hominids have been found here, up to and including one complete skeleton of *Homo sapiens*, dated to 17,000 years ago. Possibly the greatest discovery of all was made by Mary Leakey, when she found fossilized footprints dating to 3.75 million years ago, proving that our pre-human ancestors walked in an upright position.

On the edge of the gorge is a museum, founded by Mary Leakey in the late 1970s, and centred around the paleoanthropological artefacts discovered in the area. Some 20 years later it was renovated and added to by the J. Paul Getty Museum. The discoveries at Olduvai Gorge have been instrumental in furthering our understanding of early human evolution.

Remains of prehistoric man were found in this archaeological site at Olduvai Gorge by Louis Leakey between 1960-63. He named the hominid fossil Homo habilis *and argued that this represented a direct link to man's ancestor* Homo erectus.

Selous Game Reserve

The sun sets over the River Rufiji in Selous Game Reserve.

Selous Game Reserve is an absolutely enormous area of some 50,000 sq km (19,300 sq mi). Large enough to be a country in its own right, it occupies 5 per cent of Tanzania, and is larger than Switzerland. Inscribed as a UNESCO World Heritage Site in 1982, sections of the reserve were first designated as a hunting area in 1905, and in 1922, when extra land was added, it was named after Fredrick Selous, a popular Victorian explorer and author. Constant additions to its boundaries have made it one of the largest game reserves in the world.

The landscape consists of rolling, grassy woodland and plains covered by unusually lush grass and tangled vegetation as well as the Rufiji River and its delta. This impressive river is the life blood of Selous, from narrow, rock sided Stiegler's Gorge to the tributaries, sand rivers, oxbow lakes, lagoons and channels of the delta, it is the main water source of the region.

Best known for its huge herds of elephants, which migrate annually across the border to Niassa Game Reserve in Mozambique, the park is home to large numbers of animals. Lions, leopards and cheetahs all thrive here, hunting antelope, wildebeest, eland and zebra. One third of all the remaining endangered African wild dogs roam freely and thrive in Selous, which also contains some of the region's last black rhinos. The river is home to hippos and crocodiles, and attracts many of the reserve's 440 species of bird.

Selous has various safari camps and lodges, mainly situated around the Gorge area, but is otherwise uninhabited. Roads here are impassable during the rainy season, but camps can be reached by plane. Safaris by boat are increasingly popular, and it is one of the only African reserves that allow safaris on foot, accompanied by an armed ranger. Few visitors come here, but those who do enter an absolutely untamed wilderness and gain a life-enhancing experience.

WHAT IS IT?
The second largest game reserve in Africa, home to a unique combination of both East and South African wildlife.
HOW TO GET THERE:
Most visitors fly into Selous from Dar es Salaam; road travel is only possible during the dry season.
WHEN TO GO:
June to November for viewing game along the rivers and January to April for bird watching.
NEAREST TOWN:
Dar es Salaam 150 km (94 mi)
DON'T MISS:
Stiegler's Gorge, boating safaris, walking safaris.
YOU SHOULD KNOW:
This is a region of malarial mosquitos and Tsetse flies.

Lake Tanganyika

Lake Tanganyika, which is situated within the Western Rift, is one of the most ancient lakes in the world. Largely surrounded by mountains, the sidewalls of the Great Rift Valley rise sharply to a height of 2,000 m (6,600 ft) from its western shore. The longest lake in the world, at 673 km (421 mi), it is also the second largest freshwater lake by volume, as well as the second deepest, and its health is vitally important to an estimated 10 million people.

Two large and many smaller rivers flow into Lake Tanganyika, which has one major outflow, the Lukuga River. The extraordinary depth of the lake, at its maximum 1,470 m (4,850 ft), prevents 'turnover' of the water, resulting in much of the lower depths lacking oxygen. However, this is a lake that is teeming with life, much of it endemic, which has evolved through millennia.

Over 1,500 species of flora and fauna from the lake have been described thus far, with new species being added each year, making it one of the richest freshwater ecosystems in the world. About 600 of these species occur nowhere else. Six species of fish dominate the open waters, including some of the finest game fish in Africa such as the Goliath tiger fish and the predatory Lates, a species related to the Nile perch.

The lake is rich with cichlid species, 98 per cent of which are endemic, and these brightly coloured fish are extremely popular within the aquarium trade. There are also numerous invertebrates here, crabs, shrimps, jellyfish and molluscs and more, again largely endemic to these waters. This is wonderful territory for researchers, anglers, divers and snorkellers – the visibility around the rocky shoreline is superb, often more than 20 m (66 ft). However, don't allow yourself to be totally dazzled by the gorgeous tropical cichlids as the lake is also home to the slender snouted crocodile.

Mount Kilimanjaro

WHAT IS IT?
The highest mountain in Africa
HOW TO GET THERE:
By air to Kilimanjaro international airport, then by road.
WHEN TO GO:
December–January is the most popular time. Avoid April, May and November when it is wet.
NEAREST TOWN:
Moshi 15 km (9 mi)
DON'T MISS:
Sunrise from Gilman's Point
YOU SHOULD KNOW:
You will need clothing for almost every type of weather.

Set in the national park of the same name in north-eastern Tanzania, Mount Kilimanjaro, a dormant stratovolcano, is the highest mountain in Africa. Gases still rise from fumaroles in Kibo crater and scientists estimate that there is a pool of magma only 400 m (1,300 ft) below the 2.4-km (1.5-mile) diameter crater. At 5,895 m (19,340 ft), Kibo is the youngest and highest of the three volcanic cones.

Despite its position near the equator and the residual warmth from the last eruption, Kibo is so high that its peak, Uhuru, remains covered in snow all year, although the amount of snow and ice is less and less year by year on average and the glaciers are retreating rapidly.

There are various climbing routes up to the three peaks: Kibo has several that may be attempted by novices, while Mawenzi should not be attempted by anyone without rock-climbing and ice-climbing skills.

Groups climb the mountain accompanied by guides and porters, stopping at mountain huts overnight. Kibo hut, the last on that cone on the Marangu route (one of the most straightforward), is at 4,720 m (15,500 ft) and most people who make it this far opt to make the final 1,175-m (3,840-ft) ascent in the dark because the scree slope is less slippery and because they get the reward of watching the sunrise from the spectacular setting of Gilman's Point on the crater rim before continuing to the top.

Mount Kilimanjaro from Kenya

The journey up the mountain takes climbers through a variety of beautiful habitats, from rainforest to bush, sparse woodland draped with eerie hanging mosses, moorland and alpine desert, bare rock and ice. On the lower slopes the mountain looms over the landscape, only to be hidden in the dense rainforest and then burst into spectacular view again as the climbers emerge.

The views across the landscapes of northern Tanzania and southern Kenya make even this challenging climb well worth every effort.

Victoria Falls

Known to the people of the Kololo tribe who lived in the area in the nineteenth century as 'Mosi-oa-Tunya' - 'the Smoke that Thunders', Victoria Falls is one of nature's greatest spectacles. The spray above it can be seen from almost 65 km (40 mi) away. The River Zambezi flows through a shallow valley across a flat basalt plateau for miles, but in some places, cracks in the basalt exposed the weaker sandstone below and the water was able to force a way through and begin to erode it. The 8 km (5 mi) of steep-sided gorges the Zambezi cuts through here represent hundreds of thousands of years of erosion.

Victoria Falls is neither the highest nor the broadest waterfall on earth, but with a single drop of 108 m (360 ft) and a width of 1.7 km (1 mi), it is claimed to be the single largest falling sheet of water. At the peak of the rainy season, more than 546 cu m (2.5 million gallons) spill over the falls per minute.

Because the gorge is so narrow, it is simple for visitors to get a spectacular view of the thundering waters from as little as 60 m (200 ft) away, if they are prepared both to brave the path along the opposite edge and to get very, very wet. The Knife-Edge Bridge affords views of the main falls, the Boiling Pot and the Eastern Cataract, while the Lookout Tree and Victoria Falls Bridge give panoramic views of the falls and gorge.

At the height of the river's spate in March to May, a plane ride along the gorge and above the falls makes an exhilarating experience and an amazing way to see one of nature's best wonders.

A close-up view of Victoria Falls

WHAT IS IT?
One of the largest waterfalls on earth, set in a spectacular gorge.
HOW TO GET THERE:
By air to Livingstone or Victoria Falls, by road or rail from Lusaka or by rail from South Africa, then by car.
WHEN TO GO:
Winter, when the flood is not at its peak but the falls are not obscured in spray.
NEAREST TOWN:
Livingstone 10 km (6 mi)
DON'T MISS:
A plane ride over the falls.

Sunrise over Lake Malawi

Lake Malawi

WHAT IS IT?
The third largest freshwater lake in Africa.
HOW TO GET THERE:
By air to Lilongwe, then overland.
WHEN TO GO:
April–October.
NEAREST TOWN:
Salima (20 km, 12 mi)
DON'T MISS:
A trip in a traditional boat.
YOU SHOULD KNOW:
The lake is divided between Malawi, Mozambique and Tanzania.

Lake Malawi is the southernmost lake in Africa's Great Rift Valley. Formed about 40,000 years ago, it is 580 km (360 mi) long at 75 km (47 miles) across at its widest point, making it Africa's third largest lake. Its crystal-clear blue waters are set amid a stunning landscape of rocky outcrops and lush wooded slopes, swamps, lagoons and reedbeds.

Formerly known as Lake Nyasa, Lake Malawi has an abundance of wildlife including chachma baboons and vervet monkeys, hippos and bush pigs, leopards, crocodiles and water monitors. Birdlife in the area includes white-breasted cormorants, which nest on several of the lake's islands.

However, it is the lake's fish that justify its inclusion on the World Heritage List. It is home to a greater variety of freshwater tropical fish than anywhere else in the world, including almost 500 species of a group called the cichlids. These species constitute almost one-third of all the species in the group and make the lake an important place for biologists to study the evolutionary processes that have occurred in an enclosed environment.

But it is not just scientists who can appreciate the riches of Lake Malawi: away from the settlements by the shore, it is a serene wildlife-watcher's paradise.

Tsingy of Bemaraha

Located some 80 km (50 mi) inland from Madagascar's west coast, much of this reserve is a mass of sharp-ridged limestone pinnacles – 'tsingy' in the Malagasy language – some rising up to heights of 50 m (160 ft) and cut through with canyons and gorges. Declared a nature reserve in 1927, this extraordinary mineral 'forest' was recognized as a UNESCO World Heritage Site in 1990 and opened, in part, to the public as recently as 1998.

These peculiar rock formations, which are unique to Madagascar, were created by erosion as the acidity of rainwater over the centuries gradually dissolved the stone of the chalky plateau. The pinnacles are so close together as to make the area virtually impenetrable by humans; yet there are many species of lemur here whose agility is entirely unaffected by the razor-sharp stone environment.

The eastern border of the reserve is defined by the Bemaraha Cliff, which rises dramatically some 400 m (1,300 ft) above the Manambolo River valley. The northern part, which is closed to the public, is a mixture of undulating hills and limestone extrusions.

Madagascar is famous for its unique diversity of wildlife – nearly 90 per cent of the species to be found on this beautiful island, the world's fourth largest, can only be found here – and the Tsingy of Bemaraha reserve itself is the only known location for a number of rare plants and animals, some of which are endangered. There are numerous springs at the base of the pinnacles and the Tsingy provides an important water catchment function for the surrounding area, particularly to the west.

WHAT IS IT?
A reserve with a unique 'forest' of limestone pinnacles.
HOW TO GET THERE:
Flights from Antananarivo to Antsalova then by road (4 wheel drive).
WHEN TO GO:
July to October.
NEAREST TOWN:
Morondava 225 km (140 mi)
DON'T MISS:
The ancient cemeteries in the Manambolo Gorge. The avenues of Baobab trees near Morondava.
YOU SHOULD KNOW:
There are no facilities within the reserve. The nearest hotel is 150 km (94 mi) away. Road travel is slow and arduous.

An aerial view of Tsingy of Bemaraha

Madagascar's Rainforests

Madagascar, the world's fourth largest island, lies in splendid isolation some 480 km (300 mi) off the south east coast of Africa, in the Indian Ocean. Its separation from Africa occurred between 150-180 million years ago, and produced the extraordinarily high levels of endemic species of flora and fauna for which the island is famed. Much of Madagascar's forest cover has been destroyed during the last hundred years – 50 per cent of it since 1950. This deforestation is directly linked to coffee cultivation: because the most fertile land is used for export crops, the local inhabitants are obliged to clear the forested slopes for their own subsistence farming.

Madagascar's remaining rainforests run from north to south down the eastern side of the island, between the mountainous central highlands and the coast. They consist of dense evergreens with a canopy of some 30 m (66 ft), within which a biological treasure trove of endemic plants and animals exist. Almost all of Madagascar's mammals are found here, including the island's star turn, 15 species and sub-species of lemur, all of which are now endangered. These remarkable, attractive creatures, known as prosimians, were evolving when the island floated free from Africa. Monkeys, which had not yet appeared, were never able to reach Madagascar, and lemurs were never able to live anywhere else.

The diversity of Madagascar's plant life is bewildering – there are at least 8,000 endemic species of flowering plants alone, and botanists are still classifying flora and discovering new species. The world needs Madagascar: Vinscristine, the drug that changed the survival rates in childhood leukaemia from 20 to 90 per cent, is just one of the drugs that came from the Madagascar rosy periwinkle. This is now extinct. We can only imagine what we could be losing each time a piece of this rainforest is lost.

The tropical rainforest and beach

Gorges of the Bras de Caverne

Gorges of the Bras de Caverne

The French island of Réunion lies some 650 km (406 mi) off Madagascar's east coast, close to Mauritius. About 65 km (40 mi) long and 45 km (28 mi) wide, it is a popular destination for adventurous tourists who are attracted by the prospect of exploring and trekking in the spectacular mountainous region in the centre of the island.

The gorges created from volcanic fractures, such as the bed of the Bras de Caverne river, have in the past made access to this region difficult and, as a result, the tropical forests of giant heathers, ferns and lichens have been preserved, unlike those in the lower lying parts of the island where they have, for the most part, disappeared. One of the biggest, and certainly the most famous and spectacular of the gorges is the Trou de Fer (Iron Hole). Over a distance of about 3.5 km (2 mi) the Bras de Caverne River plunges down almost 930 m (3,050 ft) over three dramatic waterfalls and then winds its way down a narrow canyon till it joins the Rivière du Mât on its way to the Indian Ocean.

A considerable number of adventure sports enthusiasts, especially in France, have taken up canyonning in recent years and the Trou de Fer, which was only discovered in 1989, has become something of a 'destination' for them – albeit a very challenging one.

WHAT IS IT?
Dramatic ravines surrounded by tropical forest.
HOW TO GET THERE:
By road from St. André via Salazie.
WHEN TO GO:
May and June.
NEAREST TOWN:
St André 25 km (16 mi)
DON'T MISS:
The Piton de la Fournaise and the Piton des Neiges volcanoes.
YOU SHOULD KNOW:
Accommodation on Réunion is quite expensive and needs to be booked well in advance.

187

The Piton de la Fournaise volcano puts on a great display.

Piton de la Fournaise

Along with Mount Erebus in Antarctica and Kilauea in the Hawaiian Islands, Piton de la Fournaise ("Peak of the Furnace") is one of the most active volcanoes on earth. It is situated in the south east corner of the French island of Réunion which lies in the Indian Ocean between Madagascar and Mauritius.

Thought to be over 500,000 years old, it is known to the locals simply as Le Volcan ("The Volcano"). There have been more than 150 eruptions recorded since the 17th Century and in the space of a year it erupted on three separate occasions. Throughout most of its history the eruptions have overlapped with those from the even larger, older, but now extinct volcano Piton des Neiges in the north west of the island.

The top part of the volcano, at a height of 2,632 m (8,635 ft), is a caldera – or crater – that is 8 km (5 mi) wide and contains a 400 m (1,312 ft) high lava shield. Most eruptions take place within the caldera and, because it is uninhabited, these cause little significant damage, though when there are eruptions outside the caldera (the most recent was in 1986) they are potentially dangerous. The caldera is breached on the eastern side into the sea; sometimes the erupting lava reaches the sea with spectacular results. Numerous craters and pyroclastic cones are to be seen within the caldera and also on its outer flanks.

It is quite easy to walk to the top of the mountain but really the view from below is the most spectacular. Piton de la Fournaise spews out orange and yellow lava day and night and the evening pyrotechnics are better than any fireworks display.

WHAT IS IT?
One of the world's most active volcanoes and Réunion's most popular tourist attraction.
HOW TO GET THERE:
By road from St-Joseph, then by foot.
WHEN TO GO:
May to November.
NEAREST TOWN:
St-Joseph 24 km (15 mi)
DON'T MISS:
A helicopter trip over the volcano.
YOU SHOULD KNOW:
Since 1978 the volcanic activity has been constantly monitored by a modern volcanological observatory.

Vallée de Mai Nature Reserve, Praslin Island

The beautiful island of Praslin lies 50 km (31 mi) north-east of Mahé, the main island of the Seychelles, and amidst the hills at its heart, lies one of the smallest, most perfect of the World Heritage Nature Reserves, itself surrounded by the Praslin National Park. This is the tropical island of one's dreams, surrounded by shimmering white sand beaches and turquoise seas, its interior hosts a wealth of flora and fauna, much of which is endemic. The climate remains steady throughout the year as it lies tranquilly outside the cyclone belt.

The Vallée de Mai covers only 18 hectares (44 acres) but it is unique, containing the remains of the palm forest that once covered the entire island, in virtually its original state. All six of the endemic Seychelles palm species thrive here, in particular some 6,000 Coco-de-Mer palms, one of the wonders of the botanical world. These extraordinary trees are the stuff of legend. Their straight, bare trunks rise to 30 – 40 m (99 – 132 ft) in height, topped by large, stiff fans of leaves and huge fruits, each about 50 cm (19.7 in) long and weighing up to 20 kg (44 lbs). These are the largest seeds on earth. Male and female trees stand next to each other, the larger male apparently protecting its mate. Their reproductive organs mirror those of men and women and they produce one or two bunches of suggestively shaped nuts each year. Germinating and growing very slowly, Coco-de-Mer palms live for hundreds of years – the oldest specimens here are over 800 years old.

The valley's forest, virgin until 1930, has many other remarkable plants and trees, but it is also home to a mass of animal life. Chameleons, geckos and snakes rustle through the undergrowth, and the two streams originating in the valley are home to endemic freshwater crabs, large freshwater prawns and the only endemic freshwater fish in the Seychelles. Over 100 species of birds flit through the trees, including the noteworthy Black parrot, which lives only here. No surprise, then, that General Gordon of Khartoum claimed, in 1881, that he had visited the Garden of Eden, and seen the Tree of Knowledge and the Forbidden Fruit – the Coco-de-Mer.

WHAT IS IT?
The only habitat for the Coco-de-Mer, whih has the largest seed in the plant kingdom.
HOW TO GET THERE:
By air or ferry boat from Victoria, on Mahé Island.
WHEN TO GO:
From May to September.
NEAREST TOWN:
Victoria 50 km (31 mi)

Dense forest in the Vallée de Mai Nature Reserve

Aldabra Atoll

WHAT IS IT?
One of the largest atolls in the world and home to around 100,000 Great Indian Ocean tortoises.

HOW TO GET THERE:
Virtually the only way is to join a cruise ship, embarking at Victoria, on Mahé Island.

WHEN TO GO:
May to November.

NEAREST TOWN:
Victoria, on Mahé Island (but it's a long way at around 1,200 km (750 mi)

DON'T MISS:
Bird watching in the nature reserve on Cousin Island; a visit to the beautiful island of La Digue; the Vallée de Mai on Praslin Island.

YOU SHOULD KNOW:
Aldabra Atoll is uninhabited and very isolated. Astove Atoll, part of the Aldabra Atoll, used to be occupied by African slaves who escaped from a Portuguese ship in 1760.

Lying in isolation in the western part of the Indian Ocean, Aldabra, at 34 km (21 mi) long, 14.5 km (9 mi) wide and 8 m (26 ft) above sea level, is the second largest atoll in the world. It consists of four raised reef limestone islands surrounding a lagoon of 224 sq km (86 sq mi) that loses two thirds of its waters during low tide. Despite being little known to outsiders, Aldabra is considered to be a natural wonder of the world by the scientific community, and was given World Heritage status in 1982.

The tidal range is between 2-3 m (7-9 ft), and large volumes of water flow in and out of the lagoon via small reef passages and three larger channels. Lying mainly within the lagoon itself are 40 smaller rocks and islands, providing nesting areas for thousands of frigate birds and red-footed boobies. Many other birds come here too, the most unusual being the Aldabra flightless rail, the only flightless bird found on any Indian Ocean island.

Aldabra's remoteness has led to high levels of endemism – 22 per cent of the 273 species of plant to be found here are endemic. Its fauna include the endangered hawksbill and green turtles, but its most famous inhabitant is the giant tortoise, of which there are some 100,000 individuals – ten times the number on Galapagos.

For almost 100 years scientists have been studying the structure, flora and fauna of the atoll, which is uninhabited other than by those working at the small research station here. The terrain is inhospitable to humans as the limestone has been eroded into many sharp spikes and water filled pits, but extensive mangroves support fish nurseries, and beneath the surface of the lagoon at high tide is a wealth of marine life, from black-tipped reef sharks to eagle rays and parrot fish that literally pour in to feed, returning to the open sea when the tide turns once again.

Aldabra Atoll

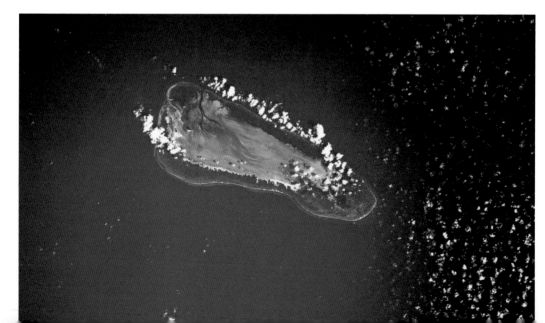

Black River Gorges National Park

The small island of Mauritius lies in the Indian Ocean, to the east of Madagascar, and its isolation has produced a quantity of endemic species of flora and fauna. The Black River Gorges National Park was established in 1994, and listed as a UNESCO World Heritage Site in 2006 in order to protect the last remaining indigenous forests of the island and the endangered species within them. Sadly, human activity, loss of habitat and natural disasters such as cyclones has caused the extinction of many of these species.

The National Park consists of cliffs and gorges carved by water over millions of years – this was once a region of active volcanoes, now long extinct. Today there is marshy heathland, dwarf upland forest, creeks, waterfalls and fantastic panoramic views over the gorges and down to the sea. There are splendid indigenous trees here, for example the extraordinary Bois de Natte, its umbrella-shaped outline luxuriantly draped with ferns, lichens and sensuous orchids. Here too is Casuarina, Colophane, Tatamaka, Tambalacoque and Ebony, but amongst the 163 endemic flora the most famous is the Trochetia, the country's national flower.

Mauritius has only 28 of its endemic bird species remaining, but the Park provides habitats for them all. Conservation programmes are in place to save the Mauritius kestrel, Pink Pigeon and Echo Parakeet, but twitchers are more likely to see White tailed tropic birds, yellow eyed canaries, Mauritius bulbuls or Mascarene martins. There are 60 km (37 mi) of marked trails that wind through the park, leading visitors to viewing points for amazing panoramic vistas, as well as to the island's highest point at Black River Peak.

WHAT IS IT?
A national park that protects the last remaining original woodland of Mauritius and much of its endangered, endemic flora and fauna.

HOW TO GET THERE:
By air to Mauritius, then by road to the Park.

WHEN TO GO:
The best time is between May and December.

NEAREST TOWN:
Curepipe 6 km (4 mi)

DON'T MISS:
The Chamarel waterfall, the seaside resort of Souillac, Casela Bird Park, a boat trip to Ile Aux Cerfs.

YOU SHOULD KNOW:
Between May and September Le Morne is a top kite- and wind-surfing destination, where manufacturers often trial the kites and boards of the future.

Black River Waterfall

The Skeleton Coast

WHAT IS IT?
A wildlife reserve in one of the earth's most inhospitable regions.
HOW TO GET THERE:
By road from Windhoek
WHEN TO GO:
Summer
HOW TO GET THERE:
Via the Ugab gate in the south
NEAREST TOWN:
Hentiesbaai 50 km (30 mi)
YOU SHOULD KNOW:
The southern area of the park is open to anyone who has obtained a permit, but the northern half is a designated wilderness area and visits are allowed only on fly-in safaris with designated companies. Supplies, such as water and petrol are available only at Terrace Bay rest camp so spares must be carried at all times.

Namibia's Skeleton Coast Park is a desolate strip of dunes, leading inland to multicoloured mountains and canyons. It is thought to be named for the skeletons of the numerous ships that have been wrecked on its shores and for the men who did not make it back to civilization. It receives less than 10 mm (0.4 in) of rain a year, but some life is able to survive here because of the frequent fogs caused by the interaction of the cold Benguela Current and sea breezes offshore and the hot dry air of the desert. Desert plants and some small animals trap the fogs' moisture while others, such as the oryx are adapted to get water from the plants that they eat and to go for weeks without water. When rain does fall, the desert temporarily bursts into bloom as plants such as lithops, which normally resemble stones, flower briefly before subsiding to wait for next year's rains.

Other animals in this remote landscape, which stretches 500 km (310 mi) south from the Kunene River, include desert elephants, which live on plants fed by rare underground springs, and, the lucky visitor might catch a glimpse of black rhino, porcupine, brown hyena, lion, ostrich, gemsbok or springbok. A wide variety of seabirds and waders can be seen along the coast.

Temperatures vary wildly between day and night and between the coast where it is always chilly and the interior, where mornings are warm but afternoons cooler.

Visitors to this otherworldly landscape are always struck by its stark beauty and desolate isolation.

An aerial view of a shipwreck, one of hundreds along the shores of the Skeleton Coast.

Etosha National Park

Zebras drinking from a water hole.

Etosha National Park in Namibia is one of the best places in which to view big game in southern Africa. Covering more than 20, 725 sq km (8,000 sq mi), it is dominated by the Etosha Pan, a vast, flat, saltpan surrounded by grassland and thorny savannah. Millions of years ago this was a lake, but today it only holds water briefly during the rainy season, attracting thousands of flamingos and white pelicans which fly in to breed. Its eerie, silvery white surface is so huge it can be seen from space, and at ground level mirages formed by reflected heat are common.

To the west of the saltpan lies Mopane bushland, and to the north east, dry forest. Around the southern part are many permanent waterholes, and it is these that provide visitors with the most wonderful opportunities to see many of the species that inhabit this park. There are thought to be more than 2,000 elephants here, 250 lions, 2,500 giraffes, 6,000 zebras and 20,000 springbok, but there are other, exciting animals too. Leopards and cheetahs stalk many different types of antelope including the endemic black-faced impala, and the Park is recognized as one of the last remaining homes of the highly endangered black rhino.

A car is needed to visit Etosha, which has a network of well maintained tracks around the edge of the pan leading from the three camps within the park to various waterholes at which the animals congregate. Each camp has its own waterhole, floodlit to facilitate night viewing. After sunset, visitors must remain inside a camp, or leave the park for one of the surrounding lodges. The waterholes are so rich with species that you might see a dozen at one viewing and the most difficult decision you will have to make is whether to stay put and wait for different species to arrive, or to drive to another waterhole altogether.

WHAT IS IT?
One of southern Africa's major wildlife reserves.
HOW TO GET THERE:
By air to Windhoek and Ondangwa, then by road.
WHEN TO GO:
May-September for game, November-March for birds.
NEAREST TOWN:
Outjo and Tsumeb 100 km (62.5 mi)
DON'T MISS:
The Haunted Forest, Batia, Okaukuejo, the Charitsaub/Salvadora/Sueda waterhole cluster.
YOU SHOULD KNOW:
Stay at a private lodge or join a tour in Windhoek if you want a guided safari. Book your entry permit well in advance.

The Namib Desert

The Namib Desert

The oldest desert on Earth, the Namib stretches for some 1,600 km (1,000 mi) along the Atlantic coast of southern Africa, within the Namib Naukluft National Park. It receives less than 10 mm (0.4 in) of rain per year and is one of the driest places on earth. Its massive red and grey dunes form at right angles to the prevailing wind and seem to march in unending ranks as far as the eye can see. Dune 7, at more than 380 m (1,250 ft), is the highest sand dune on the planet.

The interaction between the dry air of the desert and moisture-laden air over the sea causes immense fogs to form, and to the north lies the Skeleton Coast, the final resting place of many ships lost in the fog and unable to escape the strong currents.

For many of the animals in the desert, the fog is a lifeline, bringing extra moisture to this arid landscape, allowing insects and small reptiles to survive. There is a surprising variety of wildlife here, with 45 species of lizards and 200 types of beetles, as well as wasps and spiders. Reptiles here include geckos and sidewinder snakes, which make a distinctive pattern of waves in the sand as they move. Birds that breed here include sand grouse and ostrich, while the mammals are represented by baboons.

From the top of one of these dunes, sunrise and sunset are spectacular events, as the dunes are 'painted' in different colours with the changing light. At the coast, the sight of the swollen sun slipping below the sea is an added bonus.

Kalahari Desert and Okavango Delta

The Kalahari Desert, which spreads over 930,000 sq km (360,000 sq mi) of Botswana, South Africa and Namibia, is a semi-arid land subject to summer rainfall that provides grazing. The only permanent river in this red-brown, dusty land is the Okavango, which runs south-east from the highlands of Angola and drains into the Okavango Delta in the north-west of the Kalahari, creating an area full of spectacular wildlife. The highlight is the Moremi Wildlife Reserve. Seasonal rainfall in the Angolan highlands leads the delta to flood in the north in mid-summer (November to December) and in the south in mid-winter (May to June), giving rise to a constantly changing landscape.

Animals that inhabit the reserves in the Kalahari include several species of antelope, brown hyenas, lions, African wild dogs, cheetahs and meerkats. Among the spectacles of this arid region are the massive communal nests of weaver birds, which drape the acacia trees.

The delta itself is home to such large mammals as African elephants, African buffalo, hippos, and black and white rhinos. Giraffes, blue wildebeest, zebras, warthogs and chacma baboons are also here, as well as species of antelope such as lechwe, topi and greater kudu. Predators and scavengers here include lions, leopards, cheetahs, hyenas and wild dogs and the waters harbour Nile crocodiles and water monitors. More than 450 species of birds have been seen here, including crested cranes and African fish eagles.

A visit to this beautiful, lush landscape, set within the surrounding desert, is an experience that will not easily be forgotten.

WHAT IS IT?
A wildlife heaven set in the middle of a giant desert.
HOW TO GET THERE:
By air to Maun, Botswana, then overland.
WHEN TO GO:
May to October.
NEAREST TOWN:
Maun 80 km (50 mi) from the Moremi Wildlife Reserve
DON'T MISS
A canoe trip on the river.

The Okavango Delta

The Swartberg Mountains

The Swartberg Mountains

WHAT IS IT?
Western Cape's highest mountain range.
HOW TO GET THERE:
By road from Cape Town or Port Elizabeth.
WHEN TO GO:
April, May, September and October are best for walkers.
NEAREST TOWN:
Prince Albert and Oudtshoorn sit north and south of the Swartberg Pass.
DON'T MISS:
The once-secret valley of Gamkaskloof, first inhabited by farmers in 1830 and only accessible by foot until 1963 when a road was finally built into the valley.
YOU SHOULD KNOW:
In winter and early spring the mountains are often snow covered.

The Swartberg Mountains are a chiefly sandstone massif of considerable rugged beauty that runs roughly east west across the Western Cape. An absolute paradise for anyone who loves the great outdoors, there are numerous popular day hikes and for the more adventurous the five-day Swartberg Hiking Trail. Almost any walk into the mountains will reveal some treasure, be it a tinkling waterfall or a crystal-clear pool. The Rust-en-Vrede waterfall, some 18 km (11 mi) from Oudtshoorn, is 80 m (260 ft) high and well worth the trip.

The Swartberg Mountains range in altitude from 700 m to a lofty 2,325 m (2,300–7,625 ft). In area they span some 5,000 sq km (2,000 sq mi) – roughly a quarter the size of Wales. This makes them manageable enough to explore but large enough to harbour hidden surprises.

There are several passes through the range, but the most famous and spectacular is the eponymous Swartberg Pass. Built by Thomas Bain in the late nineteenth century, it somewhat tortuously links the towns of Oudtshoorn in the south with Prince Albert in the north. It's 27 km (17 mi) of winding switchbacks with jaw-dropping views at every turn. At the top, some 1,583 m (5,200 ft) above sea level, travellers are rewarded with quite spectacular views over the Little Karoo to the south and the Great Karoo to the north.

The vegetation of these mountains is incredibly varied, and while spring is the showiest season, early autumn is when the many kinds of protea burst into bloom. Adding to the display, sunbirds and sugarbirds are drawn to their nectar rich flowers. More than 130 bird species have been recorded, pied kingfishers and three kinds of eagle among them. More surprising is that there are also antelope here – in particular the klipspringer, or 'rock jumper'. This shy, dog-sized creature can seemingly skip up almost vertical rock faces. Another remarkable inhabitant of these mountains is the Rock dassie – or Cape hyrax. Although it looks much like an oversized guinea pig, it is believed to be a relative of the elephant!

Hermanus and Walker Bay

Nestled at the heart of Walker Bay, Hermanus is a jewel of a resort. One of South Africa's oldest, it was founded by Hermanus Pieters in the early nineteenth century. Its popularity grew steadily and today it is one of the most attractive destinations along South Africa's self-styled Riviera.

With the blue waters of the Atlantic before it, the inspiring Overberg Mountains behind and golden beaches stretching north and south, Hermanus is breathtakingly beautiful. But if that were not enough to draw the crowds, it can also lay claim to being the 'whale capital of the world' – offering the best land-based viewing of these awesome animals anywhere in the world.

In fact Hermanus is the only town in the world with an official 'whale crier' who can be seen wandering the streets and advertising the arrival of the town's most welcome visitors with a blast of his horn.

The whale watching season typically runs from April to October, when these giant denizens of the deep sojourn in the shallow, warm waters of Walker Bay to breed. At times almost 100 females and their calves congregate in the bay. A 12 km (9 mi) cliff path stretches from one side of town to the other and provides numerous vantage points. Frequently the whales come within just a few metres of the cliffs offering spectacular views and irresistible photo opportunities. Telescopes by the Old Harbour Museum, right in the heart of town, afford even closer views of these majestic creatures.

The whales are Southern Right whales (*Eubalaena australis*) – so-called because the whalers considered them the 'right' whales to hunt. Right whales are baleen whales; instead of teeth they have brush-like plates that they use to sieve their food from the water. Easily identified by their lack of a dorsal fin, these giants can grow 11-18 m (35-60 ft) in length and weigh 30-80 tonnes.

Although whale watching is what brings most people to Hermanus, the town is not short on attractions. The inviting white sands of Grotto Beach, the botanic delights of the fynbos and the delicious produce of the local vineyards make Hermanus irresistible at almost any time of year.

WHAT IS IT?
A spectacular seaside resort with great whale watching.
HOW TO GET THERE:
By road or train from Cape Town
WHEN TO GO:
Early autumn, March to April, offers the best weather. April to October is best for whale watching.
NEAREST TOWN:
Cape Town 90 km (56 mi)
DON'T MISS:
The beautiful Hemel-en-Aarde valley, where you can sample some of South Africa's finest wines.

A group of Southern Right whales (Eubalaena australis) *on the surface off Hermanus*

The Cape Floral Region

WHAT IS IT?
Home to one of the richest collections of plant life to be found anywhere in the world.
HOW TO GET THERE:
By air to Cape Town, then by road along the N2.
WHEN TO GO:
Flowers bloom all year but the season peaks between August and October.
NEAREST TOWN:
The region includes many towns including Cape Town to the west.
DON'T MISS:
See Southern Right whales from boat or shore at Hermanus, a 90-minute drive from Cape Town.
YOU SHOULD KNOW:
Flowering begins in the Springbok area of the Northern Cape and spreads southwards as the weather becomes warmer. The flowers are at their best during the hottest part of the day from 11 am to 3 pm.

The Cape Floral Region (CFR) in southwestern South Africa is a botanical Garden of Eden, blessed with an unsurpassed wealth of plant life, including a multitude of species found nowhere else in the world. The CFR comprises the smallest and the richest of the world's six floral kingdoms – and is the only one to be contained within a single country. So rich in diversity is this region that is has been declared one of South Africa's seven World Heritage Sites by UNESCO.

The total area of the CFR extends to nearly 90,000 sq km (35,000 sq mi), making it only a little larger than Scotland, and yet it contains three per cent of the world's plant species. In fact, with around 9,000 different species, 70 per cent of which are unique, this thin coastal strip of southern Africa boasts the highest density of plant species found anywhere in the world.

What enables this tiny corner of Africa to host such an abundance of plant life is its incredible variety of habitats. These range from coastal dunes to rugged mountains, fertile plains to semi-arid shrub lands. The dominant vegetation here is 'fynbos' – Afrikaans for fine bush – and among it four kinds of plant dominate: proteas, ericas, restios and geophytes.

Proteas, such as the king protea, South Africa's national flower, typically have large, beautiful blooms. Ericas, or heathers, are far less showy with their tiny leaves and bell-like blooms. Even more unassuming are the restios, reed-like grasses that are among the oldest plants of the fynbos. The geophytes, however, are far more eye-catching, comprising stunning orchids, such as the rare red disa, as well as lithe and lovely arum lilies.

Although a few plant enthusiasts are drawn to the region in search of the many rarities – by far the majority of visitors come to the Cape Floral Region to enjoy the breathtaking expanses of colour when the fynbos burst into bloom each spring.

Pincushion protea flowers (Leucospermum reflexum) grow in the Cape Floral Region of South Africa.

The Drakensberg Mountains

The Drakensberg Mountains

Listed as a UNESCO World Heritage Site in 2000, the Drakensberg, the Dragon's Mountain, is a bluish, spiky escarpment of rock that in part forms a natural boundary between South Africa and the kingdom of Lesotho. The highest range in southern Africa, the Drakensberg separate the coastal lowlands of KwaZulu Natal from the high interior. Several of the peaks tower above 3,000 m (9,843 ft) and the highest – Thabana Ntlenyana reaches 3,482 m (11,422 ft).

This steep land is cut through by streams and rivers, creating a spectacular landscape of gorges and river valleys. Among the most popular attractions is the Tugela Falls in the Royal Natal National Park. These five falls make up the second highest waterfall on the planet, dropping 947 m (3,110 ft) into the 'amphitheatre', with an average flow of 1 cubic metre (50 cu ft) a second.

While the higher mountain areas are a paradise for hikers, there are several game reserves and wildlife parks within the area covered by the Ukhahlamba-Drakensberg World Heritage Site, offering protection to a wide variety of animals in a range of landscapes, including nearly 300 bird species, several of which are extremely rare, and 48 species of mammal, as well as more than 2,150 species of plants.

WHAT IS IT?
A 1,000-km (600-mi) mountain range in southern Africa.
HOW TO GET THERE:
By road from Pretoria for the north, from Durban for the south.
WHEN TO GO:
November to March
NEAREST TOWN:
Ladysmith 70 km (48 mi)
DON'T MISS:
The rock art of the San people, depicting their relationship with the animals they hunted.
YOU SHOULD KNOW:
It can get very cold in winter.

The Cango Caves

The Cango Caves contain some of the most stunning subterranean scenery to be found anywhere in the world. Situated along South Africa's famous Garden Route, these remarkable caves have a long history both in the making and as one of the country's premier tourist attractions.

The caverns formed over millions of years, as water percolated through a narrow ridge of Precambrian limestone that runs parallel to the Swartberg Mountains. They form an interlinked system that stretches for over 5 km (3 mi). The largest of the caverns measures an echoey 107 m (350 ft) across and 16 m (52 ft) high. Impressive though this is, it is not the caves' size but their remarkable contents that suck thousands of visitors underground every year. For the Cango Caves contain a truly wondrous showcase of natural art, created by the limestone-laden water that has seeped and dripped its way through these voids over the millennia.

Many of the caves bear evocative names, such as the Fairy Queen's Palace and the Throne Room, and visitors are encouraged to apply their imagination to the wondrous sights they encounter. These include everything from impressive collections of stalactites and stalagmites some joined to form mighty stone columns to more unusual helictites, twiggy stone formations that grow in all directions. More impressive still are the subtly coloured flowstones that resemble frozen rivers, and the almost unbelievable stone curtains that hang before your eyes like petrified waterfalls.

Visitors can choose between an hour-long exploration of eight chambers or a 90-minute Adventure Tour that involves some steep climbs and a good deal of wriggling though narrow passages. Whichever tour you chose, however, the Cango Caves will not fail to amaze, and for summer visitors their more or less constant 18 °C (64 °F) will come as a welcome respite from the burning heat above.

One of the many amazing formations in the Cango Caves

Duiker Island

Duiker Island is a small rocky protuberance that lies just a short boat ride away from the popular fishing settlement of Hout Bay, in the Western Cape. Despite the island's name, visitors to this rocky refuge won't find any small antelope here. Instead, they will come face to face with a huge colony of Cape fur seals (*Arctocephalus pusillus*) a species of sea lion – up to 5,000 of them.

The sea that churns around the island may look blue and inviting, but it is often disappointingly chilly, due to the Benguela Current that carries icy water north from the Antarctic. This cold water, however, provides plenty of fish for the seals to hunt. What is in short supply, however, are safe refuges where the seals can clamber onto dry land. And it is for this reason that Duiker Island becomes so over-populated.

Most of the seals that gather here are immature males. But a number of females do raise their young here, and visitors in December may be lucky enough to catch sight of a black-coated pup still too young to swim.

Fur seals differ from so-called true seals in that they have external ears and they can rotate their rear flippers forwards and so more easily walk and climb on land. But they remain most at home in the water. They learn to swim from about six weeks and adults can reach speeds of up to 17 kph (10 mph) in pursuit of prey. Seals seem to enjoy the water in the way dolphins do, and as they dive and twist around visitors' boats they often appear to be performing for the audience's benefit.

Although it is the seals that steal the show, visitors to Duiker Island may also be rewarded with views of numerous seabirds – including the increasingly rare bank cormorant.

WHAT IS IT?
A tiny offshore island, home to thousands of Cape fur seals.
HOW TO GET THERE:
By boat from Hout Bay.
WHEN TO GO:
Seal numbers are highest January to March.
NEAREST TOWN:
Hout Bay.
DON'T MISS:
The World of Birds at Hout Bay – the largest bird park in Africa.
YOU SHOULD KNOW:
Boat trips to the island last between 40 minutes and 1 hour.

Cape fur seals on Duiker Island

*The interior of one of the
Sudwala caves*

The Sudwala Caves

The Sudwala Caves are believed to be the oldest caves in the world, making them an irresistible destination for anyone travelling through the Mankelekele Mountains of Mpumalanga. Geologists estimate that they began forming about 240 million years ago, after stress fractures cracked the mountains' 3,800 million year old Precambrian dolomite. Water soon found its way through the fractures, corroding the dolomite and creating the great caverns that today house a breathtaking subterranean tableau of stalactites, stalagmites, flowstones and dripstones.

A welcome refuge since prehistoric times, in 1914 the caves were first exploited commercially when the bat guano they contained was dug out and sold for fertilizer. It wasn't until 1966, however, that landowner Philippus Rudolf Owen opened them to the public.

The cave entrance itself is remarkably discreet, being set in the side of the mountain at the top of a short stone stairway and framed by a wrought iron facade. The main caverns, reached by a level path, are large, airy and unusually dry. This is due in part to the refreshing breeze that blows through the caves – the source of which remains one of the cave's secrets. The temperature is a cool and constant 17 °C (63 °F).

The main cave – the P. R. Owen Hall – is a truly cavernous 70 m (230 ft) across, and is the largest dolomite chamber in the world. Its ceiling disappears some 37 m (120 ft) up into the darkness.

Atmospheric lighting enhances the caves' many impressive formations, and the echoey silence is frequently punctuated by squeals of delight when visitors encounter the terrifying 'Screaming Monster', the remarkable 'Lowveld Rocket', or the towering 'Samson's Pillar'.

Although the cave system is believed to be more than 30 km (18 mi) long, the one-hour daily tours only explore the first 600 m (2,000 ft) or so. For the more adventurous, the once-a-month, five-hour Crystal Tour takes visitors 2 km (1.2 mi) through the cave, with the tour culminating at a chamber glittering with crystals of aragonite.

The Witwatersrand

From the air, the Witwatersrand is easily overlooked. A small and quite unremarkable range of sedimentary hills, it forms the watershed between the rivers Vaal and Olifants in what is now the province of Gauteng.

But the Witwatersrand isn't renowned for its scenery, or even its wildlife. A clue to its claim to fame lies in its name. Often shortened simply to 'the Rand', this region gave its name to South Africa's currency – and for good reason. For there is gold in these Witwatersrand hills – lots of it. In fact, around 40 per cent of all the gold ever mined has come from this small area.

Witwatersrand translates literally to 'white water reef'. And the gold here occurs in thin bands, called reefs, mined at depths of around 3,000 m (10,000 ft).

Mining began here in earnest in 1886, with the discovery of the 120 km (75 mi) Main Reef that runs from Boksburg to Randfontein. Although many of the older mines are close to exhaustion, this area still produces most of South Africa's gold.

No visit to the Rand would be complete without a visit to a gold mine. Gold Reef City, just 6 km (4 mi) south of Johannesburg, has tourist attractions aplenty. Crucially it has both a museum, where you can learn about the history of gold and the special geology of this area, and an original mineshaft that has been kept in working order.

Tours run several times a day and visitors are given a hard hat and a torch before getting into an authentically clangy lift and descending 226 m (740 ft) to level 14. The mine itself originally plunged more than 3,000 m (10,000 ft) deeper, but today levels 19-57 are under water. For most visitors, however, level 14 is deep enough.

While underground you really get a sense of what life was like for a gold miner. You also get a glimpse of the world's deepest pub and learn a few words of the miner's remarkable language called Fanagalo. Developed in 1910 to help workers from different nationalities talk to each other, it comprises 2,000 words – 500 of which are expletives!

WHAT IS IT?
The richest gold-producing region in the world.
HOW TO GET THERE:
By road from Johannesburg.
WHEN TO GO:
There is plenty to see all year.
NEAREST TOWN:
Johannesburg.
DON'T MISS:
The Apartheid Museum at Gold Reef City.
YOU SHOULD KNOW:
The mine tours and the Apartheid Museum may not be suitable for young children.

Gold mining in the Witwatersrand region.

Boulders Beach – African penguins

WHAT IS IT?
One of the largest mainland colonies of African penguins.
HOW TO GET THERE:
A short walk or drive from Simon's Town.
WHEN TO GO:
The penguins are there all year but Simon's Town has an annual 'penguin festival' one weekend in September and the birds breed March to May.
NEAREST TOWN:
Simon's Town.
DON'T MISS:
The Cape Point Nature Reserve.
YOU SHOULD KNOW:
For good reason this area was once called the Cape of Storms and it can be very windy.

African penguins waddling on the beach.

Nestled on the shores of False Bay, on the east coast of the Cape Peninsular, lies Simon's Town, a historic settlement of great character and charm. The town's breathtaking views of sea and mountain are good enough reason to make the short drive south from Cape Town. But the reason visitors are drawn here in their hundreds lies just a short walk out of town.

South Africa undoubtedly offers some of the best wildlife experiences in the world. But here you can get up close and personal with perhaps the last creature in the world you would associate with Africa. For here among the bush and boulders of the beach is one of the world's largest colonies of African penguins (*Spheniscus demersus*).

Wide wooden boardwalks provide easy, if sometimes crowded, access to the site. Often you will hear the birds before you see them – for the males produce a raucous braying call that gave rise to the species' original name: jackass penguin.

With around 2,500 of these birds residing here you are certain to get some marvellous close encounters with these 50cm (20 in) dapper black and white birds. Like all penguins, African penguins are quite flightless, having traded mastery of the air for that of water. Somewhat comical while they are waddling about on land, once in the water, the penguin's physical shape begins to make sense as its stubby wings power its torpedo-shaped body through the water at tremendous speed.

The first penguins began breeding here as recently as the 1980s, and since then the colony has grown incredibly quickly. Most of the birds are concentrated on Foxy Beach at Boulders. But there are always some along the neighbouring beaches and Boulders is more or less the only place in the world where you can swim with penguins – even if the water is sometimes a little chilly.

Lapalala Wilderness

A White rhinoceros

The lyrically named Lapalala Wilderness lies within the UNESCO Waterberg Biosphere Reserve, in Limpopo Province, just a three and a half hours' drive from Johannesburg. Despite its name, Lapalala is actually a privately owned nature reserve, created from the consolidation of 19 farms between 1981 and 1999. Currently some 360 sq km (140 sq mi) in extent, there are plans to extend the reserve still further.

The Lapalala Wilderness is characterized by endless vistas of upland plains and rugged hills, dissected by craggy ravines. The predominant vegetation here is so-called bushveld – grassland, punctuated by dense clusters of trees and tall shrubs. Bringing the whole area to life are the 90 km (56 mi) or so of rivers and streams that course through it, chief of which is the Palala River with its clear pools and noisy rapids.

Within this largely unspoiled landscape, visitors can encounter the wildlife both from the seat of a Land Rover, or by foot on guided walks. There are buffalo, hippo, crocodile, zebra, leopard, baboons and many kinds of antelope here as well as over 280 species of bird.

But Lapalala's 'A-list' is without doubt its black and white rhino. Hunted dangerously close to extinction, both species have only been saved by the strenuous efforts of conservationists such as Lapalala's Clive Walker.

Black and white rhino are easy to tell apart – but not for the reason suggested by their names. Black rhino (*Diceros bicornis*) are the smaller species and have a hooked upper lip, which they use to grasp the leaves, and shoots that they eat. White rhino, (*Cerototherium simum*) by contrast, have very wide mouths, which they use to tear off great mouthfuls of grass. It was a corruption of the word 'wide' which in Afrikaans sounds like 'white', that led to them being called white rhino, when in reality they are much the same colour as black rhino.

To be able to have a close encounter with both these species in a single day leaves visitors with memories to last a lifetime and makes Lapalala a truly special place.

WHAT IS IT?
A privately owned game reserve.
HOW TO GET THERE:
By road or bus from Johannesburg.
WHEN TO GO:
There is plenty to see all year.
NEAREST TOWN:
Vaalwater 50 km (30 mi) to the southwest.
DON'T MISS:
The Waterberg Environmental Centre, Melkrivier.
YOU SHOULD KNOW:
There is a charge to enter the reserve. Game drives and guided walks may need advance booking.

Table Mountain

WHAT IS IT?
A mountain that dominates the city around it.
HOW TO GET THERE:
On foot or by cable-car from Cape Town.
WHEN TO GO:
Clear days in summer.
NEAREST TOWN:
Cape Town.
DON'T MISS:
The amazing views from the top.
YOU SHOULD KNOW:
Even on the warmest day, take a coat as the temperature drops when the mist forms.

Almost at the southern tip of Africa, Table Mountain provides a stunning backdrop to the city of Cape Town, which nestles around it. Its level plateau is roughly 3 km (2 mi) across, with the Lion's Head to the west and Devil's Peak to the east. The name derives from the mists that form suddenly, spill over the edge and slide down the mountain sides like a table cloth. The mountain is part of the larger Table Mountain National Park.

Most visitors take the cable-car up to the western end of the plateau, although there are also many walking trails and climbing routes. The highest point of the mountain, at 1,086 m (3,563 ft), is Mclear's Beacon, at the eastern end. Numerous boardwalks and designated paths allow exploration of this beautiful wilderness without damaging it. More than 1,470 plant species have been found on this sandstone giant, many of them belonging to the flora called fynbos. There are also several species of proteas. Animals that can be seen here include the rock hyrax, or dassie as it is known locally, mongoose, baboons, grysboks, snakes and porcupines. There is also a project to reintroduce klipspringers (dwarf antelopes) to the region and several were released on the mountain in 2003.

It is not just the close-up views of nature that make the trip up the mountain worthwhile: the views over the city, and along the coastline, are magnificent.

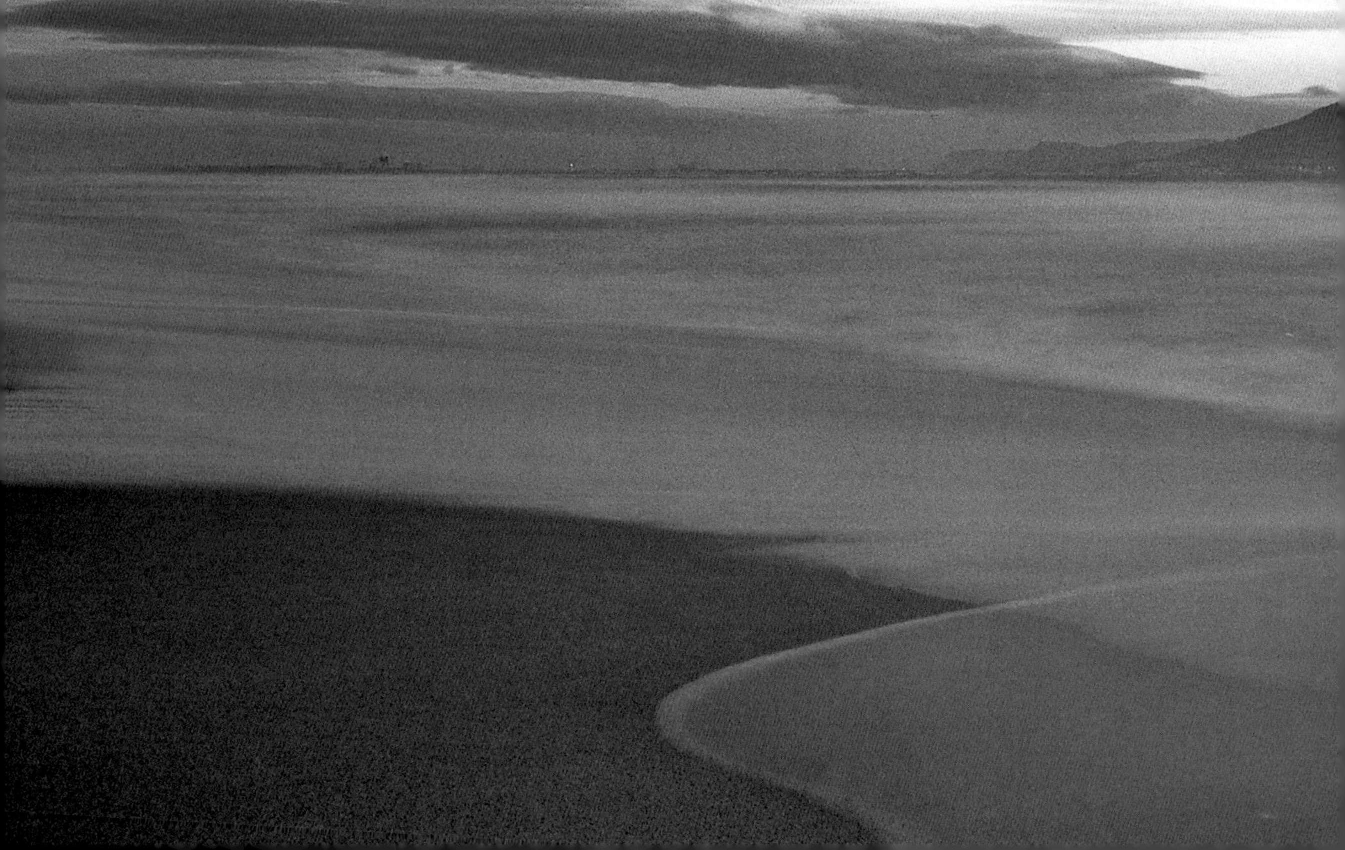

Namaqualand daisies in bloom

Little Namaqualand

Little Namaqualand is a sunburned, semi-arid region of some 60,000 sq km (23,000 sq mi) that lies south of the Orange River, in South Africa's Northern Cape Province. It is a winter-rainfall desert, with much of the area receiving less than 150 mm (6 in) of rain each year.

Along its rugged western shores the cold Atlantic breakers pound, and sea mists frequently roll in, gripping the region in a clammy embrace. Alluvial diamonds have been found on this coast, but these crystalline beauties are no match for the true gems of Namaqualand – its flowers.

For although this region is dry and almost lifeless for nine months of the year, with the spring comes a transformation that is as beautiful as it is remarkable. Late winter rains awake the life that is lying just beneath the surface, and all at once the land is awash in a sea of colour. Flowers of every hue imaginable, almost simultaneously burst into bloom creating a spectacle that is in every sense of the word, wonderful.

Most of the flowers are various species of daisy, but home to some 3,000 species – nearly half of which are found nowhere else – Namaqualand is truly a plant-lover's paradise. Although most of the plants here are ground hugging, two larger ones worth searching out are the halfmens and the quiver tree. The rare halfmens – or half-person – is a triffid-like succulent that bends to face the sun as it grows. Taller still is the remarkable quiver tree, so named because Bushmen use its branches to make quivers for their arrows. This distinctive plant is often the tallest plant around, and as a result is popular with birds. Sugarbirds feed on the flowers, weaverbirds nest in its branches and hawks use it as a welcome vantage point from which to spy prey.

For those visitors who arrive in Namaqualand 'out of season' this unique landscape still has much to offer. Aside from the uncountable number of succulents, the desert itself also possesses a special beauty, with its shattered landscape of billion-year-old granite and huge over-arching skies that at night twinkle with stars as bright as any earthly diamond.

WHAT IS IT?
A desert that bursts into bloom each spring.
HOW TO GET THERE:
By road up the N7 from Cape Town.
WHEN TO GO:
July to October.
NEAREST TOWN:
Springbok is the region's main town.
DON'T MISS:
The Geogap Nature Reserve in Springbok.
YOU SHOULD KNOW:
During the spring you can telephone 'flower hotlines' to discover where the best blooms are. The area becomes very busy when the flowers are in bloom.

Cape Cross Seal Reserve

There are nine species of mammals known as fur seals, which are, in reality, a species of sea lion. The Cape fur seal is the largest species and Cape Cross (Kaapkruis) Seal Reserve is its main stronghold and the largest of the 24 breeding colonies along this coastline. The cape's name derives from the cross that was erected here by the explorer Diego Cao in 1486 to claim the land for Portugal.

At its height, Cape Cross Seal Reserve supports between 80,000 and 100,000 seals, but in years when food is scarce, the number of seals is often lower.

Each summer, the reserve is home to the spectacle of the seals breeding season. The bull seals are first to arrive, usually in October, and they will fight for and establish breeding territories. When they first arrive, the bulls weigh up to 360 kg (800 lb) but lose a proportion of this during their enforced stay on the beach.

The pregnant cows arrive in November or December and join a bull in his territory. Depending on his strength, position on the beach and ability to prevent his cows being taken by other males, a bull will have a harem of between 5 and 25 cows. Within a week of giving birth to their single pups, the females are fertile again.

At birth, the pups are black and weigh 5-7 kg (11-15.5 lb). They will continue to suckle for almost a year, until their mother leaves them to return to the beach to give birth to the next year's pup. Until the bulls leave the beach, the pups are vulnerable during territorial fights and once their mothers leave them in order to feed, they are at risk from hyenas or jackals. They will remain on the beach until they are able to go to sea with their mothers and will start to eat fish at about five months.

Whether you witness the enormous bull seals fighting for territory and cows or the thousands of appealing pups, the sheer number of seals here is almost overwhelming.

WHAT IS IT?
The largest breeding colony of Cape fur seals in the world.
HOW TO GET THERE:
By road from Hentiesbaai on the C34
WHEN TO GO:
November–January.
NEAREST TOWN:
Hentiesbaai 70 km (45 mi)
YOU SHOULD KNOW:
Do not walk among the seals: the males are aggressive at all times and the females will become so if they see you as a threat to their young.

Cape fur seals along the shore at the Cape Cross Seal Reserve.

The MalaMala Reserve

WHAT IS IT?
A privately owned game reserve.
HOW TO GET THERE:
By air from Johannesburg to MalaMala Airfield, or by road from Johannesburg.
WHEN TO GO:
There is plenty to see all year. September to March can be very hot.
NEAREST TOWN:
Newington 19 km (12 mi) west.
DON'T MISS:
Sun City, South Africa's Las Vegas in the veldt.
YOU SHOULD KNOW:
To visit MalaMala you must be resident in one of the reserve's lodges. The area is malarial.

The MalaMala Game Reserve is a 160 sq km (62 sq mi) wildlife sanctuary located in Mpumalanga Province. Established in 1927, MalaMala lays claim to being the oldest game reserve in South Africa. At one time it was a hunter's paradise for those seeking to bag the 'Big Five', but since 1964 the only shooting that has been done here has been done by tourists with cameras.

Much of MalaMala is textbook African savannah, replete with an impressive inventory of wildlife species – the richest anywhere on the continent. If that were not enough, MalaMala holds further aces that make it one of the premier game viewing destinations in the world.

First is its sheer size, guaranteeing visitors a rich and varied habitat. Second is the fact that it fortuitously shares a 19 km (12 mi) unfenced border with the Kruger National Park. This simple accident of geography benefits the reserve enormously. Thirdly, MalaMala is blessed with the life-giving waters of the Sand River. Some 20 km (13 mi) of this perennial river flows north-south through the reserve, drawing huge herds of grazing animals to its banks – not to mention the numerous predators that hunt them.

MalaMala Game Reserve at sunrise

To allow the animals approaching from the Kruger National Park free access to the river, all the MalaMala camps are on the western bank, and throughout the reserve human density and impact on the land is kept to an absolute minimum.

The results of this single-minded management are writ large in the reserve's viewing statistics. Typically, lion, leopard, elephant, rhino and buffalo make an appearance here 335 days every year. So for visitors on a once-in-a-lifetime trip to see Africa's 'Big Five', MalaMala is unlikely to disappoint.

Visitors staying on the reserve are provided with their own personal guide and local Shangaan trackers. These experts know the area and its inhabitants intimately. Whether by open top Land Rover or on foot – with an armed ranger – by day or night, these guides will help guarantee an unforgettable experience not least of which is an unrivalled opportunity to photograph the best of Africa's wildlife.

The Wonder Cave

The Wonder Cave in Kromdraai, Gauteng, is the third largest cavern in South Africa and an attraction that easily lives up to its name. Thought to be around 2 million years old, it was discovered in the late 19th century by miners excavating limestone to make cement. It was only opened to the public, however, in 1991.

The cave itself comprises a single, vertigo-inducing void, measuring some 46,000 cu m (1,600,000 cu ft). For the claustrophobic, therefore, it offers possibly the perfect underground experience. Visitors begin their subterranean sojourn via a 90-step metal stairway, followed by a short lift ride to the cave floor. Once there the walkways are wide and relatively flat. Despite its size, the Wonder Cave still has a slightly damp, musty smell, and on summer days when the temperature can be over 25 °C (77 °F), the cave's ambient 16 °C (60 °F) can feel suddenly chilly.

Formed by the erosion of limestone by underground water, the cave contains a dazzling display of beautifully presented dripstone formations. The scale of everything here is astonishing – there are 14 or so stalagmite and stalactite formations all over 15 m (50 ft) high and most of which are still growing.

There are also a huge number of imaginatively named flowstone formations that are creatively lit for maximum effect. Some, such as the figure of the praying Madonna, are so realistic that it seems impossible that they can be the purely accidental creations of limestone-laden water.

WHAT IS IT?
A remarkable underground cavern.
HOW TO GET THERE:
By road from Krugersdorp.
WHEN TO GO:
Open Mon-Fri 8am to 5 pm (last tour 4 pm) Sat, Sun and Public holidays 8 am to 6 pm, (last tour 5 pm).
NEAREST TOWN:
Krugersdorp 10 km (6 mi), Johannesburg, 50 km (30 mi)
DON'T MISS:
Displays of early hominids at 'The Cradle of Humankind', Sterkfontein.
YOU SHOULD KNOW:
Entrance is by guided tour only for which there is a small charge.

EUROPE &
THE MIDDLE
EAST

Kongsvegen Glacier

Svalbard Archipelago

The remote archipelago of Svalbard is in the Arctic Circle, at the point where the Gulf Stream current sinks. The islands are a frozen white wonderland of barren mountains, glaciers, fjords and ice caves, inhabited by as many polar bears as humans (about 2,500 of each).

Svalbard is the northernmost part of the kingdom of Norway, 565 km (353 mi) to the north of the mainland, about halfway to the North Pole. It was probably known to the Vikings in the 12th Century but was officially discovered by William Barents in 1596. During the 17th and 18th centuries, Spitzbergen, the largest of the islands, grew into an important whaling station as well as attracting animal trappers. By the 20th century, whale stocks had become so depleted that coal mining replaced whaling as the main occupation. Today there is still a small coal mining community.

The archipelago consists of three large islands – Spitzbergen, Nordaustlandet and Edgeøya – and numerous smaller ones, covering an area of about 61,000 sq km (23,550 sq mi), of which 60 per cent is covered by glaciation. Most of Spitzbergen's 2,500 inhabitants live in the main settlement of Longyearbyen; the other islands are nature reserves, largely uninhabited except by scientific researchers.

A trip to Svalbard is a uniquely rewarding experience. You can test your stamina on a wilderness camping expedition, try your hand at dog sledging, and explore the ice caves beneath the glaciers as well as snowmobiling, skiing, horse riding and kayaking. You cannot fail to encounter several polar bears, which roam around freely here, even occasionally wandering into the settlements. The islands are also a haven for Arctic foxes, reindeer, walruses and seals. You can take boat trips to see whales, dolphins and seals, and in the summer watch the thousands of seabirds, including puffins, which congregate along the cliffs to breed.

Trondheimsfjord

The Trondheimsfjord is the third longest fjord in Norway. It winds its way 130 km (80 mi) inland through a lovely region of forested hills, the end of the Pilgrim Route from Oslo, and creates a natural boundary between south and north Norway. The lowlands to the south and east provide some of the best agricultural land in Norway, while to the west there is a wonderful view of the rugged hills of the Fosen peninsula.

The fjord has an average depth of 400 m (1,300 ft) with a deep point of 617 m (2,024 ft). It is ice-free in most parts all year round and is a unique cold-water marine habitat with more species than any other fjord in Norway. The inexplicable discovery of coral sea bushes and trees 1-2m (3-6 ft) high, as well as a coral reef and rabbit fish, normally found only in much deeper water, has stirred great excitement among marine biologists. The fjord also provides some of the best fishing in Norway.

A 50 km (30 mi) stretch of wetland and mudflat along the northeast side of the fjord and Tautra, an island bird sanctuary, are important staging posts for migrating pink-footed geese and numerous seabirds. In the spring more than 20,000 birds stop over around Trondheimsfjord, including waders, songbirds and several rare species. The surrounding forests shelter many attractive woodland birds, and in the south-west coastal region you can see buzzards, eagles and crossbills.

The Trondheimsfjord is connected to the Beistadfjord, at Skarnsund Sound where there is one of the world's longest cable-stayed bridges, a spectacular award-winning construction. The scenic terrain around the fjord is wonderful walking and horse-riding country, and the fjord itself is a diving and fishing paradise.

WHAT IS IT?
An unusual marine and birding environment.
HOW TO GET THERE:
Plane, train, road or boat to Trondheim.
WHEN TO GO:
April to September.
NEAREST TOWN:
Trondheim
DON'T MISS:
The tiny island of Munksholmen ("monk's haven"), once the site of a Benedictine monastery and then a prison – a popular hangout for Trondheimers to swim and relax.
YOU SHOULD KNOW:
A coastal express boat runs every day of the year between Bergen and Kirkenes, calling at Trondheim on the way.

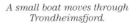

A small boat moves through Trondheimsfjord.

Jostedalsbreen Glacier Field

WHAT IS IT?
A scenic feast of an ice world.
HOW TO GET THERE:
From Oslo or Bergen, fly to Sogndal airport then take the Jostedal bus; or car/bus/train plus ferry to Sogndal. The easiest way to get to Jostedal is to use the "glacier buses", which run frequent connecting services from all the towns in the region to Jostedal.
WHEN TO GO:
End May to mid September.
NEAREST TOWN:
Sogndal.
DON'T MISS:
Ramnefjellsfossen, unofficially the third highest waterfall in the world, total drop 818 m (2,680 ft) fed by the Jostedal icefield.
YOU SHOULD KNOW:
There are hidden crevasses on the ice field; it can be incredibly dangerous and you must not walk, climb or ski on the glaciers without a guide.

Jostedalsbreen is the largest glacier in Europe, a massive ice plateau of over 480 sq km (185 sq mi), more than 60 km (37 mi) long, with ice up to 600 m (1,970 ft) thick. The ice field covers almost half of the Josdtedal National Park, a beautiful wilderness area on Norway's west coast between Sognefjord and Nordfjord – two of the longest fjords in the world. Here you will find some of the world's most awe-inspiring scenery, carved out of the terrain by thousands of years of constant glacial activity.

The ice field is an incredible labyrinth of deep icy crevasses and outcrops. There are 22 valley branches (or "arms") running down from the ice plateau as well as some smaller separate glaciers. The most accessible of the arms are Briksdalsbreen, Kjenndalsbreen and Nigardsbreen – the experience of walking along the blue ice crevasses of these dynamic wonderlands, sheer ice walls towering above you, is a thrill quite unlike any other.

Glaciers are an awesome natural phenomenon – a constantly moving mass of ice slides remorselessly down from the ice field, shifting the rock and sediment in its path as it scoops out an ever-deepening valley, an endless stream of water flowing out from beneath it into the eerily still milky green glacial lake at its end.

Jostedal contains an astounding variety of scenery as well as the ice field, ranging from tranquil wooded valleys of alder and birch trees to bleak mountain peaks, and a barren moraine plain of shifting sands – the Fåbergstølsgrandane "sandur" – composed of sediment deposited by rivers flowing from one of the glacier's arms.

As you trek along the ancient cattle tracks, once used by herdsmen, you feel as though you are roaming through different countries and changing seasons. And when you reach the ice field, you step onto an entirely different planet.

The snout of the Jostedalsbreen glacier

The Maelstrom

The fictional Maelstrom, invented by that master of horror stories, Edgar Allen Poe, really does exist. It is the most ferocious of several powerful tidal currents in the waters around the Lofoten Islands in northern Norway.

The rugged Lofoten archipelago sticks straight out into the Atlantic Ocean, separated from the mainland by the Vestfjord, a 40-60 m (130-200 ft) deep, 5 km (3 mi) wide strait. Twice a day, the tides cause the waters of the Vestfjord to run back against the main stream, stirring up the Maelstrom (known as the Moskstraumen to the locals) – great whirlpools that swirl at speeds of up to 6 knots. The Moskstraumen is one of the most forceful eddies in the world, an amazing sight which fascinates and terrifies in equal measure.

"Those who sail at the wrong time are suddenly snatched down into spiralling abysses", wrote Olaus Magnus, a 16th century Swedish mapmaker; and, in 1591, the district bailiff recorded: "... the waves and breakers ... roll in as high as mountains".

The local people tend to play down dramatized accounts of the Moskstraumen – they are grateful for its existence, and treat it with the utmost respect. For, even though it has taken its toll of the islanders' lives, it also washes in the great shoals of fish on which their livelihoods have always depended.

Apart from the unforgettable experience of the Maelstrom itself, the Lofoten Islands are one of the most scenically beautiful parts of Norway, in range of both the Northern Lights and the Midnight Sun. Wander along white sand beaches and clamber through the mountains, enjoying wonderful views and an exhilarating sense of space and freedom; and explore the dramatic coastline by boat, marvelling at the skills of the fishermen as they negotiate their way through the temperamental seas.

The ferocious whirlpools of the Maelstrom (Moskstraumen)

WHAT IS IT?
A spiralling watery abyss.
HOW TO GET THERE:
Fly to Oslo then domestic flight to Svolvær or Leknes. Or, take the coastal boat that runs between Bergen and Kirkenes. Or, road, rail or air to Bodø then take ferry to Moskenes or express passenger boat to Svolvær.
WHEN TO GO:
September to April to catch the Northern Lights. May to July for the Midnight Sun.
NEAREST TOWN:
Svolvær, Sørvågen, Leknes
YOU SHOULD KNOW:
The word "maelstrom" was first introduced into English from Nordic by Edgar Allen Poe, in his 1841 story "A Descent into the Maelstrom". He based the story on his knowledge of the Moskstraumen. The Moskstraumen was also the inspiration for Jules Verne's *Twenty Thousand Leagues under the Sea*. (Both authors describe it, inaccurately, as a single great whirlpool).

Geirangerfjord

WHAT IS IT?
Simply the most beautiful fjord in the world.
HOW TO GET THERE:
Fly to Ålesund. Drive along the Ørneveien to Geiranger.
WHEN TO GO:
May to September.
NEAREST TOWN:
Geiranger
DON'T MISS:
The Golden Route tour – incredible scenic drive along hairpin bends past the Trollveggen, the tallest vertical rock face in Europe. The cliffs of Runde – an island sanctuary for more than half a million sea birds.
YOU SHOULD KNOW:
Geirangerfjord is one of Norway's most visited tourist attractions.

The Geirangerfjord is considered the archetype of fjords – the most scenically beautiful fjord of all in a fairytale region of sublime natural beauty. Geiranger is part of the intricate Norwegian fjord system that stretches from Stavanger in the south 500 km (300 mi) northwards along the western coast. The terrain here has been shaped by glaciation to create some of the most outstanding scenery in the world.

Geirangerfjord is a 15 km (9 mi) long stretch of deep blue water, branching off from the Storfjord in a narrow, winding ravine of hairpin bends and sheer crystalline rock escarpments. The cliff face is up to 1,400 m (4,600 ft) high and plunges 500 m (1,640 ft) below sea level. A series of spectacular waterfalls cascade down the sides of the ravine. The most famous are the Seven Sisters and the Suitor, facing each other on opposite sides of the fjord, and the Bride's Veil, so called because, when backlit by the sun, it gives the impression of a thin veil trailing over the rocks.

The surrounding scenery is breathtaking – a landscape of rugged, ice-capped mountains, glacial lakes, and deciduous and coniferous forests traversed by rivers. Along the sides of the fjord, you will see many abandoned smallholdings – historic traces of the way the people of this region scratched a living from the soil before the days of mass tourism. These ramshackle dwellings are in isolated shelves of land along the escarpments; some of them are surrounded by such steep slopes that they can only be accessed by ladder from a boat. When the farmers wanted to avoid the taxman, they simply drew up their ladders and relied on nature to protect them from the authorities.

The spectacular Geirangerfjord

Lofoten Islands

West of mainland Norway, the Lofoten Islands lie more than 67° north of the equator, within the Arctic Circle. Despite this, they have a relatively mild climate because of the warm waters of the Gulf Stream.

There are five main islands – Austvågøy, Gimsøya, Vestvågøy, Flakstadøya and Moskenesøya – and three smaller ones – Vaerøy, Røst and the tiny islet of Vedøy. They are mountainous, with wooded hillsides and are fringed with pretty bays and beautiful white, sandy beaches.

The islands are surrounded by rich waters that support vast colonies of breeding seabirds, including puffins, kittiwakes, razorbills, red-necked phalaropes and Arctic terns, as well as white-tailed sea eagles. Rare birds like capercaillie and black grouse can sometimes be spotted. In summer, sperm whales can be found offshore, while orca follow the herring to this area in early autumn. Seals and otters can also be seen and there are moose on Austvågøy.

One of the biggest deepwater coral reefs, the 40-km (25-mi) long Røst Reef is just west of Austuagoy and off the coast of Moskenesøya lies the vast whirlpool, the Maelstrom.

The spectacular ruggedness of these islands makes them popular with climbers and hikers, and the beautiful coastline is a favourite destination for cyclists. In midsummer, this beautiful area becomes even more magical, as for more than seven weeks, the sun remains above the horizon.

A fisherman's cottage and mountain are reflected in a bay on Vestvågøy.

WHAT IS IT?
A northerly archipelago of surprising beauty.
HOW TO GET THERE:
By ferry or air from Bodø, ferry from Narvik or by road via Narvik.
WHEN TO GO:
Late May to early July for the Midnight Sun; the best weather is from April to September.
NEAREST TOWN:
Narvik 140 km (90 mi)
DON'T MISS:
The Midnight Sun
YOU SHOULD KNOW:
The sun does not rise for weeks in midwinter.

Folgefonni (Folgefonna) Glacier

WHAT IS IT?
A glacier adventure playground.
HOW TO GET THERE:
Fly to Bergen. 3-hour drive to Odda.
WHEN TO GO:
Year round skiing. May to September for hiking.
NEAREST TOWN:
Odda 3 km (under 2 mi)
DON'T MISS:
The cheese factory in Odda, where you can buy wonderful goat's cheeses.
YOU SHOULD KNOW:
Like all glaciers, Folgefonni is more dangerous than it looks. Always go with a certified guide.

The Folgefonn peninsula is a captivating region of dramatic mountains, forests and lakes between the Hardanger and Sor fjords about 150 km (95 mi) south-east from Bergen on the west coast of Norway. The area has been designated a National Park to protect The Folgefonni ice cap – the third largest ice cap in Norway.

The ice cap is composed of three adjoining glaciers, which blanket 203 sq km (78 sq mi) of the peninsula in a layer of ice up to 145 m (476 ft) thick. A film of water between the ice and the rock collects sediment and clay; in the summer, melting ice mixed with this watery sediment flows into the fjords giving them their unique green tint.

The largest of the three glaciers, and the only plateau glacier, is Sønde (South) Folgefonni, which extends over 168 sq km (65 sq mi), and contains the highest point of the region at 1,662 m (5,451 ft). Sønde Folgefonni is the safest of all the glacier plateaus with its gentle slopes, so it is the ideal place to practise glacier walking and cross-country skiing.

As long ago as the 19th Century, the ice cap was already attracting visitors and the nearby town of Odda became one of Norway's leading tourist destinations. In 1902 a riding path was constructed across the glacier. This Turistvegen (Tourist Path), together with three huts for sheltering in, has recently been restored for riding and walking across the ice cap. There are several paths leading up to the edge of the glacier, mostly on the west side since the eastern and southern slopes are far more forbidding.

Summer or winter, the stunning purity of Folgefonni's glacier landscape cannot fail to thrill even the most jaded senses and restore a sense of wonder in the power of nature.

Aerial view of Folgefonna Glacier

Reindeer migration

A herd of reindeer

Reindeer (*Rangifer tarandus*) are the domesticated cousins of the caribou of North America. As their name suggests, they are members of the deer family. They are large animals with broad hooves well adapted to walking on soft – often snow-covered – ground. Unlike some deer species, however, both sexes grow antlers that the males use to battle rivals during the breeding season or rut.

It is believed that caribou were first domesticated in Europe around 5,000 years ago. It is also thought that all domestic reindeer descended from these animals, as recent attempts to domesticate caribou have failed.

Throughout the Arctic the lives of many native peoples are closely entwined with these hardy animals. In Scandinavia the Sámi people have herded reindeer for centuries, relying on their meat for food, their skins for clothing and shelter, and their strength to carry their belongings on their nomadic wanderings.

For the Sámi time is divided into seasons, each one being defined by the reindeer and the climate. During the summer months the reindeer live on the coast, even swimming out to nearby islands. Here the grass is rich and the herd, especially the newborn calves, fatten up for the hard winter ahead.

As autumn approaches the migration inland begins. The reindeer have traditional breeding grounds where the annual rut takes place and usually they will return to the same rut area each year.

Winter lasts from October through April, of which around eight weeks are passed in total darkness. Exactly where the reindeer spend these harsh months will depend on snowfall and the availability of their winter food – lichen.

When at last spring returns, the herds move back towards the summer pastures where the females will give birth to their calves.

WHAT IS IT?
A twice a year migration of reindeer and their herders.
HOW TO GET THERE:
By air to Ivalo, then by road.
NEAREST TOWN:
Utsjoki, Finland.

The Midnight Sun over Lake Kallavesi in Finland

The Midnight Sun

There can be fewer more romantically appealing destinations than the 'land of the midnight sun'. But where exactly is this sunshine state? Paradoxically, it is to be found in the chilly polar regions. It's a phenomenon that occurs both north of the Arctic Circle and south of the Antarctic Circle. But as there are no permanent settlements south of the Antarctic Circle, most midnight sun seekers head north.

For six months of the year the earth's north pole is tilted towards the sun. Close to the summer solstice – 21 June – this inclination is at its maximum, and the sun shines directly on the North Pole and down to a latitude of 66°34' – the Arctic Circle. If you travel north of this line at this time, you will see the sun dip towards the horizon, but not slip below it.

More than a quarter of Finland lies above the Arctic Circle, making it a perfect place to experience this magical phenomenon. In fact, at Finland's northernmost town, Utjoki, the sun does not set for a period of 73 days during summer.

Many visitors can find it difficult to sleep when the natural pattern of day and night is so disturbed. But the locals seem to revel in the experience, and an almost festive spirit breaks out throughout Finland. This reaches a climax with the midsummer celebrations. Everywhere is decorated with birch branches and flowers and midsummer bonfires – called *kokko* – are lit. It's a time of great celebration and euphoria.

When you have had enough of partying, a walk beside a beautiful lake at midnight, among the soft shadows cast by a low and luminous sun will provide an experience never to be forgotten.

WHAT IS IT?
A period of time when the sun never sets.
HOW TO GET THERE:
To reach Utjoki, Finland's most northerly town, fly to Ivalo and then travel by road on the E75.
WHEN TO GO:
16 May to 27 July at Utjoki.
NEAREST TOWN:
Utjoki is 165 km (102 mi) north of Ivalo on the E75.
DON'T MISS:
Look out for special summer concerts held outdoors at night.
YOU SHOULD KNOW:
Refraction of sunlight makes it possible to experience the Midnight Sun up to 80 km (50 mi) south of the Arctic Circle for a few days each year. Mosquitoes are a nuisance during the summer in northern Finland.

Åland Islands

The Åland Islands comprise some 6,500 emerald shards, scattered in the blue waters of the Baltic at the mouth of the Gulf of Bothnia. Although part of Finland, the islands have retained a unique degree of independence and autonomy. Åland has its own flag, its own stamps and its own vehicle licence plates, even its own top internet domain! Another curious idiosyncrasy is that the language spoken here is Swedish.

The archipelago is home to some 26,700 souls, spread among 65 of the islands. Just under half of the population live in and around Mariehamn, the islands' only town. Founded in 1861, this is the centre of the shipping and tourist industries and is home to the Landskapsregering – the local seat of government.

For many visitors, the islands provide an invitingly peaceful retreat to a world where time is measured by the tides and seasons. It's a place of tranquil beauty where every sunrise and sunset over the archipelago provides a photo opportunity not to be missed. What the islands lack in drama they more than make up for in their gentle beauty and the ease with which they can be explored. Hire a rowing boat and you'll soon find a beach all to yourself – perhaps even a whole island.

From May to August Åland captures more sunshine than any of its Nordic neighbours, making it a popular holiday destination. But for hardier types a winter visit here is rewarded with the opportunity to experience long-distance skating or ice-boating through the ice-sheets that form around the smaller islands and skerries.

At any time of the year visitors can enjoy the medieval castle of Kastelholm, the Jan Karlsgården farm museum, or the maritime museum complete with the *Pommern*, a historic sailing ship built in Glasgow at the beginning of the last century.

The view from Kokar Island, the largest of the Åland Islands

WHAT IS IT?
An archipelago in the Baltic Sea.
HOW TO GET THERE:
By boat: two and a half hours from Grisslehamn or Kapellskär, Sweden, or about 5 hours from Turku, Finland.
WHEN TO GO:
There is plenty to see and do all year.
NEAREST TOWN:
There is only one town on the islands: Mariehamn.
YOU SHOULD KNOW:
The islands are very popular in summer; prior booking of accommodation is essential.

Lake Inari

WHAT IS IT?
The largest lake in Lapland.
HOW TO GET THERE:
The nearest airport is in Ivalo. Inari is over 15 hours by bus from Helsinki.
WHEN TO GO:
May to July for the Midnight Sun. The lake is frozen from November to June.
NEAREST TOWN:
Ivalo, 45 km (28 mi) south.
DON'T MISS:
The Inari Sámi Museum, devoted to the culture of the indigenous Sámi people. In addition to the indoor exhibition, there is an outdoor museum featuring traditional Sámi dwellings. Entrance fee, open daily except Monday from 10 am to 5 pm (longer in the summer).

Situated on the 69th parallel, deep inside the Arctic Circle, lies Finland's third largest lake – Lake Inari. The sixth largest in Europe, Lake Inari is actually more like a small sea. Measuring around 1,000 sq km (386 sq mi), by the time you have sailed out to its often choppy centre, the shore will have long disappeared. Almost completely frozen for more than half the year, the last of the winter ice usually melts away by the second week of June. But even on the warmest days the water temperature only just makes it into double figures.

The Finnish name for Finland, Suomi, means 'land of lakes' – Lake Inari is, by contrast, a 'lake of lands' with over 3,000 islands peppering its surface and providing a fascinating waterborne tableau for visitors to explore.

Cruises are a popular way to enjoy the lake – although for the more adventurous all manner of watercraft, from small motorboats to kayaks, are available for hire. Around the lake's 2,776 km (1,725 mi) rocky and rugged shoreline there are numerous discoveries to make.

At Ukonkivi there is an old sacrificial site that the Sámi people used to ensure good fishing. And when their catches were good they would store the surplus in ice caves such as the one on Iso-Maura that stays frozen all year. Fish remain one of the lake's more abundant resources, with whitefish, trout and Arctic char the most common species. More obvious are the mergansers and red-throated divers that come here to fish and whose hauntingly strange calls float across the water.

Visitors in summer can enjoy the delights of Lake Inari by day or night as from May to the end of July the sun never completely sets. The temperature at this time can reach a warmish 13 °C (55 °F). But it doesn't last long. And then when the ice freezes in November the lake is plunged into the one-and-a-half-month-long *Kaamos*, or dark season.

A few of the more than 3,000 islands that pepper the surface of Lake Inari.

Sweden's Lakeland

A Lakeland view

Sweden's Lakeland region covers a vast area blessed with beautiful countryside, picture-perfect villages and vibrant metropolitan areas. But above all, the lakes take centre stage. The largest of which are: Vänern, Vättern, Mälaren, Hjälmaren and Siljan.

More like a small inland sea, Vänern, Sweden's largest lake and the third largest in Europe, extends to around 130 km (80 mi) by 70 km (43 mi) at its longest and widest points. It's a freshwater paradise for anyone who enjoys any kind of watersport, from sailing to swimming, waterskiing to windsurfing.

A short drive east lies Lake Vättern, Sweden's second largest lake and one whose water is so clean the locals claim you can drink it. The lake is also home to some of the best salmon and char fishing in Europe. The area around the lake is home to hot air ballooning festivals and there is also an annual 300 km (186 mi) cycling race around the shoreline in June called the Vätternrundan.

From the castle of Läckö, constructed in 1298 on Lake Vänern, to the island of Sollerön in Lake Siljan, where there are Viking graves, Swedes think of this area as their 'cradle of culture'. Truly there is so much to see and do in this vast area that it is difficult to know where to begin.

But one of the best ways to explore the watery theme of Swedish Lakeland is to take a trip along the amazing Göta Canal that links Lake Vänern to the Baltic. It takes about eight-days to cruise from Mem in the east to Sjötorp in the west. During that time you'll navigate some 240 km (150 mi) of canal and pass through 58 locks. But most importantly you'll have savoured one of the true delights of the region.

WHAT IS IT?
A huge area of Sweden, home to numerous lakes including one of the largest in Europe.
HOW TO GET THERE:
By road from Stockholm or Göthenburg.
WHEN TO GO:
Spring to autumn offers the best weather.
NEAREST TOWN:
Göthenburg is about 50 km (30 mi) south of Lake Vänern.
YOU SHOULD KNOW:
The Göta Canal is open from May through to September.

Maelifell

WHAT IS IT?
A volcanic cone.
HOW TO GET THERE:
The bus to Kirkjubaejarklaustur from Reykjavik takes 5 hours.
WHEN TO GO:
Spring to autumn.
NEAREST TOWN:
Kirkjubaejarklaustur
DON'T MISS:
The 62 m (200 ft) high waterfall Skogafoss at Skogar.
YOU SHOULD KNOW:
Maelifell can only be reached either on foot or by 4 wheel drive.

In a country full of remarkable volcanic creations, one of the more unusual is Maelifell. It's an unnaturally uniform cone that rises from a barren desert of laval ash. It was created by an eruption under the Myrdalsjökull glacier in southern Iceland. Its cone is made up of 'tuff', a mixture of solidified ash and other volcanic debris, and rises some 200 m (650 ft) above the plain.

About 10,000 years ago Myrdalsjökull, Iceland's most southerly, and fourth largest, glacier, finally loosened its icy grip on Maelifell, exposing this pointy little peak to the Icelandic sun. As a consequence, this mysterious cone became clothed in a soft coat of moss. The moss, grimmia, is one of the 500 kinds of moss that make up a large percentage of Iceland's rather uninspiring 1,300 plant species. Grimmia thrives on laval soils, but what is most remarkable about it is its colour. Where the soil is dry it grows a somewhat inconspicuous silver-grey colour. But where the soils are moist, as they are on Maelifell, grimmia turns a bright, almost luminous green.

Surrounded by the dusty Maelifellsandur Desert, Maelifell's feet are washed by the numerous braided rivers and streams that flow from Myrdalsjökull. It's a quite otherworldly landscape presided over by the silent green cone of Maelifell.

Maelifell hasn't erupted for over 10,000 years, long enough for even the most conservative volcanologist to confidently consider it extinct. But a little further south, still underneath the ice of Myrdalsjökull, lies Katla, one of the most active volcanoes in Iceland. Katla last erupted in 1918 and experts believe that another eruption could occur very soon.

Grimmia thrives on the slopes of Maelifell.

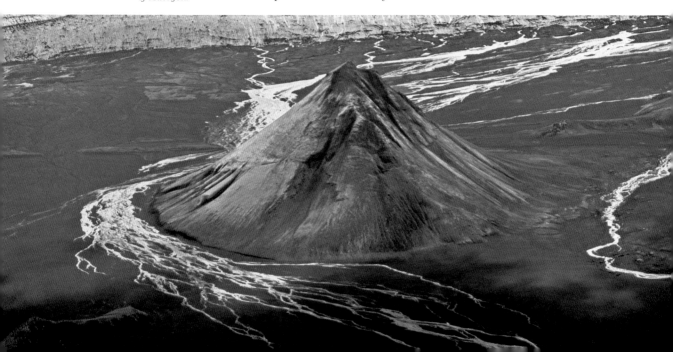

Vatnajökull

One of the most eye-catching features of almost any map of Iceland is the huge white mass covering the southeast of the country. This is Vatnajökull. Covering more than eight per cent of the country, and measuring 8,100 sq km (3,100 sq mi), it is not simply the largest glacier in Iceland, it is the largest in Europe. With an average thickness of 400 m (1,300 ft) – but in places extending to 1,000 m (3,200 ft) – Vatnajökull contains a mind-boggling 3300 cu km (791 cu mi) of ice.

Beneath the glacier's uniformly white surface lies an undulating plateau of valleys and gorges, and like most of Iceland it's an area of high volcanic activity. Beneath the ice the Grímsvötn lakes sit above a huge magma chamber that erupted as recently as 2004, sending up plumes of ash and sulphur dioxide that were detected as far away as Norway.

When eruptions occur beneath the glacier they can actually lift the ice like a fluffy white blanket, allowing huge quantities of water to rapidly escape. The ensuing floods that followed an eruption in 1996 actually washed away part of Iceland's ring road. And because of the potentially devastating consequences of such glacial 'runs', Vatnajökull is monitored very closely. It has also been receiving more attention of late as, scientists have been examining it for signs of global warming.

Vatnajökull lies within the Skaftafell National Park and every year thousands of visitors come to hike, ski, sled and skidoo over its surface. Nearby are the equally enticing Jökulsarlon Lagoon with its flotillas of icebergs, and Öraefajökull, at 2,110 m (7,000 ft), Iceland's highest mountain.

WHAT IS IT?
The largest glacier in Europe.
HOW TO GET THERE:
By road from Hofn. Hofn has an airport and is an 8 hour bus ride from Reykjavik.
WHEN TO GO:
The months May to August offer the most benign weather.
NEAREST TOWN:
Hofn lies a few kilometres to the east of the glacier.
YOU SHOULD KNOW:
Traversing the glacier is potentially dangerous, especially in winter.

The Vatnajökull glacier is the largest glacier in Europe. There are several volcanoes beneath the glacier which form these volcanic glacier lakes.

The sapphire blue water of the Blue Lagoon is heated geothermally.

Blue Lagoon, Reykjanes Peninsula

Unless arriving by boat, most visitors to Iceland touch down at Keflavik, 70 km (43 mi) southwest of the capital Reykjavik. Keflavik perches right at the tip of the Reykanes Peninsula, a rugged, rocky finger of land that curls upwards, as if beckoning visitors to its shores. From the air the lunar-like landscape appears dark and moody, but set right in this heart of darkness shines a sapphire gem – the Blue Lagoon.

Iceland is often referred to as the land of ice and fire, and with good reason. Geothermal activity is everywhere, from bubbling lava to gushing geysers. One of the more benign benefits of all this volcanism is the Blue Lagoon, a huge pool of mineral-rich seawater, and heated geothermally to a comfortable 36-39 °C (97-102 °F).

Privately owned, the site has been tastefully developed into a luxury spa, a giant geothermal hot tub, where visitors can soak away their cares in a uniquely Icelandic way. The milky blue waters are suffused with silica and other minerals, which together are claimed to benefit the skin in numerous ways. In particular the waters are said to be particularly efficacious for sufferers of psoriasis, and attached to the spa is a clinic where various treatments are available.

In addition to a relaxing wallow in the shallow lagoon, guests can enjoy a sauna, which overlooks the lagoon, a cosy steam bath that is carved into a lava cave, or stand beneath a Blue Lagoon waterfall for an energizing aqua massage. And once dry and refreshed you have the option of visiting the café, restaurant or gift shop, from where you can take some of the Blue Lagoon's mineral magic away with you.

WHAT IS IT?
A geothermal, mineral rich pool.
HOW TO GET THERE:
By road 40 km (25 mi) from Reykjavik or 22 km (14 mi) from Keflavik. There is a bus service, but many tour operators offer tours to the site.
WHEN TO GO:
The Blue Lagoon is open all year. From 1 June to 31 August it opens 7.30 am to 9.00 pm and you can stay in the water until 9.45 pm.
NEAREST TOWN:
Keflavik 23 km (14 mi) west.
DON'T MISS:
The Rift, a fascinating geological museum at nearby Eldborg.
YOU SHOULD KNOW:
There is an entry charge and towel, costume and robe hire are extra.

The Great Geysir

Iceland may not have bequeathed many words to the world, but one that surely springs to mind is 'geyser'. Throughout the world 'geyser' is used to describe any hot spring that periodically ejects a column of steaming water into the air. In Iceland, however, it refers to just one: the Great Geysir.

The first record of the Great Geysir dates back to 1294. After a powerful earthquake had shaken the western lowlands in the Haukadalur valley, hot springs formed, some of which began to spout. Over the centuries more earthquakes shook the valley and the power of one of its spouting springs – the Great Geysir – became legend.

Sadly, in recent times the Great Geysir's power has waned. There was hope that it might reawaken when, on Iceland's national holiday, 17 June 2000, a quake that measured 6.5 on the Richter scale hit the area. But it was not to be.

For centuries the cause of the Great Geysir's steamy outbursts was thought to be supernatural. And although today the science is well understood, it is difficult to watch a geyser erupt without feeling a connection with a power that is as old as earth itself.

At Geysir there is a water filled natural 'pipe' that runs over 20 m (65 ft) under ground. At this depth pressure from above allows the water to reach 120 °C (248 °F) without boiling. Higher up the pipe, however, the pressure is less, so the water can boil more easily. As it turns to steam it forces the water above it out of the pipe. This then causes a chain reaction. The rapid reduction in pressure on the super-heated water below results in it explosively turning into steam, sending the water above it up into the air. The expelled water then slowly trickles back into the pipe and the process begins again.

WHAT IS IT?
A hot spring that periodically expels steam and water into the air.
HOW TO GET THERE:
By road from Reykjavik.
WHEN TO GO:
All year – but winters can be cold.
NEAREST TOWN:
Reykjavik 75 km (46 mi) to the south west.
DON'T MISS:
The impressive waterfall at Gulfoss.
YOU SHOULD KNOW:
Although the Great Geysir now seldom erupts, just 50 m (165 ft) away another geyser called Strokkur is reliably active, producing jets up to 30 m (100 ft) high every ten minutes.

An eruption of Strokkur geyser, near the Great Geysir from which the word geyser originates.

Laki

WHAT IS IT?
A volcanic fissure with numerous craters.
HOW TO GET THERE:
A bus service from Kirkjubaejarklaustur that takes approximately three hours.
WHEN TO GO:
Spring to autumn.
NEAREST TOWN:
Kirkjubaejarklaustur
YOU SHOULD KNOW:
There are no facilities at Laki.

Laki, or Lakagígar, which means 'the craters of Laki', is a huge volcanic fissure that lies southeast of the Vatnajökull glacier – the largest glacier in Europe. The fissure is itself some 25 km (16 mi) long, and punctuated by around 100 crater cones, the largest of which is around 100 m (330 ft) high. Resembling a poorly healed wound, this ragged scar runs southwest to northeast through a desolate, otherworldly landscape, composed of reddish grey basalt lava softened only by a green patina of moss and lichen.

In a country not short of volcanic spectacle, Laki's peacefully dormant craters remain powerfully attractive. For Laki has an explosive past whose infamy is indelibly etched into Icelandic memory.

In 1783 this fissure erupted with incredible ferocity, ejecting 15 cu km (3.6 cu mi) of liquid basalt and creating the largest lava field ever produced by a single eruption. But worse was to follow. As the lava slowly smothered the ground, rising into the air was a far deadlier cloud of toxic gas.

A lethal mixture of fluorine and sulphur dioxide, this noxious cloud killed over 50 per cent of the livestock on Iceland. A terrible famine then followed in which around 10,000 Icelanders starved – around a fifth of the population. The tragedy was of such proportions that the Danish government, which at the time administered Iceland, even planned the evacuation of the remaining population to Jutland.

Due to its isolated location, and the nature of the terrain any visit to Laki needs to be well planned. The lava fields are, however, relatively easy to traverse on foot, while the more ambitious can go by horse or mountain bike. Whatever your mode of transport, the trip will reward you with some outstanding scenery and a special sense of unity both with the creative forces of planet earth and the history of the Icelandic people.

An aerial view of the volcanic fissure in the region of Lakagígar

Aurora Borealis

The aurora borealis is Nature's very own lightshow, a shimmering stream of coloured light that suffuses the night sky. Visually stunning, part of an aurora's beauty lies in its ephemeral nature. You can never be sure when you will see one and you can never be sure what kind of display you will witness. Sometimes an aurora can be a disappointingly monochrome, diaphanous cloud. At others a pulsating psychedelic curtain of colours.

This remarkably sci-fi phenomenon has an equally remarkable sci-fi explanation. It occurs when electrically charged particles, travelling at speeds of up to 1,200 km (750 mi) per second on the solar wind, are captured by the earth's magnetic field. As these particles are drawn down towards the poles they hit the ionosphere and collide with the gases in the atmosphere. These collisions produce photons –light particles that glow red, green, blue and violet. The result is a shimmering sky show known as the aurora australis in the southern hemisphere and the aurora borealis, or northern lights, in the north.

Auroras appear over the poles in what are described as auroral ovals. These ovals dip further south when the solar winds are stronger, but most auroras are seen at latitudes higher than 65ºN – which includes all of Iceland.

Viewing is best on crisp clear evenings in winter, away from the glare of city lights, when the nights are long and dark. Although visually spectacular, the light of an aurora is dimmer than starlight – so if you cannot see any stars you are unlikely to see the northern lights.

WHAT IS IT?
An electric display of atmospheric fireworks.

HOW TO GET THERE:
To see the aurora borealis in Iceland you must fly to Reykjavic.

WHEN TO GO:
The best months are October to March, late autumn being the best time of all.

NEAREST TOWN:
Get as far away from town and its light pollution as possible.

DON'T MISS:
Haukadalur Valley, 193 km (120 mi) north of Reykjavic, the home of the Great Geysir.

YOU SHOULD KNOW:
Aurora 'forecasts' can be found on the internet, search for 'spaceweather'. For much of the summer the Icelandic sky never really gets dark enough to see the aurora.

Horses are unfazed by the aurora borealis.

Þingvellir

WHAT IS IT?
Home of the world's oldest parliament and a rift valley set within a national park.
HOW TO GET THERE:
By road from Reykjavik.
WHEN TO GO:
All year – although more enjoyable in summer.
NEAREST TOWN:
Reykjavik, 49 km (30 mi) southwest.
YOU SHOULD KNOW:
Entry is free. There is a visitor's information centre, with café and bookshop.

Þingvellir, pronounced 'Thingvellir', is one of the so-called 'Golden Circle' attractions of Iceland, a collection of natural wonders and historical sites located within striking distance of Reykjavic. Þingvellir is, however, a collection of attractions itself, comprising the Parliamentary Plains, a rift valley and Lake Þingvallavatn, all encompassed by the oldest national park in Iceland.

The Parliamentary Plains are perhaps Þingvellir's greatest claim to fame. These were home to the Althing, the oldest parliament in the world. Established in 930AD, it met annually until 1789 when an earthquake caused the plain to slip by a metre (3 ft) and proceedings were moved to the current capital, Reykjavik.

It is no coincidence that Þingvellir is also of great geological interest, located at the centre of a tectonic tug-of-war between the continental plates of Europe and North America. Þingvellir and the Great African Rift Valley are in fact the only places on earth where the effects of two major plates drifting apart can be observed – albeit only by the patient. For the valley here is estimated to be expanding by about 7 mm (0.28 in) each year.

To the south of the rift lies Lake Þingvallavatn, Iceland's largest natural lake with an area of nearly 84 sq km (32 sq mi). Interestingly, at its greatest depth of 114 m (375 ft), it lies 13 m (43 ft) below sea level. As well as its natural beauty, the lake's clean, cool waters are popular with anglers as they are home to good numbers of at least four species of char and brown trout.

As well as being historically significant, Þingvellir is very beautiful. With rugged hills, some snow-capped, framing the valley, through which rivers and streams wind in and out, it is easy to appreciate why it was chosen as Iceland's first national park in 1928. Its value was further recognized in 2004 when it also became a UNESCO World Heritage Site.

An aerial view of Þingvellir

The Greenland Ice Sheet

The Greenland Ice Sheet is a vast body of ice covering roughly 80 per cent of the surface of Greenland. It consists of layers of compressed snow, which date back for more than 100,000 years. It is 2,400 km (1,500 mi) long from north to south, 1,100 km (690 mi) wide at its greatest width and 2-3 km (1.24-1.86 mi) thick. There are other ice masses in Greenland covering almost 100,000 sq km (38,600 sq mi) around the periphery.

Ariel view of the Greenland Ice Sheet

The ice in the current ice sheet is 110,000 years old. Scientists believe that if global warming continues at the current rate, the entire sheet will melt in a few hundred years. If all 2.85 million cu km (684,000 cu mi) of ice melts, global sea levels will rise by 7.2 m (24 ft). This would swamp most coastal cities in the world and drown several small island countries such as Tuvalu and the Maldives as well as low-lying countries, such as Bangladesh and The Netherlands.

The massive weight of the ice has depressed the central area of Greenland; the bedrock surface is near sea level over most of the interior of Greenland, but mountains occur around the periphery, with two north-south elongated domes that reach a height of 3,290 m (10,800 ft). The ice margin just reaches the sea near Melville Bay, southeast of Thule. Outlet glaciers, which are like tongues of the ice sheet, move through valleys around the periphery of Greenland to calve off into the ocean and produce the icebergs that occur in the North Atlantic shipping lanes. In winter, the ice sheet takes on a strikingly clear blue/green colour. In summer, the top layer melts, leaving pockets of air in the ice that make it appear to be bright white.

The area of melting in 2002 broke all previous records, and the ice sheet is now estimated to be melting at a rate of 239 cu km (57 cu mi) per year. When the melt water seeps down through cracks in the sheet, it accelerates the melting and allows the ice to slide more easily over the bedrock below, speeding its run to the sea. If the ice were to disappear, Greenland would appear as an archipelago.

WHAT IS IT?
The second largest ice body in the world, after the Antarctic Ice Sheet.
HOW TO GET THERE:
Fly to Nuuk - the capital of Greenland.
WHEN TO GO:
Summer season.
DON'T MISS:
The Jakobshavn Isbræ outlet glacier, which at its terminus, flows at speeds of 20-22 m (66-72 ft) per day.
YOU SHOULD KNOW:
In the past decades scientists have drilled ice cores here up to 3 km (2 mi) deep and as a result have gleaned the most valuable record to date of past climates, ocean volume, volcanic eruptions, desert extent and even forest fires.

Massive icebergs from Ilulissat Kangerlua Glacier (Jakobshavn Icefjord) floating on calm seas in Disko Bay.

Ilulissat Icefjord

Located on the west coast of Greenland, 250 km (156 mi) north of the Arctic Circle, Greenland's Ilulissat Icefjord is the sea mouth of Sermeq Kujalleq, one of the few glaciers through which the Greenland ice cap reaches the sea. It is also one of the fastest moving – 19 m (62 ft) per day – and most active glaciers in the world. Annually it calves over 35 cu km (8.4 cu mi) of ice, i.e. 10 per cent of the production of all Greenland calf ice and more than any other glacier outside Antarctica. It is an outstanding example of a stage in the earth's history: the last ice age of the Quaternary Period.

The combination of a huge ice sheet and a fast moving glacial ice stream calving into a fjord covered by icebergs is a phenomenon only seen in Greenland and Antarctica. Ilulissat offers scientists and visitors easy access for close viewing of the calving glacier front as it cascades down from the ice sheet and into the ice-choked fjord. The wild and highly scenic combination of rock, ice and sea, along with the dramatic sounds produced by the moving ice is an astonishing natural spectacle and, combined with the northern lights, makes Ilulissat a 'must-visit' destination.

The aurora borealis or northern lights is a celestial display of greens, yellows and reds that leave you spellbound by their extraordinary beauty as they shimmer against the inky backdrop of a starry night sky. In summer you can take a midnight cruise to the ice fjord and see the midnight sun with the warm red colours reflecting in the gigantic icebergs while you enjoy a late Martini on 'the real rocks'!

WHAT IS IT?
The glacier through which the Greenland Ice cap reaches the sea.
HOW TO GET THERE:
From Copenhagen fly to Kangerlussuaq, from there fly on to Ilulissat.
WHEN TO GO:
April to August for the midnight sun.
NEAREST TOWN:
Ilulissat, on the sea border of the fjord.
DON'T MISS:
The aurora borealis - the northern lights - a mesmerizing display of lights in the Arctic night sky.
YOU SHOULD KNOW:
The glacier has been studied for 250 years and has recently been instrumental in helping our understanding of climate change.

The Krimml Falls

One of the greatest attractions in Austria is the Krimml Falls on the western edge of the Hohe Tauern National Park. The Krimml is the biggest waterfall in Europe and ranks in the top eight great waterfalls of the world. It falls a total distance of 380 m (1,246 ft) in three dramatic drops, each of more than 100 m (330 ft), connected by twisting rapids. The incredible thunder of the water as it comes crashing down at the rate of 7 cu m (250 cu ft) per second is truly awesome.

Krimml flows through a narrow wooded valley in the heart of a dramatically beautiful glaciated region of the eastern Alps – there are more than 300 mountains over 3,000 m (9,850 ft) high, and the tallest mountain in Austria, the Grossglockner, at 3,798 m (12,460 ft). A tenth of Hohe Tauern is covered in glacial ice, the mountains are permanently snow-capped, and winter here can last for up to eight months.

The 4 km (2.5 mi) long trail to the top of the falls, the headwaters of the River Salzach, takes you through a dazzling landscape of mountain and forest, which you view through a fine haze of water, sprayed up in great clouds by the force of the Krimml. The path is extremely steep in places and it takes about one and a half hours to complete the entire route. However, it is well worth persevering to reach the viewing point at Bergerblick – you will be rewarded with an amazing sense of achievement and the most superb view.

In winter, the slopes above Krimml village are a popular skiing resort and the waterfall is frozen into a bizarre static ice cascade.

The Krimml Falls

WHAT IS IT?
The largest waterfall in Europe.
HOW TO GET THERE:
Fly to Salzburg or Innsbruck. Road or rail to Zell am See, 50 km (30 mi) away. Steam train trip recommended from Zell am See to Krimml.
WHEN TO GO:
At its most amazing in the spring.
NEAREST TOWN:
Krimml 4 km (2.5 mi)
DON'T MISS:
Franz-Josefs-Hohe, the most beautiful spot in the whole area, on the edge of the Pasterze – the longest glacier in the eastern Alps. In the east of Hohe Tauern is the unspoilt Rauris valley, where there is a colony of bearded vultures whose droppings make the lichens on the cliffs grow bright red.

YOU SHOULD KNOW:
The Krimml Falls is one of the most popular tourist resorts in Austria so be prepared for plenty of company. Most people can't be bothered to climb the entire way – by the time you reach Bergerblick you should have left most of them behind.

Spring flowers in a meadow below Kaisergebirge in North Tyrol

North Tyrol

The fairytale alpine scenery of North Tyrol is the stuff of picture books – swift mountain rivers tumbling down forested slopes, fertile pastoral valleys dotted with smallholdings and villages, ice-clad peaks and sparkling glacial lakes. This beautiful region is a sports paradise for anyone who enjoys the outdoors, with its panoramic landscapes, pure mountain air and sparklingly clean bathing lakes.

Wildspitze, the second tallest mountain in Austria is 3,374 m (10, 980 ft) high. Its slopes are glaciated but otherwise straightforward, which makes it perfect for ice climbing. There are more than 700 other mountains over 3,000 m (9,840 ft) high, so this is great climbing territory. In winter, there is terrific downhill and cross-country skiing at world famous resorts like Kitzbühel and St Anton am Arlberg; in the warmer months you can go white water rafting and kayaking as well as trekking, horse riding and mountain biking.

Above all, the scenic beauty of the landscape makes the Tyrol idyllic walking country, with more than 15,000 km (9,375 mi) of trails to roam. You will find walks at all levels of difficulty to match your fitness, and there are numerous mountain huts in which to shelter or spend the night.

The Adlerweg (Eagle Walk) is a 280 km (175 mi) route that wends its way across the Tyrol in 23 sections, with side paths branching off it and easy bypasses of the more precipitous parts. For those in search of peaceful communion with nature there is the St James Pilgrimage trail, with abbeys and monasteries that you can stay in.

Tyroleans are intensely proud of their regional identity and language, and are renowned for their warm hospitality and hearty cooking. The Tyrol has many cultural attractions as well as natural ones; it is one of the most charming regions of the Alps.

WHAT IS IT?
A picturebook land of lederhosen and schnapps.
HOW TO GET THERE:
Fly to Innsbruck.
WHEN TO GO:
Time of year depends on your sports interest.
NEAREST TOWN:
Innsbruck.
DON'T MISS:
Innsbruck's historic town centre; the centennial garden of Swarovski Crystal World in Wattens 15 km (9 mi) east of Innsbruck designed by Andre Heller.
YOU SHOULD KNOW:
After World War I, the Tyrol was divided between Italy and Austria. North and East Tyrol are in Austria, separated from each other by a 20 km (12 mi) strip of land, while South Tyrol, an autonomous German-speaking region of Italy, borders onto both.

Eisriesenwelt Ice Caves

The Eisriesenwelt is the largest accessible ice labyrinth in the world, with more than 40 km (25 mi) of explored passageways. Its entrance is a gaping hole in the side of a sheer rock face at an altitude of 1,640 m (5,380 ft). The caverns are lined in ice 20 m (65 ft) thick and are elaborately ornamented with stunning ice stalactites, stalagmites, columns, domes and waterfalls. They have romantic names from Norse mythology – Odin's Room, Frigga's Veil, Hall of Hymir – in a reference to the Ice Giants of Norse legend who opposed the rule of the gods.

Opposing air currents keep the ice frozen all year round. In the winter, cold air blows into the cave entrance, freezing the water from the melting snow that has dripped into the labyrinth through the summer. In the warmer months, cold air from deep inside, in its attempt to flow out, prevents the ice near the entrance from melting.

High in the mountains, the Eisriesenwelt was only known to hunters and poachers, and was not formally "discovered" until 1879. And it was not until 1912 that Alexander von Mörk, a famous speleologist (cave expert), alerted the world to its significance. His ashes are interred here, in an urn in the Mörk Cathedral, an ice chamber set 35 m (120 ft) above the cave floor.

The Eisriesenwelt was opened to the public in 1920 and rapidly became one of the most popular tourist attractions in Austria. At first, people had to undergo a strenuous one and a half hour climb up to the caves but in 1955 a cable car was built, so now it only takes a matter of minutes. There is a spectacular view of the Hohe Tauern Mountains from the cave entrance.

WHAT IS IT?
"World of the Ice Giants".
HOW TO GET THERE:
Fly to Salzburg. Road or rail to Werfen, about 40 km (25 mi) south, then a bus to Eisriesenwelt.
WHEN TO GO:
Open May to October.
NEAREST TOWN:
Werfen 5 km (3 mi)
DON'T MISS:
Hohenwerfen Fortress, near Werfen – a 900 year-old fortress and prison with falconry.
YOU SHOULD KNOW:
A tour of the cave lasts 75 minutes so remember to wear warm clothes to protect you against the freezing temperature inside.

Ice formations in the Eisriesenwelt ice cave

239

*Hallstättersee as seen from
Mount Krippenstein*

Salzkammergut

WHAT IS IT?
"The land of white gold" – stunningly scenic region for outdoor land and water activities.

HOW TO GET THERE:
Fly to Salzburg or Linz. Road or train to Vocklabrück or Bad Ischl.

WHEN TO GO:
Any time, although, unless you are going for the skiing, the summer months are probably best to fully appreciate the scenic beauty and enjoy the waters of the lakes.

NEAREST TOWNS:
Vocklabrück, Bad Ischl.

DON'T MISS:
The Hallstatt salt mines, with huge underground salt lake; the Beinhaus – an ossuary, stacked with decorated skulls and bones, each engraved with their identity and date of death; the Dachstein ice and limestone caves. Pastry shops and health spas of Bad Ischl.

YOU SHOULD KNOW:
The artist Gustav Klimt spent many summer holidays in Salzkammergut and used Attersee (Lake Atter) as a source of inspiration for his landscape paintings.

Salzkammergut is a World Heritage Landscape, famous for its enchanting scenery of lakes, mountains, and picturesque villages. It is arguably the most beautiful region in the whole of Austria, where, in the days of the Hapsburg Empire, the emperors and noble families used to take their holidays.

The word "salzkammergut" means "estate of the salt chamber"; salt has been quarried here since the Bronze Age without defacing the landscape. In fact, the salt (or "white gold") trade has only added to the region's charm since it led to enormous wealth, reflected in the fine architecture of the historic towns here. The government had a monopoly on the trade and Salzkammergut was banned to outsiders until the 19th century in case they were salt smugglers.

The oldest salt mine in the world is here, in the village of Hallstatt. This unbelievably quaint 17th century toy town, with its own waterfall, is squeezed precariously between the brink of the 135 m (440 ft) deep Hallstättersee (Lake Hallstaetter) and the precipitous slopes of the Dachstein mountains.

The largest lake in Austria – Attersee – is one of the 76 beautiful lakes in Salzkammergut. It covers an area of 46 sq km (18 sq mi) and is famous for its pure water and easterly "Rosenwind", which wafts the scent of roses from nearby castle gardens across its waters. Perhaps the most scenically beautiful lake is Altausseersee, known as the "ink pot" for its dark blue water. And a visit to the tiny Toplitzsee, hidden deep in the mountain forest, with its murky but fascinating connection to Nazi weapons testing, stashing of gold and counterfeit currency, is a must.

Whatever the season, the picture postcard scenery of Salzgammerkut will make your spirit soar; you cannot help but be exhilarated by the pure air, clear water and breathtaking views.

The Rhône Glacier

The once-mighty Rhône Glacier, high in the Dammastock mountains, is not only one of the best known glaciers in the world, but one of the most endangered, too. Seen from a distance, the grey wedge in the side of the valley above the Gletsch is still impressive, yet only 150 years ago, it reached the edge of the village. Between 1996 and 2006, it shrank by 50 m (165 ft) and in the last 150 years has receded 2.5 km (1 mi) and is 450 m (1,476 ft) higher up the valley. It is estimated that the last 9.5 km (6 mi) may be gone before the end of the twenty-first century as the process speeds up.

Access to the glacier is via the Belvedere Hotel, just west of the switchback Furkapass. As you get nearer to it, its colour changes from grey to a pale sky blue. A trail and wooden steps lead to the face of the glacier, and to the 'ice cave', an artificial tunnel carved deep into the glacier. Some 30-40 m (98-131 ft) of tunnel have to be cut each year to compensate for the glacier's movement down its valley. Inside, the light is a startling deep blue-green and the air is cool but still. Despite the creaks of the ice as it shifts and the occasional cracking sounds, and the knowledge that this mammoth glacier may not be here much longer, there is a sense of serenity and calm.

WHAT IS IT?
One of the best known glaciers in the world.
HOW TO GET THERE:
By road via the Furkapass or Grimselpass
WHEN TO GO:
Spring to autumn.
NEAREST TOWN:
Andermatt 26 km (16 mi)
DON'T MISS:
A walk through the ice cave.
YOU SHOULD KNOW:
The roads are very steep and twisting.

The upper section of the Rhône Glacier

The Matterhorn

WHAT IS IT?
An instantly recognizable mountain.
HOW TO GET THERE:
By road to Tasch, then by train to Zermatt, and on foot or by ski lift from there.
WHEN TO GO:
The best time for climbing and hiking is July to September.
NEAREST TOWN:
Visp (40 km, 25 mi)
YOU SHOULD KNOW:
Cars are not allowed in Zermatt village.

The Matterhorn mountain is reflected in Lake Rifflesee above Zermatt. The Matterhorn is the seventh highest mountain in the Alps and one of the most often photographed mountains in the world.

Lying on the border between Switzerland and Italy, the iconic 4,478-m (14,693-ft) Matterhorn (Monte Cervino in Italian) is perhaps the most widely recognized mountain in Europe. It's four faces – facing north, south, east and west – remain almost snowless because they are so steep. The snow instead feeds the glaciers that lie at the foot of each face. It was first climbed in 1865, by the route that is most commonly used today, the Hörnli ridge above the Swiss village of Zermatt. Although about 3,000 people a year attempt the climb, many have to turn back because it requires a great deal of strength and stamina. The other major route is from the Italian side.

Renowned as a winter skiing area, the lower slopes of the mountain are also excellent for hiking in summer, with stunning views, larch forests, alpine meadows and mountain tarns. One of the most amazing views on offer is that from the Gorner Grat ridge across the Gorner Glacier with the backdrop of the Monte Rosa, the Dorn, the Breithorn and the Matterhorn behind. The ridge can be reached on foot or by the railway.

The Schwarzsee, or Black Lake, to the north of the mountain is a worthwhile destination in itself, and also offers closer views of the mountain and spectacular views across the valley, too. The high meadows have lovely alpine flora in spring and are home to marmots and a range of alpine birds.

Gimmelwald

The landscape surrounding the tiny hamlet of Gimmelwald is breathtaking. Perched high up on the Schilthorn, it looks east across the Lauterbrunnen valley towards the Jungfrau, Münch and Eiger. In both summer and winter, it is picture-postcard Switzerland. It is a traffic-free, television-free paradise: the only access is via the Luftseilbahn Stechelberg-Mürren-Schilthorn cable-car or on foot. The walk from Stechelberg or Mürren takes about an hour and a half: from the former it is uphill and from the latter downhill.

From the top of the 2,970-m (9,744-ft) Schilthorn, the panoramic views encompass, the Jungfrau range and Titlis and the Juras, the Black Forest. On clear days, Mont Blanc, some 110 km (70 mi) away can just be seen. The cable-car goes to the mountaintop, but the Schilthorn hike takes you through a range of scenery that is almost unimaginable – steep, narrow gorges carved by streams, waterfall, huge boulders left lying by glaciers, alpine meadows, scree slopes, pinewoods, craggy peaks, U-shaped valleys, rounded ridges in which you can see the scars left by the ice and always, the snow-tipped mountains filling the view.

Sometimes, when the valleys below are filled with cloud, it can seem like there is nothing there, except you and the mountains.

The village of Gimmelwald

WHAT IS IT?
A delightful Alpine landscape with breathtaking views.
HOW TO GET THERE:
By road to Stechelberg or train to Mürren, then on foot or by cable-car.
WHEN TO GO:
At any time.
NEAREST TOWN:
Interlaken 14 km (8 mi)
YOU SHOULD KNOW:
The trail up to the village is sometimes closed in winter because of the risk of avalanches.

The Reichenbach Falls

The five cascades that make up the Reichenbach falls have a total drop of some 250 m (820 ft) and the Upper Falls are one of the longest individual cascades in the Alps. The lower falls, where the noise of the water crashing onto the rocks is overwhelming, are within walking distance of the village, but the train ride to reach the upper falls is a must, as it criss-crosses the rushing waters below. In seven minutes, it whisks you up 244 m (800 ft). A narrow trail leads to the top of the falls, where it is far quieter than at their foot. From the mountain rescue hut, a trail leads round to good spots for viewing the spectacular falls and the Hasli Valley.

The falls are a wonderful sight in late spring and early summer, as the waters rush, splash and tumble down the shining black rocks into the gorge and clouds of spray rise like smoke. However, the falls are as well known for their literary connection: on the other side of the falls, accessed via a little footbridge, is a white star marking the place where, in Conan Doyle's *The Adventure of the Final Problem*, Sherlock Holmes and Professor Moriarty grappled before falling together into the 'boiling pit'.

WHAT IS IT?
One of the highest waterfalls in the alps.
HOW TO GET THERE:
By funicular railway from Willingen
WHEN TO GO:
The funicular operates only from mid-May to the beginning of October. May to July is the best time to see the falls.
NEAREST TOWN:
Meiringen 2 km (1 mi)
YOU SHOULD KNOW:
The annual Sherlock Holmes commemoration is on 4 May.

The Reichenbach Falls, near the village of Meiringen

Lake Lucerne

Lake Lucerne (in German, Vierwaldstättersee) and its surroundings form the image that most people picture when they think of Switzerland. Surrounded by mountains and beautiful lakeshores, it is also one of the most important places in the country's history: the Rütli meadow, where the people of the area first swore the oath that began the Swiss Confederation and its defiance of the Hapsburgs, is near its shores.

Three iconic mountains around the lake are Mt Pilatus, where according to legend Pontius Pilate is buried, the Bürgenstock and the Rigi, which so fascinated Turner that he painted it in its different moods and at different times of day. At sunset, it can appear a brilliant red.

Although it is possible to drive around most of the lake's shore, by far the most popular way to get from place to place is to take one of the many steamers that criss-cross the lake.

The most popular way to get up Pilatus is via the world's steepest cogwheel railway, which operates when the route is free of snow, and there are aerial gondolas and cableways that operate all year. The views north-east across the lake from the top are spectacular: as well as the lake, there are mountain pastures, spruce forests and the Rigi. The latter has many hiking trails and the top can be accessed by cable car or rack railway. Sunrise over the the Zugspitz, as the light floods across mountains and sneaks into valleys, is a stupendous sight.

WHAT IS IT?
A beautiful lake in central Switzerland.
HOW TO GET THERE:
By road from or rail from Zürich.
WHEN TO GO:
Summer.
NEAREST TOWN:
Lucerne, on the lake's edge
DON'T MISS:
The views from Mount Pilatus.

Mountains and trees border Lake Lucerne.

Eiger and Mönch

The Eiger

High in the Bernese Oberland, at the eastern end of the Jungfrau range, the Eiger is one of the best-known – and most notorious – mountains in the world. Climbing its north face is still a byword for attempting the impossible, even though the feat was first achieved in 1938. The relatively easy route up the west flank was first accomplished in 1858, but even that is for serious climbers only. At 3,970 m (13,025 ft), it is 188 m (617 ft) shorter than the nearby Jungfrau. As you approach on the train from either direction, the north face, or Eigerwand, dominates the valley below.

Both routes have become more hazardous in summer over recent years: warmer temperatures and less snowfall have reduced the amount of ice and rock falls are more common: in 2006, some 700,000 cu m (24,719,800 cu ft) sheared off the north face in one massive rock slide.

The Eiger Trail runs from Wengen to Alpiglen and takes in both a walk near the base of the north wall and the Eiger glacier. To walk the full trail takes a day's strenuous effort, but the short section from the Eigergletscher station to Alpiglen takes less than three hours, according to the authorities.

Switzerland's high alpine meadows

The high meadows of the Alps remain some of the most unspoiled landscapes in Europe. They are internationally important for the unique groups of plants they contain. Among the best areas are the Parc Naziunal Svizzer – Switzerland's only national park – near Engadin in the east, around Wengen in the Bernese Oberland and in the area around the Matterhorn in the south. Under feet of snow during winter, it is amazing that any delicate plants survive here, but in early summer, watered by the melting snow, a riot of flowers appears: blue and yellow gentians, lady's slipper orchids, the rare edelweiss and bellflowers carpet the dry meadows for a brief period. Up here, no fertilizers are used and these tiny plants grow as they have for thousands of years. Even higher up, wet meadows, small lakes with ice-cold water and bogs are fed by water from the melting glaciers. One of the most famous tarns – lakes that form in the base of glacial cirques – is the Schwarzsee below the Matterhorn.

The scenery in these areas is, of course, spectacular, as they are dominated by the mountains above with views over the forests and valleys below.

Wildlife that may be spotted within or from these meadows and the high slopes above includes marmots, chamois, wild goats, ibex and elk. In the national park, golden eagle and reintroduced Egyptian vulture may be seen. The flower-meadows attract a wonderful array of butterflies. Up around the moraines of glaciers, a variety of rare birds such as alpine accentors, alpine choughs, and snow finches, ring ouzels and water pipits may be seen.

WHAT IS IT?
A unique landscape, filled with flowers and wildlife.
HOW TO GET THERE:
By hiking in the areas below the glaciers.
WHEN TO GO:
Early summer.

Mountain lake in Switzerland's high alpine region

The Yorkshire Dales

The Yorkshire Dales, located in the north of England, straddle the central Pennines in the counties of North Yorkshire and Cumbria. This is a landscape of dark fells, steep sided green valleys criss-crossed with dry-stone walls, the countryside scattered with solid stone farmhouses and field barns. Modest hills look like majestic peaks, especially when clothed in snow, and after heavy rain small streams have the power of mighty rivers.

The area was designated a national park in 1954 and 10 million visitors come each year to marvel at the verdant landscape, to walk and to paint and to enjoy Yorkshire's famous hospitality.

There are four large Dales within the 1760 sq km (680 sq mi) of the park with a host of smaller Dales meandering off into rocky gorges below the fells. Wensleydale, carving a path through the

middle of the dales, is broad and wooded, known for its castles and waterfalls and the famous cheese made at the Wensleydale creamery near the village of Gayle.

Swaledale to the north is narrow and steep sided, a wild and desolate valley, topped by sweeping moorlands. Tan Hill, here, has given its name to a very successful variety of hill sheep.

Wharfedale in the heart of the Dales is long and winding, its valley floor studded with pretty villages. The Cow and Calf Rocks on the moors towards Burleigh Woodhead give breathtaking views over moor and valley. To the west, Ribblesdale is a valley of rolling countryside, limestone gorges and towering peaks. From the summit of Ingleborough Hill, on a clear day, you will see as far as the Isle of Man to the south west.

WHAT IS IT?
An area of deep valleys and high fells.
HOW TO GET THERE:
From Leeds go to Otley, take A65 to Skipton where the B6265 will lead you into the Dales.
WHEN TO GO:
Springtime with primroses, trees leafing and lambs gambolling.
NEAREST TOWN:
Hawes is the largest town within the Dales.
DON'T MISS:
Thorpe, the "hidden village" of Wharfedale where the Navvy Noddle Hole Cave has yielded remains of reindeer and bears from the ice age.
YOU SHOULD KNOW:
Members of a Halifax Church Choir composed Yorkshire's "National Anthem" – 'On Ilkla Moor baht' at' while they picnicked on the moors at Wharfedale.

Dungeness

A small fishing boat on the shingle beach

Denge Marsh in Kent reaches the sea in a remote, flat shingle headland. This is Dungeness – a vast shingle landscape, dominated by a massive nuclear power station built here in the 1960s. The stones reach to the horizon, studded in springtime with great creamy clumps of sea kale and glossy stands of wild spinach, then later in the year white bladder campion and yellow horned poppies. Wooden habitations, some no bigger than shacks, are scattered hither and thither, many concocted from old boats. The remains of long dead lobster pots and heaps of tarry rope are part of the scene. It is quite magical in a stark, Kafkaesque way.

Two lighthouses stand within view of each other – one took over active duty from the 1904 "old lighthouse" which is privately owned and open for visits. For fifty years its huge one million candle power light shone out over the English Channel and could be seen twenty miles away, but when the nuclear power station came on stream in the early sixties it was made redundant and auctioned off. Chipped masonry shows the Germans used the lighthouse for machine gun target practice. You can climb up the 169 steps to the giant lens and from the balcony, gaze at France across the channel.

Colonies of sea birds and a myriad of rare visitors, such as the Tundra Bean goose and the Pomaine skua, congregate here at the RSBP Reserve. This is one of the largest expanses of shingle in the world and home to many unique insects and butterflies.

One feature of the landscape, much enjoyed by visitors and known by anglers as 'the boil', is where the waste hot water and effluents pumped into the sea from the nuclear power station attract seabirds from miles around.

WHAT IS IT?
The headland of a shingle beach.
HOW TO GET THERE:
From Lydd in the north west or from New Romney via Littlestone on Sea, along the coast.
WHEN TO GO:
The bleak other-worldliness of Dungeness makes it unusually beautiful throughout the seasons.
NEAREST TOWN:
New Romney 12 km (8 mi)
DON'T MISS:
Prospect Cottage with its driftwood/flotsam garden created by the film director Derek Jarman.
YOU SHOULD KNOW:
TThe New York Times once stated 'If Kent is the garden of England, Dungeness is the back gate'.

The Seven Sisters

These cliffs are formed on the south coast of England, where the chalk south coast plain ends abruptly at the sea. This plain is a chalky landscape of rolling arable fields and dry valleys, with close-cropped grassland on scarps sparsely settled with small hamlets and farmsteads built of flint and brick. Roman and ancient drove roads are common and there are many prehistoric remains with Neolithic and Bronze age barrows and Iron Age hill forts.

The spectacular white chalk cliffs are composed of the limey skeletons of small marine organisms, which were laid down in sedimentary layers, with silica laid down in nodules within the chalk to form flint. All these layers have been contorted and lifted by the movement of the continental drifts and then corroded by the sea to form cliffs.

One of the most famous cliffs here is called Beachy Head – supposedly from the French *beau chef* or 'lovely head' – sadly infamous for its suicide leaps. From there to Cuckmere Haven the elements have carved out the bright white Seven Sisters – West Hill Brow, Baily's Hill, Flagstaff Point, Bran Point, Rough Brow, Short Brow and Haven Brow, ending where the river Cuckmere runs into the sea at Cuckmere Haven. Walking tracks from Beachy Head lead across the hilltops and across the Seven Sisters County Park.

This whole area, which is the south eastern end of the South Downs, is popular with cyclists, walkers, kite fliers and hang gliders with both quite challenging walks or more leisurely strolls through Friston forest or down through Birling Gap.

WHAT IS IT?
Sheer chalk cliffs on the South Coast of England
HOW TO GET THERE:
The A21 from junction 5 of the M25 to Tonbridge – then the A26 to Uckfield – and the A22 to Eastbourne.
WHEN TO GO:
Good for walking all year.
NEAREST TOWN:
Eastbourne 3 km (2 mi)
DON'T MISS:
The Long Man of Wilmington – a chalk figure cut into the clay hillside north of the cliffs.

The Seven Sisters

The Lake District

Lying in the north-west of England, the Lake District is one of the best-loved landscapes in the country and has been celebrated in poetry and literature – from Wordsworth's *Daffodils* to Ransome's *Swallows and Amazons* – and art. It is the highest area in England, and its fells are wonderful hiking territory. The U-shaped valleys that radiate out from the centre of the area were carved out of the rock by glaciers during the last ice age. Where the underlying rock is soft, the valleys and hills are gentle, but in the middle where the rocks are volcanic the skyline is full of jagged edges where the grinding ice ripped rocks apart.

The higher fells, like Scafell Pike, Helvellyn, Skiddaw and Great Gable are challenging hikes and not for the beginner, but the softer areas near Windermere itself are easier.

Windermere is the largest lake in England, and Wast Water the deepest. Windermere, Derwentwater and Coniston Water are popular for boating, and can get busy, but the more remote lakes are far more peaceful. Higher up are smaller tarns that sit in glacial cirques.

The Lake District is not large, only 56 km (35 mi) across at its widest, but its sheer variety of scenery – from rolling hills to rugged moorland and bare jagged rock and from peaceful lakes to rushing mountain streams – and the continually changing light as clouds rush across the landscape make this area so dramatic and so beautiful.

Buttermere Fell

Dartmoor

Sprawling across Devon, in south west England, between the towns of Plymouth and Exeter, Dartmoor is as starkly beautiful as it is historically fascinating. Occupying 4,700 hectares (11,610 acres) of desolate wilderness: heather-strewn moors, barren bog land and mile upon mile of raw granite, this is the place to come for a sense of Nature at her most stoical.

At its centre is Dartmoor Forest where you can find the famous wild ponies, ancient weather-chiselled tors (flat granite hilltops), and, if you catch the right weather, you will see the mist coming down, imbuing this desolate terrain with a bleak and magical beauty. But be warned, it is easy to lose your way and bottomless bogs and stinking mires are never far away.

Dartmoor was once home to many Bronze Age settlers whose artefacts can be viewed all over the area, particularly to the east at Grimspound. Man's more recent contribution comes in the form of Dartmoor Prison, in Princetown, originally built for the POWs captured in the Napoleonic Wars. And, at nearby Wistman's Wood, it is not hard to picture the druid gatherings that are thought to have taken place amongst the gnarled old trees.

In literature, it is Sir Arthur Conan Doyle who captured the spirit of Dartmoor best with his grimly transfixing 'The Hound of the Baskervilles'. Within its pages the reader can absorb the dark tales and sinister myths that linger on the Moor. 'So vast and so mysterious,' he mused. The tumbling streams in the forest, the trout that swim under Fingle Bridge, the solitary kestrels and the crazed buzzards circling overhead; all against the grim presence of the prison and the endless, beguiling view from the heights of High Willhays. There is the creeping possibility that maybe, if you get in too deep, you might become lost here forever.

Heather covers the ground near a knoll on Dartmoor.

WHAT IS IT?
Southern England's greatest expanse of wilderness.

HOW TO GET THERE:
From London it is a 281 km (174 mi) journey west to Exeter at the north-eastern edge of the moor. Trains run regularly from London (Paddington).

WHEN TO GO:
Any time of year is good, but November to February is especially atmospheric.

NEAREST TOWN:
Tavistock is the largest of Dartmoor's towns.

DON'T MISS:
The cream teas offered in the Moor's idyllic villages.

YOU SHOULD KNOW:
High Willhays is the highest point at 621 m (2,037 ft) above sea level. The pockets of trembling earth are known as 'featherbeds' – this underfoot-wobbling sensation is caused by waterlogged peat.

257

One of the caves at Wookey Hole

Wookey Hole

The caves and caverns of Wookey Hole on the edge of the Mendip Hills are an exciting and folklore-filled area. The ancient river Axe, over many thousands of years, carved these caves into the limestone escarpment of the Mendips. The caves are thought to have been inhabited for at least 70,000 years, as they were safe, dry and easy to defend.

They first gave shelter to Stone Age man, and much later to the Celts, who farmed the fertile valley floors. Later still, the Romans subdued the Celts, built a villa here and mined the hills for lead. The name Wookey is thought to come from the Old English *wocig*, meaning animal trap, as the caves were inhabited alternately by hyenas and man between 35,000 and 25,000 BC. Hyenas would have chased their prey over the limestone escarpment in which the caves are formed. Bones of other tropical and Ice Age animals, such as rhinoceros, bear, mammoth and lion have been found in the hyena den, along with human flint tools.

The action of the river on the limestone has carved out more than 25 chambers and pools, linked by the subterranean river Axe, all discovered during the 20th century by a series of novel diving expeditions – and there is still more exploration pending.

One of the cave's most notorious dwellers was the 'witch' in the Witch's Parlour Cavern, who was supposedly turned to stone whilst guarding the caves on the river shore, by a monk from Glastonbury. He blessed some of the river water, sprinkled it over her and she turned into a block of stone.

The river Axe has made other caves such as Swildon's Hole and St Cuthbert's Swallet, and after exiting Wookey Hole, its waters are used for making paper in England's oldest, handmade paper mill, situated on the site of an old corn mill circa 1086.

Nearby are Cheddar Gorge, and Ebbor Gorge, a Site of Special Scientific Interest and a quieter spot than Wookey.

WHAT IS IT?
Natural limestone caves, caverns and flooded chambers formed by the River Axe in south east England.
HOW TO GET THERE:
Train from London Paddington to Bristol - or by car or coach direct to Wells where there will be buses to Wookey Hole.
NEAREST TOWN:
Wells 4.8 km (3 mi)
WHEN TO GO:
All year round.
DON'T MISS:
Wells Cathedral and Glastonbury Tor.
YOU SHOULD KNOW:
This is the home of the delicious Cheddar cheese.

The Jurassic Coast

This, the first British World Heritage Site, is 152 km (95 mi) of coast, recording 185 million years of ancient history through the Triassic, Jurassic and Cretaceous geological periods that comprise the Mesozoic Era. It stretches from the Orcombe Rocks in East Devon through to Studland Bay and Poole in West Dorset.
The cliff exposures along this coast provide an almost continuous sequence of rock formations spanning the Mesozoic Era. The area's important fossil sites and classic coastal geomorphologic features have greatly contributed to the study of earth sciences for over 300 years.

The Triassic period is seen from Exmouth to Lyme Regis, then the Jurassic from Lyme Regis to Swanage, and finally the Cretaceous period through to Studland Bay and into Poole harbour.

This area is also rich in wildlife with large populations of avocet, dark bellied Brent goose, Slavonian grebe and the little tern at Chesil beach. The Lulworth Skipper butterfly can be spotted amongst the early spider orchid, gentian, wild cabbage and the Nottingham catchfly. There is a long history of mining for shale, and local stone from Portland, Beer and Purbeck have been used throughout the UK for building work.

The Jurassic Coast, and in particular Lyme Regis and Charmouth with their clay based old tropical seas with soft, muddy and often stagnant lower levels, was perfect for preserving shells, bones and even soft tissue of long dead prehistoric creatures. Imagine the excitement of discovering green ammonites and 197 million-year-old Belamnite Marl alongside other vertebrate and invertebrate marine and terrestrial fossils, and even ancient fossilized footprints.

WHAT IS IT?
152 km (95 mi) of corroding south England coastline, showing ancient geological strata and fossils.
HOW TO GET THERE:
By train from London (Paddington) to Poole, Dorchester or Honiton or by road from London via the M3/A303 to Honiton.
WHEN TO GO:
All year round (busy in the summer months).
NEAREST TOWN:
Bridport 2.4 km (1.5 mi)
DON'T MISS:
Portland – a small island joined to Weymouth by a causeway and also The Fleet lagoon at Chesil Beach.
YOU SHOULD KNOW:
Between Abbotsbury and Chesil Beach there is a tiny unused chapel on a hill called St Catherine's where spinsters come in November to wish for husbands.

Durdle Door on the Jurassic Coast

The Peak District

WHAT IS IT:
A large area of hillscapes.
HOW TO GET THERE:
The M1 motorway runs to the east and north of the National Park and from junctions 33 the A57 runs through the city of Sheffield and into the north of the Park which is also crossed by several major roads.
WHEN TO GO:
All year round.
NEAREST TOWN:
Ashbourne 10 km (6 mi) from Dovedale in the south Peak district.
DON'T MISS:
Mam Tor (Shivering Hill) the views from the cliff face at the top are stupendous.
YOU SHOULD KNOW:
Charlotte Bronte stayed at Hathersage Vicarage, in the heart of the Peaks, and incorporated both vicarage and village in *Jane Eyre*.

The Peak District stretches from the beautiful town of Ashbourne in the south to the craggy and remote High Peak District west of Sheffield. This, the first established of the National Parks, reaches deep into six English counties – Derbyshire, Cheshire, Staffordshire, South Yorkshire, West Yorkshire and Greater Manchester, but to most people The Peaks mean Derbyshire.

Rock dominates the landscape, in its pinnacles and spires and airy limestone crags that overhang the deep dales, whose greenness is counterpaned with grey-white dry stone walls and wandering threadlike rivers. The central core is the White Peak, limestone country, scarred everywhere by the green gorges of the dales. Surrounding this is an area of shale and thin sandstone through which rivers such as the Derwent and the Goyt have carved their wider, flatter valleys, and embracing all is the Dark Peak, sombre and forbidding, the gritstone rock rising to a moorland plateau – the lonely domain of red grouse and hardy sheep. Here are the Roaches – last bastion of the Pennines – never rising to more than 518 m (1,700 ft) but with their fantastic ridge battlemented with weird, weathered shapes, this is a hugely impressive site.

Stone is everywhere in the architecture and the landscape, yet in contrast to this, the countryside is gentle, green and lush. Dove Dale is a wooded, utterly beautiful part of the valley of the Dove just to the north of Thorpe. Every part of the little river's course is extraordinarily pleasant and much of it can be followed by footpath. Thankfully, there are no riverside roads.

Nether Tor in the Peak District

The Severn Bore

The Severn Bore is a surge wave that forms in the funnel-shaped Severn estuary and travels upstream as a sequence of three or four unbroken waves. At a certain point it splits in two and then rejoins. It is a fascinating sight to see the river suddenly reversed as the incoming tidal wave overcomes the natural flow of the water and flows upstream.

The height of each bore is unpredictable mainly due to the height and speed of the incoming tide entering the narrowing and shelving estuary. Other influences are the amount of fresh water in the river, atmospheric pressure and wind direction. Strong winds from the Atlantic increase the bore's height. The largest bores tend to follow the highest tides, which occur a few days after new and full moons, the biggest coming from February to April and August to October, the spring and autumn equinoxes. The record height for a bore is 2.75 m (9 ft).

The best vantage points to witness this phenomenon are between Minsterworth and Lower Parting and it is a thrilling sight given the sheer power of the water, the increasing roar as it advances and the dramatic change in river level once the bore has passed. Those who live and work on the river know well the cries of "Tide ho" as it approaches. About a dozen times a year the bore is big enough to be ridden. Dave Lawson, a local surfer holds the record – 9 km (5.7 mi) for the longest wave ride.

WHAT IS IT?
A naturally occurring tidal wave.
HOW TO GET THERE:
From Oxford in the east, take A40 west to Gloucester or from north of England take M5 towards Bristol and turn off at Gloucester.
WHEN TO GO:
A few days after the spring or autumn equinox the bore is likely to be at it's most dramatic.
NEAREST TOWN:
Gloucester 4 km (3 mi)
DON'T MISS:
The beautiful Cotswold countryside around Stroud just south of Gloucester.
YOU SHOULD KNOW:
The Severn is England's longest river rising in Wales and meandering 350 km (220 mi) through Powys, Shrewsbury, Worcester and Gloucester to the Bristol Channel.

*Nant Franton Valley
in Snowdonia*

Snowdon and Snowdonia

At 1,085 m (3,560 ft), Snowdon is the highest mountain in Wales, and the fourth highest in the British Isles. The Snowdonia National Park was formed in 1951 to protect an area 56 by 80 km (35 by 50 mi), which covers most of north-west Wales.

Snowdon itself is one of the most popular mountains in Britain for climbers, but the less energetic can get to the summit by catching the Snowdon Mountain Railway from Llanberis in the west. There are half a dozen routes up the mountain, so pick one that suits your ability. There are also walking, hiking, pony and mountain-biking and cycling trails lower down the mountain and throughout the park.

The views from the top of the mountain are unbelievable, but there is also stunning scenery lower down, from woodland to secluded valleys with gushing waterfalls. The weather can often be worse up in the high peaks, so if the weather forecast is not good, other activities such as white-water rafting, sailing and pony trekking are on offer. There are 37 km (23 mi) of sandy beaches to enjoy on the Lleyn peninsula.

The park is home to a wide variety of wildlife, including otters in the lower rivers, a good range of butterflies in the wildflower meadows, important populations of the minute lesser horseshoe bat, buzzards, peregrine falcons and many smaller species of birds, and the feral goats that have roamed the area for at least 10,000 years.

WHAT IS IT?
Wales's highest mountain, set in a stunning landscape.
HOW TO GET THERE:
By road from Caernarfon or rail from Llanberis.
WHEN TO GO:
April to October
NEAREST TOWN:
Llanberis 5 km (3 mi)
DON'T MISS:
The amazing views from the summit.
YOU SHOULD KNOW:
It takes about five hours to get to the top of the mountain on foot.

Fingal's Cave

Fingal's Cave is on the tiny island of Staffa, which is just west of the Isle of Mull in the Inner Hebrides, off the west coast of Scotland. Approached over the water, Staffa looks as if a giant hand has reached into the Atlantic pulling it upwards and outwards, stretching it like black rubber. The dark and elegant symmetry of the hexagonal columns which surround the island, flanking the entrance and interior of Fingal's cave, baffles description and caused the famous naturalist Sir Joseph Banks, when he 'discovered' the cave in 1772, to exclaim 'compared to this, what are the cathedrals and palaces built by men!'

The cave is 20 m (66 ft) high and 69 m (226 ft) deep. Six-sided, black basalt formations create a spectacular forest of columns, some 11 m (36 ft) tall, and the eerie sounds of the waves rising and falling against the glossy dark pillars do give the place the atmosphere of a natural concert hall.

The columns were created after a mass of hot lava from an ancient lava flow cooled, forming hexagonal patterns as it cracked and shrank (in a similar way to drying mud) and slowly extended down into the mass of lava to form the pillars subsequently exposed by erosion.

The cave is named after Finn MacCool, a hero of Celtic folklore who is supposed to have built the Giant's Causeway – a collection of some 40,000 basalt columns on the north east coast of Antrim, Ireland, which was once joined to Fingal's Cave. Only sheep live on Staffa. It is a speck in the ocean but the stark and lonely beauty of the place and the wondrous sight of the 'Cathedral of the Sea' attract visitors from around the world.

WHAT IS IT?
A sea cave formed within tertiary basalt lava flows.
HOW TO GET THERE:
Car ferries from Oban and Lochaline on the Scottish mainland to Mull, then by boat from Ulva Ferry Pier on the west side of Mull.
WHEN TO GO:
Spring, when the cliff tops are a mass of wild flowers.
NEAREST TOWN:
Tobermory 32 km (20 mi) from Ulva Ferry.
DON'T MISS:
The sweeping views of Ben More, the highest mountain on Mull, from the sea as you set sail from Ulva Ferry.
YOU SHOULD KNOW:
The cave's Gaelic name 'Uamh-Binn' means 'cave of melody' and inspired Felix Mendelssohn to write his *Fingal's Cave* overture.

Basalt columns flank the entrance to Fingal's Cave.

Loch Fyne

WHAT IS IT:
Scotland's longest sea loch.
HOW TO GET THERE:
From Glasgow A82 to Arrochar, then A83 to the head of the Loch.
WHEN TO GO:
Avoid the midges in July and August.
NEAREST TOWN:
Inveraray, beside the north west shore of the Loch.
DON'T MISS:
Feasting on oysters whilst watching the sunset.
YOU SHOULD KNOW:
During WWII over half a million troops were trained in amphibious landing techniques on the shores of Loch Fyne prior to the D-day landings.

Loch Fyne, on the west coast of Argyll and Bute, is Scotland's longest sea loch – 64 km (40 mi) long. It carves its way north into the heart of the western highlands where the hills, the sea and the sky, together with the pellucid light, make it one of the most beautiful places in the world.

This is barely an hour and a half by car from Glasgow airport on roads through some of the finest scenery in Scotland. Dolphins visit these waters, seals laze around on the rocks, otters live here year round and even basking sharks sometimes frequent the lower stretches of the Loch during the summer months. The Loch is heaven for divers. The marine life is superb, with squat lobster, scallops, large whelks and edible crabs. Feather starfish and brittle starfish are everywhere. Near Kenmore Point is Stallion Rock, a vertical overhanging rock that rises from the seabed 30 m (98 ft) below. Here are found sea squirts, anemones and large, brilliantly coloured sponges.

The pretty little 18th century town of Inveraray lies on the west side of the loch with its famous castle, which has been the residence through the centuries of the Dukes of Argyll. It is one of Scotland's classic romantic castles, with splendid ducal state apartments, furniture and family portraits. The neat, whitewashed town has several handsome classical buildings and a famous tweed shop. North of Inverary, at the very head of the loch, is the Ardkinglas Woodland Garden with exotic azaleas, rhododendrons and superb conifers, some over 61 m (200 ft) tall.

Loch Fyne and surrounding hills

The Highlands

The Highland Line in Scotland, the divide between the smooth Lowlands and the sudden lifting of the mountains, runs from the south end of Loch Lomond towards Aberdeen and around to Inverness. Cross this line going north and you are in what many people think of as the 'real' Scotland.

Here a dramatically stark beauty characterizes one of Europe's last great wilderness areas where solitude, space and silence can be found in abundance. Narrow roads twist through mountain passes, beside the lochs, with cloud-shrouded summits rearing overhead. Ruins of old dwellings remain, testimony to the times, before the Highland Clearances, when the landlords drove the people from the land in favour of more profitable sheep farming.

The majestic mountain pass of Glen Coe is a towering and sombre landscape. It was here on a February night in 1692 that the Campbells slaughtered forty members of the MacDonald clan on secret government orders, leaving many others to die of exposure in the frozen hills. To the east, Rannoch Moor occupies 388 sq km (150 sq mi) of uninhabited peat bogs, lochs, heather hillocks, lumps of granite and a few Caledonian pines.

Speyside, the region surrounding the River Spey, east of Inverness in Morayshire, is synonymous with whisky. There are more whisky distilleries in this small area than any other part of the country. The grand malt whisky names such as Glennfiddich, Glenlivet, Macallan and many more, dot the whisky trail all the way to the sea.

The north-western Highlands with its tattered coast is a wild and lonely place and, for many, the finest part of Scotland. Serrated by fjord-like sea lochs, the coastline is scattered with windswept, white-sand beaches and rugged mountains sweeping up from the shoreline. When the sun shines, the sparkle of the sea, the richness of colour and the clarity of the views out to the Hebrides are simply irresistible.

Spring arrives in the Highlands – Glen Etive

WHAT IS IT?
A mountainous region of northern Scotland.
HOW TO GET THERE:
Fly or drive to Glasgow or Edinburgh and head north.
WHEN TO GO:
August for the purple heather clad hills.
NEAREST TOWN:
Inverness, over a hundred miles from any other Scottish settlement, is the only "city" in the Highlands.
DON'T MISS:
The Highland Games, held all over Scotland between May and mid-September. Tossing the caber is the most spectacular event, when the athlete must run carrying an entire tree trunk and throw it end over end.
YOU SHOULD KNOW:
That a true Scottish breakfast consists of sausage, bacon, egg, black pudding (blood sausage) and potato scones followed by kippers, smoked haddock or kedgeree.

A valley in the Cairngorms

The Cairngorms

The Cairngorm Mountains lie in the Cairngorm National Park, which is often described as having some of the most spectacular landscapes in Britain, from the wild tundra of the high mountaintops to the seclusion of ancient pinewoods and heather. Here, too, is moorland, vivid with summer colour, and grand glens and rivers all scarred by glacial action.

The name Cairngorm derives from the Gaelic for 'The Blue Hills' while the range of mountains were called Monahd Ruahd or 'The Red Hills' due to the reddish hue of their granite composition. The eighteen mountains are part of the Munros and are amongst the highest in the country. They were formed in the last ice age with static ice caps shaping the rounded mountaintops and they are drained by the Dee and Spey rivers and the latter's tributaries, the Feshie and the Avon.

There is little population due to the harsh climate, with snow on the hills – sometimes until August, but the wildlife is wonderful. Here are red and roe deer, the only wild reindeer in Britain, mountain hare, pine marten, red squirrel, wild cat and otter all surveyed by the magnificent golden eagle, ospreys, ptarmigan, the rare cap dotterel, with snowy owl, purple sandpiper and Lapland bunting seen on occasion.

The valley, the Lairg Ghru Pass, is an old drovers' route to the Lowlands and the mighty salmon-laden River Spey runs down to the sea overlooked by Cairngorm itself, and other rivers supply the pure water for malt whiskies such as Glenlivet. A funicular railway has recently been opened to the Ptarmigan centre, 150 m (490 ft) from the summit of Cairngorm, giving easy access for hill walkers, winter sports enthusiasts, climbers, birdwatchers and deer stalkers. Fly-fishing and hang gliding are amongst other pursuits but it must be remembered that the Highlands can be a dangerous and hazardous place with unpredictable weather.

WHAT IS IT?
A mountain range in the Highlands of Scotland.
HOW TO GET THERE:
By train, air or road to Aberdeen then take the A93 to Braemar, which is in the Cairngorm National Park.
WHEN TO GO:
All year round.
NEAREST TOWN:
Aberdeen 96 km (60 mi)
DON'T MISS:
The single malt whiskies.
YOU SHOULD KNOW:
The unpredictable weather can be dangerous especially in the winter.

Loch Ness

Loch Ness (Scottish Gaelic: Loch Nis) is a deep freshwater loch in the Scottish Highlands, forming the north-eastern end of a geological fault called the Great Glen, which runs from Inverness down to Fort William. A continuous waterway is formed by the Caledonian Canal joining Inverness to Loch Ness at the north-eastern end – and at the southern end, joining Loch Oich to Loch Lochy, finally reaching Fort William and the west Coast at the junction of Loch Lynnhe and Loch Eil.

The Loch is probably best known for the alleged sightings of what is known as the Loch Ness Monster, fondly nicknamed 'Nessie', but is itself a true spectacle, being the largest body of water in the Great Glen and the second deepest loch in Scotland, some 230 m (754 ft) at its deepest. However, the water is murky as a result of the high peat content of the surrounding soil, thus making sightings of Nessie difficult!

The Great Glen, which effectively divides the Highlands in half, is one of Britain's major geographical features, containing its highest mountain as well as its greatest lake by volume. When the last Ice Age retreated some 10,000 years ago, the land, no longer weighed down by the ice sheet, rose to form the basin of this magnificent loch, 16 m (52 ft) above sea level.

Apart from tourist boat trips on the loch to try to see the elusive monster, the loch acts as a reservoir for hydroelectric power. At the southern end its only island, called Cherry, is thought to be a 'Crannog', an Iron Age man-made island for protection purposes.

WHAT IS IT?
Britain's largest lake by volume.
HOW TO GET THERE:
By air, road or train to Inverness then the A82 runs down its northern edges.
WHEN TO GO:
It has a different beauty in every season but the surrounding countryside is especially good in clear weather – avoid the midges in July and August.
NEAREST TOWN:
Inverness 6 km (4.5 mi) on the North Sea north east of the Loch.
DON'T MISS:
Ben Nevis, Britain's highest mountain, near Fort William, is easily visible in good weather.
YOU SHOULD KNOW:
The BT Tower in London at 189 m (620 ft) would be completely submerged in the Loch.

Loch Ness: looking for Nessie.

Smoo Cave

Smoo Cave is east of the village of Durness on Scotland's north coast, sheltered from the Atlantic by the Cape Wrath peninsula. Reminiscent of the Shetlands, it is set into dramatic limestone cliffs with swirling sea birds diving for food, puffins nesting in their burrows and seals in the crashing waves below.

Smoo Cave itself lies at the inner end of a narrow inlet eroded into the limestone, which is here lying almost horizontally, and contains a record of human occupation during several periods of historic and prehistoric time. Access to the cave is down a steep path, where you will find signs of an old midden (refuse-heap) just inside the entrance. Recently excavated (1992), the upper layers showed artefacts from the Iron Age, making this one of the most northern habitation sites in the British Isles. The midden was also packed with shells showing eating habits, and deeper levels have older deposits. The base is thought to be Mesolithic, when the earliest inhabitants came to the Highlands.

Passing through from the main cave to a smaller cave, the river Allt Smoo noisily pours in through a gap and falls 24 m (80 ft). Cross the river again and climb up to a ledge, from which you get good views of the waterfall – in the enclosed space, the noise is quite deafening. There are other, smaller caves thought to be side caves of Smoo Cave, called Glassknapper's and Antlers, and there are yet more adjacent sites and collapsed caves to be investigated.

A delightful way to approach Smoo Cave is to drive past Balnakiel Craft Village to the west of Durness and park beside the beach – walk over the golden sands on one side and the sea on the other and a well defined path takes you up over the cliffs, viewing the wildlife, on a circular route to Durness village and the caves.

A waterfall in Smoo Cave

Ben Nevis

The massive bulk of Ben Nevis looms above the town of Fort William, its 1,343 m (4,406 ft) top often obscured by clouds. It is known simply as "The Ben" to the 75,000 hikers and climbers who come each year to walk the track to the summit or to conquer the vertiginous cliffs of the north face, riven with buttresses, ridges and pinnacles.

Ben Nevis from the Caledonian Canal at Corpach near Fort William

The pony track or tourist path that leads to the summit begins in Glen Nevis at Achintee on the south side of the mountain about 20 m (66 ft) above sea level. The dappled woodland of pine, oak and birch opens out to heather moorland, tufted hair grass and peaty bogs, climbing steeply to 570 m (1,870 ft) where the path skirts the small Lochan Meall an t-Suide then continues zigzagging up the rounded dome of the upper mountain through deer grass and weather-shattered scree.

The summit is a 100-acre plateau with mosses and lichens, many of which are arctic/alpine, forming a dense covering on the boulder-strewn ground. Ben Nevis is a delight for bird lovers. The snow bunting and ptarmigan prefer the higher parts of the mountain, as do Golden eagles, ravens, kestrels and buzzards. Lower down in the wooded areas siskins, warblers, flycatchers and owls are to be found.

The highest point is marked with a solidly built cairn. The ruins of an observatory, which was permanently staffed between 1883 and 1904, has an emergency shelter built on the top of the tower for those caught out by bad weather and is the highest man-made structure in Britain. On a clear day the views from the top of The Ben are magical – to the east Aonach Mor, beyond, to the south, the rocky ridge of the Mamores and still further, the mountains of Glen Coe.

WHAT IS IT?
The highest mountain in Scotland and in the UK.

HOW TO GET THERE:
By rail or road (A82) from Glasgow to Fort William.

WHEN TO GO:
Avoid the midge season – July and August.

NEAREST TOWN:
Fort William 1 km (0.5 mi) from the start of the pony track.

DON'T MISS:
The Ben Nevis Race from Fort William to the summit and back again, held annually on the first Saturday in September.

YOU SHOULD KNOW:
In 2006 a piano was unearthed from a cairn on the summit of Ben Nevis. It had been carried there for charity by removal men from Dundee, twenty years earlier!

*The basalt columns that form
the Giant's Causeway*

The Giant's Causeway

The Giant's Causeway was formed about 60 million years ago when a massive volcanic eruption poured out almost unimaginable amounts of molten rock – magma. As this magma cooled, it shrank cracking into the mostly hexagonal pillars of basalt we see today. Some 37,000 of the columns remain. In places, the solidified lava flow is 28 m (92 ft) deep and the tallest columns are 12 m (36 ft) high. The tiny Hebridean Isle of Staffa to the north has similar formations, which are part of the same massive lava flow and legend has it that the causeway was built by the giant warrior, Finn MacCool so he could reach his lover there. According to another version of the legend, he was trying to reach another warrior, Benandonner.

The only UNESCO World Heritage Site in Northern Ireland, the causeway is set in a lovely landscape of seabird cliffs, sea caves and sandy bays. These rocks have been eroding almost since they were formed, ground down by ice, wind and waves into a variety of shapes, including the Giant's Boot and the Pipe Organ.

As you scramble about on these slippery stones, look out to sea to the north where they would once have stretched, and imagine the scene when that expanse of water was a sea of flowing molten magma.

WHAT IS IT?
A basalt formation that resembles a set of steps for giants.
HOW TO GET THERE:
By road or along the Causeway Coastal Cliff Path.
WHEN TO GO:
Spring or summer.
NEAREST TOWN:
Bushmills 3 km (2 mi)
YOU SHOULD KNOW:
Sensible footwear is a must.

Lough Neagh

A shallow lake with a maximum depth of 25 m (82 ft) but averaging only 9 m (30 ft), Lough Neagh, in the centre of Northern Ireland is – at 390 sq km (150 sq mi) – the largest lake by area in the British Isles. Five of the six counties of Northern Ireland border its shores and the lake is fed by the Upper Barn, a river running up from the south, the Blackwater and several other streams draining to the north through the Lower Barn. There are a number of trout and eel fisheries on its shores and fishing is a popular leisure pursuit.

Ancient deposits in Toome Bay, on its north-western shore, have yielded the oldest recorded human artefacts in Ireland. Mesolithic humans are believed to have first appeared in Ireland (c. 6,000 B.C.) near the lake, and Neolithic remains have also been found locally. According to a local legend, the lake occupies the site of a flooded town and buildings may sometimes be seen through the water. In 1959 flood-control works significantly lowered the lake's level, but no confirmed sightings have yet been made!

Bird watchers are attracted to Lough Neagh due to the number and variety of birds which winter and summer in the bog lands and shores around the lough. The traditional working boats on Lough Neagh were wide-beamed, 4.9-6.4 m (16-21 ft) long, clinker-built and sprit-rigged. Smaller, flat-bottomed cots were also used. Old barges called 'lighters' were used up to the 1940s to transport coal over the lough and adjacent canals and log boats (*coití*) were the main means of transport until the 17th century. Few traditional boats are left now, but on the southern shore of the lough a series of working boats are being rebuilt by the Lough Neagh Boating Heritage Association. There are several islands in the lough including one called Coney Island.

WHAT IS IT?
The largest lake by area in the British Isles.
HOW TO GET THERE:
Flights and ferries to Belfast then take the M2 and A26 to Antrim.
WHEN TO GO:
The wild life is of interest especially in migration times.
NEAREST TOWN:
Antrim is on the north-east shore of the lake.
DON'T MISS:
The beautiful north-east coast of Ireland.
YOU SHOULD KNOW:
There is an ancient legend that the Isle of Man was formed after the depression forming Loch Neagh was ripped out, used as a missile during a fight between giants, and thrown into the Irish Sea by mistake.

Gulls and terns over Lough Neagh

The Mountains of Mourne

WHAT IS IT?
A range of mountains in the south east of Northern Ireland.
HOW TO GET THERE:
Flights or car ferries to Belfast then drive south on the A1 to Newry, east of the Mourne Mountains.
WHEN TO GO:
Has interest for enthusiasts at most times of year.
NEAREST TOWN:
Newry
DON'T MISS:
The Ben Crom reservoir upstream from the older, Silent Valley reservoir, surrounded by bog land and scree slopes.

The granite slopes of the Mourne Mountains of County Down in the south east of Northern Ireland are situated in an area of outstanding natural beauty with the highest peak, Slieve Donard at 849 m (2,285 ft). Slieve is an Irish word derived from sliahb, meaning mountain.

Slieve Donard's grey rocky slopes rise up from the largest Irish dune heath and beach, edging the south and eastern sides of the Mourlough National Nature Reserve. This is home to many species of wildfowl, including ring ousel and red grouse, waders and a good haul-out site for grey seals. It also has varied wild flowers and butterflies, amongst them the rare Marsh fritillary.

From the top of Slieve Donard one can see the Isle of Man and the Stranford Lough. Also to the north is Lough Neagh, the large inland sea of 390 sq km (150 sq mi) famous for its eels, which are both eaten locally and exported. Evidence of human activity has been found from the Mesolithic period (7,000 – 3,500 BC) to the Neolithic age, through the Bronze Age all the way to modern day.

The raw beauty of this mountain was the inspiration for the song by Percy French whose end of verse line – 'Where the Mountains O'Mourne sweep down to the sea' makes it the most famous mountain in Ireland.

Another interesting feature of this mountain range, which is visited by hill walkers, cyclists and rock climbers, is the Mourne Wall. This is a 35 km (22 mi) dry stone wall that crosses the twelve summits of Mourne, and was originally built to define the boundary of a 36 sq km (14 sq mi) plot of land, including the two big artificial lakes in the Silent Valley that supply water to Belfast.

At Newcastle, the main town on the southeast sea border of the mountains, one can enjoy yachting, golfing and pleasure fishing.

The fertile pastureland around the Mourne Mountains

The Dingle Peninsula

The northernmost of the five peninsulas that project out into the Atlantic like fingers at the south-west tip of Ireland, the Dingle Peninsula (Corca Dhuibhne) is the westernmost point of mainland Ireland. It lies on a sandstone ridge that also forms the Slieve Mish mountains in the east of the peninsula and Mount Brandon, Ireland's second highest mountain at 953 m (3,127 ft).

Often beset by the weather that the North Atlantic throws at it, this wild landscape is known for its spectacular scenery with stunning views of the Great Blasket Island, Dingle Bay and across Castlemaine Harbour to MacGillicuddy Reeks. Described by many as one of the most beautiful landscapes on Earth, it has rocky outcrops and rugged cliffs, soft rounded hills with forests, beautiful alpine-arctic flora higher up and wide sandy beaches. There is a magnificent view around almost every corner. Off the beaten track, there are many side roads and paths that allow visitors to explore this breathtaking countryside at their leisure.

In spring and early summer, seabirds such as gannets nest on the cliffs, while Fungie the dolphin has lived in the harbour since 1984.

Popular activities include walking, boat trips out to the Great Blasket Island, swimming, surfing, walking or horse-riding through the edge of the surf. There are also hundreds of archaeological sites to visit.

WHAT IS IT?
The most westerly point of Ireland.
HOW TO GET THERE:
By road.
WHEN TO GO:
Summer but pack a raincoat!
NEAREST TOWN:
Dingle
DON'T MISS:
Fungie the dolphin.
YOU SHOULD KNOW:
The drive from Dingle over the Connor Pass is not for the faint-hearted.

The rocky coast at Slea Head on the Dingle peninsula

The fabled Kerry coastline

Kerry Coastline

The map makes the south west of Ireland look like a series of daggers stabbing the Atlantic Ocean. This is Kerry, where jagged peninsulas thrust into deep-water bays and where the rugged landscape is softened by the benign warmth of the Gulf Stream. Greenery cloaks even the most exposed rocky hillsides, and the lee of every outcrop shelters an explosive flourish of wild flowers and broadleaf woods. Kerry is a legend of tranquil beauty stretching from the Shannon estuary to the western entrance to Bantry Bay, and its towns and villages like Tralee, Dingle, Killarney, the Skelligs and Sneem trace the geography of international poetic imagination. Swimming in the rich gold of vast Atlantic light, Kerry's deepest green stands fast against scudding weather that frequently brings four seasons in a day.

From the county town, Tralee, the spectacular coast of sheer-black cliffs yields to deserted, sandy coves like Ballybunion or Ventry, safe harbours like Dingle town, and mighty strands like Inch and Annascaul – protected as wildlife sanctuaries, but whose elemental appeal provides equal balm to human visitors. The Dingle Peninsula Gaeltacht – where Gaelic is the usual local language – stands at its tip, opposite Great Blasket Island some 5 km (3 mi) offshore and the most westerly point of Europe.

South Kerry is known worldwide for the Lakes of Killarney and the Ring of Kerry, a 179 km (112 mi) circuit of the Uibh Rathach (Iveragh) Peninsula. It's a region of secluded coves rising up to Ireland's highest mountains, Macgillycuddy's Reeks, whose northern flanks drop straight down to the blue necklace of Killarney's fabled lakes. You can take a pony and trap 10 km (6 mi) from Kate Kearney's Cottage through the wild and rugged Gap of Dunloe; or take a boat to the Skellig Islands from Cahersiveen or Ballinskelligs to see the breeding sanctuary of 20,000 pairs of gannets.

WHAT IS IT?
A coastline whose panoramic beauty is protected by World Heritage status.
HOW TO GET THERE:
By air to Shannon, Cork or Kerry; then by road.
WHEN TO GO:
All year round.
NEAREST TOWN:
Tralee (N), Killarney (mid) or Sneem (S) are good regional bases.
DON'T MISS:
The Dingle Peninsula.
YOU SHOULD KNOW:
The Ring of Kerry is extremely crowded during summer.

Aillwee Cave

In sight of Galway Bay, the north coast of Co. Clare is a scarred limestone plateau called the Burren. It's bleak, flat and inhospitable even to sheep. Only the occasional tuft of greenery breaks the 40 shades of lichen-stained grey that spreads for miles of cracked rifts and deep fissures. The weird landscape is unique on earth (US astronauts trained here until they discovered it wasn't really like the moon at all), but it hides something more extraordinary. Aillwee Cave is the sole entrance to a vast underground complex from which you can explore the Burren from below.

The Burren is a unique limestone plain in the west of Ireland.

Ailwee leads through a tunnel into a succession of caverns, carved by rain and torrential streams seeping through the surface rock over millions of years. Raging water created cathedrals like Midsummer Cavern, pillared with 5,000 year-old stalagmites, tube-like passages, galleries of bare rock, and chambers like Mud Hall, whose knobbly stalagmites took 8,000 years to reach their present enormity. You walk over bridged caverns and under waterfalls, past shallow excavations hollowed out by bears as hibernation pits, before they became extinct in Ireland 1,000 years ago. Bear Haven marks the recent discovery of fossil bear bones in situ.

Throughout the system – at present, over 1.3 km (0.8 mi) are lit and monitored for visitors' safety – one of the strangest features is the roof. You look up to see the roots of many rare plants hidden in the fissures of the Burren above. In the open air, the biting stringency of Atlantic winds inhibits everything but the hardiest alpine flora; but deep in the fissures where light may reach but humans cannot see, and protected by their rocky prison, are colonies of plants, mosses and lichens that properly belong in a Mediterranean climate, including some very rare orchids. The geological oddities of Aillwee enable you to get close and personal.

WHAT IS IT?
A limestone cave system.
HOW TO GET THERE:
Take the Corkscrew Road from Ballyvaughan; after 2 km (1.25 mi) turn left on R480 S towards Lisdoonvarna. Aillwee Cave is off to the right after 3 km (2 mi).
WHEN TO GO:
January to November. Try to avoid summer crowds.
NEAREST TOWN:
Ballyvaughan 5 km (3 mi)
DON'T MISS:
The Poulnabrone Dolmen on the way to the Cave.
YOU SHOULD KNOW:
If you find an orchid, don't touch it and never reveal its exact position.

Donegal Bay

WHAT IS IT?
A seascape of towering cliffs and pristine sandy coves.
HOW TO GET THERE:
By car/bus to Donegal City or any other town lining the Bay.
WHEN TO GO:
Year-round.
NEAREST TOWN:
Best bases are Bundoran (S) and Killybegs (N).
DON'T MISS:
Slieve League.
YOU SHOULD KNOW:
Peat is 4,000 year-old, bog-preserved moss.

Donegal Bay is Ireland's largest bay, a half-moon with the highest cliffs in Europe. Its beaches and coves are among the world's cleanest, and best for surfing. It is ringed with small towns and villages where Ireland's most traditional crafts still flourish, including its biggest fishing fleet at Killybegs. Above all, it is washed by the luminous immensity of sky and water merged in a restless kaleidoscope of panoramic beauty. If there is majesty in nature, this is it.

Donegal Bay lies in north-western Ireland, and funnels the predominant westerly winds of the Atlantic Ocean onto Rossnowlagh and Bundoran, two beaches on its southern side renowned for the championship consistency of their waves. Bundoran Town is a popular resort, but from here, the 'Rougey Walk' leads you on a typically spectacular combination of clifftop and cove, past the Fairy Bridges – cliff arches carved by pounding waves – and Wishing Chair rock to the vista of Tullan Strand, a flawless arc of white sand below the cliffs.

Just past the bustle of Killybegs on the northern side is Kilcar, the gateway to the Donegal Gaeltacht, one of the few regions where Gaelic is freely spoken. From nearby Teelin a path leads to Bunglass Point, 307 m (1,007 ft) high, and epic views across the Bay to Sligo. The path continues along One Man's Pass, a 3 km (2 mi) ridge of rock and peat bog, studded with small lakes, that rises and narrows until both sides fall sheer into the waves crashing into fingerstacks of rock at the foot of Slieve League, a precipitous 598 m (1,961 ft) drop. You can see clouds literally forming below you, and marvel as they coalesce and sweep up and over your head into the forested clefts and peat bogs on the way to the megalithic complex at Malin More, Donegal's most westerly headland. It is a huge and mystic beauty to behold.

Horn Head and Donegal Bay

Møns Klint – the Cliffs of Møn

Møns Klint are awe-inspiring chalk cliffs that stand proudly along the eastern coast of Høje Møn in the Baltic Sea. Extending for some 6 km (3.7 mi), at their highest they tower 128 m (420 ft) above the crashing waves. The sheer majesty of these cliffs, rising white out of clear blue water, draw tourists from all over Europe to this faraway corner of Denmark.

The chalk formed over 70 million years ago from the skeletons of tiny creatures that lived in the warm sea that once covered Denmark. During the Cretaceous period this sea receded and the land rose. Then during the last Ice Age, glaciers scraped off a thick layer of the chalk and crushed it together, creating Høje Møn. Since then the sea has been busily trying to undo the glacier's work, cutting into the island's shoreline and sculpting the cliffs we see today.

Although the results have been dramatic, the sea's erosive efforts are relentless. In 1994 the highest part of Møns Klint, the Sommerspir, crumbled into the Baltic, and in 2007 an even larger slip created a 300 m (1,000 ft) peninsula of chalk debris and uprooted trees.

Behind this battle zone lie the peaceful woods of Klinteskoven, and a little further off is Aborrebjerg, which at 143 m (470 ft), is one of the highest hills in Denmark. The chalky soil here provides the perfect conditions for many rare plants. Eighteen of Denmark's 35 species of orchid can be found here, including the tall lady orchid that flowers in early summer.

Much of the cliff area is protected and there are many marked paths for walkers, riders and cyclists to explore. There is also a series of wooden stairways down which you can descend to the feet of these awesome cliffs. Since 2,002 the cliffs can boast another star attraction: nesting peregrine falcons (*Falco peregrinus*). Capable of diving at 180 kph (111 mph), these amazing birds can now often be seen hunting their feathered prey in the skies above Møns Klint.

Møns Klint

WHAT IS IT?
Impressively sheer chalk cliffs.
HOW TO GET THERE:
By road from Copenhagen.
WHEN TO GO:
Spring to autumn offers the best weather.
NEAREST TOWN:
Stege is about 15 km (10 mi) southwest of the cliffs.
DON'T MISS:
The new GeoCenter geological museum that opened in 2007.
YOU SHOULD KNOW:
As many as 100,000 visitors flood the area in July. Møns Klint is being eroded at the rate of 20-40 cm a year, and experts estimate that in 10,000 years the entire island will have been reclaimed by the sea. So book early to avoid disappointment!

277

Middle Rhine Valley

WHAT IS IT?
A river gorge of global mythic significance.
HOW TO GET THERE:
Car/train/boat from Koblenz (N) or Bingen (S).
WHEN TO GO:
April to October.
NEAREST TOWN:
Any of the many small towns lining the gorge.
DON'T MISS:
Wine-tasting at Rudesheim or Bacharach.
YOU SHOULD KNOW:
Lorelei was Marilyn Monroe's name in the film *Gentlemen Prefer Blondes*.

The river Rhine is over 1,300 km (807 mi) long. The Middle Rhine is what people call the 65 km (40 mi) gorge that carries the river between Bingen and Koblenz. This short stretch, where the water bullies a meandering path through unyielding slate mountains, is Germany's single, most iconic, geographical feature – but for all its physical drama, it is in fact a cultural landscape. Man, not nature, fashioned the Middle Rhine Valley.

The Rhine Gorge hems in the river between steep walls up to 200 m (656 ft) high. Castles, villages and cities punctuate the vineyard trellises that crowd the terraces on both banks. Trees and shrubs cling to bizarre rock formations that loom high above the Lilliputian river traffic. Whatever gullies or rock inclines too steep to exploit remain, are filled with local flora and fauna, which have adapted themselves to accommodate this extraordinary symbiosis of man and nature. Whether you see the gorge from a car, train or boat, you participate in what UNESCO cited as 'the continuous evolutionary nature of the cultural environment' of the Middle Rhine. For 2,000 years, it has been a highway for commerce and tourism, and a factory for both. Its importance can be measured by the number of castles, ruined or restored, that command the heights. The wildness of the gorge and the ruins combine to stimulate your imagination with ideas of ferocious battles and mythic chivalry: the feeling of desolation called 'Rhine Romanticism'. Nothing inspires this more than the fabled Lorelei Rock, opposite the town of St. Gaur, where sirens sang sailors to their doom. Sadly, there's no Little Mermaid (to the chagrin of visitors) – the siren song is that of the current, because the Lorelei's massive bulk marks the narrowest point of the River between Switzerland and the North Sea.

There are hundreds of good reasons to see the Middle Rhine. Take a boat if you can, because with the right ticket you can stop off as many times as you like.

Katz Castle and Lorelei Rock

Erzgebirge

Virtually unsettled and covered with dense forest, the Erzgebirge gained its name (it means Ore Mountains) only in the 15th century, when the discovery of silver and tin deposits brought a flood of settlers to found its towns and cities. For 130 km (81 mi) along the German-Czech border, you can see the recovering scars of hundreds of former quarries and mine workings, and the wealth that exceptional mineral resources brought to the region reflected in its mining towns like Oberweisenthal, Annaberg-Buchholz, Schneeberg and Sieffen. Now, with its mineral riches exhausted, the Erzgebirge's regeneration is protected by its status as a Biosphere Reserve, and one of Germany's loveliest mountain landscapes has been restored to its natural beauty.

You can follow the Ridge Trail for 197 km (122 mi) from Klingenthal in the Vogtland/Erzgebirge nature reserve. Gently rolling hills of forest alternate with moorland, colourful meadows and placid stream beds. It is an elemental but austere landscape, its remoteness a perfect habitat for rare animals and plants. The mountains rise ever higher towards the Trail's end at Altenberg to the south. The numerous peaks around Fichtelberg 1214 m (3,983 ft) – it has a splendid cable car – make this part of the Erzgebirge a magnet for winter visitors. Not only does the landscape and microclimate lend itself to the snowy magic of fairytales, but the region is famous for its wood-carved toys, intricate fretwork, and every kind of Christmas decoration. The industry began as a desperate measure by former mining communities when the silver ran out. Now every local industry depends on encouraging the Erzgebirge as a whole to recover its pristine variety of fauna and flora: even the spruce planted for generations for mining use is being replaced with a mixture of broadleaf trees, the way it used to be.

The beautiful landscape of the Erzgebirge

WHAT IS IT?
A mountain range of exceptional beauty in both summer and winter.
HOW TO GET THERE:
By car/bus to Seiffen (N) or Oberweisenthal (S).
WHEN TO GO:
Year-round (but the region is most crowded in winter).
NEAREST TOWN:
Zwickau 20-30 km (12-19 mi) from the central range of hills.
DON'T MISS:
Seiffen, centre of the wooden toy industry.
YOU SHOULD KNOW:
Reifendrehen (carving toy animals from wooden hoops) is a skill unique to the Erzgebirge. So is Spanbaumchen-Stechen (carving wooden trees with intricate curly branches).

281

Pillar-like sandstone rock formations are a result of erosion by the Elbe River and its tributaries.

The Bastei Rocks in the Elbe Valley

South east of Dresden lies one of Europe's biggest sandstone canyons. Carved by the river Elbe and its tributaries over 100 million years into a bizarre assembly of soaring stone finials, mesas and buttes, its gloomy crags overhang the graceful curves of the water up to 400 m (1,312 ft) below. The tallest trees are dwarfed by the huge boulders on which they totter, and one spectacular vista opens into another all the way to Bad Schandau on the border with the Czech Republic, where the Elbe rises in Bohemia. Between April and October, riverboats ply between Dresden and Bad Schandau so that awe-struck visitors can enjoy feeling puny in the face of nature at its most romantic and darkly majestic.

This feeling is most intense at the Bastei ('Bastion') Rocks, a series of needle-like sandstone spires 170 m (558 ft) high standing sentinel along the ravines and gorges hacked out of the canyon's walls. You can cross the rocky pinnacles on graceful, stone bridges built in the mid-19th century; or the river itself on the 305 m (1,000 ft) high Bastei Bridge, which offers the most magnificent view of all across the Elbe Valley and its extraordinary massif. Close to the bridge, a path weaves more than 700 mossy steps deep down the gorge called the Swedish Holes (a hideaway created when Swedish troops pillaged Saxony during the Thirty Years War of 1618-48), past a gurgling stream and pond, into a hollow, lined with metal seats that face a soaring backdrop of dark firs and beech flickering green against towers of crags. This is the Felsenbuhne Rathen, a natural amphitheatre specializing in open-air, summer productions of operas and adventure stories as eerie and fearsome as the setting.

Crossing the bridge leads you to the Konigstein Fortress, its colossal scale and severity in perfect harmony with the jagged landscape. From its heights, you can see a panorama of rolling hills, winding river, imposing peaks and table mountains like Lilienstein and Pfaffenstein. Locals call it Sachsische Schweiz – Saxon Switzerland, and the region is protected as the Elbe Sandstone Massif Nature Reserve.

Frankische Schweiz

Defined by the Regnitz and Main rivers to the west, and by the river Pegnitz to the east, the rolling vales and dolomitic outcrops of the Frankische Schweiz certainly do resemble Switzerland; but this region of northern Franconia is a distillation of a Swiss picture postcard. Green pastures follow the contours of coppiced hills, and lanes wind through the floor of a hundred steep valleys where cows contemplate prohibited fields of waving barley. Streams bite deep in the fertile loam, and then disappear in a jumble of rock into the limestone plateau below. Millennia of weathering have broken down the limestone into huge outcrops where goats rule; into cliffs where water falls in splashy profusion; and into cathedrals of cave systems full of stalactites and stalagmites. The best of these are the Binghohle at Streitberg, and the Teufelshohle ('Devil's Hole') at Pottenstein. It is the contrast of pastoral domesticity in the fields and woods, and this rocky terrain breaking out in bizarre and dramatic formations that makes the region so scenic and intriguing.

Such a pleasing landscape makes wonderful walking, and there are 4,000 km (2,500 mi) of marked trails. The region is centred on the lovely and ancient towns of Gossweinstein and Behringersmuhle, which actually does have a working water mill. They are typical of the prettiest towns, all of which lie along the rivers Wiesent, Ailsbach, Puttlach and Trubach. All tell a story of a dramatic cliff with perhaps a castle or ruin on it, overlooking calm valleys and orchards, with caves, river and forest for variety. But the region has even greater treasures, like the eagle owls, boar, and red and fallow deer in the woods; bats in the sanctuary of the caves; and true rarities like the Turk's Cap lily and Lady's Slipper orchid, among others growing in the thousands of hidden beauty spots.

WHAT IS IT?
A pastoral upland plateau of gentle hills and dramatic rock formations.
HOW TO GET THERE:
By train/bus/car to Nurnberg (S), Bamberg (W) or Bayreuth (N).
WHEN TO GO:
Year-round.
NEAREST TOWN:
Forchheim.
DON'T MISS:
The colours of spring and autumn; the medieval city of Bamberg.
YOU SHOULD KNOW:
Frankische Schweiz has the highest density of private breweries in the world (72).

The sun will chase away the early morning mist.

The Helgoland Cliffs

The island of Helgoland is a geological oddity – a block of red sandstone 70 km (43 mi) out in the open sea, quite unlike anything else on the whole of the continental North Sea coast. It dates from the early Eocene geologic age, and is younger than, and layered on top of, a much thicker bedrock of the same white chalk that includes the white cliffs of Dover in England, and the cliffs of German and Danish islands in the Baltic Sea. One thousand years of weathering has eroded and submerged all the dunes and marshes that used to connect it almost to the mainland. Only the small island of Dune remains, an offshore sandspit that serves as Helgoland's airstrip.

Helgoland is a triangle that appears to be heaving itself out of the water. On the north, west and southwest, 50 m (164 ft) cliffs cut a rosy pink line against the blue steel of the sea. On the southwest, they keep plunging below the waterline for another 56 m (184 ft). Part of this spectacular vista is the Lummenfelsen wildlife reserve, set aside as the breeding habitat of 2,000 guillemots and thousands of razorbills, northern gannets, and gull species. At the beginning of June, you can witness the amazing sight of young guillemots, still unable to fly, hurling themselves off a 60 m (197 ft) cliff and landing unharmed only by means of a miracle of optimism. At the north end of the cliff path, where the lighthouse sits in a sandy cove full of basking seals, is Lange Anna (Tall Anna), a 47 m (154 ft) freestanding pillar of red sandstone.

What makes Helgoland so very special is its climate. It gets the full benefit of the Gulf Stream without a large landmass to retain cold. So the two long beaches of fine sand on Dune resemble the Caribbean, with palm trees nodding in the turquoise sea. It is the sunniest place in Germany, and with winter temperatures frequently 10 °C (18 °F) higher than Hamburg, warm enough to grow figs.

The steep coast of Helgoland with Lange Anna to the right

Thuringian Forest

The unspoilt 'green heart' of Germany

Known as the 'green heart' of Germany, an upland corridor of emerald forest some 20 km (12.5 mi) broad stretches 60 km (37.5 mi) south east from Eisenach to Greiz. This highland plateau is the core of the greater 4,725-sq-km (1,824-sq-mi) Thuringian Forest, and it includes its most dramatic, unspoilt and beautiful natural scenery. Bounded by fault lines, its hills rise in steep scarps directly from the dense spruce and broadleaf forest; the canopy occasionally broken by brightly flowered pasture where the inhabitants of ancient hamlets still work smallholdings. Weaving along a ridge connecting the highest peaks in this pastoral idyll is part of the legendary Rennsteig Trail, which runs from Horschel (5 km [3 mi] from Eisenach) to Blankenstein, 168 km (105 mi) away on the upper Saal river. The Rennsteig has been a geographical and political border as well as a highway for over 1,000 years, but it has been relatively inaccessible until recently. As a result, despite the crowds of summer visitors, its natural ecology has revived wonderfully, and the region is a wildlife haven. Each season reveals a new beauty, and opens new vistas of panoramic magnificence.

The almost mythical status of the Thuringian Forest was confirmed by the intimacy with it of Germany's finest philosophers and artists – like Goethe, Schiller, Cranach, Luther, Liszt and J.S.Bach, who was born in Eisenach. When you stand before the Thuringian highlights like the 'fairy grottoes' of Saalfeld – a former alum mine and cave system whose myriad minerals have been transformed by 400 years of disuse into a diamante rainbow – or the Trusetal waterfall, it's easy to share their mixture of joy and humility in nature. Rather less so, when you see, next to the romantic waterfall, the Trusetal Gnome Park exhibition of garden gnomes!

WHAT IS IT?
A highland plateau of forest and upland pasture.
HOW TO GET THERE:
By train/car to Eisenach (N) or Blankenstein (S)
WHEN TO GO:
Year-round.
NEAREST TOWN:
Zella-Mehlis 5 km (3 mi) from Rennsteig and Ilmenau are good bases.
DON'T MISS:
The summer toboggan runs at Brotterode and Inselberg.
YOU SHOULD KNOW:
Martin Luther translated the Bible into German in Eisenach.

Watzmann massif reflected in Königssee.

Berchtesgaden Alps

Berchtesgaden National Park, in the far south-east of Bavaria and on the border with Austria, is the only alpine national park in Germany and is popular with walkers, hikers and climbers. Within it lie the Watzmann massif, the third highest mountain in the country, and the Königssee, a beautiful glacial lake. The slopes of the glacial valleys are carpeted with dense forest, separated by deep gorges while the valley bottoms make an idyllic farmland.

As its name suggests, the Königssee (King's Lake) was popular with the Bavarian royal family, and it is still a popular place for recreation today. It remains peaceful because the only powered boats allowed on it are electric: its water is reputed to be the cleanest in Germany. Its 5.2 sq km (2 sq mi) of beautiful clear waters reflect the mountains that surround it on all sides and canoeing is a favourite activity here. Looming over the lake is the Watzmann massif, a popular challenge for experienced climbers only.

The National Park, which covers 210 sq km (81 sq mi) was declared a UNESCO Biosphere Reserve in 1990 because of its alpine landscape and its wildlife, which includes griffon vulture, bearded vulture, golden eagle, chamois, red fox and roe deer.

A popular hike for many is up the 1,835-m (6,020-ft) Kehlstein. Most famous as the site of Hitler's command complex and the Eagle's Nest retreat, the top of this peak provides stunning views across the valley.

WHAT IS IT?
A mountainous region in the south-east of Bavaria.
HOW TO GET THERE:
By road from Munich.
WHEN TO GO:
Summer.
NEAREST TOWN:
Berchtesgaden 5 km (3 mi)
DON'T MISS:
The view from the top of the Kehlstein.
YOU SHOULD KNOW:
The Watzmann is a very tough climb, and should be undertaken only by climbers who have achieved the necessary levels of expertise.

Bodensee

Better known as Lake Constance, Bodensee has been synonymous since Roman times with unsurpassed natural beauty. It's a freshwater lake 63 km (39 mi) long and 14 km (9 mi) at its widest, and it nestles at an elevation of 395 m (1,296 ft) between the mountains of Germany, Switzerland and Austria. From Bregenz in the Vorarlberg, where the nascent Rhine feeds it, to Schaffhausen in the west, where the river crashes out of the lake via the Rhine Falls, Bodensee is a magnificent panorama of snow-capped mountains backing hills greened with woods and fields, reflected in the endless waterscape. East to west, it's a continual highlight.

The Lake was actually formed by the Rhine Glacier during the Ice Age, but its effortless beauty now owes nearly as much to subsequent human activity. Its shores are lined with orchards, vineyards, meadows and pastures, occasionally interrupted by the colourful roofs of ancient towns and villages, some of them on bijou islands like Lindau, a medieval town of intricate lanes and crooked towers that appears to sail on the water. At the other end of Bodensee, near Konstanz, is the 'Flower Island' of Mainau. Here, in 1827, Prince Esterhazy realized that the lake's summer microclimate (it's considerably warmer than any of its surroundings) was perfect to create the profusion of sub-tropical trees, fruits and plants for which Mainau is still famous. Reichenau, a haven of solitude in the Untersee, the western bowl of Bodensee between Konstanz and Schaffhausen, has an ancient monastery; and Meersburg, on the Baden-Wurttemberg mainland a ferry-ride from Konstanz, is a typically lovely resort town of half-timbered houses and Germany's oldest schloss.

Many, varied, and lovely are all these places – but it is the lake itself that adds grandeur to their picturesque charms. Bodensee provides the elemental magic of mountains and big water to what would otherwise be miniature human triumphs.

WHAT IS IT?
A mountain lake.
HOW TO GET THERE:
By air/rail/bus/car to Konstanz.
WHEN TO GO:
Year-round.
NEAREST TOWN:
Konstanz, Uberlingen, Meersburg or Lindau are good local bases.
DON'T MISS:
The Rhine Falls (best approached from Schaffhausen on the Swiss side).
YOU SHOULD KNOW:
There is a car ferry across the middle of Bodensee, from Friedrichshafen to Romanshorn in Switzerland.

Bodensee with Swiss mountains in the background

Rügen

It's only 51 km (32 mi) long and 43 km (27 mi) at its widest, but Rügen, the Baltic island close to Germany's northeast border with Poland, has an astonishing 574 km (357 mi) of coastline. Inevitably, the long strands of white sand backed by ancient woodlands and gleaming lakes, have made Rügen one of Germany's most popular holiday resorts for generations of visitors. Much more remarkable is that the island has preserved its greatest natural treasures intact. Nature parks protect three distinct – and rare – aspects of the Baltic coastline; and guard the pastoral idyll of Rügen's interior against over-enthusiastic development.

Biggest (22,500 hectares) and most important is the Biosphere Reserve of Southeast Rügen, a region of peninsulas, small islands, hooked spits, and sand bars barely submerged beneath shallow, inland waters. It includes the Granitz forest, the Monchgut peninsula and Vilm, a small island whose oak and beech forest has remained untouched for whole centuries, and whose unique delights can only be visited by appointment. Hiddensee, a long, thin island within the West-Pomeranian Boddenschaft Reserve at the other side of Rügen, shares a similar landscape of dunes, forests, salt marshes, and lagoons of brackish water typical of the Baltic. The ratio of salt to fresh water makes these 'Bodden' invaluable habitats to millions of migratory birds. Every autumn, around 30,000 cranes arrive in one of Europe's most dramatic avian spectacles. Cars are forbidden on Hiddensee, and its isolated wetlands are a habitat for some of the rarest flora and fauna in the world. Here, earth and water merge under the piercing clarity of huge, northern skies.

One of Rügen's loveliest walks takes you through the Jasmund Reserve on the east coast. The Königsstuhl (King's Chair) is the highest point of Germany's only pure white, chalk cliffs. At 10 km (6 mi) long and up to 117 m (384 ft) high, the cliffs illustrate the dynamics of coastal erosion – and there's a visitor centre of exceptional interest and quality that helps explain this and the other features that make Rügen so special.

The beautiful coastline of Rügen

The Spreewald

*Canoeing on the Hauptspree
in Spreewald.*

Just 100 km (62 mi) south of Berlin is a huge nature reserve 75 km (47 mi) long and 15 km (9 mi) wide. It is a lowland of water meadows and broadleaf woods developed 20,000 years ago during the Ice Age, intersected by 970 km (606 mi) of streams and water courses, and unique in central Europe. Incredibly, so close to Germany's capital, it has resisted history: its people, the Sorbs, one of only two recognized minorities with their own ancient customs, dress and still-spoken language, and its landscape have both remained intact and untouched. The Spreewald is a paradise of benign wilderness given over to thousands of very rare species of plants and animals.

However you reach the Spreewald region, you need a boat to travel within it. There are thousands of waterways (called 'fliesse'), broad and narrow, and punts are the usual transport for local farmers as well as visitors. Motor boats are discouraged because they are noisy – and the Spreewald demands maximum attention from all the senses. You hear, touch and smell the rushes bowing on the breeze, the gurgle of water and creaking wood of the punt, overlaid with the snap of wings as storks, hoopoes, cranes and curlews lift off in sudden, flapping urgency. The more you listen, the more the watery stillness comes alive with the sound of living things. Thousands of butterflies dart in the leafy canopy of poplars, oak-trees and the slender alders that dapple the sunlight over the streams. Fish leap; dragonflies dart and hum; birds sing their glory. Lilies float companionably, and wild flowers dot every leafy corner of the marshy labyrinth.

Take a canoe or a kayak, or hire a punt (perhaps with a guide to identify the flora and fauna), or ride a bicycle, or stroll, or hike. There's no public transport. The Spreewald succeeds in being remote even in the middle of an industrialized society.

WHAT IS IT?
A Biosphere Reserve of interlinked waterways and water meadows.
HOW TO GET THERE:
By car to Burg (Spreewald); by train/bus/car to Lubben or Lubbenau. These are the three best centres to explore the region.
WHEN TO GO:
Year-round.
NEAREST TOWN:
Burg, Lubben and Lubbenau.
DON'T MISS:
The museum village of Lehde near Lubbenau.
YOU SHOULD KNOW:
The Spreewald is famous for giant cucumbers and gherkins.

The Harz Mountains

WHAT IS IT?
A mountain Biosphere Reserve with a legendary moorland plateau.
HOW TO GET THERE:
Train to Bad Harzburg; then car/bus to Torfhaus (for Goethe Trail up the Brocken).
WHEN TO GO:
Year-round.
NEAREST TOWN:
Wernigerode 10 km (6 mi)
DON'T MISS:
The medieval town of Quedlinburg; the view from Rosstrappe, nr Thale.
YOU SHOULD KNOW:
Dwarf birches, the Brocken anemone, and emerald dragonflies are Ice Age relicts – some of the many species preserved by the isolation of the Harz.

For 100 km (62 mi) across central Germany, the Harz Mountains divide the northern lowlands from the southern uplands. The region has benefited from 20th century politics, which left it virtually uninhabited, and provided its 27,400 hectares of evergreen and broadleaf woodlands, its marshes, alpine meadows, cliff-faces, waterfalls and gorges with the ideal opportunity for regeneration. The entire mountain range is now a protected nature reserve, but its centrepiece is the Upper Harz plateau, the 65 sq km (25 sq mi) circling the rounded granite peak of the Brocken, the highest at 1,142 m (3,746 ft) in the Harz. Shrouded in mists 300 days a year, the Brocken's harsh appearance inspired Goethe to recreate its wild atmosphere in the nightmares of Faust; and a rock shelf in Thale, a small town overlooking the dramatic Bode Valley nearby, is called the Hexentenplatz, the place where witches dance every Walpurgisnacht (1st May), before flying off to meet the devil on Brocken.

If the high moors are austere, the surrounding forests of rowan, maple and beech frame more than 100 lakes that are often linked in systems of torrent streams and thin strands of waterfalls. Their splashing echo traces the course of the Bode River out of the mystery and magic of the Upper Harz to a landscape of fairy-gothic romanticism. The force of the water has cut whole cave systems in its scramble round jagged outcrops of granite, imperturbable in the yielding limestone. Most spectacular of the dripstone caves found everywhere in the Harz are here, in Rubeland, near Wernigerode. The Baumannshohle plays host to music festivals in its colossal 60 x 40 m (197 x 131 ft) 'Goethe Hall' cavern; and the nearly equally huge Hermannshohle features a dazzling arrangement of stalactites and stalagmites, rich with the sparkle of mineral crystals.

The Harz and the Bodetal are stunning in every season. Just remember, however crowded it may seem near attractions like the charming narrow gauge railway system, you only need to step a few metres away to enjoy the sylvan solitude that truly belongs to the lynx, marten, red and fallow deer, and the myriad birds for which it is home.

A winter landscape on the Brocken

Schwabische Alb

Scenery of the Schwabische Alb

South and east of Stuttgart, the Schwabische Alb is a highland plateau 220 km (137 mi) long and about 50 km (31 mi) wide. The landscape is a combination of bizarre rock formations and gently rolling slopes of light forest and sparse juniper shrubs where sheep nibble. There is almost no surface water, because the region's limestone is the residue of what was once a sea-bed, and weathering has created an entire system of subterranean rivers and caves. Not only does the region bear easily visible witness to 200 million years of geology; it is a paradise for rare fossils like those of the dinosaurs, giant squid, monsters up to 18 m (59 ft) long, crocodiles, pterodactyls and sea lilies that you can see in local museums. Children still make lesser finds in their back yards.

The western edge of the Schwabische Alb is a steep cliff, 300 m 984 ft) high, of wooded crags called the Albtrauf, an escarpment 180 km (112 mi) long from which you gaze imperiously towards the Black Forest. The Alb shelves gently to the east and south, where its boundary is the newborn Danube. Geologists have described the area in between as an underground barrel supplying warm, mineral-rich water from deep in the earth to the springs that justify the fame of the region's many thermal baths and health resorts. Of these, none is more famous or spectacular than the Blautopf, or Blue Pot. Below the lake – of intense, silicon blue without parallel in Europe, the spring rises 30 m (98 ft) from the start of a river cave. It is the entrance to a system of passages and cathedral-size caverns running for over 5 km (3 mi), before the water gushes out of the ground as the source of the Danube.

Some of the Alb's smaller caves, well above the water table, still show the marks of human habitation 30,000 years ago. Hohlenstein-Stadel and Gleissenklosterle are just two where you can see cave art of really high quality.

WHAT IS IT?
A Jurassic limestone plateau significant for its major fossil finds.
HOW TO GET THERE:
By car/bus/train to Ulm or Reutlingen.
WHEN TO GO:
Year-round.
NEAREST TOWN:
Blaubeuren 16 km (10 mi) W of Ulm on B28.
DON'T MISS:
The Apokalypse cavern, 170 m (558 ft) long, 50 m (164 ft) wide, 50 m (164 ft) high.
YOU SHOULD KNOW:
The region was once one of the most volcanic on earth.

Bayerische Wald

The oldest of Germany's national parks, the Bayerische Wald winds around the Bavarian forest peaks of Falkenstein, Rachel and Lusen along the border with the Czech Republic. In partnership with the neighbouring Sumava National Park in the Czech Republic, it is the largest protected forest area in central Europe. Nowhere else between the Atlantic Ocean and the Ural mountains has a major forest been returned completely to nature. No human lives there; and no human intervention is allowed to shape the development of the forest in any way. With no agriculture, husbandry or commercial logging, the forest has regenerated a wide variety of habitats among its many wet valleys, streams, bogs, moors and meadows. Rare species like the lynx, black stork, eagle owl, pygmy owl, three-toed woodpecker, and Bohemian gentian have returned, among hundreds of others. In some places, huge tracts of spruce lie in rotting tumbles, shrouded in moss and undergrowth: your heart sinks until you see the evidence of a whole new kind of forest emerging from centuries of commercial exploitation which have left it vulnerable to the ravages of the bark beetle, agent of the devastation. As the bark beetle kills off the spruce, nature is replacing them with the truly native beech, mountain ash, rowan and other deciduous species, which in turn are attracting even greater varieties of flora and fauna.

You can witness this unique landscape along 300 km (187 mi) of walking trails and 200 km (125 mi) of cycling paths. The Hochwaldsteig takes you (via Jacob's ladder) to the 1,373 m (4,503 ft) rock dome of the Lusen, above the tree line; the Watzlikhain, near the Zwieslerwaldhaus sanctuary, is a forest wilderness discovery path; and the Igelbus (the national park bus) will drop you at the Seelensteig, a trail of such contemplative beauty that will crush your inner demons. But when you come to Bayerische Wald for the first time, visit the information centre at Neuschonau for one-to-one advice on how best to enjoy your personal enthusiasms, and a first-class children's discovery room.

A trail leads through the Bayerische Wald

WHAT IS IT?
A forest Biosphere Reserve with a unique no-intervention policy.
HOW TO GET THERE:
By car/train (the 'Waldbahn') to Zwiesel, Eisenstein, Grafenau or Frauenau; then by bus (ask for the Bayerische Wald-ticket).
WHEN TO GO:
Year-round.
NEAREST TOWN:
Eisenstein/ Neuschonau (N), Grafenau (S).
DON'T MISS:
The 7 km (4.4 mi) loop through the wilderness enclosure where the Lynx Project is flourishing; from the Hans-Eisenmann-Haus at Neuschonau.
YOU SHOULD KNOW:
The spruce bark beetle is under 6 mm (1/5 in) long. Just 50 can kill a fully-grown tree in 8 weeks.

Nordlinger Ries

North of the Danube, in the Donau-Ries district of Bavaria, lies the depression of Nordlinger Ries. It is the impact crater of a huge meteorite that struck the region almost 15 million years ago, circular in shape and 25 km (16 mi) in diameter. The bottom of the crater is 100-150 m (328-492 ft) below its rim, and the city of Nordlingen, itself defined by its still-complete, circular medieval wall, lies in the middle of the crater.

Until 1960 the Ries was believed to be of volcanic origin. Then, scientists found direct evidence of the shock-metamorphic effects of a meteor strike. The high temperature of the strike caused laminations and welding in the local sandstone, creating tektites, identifiable by their glassy spatters of molten material. But the conclusive proof was the discovery of coesite, a variety of shocked quartz that occurs only when a force as powerful as a meteor causes microscopic deformations in minerals. While celebrating, they realized that the ancient town church of Nordlingen was itself made out of a huge chunk of coesite.

Visitors can see details of the meteor strike and subsequent local geology at the Ries Crater Museum in Nordlingen. But you get a better idea of the colossal impact 12 km (7.5 mi) south of Nordlingen, where the crater rim outside the village of Monschdeggingen rises in a steep escarpment, and even now the grass is broken by rocky outcrops containing coesite and tektites. From here you get a vision of nature that is almost too powerful for easy contemplation: it is simply awesome.

WHAT IS IT?
A huge meteorite impact crater.
HOW TO GET THERE:
By car/train/bus to Nordlingen.
WHEN TO GO:
Year-round.
NEAREST TOWN:
Nordlingen (about 12 km [7.5 mi] to anywhere on the rim).
DON'T MISS:
The medieval town church and steeple of St Georg, made of coesite.
YOU SHOULD KNOW:
Nordlingen is twinned with Wagga Wagga, Australia.

Ofnet cave area of Nordlinger Ries

Wimbachklamm

The Bavarian Alps, tucked away in Germany's south-east on the Austrian border, are the definition of a romantic landscape. Snowcapped mountains plunge into the patchwork of fields that chequers deep green valleys. Steep rock faces thrust out of dense forest, and every rocky outcrop gives way to a fresh panorama of waterfalls, grey scree, and the serried green of larch, spruce, pine and beech. In the heart of this fairytale setting – itself protected for its pristine beauty in the 210 sq km (81 sq mi) Berchtesgarden National Park – is Wimbachklamm, a slab-sided gorge of authentically Wagnerian drama.

Wimbachbrucke, where you arrive by bus or car, is one of the main entrances to the Park as a whole. Inside, you pay a small fee to enter the Wimbachklamm itself, and follow the trail into and up the gorge. Almost immediately, your hearing is drowned by the rushing torrent of the Wimbach as you take a couple of turns out of sight into wilderness. The trail becomes a wooden stairway hugging the rock face rising on either side. Jagged crags spit out mountain streams and crowd higher and closer together until what seemed a canyon is a ravine, twisting and turning upwards in exhilarating majesty. Just when the climb is becoming as exhausting as the brilliant view, the river disappears beneath a rock bed, and you must climb a further 2 km (1.25 mi) before you reach a more gentle incline, and emerge into an alpine pastoral of woods and meandering stream that leads to the hut called (wittily) Wimbachschloss, and summertime refreshments. After 10 km (6 mi), they will be welcome.

Wimbachklamm has the dramatic intensity of the very best German poetry and opera. It is a truly classic German landscape, and truly beautiful.

Small waterfalls in Wimbachklamm

Ardennes Peaks

Boating is a popular activity on the scenic River Meuse.

The Ardennes is a rugged wilderness landscape, stretching east from France across Luxembourg and Belgium and on into Germany. The highest part, the Hautes Fagnes (High Fens) in the German-speaking far east of the country, is an expanse of windswept heathland popular with skiers, but the most scenic corner lies further west between Dinant, La Roche-en-Ardenne and Bouillon. Here the river valleys and deep, wooded, winding canyons reach up to high green peaks, sublimely and inspiringly beautiful.

The Ardennes' cave systems are also a major attraction, carved out by underground rivers that, over the centuries, have cut through and dissolved the limestone of the hills, leaving stalagmites and stalactites in their dripping wake.

The gateway to the most scenic area within the Ardennes is Namur, sited at the junction of the Sambre and Meuse rivers (known as the 'Grognons' or 'Pig's snout') with its massive hilltop citadel, once one of the mightiest fortresses in Europe and accessible by an exhilarating cable car ride. The town also boasts some good museums, restaurants and nightclubs. From Namur, the Meuse passes through a landscape of gently wooded slopes, interrupted by steep escarpments and jagged crags capped by ruined castles. This area draws rock climbers in their droves.

The little town of Rochefort, some 50 km (31 mi) south of Namur, is a good centre for exploring the Ardennes and an attractive base for cyclists and walkers. This is lovely countryside with thickly wooded hills, river valleys and plenty of castles.

At Han-sur-Lesse just east of Rochefort, is a wild animal reserve containing animals that have inhabited the Ardennes since prehistoric times – bison, bears, deer and wild boar.

WHAT IS IT?
Hills in southern Belgium.
HOW TO GET THERE:
From Brussels head south east to Namur.
WHEN TO GO:
Spring and summertime for walking, cycling and canoeing.
NEAREST TOWN:
Namur 60 km (37.5 mi)
DON'T MISS:
The Tresor du Prieure d'Oignies, housed in a convent at Namur, is a unique collection of exquisitely beautiful gold and silver.
YOU SHOULD KNOW:
The Ardennes have more than 800 km (500 mi) of ski trails.

The Aven-Armand Cave

WHAT IS IT?
An amazing cave full of stalagmites.
HOW TO GET THERE:
By road from Nimes
WHEN TO GO:
Any time except
December–February, when it is shut.
NEAREST TOWN:
Meyreuils 8 km (5 mi)
DON'T MISS:
The spectacular stalagmites.
YOU SHOULD KNOW:
There is now a funicular railway,
making visiting the cave far less
strenuous.

Home to the biggest known stalagmite in the world, the cave of Aven-Armand was discovered in 1897 by Louis Armand, a local blacksmith. Located within the Cévennes National Park, this limestone karst cave is reached by two deep chimneys. It is vast, 45m (150 ft) high, 60 m (200 ft) wide and 110 m (360 ft) long. It's collection of hundreds of stalagmites is known as the Virgin Forest, and tour guides lead visitors though the forest, showing the more famous structures, such as the Cauliflower, the Jellyfish, the Turkey and the Palm Tree. At least 400 of the stalagmites are more than 1 m (3 ft) high, many of them top 20 m (66 ft) and the tallest is over 30 m (100 ft) from its base to its tip.

Many of the stalagmites are of a particular shape, known as plate-stack or Palmtrunc, with broader tops, reminiscent of the trunk of a palm tree. They form in this way because the height of the cave allows drops of water to accelerate so they hit the top of the stalagmite with a splash. Because the cave is relatively near the surface, the amount of water dripping seeping through from above varies greatly depending on the amount of rainfall: the narrower parts of the structures form when there is little water and the broader parts when it is very wet.

A visit to this eerie place, where stalagmites loom at you from the darkness, and the background drip, drip, drip of water reminds you that they are still being formed, is an experience not to be forgotten.

Twenty metre- (66ft-) high stalagmites grow in the underground cavern of Aven-Armand.

The Garlaban Massif

Looming over Aubagne, and easily visible from much of southern Provence, the blue-white limestone rock of the Garlaban towers into the skies above the Plan d'Aigle. It was used in ancient times as a landmark by Greek and Roman sailors approaching the port city of Massalia (Marseille).

The slopes were heavily forested until the 20th century, but a series of severe forest fires means that the lower slopes are now chiefly covered in the rough scrub known locally as *garrigue*, where the air is scented in summer with such herbs as rosemary, wild thyme, lavender and artemisia. The bare higher reaches of the massif loom starkly over the secluded valleys below.

The Garlaban itself is 714 m (2,343 ft) although the peak of the range is the Butte des Pinsots at 729 m (2,392 ft). Other well-known peaks are Tête Rouge, which resembles a head and is red because of the bauxite in its soils, and Taoumé.

The author Marcel Pagnol was born in nearby Aubagne in 1895. From 1903 his family had a holiday home in the hamlet of La Treille at the west of the massif, and he returned to the beautiful wild landscape that he loved again and again in his books, evoking its magic and scenery. The *leitmotif* of a lack of water runs through Pagnol's work in his childhood reminiscences, *La Gloire de mon Père* and *Le Château de ma Mère* and, particularly, in the novels *Jean de Florette* and *Manon des Sources*, in which the need for water triggers murder, madness, revenge and suicide.

The Garlaban Massif near Aubagne

WHAT IS IT?
A limestone range that is the epitome of the southern Provençal landscape.
HOW TO GET THERE:
From the N96 between Aubagne and Roquevaire.
WHEN TO GO:
Late spring, early summer or early autumn as the height of summer is extremely hot.
NEAREST TOWN:
Aubagne 5 km (3 mi)

The Pain du Sucre and the River Orne in Suisse Normande

Suisse Normande

While not as mountainous as its name might suggest, the area known as Suisse Normande (Norman Switzerland) is a picturesque mix of rugged cliffs, lush valleys, wooded hills and dramatic gorges, set among the tranquil agricultural land for which Normandy is famous. It centres on the gorge of the River Orne, which created a deep gorge popular with canoeists and rock climbers alike. There are several routes within the region: the Route des Crêtes follows the line of its peaks, such as the Pain du Sucre and Rocher des Parcs, while the main circuit sometimes follows the river and at others detours into gorges and past rocky cliffs. The highest point is the Oëtre Rocks (Roches d'Oëtre), a spectacular outcrop high above the gorges created by the area's second river, the Rouvre.

This area has been inhabited for many thousands of years: there are several menhirs around, and there is a museum in an ancient iron-ore mine in Saint-Rémy exploring the region's 650 million years of geology and history from how its granite was formed, the arrival of the dinosaurs, how the landscape has been shaped to the history of man in the area.

This is a sporting paradise, with hang-gliding and parascending, horse-riding and mountain biking all on offer as well as numerous places for walking or more strenuous hikes.

Gorges du Tarn

The Gorges du Tarn have long been considered one of the most beautiful sights in France. Over millions of years, the River Tarn has found itself a route through the limestone of the Grands Causses, slowly eroding away the soft stone, forming steep cliffs and spectacular scenery. Starting at Mont Lozère in the Cévennes, the river runs some 370 km (230 mi) to Moissac in a westerly direction before joining the Garonne, but it is the section through the Grands Causses, particularly the Causse du Larzac, for which it is best known. This 60-km (37-mi) stretch is truly breathtaking, especially from the roads that switch back and forth as they climb up the high walls of the valley. The aptly named Point Sublime is one of the best places to stop to catch the views, and perhaps to catch your breath.

A new attraction in the area is the bridge across the valley near Millau. Cars soar 270 m (885 ft) above the river, giving the passengers a view across the whole valley.

However, for those with no head for heights or no need for speed, there are other ways to explore the gorge: it is possible to take a trip on a glass-bottomed boat to watch the rocks drift past beneath you, walk along the riverside footpath or paddle your way downstream by canoe, looking out for the owls and birds of prey that play in the updraughts. From this perspective, you get a true sense of the scale of this valley, which dwarfes the buildings and people within it.

WHAT IS IT?
A spectacular gorge in south-western France.
HOW TO GET THERE:
By road from Toulouse or Montpellier.
WHEN TO GO:
Summer.
NEAREST TOWN:
Millau
DON'T MISS:
The drive over the new Millau viaduct.
YOU SHOULD KNOW:
The river can gain height rapidly after heavy rains.

White limestone cliffs enclose the River Tarn in the Gorges du Tarn, in the Languedoc region of southern France.

Côte d'Alabâtre

WHAT IS IT?
A stretch of chalk cliffs and beautiful rock formations.
HOW TO GET THERE:
By road from Dieppe or Le Havre.
WHEN TO GO:
Any time of year.
NEAREST TOWN:
Fécamp 20 km (12 mi)
DON'T MISS:
Walking through the Porte d'Aval.
YOU SHOULD KNOW:
The cliffs are crumbly and rock falls are a hazard.

The Côte d'Alabâtre, or 'Alabaster Coast' is, in fact, not alabaster, but a line of chalk cliffs on the coast of Normandy, west of Dieppe. They are part of the same formation of Cretaceous chalk that makes up the Seven Sisters and the White Cliffs of Dover on the other side of the English Channel. They were formed more than 65 million years ago, from the fossil skeletons of billions and billions of creatures that lived in shallow warm seas. Once, they covered most of Britain, but still extend as far north as Yorkshire and as far south as the Paris Basin. The chalk is so much a feature here that the coast's hinterland is called the Pays de Caux, from the Norman word for chalk. The principal towns on the coast are Fécamp and Etretat, where the most spectacular cliff formations are to be found. The western cliff, the Falais d'Aval, has been scoured into an arch, called the Porte d'Aval, by the waves. From its clifftop, visitors can see more rock formations, including l'aiguille, the needle, a soaring sea-stack. Other arches here are the Porte d'Amont and the Manneporte. At low tide visitors can walk through the arches.

The area was a favourite place for the Impressionists and other painters, including Degas and Matisse, and they painted the cliffs and surrounding countryside many times. Literary connections include Victor Hugo and Guy de Maupassant, who likened the Porte d'Aval to an elephant dipping its trunk into the sea. In summer it is still bustling with tourists, but in winter it is a spectacular, lonely place to watch the waves crashing into the cliffs.

The Porte d'Aval is a natural arch off the coast of France near the town of Etretat.

The Caves of the Dordogne

The limestone plateau that the river Dordogne flows through is riddled with caves. As well as those with prehistoric paintings for which it is rightly famous, many of them have spectacular stalactite formations. Padirac, in the Causse de Gramat is an immense group of caverns, accessed via two lifts that descend to the bottom of the 100-m (330-ft) chasm, then a vertiginous walkway, followed by a boat down the low-roofed river and across the underground lake with its stalactite-encrusted ceiling to reach the caverns, including the Grand Dôme. In places the roof of the cave is only 7 m (23 ft) from the surface above, so this cave is very wet after rainfall. The entire cave system is dripping with water and covered with lichens. Lacave is a less well-known but equally fascinating cave nearby.

One of the many caves in the Dordogne

To the west, the river Vézère's gorge is another hot spot for caves. The Grand Roc is riddled with a network of caves, full of spectacular stalactites, with such names as 'rabbit's ear' and 'serpent's nest'. Geologists have estimated that the caves must have been formed about 60 million years ago and that the stalactites have taken many hundreds of thousands of years to form. The ceilings of the caves are very low, so this is not one for those who suffer from claustrophobia. A short distance to the north-west is Carpe Diem, whose 200-m (660 ft) length is crammed with stalactites and stalagmites.

The sites where our ancestors painted the animals they hunted are justifiably popular, but these caves where nature's work is evident, are also definitely worth a visit.

WHAT IS IT?
A group of natural caves filled with rock formations.
HOW TO GET THERE:
By road from Bergerac.
WHEN TO GO:
Summer.
NEAREST TOWN:
Rocamadour for Padirac 9 km (5.5 mi) and Lacave (3 km (8 mi), Les Eyzies for the Grand Roc 1 km (0.5 mi) and Carpe Diem 2.5 km (1.5 mi)
DON'T MISS:
The Grand Dôme.
YOU SHOULD KNOW:
Many of the caves are closed out of the peak tourist season.

The Mountains of the Auvergne

WHAT IS IT?
Chains of volcanoes in southern France.
HOW TO GET THERE:
By road from Lyon.
WHEN TO GO:
Any time of year.
NEAREST TOWN:
Clermont-Ferrand 10 km (6 mi)
DON'T MISS:
The cable-car ride and walk to the top of the Mont Dore.
YOU SHOULD KNOW:
Cycling on the Puy-de-Dôme is restricted to a few hours a week, when the road is closed to all other traffic.

The Auvergne is well known for the beauty of its wooded slopes and rocky peaks, particularly those of the Monts Dômes (also known as the Chaine des Puys) and the Monts Dore. What many do not realize, however, is that this stunning landscape in the Massif Central is a result of relatively recent volcanic activity. The youngest, and highest, volcano in the Monts Dômes is the Puy-de-Dôme, which last erupted less than 8,000 years ago. This stunning mountain, with its double crater, is one of the most popular sights in France. A steep road spirals most of the way up the mountain, but the original Roman zigzag track to the top of this 1,464-m (4,803-ft) peak is popular with hikers. From the edge of the inner crater, the views north and south over the lava domes and cinder cones of the rest of the chain are stunning.

To the south-west, the Monts Dorés are also volcanic. There are three main volcanoes – the Puy de Sancy, the Puy de l'Aiguiller and the Banne d'Ordanche, which dominate a landscape of woodland, lakes, rivers and waterfalls. This area was popular with the Romans because of its thermal springs and curative waters. There are still spas here today and the mineral-laced waters are exported the world over.

The Parc Natural Régional des Volcans d'Auvergne is vast. It stretches from the Monts Dômes in the north to the Monts du Cantal in the south. This beautiful landscape is popular for hiking, canoeing and sailing in summer and skiing and snowboarding in winter.

Volcanic cones in the Puy-de-Dôme

Meuse Valley and the Ardennes Forest

The River Meuse at Monthermé in the Ardennes

Although in its lower reaches nearer the North Sea, the Meuse is industrialized, in its higher reaches, it runs through beautiful landscapes on the border between France and Belgium. The Ardennes, whose name comes from the Celtic for deep forest, is a wild land of dramatic valleys and hills carpeted with deciduous forests. The Meuse makes sweeping double meanders in the area around Monthermé and Revin, and this is generally thought to be the most spectacular part of the river valley. The steep valley sides generally mean that agriculture is difficult, and the river cannot be navigated by boats of any great size, so the area remains sparsely populated and it is very easy to escape what few other people there are. The area abounds in wildlife, such as boar and deer, although they are not easy to spot. There is also a wide variety of forest birds. There are numerous hiking trails that lead up into the hills, and up to viewpoints like Mont Malgré-Tout above Revin. The warped and twisted granite rock formations that line the gorges of the area – including the rather obviously named Roche à Sept Heures – appeal to climbers of all abilities and the lack of commercial traffic on the rivers makes the Meuse popular with canoeists.

WHAT IS IT?
An area of beautiful landscapes on the border of France and Belgium.
HOW TO GET THERE:
By road from Charleroix or Reims.
WHEN TO GO:
Summer
NEAREST TOWN:
Monthermé
YOU SHOULD KNOW:
The hunting season runs from mid-October to mid-January.

Cirque de Gavarnie

In the high Pyrenees, and within the Parc National des Pyrénées, just below the French/Spanish border, the Cirque de Gavarnie is a spectacular, natural horseshoe shaped amphitheatre, which boasts Europe's tallest waterfall, at 422 m (1,384 ft). Gouged out of the rocks of the Pyrenees by an ancient glacier, the 800-m (2,625-ft) base of the cirque is littered with terminal moraine and the floor of the valley carved out by the glacier and the river is strewn with larger rocks, some house-sized, left high and dry as the glacier retreated. As you get nearer the base of the waterfall, the woodland gives way to allow you to gaze up at the towering cliffs around you. Eleven of the peaks around the cirque soar to over 3,000 m (10,000 ft) and lead up to the sharp crests that separate France and Spain.

Gavarnie used to be on one of the pilgrimage routes from France to Santiago de Compostella, and there are several good walking and hiking trails, in and around the valley, offering spectacular vistas and glimpses of wildlife such as isards (the Pyrenean version of chamoix), the comical whistling marmots and birds such as golden eagle, lammergeier, griffon vulture, honey buzzard, alpine accentor, water and rock pipits, alpine chough and raven. In the river valley, dippers and wallcreepers may be seen and little owl and black woodpecker heard. There are also spectacular butterflies in summer.

The Cirque de Gavarnie in the Pyrenees boasts Europe's tallest waterfall.

WHAT IS IT?
The most spectacular glacial cirque in Europe.
HOW TO GET THERE:
By car on the scenic D921 to the village of Gavarnie, then by mule or on foot.
WHEN TO GO:
Early summer for the wildflowers, early-mid September for the birds.

NEAREST TOWN:
Luz-St-Sauveur 20 km (12 mi)
DON'T MISS:
The Brèche de Rolande, a 100-m (600-ft) breach in one of the crests above the cirque, created, according to legend, by Charlemagne's nephew.
YOU SHOULD KNOW:
The ground at the base of the cirque can be treacherously soggy when the waterfall is in full spate.

Gorges de l'Ardèche

Rising in the Ardèche mountains in the department of the same name, this short river flows roughly south-eastwards until it flows into the Rhône a few kilometres from Pont St-Esprit. The most scenic section is between here and Vallon-Pont-d'Arc, where it flows rapidly through the Gorges de l'Ardèche. This area has one of the most rugged landscapes in France, with cliffs that reach 300 m (1,000 ft) in places. In some stretches, the sides of the gorge are a brilliant white, while in others they are in shades of ochre. One of the most famous features is the Pont d'Arc near the head of the gorge, a 60-m (200-ft) arch spanning the river, evidence that thousands of years ago the river flowed through underground caverns here, before erosion weakened their roofs and they collapsed. One day, this final remaining arch, too, will fall into the river that created it. The best way to see the gorge is from the road that parallels the top of the cliffs for most of the gorge's length and offers frequent viewpoints, such as the Belvédère de Gournier.

More evidence of the effects of water can be seen in the area around the gorge, in the many stalagmite-rich caves, such as the Aven d'Orgnac a few kilometres to the south and the Grotte de la Madeleine, which can be accessed from the clifftop road.

The Pont D'Arc over the Ardèche River

WHAT IS IT?
A 32-km (20-mi) limestone gorge in the south-east of France.
HOW TO GET THERE:
By road from Orange or Avignon.
WHEN TO GO:
Spring to autumn, but the best time for kayaking down the river is from May to June.
NEAREST TOWN:
Vallon-Pont-d'Arc 5 km (3 mi)

The Camargue

A vast, beautiful expanse of wild marshland and lagoons on the Mediterranean's Golfe du Lion, the Camargue is a protected area full of wildlife. It is formed by silt deposited by the Grande and Petit Rhône rivers as they reach the sea and is continually encroaching into the Mediterranean. The northern part and the edges were turned over to agriculture, primarily red Camarguais rice, in the middle of the twentieth century, but the central part, sheltered from the sea by sand bars, remains as a haven for wildlife. The Étang de Vaccarès was declared a regional park in 1927 and was incorporated into the Parc Régional de Camargue in 1972.

The Camargue covers an area of 930 sq km (360 sq mi). The briny lagoons (*étangs*) and reed marshes are home to thousands of birds and also provide a haven for migrants, with a total of more than 400 species of birds having been recorded here. The symbol of the area is the greater flamingo, of which some 13,000 breed on the Étang Fangassier. Mammals in the area include badgers, beavers and wild boar.

The other animals for which the area is famous are the white horses and the black bulls. The bulls roam free, guarded by *gardiens*, who ride tamed Camarguais horses.

The area has been exploited by humans for thousands of years, for agriculture and for extracting salt and some of the dykes created for water-control purposes give access to the inner marsh. It is also possible to explore by canoe or you can hire a horse.

The Camargue is famous for its white horses.

The Dordogne River

The Dordogne River

At almost 300 km (200 mi) in length, the Dordogne is not France's longest river, but it does flow through some of the most spectacular and varied landscapes in the country. It rises just west of the Puy-de-Dôme in Auvergne's Monts Dore, and winds its way through the countryside until it joins with the Garonne and discharges into the Atlantic Ocean. Among the most beautiful, and popular, stretches of the river is the Vallée de la Dordogne, west of Souillac, around where it enters limestone causse country. The surrounding land is some of the most unspoiled in France, even though it has been inhabited for many thousands of years, as can be seen from the amazing number of caves in the region with prehistoric paintings. Over hundreds of thousands of years, the Dordogne and its tributaries have carved their way through the soft stone plateaux, and the sheer cliff walls tower over the river below, only suddenly to give way to picturesque farmland before sharply rising again, to rocky outcrops often topped by a small château. The whole area has recently been made into a national park in order to protect its beauty.

Some of the roads that loosely follow the river are frankly terrifying and a gentler alternative is to kayak downstream for a few kilometres on one of the easier stretches or, in summer, go on a trip on a *gabarre*, a type of boat typical of the region. As you drift along you will pass pretty villages that shelter under crumbling cliffs, farmland and wooded slopes.

Downriver, the widening Dordogne flows through wine country and the rich landscape is clothed with vineyards and farmland until it reaches Bordeaux and the sea.

WHAT IS IT?
A river valley with spectacular scenery.
HOW TO GET THERE:
By road from Clermont Ferrand or Toulouse.
WHEN TO GO:
Spring to autumn.
NEAREST TOWN:
Martel 5 km (3 mi)
DON'T MISS:
The prehistoric cave paintings.
YOU SHOULD KNOW:
The area that the British call the Dordogne is known to the French as Périgord.

The Caves of Languedoc-Roussillon

WHAT IS IT?
A variety of spectacular caves.
HOW TO GET THERE:
By road.
WHEN TO GO:
Summer.
NEAREST TOWN:
St-Guilhem-le-Désert for the Grotte de Clamouse 3 km (2 mi), Courniou for the Grotte des Devèze 0.5 km (0.3 mi), Ganges for the Grotte des Demoiselles 4 km (2.5 mi), Limousis for the grotto of the same name 1 km (0.6 mi), Mialet for the Grotte de Trabuc 1 km (0.6 mi) and Fontrabiouse for its namesake 1 km (0.6 mi).
YOU SHOULD KNOW:
Many of the caves are closed in winter.

The limestone hills of this diverse region of south-western France are rich in spectacular caves. Many have been known about for centuries, but some for only a few years, such as the Grotte de Clamouse, which was discovered only in 1945 and whose full extent has yet to be explored. There are dozens of them, so a few will serve to show their variety. In the west, Fontrabiouse's 1 km (0.5 mi) of tunnels lead to spectacular coloured formations that shimmer in the light while in the east, the Grotte de Trabuc is the largest cave in the Cévennes. In Aude, the Grotte de Limousis has eight halls with rock and crystal formations. Perhaps the best known caves in the region, and certainly the most spectacular lie in Hérault. The Grotte de la Devèze lies within the Parc Régional du Haut-Languedoc and is renowned for its smooth, delicate limestone formations. To the north of the park is the Grotte des Demoiselles, the fairies' cave, and to the east is the Grotte de Clamouse. The former is accessed via a funicular and the trail through it clambers in and out of the chamber and formations, to the giant Salle de Vierge. The latter is a vast complex with every kind and shape of stalagmite and stalactite, with columns where they have met in the middle, and draperies that range from massive 'curtains' to delicate lace-like structures. In the Red Niagara Chamber the cascading stone is stained red with minerals deposited over the millennia.

One of the many fantastic caves of Languedoc-Roussillon

Les Cascades du Hérisson

Set at the edge of the Parc Naturel des Haut Jura near the Swiss border is one of France's hidden beauties, the Cascades du Hérisson, a group of thirty-one waterfalls that drop the waters of the lakes above them 600 m (1,960 ft) in just 3.5 km (2.2 mi). The two largest cascades are l'Eventail (the fan) and le Grand Saut (the great leap), which are 65 and 60 m (213 and 196 ft) respectively. The name Hérisson comes from the Greek for sacred and the Celtic for water. The path along the river valley from Doucier takes you through beautiful woodland scenery, accompanied by the constant gurgle of water. As you approach the falls, the gurgle grows to an overwhelming roar. The lowest fall, the Cascade Girard, is 35 m (115 ft) of tumbling water, rushing over the rocks. The path leads up from one waterfall to the next, each one more beautiful than the last until you finally reach the Cascade de l'Eventail at the top. The river is fed by waters from the lakes high in the mountains here – and various trails lead to them, and further up to the Pic d'Aigle for an amazing panoramic view over this beautiful region. In the Grand Saut, the water drops into a deep pot, and it is possible to walk behind the curtain of water, while the Gour Bleu is a limpid blue pool where the water temporarily halts in its mad rush down the mountainside.

Farther back down the valley is a cave set in the side of the cliff, the Grotte Lacuzon, which can be reached with care.

WHAT IS IT?
One of the most spectacular sets of waterfalls in Europe.
HOW TO GET THERE:
By road from Besançon to the hamlet of Doucier, then on foot or on the GR 559 long-distance footpath.
WHEN TO GO:
Late spring is best.
NEAREST TOWN:
Champagnole 25 km (15.5 mi)
YOU SHOULD KNOW:
Good walking shoes are a must because the trail is rough in places, and often slippery. The walk takes 2 ½–3 hours each way.

The Cascades du Hérisson

Mont Blanc

Set high in the Alps, on the border between France and Switzerland, at 4,807 m (15,771 ft), Mont Blanc is Europe's highest mountain. Sometimes called la Dame Blanche, the White Lady, by the French, it is, naturally, popular with serious climbers. The scenery around the mountain is beautiful, with alpine meadows, gorges, waterfalls and glaciers, including the Mer de Glace, the second-largest glacier in the Alps. To the north-west of the mountain, the waterfalls of the Gorges de la Diosaz are thought by many to be the most beautiful in France.

The world-famous resort of Chamonix-Mont-Blanc has long catered for skiers, but the area is now also important for summer sports and activities, including white-water rafting, hiking (there are more than 310 km (195 mi) of trails in the area, mountain biking, donkey trekking, skiing on the glaciers, dog-trekking and paragliding. A network of cable-cars allows access to the upper slopes, but the most spectacular way to see the area is by helicopter.

The flora and fauna are typical, with a profusion of spring flowers in the meadows in June and marmots and chamois on the higher slopes.

Whether or not you wish to tackle climbing Mont Blanc itself, this is a special place, with beautiful scenery and plenty to do and see.

WHAT IS IT?
Europe's highest mountain.
HOW TO GET THERE:
On the route des Hautes Alpes to the Chamonix-Mont-Blanc resort or via the Mont Blanc tunnel from the south.
WHEN TO GO:
At any time.
NEAREST TOWN:
Megève 15 km (9 mi)

Les Gorges du Verdon

WHAT IS IT?
The largest canyon in Europe.
HOW TO GET THERE:
By road from Avignon or Nice.
WHEN TO GO:
In good weather in summer.
NEAREST TOWN:
Castellane (12 km, 7.5 mi)
DON'T MISS:
The spectacular views.
YOU SHOULD KNOW:
The road is treacherous.

The second largest canyon on earth, after the Grand Canyon, the Gorges du Verdon are a spectacular sight in the north of Provence. Known only to the locals until 1905, the gorge was 'discovered' by the caver Edouard Alfred Martel and rapidly became a tourist attraction. Its proximity to the Provençal coast made it an ideal place to retreat during the heat of summer. Millions of years ago, this area was under a forerunner of the Mediterranean Sea and layer upon layer of limestone and then coral were deposited over the whole area. After the region was lifted up because of the northwards movement of Africa, the land was crumpled and cracked, allowing water and ice to find their way through faults in the soft rock, creating caverns and underground rivers, whose ceilings finally collapsed, slowly etching out this deep, v-shaped valley.

The gorge is only about 20 km (12 mi) long, but the roads that climb the two sides of the valley are so winding that the whole circuit is more than 130 km (80 mi). The most famous viewpoint is the Belvédère de la Maline, although there are other stopping points around the gorge. The roads, especially that round the southern side of the gorge are full of switchbacks and tight turns, and a much more relaxing way to appreciate the views is to kayak along the river instead.

The stunning scenery of the Gorges du Verdon

However, this area's main draw is its rocky cliffs and sheer drop, which are also very popular with rock climbers. There are more than 1,500 different climbs in the area, most of them far too difficult for beginners. There are also several designated hiking routes through the gorge, including the Sentier de l'Imbut, Sentier du Bastidon and that named after the valley's discoverer, the Sentier de Martel.

However you choose to spend your time in this beautiful landscape, you will not forget it easily.

The Bohemian Forest

The landscape of the Bohemian Forest

The Bohemian Forest is a low mountain range in central Europe, extending from the Czech Republic on one side, to Germany and Austria on the other, thus creating a natural border between the countries.

This heavily forested range, with its unforgiving climate, is one of the oldest in Europe and is the divide of the watershed between the North Sea and the Black Sea. The peaks have been eroded by the climate into rounded forms with few rocky parts, and have peat bogs and high plateaux at about 1,000 – 2,000 m (3,300 – 6,560 ft). The highest peak in the range is Grober Arber reaching 1,456 m (4,775 ft).

From the waters collected in the Bohemian Mountains spring, the rivers Vltave, Otava and Uhlava, and with the heavy winter snows, the peat bogs and the Lipno dam, this region is an important source of water for central Europe – other glacial lakes add to the aesthetic value

The origins of this forest go back to about 400 BC, when it was inhabited by the Boii people. These were ancient Celts from Gaul, Northern Italy, Bohemia, Moravia and Slovakia. The name Bohemia comes from the Latin for 'the home of the Boii'. Nowadays these forests have a complicated history as they were part of the Iron Curtain and the previously sparsely populated areas were stripped of habitation allowing the forest to become dominant. This turned farmed areas into forest with preserved and unspoilt ecosystems.

Today the Bohemian Forest is a popular holiday destination for its hiking and biking possibilities, and skiing in the winter, both downhill and cross-country. The region has industries such as coal, graphite, kaolin and granite extraction and, more glamorously, glassmaking and schnapps production.

WHAT IS IT?
Natural wild forest in Central Europe covering several countries.
HOW TO GET THERE:
Czech Republic – fly to Prague, take the E50 to Plzen then the E53 to Klatovy continue to the forest. Germany – fly to Nuremburg; take the E 56 to Regensburg then the E53 into the forest.
WHEN TO GO:
At any time but best in summer for hiking and all outdoor sports, in winter for skiing.
NEAREST TOWN:
In the Czech Republic, Klatovy 20 km (12.5 mi). In Germany, Regensburg 18 km (11.25 mi)
DON'T MISS:
Lipno, an artificial reservoir lake in the Czech Republic on the southern edge of the Sumava.
YOU SHOULD KNOW:
Folklore etymology suggests the name Sumava derives from the words meaning 'noise of wind in the trees'.

Balcarka Cave

WHAT IS IT?
An intricate maze of subterranean passages and vaults.

HOW TO GET THERE:
Train from Brno to Blansko. A few buses from Blansko or 2km (1.25 mi) walk from Skalni Mlyn.

WHEN TO GO:
May to September.

NEAREST TOWN:
Blansko 8 km (5 mi)

DON'T MISS:
The summer music concerts in the Katerinska Cave nearby.

YOU SHOULD KNOW:
Subterranean temperatures are very cold –8 °C (18 °F) , so be prepared.

The Balcarka Cave is in the northern part of the Moravian Karst, which is 100 sq km (62 sq mi) of beautiful, heavily wooded, hilly terrain to the north of Brno, honeycombed with more than a thousand caves. Discovered in the 1920s, this is a two-storey cave, a maze of rambling corridors connected by chimneys and high domes with extraordinarily colourful stalagmites and stalactites. The spectacular effects have been created by the drip of acidic rainwater through limestone, slowly dissolving it. The natural entry portal is an important archaeological site. Bones of Pleistocene animals and tools made of flint and bone from the late Stone Age were found here, but for the visitors who flock to this place the big draw is nature's subterranean decorations on the walls and ceilings.

Unlike the other, better known caves around here, you do not need to buy your ticket in advance for Balcarka. There is a guide to take you through the 'Halls'.

The entry hall leads through an artificial tunnel to a 10 m (33 ft) high circular gorge covered with sparkling sinter cascades. This leads into the biggest hall of the labyrinth, Large Foch's Hall, where the ceiling is decorated with transparent stalactites and sinter curtains. The most beautiful chambers, the Gallery and the Natural Hall follow on from here; the stalactite decorations on the walls and ceilings are very rich and clear.

From here, continue into the Destruction Hall, created by the ceiling collapsing and containing the Madonna Cactus stalactite waterfall, to finally reach the Hall of Discoveries, where the walls are covered in "Nickaminek", a calcic pulpy substance.

Balcarka Cave

Macocha Gorge

This is a wonderful area of Moravian Karst with a multitude of caves, underground streams and dead-end valleys. The karst's best-known features are the Punkva Cave and the Macocha Gorge, located north of the city of Brno, in the Drahanska Highlands. The Macocha Gorge, from the Czech 'Propast Macocha' – literally 'the 'stepmother gorge', is also known as the Macocha Abyss. Part of its beauty is that it is formed by a roof collapse of an underground cave forming a 'light hole' filtering light down into the abyss below.

Macocha Gorge

The history of the name 'stepmother' comes from a 17th century legend of a widower living with his son. On remarrying, his new wife bore him a child, but wishing to be rid of her stepson, she threw him over the abyss. Fortunately he was caught in the branches below and saved by local woodcutters. Hearing the woodcutters' story, the village people of Vilemovice threw the stepmother over the abyss and killed her.

The gorge is a 'doline' or sinkhole, 139 m (455 ft) deep, the deepest of this type in Central Europe. The limestone from which it is formed is 350 – 380 million years old and there are as many as 1,000 caves that have been discovered in this region. These are referred to as the Amateur caves.

This area forms part of the Punkva Natural Reserve and is not open to traffic, but tourists and hikers can see the interiors and the beautiful stalagmites and stalactites of the Punkva caves on the Punkva River, which lead to the bottom of the Macocha gorge. Take a trip on an electric boat on the green waters of the river, through the Macocha caves and the nearby Katerina Cave, with a stop over in the Masaryk chamber.

WHAT IS IT:
Natural limestone gorge.
HOW TO GET THERE:
Flights, trains, buses to Bratislava or Brno then take the E461 to Lipuvka, the 374 to Blansko and on to Vilemovice, which is in the Moravian Karst.
WHEN TO GO:
May to September
NEAREST TOWN:
Brno 40 km (25 mi)
DON'T MISS:
Balcarka Cave
YOU SHOULD KNOW:
In 1805, on a site near Brno, Napoleon, Emperor Francis I of Austria and Tsar Alexander 1 of Russia fought the Battle of Austerlitz, one of the bloodiest battles of the period.

Biebrza National Park

WHAT IS IT?
A Ramsar protected wetland of international importance.
HOW TO GET THERE:
The marshes are a 200 km (125 mi) drive from Warsaw.
WHEN TO GO:
Spring to autumn is best. Winters can be very cold.
NEAREST TOWN:
The small town of Gugny is right in the park.
DON'T MISS:
The primeval forest of Bialowieza National Park, on the border between Poland and Belarus.
YOU SHOULD KNOW:
The wildlife of the marshes also includes mosquitoes and ticks.

The Biebrza marshes in Podlaskie, northeast Poland, are widely considered to be the most unspoilt and valuable expanse of peat bog in Europe. And while the words 'peat' and 'bog' may lack the pizzazz of 'piste' and 'beach', the Biebrza marshes offer a unique opportunity to step into a landscape that is both ancient and largely unchanged. Incredibly peaceful and unpopulated, the marsh and the National Park that surrounds it are home to an incredible wealth of wildlife.

The Biebrza National Park runs southeast to northwest for roughly 90 km (56 mi), from the Biebrza River's confluence with the Narew River up towards Poland's border with Belarus. In total it covers an area of nearly 600 sq km (230 sq mi) and is the largest of Poland's national parks. Often referred to as the region's 'Green Lungs', the park comprises large areas of forest and agricultural land, but it is the 255 sq km (100 sq mi) of wetland – the Biebrza marshes – that form the soggy treasure at its heart.

Biebrza is a mecca for myriad bird species that flock here as soon as spring unlocks the marshes. Over 180 species breed here, including around 20 of the 56 most threatened species in Poland. From eagles to egrets, bitterns to bearded tits, Biebrza is a veritable who's who of the bird world.

As well as its incredible bird life, and enough rare plants to bring out the botanist in anyone, the park also includes some pretty mouthwatering mammals. Among the 48 species that live here are elk, wolf, beaver, otter, fox, pine marten, roe deer and wild boar.

Aside from the wetland's undoubted natural beauty, Biebrza also has a fascinating history due in part to its location in an area where borders have often changed. Scratch the surface and you'll discover influences coming from many different cultures and religions, including picturesque churches, roadside crosses, ancient wooden houses, and even a 19th century Tsar Fortress, preserved at Osowiec.

The Great Masurian Lakes

WHAT IS IT?
A vast area of lakes, marshes and forests in north-eastern Poland.
HOW TO GET THERE:
By road from Warsaw or Gdańsk.
WHEN TO GO:
Summer
NEAREST TOWN:
Elblag 22 km (14 mi)
DON'T MISS:
Augustow forest.

The Great Masurian Lakes in north-eastern Poland are one of the highlights of the region. Known as the land of a thousand lakes, the area encompasses the largest stretch of fresh water in Europe, as well as beautiful forests and hills and extensive farmland. There are 45 major lakes, which are joined by twelve canals and eight rivers, as well as many smaller lakes, in an area that stretches some 290 km (180 mi) east from the Vistula to the border with Lithuania. Roughly 15 per cent of its 52,000 sq km (20,000 sq mi) is water.

The largest lake is Lake Sniardwy which, like the others in the region, is glacial in origin. They are rich in wildlife, and the birdlife here includes black storks, bitterns and herons. At the Lake Luknajo Reserve the largest breeding population of Mute swans, which are rare this far east, can be seen in summer.

Two of the largest remnants of ancient forest – Augustow and Pisz forests – are here. Augustow forest has beavers, bison, boar, elk and wolves. The Pisz forest is strewn with lakes that are dotted with islands, perfect for messing about in boats and birdwatching, while on land there are many trails for walking, hiking and cycling. The lakes are criss-crossed by boats.

In this tranquil, scenic landscape, it is possible to spend hours in peace, drinking in its beauty at your own pace.

Sajno Lake in the Great Masurian Lakes district

Smocza Jarma

Set right in the heart of Kracöw, Poland's ancient royal capital, lies Poland's best known cave: Smocza Jarma – the Dragon's Den. A multi-chamber limestone cavern, it draws nearly a quarter of a million tourists down into its dark, dank depths every year.

Smocza Jarma's appeal, however, derives not from any special subterranean merit, but more from its links with the supernatural. For it is the cave's association with the 'Legend of the Wawel Dragon' that ensures its undying popularity.

As with most legends, this one exists in several versions. But the most popular has it that a long time ago an evil dragon took up residence in the cave on Wawel Hill. For years the fire-breathing beast caused mayhem and murder until a local cobbler came up with a clever plan. He stuffed an animal skin with sulphur, and threw the offering into the cave mouth. Next morning the dragon hungrily gobbled the gift. Soon the sulphur was burning its throat so badly that the doomed beast began to drink the Vistula dry – until eventually its stomach exploded.

During the sixteenth and seventeenth centuries the cave had a second, equally colourful claim to fame, when a house of ill repute was established within it. But for most of the Polish people, the cave will forever be the legendary Dragon's Den.

Today an impressive fire-belching statue of the Wawel Dragon stands at the entrance. From here you descend a dizzying flight of a hundred or more steps into the cave. As you go deeper the air quickly becomes chill and suffused with the damp smell of moist and musty rock.

Although the cave originally had but one entrance, today it has two: the original and another made in the nineteenth century as part of a well excavation. These two points are connected by three large limestone chambers. These extend up to 15 m (50 ft) high and some 276 m (900 ft) in length and take about 20 minutes to explore. There is also a side passage discovered as recently as 1974 that leads underneath the cathedral.

WHAT IS IT?
The best-known cave in Poland.
HOW TO GET THERE:
Fly to Kraków. The cave is in the heart of the city, on Wawel Hill.
WHEN TO GO:
The cave is open 10 am to 5 pm from May to October.
NEAREST TOWN:
Kraków.
DON'T MISS:
The Royal Castle and Wawel Cathedral.
YOU SHOULD KNOW:
In summer it's best to go early to avoid lengthy queues.

Bialowieza Forest

WHAT IS IT:
A vast belt of virgin forest.
HOW TO GET THERE:
Two hour bus ride from Bialystok
in Poland.
WHEN TO GO:
Spring, summer or autumn.
NEAREST TOWN:
Locally in Poland Hajnvka 2 km
(1.25 mi) or Brest in Belarus
70 km (44 mi).
DON'T MISS:
Great Mamamuszi – at 34 m
(112 ft) high with a circumference of
690 cm (22 ft 6 in) at its base, it is
the thickest oak tree in the forest,
with a beautiful column-like trunk.
YOU SHOULD KNOW:
In 1639 King Wladyslaw IV Waza
issued the "Bialowieza Forest
Decree" freeing all peasants living in
the forest, in exchange for their
service as royal hunters.

This enchanting place, the last remnant of the primeval forest which once cloaked Europe from the Atlantic coast to Russia, survives in one of the world's most polluted countries, Belarus, and continues into Poland. Bialowieza shelters hundreds of native bison, a once plentiful species that provided food for prehistoric Europeans, as well as subject matter for primitive cave paintings. The European bison – or wisent – became extinct in the wild 100 years ago, having been hunted almost to extinction by famished soldiers in the First World War. With careful reintroduction they are now flourishing with a population figure of over 1,800.

Elk, wild Tarpan horses and hundreds of varieties of flora and fauna are to be found in this forest. Covering an area of some 126,300 hectares (312,000 acres), it is situated 100 km (62 mi) south east of Bialystok, with the Belarus/Poland border running through it.

For centuries Bialowieza was a private hunting ground for Polish kings, Russian tsars and Belarussian princes, but in the 1920s the Polish Government turned large sections of it into a national park, accessible only on foot or by horse-drawn carriage, in order to protect the wildlife.

The forest's endless depths seem serene and peaceful but the atmosphere will suddenly change as huge trunks of hornbeam, spruce and oak loom up and swell into a dark canopy, pierced here and there by slivers of sunlight. There is a famous thicket of huge oaks, 40 m (131 ft) high, very different from the smaller oaks of England, with many of the trunks having diameters of over 6 m (20 ft).

*Wild garlic covers the forest
floor in Bialowieza Forest.*

The Balkan Mountains

The Balkan Mountains

The Balkan Mountains, or *Stara Planina*, extend some 560 km (350 mi) from eastern Serbia, through northern Bulgaria, to Cape Emin, which lies to the north of Burgas, on the Black Sea. The highest peaks are in the central section, and include Mount Botev, at 2,376 m (7,795 ft), as well as 20 others that pass the 2,000 m (6,600 ft) level. Rivers from the Balkan Mountains mainly flow north to the Danube, or south to the Aegean Sea, and 20 passes and several railway lines cross the range.

The region is notable for its flora and fauna, and includes nine nature reserves, four of which are UNESCO Biosphere reserves. Ancient forests of hornbeam, beech, spruce, fir and durmast cloak the slopes of the Central Balkan National Park, giving shelter to ten species and two sub-species of flora that are endemic. Edelweiss grows here, 256 species of mushroom can be found, and 166 species of medicinal plant. The mountains are full of birds – 224 different species – making the region a magnet for twitchers. The scenery is varied: there are very lovely, high, mountain meadows filled with wild flowers, waterfalls that tumble and splash down almost vertical rock faces, deep, mysterious canyons and exciting caves.

These mountains have been inhabited for centuries and there are several towns enabling the visitor to discover the region's cultural and historical heritage. It is also known for its monasteries, some of which were founded as long ago as the 12th century. Within their walls lie many treasures – icons, frescoes and fabulously carved wooden iconostases. During the 19th century many monks were actively engaged in the national liberation struggle, and many of the monasteries were destroyed and later restored.

WHAT IS IT?
A range of mountains extending from Serbia to the Black Sea.
HOW TO GET THERE:
By road or train.
WHEN TO GO:
July, August and September.
NEAREST TOWN:
There are many towns and villages in these mountains.
DON'T MISS:
The historic monasteries and their treasures.
YOU SHOULD KNOW:
Even during the summer the weather is unpredictable.

The Pirin Mountains

WHAT IS IT?
A smallish mountain range containing glorious Alpine scenery rich with flora and fauna.
HOW TO GET THERE:
By road.
WHEN TO GO:
All year round.
NEAREST TOWN:
Many towns and villages surround the Pirin Mountains, but Bansko, at the entrance to the National Park, has the best tourist facilities.
DON'T MISS:
The spa resort of Sandanski; Melnik.
YOU SHOULD KNOW:
The climate in the Pirin Mountains differs dramatically according to altitude. The high mountains can have snow for eight months of the year, whilst the southern foothills are sub-Mediterranean.

This rugged mountain range in southwest Bulgaria is notable not only for its limestone and granite landscapes, but also for its rich and diverse flora and fauna. Most of the area is a protected National Park, and was listed as a World Heritage Site in 1983. Extending some 60 km (37.5 mi) from northeast to southeast, the range is between 25 km (16 mi) and 40 km (25 mi) wide. Pirin has abundant rivers, and the main ridge forms the watershed between the catchment area of both the Mesta and the Struma Rivers.

The highest peak, Vihren, is 2,914 m (9,616 ft), and a further 60 peaks rise above 2,500 m (8,250 ft). This is a wonderful Alpine landscape of marble and granite mountains, and spectacular glacial lakes situated in deep cirques. The largest and deepest of these is the Popova Lake, but there are about 180 others, all crystal clear and surrounded by snow-caps.

Pirin can be divided into three parts, both geographically and geologically: north, central and south, Alpine, sub-Alpine and tree line, and it is this diversity that has produced such a rich flora and fauna. There are unique stands of ancient pine and fir, and over 1,300 plant species including 18 that are endemic. Several of the 175 vertebrate species breeding in these mountains are rare or endangered. Mammals include Brown bear, Grey wolf, jackal, Pine marten and Rock marten, while birds include Golden eagle, Spotted eagle, Eagle owl and capercaille.

The Pirin Mountains have something for everyone. Trekkers and hikers enjoy the summer beauty, and in winter there are ski resorts and other sporting activities. In southern Pirin, near the Greek border, there are wine tasting trails – the pretty, whitewashed village of Melnik is said to produce the best wine in the country.

Some of the peaks in the Pirin Mountains

Hortobágy National Park

Hortobágy National Park is the largest continuous stretch of grassland in Europe. It is 800 sq km (300 sq mi) of salt marsh, grassland, and wetland around the River Tisza in the Puszta (steppe) of eastern Hungary – a stark, daunting land of fierce winds, extreme temperatures and haunting mirages.

Wetlands in the Hortobágy National Park

The landscape appears to stretch forever, a strangely varied mosaic of vegetation merging into a vast sky, without any sign of human occupation other than the occasional traditional well or shepherd's hut, which may, disconcertingly, appear to be hanging in the sky as a result of the weird visual distortions often experienced here.

Ancient domesticated animals graze freely on the plain – flocks of indigenous Racka sheep, with their threatening V-shaped screw horns; curly-furred Mangalica pigs, descendants of semi-wild Siberian pigs; and huge horned Hungarian grey cattle, water buffalo and Nonius horses. The Nonius horse originated in the Puszta. A fecund young stallion called Nonius, captured from the French during the Napoleonic Wars, was sent here for breeding in 1816. He mated with 368 of the local Hortobágy mares and his progeny are world famous.

Hortobágy is renowned for its birdlife, including the increasingly rare Great Bustard – one of the largest birds in the world, over 1 m (3 ft) tall and weighing in at up to 20 kg (42 lb). The flocks of migrating birds are an incredible sight and sound, particularly wave after wave of tens of thousands of cranes – one of nature's most awe-inspiring ornithological experiences.

What, at first sight, looks like a bare windswept plain is not only one of the most important and diverse bird habitats in Europe – with over 330 species – but also a fascinating pastoral environment. The Puszta sustained a nomadic society of herdsmen for more than two millennia and in Hortobágy you will discover a rich cowboy folk culture with a long tradition of harmonious human and animal interaction.

WHAT IS IT?
A unique birdlife and pastoral region with cowboy culture.
HOW TO GET THERE:
Fly to Debrecen.
WHEN TO GO:
The autumn months are best for birds as well as temperate weather.
NEAREST TOWN:
Debrecen 38 km (24 mi).
DON'T MISS:
Taking one of forty treatments in the medicinal thermal baths of Debrecen. The Déri Museum – richly stocked with treasures from eastern Asia and famous sculptures and paintings as well as local folk art.
YOU SHOULD KNOW:
Puszta translates as "bleak" or "bereft". The Puszta has a fascinating history. It is well worth researching this before you visit to fully appreciate both the landscape and the culture here.

Lake Balaton in the evening light

Lake Balaton

WHAT IS IT?
"The Hungarian Sea" – sports and beach resort.
HOW TO GET THERE:
Fly to Budapest and then take a train or fly direct to Sármélleck Airport, situated at the western end of Lake Balaton.
WHEN TO GO:
June to end August although aficionados enjoy winter holidays there as well.
NEAREST TOWNS:
Keszthely, Tapolca, Balatonfüred, Siofok.
DON'T MISS:
The "stone sea" – extraordinary rock formations at Szentbékkálla; the Lake Cave at Tapolca.
YOU SHOULD KNOW:
Lake Balaton is a major centre for sporting activities, especially sailing, yacht racing, angling, riding and cycling. Every year, for a week in July, artists from all over the world gather to perform traditional music and dance at The Golden Cockle International Folklore Festival in Síofok.

Lake Balaton, 80 km (50 mi) southwest of Budapest, is the largest lake in central Europe. It is 77 km (48 mi) long, has more than 170 km (106 mi) of shoreline, and covers an area of 592 sq km (229 sq mi). Hungary is a landlocked country, and Lake Balaton, with its miles of wonderful beaches, safe swimming, and clean water at a summer temperature of 25 °C (77 °F) , has always served as a superb "seaside" holiday resort. It is surrounded by lovely varied countryside for walking, cycling and bird watching, with towns and villages steeped in history. The lake is in the heart of the wine-growing region, which, for some, adds to its charms.

The southern shore is one long uninterrupted beach with coastal resorts catering for everyone. It is especially suitable for family holidays since the gentle incline of the shore makes it ultra-safe for children to play in the water. To the south west, there are the unique wetlands of Kis-Balaton – a conservation area of marshlands and reed beds, a paradise for nature lovers and bird watchers.

The northern shore, where the water is deeper, is far less developed. Here is Balaton Uplands National Park, a beautiful hilly region of gorges, forests, and meadows, formed by volcanic activity; the 5 km (3 mi) long nature reserve of Tihany peninsula – famous for its beautiful Benedictine abbey and twin-towered church – with its own inner lake and geyser cones; and the town of Badacsony with its extraordinary dormant volcanoes. Balatonfüred is worth a visit for its renowned thermal spas and Hévíz for the largest thermal lake in Europe. To the west, the quaint university town of Keszthely has incredible views.

Balaton is also a popular winter resort, when the surface of the lake freezes and the daring (or foolhardy) skate on it.

Baradla-Domica Caves

The Baradla-Domica Cave system is not only by far the largest but also one of the most beautiful cave systems in Central Europe. It extends for about 21 km (13 mi), crossing under Hungary's north-eastern border with Slovakia, in the heart of the magnificent World Heritage karst landscape of Central Europe, where there are more than 700 caves.

The Baradla is one of the most renowned and researched caves in the world. There is plentiful archaeological evidence that its halls were inhabited by prehistoric man, and in the Middle Ages people used it as a source of rocks, driving carts in to be loaded up. It was first written about in 1549, and the world's first known cave map, based on a 2 km (1¼ mi) section of it, was made in 1794. Tourism and geological research began in earnest in Baradla in the mid-19th century, and, in 1932, it was established that Baradla and Domica were in fact separate entrances to the same cave, with the underground River Styx running between them.

The cave system, which is on three levels, began to form about 2 million years ago. Water started to seep into cracks in the 230 million year-old limestone rock, gradually dissolving it and depositing sediment to create a vast fairyland of underground halls and passages decorated with a staggering display of stalagmite forests and fantastic dripstone figures of all colours, shapes and sizes. The caves contain the world's tallest stalagmite 32.7 m (107 ft), a 13 m (43 ft) long stalactite, an ice abyss, a lake, and two underground rivers. It is also a habitat for 465 different creatures, ranging from unicellular organisms to crabs and bats.

WHAT IS IT?
A subterranean fairyland.
HOW TO GET THERE:
Fly to Budapest. Fast train to Miskolc, 50 km (30 mi) from Aggtelek National Park.
WHEN TO GO:
Any time. Open all year.
NEAREST TOWN:
Miskolc 50 km (30 mi).
DON'T MISS:
Other unique caves in the area – Vass Imre and Béke.
YOU SHOULD KNOW:
The border between the Hungarian and Slovakian sections of the cave is blocked by an underground iron gate. Baradla is the better-known and larger section. However, if you only tour the Baradla, you miss some fantastic sights as well as the experience of a boat ride on the subterranean River Styx, so it is worth crossing the surface border (which is very quick and easy) to enter the cave from Domica as well.

Interior of the Baradla-Domica cave system in the Aggtelek National Park which straddles the border between Hungary and Slovakia.

The Curonian Spit

WHAT IS IT?
"Only sand, sand and the sky" –
Thomas Mann.
HOW TO GET THERE:
Fly to Vilnius, then bus to Klaipéda
and ferry across to Smiltyné.
WHEN TO GO:
Sea climate with a late spring and
long autumn.
NEAREST TOWN:
Nida.
YOU SHOULD KNOW:
The best way of exploring the Spit is
by bike, which can be hired in any of
the villages. It is worth delving into
Curonian Spit's fascinating history to
get the most out of your visit here.

According to Baltic legend, the girl giant Neringa took pity on the fishermen, who were being bullied by the god of storms; she flung an apronful of sand out to sea to create the Curonian Spit and the sheltered fishing waters of the Curonian Lagoon.

This extraordinary 98 km (61 mi) spit, lined with woods and dotted with fishing villages, is at least 5,000 years old, with the highest shifting sand dunes in Europe – up to 60 m (200 ft) tall. It heads northward from Russia's Sambian peninsula, the first 46 km (29 mi) being Russian territory. The remainder is the Lithuanian municipality of Neringa, which meets the mainland port of Klaipéda at its northern tip, separated only by a narrow strait – the exit for the waters of the Curonian Lagoon. The width of the spit varies from just 400 m (0.25 mi) to nearly 4 km (2.5 mi). A single road runs along it passing through nine small fishing communities with traditional blue- and brown-painted timbered and tile houses. Both Russian and Lithuanian parts are National Parks, and the entire spit is a World Heritage Site.

Towards the end of the 19th century, Neringa was discovered by artists, writers and bohemians. Gradually they have taken over from fishermen as mainstays of the communities, renovating the old houses and protecting the landscapes and wildlife. Elks and wild boar live among the pinewoods, and from August to November the skies are filled with wave after wave of hundreds of thousands of migrating birds of more than 200 species.

The Curonian Spit is one of the most curious and charming places in Europe, where you really do feel in harmony with nature as you wander among pine and birch woods by the calm waters of the lagoon or clamber through the emptiness of the massive dunes on the wild Baltic shore.

The shifting sand dunes
of the Curonian Spit

Butrint National Park

With the Ionian Sea at its western extreme and the Greek border to the south, Butrint National Park is a remarkable area in south-western Albania. Not only does it contain a unique wetland ecosystem and a wealth of diverse habitats, but also the ruins of the ancient city of Buthrotum. Within the park's boundaries, the ancient city and part of the surrounding area of lakes, including the southern part of Lake Butrint, is a UNESCO World Heritage Site, while the surrounding wetlands are protected under the Ramsar Convention.

The landscape is outstanding and very varied. The woods consist mainly of oak, elm, ash, white poplar and laurel, and on the Ksamili Peninsula and islands there are areas of typical Mediterranean maquis. Of the 90 plant species recorded here, 32 are listed in the Albanian Red Data book. The wetlands, however, are the dominant feature, with brackish lagoons, salt and fresh water marshes, reed beds, rivers, channels and a rocky shoreline. These unspoilt habitats support large numbers of birds, some of which are threatened, and 105 species of fish for which the lagoons are an important spawning ground, nursery and migration route to the sea. Butrint is particularly known for its reptiles and amphibians, including the Epirote frog and the Balkan sand lizard, and holds the highest number of species recorded on any Albanian site.

The main human activities here are fishing and mussel farming, as well as some agriculture. At present, most of the tourism is concerned with the main archaeological site, which has been occupied since the 8th century BC, and is elegantly situated by the placid, blue waters of the Vivari Channel and Lake Butrint. However, plans are afoot to develop the eco-tourism potential of the wetlands, as well as to encourage wintertime twitchers.

Butrint National Park

WHAT IS IT?
A national park containing wetlands of global importance as well as the site of the ancient city of Buthrotum.
HOW TO GET THERE:
By road, or by ferry from the Greek island of Corfu.
WHEN TO GO:
During the summer months, although winter is the best time for bird watching.
NEAREST TOWN:
Saranda 19 km (12 mi)
DON'T MISS:
The archaeological site of Buthrotum.
YOU SHOULD KNOW:
The ruins at Butrothum date from the Bronze Age, continuing through the Greek, Roman, Byzantine, Venetian and Turkish eras to the 18th/19th century.

Transylvanian Alps

WHAT IS IT?
Count Dracula's stamping ground.
HOW TO GET THERE:
Fly to Bucharest.
WHEN TO GO:
May to October (unless you are going specifically for winter sports). Winters are extremely cold.
NEAREST TOWNS:
Brasov, Zarnesti, Sibiu, Petrosani.
DON'T MISS:
Sighisoara, a World Heritage Site – an atmospheric medieval town with breathtaking battlements and spires.
YOU SHOULD KNOW:
The word "Transylvania" is derived from Latin *trans silva*, meaning "across the forest".

The legendary land of the vampires is surrounded by rugged mountains, of which the highest and wildest are the Transylvanian Alps – the barrier between Transylvania and southern Romania. They are over 2,000 m (6,560 ft) high, with peaks rising to more than 2,500 m (8,200 ft), and are the most remote and impressive range of the 1,500 km (900 mi) arc made by the Carpathian Mountains of Central Europe.

The Transylvanian Alps are one of the last remaining undeveloped regions of Europe, extending for 360 km (230 mi) westwards from the Prahova River to the River Timis. The mountains slope gently down to Transylvania in a romantic idyll of flowering meadow valleys and bubbling streams, overlooked by fairytale castles (including Brad – Count Dracula's family seat);

sheep graze contentedly and medieval wooden villages nestle in the hills. In stark contrast, the wild south-facing slopes are jagged limestone escarpments, incised with ravines and covered with menacing pine forests in which bears, lynx and wolves still prowl.

From the Prahova valley, you can climb the weathered rocks of the Bucegi massif, where wild animals roam, eagles soar above you, and the only other people are local shepherds. The astoundingly beautiful Piatra Craiului – a razor-like limestone ridge – has a precarious 18-km- (11-mi-) long path that leads through a dramatic landscape of pitted slopes, scarred with caves and gorges, into the heart of the mountains, the Fagaras massif and Mount Moldoveanu, the highest mountain at 2,544 m (8,344 ft). To the west of Fagaras is the breathtaking landscape of Retezat National Park, where the terrain has been transformed by glaciation into massive peaks, glacial lakes, rivers and primeval forest.

The joy of exploring the Transylvanian Alps is their aura of remoteness, the incredible scenic contrasts and the sensation of time-warping into the Middle Ages.

The Danube Delta

The Danube Delta is the largest continuous marshland in Europe, a huge wilderness of utterly isolated waters with expansive skies and almost unpopulated landscapes. Shared between Romania and Ukraine, the delta formed where the waters of the Danube flow into the Black Sea. Reeds, which create floating or fixed islands, dominate its marsh vegetation.

Classified into twelve different habitats, ranging from lakes to wet meadows to forests on slightly higher ground, the area was declared a Natural World Heritage Site in 1991 and is internationally significant for birds, both breeding and migratory. Over 300 species of birds have been recorded here, among them cormorants, pelicans, herons, storks, swans, falcons and harriers.

The floating islands are also one of the last refuges of the European mink, wildcat, freshwater otter and stoat not to mention the huge variety of freshwater fish found here including sturgeon. Permission is needed to visit specific nature reserves, which are closed during the bird-breeding season.

The scattered small villages around the delta are also fascinating and timeless microcosms in themselves. Home to a variety of peoples – Ukrainian, Russian, Lipovan, Bulgarian, Moldovan, Turkish and Gagauz – these fishing and farming communities have changed very little from former times.

A pelican colony in the Danube Delta

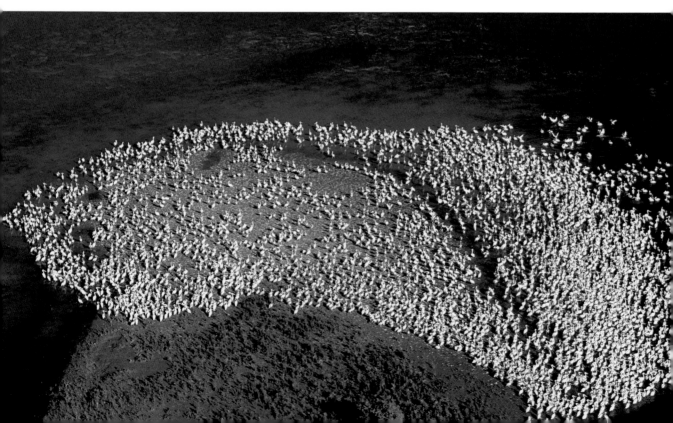

Dobsiná Ice Cave

Dobsiná, a karst formation between seven and nine thousand years old, is one of the most significant ice caves in the world. It is situated in the Slovensky Raj (Slovak Paradise) National Park, a beautiful region of eastern Slovakia.

The cave was officially discovered in 1870 by Eugene Ruffini, opened to the public just one year later, and, in 1887, was the first show cave to be lit by electricity. In fact, it had been known to the locals for generations as the Studená Diera (Cold Hole). In the 18th century some dragon's bones were found there, causing a great stir. It turned out that the bones belonged to a bear, but the myth of the cave as a dragon's lair persisted for many years.

Dobsiná is 1,388 m long (4,550 ft), with 475 m (1,560 ft) open to the public. Its north facing entrance is at an altitude of 970 m (3,180 ft), from where the cave descends straight downwards. This ensures that the interior remains a constant 0 °C to -1 °C (32 °F to 30 °F), whatever the external temperature – warm summer air cannot flow downwards, and in winter, the freezing north wind prevents air escaping upwards.

At the entrance, you are immediately startled by a cold blast. The icy passage walls are smooth to the touch and, in the course of your descent into the cave, you pass by a stunning array of frozen stalactites, stalagmites and waterfalls.

The largest chamber is the 120 m (395 ft) long Big Hall, with a 12 m (40 ft) high ceiling, a floor covered in ice, 26.5 m (87 ft) thick, and walls dripping with extraordinary ice formations. In places, the floor is smooth enough to have been used as a popular skating rink. In the spring, a shimmering layer of frost crystals makes the entire ceiling sparkle like a fairy palace.

Dobsiná Ice Cave in eastern Slovakia was included in the UNESCO List of World Natural Heritage Sites in 2000.

WHAT IS IT?
One of the largest ice caves in Europe.
HOW TO GET THERE:
Fly to Poprad. Regular buses from Poprad to Dobsiná cave entrance.
WHEN TO GO:
Open May to September.
NEAREST TOWN:
Dobsiná.
DON'T MISS:
The spectacular Spis Castle, the largest gothic castle in Central Europe, a World Heritage Site 50 km (30 mi) to the east.
YOU SHOULD KNOW:
Dobsiná Cave is estimated to hold 110,000 cu m (3,884,100 cu ft) of ice.

Ochtinská Aragonite Cave

WHAT IS IT?
Incredibly rare subterranean phenomenon.
HOW TO GET THERE:
Fly to Kosice. Then by road to Roznava.
WHEN TO GO:
April to October.
NEAREST TOWN:
Roznava 20 km (12 mi).
DON'T MISS:
Zadielska Dolina, a breathtaking karst canyon 26 km (16 mi) east of Roznava.
YOU SHOULD KNOW:
Aragonite forms naturally in almost all mollusc shells and coral skeletons. Mother of pearl is built up from alternate super-thin layers of aragonite and organic matter. These layers split the light so that it is reflected back with an iridescent rainbow sheen.

Of the thousands of caves in Slovakia, twelve of which are open to the public, the Ochtiná Cave is recognized as being incomparable. It exemplifies an incredibly rare phenomenon – the creation of aragonite. It is one of only three publicly accessible aragonite caves in the entire world (the others are in Mexico and Argentina). This World Heritage Site, discovered by chance during a geological survey in 1954, but not opened to the public until 1972, is situated in the karst limestone region of Slovensky Kras near Roznava in southern Slovakia.

Aragonite, like limestone, is basically chalk (calcite), although it looks entirely different. Its structure is so unstable that its delicate crystals can only form, without immediately collapsing, under very precise conditions of temperature and pressure. At certain combinations of high pressure and low temperature in an enclosed space – the sort of conditions that may occasionally be found underground – a magical chemical transformation takes place and ordinary looking limestone sediment, instead of forming stalactites and stalagmites, metamorphoses into delicate aragonite twigs and flowers.

In Ochtiná, there is a staggering amount and variety of aragonite ornamentation in three distinct formations – kidney-shaped clusters, needles and spirals – in a medley of colours, ranging from bluish-white to dark red.

The most beautiful of the many attractions is the Milky Way Hall – named after the clusters of pure white aragonite that have formed an incredible sparkling trail along the ceiling, shining like stars. Although only 300 m (980 ft) long, with 230 m (755 ft) open for viewing, the sublime natural beauty of Ochtiná is overwhelming. It is an extraordinary wonder of nature.

Vysoké Tatry (High Tatras)

Although they only stretch for 26 km (16 mi), the Vysoké Tatry rival any mountain range in Europe for their challenging terrain, stark beauty and breathtaking views – a perfect version of the Alps in miniature. They rise in the eastern part of Tatras National Park, which covers 750 sq km (290 sq mi) of the border area between Slovakia and Poland, and are the only mountains of a truly alpine character in Slovakia. They are the highest and northernmost mountains of the 1,500 km (900 mi) long Carpathians that curve round Central Europe from Austria to Romania.

There are eleven narrow jagged peaks of more than 2,500 m (8,200 ft), with Gerlachovsky Stit at 2,655 m (8,710 ft) being the highest point in the whole of the Carpathians. Successive glaciations over tens of thousands of years have carved out a breathtaking granite landscape of deep rounded valleys, exquisite mountain lakes, waterfalls and dramatic 1,000 m (3,280 ft) tall cliffs that soar straight up, seemingly out of nowhere, from the completely flat terrain of the Liptov Plain.

The climate of the Vysoké Tatry is unique. The mountains impede the movement of Central European air masses, which makes for extreme temperatures ranging from -40 °C (-40 °F) in winter to 33 °C (91 °F) in summer. The weather is exceptionally volatile, with sudden dramatic changes in conditions – the possibility of sudden summer snowfalls adds an extra thrill to climbing here.

There is a rich variety of flora and fauna, including bears and wolves, and there are 600 km (375 mi) of well-maintained trails leading through all the valleys and to the summits of ten of the mountains. The high mountain character of the Vysoké Tatry combined with their accessibility makes them the perfect place for skiing, hiking and climbing enthusiasts.

WHAT IS IT?
The "smallest big mountain range in the world".
HOW TO GET THERE:
Fly to Poprad or to Bratislava (4 hours by car or train to Poprad).
WHEN TO GO:
All year depending on activity.
NEAREST TOWN:
Poprad 25 km (16 mi)
DON'T MISS:
Eating halusky, a traditional dish of pasta with sheep's cheese and bacon. Seeing Belianska Cave with its eight species of bat.
YOU SHOULD KNOW:
There are no trails up Gerlachovsky Stit and it must be climbed with the help of a guide.

High Tatras Mountains – the Alps in miniature

A small town perches on the shores of Lake Ohrid.

Lake Ohrid

This is the oldest lake in Europe, with a natural ecosystem so rare, it's often called a 'museum of living species'. Three million year-old Lake Ohrid is so deep – 288 m (945 ft) – that it survived the Ice Age, along with many of the creatures in its waters. Ten of its 17 fish species exist nowhere else in the world – and one of them is the Koran (Ohrid trout), a fabled delicacy since Roman times, and a fish whose meat is red during the winter, and white in the summer. Its future, and the future of the lake as a World Natural Heritage Site, depends on the ability of Albania and Macedonia, who share the 88 km (55 mi) shoreline, to co-ordinate their efforts to maintain the long-term ecological stability of its 358 sq km (138 sq mi).

Lake Ohrid is a mountain lake set at 693 m (2,273 ft). This height, plus the microclimate driven by its exceptional depth, and position close to the Mediterranean, makes its reed beds and wetland areas, and every other kind of habitat among its rocky coves, beaches, and cliff sections, very special for both endemic and migratory species. Lake Ohrid's crystal clear water – you can see to a depth of over 20 m (66 ft) – rises in giant springs on the south shore at the foot of a 2,265 m (7,429 ft) mountain, part of a thickly forested Macedonian National Park containing bears, wolves, and wild boar. The water originates in neighbouring Lake Prespa, 153 m (502 ft) higher (and also shared between Albania and Macedonia), and is purified during its underground limestone transit. But Ohrid is drained by just one river, the Drin, which empties into the Adriatic 110 km (69 mi) away, and its enormous depths take 70 years to exchange. Now that precarious eco-stability is threatened – by a relatively massive increase (from 50,000 to 170,000 in 20 years) in the shoreline population; by largely uncontrolled tourism; and by the diversion, in 1963, of the River Sateska into the lake. The Sateska alone has dumped huge quantities of silt, and tonnes of rubbish and toxic waste, into the fragile ecosystem that attracts tourism, and supports the local fishing economy.

Around Pogradec, a lovely and ancient resort on the Albanian lakeshore, close to the border where Macedonia's National Park begins, you can see both the necessity for a coherent biodiversity conservation programme, and – everywhere – the signs of transborder co-operation, as Albanians and Macedonians demonstrate a willingness to ignore borders and work in tandem to preserve their truly precious lake, for all of us to enjoy.

WHAT IS IT?
Europe's oldest lake, and the only one to survive the Ice Age.
HOW TO GET THERE:
By air to Tirana, Albania, then taxi/taxi-van/bus to Pogradec.
WHEN TO GO:
April to October.
NEAREST TOWN:
Pogradec, on the lake shore, close to some of Ohrid's most beautiful and varied scenery.
DON'T MISS:
The 4th century BC monuments engraved in the rocks at the village of Selca e Poshteme (believed to be the ancient Pelion, seat of King Klit).
YOU SHOULD KNOW:
The Albanian Adriatic is Shakespeare's Illyria, a byword for natural beauty.

Skocjan Caves

The Skocjan Caves are the most famous site in the world for the study of karst (water-soluble rock) phenomena. The Reka River runs through the limestone terrain of Kras, in southwest Slovenia, disappearing underground for 34 km (21 mi). Over thousands of years, the river has dissolved the surrounding rock to create a magical subterranean world of thundering waterfalls, still lakes and turbulent rivers in a fantastical setting of multicoloured stalactites, stone curtains, dramatic sinkholes, collapsed dolines (valleys) and natural bridges.

The sheer scale of the Skocjan caves is overwhelming. It is a huge labyrinth of eleven interconnected caves, some more than 200 m (655 ft) deep. There are 6 km (4 mi) of cave passages, with an immense hall 146 m (480 ft) high and a vast subterranean gorge 2.6 km (1½ mi) long and over 100 m (330 ft) high. There are 25 underground cascades, including a waterfall 163 m (535 ft) high. Among the many incredible sights are the Paradise Hall, draped with exquisite coloured stalagmites and stalactites, and the Organ Hall, with its spectacular dripstone formations.

The caves are in a protected area of 413 ha (1,020 acres) and are a habitat for the cave salamander (*Proteus anguinus*), endemic beetles, crabs, and huge breeding colonies of bats. The River Reka has extremely variable water depths. After heavy rain, the sight and sound of the booming, turbulent water as it is sucked underground from the valleys of Mala Dolina and Velika Dolina can be quite terrifying.

The incredible variety of the formations here have been documented since ancient times and are a constant source of fascination for geologists – the karst here is known as "original" or "classical" and is the paradigm for karst phenomena everywhere. Skocjan is a true wonder of the world.

The Skocjan cave system is one of the largest in Europe and has many underground canyons, 5 km (3 mi) of underground passageways and many waterfalls.

WHAT IS IT?
A fantastical labyrinth of interconnected caves.
HOW TO GET THERE:
By road – Ljubljana-Koper Highway, exit to Divaia. By train – from Ljubljana to Divaia. From station follow signed path, 35 minutes walk to Skocjan.
WHEN TO GO:
Anytime, but for a dramatic experience avoid high summer when the river is at its lowest.
NEAREST TOWN:
Divaia 3 km (2 mi)

DON'T MISS:
Exploring the archaeological sites in the village of Skocjan, which was once a fort.
YOU SHOULD KNOW:
The technical word karst used by geologists everywhere to describe this kind of limestone scenery is a corruption of Kras – the region where karst phenomena were first investigated. Similarly, the word doline – the geological word for a steep sided, flat bottomed depression – is the Slovenian word for "valley", taken from Mala Dolina (Small Valley) and Velika Dolina (Big Valley) where the River Rika goes underground.

Mount Triglav & The Julian Alps

WHAT IS IT?
Outstandingly beautiful mountain scenery for winter and summer sports and outdoors adventure.
HOW TO GET THERE:
Fly to Ljubljana
WHEN TO GO:
All year. Excellent snow sports in the winter season.
NEAREST TOWNS:
Bled, Tolmin, Kobarid, Bohinjska, Bostrika, Kranjska Gora
DON'T MISS:
The Triglav Lakes Valley, a high mountain valley to the south west of Triglav, also known as The Sea of Stone, with ten lakes surrounded by dramatic karst (limestone) scenery.
YOU SHOULD KNOW:
Although it is possible to hike to the top of Mt Triglav in one day, the more scenic routes take two or three, staying in huts on the way.

This little known region of northwest Slovenia, named after the Julian dynasty of Roman emperors, is a fairytale land of romantic castles and medieval villages set in a spectacular landscape of soaring peaks and deep gorges, with thundering waterfalls, clear rivers and mountain lakes. The rugged white limestone mountains rise up out of thick forests and wildflower meadows that, in winter, are transformed into a snowbound wonderland. The Julian Alps extend over an area of 4,400 sq km (1,700 sq mi) creating a natural land barrier between Italy and Slovenia.

The colossal Mt Triglav stands between the rivers Soca and Sava in the middle of Triglav National Park. It has the highest summit in the Julian Alps at 2,864 m (9,394 ft), with panoramic views over the exquisite alpine valleys that spread out like a fan below. Just below the summit is the Triglav glacier, where there is a chasm of ice more than 280 m (920 ft) deep. The north face is a difficult and dangerous climb for experienced mountaineers but there are also trekking routes to the summit for the amateur. From the top, you can see all the way from Austria to the Adriatic Sea. Mount Triglav is an important symbol of national identity, and its outline appears on the Slovenian flag and the 50-cent euro coin.

There are two famous lakes on the edge of Triglav National Park – the sublime Lake Bled, with its legendary castle and island church, and, high in the mountains, the unspoilt Lake Bohinj, renowned for its intense dark blue water. It is the largest lake in Slovenia, 3.3 sq km (1.3 sq mi), surrounded by beautiful scenery, with the 60 m (200 ft) tall Savica waterfall crashing down in the forest nearby.

Morning sun on Mount Triglav

Carpathian Mountains

Always remote, and never touched by mass tourism, the Carpathian Mountains of southwest Ukraine are a treasury of European natural resources. Between Poland, Slovakia and Romania, they form a corridor 280 km (175 mi) long and roughly 100 km (62 mi) across, in which one of Europe's oldest landscapes stands intact as nature intended, a sanctuary for many of its rarest species, and guardian of a huge proportion of endemic flora and fauna. They are famously beautiful: the rounded peaks and wide ridges of their central spine are covered with sub-alpine and alpine meadows called *polonyny*, for millennia the summer grazing grounds of nomadic herders. Between and below them are the spruce and fir forests, crowding the rocky spurs of countless ravines, where mountain torrents have carved their path either side of this European watershed. Lower down, beech fills the steep valley slopes, along with extremely rare Carpathian cedars and berry yew trees that are 4,000 years old (there is a 206 hectare (509 acre) reserve for them near Kolomyia), as well as maple, oak, mountain elm, hornbeam, and others that have disappeared elsewhere in the Carpathians. At every level, rarity in abundance is the hallmark of the hundreds of flower species that mark the seasons; just as the presence of lynx, wolf, bear, bison, elk, salamander, and a host of rare birds like grey herons, indicates the pristine state of this region of the mountains.

The Ukrainian Carpathians' tranquil joys are typified by the Chornohora massif round the small town of Yaremche, south of Ivano-Frankivsk. Between Yaremche and Mt. Hoverla, at 2,061 m (6,760 ft) the highest in Ukraine, you can sample the very finest from top to bottom: alpine flora in the *polonyny*, the tranquility of the forests, the Prut river crashing out of the mountain into the Yaremche canyon, and the series of cascades leading to the 80 m (262 ft) Probiy falls. There are dozens of other equally beautiful places in the region – and dozens of astonishing cave systems, panoramas, bizarre rock formations, and particular wonders. The one that really impresses visitors is that the very few people who live in the region are as friendly and hospitable as their fairy-tale wilderness home is spectacular.

The white flowers of the Carpathian bellflower (Campanula carpatica)

WHAT IS IT?
A remote section of virgin mountain range, where natural beauty and rarity of species are the norm.
HOW TO GET THERE:
By air/train to Ivano-Frankivsk or Chernovtsi; then bus/car.
WHEN TO GO:
April to October.
NEAREST TOWN:
Kolomyia (E), Khust (W)
DON'T MISS:
Narcissus Valley in the Khust massif – 80 hectares carpeted with wild narcissi.
YOU SHOULD KNOW:
'Brynza' is the very strong cheese made in the *polonyny* by the Hutsul nomad shepherds, to while away their summer vigils.

337

Mount Etna towers over the town of Taormina.

Mount Etna

Mount Etna's looming presence can be felt over a large area of north-eastern Sicily. It is more than 30 km (19 mi) across the base, and 3,323 m (10,900 ft) high. There is usually some geothermal activity somewhere on the mountain, and more major events happen every few weeks or months. The structure of the volcano is complex, and eruptions are not confined to the main crater. Unlike many volcanoes, Etna produces more than one type of eruption – in some, lava flows quickly down the sides of the mountain while in others it spits out gas and launches gobbets of magma high into the air, making particularly spectacular displays at night. The ancient Greeks ascribed its activity to monsters and giants imprisoned under the mountain by Zeus, while the Romans thought it might be Vulcan's workshop.

Eruptions from the multiple vents on the mountain's flanks have created numerous smaller peaks and valleys, such as Monte Spagnolo and Monte Gallo: these are delightful places to hike. Protected from development, the wooded slopes can be explored along a maze of nature trails and are home to wild cats, porcupines, a variety of reptiles and golden eagles. In winter, is is a paradise for skiers.

Because of the ever-present danger of volcanic activity almost anywhere on the mountain's higher slopes, climbing to the summit is forbidden. During eruptions, or if the network of seismometers that sense the mountain's every breath indicates that activity is imminent, roads and paths will be subject to closures, especially downwind.

Despite the risks that Etna poses to the people who live around its base, this beautiful mountain and its stunning scenery are well worth a visit.

WHAT IS IT?
Europe's largest active volcano.
HOW TO GET THERE:
By road or rail from Catánia.
WHEN TO GO:
Any time of year.
NEAREST TOWN:
Piedimonte Etneo
DON'T MISS:
The view at night during an eruption.
YOU SHOULD KNOW:
Roads and paths on the mountain are subject to closures during eruptions.

Vesuvius

Probably the best-known volcano in the world, Mount Vesuvius towers over the Bay of Naples. The view from its summit is magnificent – on a clear day, the whole of the Bay of Naples spreads before you, from Sorrento to Ischia.

Vesuvius is most famous for the eruption of 79 AD, which caused the total destruction of the towns of Pompeii and Herculaneum. It has erupted more than 50 times since then, most recently in 1944, and is one of the most dangerous volcanoes in the world. Although there is no indication that it will erupt in the immediate future, it is inevitable that one day it will wreak havoc again.

The volcano is around 13,000 years old and countless eruptions have given the summit a distinctive "humpbacked" shape of a cone within a cone. The present summit is 1,282 m (4,202 ft) high and is almost completely encircled by the steep rim of a caldera at 1,133 m (3,716 ft), created out of the earlier collapse of a much higher summit.

Apart from the lava scars running down its sides, the mountain is green and fertile, its lower slopes covered in vineyards. The surrounding area is a National Park with a network of paths, as well as a road that takes you to within 200 m (650 ft) of the summit.

You can explore historic Pompeii – a town frozen in time. The buildings and inhabitants were perfectly preserved under 10 m (30 ft) of lava, buried and forgotten for nearly 1,600 years. The town was uncovered again during rebuilding work after a devastating eruption in 1631, but it was not until 1748 that archaeologists started to excavate it systematically.

Today, more than 3 million people live in the immediate vicinity of Vesuvius – a cause of great concern.

WHAT IS IT?
Probably the world's best known active volcano.
HOW TO GET THERE:
By train/bus/taxi from Naples.
WHEN TO GO:
At its best between April and June.
NEAREST TOWN:
Naples 9 km (5.6 mi)
DON'T MISS:
Herculaneum, less well known but just as, if not even more, interesting than Pompeii.
YOU SHOULD KNOW:
It is estimated that, at times during the 79 AD eruption, the ash column from the top of Vesuvius shot 32 km (20 mi) into the stratosphere and 4 cubic km (1 cubic mi) of lava was emitted over a period of 19 hours.

Mount Vesuvius and Naples at dawn

Lake Garda

The Italian lakes are renowned for their sublime beauty, and Lake Garda is the star. It is the largest lake in Italy, 370 sq km (143 sq mi) and 346 m (1,135 ft) deep, with spectacularly blue water and landscapes full of contrast and colour. It lies in an alpine region, halfway between Venice and Milan, in a moraine valley formed by glaciation from the last ice age. It has an exceptionally mild microclimate that supports year round green vegetation. The Lake acts as a giant solar panel and the heat is prevented from escaping by the surrounding mountains.

From its northern tip, for about two thirds of its length, Lake Garda is a narrow fjord, enclosed by mountains and dominated by the verdant ridge of Monte Baldo, 2,078 m (6,815 ft) high, on its eastern shore. Steep limestone escarpments, covered in woods and pasture, sweep down to the edges of the lake. Winding roads and paths snake their way through isolated villages, past castles and ancient churches perched perilously on the rocky slopes.

Towards the south, it feels much more Mediterranean. The lake suddenly opens out, widening to 17 km (11 mi) across and the landscape is transformed into gently rolling hills with citrus trees, vines, oleander and bougainvillea. The ancient town of Sirmione juts out on a peninsula at the southern edge, with its quaint cobblestone streets, fairytale 13th century castle and thermal springs. There are Roman remains here including the villa of the love poet, Catullus.

The Brescia Riviera on the western shore is a well-known holiday hideout for the wealthy and Lake Garda is one of the top resorts in Europe for sailing and windsurfing.

Charybdis

The island of Sicily is separated from the Calabrian coast of Southern Italy by the treacherous waters of the Strait of Messina – the Scylla and Charybdis of Greek legend.

This 32 km (20 mi) long strait connecting the Ionian Sea to the Tyrrhenian Sea is only about 90 m (295 ft) deep but its turbulent water has such strong currents that they rip the seaweed off the ocean bed. Two opposing currents switch direction every six hours creating a whirlpool of complex wave patterns – this is Charybdis, the voracious daughter of Poseidon and Gaia, who lives under a giant fig tree on a mythical rock in the strait. Four times a day, she swallows the water and spits it out again.

The sea monster Scylla hides in a cave in the rugged Calabrian cliffs making terrible howling noises. She has twelve legs and six snake-necked heads with three rows of teeth in each. The Strait is only just over 3 km (1.9 mi) wide at its narrowest point so, in Odysseus's attempt to avoid both Scylla and Charybdis, he was "caught between a rock and a hard place".

The mirage of Fata Morgana adds to the mythical aura of Messina. A layer of cold air becomes trapped below warm air, making images on the horizon appear elongated, spiky and elevated. The buildings on the opposite shore are transformed into fairy palaces emerging from the waters of the strait.

The history of Messina is a tragic one – from plague and cholera epidemics to earthquakes and war. The earthquake of 1908 flattened the city, and Allied bombing raids of 1942 destroyed it again. There are plans to build a suspension bridge across the Strait of Messina so that travellers will no longer have to face the choice between Scylla and Charybdis.

Cape Peloro and the Strait of Messina

The Blue Grotto

The Blue Grotto

The southern Italian isle of Capri, beloved of the emperors Augustus and Tiberius, lies off the Sorrentine Peninsula at the south of the Bay of Naples. It is predominantly made of limestone and this soft rock has allowed the sea to carve numerous sea caves into its cliffs. The most famous of these is the Blue Grotto, on the south coast, which the emperors supposedly used as a private bath. Once under the low entrance to the cave, visitors are surrounded by blue light that fades as the cave recedes away into the darkness. But where does the eerie blue light come from? It is, in fact, sunlight getting into the cave though another, submerged, entrance and being reflected off the white limestone and sand on the cave's floor, so lighting the water from underneath. If the entrance to the cave were higher, sunlight would get in that way, too, and drown out the magical blue glow.

Depending on the height of the waves, guides on the boat trips, that are the only way to get into the cave, may ask visitors to lie down in the boat to avoid bumping their heads. If you shut your eyes on the way through the entrance, the effect of the blue around you as you open them is even more startling.

WHAT IS IT?
A remarkable accident of nature.
HOW TO GET THERE:
By boat from Naples or Sorrento to Capri's Marina Grande, then a local boat trip.
WHEN TO GO:
Summer.
NEAREST TOWN:
Capri town 3 km (2 mi)
YOU SHOULD KNOW:
The guides sometimes sing in the caves.

343

Stromboli

Stromboli is the summit of a volcanic mountain sticking 926 m (2,950 ft) out of the Tyrrhenian Sea. The rest of it is submerged to a depth of 1,500 m (5,000 ft). It is the most remote of the Aeolian Islands, a volcanic archipelago off the northern coast of Sicily, about 50 km (30 mi) from the Italian mainland.

"The Lighthouse of the Mediterranean" is one of the most active volcanoes on the planet – it has been in a state of more or less constant eruption for the past 2,000 years. The volcano stands alone in the middle of the sea, emitting a constant plume of steam from its cone. At night, there is the awesome spectacle of its flame shooting into the sky, like a giant firework.

Constant minor explosions throw incandescent blobs of lava over the crater rim several times an hour, and the term "Strombolian eruption" is used to describe this sort of volcanic activity anywhere.

Amazingly, this tiny island, only 12.6 sq km (5 sq mi), is inhabited by about 500 people, who live philosophically in the shadow of the volcano in two villages and several tiny hamlets perched on its slopes. The views from the upper slopes are stunning – rugged cliffs tower above the black sand beaches and you gaze across a clear blue sea dotted with islands.

Throughout Stromboli's long history, large eruptions and lava flows have been rare. There was one in 2002 for the first time in 17 years, which created the Sciara di Fuoco (Slope of Fire), a horseshoe-shaped crater, and caused two landslides and several tsunami waves up to 10 m (33 ft) high. In February 2007, two new craters opened, with lava flowing into the sea from one of them. Since then, Stromboli has been under extra surveillance.

Steam rises where lava flows into the sea on Stromboli.

Marmolada

The massive ridge of Marmolada dominates the Val di Fassa, a fairy-tale land of flower-filled meadows, lakes and spiked mountain peaks in the eastern Alps of Northern Italy. "The Queen of The Dolomites" rises up from the Fedaia Pass to its summit of 3,344 m (10,972 ft) at Punta Penìa, towering over its neighbours, which themselves are some of the region's most impressive mountains.

Marmolada runs east to west with five separate peaks and the only large glacier in the Dolomites – the most extensive ice formation in the whole of the eastern Alps. In both winter and summer, it is a superb natural playground for sports enthusiasts. Along its south face, there is a wall of sheer cliffs several kilometers long – an irresistible challenge for climbers. The gentle glaciated slope of the north side, still snow-covered long after it has melted elsewhere, is famous for the freedom of off-piste skiing. The countless ridges and passes are ideal terrain for mountain cycling and the outstandingly beautiful countryside and sublime landscape views make it a joy for para-gliders and hill walkers.

The group of mountains around the Val di Fassa are geologically complex. Unusually, the dolomite rock, from which the mountains get their name, is interspersed with volcanic lava ridges. The black rock of the lava stands out in striking contrast to the white dolomite and the bluish sheen of the glacier to create a uniquely fascinating landscape. At sunset, the phenomenon of *enrosadira* suffuses the mountains so that the entire landscape is lit up with a magical rose-tinted hue.

The Italian Dolomites and the Serauta peak from the summit of the Marmolada.

WHAT IS IT?
A five-peaked mountain and glacier in the Dolomites.
HOW TO GET THERE:
Fly to Bolzano, Verona, Venice, Milan. Rail/road to Bolzano or Ora, 37 km (23 mi) or 45 km (28 mi) from Val di Fassa.
WHEN TO GO:
Time of year depends on your interests.
NEAREST TOWN:
Canezei (and villages Alba and Penìa) in Val di Fassa
DON'T MISS:
A trip to Lake Misurina.
YOU SHOULD KNOW:
Marmolada was the scene of fierce fighting between Austria and Italy in the First World War with a huge number of casualties. There is a war museum and memorial and you can explore the remains of the "City of Ice", an extraordinary labyrinth of tunnels built by the Austrians, where war artefacts are still regularly unearthed.

345

Plitvice Lakes National Park

The Plitvice Lakes

In the heart of the forbidding forests of Croatia's Dinaric Mountains – marked on old maps as "The Devil's Garden" – there is an enchanting valley. Here is one of the most outstanding natural wonders in Europe – the Plitvice Lakes.

These are sixteen interconnected naturally terraced lakes. At each terrace, water gushes out through hundreds of holes in the porous wall as well as spilling over the lip, cascading into the lake below in never-ending streams of sparkling clear water. The exquisite colours of the lakes – azures, blues and greens – are constantly changing according to the sunlight and the quantity of mineral deposit in the water.

The terraces are made from travertine – a weird rock-like substance composed of limestone sediment (deposited by the mountain streams) mixed with algae and mosses. The travertine builds up in layers around the vegetation, petrifying it and creating bizarre shapes as it hardens. At Plitvice, the travertine has built up so thickly it has formed natural dams, which have led to the creation of the lakes.

The lakes are in two separate clusters, extending over 8 km (5 mi), and covering an area of 2 sq km (¾ sq mi). The upper part of the valley contains twelve lakes, ending in Veliki Slap (Big Waterfall), a dramatic waterfall that spills over a sharp drop into a sheer canyon 70 m (230 ft) below. This canyon contains four more lakes, which finally become the River Korana.

The beauty of the lakes is breathtaking at any time of year. The forest is blanketed in snow in winter and has long hot Mediterranean summers. It supports an exceptional diversity of plants and wildlife, harbouring deer, wild boars, wolves and bears. It is reputed to be the most beautiful spot in Europe and is a World Heritage Site.

WHAT IS IT?
A group of 16 interconnected lakes.
HOW TO GET THERE:
Fly to Zagreb. Road from Zagreb to Dalmatia 140 km (88 mi).
WHEN TO GO:
Anytime.
NEAREST TOWN:
Slunj 35 km (22 mi).
DON'T MISS:
Barac's Caves 6 km (4 mi) east of Rakovika near the village of Nova Krslja.
YOU SHOULD KNOW:
The forest around the Plitvice Lakes was a central theatre in the Croatian War of Independence. Soldiers from both sides took up positions in the caves and mined the forest. One of the first priorities of the new government was to clear the Lakes and surrounding woods of unexploded munitions.

The Blue Cave

Bisevo is one of the thousands of limestone islands that are strewn the length of Croatia's Dalmatian coastline. It is tiny, at less than 6 sq km (2.5 sq mi) in area, it is a rocky outcrop that supports a small population. Like many other islands in the area, it has sea caves, which can be visited by boat. The most famous of these is the Blue Cave (*Modra spilja*) in Balun Cove.

Originally, the only way to enter the cave was by diving through the undersea entrance but more than 100 years ago, an artificial entrance was added to allow boats to enter. The light is at its best in early July and early September, between 11 am and noon. Bright, sunny, calm days are the best; the colour will not be so intense under overcast skies or when the water is rough.

The effect is created by sunlight entering the cave through an underwater entrance and being reflected by the white floor up through the 20 m (66 ft) of water and creating a glorious blue colour through scattering the blue part of the spectrum. Whatever the reason for the effect, it is magical and well worth a trip.

WHAT IS IT?
A sea cave filled with unearthly blue light.
HOW TO GET THERE:
By boat, from Split or Hvar to Vis, then a boat trip.
WHEN TO GO:
It is at its best in early July and early September.
NEAREST TOWN:
Komiza, Vis 5 km (3 mi)
YOU SHOULD KNOW:
Because so many boats visit the cave, swimming is no longer allowed.

Visitors enter the famous Blue Cave

Dalmatian Coast

WHAT IS IT?
Magnificent and varied concordant coastline and popular holiday destination.
HOW TO GET THERE:
Fly to Zagreb. Domestic flight to Split or Dubrovnik, or high-speed train to Split. Jadrolinija coastal ferry plies the waters between Dubrovnik and Rijeka.
WHEN TO GO:
April to October.
NEAREST TOWNS:
Rijeka, Zadar, Split, Dubrovnik.
DON'T MISS:
Dubrovnik, described by Byron as "the pearl of the Adriatic". The island of Mjlet's two interconnected salt-water lakes, Malo Jezero and Veliko Jezero, and 12th century Benedictine Monastery.

The rugged Dalmatian coastline is an exquisite stretch of more than 1,780 km (1,100 mi) of intricate coves, channels and inlets, fringed by a complex network of more than a thousand islands. It runs along the eastern shores of the Adriatic Sea, from the island of Rab in the northwest to the Gulf of Kotor in the southeast, with a hinterland that is only 50 km (30 mi) at its widest point.

There are hundreds of glorious unspoilt beaches, seven national parks and some of the most beautiful medieval towns and villages in Europe. From space, the Adriatic is the bluest patch of sea on the planet.

Each island has a unique charm of its own. The stark white karst (limestone) cliffs of the barren "Robinson Crusoe" Kornati islands stand out in spectacular contrast to the cobalt blue seas. Krapanj, famous for its sponges, is a peaceful haven for a secluded holiday. Hvar is the place for celebrity spotting, and the beach of Brac is renowned among surfers. The green, hilly island of Korkula was Marco Polo's birthplace, and the beautiful forests of Mjlet are a National Park.

The extraordinary geological complexity of the Dalmatian coastline is the result of "concordance". Where two bands of rock run parallel to the coast, the outer band may be harder than the inner. The surface of the hard outer rock cracks at weak spots, allowing water to seep in, which dissolves the softer rock from the inside. Inlets, and coves with characteristic narrow entrances are formed, and islands break away from the mainland.

A boat near Dugi Otok on the Dalmatian coast

named "Destination of the Year" by National Geographic magazine, and the Dalmatian Coast has a growing reputation as "the New Riviera". With its balmy Mediterranean climate, magical beauty and fascinating history, one can see why.

Marble Cave

When you enter the Mermerna Pecina (Marble Cave), you will encounter an incredibly rare and beautiful phenomenon – the metamorphosis of limestone to marble. Fluctuations in underground temperature and pressure transform the basic structure of the limestone. Its crystals are forced into different arrangements, changing into aragonite, and eventually, marble. This process is happening in front of your eyes in the Marble Cave. You are in a magical realm of coloured marble, bizarre aragonite crystals and speleothems ("cave ornaments" – such as stalactites and stalagmites).

The entrance to the cave was discovered in 1966 by Ahmet Diti while he was building an extension to his house in the village of Donje Gadimlje. It was full of silt and was not opened to the public for another ten years. Much of it remains unexplored and there are entire passages, still choked up with mud and gravel, waiting to be discovered.

So far, a total length of 1,260 m (4,130 ft) has been uncovered, and 440 m (1,440 ft) is open to the public. There are four separate sections: The Entrance and the Western, Northern and Eastern Galleries. The ceilings are covered in stalactites and there are massive pillars, up to 5 m (16 ft) high, which are ornamented with weird spikes. The variety of speleothems is astounding, especially in the Northern Gallery, where the ceiling is covered in stalactites that look like organ pipes, draped with almost transparent sheets of limestone, in folds like curtains. The various rock forms are in a spectrum of colours from white aragonite crystal to deep red. You can only gaze and marvel at the amazing processes that are continually at work deep underground.

WHAT IS IT?
A karst limestone cave, much of it still unexplored.
HOW TO GET THERE:
From Belgrade 360 km (225 mi)
From Skopje 65 km (41 mi)
WHEN TO GO:
April to October (closed outside these months).
NEAREST TOWN:
Pristina 20 km (12 mi)

Durmitor National Park

Durmitor National Park & Tara Canyon

The Tara River flows through a spectacular canyon 1,300 m (4,260 ft) deep – the second deepest in the world after the Grand Canyon of Arizona. The river current is unbelievably fast and there are 21 rapids, some of them dangerous. The canyon cuts a path 80 km (50 mi) long through the scenic meadows and forests of Durmitor National Park in northwest Montenegro.

The Park is a 390 sq km (150 sq mi) World Heritage Site of breathtaking beauty, shaped by the effects of glaciation. It is a rugged plateau of forests and meadows, incised with gorges and underground rivers, overlooked by permanently snow-capped mountains with lakes, streams and bubbling springs. It is bordered by canyons on three sides, with the wondrous Durmitor massif, 2,552 m (8,370 ft) high, towering up as though to touch the sky.

The 18 glacial lakes – known as Gorske Oci (Mountain Eyes) – are an outstanding feature of the landscape. Nowhere else in the world are there so many in such a compact area. The most famous is Crno (Black) Lake at an altitude of 1,416 m (4,644 ft). It is fed by mountain streams, which in summer become a waterfall, and is in fact two lakes interconnected by a narrow channel. Crno nestles in a dense conifer forest, which causes the reflection from the water to be an intense dark blue-green colour.

The Montenegrin mixed Mediterranean and Continental climate makes Durmitor a rich habitat for over 1,300 plant species and the dense forests still harbour brown bears, wolves, lynx and jackals. The mountains are renowned for the superb skiing and variety of slopes to climb, while few white water rafters can resist the challenge of the Tara River Canyon.

WHAT IS IT?
Natural landscape, river, lakes and the second deepest canyon in the world.
HOW TO GET THERE:
Fly (or train from Belgrade) to Podgorica, then by road to Zabljak.
WHEN TO GO:
December to March for skiing. May to September for summer season.
NEAREST TOWN:
Zabljak.
DON'T MISS:
A trip to the coast to visit the World Heritage Site of Kotor on the Boka Kotorska fjord.
YOU SHOULD KNOW:
Montenegro gets its name (Black Mountain) from the dark mountain forests that cover most of it. It gained its independence from Serbia in July 2006.

Garajonay National Park

This national park and UNESCO World Heritage Site in the middle of La Gomera forms a marked contrast to anywhere else in the Canary Islands. Set on the volcanic peaks of the same name, it is a lush escape from the nightlife of the other islands. About 70 per cent of its 40 sq km (15.4 sq mi) is covered in laurisilva (with laurel-like leaves) forest, sustained by numerous springs, streams and the humid fog that frequently visits the heights of La Gomera. This forest is a remnant of the subtropical rainforest that covered large swathes of southern Europe millions of years ago but died out during the ice ages. There are also cedar woods, and Azores laurel, Canary holly and Canary willow. The evergreen trees are cloaked in moss, and often shrouded in the fog brought by the Atlantic trade winds. As you explore the park, you will climb up and down hillsides and cross streams on little wooden bridges. It is necessary to keep an eye on where you are putting your feet, but don't forget to look around you at the woodlands and the occasional glimpses of more distant views. As you near the top, you will see the area of Los Roques and eventually will see Teide, on neighbouring Tenerife, in the distance.

This unusual, and beautiful park is well worth a day trip from the other islands in the group.

WHAT IS IT?
A reserve guarding one of the oldest ecosystems in Europe
HOW TO GET THERE:
By plane to La Gomera airport or ferry, then by road and on foot.
WHEN TO GO:
Any time of year.
NEAREST TOWN:
San Sebastian de la Gomera
12 km (7.5 mi)
YOU SHOULD KNOW:
The road up to the park is vertiginous.

Curving trees in Garajonay National Park on the island of La Gomera

351

Picos de Europa National Park

A massive national park located in the Cordilla Cantabrica and shared between the provinces of Cantabria, Asturias and Léon, the Picos de Europa (Peaks of Europe) is also a UNESCO Biosphere Reserve because of the importance of its wildlife. Among the rare species that live here are brown bears, wolves, capercaillies and lammergeier, while buzzards, choughs and the mountain deer known locally as rebeccos are more common.

The limestone rocks of the area have been shaped by the action of glaciers and rivers, creating a typical limestone karst landscape with some of Spain's deepest cave systems, of which new ones are continually being discovered.

The narrow gorge carved by the River Cares between two of the mountain ranges in the park is a draw for many visitors because it can be reached via the aerial tramway between Fuente Dé and the village of Caín. The river itself has been canalized, but the pathway alongside offers views of its 1.5-km (1 mi) depths.

The area is extremely popular with climbers as the varied landscape offers pitches of different levels of difficulty. One of the most spectacular formations is the Naranjo de Bulnes in the central massif, which offers 500-m (1,550-ft) multi-pitch climbs.

WHAT IS IT?
A huge national park set in a stunning landscape.
HOW TO GET THERE:
By road from Santander or Oviedo.
WHEN TO GO:
Spring to autumn.
NEAREST TOWN:
San Vicente de la Barquers 20 km (12 mi)
DON'T MISS:
The chance to spot brown bears.

Lake Ercina in the Picos de Europa National Park

Sierra Nevada National Park

WHAT IS IT?
A national park in the far south of Spain.
HOW TO GET THERE:
By road from Granada or Almería.
WHEN TO GO:
Any time of year.
NEAREST TOWN:
Orjiva (3 km, 2 mi)
DON'T MISS:
The O Sel Ling Tibetan Monastery.
YOU SHOULD KNOW:
Bring sunscreen, even in winter.

In southern Andalucia, within just a few kilometres of the Costa del Sol, lies the second highest mountain range in Europe, the Sierra Nevada. Two of Spain's highest mountains – Mulhacén at 3,482 m (11,420 ft) and La Veleta at 3,394 m (11,140 ft) are to be found here. Surprisingly for somewhere this far south, the mountains can be snow-covered and the weather icy-cold from November to April. High in the mountains, visitors will find glacial lakes, alpine meadows and scree slopes, which give way lower down to pine forests, cut by waterfalls and deep gorges, woodlands of oak, sweet chestnut and maple, scrub and then the fertile lands of the Alpujarras in the south.

Because of the sierra's isolation from other similar high mountain ranges, a large proportion of its plants are species or subspecies that occur nowhere else.

The area is a draw for birdwatchers: birds that breed here include Bonelli's and golden eagles, peregrine falcons and griffon vultures. Hoopoes, green woodpeckers and golden orioles inhabit the woodland on the lower slopes while in the higher areas red-billed choughs, alpine accentors and rock thrushes can be seen and the song of skylarks is everywhere. The Spanish ibex is ubiquitous higher up, while in the woods below wild cats, boars, badgers and beech martens may be found.

Mulhacén itself takes a couple of days to scale, but lower down a network of footpaths and tracks criss-crosses the area allowing access for the walkers, trekkers, horse-riders and mountain bikers who are drawn to explore this beautiful area.

The peaks of Alcazaba and Mulhacén in the Sierra Nevada mountains

Fuerteventura's interior

The desert-like scenery of Fuerteventura's interior

Like the other islands in the Canary group, Fuerteventura is volcanic. However, it is so old – perhaps 30 to 35 million years old – that its volcanic rocks have been weathered smooth over much of the island, exposing the sedimentary rocks on which the volcano was built. Away from the resorts, the island is peaceful and can be explored by the paths than run round the coast, or by 4 wheel drive to reach the interior or the wild areas in the south. While many volcanoes are quickly colonized by plants, Fuerteventura's interior is so dry that there is little plantlife, except lichens, and there are few animals, except small reptiles like the Haria lizard and the East Canary Gecko, which has the ability to change colour like a chamaeleon.

The landscape of Fuerteventura is a mixture of eroded pumice, rocky grounds and lava flows – the volcano is dormant, not extinct and there have been minor eruptions in recent times, geologically speaking. Hiking across it reveals a strange lunar landscape of rocks that look as if they have been sandpapered. In summer, when the rocks are warmer, they turn redder.

The highest point is Jandia's Pico de la Zarza at 807 m (2,647 ft) in the southern part of the island. A climb to the peak gives rewarding views over the beautiful landscape, but it is tough going because of the wind that almost always blows across the island and it can be hazardous if the mist forms.

WHAT IS IT?
The oldest island in the Canaries.
HOW TO GET THERE:
By plane or ferry to Puerto del Rosario.
WHEN TO GO:
Any time of year.
NEAREST TOWN:
Puerto del Rosario.
YOU SHOULD KNOW:
Fuerteventura means strong wind.

Sierra Madrona and the Valle de Alcudia

WHAT IS IT?
A beautiful mountain range and valley.
HOW TO GET THERE:
By road from Córdoba.
WHEN TO GO:
Spring to autumn.
NEAREST TOWN:
Puertollano 20 km (12 mi)

An Iberian lynx
(Lynx pardinus)

Part of the Sierra Morena, the mountain range that divides Andalucía from the Castilian plateau, the Sierra Madrona is an important refuge for the Iberian lynx and wolves. The scenery is beautiful, rather than awe-inspiring – the highest peak in the range is Bañuleas at 1,324 m (4,340 ft). The slopes are covered with unspoiled forests of oak, holm oak and cork oak – with some large specimens thought to be at least 100 years old – punctuated by deep gullies and waterfalls. There are also numerous strawberry trees (*Urbutus unedo* or *madroño*), which the range is named after, and olive groves. The valley to the north, the Valle de Alcudia, is the landscape through which Miguel de Cervantes' hero, Don Quixote, journied. A huge forest carpets the valley's sides, while in early summer the floor is covered with fields of scarlet poppies. This landscape, widely acknowledged to be among the most beautiful of this part of inland Spain, offers plenty of tracks and trails for walkers, long-distance hikers, horse-riders and mountain bikers, as well as climbing in the mountains themselves. The region's rivers and lakes are popular for kayaking and the area is also known for its thermal springs. This area has been inhabited for thousands of years and among the attractions here are palaeolithic remains at the lovely Retamar Lake and several cave-painting sites.

Monfragüe National Park

Not far from the Portuguese border, Monfragüe is a lovely area of woodland, pastures and scattered cork and holm oaks – this landscape is known locally as *dehesa* – and higher, craggy peaks, set around a vast reservoir, the Embalse de Torregon. It covers some 170 sq km (65 sq mi) and is one of the natural highlights of Spain. As well as being an area of outstanding beauty, it is a UNESCO Biosphere Reserve. Mammals here include wild cats, Iberian lynx, wild boar, otters and red, roe and fallow deer. But it is the birds of prey that make Monfragüe special. Not only does it have the largest breeding colony of the extremely rare Black vultures, with upwards of 200 pairs, but it has ten pairs of Spanish Imperial eagles. Two other species of vulture, four other species of eagles and three kites also breed here. Large numbers of wildfowl also nest here by the rivers and the reservoir. The rarest bird in the park, however, is the Black stork, which constructs its nest high in the crown of trees. The best spot to see the nesting vultures and storks is the canyon near the Pena Falcon cliff.

Even those who are not natural birdwatchers will not fail to be enthralled by this beautiful park.

WHAT IS IT?
A beautiful area of landscape with rich wildlife.
HOW TO GET THERE:
By road from Salamanca.
WHEN TO GO:
April to October.
NEAREST TOWN:
Plasencia 20 km (12 mi)
DON'T MISS:
The birds of prey.

The River Tajo flows between jagged peaks in Monfragüe

Cabañeros National Park

WHAT IS IT?
A national park in central Spain.
HOW TO GET THERE:
By road from Toledo or Ciudad Real.
WHEN TO GO:
Spring or autumn.
NEAREST TOWN;
Retuerta del Bullaque 7 km (4.5 mi)
YOU SHOULD KNOW:
Visits to the central reserve must
be pre-booked.

Perched in the Montes de Toledo southwest of the city of the same name, this national park covers 390 sq km (150 sq mi) of low hills, mountains and woodlands. The species that live here are perfectly adapted to a harsh existence on poor soils and with extremes of weather, ranging from freezing cold with howling winds in winter to baking hot in summer. Trees here include stands of the prickly-leaved holm oak, as well as cork oak, which are interspersed with Mediterranean scrub and lush pastures.

The area is important for wildlife, with a large number of species that occur nowhere else in the world, and offering a protected area for the second largest breeding colony of black vultures in the world, griffon vultures, black and black-shouldered kites, black and white storks, golden and imperial eagles, Montagu's harriers and eagle owls, which feed on the smaller animals supported by this diverse landscape. Smaller birds that can be seen in spring and summer include rollers and brightly coloured bee-eaters. You are far more likely to hear a hoopoe's characteristic oop-oop call than you are to see one of these shy and surprisingly well-camouflaged birds. Among the 45 mammal species seen here are wild boar, red and roe deer and the extremely rare Iberian lynx. The outer parts of the park are open access, but trips to the main reserve must be pre-booked: it can be visited on guided tours either on foot or in a jeep.

The meadows of Rana de Santiago and the Sierra del Chorito range in Cabañeros National Park

The Rock of Gibraltar

Probably the most famous rock in the world, the Rock of Gibraltar rises 426 m (1,396 ft) from sea level to tower over the narrow body of water that separates Europe from north Africa, namely the Strait of Gibraltar. In mythology, Hercules pulled Spain and Africa apart, and from time immemorial, the two mountains on either side of the Strait, the Rock and Djebel Moussa, have been known as the Pillars of Hercules.

In reality, the Rock is a monolithic limestone promontory, linked to Spain by a narrow, sandy isthmus. Formed by the collision of European and African tectonic plates, a subsequent shift enabled the Atlantic Ocean to break through, creating the Mediterranean Sea. The location of the Rock is of extreme strategic importance: transferred to Britain by the Treaty of Utrecht, in 1713, it has, since then, played a major part in the protection of the Mediterranean seaways during times of war.

Covering some 6.5 sq km (2.5 sq mi), the eastern side is formed by almost sheer cliffs, with sandy beaches at the base. The western side is a much gentler slope, the lower half being the city, while the upper half is a nature reserve, home to some 250 Barbary macaques (more often known as apes) that are the only wild monkeys in Europe.

The range of flora and fauna on the Rock is surprisingly rich and includes endemic species such as Gibraltar thyme, candytuft and chickweed. As well as the macaques, there is the endemic Barbary partridge, and as it is on the migration route, this is a great place for twitchers. Sea mammals such as dolphins, Pilot whales, orcas and even Sperm whales can be seen here too – for such a tiny, infertile territory, Gibraltar is of considerable interest.

The Rock of Gibraltar

WHAT IS IT?
A monolithic rock that stands at the meeting point of the Mediterranean and the Atlantic.

HOW TO GET THERE:
By air, by sea or by road from Spain.

WHEN TO GO:
The climate is pleasant throughout the year.

NEAREST TOWN:
Gibraltar, on the Rock itself.

DON'T MISS:
Europa Point Lighthouse; Nelson's Anchorage; the Moorish Castle; St. Michael's Caves.

YOU SHOULD KNOW:
The interior of the Rock is an enormous and famous labyrinth of fortified tunnels, built to defend the Rock against invaders.

WHAT IS IT?
The remnants of a volcano.
HOW TO GET THERE:
By boat from the Greek mainland or other Greek islands or by plane from Athens or Thessaloniki.
WHEN TO GO:
Spring to autumn.
NEAREST TOWN:
Heraklion, Crete 123 km (76 mi)
DON'T MISS:
The excavations at Akrotiri.

Santorini

Rising from the blue waters of the Sea of Crete in the eastern Mediterranean, the picture-postcard multicoloured cliffs of Santorini (Thera, or Thira) belie their cataclysmic past. As your boat or plane approaches the island, it is a sobering thought that the circular bay was once the heart of a volcano. In around 1650 BC, a massive eruption emptied the chamber below the volcano of magma with such speed and force that the entire mountain collapsed into the void left behind. It is estimated that 30 cubic km (7 cubic mi) of magma must have been thrown out to create a bay this size. The traces of previous eruptions can be seen in the coloured bands of rock on the island's cliffs: each one is a layer of compressed ash ejected in one eruption. The little island in the middle of the bay is evidence of more recent volcanic activity, where a new volcano has formed in the heart of the old one.

It has long been thought that the eruption of Thera could be connected with Plato's legend of the lost island of Atlantis, even though his land was located in the Atlantic Ocean. Evidence now suggests that he may have been relating a tale, corrupted over more than 1,200 years, of the destruction of the Minoan civilization on Crete by a tsunami created when the mountain collapsed.

Whether the eruption of Santorini was the basis of the legend or not, this is a beautiful island with spectacular scenery.

The island of Santorini at sunset

Loggerhead Turtles, Zakynthos

Of the eight species of sea turtle swimming the oceans today, the Loggerhead (*Caretta caretta*) is the largest. Recognizable by its big head, reddish-brown shell and yellow underside, an average Loggerhead weighs more than 100 kg (220 lbs) and is 120 cm (4 ft) in length. Greece is the only country within Europe where these turtles nest, and the sandy beaches of Laganas Bay, on the island of Zakynthos, host the largest nesting colony of this endangered species.

Little is known about the life of sea turtles, particularly the males. We do know that they live for about 60 years, reaching reproductive age at about 30, and that Loggerheads make the longest migration journeys of all sea turtle species. Their strong jaws can easily crush their food – largely shellfish or jellyfish. Nesting females can be tagged to provide information about migration routes, but males never leave the sea.

At night, between June and August, the female Loggerheads drag themselves up the beach to lay some 200 eggs in nests of 40 – 60 cm (1ft 4 ins – 2 ft) deep, which they cover with warm sand. This process is repeated three or four times each season. About eight weeks later, the eggs hatch, and the hatchlings scrabble up through the sand and dash to the sea. After this their lives are unknown until, some 30 years later, the females return to the same beach to reproduce.

In 1999 a National Marine Park was established in southern Zakynthos to protect about 6 km (4 mi) of separate, sandy beaches where about 900 turtles come to nest each year. Sadly, by 2004, the management body had ceased to function, and so many violations of the protection laws were occurring that the European Commission began legal action against the Greek authorities, who appear to feel that tourism is more important than protecting these desperately important breeding sites.

Loggerhead turtle hatchlings heading for the sea.

WHAT IS IT?
The only European nesting grounds of the Loggerhead turtle.
HOW TO GET THERE:
By plane or boat to the island, then by car.
WHEN TO GO:
Between June and October for the Loggerhead's reproductive season.
NEAREST TOWN:
Keri.
DON'T MISS:
The Blue Caves on the Skinari Cape; the Venetian Castle in Bohali; the Monastery of St George at Gremna; the Strofadia islands 35 km (22 mi) south of Zakynthos.
YOU SHOULD KNOW:
Many restrictions apply to the protected areas, which include boating and water sports within the sea itself.

*Mount Olympus in
northern Greece*

Mount Olympus

Steeped in ancient history, Mt Olympus is the highest mountain in Greece. Once home to the appallingly behaved principal ancient Greek gods, this is where Zeus stood to fling thunderbolts at anyone who displeased him. The archaeological museum at Dion is where Alexander the Great made sacrifices to the Olympian gods before setting off to conquer lands as far away as India. The lower slopes of the mountain have a rich variety of plants: more than 1,700 species have been identified here. It became Greece's first national park in 1937 and is especially rich in wildflowers in late spring. The sides of the mountain are cloaked in forests of beech, cedar, oak and pine, in which bears, lynx and wolves roam.

In ancient times, it was forbidden for humans to set foot on this mountain but the restriction was lifted centuries ago. The highest of the eight peaks, Mytikas (or nose) was first reached in 1913 by the local Christos Kakalos and Swiss mountaineers Frederic Boissonas and Daniel Baud-Bovy.

The hike from Litochoro at sea level up this 2,919-m (9,570-ft) giant and back takes most people two days. There are many trails up the mountain and refuges to stay at overnight, although you may need to book in summer.

The climb is not difficult in itself, but the mountain can be hazardous in bad weather. The beautiful scenery and stunning views make the effort worthwhile.

The Samaria Gorge

The Samaria Gorge

The Samaria Gorge is a spectacular geological feature in western Crete that is also important in the island's history. It is Crete's only national park. This gash in the White Mountains drops 1,250 m (4,100 ft) in 16 km (10 mi). For thousands of years, its secret tracks have provided a last hiding place, and secret base, for the locals to go when invaders strike. Today, its well trodden, if still tricky, path is a must-do for visitors to the island.

Most people get the bus from Chania to Omalos at the top of the gorge and then pick up a boat ride at Agia Roumeli to return to Chania. The first section of the trail is a steep descent of 1,000 m (3,300 ft) in less than 2 km (1 mi), down a feature known as the Wooden Stairs. The other 14 km (9 mi) is a relatively easy descent of 250 m (800 ft), and it is much easier to appreciate the spectacular scenery and wild flowers. The old village of Samaria, half-way down the gorge, is also a good place to catch your breath and take in the delightful views, before making the final descent towards the Iron Gates, where the sides of the gorge narrow dramatically to leave a passage a mere 3 m (10 ft) across.

Late spring, when the wild flowers are at their best, is the best time to undertake this hike: the gorge is not opened until the river has stopped flowing and in the height of summer, the heat in the gorge can be stifling. For this reason, an early start is a good idea, so that you spend as little of the four to seven hours the descent takes in the heat of the day.

WHAT IS IT?
A spectacular 16-km (10-mi) gorge in the west of Crete.
HOW TO GET THERE:
By bus from Chania to Omalos.
WHEN TO GO:
Late spring,
NEAREST TOWN:
Omalos
DON'T MISS:
The views.
YOU SHOULD KNOW:
It is advisable to take plenty of water and a snack or two.

367

*Snow covered Mount Ararat –
said to be the site of the
landfall of Noah's Ark.*

Mount Ararat

Lying in the far east of Anatolia, Mount Ararat (Agri Dagi) is worth taking the trouble to visit, both for its beauty and its importance in the Bible, as it is the site where the Book of Genesis says that Noah's Ark came to rest after the great flood. The higher of this volcano's two peaks, Buyuk Agri, is the highest in Turkey, at 5,137 m (16,854 ft). Mount Ararat is not extinct, merely dormant: the last eruption was in 1840.

In 2004 the area around and including Mount Ararat was designated as the Kackar Mountains National Park, but access to the mountain is by permit only for foreign visitors because this is a politically sensitive area. Permits must be applied for at least two months before a proposed visit through a registered tourist agency that operates treks. However, reaching the summit of the mountain makes all the hassle worth while. The views from the snow-covered peak – across to Iran and Armenia and west across the plain – are spectacular.

Climbs leave from the village of Eli, at the foot of the south-west flank of the volcano and normally take five to six days for the ascent and descent. The climb is strenuous and the top part of the mountain is permanently covered in snow and ice, and it is not for the inexperienced!

WHAT IS IT?
A spectacular dormant volcano in eastern Turkey.
HOW TO GET THERE:
By air to Van, then by road.
WHEN TO GO:
The climbing season is from June to September.
NEAREST TOWN:
Doguveyazit 10 km (6 mi)
DON'T MISS:
The views from the summit.
YOU SHOULD KNOW:
Cloud tends to gather in the afternoon, so the final summit should be attempted in the morning.

Göreme National Park

In the heart of Cappadocia, Göreme National Park has one of the strangest landscapes on earth. Over millions of years, volcanoes in the area covered the land with thick layers of soft tuff stone, which were then covered with layers of lava that hardened and sealed the top. Eventually, water broke through and the soft rock below became subject to weathering, and wind, snow and rain have carved it into conical pillars, towers and needles of varying colours and heights of up to 40–50 m (130–165 ft). The volcanic plain once covered some 10,000 sq km (3,850 sq mi) of landscape and the park now protects the central 95 sq km (37 sq mi). The soft rock is also easily carved by humans and over the centuries many of the pillars, the so-called fairy chimneys, have been turned into homes or churches, and the latter are famous for their Byzantine murals.

Away from the villages, the landscape is best explored on foot or by bicycle. A popular walk is the 12-km (7.5-mi) circuitous path to Üçhisar through the Uzundere Valley. The valleys are dominated by the volcanoes that produced the landscape, such as Erciyas Dag and Hasan Dag.

Up in the hills of this spectacular valley, wolves and beech martens can sometimes be spotted, and badgers, foxes and hares also inhabit the park.

Although it is expensive, a popular way to get a grasp on the whole landscape – and to get amazing photographs – is to take one of the many balloon trips on offer. Drifting over this weird landscape on a clear, still morning is a magical experience.

WHAT IS IT?
A strange eroded landscape.
HOW TO GET THERE:
By road from Kayseri
WHEN TO GO:
Spring to autumn.
NEAREST TOWN:
Üçhisar (3 km, 2 mi)
DON'T MISS:
A balloon ride over the area.
YOU SHOULD KNOW:
Although the volcanoes are now extinct, earth tremors can occur.

The strange landscape near Göreme is formed by the erosion of volcanic tuff. Some of these pinnacles were carved out to provide troglodyte dwellings.

Demirkazik

WHAT IS IT?
The highest peak in the Taurus Mountains.
HOW TO GET THERE:
By road from Adana or Kayseri.
WHEN TO GO:
July to September.
NEAREST TOWN:
Demirkazik village.

Demirkazik, at 3,756 m (12,323 ft) is the highest peak in the Taurus Mountains, which run along 560 km (350 mi) of southern Turkey's south-east coast. This portion of the chain is known locally as Aladaglar, the crimson mountains. There are various well-known climbing routes on the mountain. The first successful ascent was made in 1927, but the dangerous north wall was not conquered until 1991. The climb to the peak is for experienced climbers only, but there are other easier routes on the lower slopes.

The Taurus Mountains are young, geologically speaking, and are still in the process of being raised as the African plate moves north, squeezing the Anatolian plate into the Eurasian plate in the north and grinding it past in the east.

Demirkazik dominates the eastern end of the Aladaglar National Park and the valley below, and it is hard to turn your eyes away. For those who are not climbers, there is a beautiful landscape to see in the region, including the pine forests, karst rock formations, pretty waterfalls, underground streams and some of the largest caves in the country and the beautiful Yedigoller, (Seven Lakes Valley). Wildlife here includes bears, lynx, wild goats and sables, although the latter, like most martens, are notoriously shy and hard to find.

The Taurus Mountains in southern Turkey

Karapinar Crater Lakes

An aerial view of volcanic Meke Gölü

The area around Karapinar in south-central Anatolia is an ancient volcanic landscape, dotted with cinder cones, lava fields and craters. There are numerous lakes within the craters in the area and two of the best known are Aci Gölü (bitter lake) and Meke Gölü (smelling lake). The former is beautiful, and at night sparkles with light, while the latter is blue-green and salty. In this dry area, they are both important sources of water for birds.

The caldera in which Meke Gölü sits was created millions of years ago in an eruption so massive that it caused the top of the volcano to collapse, while the eruption that caused the 300-m (1,000-ft) cinder cone in the middle is much more recent, occurring about 9,000 years ago. The caldera is about 4 km (2.5 mi) in circumference and up to 12 m (40 ft) deep in places.

Everywhere you go in Turkey, you will see blue glass beads called *Nazar Boncugu* that ward off the evil eye and Meke Gölü is said to be the country's own version.

In a geologically active land, prone to earthquakes, people have long been aware of their surroundings: a wall painting at nearby Çatalhöyük showing a volcanic eruption has been dated to about 6200 BC.

Although off the beaten track, these beautiful lakes are well worth a detour.

WHAT IS IT?
Lakes in ancient volcanic craters.
HOW TO GET THERE:
By road from Könya
WHEN TO GO:
Summer
NEAREST TOWN:
Karapinar 10 km (6 mi)
DON'T MISS:
A swim in the waters of Aci Gölü.

371

Nemrut Dagi

WHAT IS IT?
An extinct volcano in eastern Turkey.
HOW TO GET THERE:
By air to Van, then by road or by train to Tatvan.
WHEN TO GO:
Summer
NEAREST TOWN:
Tatvan 15 km (9 mi)
DON'T MISS:
The views over Lake Van.

Nemrut Dagi, a volcano at the western end of Lake Van, is named after Nimrod, the mighty hunter who, according to legend ruled here in ancient times. It is now 3,050 m (10,000 ft) high, having lost its top 1,400 m (4,600 ft) in an eruption some 6,000 years ago. The lava blocked the river running round its base and led to the creation of Lake Van. The volcano's caldera, which is an oval is roughly 7 by 8 km (4.3 by 5 mi). Two craters, evidence of more recent, if smaller, eruptions, have lakes within them.

The views from the crater rim over Lake Van are amazing. Once into the crater, you will find a different, and totally unexpected, world: in contrast to the arid slopes of the mountain, there is vegetation including juniper, aspen and beech. The crater lakes provide a stopping-off point for a variety of birds.

The larger, crescent-shaped lake – Sogukgöl – is cold, except for some hot springs towards the middle of the caldera, while the waters of the smaller – Sicakgöl – are warm, indicating that the rocks below are still hot, although whether this is because of continuing volcanic activity deep down or residual heat is not clear. It is an ideal place for a swim after a dusty climb.

A panoramic view from the summit of Nemrut Dagi

The Chimaera

To the ancient Greeks, the Chimaera was a fire-breathing monster with the head and front paws of a lion, the body of a goat and the tail of a serpent, and this name long ago attached itself to this astonishing site, where flames spontaneously ignite as gas emerges from fissures in the bare rocks.

The Chimaera is a stiff 30-minute walk up a steep, and in places slippery, path from the car park north of the hamlet of Çirali. At its foot are the scant remains of a temple to Hephaistos, the Greek god of fire. The phenomenon is eerie during the day, but is best seen at night and a popular time to make the trip is just before sunset, although this entails a torchlight scramble back down the path.

The gases are released as a result of geological processes deep in the Earth below as the Anatolian plate is squeezed between the African and Eurasian plates. Although methane has been detected in the gas, its exact composition is unknown and if you put out one of the flames, it will soon reignite itself.

A couple of miles to the south, along the beach where loggerhead and green sea turtles nest, or along part of the inland route of the Lycian Way, is the ancient site of Olympos, with ruins from the second century BC to the twelfth century AD, including an ancient theatre, church, rock-cut tombs and parts of a villa and aqueduct. Out of the high tourist season, wildlife on the stream here includes turtles, kingfisher and water rails.

The surrounding landscape of the Olympos Beydaglari National Park is full of forested hillsides, secluded valleys and craggy peaks, and on some of the higher slopes red squirrels are sometimes seen.

The Chimaera is an area of permanent gas vents, about two dozen in total, that ignite spontaneously.

WHAT IS IT?
An amazing phenomenon where the hillside appears to be on fire.
HOW TO GET THERE:
By road, taking the road marked 'Çirali 7, Yanartas, Chimaera' off the A400 south from Antalya to Kumluca.
WHEN TO GO:
In autumn, out of the main tourist season
NEAREST TOWN:
Kumluca 26 km (16 mi)
DON'T MISS:
The ruins of nearby Olympos and the beautiful beach
YOU SHOULD KNOW:
During the day, it is not always obvious where some of the smaller flames are, so be careful where you tread.

Trees in bloom on the rocky shores of Lake Van in eastern Turkey. The snow-capped peak of Mount Suphan lies in the distance.

Lake Van

Formed when a lava flow from Nemrut Dagi blocked the river running through this lowland basin, Lake Van (Van Gölü) is an important stopover for migrating birds on their way to and from Africa, as well as providing valuable breeding grounds for many species of wildfowl and waders, which nest on the islands in the lake, and a small colony of great bustards. Birds that can be seen here include flamingos, spoonbills, pelicans, kestrels and night herons.

Lake Van has no outlet and loses water only through evaporation and is a strongly alkaline soda lake. Although it is slightly soapy to the touch, it is fun to float around in its waters in the quiet areas away from the lakeside towns.

High mountains surround this picturesque lake, which has a surface area of nearly 4,000 sq km (1,550 sq mi), is 119 km (74 mi) across at its widest and nearly 200 m (660 ft) deep in some places. The water level fluctuates with the seasons.

The area has two animal claims to fame. The first is the local Van Kedisi cats, which have an odd genetic mutation that gives them one blue eye and one gold and a love of water. The other is the Van Gölü Canevan, a dinosaur-like monster that lurks in the lake and has been spotted on a few occasions since the 1960s. Like the Loch Ness Monster, it is elusive.

WHAT IS IT?
A beautiful inland sea, rich in wildlife.
HOW TO GET THERE:
By air or rail to Van.
WHEN TO GO:
Summer or during the bird migration seasons.
NEAREST TOWN:
Van 4 km (2.5 mi)
DON'T MISS:
A ride across the lake in the train ferry.
YOU SHOULD KNOW:
Bring mosquito repellant.

Pamukkale

Visible from kilometres away, the dazzling 100-m (330-ft) white cliff of Pamukkale is one of the geological wonders of the world. Water from hot springs on the volcanic plateau above bubbles out of the ground at 35 °C (95 °F) streams down the side of the cliff, depositing calcium carbonate in the form of blinding white travertine as it cools and creates strangely shaped terraces and pools as it goes.

Pamukkale means 'Cotton Fortress' and according to legend the white cliffs were created when the giant Titans left their crop of cotton out to dry. Over thousands of years, the terraces have grown out from the cliff like a magical giant staircase or solid waterfall. Everywhere you go, you are accompanied by the sound of splashing water.

Because of earlier damage to the soft, porous rock, only a few terraces are open to the public, but paths lead right round the site. At the top of the cliff, it is possible to bathe in the town's thermal baths, which include the original sacred spring. As you swim about, you can see the water bubbling out of the ground beneath you.

The site, and the supposedly health-giving effects of the water, have been known about for thousands of years and the ruins of ancient Hierapolis, which grew up around the spring, dot the top of the cliff. Close to the baths is the Plutonium, a grotto sacred to the god of the underworld. From the grille that prevents entry, you can hear rushing water and the hiss of the poisonous gas that escapes from the ground here.

WHAT IS IT?
A shining white cliffside with amazing rock formations.
HOW TO GET THERE:
By road from Denizli
WHEN TO GO:
Any time of year.
NEAREST TOWN:
Denizli 20 km (12 mi)
DON'T MISS:
A swim in the thermal baths.
YOU SHOULD KNOW:
Climbing on the terraces and pools is forbidden.

The terraces of Pamukkale

The Forest of the Cedars of God

Forest of the Cedars of God

The Cedars of Lebanon have been venerated throughout history. In ancient times, they grew in profusion across the land, but today the trees that grow on the slopes of Mount Makmel, which towers over the Qadisha Valley, are some of the last survivors of those forests. Known as Arz el-Rab or the Cedars of God, this precious grove of trees grow at an altitude of over 2,000 m (6,562 ft) and was listed as a UNESCO World Heritage Site in 1998.

The Cedar of Lebanon (*Cedrus libani*) is a coniferous, evergreen tree that is both very slow growing and very long lived. Although there are fewer than 500 trees protected on these slopes, 12 of them are well over 1,000 years old. They have large trunks, some reaching 14 m (46 ft) in circumference, and are up to 35 m (115 ft) high. Their shape is dependant on density – taller and straighter in higher densities, but producing spreading, horizontal branches where they have the space.

Over thousands of years, these beautiful trees have been prized by every civilisation, and their exploitation is the reason that relatively few remain today. The Phoenicians used the wood for ship building, the resin was used by ancient Egyptians in the mummification process, Moses commanded Jewish priests to use the bark in circumcision ceremonies, and cedar wood was also used by the Romans, Greeks, Persians, Assyrians and Babylonians.

Cedar of Lebanon is mentioned in many ancient works of literature, including 75 references in The Bible, and the Qadisha Valley, at the foot of this protected grove, has been the home of monastic communities since the beginning of Christianity. Since 1985 a reforestation programme has been underway, but the results will not be appreciable for several decades to come.

WHAT IS IT?
A forest of deep religious significance, containing some of the last and most ancient of the Cedars of Lebanon.
HOW TO GET THERE:
By road.
WHEN TO GO:
It is beautiful at all times of year, particularly in winter, when the trees look superb under a covering of snow.
NEAREST TOWN:
The village of Bqaa Kafra is close to the Forest of the Cedars of God. Or Beirut, 121 km (76 mi)
DON'T MISS:
The monasteries of the Qadisha Valley.
YOU SHOULD KNOW:
The Cedar of Lebanon is the country's national emblem. It is only possible to visit the forest with an authorised guide.

Mount Hermon

Uncomfortably divided between Syria and Israel, and overlooking Lebanon, Mount Hermon, known in Arabic as Jabal Ash Shaykh, is something of a political hot potato. The southern and western slopes were captured by Israel in 1967, and unilaterally annexed in 1980. Syria controls the highest peak, where they have a military observation post, and there are also plans for developing a multi-billion dollar ski resort. Israel already has its only ski resort here, a popular getaway for thousands of Israelis, who can hike in lovely countryside in the summer months and enjoy skiing and other winter sports during winter and spring. Israeli Security Forces have a heavily guarded observation post at Mitzpe Shelagim.

Mount Hermon, which stands at the northern tip of the Golan Heights is, in fact, a group of mountains with three separate summits, the highest of which rises to 2,814 m (9,230 ft), and is in Syrian hands. The mountain is crucially important to the people who live in this most politically sensitive part of the world, not only for political reasons but also because its height traps a great deal of precipitation in an area which is otherwise extremely arid.

All three of the peaks are snow covered for much of the year, and even in the middle of summer there will be snowy areas at the highest points. Formed from limestone and riven with faults and channels, meltwater and rain feed down into the mountain springs from which water pours almost all year round. The resulting streams feed into the Jordan River, and the slopes beneath the snow line abound with plant life. Pine, oak and poplar trees are abundant, and the foothills are farmed extensively with vineyards, olive groves, orchards, nuts and vegetables.

WHAT IS IT?
A cluster of mountain peaks of great political, geographical and religious significance.
HOW TO GET THERE:
From Syria, Israel or Lebanon.
WHEN TO GO:
All year round.
NEAREST TOWN:
On the mountain itself are the Israeli town of Neve Ativ and the Druze town of Majdal Shams.
DON'T MISS:
The magnificent views.
YOU SHOULD KNOW:
Bring some warm clothes with you – even in mid-summer the evenings are chilly.

Mount Hermon

The Dead Sea

The name the Dead Sea conjures up images of people trying to sink, arid landscapes, salt flats and the history that was made, and still is, along its shores. Any description of it contains superlatives, e.g., it is the deepest exposed point on the earth's surface and it is the deepest hypersaline lake on the planet. However, contrary to popular belief, it is not the saltiest water on the planet: Lake Asai in Djibouti and Don Juan Pond in western Antarctica both have greater salinity. It is the salt that prevents the lake harbouring anything but extremely hardy bacteria and microbes.

It lies on the border between Jordan, Israel and the West Bank in the Jordan Valley, the northern extension of Africa's Great Rift Valley. It is so salty because it has no outlet and receives minimal amounts of rain. Most of the water entering the lake is rich with minerals, including salt, and when the water evaporates, the salt remains. In recent years, the flow in the Jordan has lessened while evaporation rates have stayed the same, so the lake is both shrinking and getting saltier. The southern part of the lake is drying out rapidly and giving way to salt flats.

Its mineral-rich muds are thought by many to have health-giving properties and there are spas and treatment centres dotted around the lake's edge.

The hills and mountains surrounding the lake are home to a variety of species that cope with the dry conditions, including camels, foxes, hares, hyraxes and ibexes. The area is also becoming known as an excellent area for birdwatchers, particularly during the migration seasons when thousands of birds of different species pass through here on their way to or from their wintering grounds in Africa.

The Dead Sea

WHAT IS IT?
A hypersaline lake set in a beautiful desert landscape.
HOW TO GET THERE:
By road from Jerusalem or Amman.
WHEN TO GO:
Spring or autumn.
NEAREST TOWN:
El Ariha 10 km (6 mi)
DON'T MISS:
Trying to sink in the salty water.
YOU SHOULD KNOW:
This is a politically sensitive area.

The Avshalom Cave

The star attraction of the Avshalom Reserve, on the western foothills of the Judean Hills, is the Avshalom Cave or Soreq Cave, the only 'showcave' in Israel. In 1968, whilst blasting was being carried out in a nearby quarry, an opening into this magnificent cave was exposed. The discovery was not made public for 9 years, during which time wooden walkways were constructed, a special lighting system was installed, and double doors were put in place at the entry and exit. All this was to protect the living formations within.

A relatively small cave, Soreq is some 83 m (273 ft) long, 60 m (198 ft) wide and 15 m (50 ft) high. What makes it unique is the sheer quantity, beauty and variety of its formations. Created millions of years ago by surface water penetrating and dissolving the limestone, once the cave had been hollowed out, the droplets, full of limestone sediments, began depositing this sediment on both the floor and the ceiling, and over hundreds of thousands of years these grew, and continue to grow, into slender stalactites and stalagmites in all sorts of unusual shapes, some as much as 3,000 years old. There are many different types of speleothems and flowstone walls that divide the cave into different chambers, and many of them are active formations, undergoing a process of continuous change.

Speleothems are extremely delicate, which is why so much work was undertaken within the cave to protect it. Even so the temperature, which was 19 °C (66 °F) when it was first discovered, has risen to 24 °C (75 °F) today, and this means that the natural processes at work here are certainly being disturbed.

WHAT IS IT?
A remarkable cave containing an enormous variety of speleothems.
HOW TO GET THERE:
By road from Jerusalem or Tel Aviv.
WHEN TO GO
All year round.
NEAREST TOWN:
Beit Shemesh 2 km (1¼ mi)
DON'T MISS:
The Romeo and Juliet formation.
YOU SHOULD KNOW:
An entry fee is payable and includes a slide show and a guided tour. On Fridays, when there is no tour, photography is permitted.

Soreq Cave

Wadi Rum

Wadi Rum is quite simply one of the most astonishingly, austerely beautiful places in the world. It fulfils every romantic notion of a desert landscape, complete with sheer, dark granite mountains, sandstone ridges rising vertically from the pink sand of the desert floor, and ancient graffiti scratched on the rocks of these vast and silent valleys.

Man has inhabited this place from Neolithic times, and the presence of freshwater springs made it a natural meeting place for caravans wending their way across the desert. In the 1st century BC, the Nabataeans settled here, before decamping to the rose coloured city of Petra. Everyone left their mark in the form of Neolithic flint axes, iron-age pottery, cave paintings and a Nabataean temple. Jabal Rum is the highest peak here at 1,754 m (5,315 ft).

On a clear day, rock climbers can see both the Saudi Arabian border and the Red Sea from the summit.

In early spring, after the rains, the desert explodes with life. Wildflowers colour the landscape – red anemones, Black iris, bright poppies and medicinal herbs abound. Eagles and buzzards wheel and drift in the sky above, just two of the 110 bird species recorded here. Ibex, gray wolves, Arabian sand cats and foxes all thrive in this region. Nomadic Bedouin still graze their herds, judging when to pack up and move on.

This is a protected environment: before entering Wadi Rum you will find the fort of the famous Desert Patrol, who police the area astride camels, wearing flowing robes and red and white headdresses, daggers at their waists and rifles across their backs. Rest under the vast, star spangled night sky sipping a cardamon coffee, and listen to the sound of silence.

WHAT IS IT?
One of the most amazing desertscapes in the world.
HOW TO GET THERE:
By road from Aqaba or Petra.
WHEN TO GO:
March, April, September, October and November.
NEAREST TOWN:
Wadi Rum village 6 km (3.75 mi)
Rashidiya 30 km (18.75 mi)
DON'T MISS:
The Seven Pillars of Wisdom mountain.
YOU SHOULD KNOW:
Wadi Rum was the headquarters of the legendary T.E. Lawrence, who named the mountain; much of the film *Lawrence of Arabia* was shot here.

The Damavand region in the Alborz Mountains

Tangeh Savashi, Alborz Mountains

The Alborz mountain range is located in northern Iran, which stretches from the Armenian border, around the Caspian Sea and ending in the east at the borders of Afghanistan and Turkmenistan. Between 60 km (37.5 mi) and 130 km (81 mi) in width, this range contains the largest of Iran's mountains, with Mount Damavand, rising to 5,670 m (18,600 ft). This peak is permanently snow covered, and the whole range endures long, cold, snowy winters, during which Iranians flock to the ski resorts that have sprung up.

The northern slopes of the Alborz are covered with deciduous trees that form the largest area of vegetation in the country. These forests are home to the Alborz Red sheep, the Orcal ram, and the endemic Iranian wild ass as well as gazelle, ibex, porcupine, badger and mongoose, and this plentiful wildlife has drawn hunters to the area for centuries.

Tangeh Savashi is a narrow mountain pass within the range, gouged out by a stream that is fed by a series of lovely waterfalls further upstream. This was once the favourite hunting ground of the Qajar king, Fath Ali Shah (1797-1834) who kept a hunting lodge on the lush grassland here. Midway through the pass, which is 1 km (0.6 mi) long and 4 m (13 ft) wide, a bas-relief can be found, depicting the king, his sons and grandsons in hunting scenes.

Carved into a niche in the mountainside by order of the king, the relief is sheltered from the worst of the weather and remains well preserved. It is, however, quite difficult to access, and involves fording the stream (which can be waist deep at times) that runs through the gorge, and clambering along a precipitous mountain path.

WHAT IS IT?
Iran's dominant mountain range, containing Qajar era relics.
HOW TO GET THERE:
By road.
WHEN TO GO:
Mid April to early June and late September to early November.
NEAREST TOWN:
Firouzkouh 15 km (9 mi)
YOU SHOULD KNOW:
As yet there is no tourist infrastructure at Tangeh Savashi, and due to the sensitive political situation it is difficult for foreigners to visit. Alborz is thought to be the home of the Peshotan, a Messiah-like figure awaited by Zoroastrians.

The Caspian Sea

Bordered by Russia, Turkmenistan, Azerbaijan, Kazakhstan and Iran, the Caspian Sea is classified either as the world's largest lake, or its smallest sea. Formed some 30 million years ago, it became landlocked about 5.5 million years ago, and has no natural outlet, apart from evaporation, other than the Manych Canal, which connects it to the Black Sea.

Forming Iran's northern boundary, the lake is fed by numerous small rivers and streams. However, Iranian rivers only provide 10 per cent of the Caspian's water – 90 per cent is supplied by only 5 rivers, the largest of which is the Volga. Despite this, the Caspian is saline, though much less so than most oceans, and this is attributed to its origin as an ancient ocean, connected to both the Atlantic and Pacific oceans.

The Caspian Sea is of major economic interest to all those who border it, but the water boundaries of the five nations has not yet been fully established. This is an energy rich area – major oil and natural gas fields have been found here, but this is not the only difficulty: there is the problem of access to international waters, currently only possible through Russia's Volga River and canal system. Finally, there is a great deal of money to be made through fishing – 90 per cent of the world's sturgeon swim in these waters, and caviar is big business.

There are about 120 species of fish in the southern part of the Caspian Sea, including seven species and sub-species of sturgeon, and Iranian caviar is renowned. The Iranian fisheries are trying to develop a sustainable resource, but sadly, over the past 20 years, stocks of all the fish here have dropped dramatically, partly due to over exploitation and partly to industrial pollution to which this enclosed body of water is extremely vulnerable.

WHAT IS IT?
By area, the world's largest enclosed body of water.
HOW TO GET THERE:
By road.
WHEN TO GO:
During the summer months.
NEAREST TOWN:
Rasht 2 km (1 mi)
YOU SHOULD KNOW:
Due to the sensitive political situation, it is difficult for foreigners to visit.

The Elburz Mountains on the Caspian Coast in Iran

Ali Sadr Cave

WHAT IS IT?
Iran's only 'showcave'.
HOW TO GET THERE:
By road.
WHEN TO GO:
March to October.
NEAREST TOWN:
Ali Sadr village, or Hamadan
100 km (60 mi)
YOU SHOULD KNOW:
Due to the political situation in Iran,
it can be difficult at present for
foreigners to visit the country.

The Ali Sadr Cave is one of Iran's most famous natural wonders, and has been a magnet for Iranian tourists since its re-discovery in the late 1970s. Situated in the Soubashi Mountains to the north of the city of Hamadan, the limestone cave is highly unusual. It is a water cave, however the water within it is more like a series of long lakes than a river. An inscription at the entrance of the man-made tunnel makes it clear that it was built during the reign of Darius 1 (521-485 BC).

Formed some 70 million years ago, the cave has been used by man for 1,200 years. Ancient tools, pottery and fascinating cave paintings depicting animals such as stags and gazelles, as well as hunting scenes, have been found here. For years the cave acted as a reservoir for people in the nearby village, but in 1978, when the water supply diminished somewhat, a local man followed the tunnel deep into the mountain in search of more.

In 1994, new areas of the cave were discovered, and in 2000 a German expedition began a new survey that eventually charted 11 km (7 mi) of canals.

On entering the tunnel, a wide passageway leads to a wharf. From here, the journey must be undertaken by boat. There are several different routes, varying between 2 m (6.6 ft) and 50 m (165 ft) in width, all of which end in a vast central atrium. Along the way the roof and walls are covered with fantastically shaped stalactites, some more than 15 m (49.5 ft) in length, and stalagmites, in extraordinary colours – purple, green, blue, red and brown. The water is absolutely crystal clear and even in dim light one can see to depths of several metres.

Rub' al Khali

WHAT IS IT?
The largest sand desert in the world.
HOW TO GET THERE:
Some tour companies offer GPS
equipped excursions into the desert.
WHEN TO GO:
Between November and February.
NEAREST TOWN:
Najran, close to the Yemeni border.
YOU SHOULD KNOW:
Saudi Arabia issues only a few,
restricted, expensive visas to visitors.

Rub' al Khali, meaning the Empty Quarter, is also known as the Great Sandy Desert. This vast area, 1,000 km (600 mi) long and 500 km (300 mi) wide, is virtually uninhabited and, until recently, largely unexplored. Formed over 2 million years ago, this great sand desert occupies over 25 per cent of Saudi Arabia, and stretches into Oman, Yemen and the United Arab Emirates.

Some 40,000 years ago this was a fertile area, covered with a number of lakes that were filled by monsoons that subsequently moved on to Egypt and India. Remnants of this era can still be seen in the perfectly fossilized teeth of hippopotamus, and the bones of water buffalo, long horned cattle, goats and gazelle – even freshwater shells have been discovered.

Today, 24 bird species, 31 plant species, arachnids and rodents are the only things that can survive the harsh environment. Nomadic Bedouin move around the outer edges, but before 300 AD, when the desertification was not as severe, caravans carrying frankincense crossed the Rub' al Khali, stopping at cities now lost in the shifting sands. At night, the temperature drops to 0 °C (32 °F) and frequently surpasses 55 °C (131 °F) at noon, and where once there was water, now there are enormous sand dunes over 250 m (800 ft) high.

Beneath this vast, inhospitable expanse of sand lies a wealth of oil, possibly the largest reserves on the planet, and the source of Saudi Arabia's fortune. Sheyba, in the centre, is a major light crude oil producing site, and the Gawwar Field is the largest in the world.

The Rub' al Khali, or Empty Quarter, is a vast sea of sand at the southern end of the Arabian Peninsula. The coastline is that of Oman.

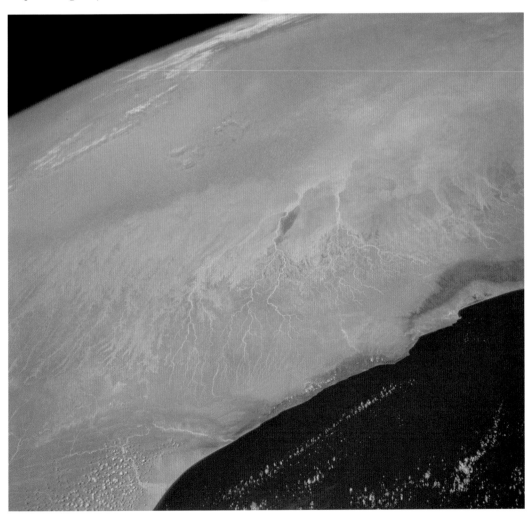

AUSTRALASIA & OCEANIA

The Twelve Apostles

Just off the coast of southern Victoria is a spectacular group of limestone sea-stacks. Originally they were known as the sow and her pigs, but were renamed in the 1950s. The howling winds and high seas of the Southern Ocean are eating away at the soft limestone walls of the coast here and these stacks are the remnants of land that has already fallen into the sea. They are under threat themselves: in the winter of 2005, one of them collapsed into the sea in a matter of seconds. The cliffs here are up to 70 m (230 ft) high and the tallest of the apostles is about 45 m (150 ft).

They are a spectacular sight from the clifftops, with the waves crashing against them. The wider area of the Twelve Apostles Marine National Park also has areas where visitors can swim, surf, kayak, snorkel or dive, if weather and wave conditions allow. Diving is permitted both on the wreck of the *Lorc Ard* and in the area of the underwater canyons known as the The Arches, where there are spectacular landscapes of seaweed-covered walls with sea fans, lace corals and sea-mosses. Sometimes there are fur seals playing here, zipping through tunnels and underneath arches.

This is rightly one of the three most popular natural attractions in Australia.

The Twelve Apostles coastline on the Great Ocean Road in Victoria.

The Wet Tropics of Queensland

In the 1980s, a battle was waged between environmentalists and the federal government on one hand and the timber industry and the state government on the other. This resulted in the addition to the World Heritage List of a 450-km (280-mile) long swathe of the coastal area of northern Queensland between Townsville and Cooktown in order to prevent any more logging in the area. What remains is a unique environment, with plants that are examples of types found on the ancient supercontinent of Gondwana. But the area is not just important as a living relic of evolution, it is also beautiful, with rugged peaks, beautiful sandy beaches, dramatic gorges, dense rainforest and Australia's tallest single-drop falls, the Wallaman Falls, near Trebonne.

Lying between the coast and the Atherton Tablelands and their dry eucalypt habitat, the forests contain eucalypts, banksias and paperbark trees, around the rivers there are swamps, and mangroves protect the coasts. Mossman Gorge, near the town of the same name, has spectacular scenery and lovely swimming holes.

This protected, pristine area, is brimming with wildlife, from cassowaries to tree-kangaroos and golden bowerbirds to yellow-bellied gliders and estuarine crocodiles. Its four national parks are havens for the animals that live in this tiny relic of a habitat that once occupied much of Australia.

WHAT IS IT?
A vast area of tropical habitat and a UNESCO World Heritage Site.
HOW TO GET THERE:
By air to Cairns, then by road
WHEN TO GO:
Any time except December to March when it is hot and humid and the roads are often impassable.
NEAREST TOWN:
Cairns
DON'T MISS:
A swim in a pool in Mossman Gorge.
YOU SHOULD KNOW:
Mosquito-repellent is a must at all times in the wet tropics; box jellyfish are a hazard in the sea in the very hot months; before swimming in any river, check with the locals that it is crocodile free.

Millaa Millaa Waterfall in the Atherton Tablelands

Mount Coonowrin, one of the Glasshouse Mountains, rises above the red soil in Queensland.

Glasshouse Mountains

A few miles in from Queensland's Sunshine Coast, a set of strange landforms dominate the plain around them. They are visible from the sea, and were given their name by Captain Cook, who thought their shimmer in the distance was similar to that of sun on glass. They are the plugs of volcanoes active some 25-27 million years ago, left standing proud of the sandstone plateau around them which has been eroded away to a depth of several hundred metres, leaving these structures, which show how the lava shrank and cracked as it cooled. Much of the area around the peaks consists of national parkland and there are trails of varying grades through eucalypt forests, plantations, scrubby gum, coastal rainforest, melaleuca swamp and casuarina groves. There is also a 22-km (14-mile) scenic Forest Drive that runs through the park and has several good lookout points.

Although several of the peaks should only be attempted by climbers, others like Mount Beerburrum, Mount Ngungun and designated tracks on Mounts Tibrogargan and Beerwah are possible for anyone who is reasonably fit.

On the way, you might see koalas, grey kangaroos and goannas (lizards), and birds include peregrine falcon, kookaburras, various cockatoos, rosellas and lorikeets. Mosquitos also abound here, so insect-repellant is a must.

From the top of these peaks, or from the Glasshouse Mountain Lookout, you get amazing views over the patchwork landscape.

WHAT IS IT?
A group of thirteen ancient volcanic plugs
HOW TO GET THERE:
By road or rail from Brisbane
WHEN TO GO:
In good weather from spring to autumn.
NEAREST TOWN:
Caboolture 20 km (12 mi)
DON'T MISS:
The view from the Glasshouse Mountains lookout.
YOU SHOULD KNOW:
Several sites here are sacred to the local Gubbi Gubbi people and are protected, so it is important to keep to the trails.

The Great Barrier Reef

The Great Barrier Reef stretches some 2,000 km (1,250 mi) from near Bundaberg in the south to the Torres Strait that separates Queensland and Papua New Guinea in the north. The main part of the coral reef sits on the continental shelf off the coast, protecting lagoons, cays and islands between itself and the mainland. There are more than 2,600 individual reefs, covering an area of 350,000 sq km (135,100 sq mi). Some 400 different types of coral give the reef its amazing colours and shapes and provide homes for 4,000 species of mollusc, 1,500 types of fish, 350 species of starfish, sea urchins and other echinoderms and uncounted types of crabs, shrimps and other crustaceans.

The most popular way to get close to the corals is by diving or snorkelling from one of the many tour boats, but glass-bottomed boats and semi-submersibles allow you to look without getting wet. Helicopter rides over the corals provide a good overview of the structure.

This marvel of nature is under a number of threats: rising sea levels, the water becoming both too warm and too acidic for the corals to survive, pollution, damage from fishing nets and anchors, the threat of drilling for oil and damage from cyclones. Sport-fishing near the reef is thought by some to be partly responsible for a cyclical problem: the crown of thorns starfish, which preys on the corals. Get there while you can.

WHAT IS IT?
The world's largest living structure.
HOW TO GET THERE:
From any of the coastal towns offering boat trips.
WHEN TO GO:
Spring to autumn.
DON'T MISS:
A ride in a glass-bottomed boat.
YOU SHOULD KNOW:
Coral is sharp!

Australia's Great Barrier Reef

Norfolk Island

Fringed by the blue waters of the Pacific Ocean, this tiny island, just 5 by 8 km (3 by 5 mi) across, has some of the most beautiful, and most precious landscapes you will ever find. Hundrds of kilometres from the nearest landmass, it has its own unique plants, including the Norfolk Island pine, as well as rainforests full of giant tree ferns. A third of the island is a national park and botanic garden that protect many of the species that are unique to the island or endangered. Walking and cycling trails allow visitors to get up close to the world's tallest tree ferns and to lose themselves in this green haven.

The island is also home to several extremely rare birds, including the Norfolk Island Green Parrot and the Norfolk Island Morepork (also known as the Boobook Owl), which was down to one female in the late 1980s before two males of a closely related species were brought to the island. The sacred kingfisher is more common and can be seen all over the island. There are also plenty of spectacular seabirds during the breeding season.

Norfolk Island's greatest jewel is, perhaps, its fringing coral reefs, which are full of brightly coloured corals and shoals of spectacular fish.

The setting sun silhouettes pine trees near Emily Bay.

Buchan Caves Reserve

Speleothem formations in the Royal Cave at Buchan

In the heart of Victoria's southern Gippsland, the Buchan Caves Reserve surrounds two of the msot spectacular showcaves in Australia: the Royal Cave and the Fairy Cave.

The 400-m (1,300-ft) Fairy Cave has several distinctive stalagmite and stalagmite formations, including the Jewel Chamber, the Grotto, the Wedding Cake, the Hall, the Bridal Chamber, the King's Chamber and the Queen Victoria Chamber. Different colours are caused by different minerals being deposited with the calcium carbonate from which the formations are made: copper makes green shades while the rusts and browns are cause by iron oxide. The Royal Cave has formations such as Niagara Falls and the Font of the Gods, a beautiful pool ringed with calcite formations.

Important archaeological finds have been made at the Buchan Caves and other caves in the area, including the fossilized bones of a horse-sized wombat and an equally large kangaroo skeleton, as well as evidence of Aboriginal occupation from about 15,000 BC.

The surrounding reserve has a variety of animals, including koalas and kangaroos, as well as more than forty species of birds, among them the currawong, whose fluting tones ring through the air, as they call out their own name.

WHAT IS IT?
A pair of beautiful limestone showcaves.
HOW TO GET THERE:
By road from Canberra or Melbourne.
WHEN TO GO:
Any time of year
NEAREST TOWN:
Buchan 1 km (0.5 mi)
DON'T MISS:
The guided tours through the caves.

The stunning landscape of the Painted Desert

The Painted Desert

North-east of the opal-mining town of Coober Pedy in the northern part of South Australia, is one of the most unusual landscapes that visitors will ever encounter. Once the floor of an ancient sea, this land has been eroding for millions of years and the different soils, gravels and rocks that make up the mesas and mountains here create a colourful landscape whose hues change from minute to minute with the changing light. The rapid changes at dawn and dusk are particularly worth seeing.

In the Moon Plains, to the south of the main part of the desert, fossils of ichthyosaurs (marine contemporaries of the dinosaurs) and other marine life have been found. There are areas of petrified wood, and evidence that the climate here was once markedly different – large boulders left by glaciers.

In the north, the road passes through plains covered with sheets of fragile gypsum.

Although remote, and desolate, this region is beautiful, with contrasting shades of rust-red, ochre yellow, rich brown and black and white. It is so photogenic that it has been used in many films, including the *Mad Max* series and *Priscilla, Queen of the Desert*. As you drive, or hike, through the area, each face of each mesa, mountain or hillock is a new delight to explore and photograph.

WHAT IS IT?
A desert that seems to change colour during the day.
HOW TO GET THERE:
By 4 wheel drive from Coober Pedy or Oodnadatta.
WHEN TO GO:
Spring or autumn.
NEAREST TOWN:
Oodnadatta 50 km (30 mi)
DON'T MISS:
A plane ride over the desert.
YOU SHOULD KNOW:
Some parts of the desert are so fragile that they are out of bounds.

Cape Byron

Cape Byron, the most easterly point in mainland Australia, was named by Captain Cook in honour of an earlier circumnavigator of the globe. Just south of the laid-back town of Byron Bay, this headland's rocky cliffs support coastal rainforest and heath, and a beautiful banksia forest. There are three trails on the headland: the clifftop path, the coastal footpath and a shady track that leads you through the bushland. Look-outs give jaw-dropping, panoramic views over the green hinterland and white sandy beaches, and out over the Pacific Ocean. The headland's geographical position – protruding into the ocean, with a steep shelf just offshore make it a great place for watching large marine wildlife from above. This area is a hotspot for the highly endangered grey nurse shark, as well as rays, hawksbill, green and loggerhead turtles, dolphins, wobbegongs, octopus and lots of subtropical fish, including clownfish. Leopard and tiger sharks can be seen here in summer, and there are occasional reports of great white sharks. The corals provide refuge for the smaller fish, anemones and starfish.

From July to November hundreds of humpback whales make their way up the east coast of Australia, singly, in small groups or in mother-and-calf pairs. Because of their size, the headland is the best place to see these massive creatures as they move sedately past. Sometimes, one can be spotted breeching in the waters of Byron Bay.

Whatever the time of year, Cape Byron is one of the loveliest spots on Earth.

WHAT IS IT?
The most easterly point in mainland Australia.
HOW TO GET THERE:
By road from Brisbane.
WHEN TO GO:
Spring to autumn, or winter for the whales
NEAREST TOWN:
Byron Bay 3 km (2 mi)
YOU SHOULD KNOW:
In May and June, the area is full of surfers.

An aerial view of Cape Byron

The Blue Mountains

WHAT IS IT?
The edge of a massive sandstone plateau.
HOW TO GET THERE:
From Sydney by road or rail.
WHEN TO GO:
Spring to autumn.
NEAREST TOWN:
Katoomba 5 km (3 mi)
DON'T MISS:
The view from Govett's Leap.
YOU SHOULD KNOW:
It is often far cooler in the mountains than it is in Sydney.

Forming part of eastern Australia's Great Dividing Range, the Blue Mountains are, in fact, the edge of the great sandstone plateau that once covered the whole of this side of the continent. Over millions of years, the soft rock has slowly been eroded back from the coast, creating a wonderful landscape of rugged cliffs, deep gullies, steep-sided valleys, waterfalls, caves and forests. In summer, the eucalypts give off the blue haze that gives this area its name. There are several national parks and state forests in the mountains: most visitors head for the Blue Mountains town of Katoomba, which lies between two arms of the Blue Mountains National Park and gives easy access to such well-known sights as the Three Sisters, Echo Point and Honeymoon Lookout. To the north lie Govett's Leap, on a high cliff and offering views over one of the most beautiful landscapes on the planet, Bridal Veil Falls, Perry's Lookout and Pulpit Rock.

To the west are the Jenolan Caves, the best known caves in the country, many of which can be visited by guided tour.

Although it took early explorers more than 25 years to find a way through the mountains, there is now a multitude of trails through the mountains and valleys, including to the Blue Gum Forest below Perry's Lookout and along the Coachwood Glen Nature Trail in the Megalong Valley Farm. There are also long distance trails and plenty of facilities for hiking, climbing, abseiling and horse-riding.

The Three Sisters, a formation in the Blue Mountains, west of Sydney

Jervis Bay

Some 150 km (90 mi) south of Sydney, is one of the most unspoiled sites in eastern Australia. An almost enclosed natural harbour, 16 by 10 km (10 by 6 mi) it was originally purchased by the government in Canberra from the New South Wales government, a large part of the area was handed over in 1998 to the local Aboriginal people and is now officially known as the Booderee National Park and Botanic Gardens, meaning 'plenty of fish' or 'bay of plenty' in the Dhurga language.

Almost the entire bay is fringed with white sandy beaches and ringed with lush green bush. The floor of the bay is carpeted with seagrasses, which provide a haven for fish, the prey of the white-tailed sea eagle, which is the guardian of the Wreck Bay Aboriginal settlement and symbol of the national park.

The bay is home year-round to a pod of wild bottlenose dolphins, who may approach boats if the mood takes them, as well as huge jellyfish that can sometimes be seen drifting in the astonishingly clear waters. There are also colonies of New Zealand and Australian fur seals. In winter, beyond the heads and in the surrounding coastal areas are ideal places to look for migrating humpback whales, dwarf minke, false killer and southern right whales.

The land around the bay has popular beauty spots such as the Hole in the Wall and Green Patch Beach and there are trails in the lovely bushland, too.

A common seadragon (Phyllopteryx taeniolatus) in Jervis Bay, New South Wales

WHAT IS IT?
An idyllic bay with white sandy beaches
HOW TO GET THERE:
By road from Sydney
WHEN TO GO:
Any time of year
NEAREST TOWN:
Nowra (40 km, 25 mi)
DON'T MISS:
A dolphin- or whale-watching trip.

South-east Queensland's subtropical rainforests

WHAT IS IT?
Wilderness areas you can get lost in.
HOW TO GET THERE:
By road from Brisbane or the Gold Coast.
WHEN TO GO:
Spring to autumn
NEAREST TOWN:
Coolangatta 20 km, (12 mi)
YOU SHOULD KNOW:
It can rain heavily in summer, sometimes.

Inland from the lights of the Gold Coast are wide areas of relatively untouched subtropical rainforests. The McPherson Range is a paradise for walkers. In the north, Tambourine Mountain is a 600-m (2,000-ft) plateau reached by a winding road that takes you between dense forests with tree ferns. Eucalypt forest clings to the hillside round the gorges and falls, such as Cedar Creek Falls and Witches Falls. The walking trails to the latter, and to Cameron Falls, have spectacular look-outs. Kookaburras are common, especially near picnic areas, and galahs may be seen flitting through the trees and you may hear sulphur-crested cockatoos. Shyer inhabitants of the area include koalas, brush turkeys, the nocturnal tawny frogmouth and goannas – species of frilled lizards.

In the south of the range, the Lamigton National Park has thickly wooded valleys with subtropical rainforest. The spectacular landscape has gorges, waterfalls and pools, caves and superb views. This is one of the best spots in the region for wildlife, with lorikeets and parrots and bowerbirds.

To the east, the Springbrook Plateau has temperate rainforest with eucalypt, and a network of trails that allow you to explore the cliffs, forests, gorges and waterfalls, such as the 109-m (360-ft) Purling Brook Falls. If there has been sufficient rain, the Waringa Pool is a great spot to cool down after a strenuous walk. Right at the southern end of the plateau is the modestly named Best of All Lookout.

A sulpher-crested cockatoo, just one of the inhabitants of the subtropical rainforests of Queensland

Lake Eyre

Named after Edward Eyre, the first European to spot it, in 1840, Lake Eyre is Australia's largest lake, sometimes. Its bed sits some 20 m (66 ft) below sea level and is at the bottom of a catchment basin that covers parts of Queensland, the Northern Territory, South Australia and western New South Wales, although only a small proporation of rainfall from any distance away reaches the lake. When dry, the floor of the basin is covered by a thick layer of salt because water from the lake is lost only through evaporation so the minerals it carries are deposited here.

It is when there are heavy rains in the immediate area of the lake that it suddenly comes alive: small creatures that have adapted to droughts that last years, suddenly emerge and thousands of birds come here to feed, bathe and breed. Flocks of pelicans, avocets, cormorants, gulls, terns and banded stilts appear as if from nowhere.

The land around the lake also springs to life, as plants burst into flower and seeds that have lain dormant for years sprout, all in a rush to complete their life cycle before the ground dries out again.

WHAT IS IT?
A vast inland salt lake in South Australia.
HOW TO GET THERE:
By road from Port Augusta.
WHEN TO GO:
April to September.
NEAREST TOWN:
Maree 50 km) 30 mi)
YOU SHOULD KNOW:
When it rains, floods can fill gullies and gorges rapidly.

Lake Eyre, the largest lake in Australia.

Rottnest Island

Rottnest was first found in 1696 by Willem de Vlamingh in 1696, a Dutch explorer who mistook the island's small marsupials (the quokka) for rats and named it Rottnest (Rat's Nest). The entire island is run as a reserve and the surrounding waters as a marine park. It sits on the edge of the Australian continental shelf and became separated from the mainland about 7,000 years ago by rising sea levels.

The island is best explored by bicycle – private cars are not allowed – and the 24-km (15-mi) circular route round the island runs through some of the most beautiful scenery, passing its small, sandy beaches in secluded coves.

Offshore, the fringing reefs are among the best in Australia, with twenty species of colourful corals and 360 species of fish, including manta rays, as well as bottlenose dolphins and sea lions. Humpback whales pass close to the island during the migration season and green and loggerhead turtles have sometimes been seen. Sea kayaking, scuba-diving, snorkelling and visiting the reef in glass-bottomed boats are all popular activities.

Land animals include a small number of reptiles – the island's thousands of years of isolation from the mainland means that several have evolved into species not found on the nearby mainland, as well as three types of frog.

The island's shores, salt lakes and swamps provide homes for a variety of birds.

This is a lovely, relaxed place to visit, where the scenery and wildlife are amazing for such a small place.

A quokka on Rottnest Island

Uluru (Ayers Rock)

Uluru is an icon of Australia: a giant red rock standing out from the surrounding desert. Like any significant landscape feature, it is a sacred site for the Aboriginals and it is a major point in the songlines of the local people, the Anangu. The rock is an inselberg, a remnant of an eroded mountain range. The national park it stands in – the Uluru-Kata Tjuta National Park, also covers the Olgas, a group of 36 other giant red rocks a few kilometres away. When the original mountain range formed, the layers of sandstone were raised from horizontal to vertical and you can see the banding in the rock. Where water gets into cracks and fissures, it erodes away deep channels that sprout waterfalls after heavy rains. Water also soaks through the sandstone, eventually to emerge again as springs around the bottom of the rock that sustain some greenery and animals, making it an invaluable source of water and food in this arid land.

The rock owes its red colour to the oxidation of iron at the surface: freshly eroded rock is grey. However, it is the more short-lived colour changes of the rock as the sun goes down, and it changes from red to purple then black (and changes in the reverse order during sunrise) that many visitors come to see.

The climb to the summit is not as easy as you might think, and the Anangu would prefer it if people did not try it. Howeve, the views from the plateau at the top are amazing. The Anangu lead walking tours around the 9 km (6 mi) base during which they tell visitors about the plants and animals here, and about their culture and dreamtime.

WHAT IS IT?
An enormous red rock in the middle of Australia.
HOW TO GET THERE:
By air or road from Alice Springs
WHEN TO GO:
Any time of year, but it can be very cold in June and July, very hot in November and December and stormy between January and March.
NEAREST TOWN:
Alice Springs 335 km (208 mi).
DON'T MISS:
Sunrise or sunset from one of the viewing areas.
YOU SHOULD KNOW:
Do not photograph the Anangu.

Uluru at sunset

Magpie Geese in Kakadu National Park

Kakadu National Park

The largest national park in Australia, Kakadu National Park lies about 150 km (90 mi) east of the Northern Territory's capital, Darwin. This tropical landscape is home to more than 10,000 insect species, kangaroos, wallabies, water buffalo, dingoes and almost a quarter of Australia's fish species. Its varied habitats include eucalypt woodland, swamp and mangroves, rainforest, heathland as well as drier areas to the south of the park. One of the main features here is the South Alligator River, which is home to large populations of both of Australia's crocodile species: the Johnston, or freshwater, crocodile, and the estuarine, or saltwater, crocodile, which can tolerate both fresh and salt water. Locally, they are known as 'salties'. These reptiles can grow to as much as 6 m (20 ft) and can be extremely dangerous. They have been observed swimming along the coast from one river to the next in order to exploit seasonal sources of food such as migrating fish.

This part of Australia is not much more than 15 degrees south of the Equator and from November to February it is extremely hot, humid and wet, and the roads can be blocked by water for days, so it is best not to visit at this time.

Highlights of the park include Barramundi Gorge, Jim Jim Falls and Nourlangie Rock.

This area was inhabited by Aboriginals long before Europeans arrived and within the park's 20,000 sq km (7,720 sq mi) are about 5,000 sites of Aboriginal art. This land was handed back to the locals several years ago and the park is jointly administered by them and National Parks Australia.

WHAT IS IT?
A vast national park in tropical northern Australia.
HOW TO GET THERE:
By air or rail to Darwin, then by road.
WHEN TO GO:
March to October.
NEAREST TOWN:
Jabiru.
DON'T MISS:
The aboriginal rock art sites.

Grampians National Park

An area of natural beauty, the Grampian Mountains are almost the last part of the Great Dividing range that for years isolated the interior of Australia from the eastern coastal plain. Spread over 1,700 sq km (650 sq mi), the national park has a wide variety of landscapes including stringybark forests, fern-filled gullies, red gums, sub-Alpine forests, woodland, heaths, wildflower meadows and swamps. It is home to a large variety of animals, including different species of wallabies, grey kangaroos, possums, gliders, koalas and echidnas. There are many birds here, including a sizeable population of emus.

The scenery is special, with many tracks and trails leading to look-outs over the valleys and lakes. Mackenzie Falls is spectacular in spring and after rains. Mountains that can be hiked here include Mount William (also called Mount Duwill) and the aptly named Mount Abrupt, but among the most popular, if strenuous walks, is to the summit of the Pinnacle.

A serious bushfire spread through the central Grampians in 2006, but the much of the vegetation here is fire-adapted and is regenerating.

Activities in the area include rafting, rock climbing, abseiling, cycling, canoeing and birdwatching. There are several roads through the park giving access to areas like the beautiful Victoria Valley, while from the central area, tracks and bushwalking trails lead into the wilderness.

WHAT IS IT?
A beautiful mountain area in western Victoria
HOW TO GET THERE:
By road from Melbourne
WHEN TO GO:
Spring to autumn
NEAREST TOWN:
Stawell 20km (12 mi)

Forested mountainside in the Grampians

Wolfe Creek Impact Crater

WHAT IS IT?
A meteorite crater.
HOW TO GET THERE:
By 4 wheel drive on the Tanami road,
then offroad.
WHEN TO GO:
May to October.
NEAREST TOWN:
Halls Creek 145 km (90 mi)
YOU SHOULD KNOW:
The Djaru Aboriginals call the crater
Kandimalal.

First spotted from the air in 1947, the Wolfe Creek Impact Crater, located in Western Australia, was formed some 300,000 years ago when a meteorite with a mass of about 50,000 kg (125,000 lb) crashed into the desert at a speed estimated at 15 km (9 mi) a second. The resulting crater is 880 metres (2,890 ft) across and was originally roughly 120 m (400 ft) deep, with a sharp rim that rises 25 m (82 ft) above the desert. Over the millennia, sand has been blown into the bottom of the crater, reducing its depth by over half. Evidence of the heat caused by the impact can be seen in the traces of quartz and rusty coloured balls that are strewn all over the desert floor here. Fragments of the meteorite itself have been found many kilometres away.

As you approach, the rim of the crater emerges – firstly as a small feature on the horizon, and then as a broad low wall. It is only when you scramble up it and gaze down into the crater that it becomes apparent what it is. It is possible to hike round the rim of the crater, and there is a path leading to the crater floor, where you will find a surprising number of plants, which can exist because the porous rocks down here can hold on to water longer than those of the desert floor above and the walls of the crater provide some rare shade in the area.

Wolf Creek Impact Crater

Buccaneer Archipelago

An aerial view of forested clifftops in the Buccaneer Archipelago

Lying just off the north-west coast of Western Australia, the Buccaneer archipelago's 1,000 islands were once part of the mainland but have been cut off by rising seas since the last ice age. Vegetation on them is scarce, except for tiny patches of rainforest and protective mangroves. Set in the blue seas of the Indian Ocean, they are known for their beautiful, isolated sandy beaches, extreme tidal range and the extraordinary 'horizontal waterfall' in Talbot Bay, caused by the tidal water building up in front of the two narrow gaps leading to the ocean faster than it can flow through them, causing a build-up of up to 4 m (14 ft) of turquoise water that rushes between the red rocks.

Despite the apparent lack of habitat, more than 100 species of birds have been recorded here, as well as eleven species of snake, a variety of lizards, rock rats, marsupials, called quolls, and bats. The crystal clear waters support corals, shellfish and small fish, as well as sharks, swordfish, sea snakes and estuarine crocodiles.

There are numerous sacred sites on the islands, some of which are still in use.

A popular way to explore the islands in depth is on a guided sea safari, camping on a different beach each night.

WHAT IS IT?
A group of some 1,000 islands off the north-west coast of Austalia.
HOW TO GET THERE:
By boat or air from Derby
WHEN TO GO:
Autumn to spring: it is extremely hot in summer.
NEAREST TOWN:
Derby 50–100 km (30–60 mi)
DON'T MISS:
The horizontal waterfall.
YOU SHOULD KNOW:
The former iron-ore mines on Kooland and Cockatoo Islands are being reopened, so you may wish to steer clear of this area.

Cradle Mountain

Cradle Mountain-Lake St Clare National Park

Part of Tasmania's Wilderness Area World Heritage Site, the Cradle Mountain-Lake St Clare National Park is a stunning area of craggy ridges and crests, valleys scooped out by glaciers, cirques and lakes, dropping down through alpine heathland, button grass, wildflower meadows, pine and beech woods to areas of ancient rainforest.

The hike up the 1,545-m (5,068-ft) Cradle Mountain and back takes about eight hours, but there are easier walks on its lower slopes and the three-hour walk around the beautiful Dove Lake is not to be missed.

Cradle Mountain is in the north of the park, and Lake St Clare – Australia's deepest freshwater lake – in the far south. The six-day hike from one to the other – known as the Overland Track – is one of the most popular in Australia, and draws walkers from all over the world. It leads through some of the wildest pristine landscapes on the island, with glacial lakes, icy streams and waterfalls and spectacular views of the mountains above. There are nine huts spaced along the 80-km (50-mi) trail, in which walkers can make overnight stops – even in summer it can be very cold at night and snow is not unheard of in the higher areas.

Other activities on offer in the park include rafting on the Franklin River, an exhilarating ride that takes you through even more beautiful areas of pristine wilderness.

WHAT IS IT?
A beautiful glacial landscape in Tasmania.
HOW TO GET THERE:
By road from Launceston
WHEN TO GO:
Spring to autumn.
NEAREST TOWN:
Sheffield 50km (30 mi)
DON'T MISS:
The views of Dove Lake.

Kiama Blowholes

On the coast of New South Wales, south of Sydney, is what is claimed to be the world's biggest blowhole. As a wave rushes in to the hole in the cliff, the air in the lower part of the hole is compressed into an inner chamber; then, as the wave starts to fall back, the compressed air expands, forcing the water up through the upper part of the blowhole and into the air with a loud 'ooomph'. The first European to see the blow hole was a whaler, George Bass, who anchored here in 1797; the Aboriginals call the blowhole Khanterintee and the town's name means, 'where the sea makes a noise'. The hole is some 7.5–9 m (25–30) feet across. There is a second, smaller, blowhole a couple of kilometres to the south.

The rough seas and winds along this part of the shore have created other beautiful forms in the cliffs, such as Cathedral Rocks, Stack Island and Fry's Cave, while a little higher up the valley is the magnificent Minnamurra Rainforest Reserve, a tiny remnant of the original flora of the area, which is particularly noted for its variety of tree ferns and for the pretty Minnamurra Falls.

WHAT IS IT?
Two blowholes in the cliffs.
HOW TO GET THERE:
By road or rail from Sydney.
WHEN TO GO:
Any time of year.
NEAREST TOWN:
Kiama
YOU SHOULD KNOW:
The larger blowhole is better in rough weather, while the smaller is better in moderate seas.

Kiama blowhole on the coast of New South Wales

Fraser Island

Stretching 123 km (76 mi) alongside Queensland's coast, Fraser Island is one of the most beautiful places on earth. Made almost entirely of sand, it is unique. Some of the dunes are up to 240 m (790 ft) high. In the lowlands, the heathlands are awash with wildflowers in spring and summer, while in the interior, ancient rainforests surround more than 100 freshwater lakes and grow alongside crystal-clear streams. Among the highlights of the island are the wetlands of the Great Sandy Strait, where dugongs and turtles may be seen, and Hervey Bay during the whale migration season, when more than 1,500 humpbacks pass through. Inland, the lakes are beautiful, particularly Lake Wabby and the lakes round McKenzie. The northern part of the island has been designated as a national park. If you drive up the eastern beach northward from the Pinnacles, you will pass the 25-km (15-mi) expanse of the Cathedrals – cliffs made of coloured sand – on your way to Indian Head, which is a great spot for looking for dolphins, sharks and whales.

Other wildlife here includes what are probably the purest strain of dingos (do not feed them: they are losing their fear of humans and there have been several fatal attacks), loggerhead turtles, manta rays, possums, bats, sugar gliders, wallabies, echidnas and several species of reptile. The most noticeable of the 200 or so species of bird here are the sulphur-crested cockatoos, because they make so much noise, although the rainbow lorikeets are rather more colourful.

Epiphytes growing on trees on Fraser Island.

The Morning Glory

The rare and beautiful Morning Glory cloud formation

The tiny outback town of Burketown, near the southern end of the Gulf of Carpentaria, has one claim to fame: it is the best place to spot the cloud formation known as the Morning Glory. Each spring, in September and October, the curious, weather enthusiasts and, especially, glider pilots, flock here to see it. No-one knows exactly why this huge roll of cloud, up to 1,000 km (600 mi) long, 1–2 km (0.5–1 mi) high and speeding along at 35–40 kph (20–25 mph) forms here at this time of year, but it has a fascination for many, especially when as dawn breaks the black smudge of cloud can be seen on the horizon, galloping towards the viewer.

The local Aboriginals call it the 'yippipee' and say that it presages bad weather, while people in Burketown say that if there is a sea breeze and high humidity the day before, the Morning Glory may occur.

For glider pilots, riding the Morning Glory is like surfing a giant wave. In effect it is the aerial equivalent of a tidal bore, with the roll of cloud forming under the crest of the wave. The updraught in front of it gives them lift, allowing them to stay up in the air far longer than they normally can when relying on thermals. Good pilots can fly along the length of it, almost touching it with their wingtip or crest the top of it and surf down the leading edge, avoiding – at all costs – the turbulent downdraft at the back.

WHAT IS IT?
A spectacular cloud formation seen in parts of Queensland.
HOW TO GET THERE:
By road from Cairns.
WHEN TO GO:
September to October.
NEAREST TOWN:
Burketown.
DON'T MISS:
A ride beside the cloud in a glider, if you get the chance.
YOU SHOULD KNOW:
The cloud's appearance is unpredictable, so plan to stay at least a few days.

Lord Howe Island

WHAT IS IT?
A tiny island group off the coast of
New South Wales.
HOW TO GET THERE:
By air from Sydney or Brisbane.
WHEN TO GO:
Any time of year.
NEAREST TOWN:
Newcastle 600 km (373 mi)
DON'T MISS:
Diving the coral reef.

Just 11 km (7 mi) long and 2 km (1.2 mi) at its widest, Lord Howe Island is the remnant of an undersea volcano that was born some 7 million years ago but most of which has now been eroded away, leaving just the peaks of Mount Gower at 875 m (2,870 ft) and Mount Lidgbird at 777 m (2,550 ft) in the south, a central lowland and some hills to the north, as well as a few outlying islands: Admiralty Islands, Mutton Bird Islands and Ball's Pyramid.

Most of the island is covered in palm forest and subtropical forest, with trees including banyans and Kentia palms, while there are also grasslands here and on the smaller islands. The island's isolation until 1878 means that many of the species of plants here occur nowhere else.

The islands are surrounded by beautiful coral reefs, with more than eighty species of coral. The lagoon between Lord Howe Island itself and the reef is a beautiful blue, protected from the ocean waves that crash against the coral.

The island is, or was until cows, sheep, goats, pigs, mice and rats were introduced, a safe place for seabirds to nest and eradication programmes are helping to raise the numbers of birds for some species. Birds that can be found here include red-billed tropicbirds and masked boobies. This is a beautiful, isolated, quiet spot where visitors really can get away from it all.

Lord Howe Island

The Bungle Bungles

Known to the local Aboriginals as Purnululu, and set in the National Park of the same name, the Bungle Bungles are a unique range of orange, black and white landforms up to 400 m (1,300 ft) high. The sandstone they are made from was laid down about 350 million years ago, and over the last 2 million years, they have been uplifted then eroded into amazing beehive-shaped domes. From the Piccaninny Creek car park, it is a short walk to Cathedral Gorge, a giant natural amphitheatre that carries people's voices round from one side to the other. The full walk through the Piccaninny Gorge requires an overnight camp and some scrambling in places, but is worth it for the stunning views of cliffs, domes, chasms and the sight of Black Rock Pool. In the north of the park, away from the domes, are two gorges: Mini Palms Gorge and Echidna Chasm. The path through the former leads you up 150 m (400 ft) to a platform for views of the palms in the valley below, their lush green contrasting with the colour of the rocks. Echidna Chasm is a narrow gorge with soaring cliffs that glow in the sunlight, leaving you almost in the dark at the bottom.

Even though it takes an effort to get to this remote spot, it is worth it: this is a unique landscape that will stay in your memory.

A range of rounded, rock towers, striped with silica and lichen.

WHAT IS IT?
A unique mountain range in Western Australia.
HOW TO GET THERE:
By road from Halls Creek
WHEN TO GO:
April–May, at the beginning of the dry season and before the peak tourist season.
NEAREST TOWN:
Halls Creek 190 km (115 mi)
DON'T MISS:
Cathedral Gorge and Echidna Chasm.
YOU SHOULD KNOW:
A 4 wheel drive is a must as the off-road section of the drive to the park has rough track, steep climbs, tight corners and creeks to cross.

Shark Bay

Shark Bay

Shark Bay is almost unique. It is one of only two or three sites where easily-identifiable decendents of some of the earliest life-forms on earth, living marine stomatolites, exist and the only place where they can easily be seen. In the very salty waters of the Hamelin Pool Marine Nature Reserve a group of strange columns, hillocks and mounds about 50 cm (20 in) high sit between the high and low tide lines. Without their ancestors, which developed some 3,500 million years ago, life on earth as we know it would not exist. These strange cushions are made up of photosynthesizing bacteria that absorb carbon dioxide and emit oxygen. Without them, our atmosphere would be unbreathable and the ozone layer that protects us from solar radiation would not exist.

Other inhabitants of the bay are the dolphins that hang out near Monkey Mia, as well as more than 10,000 dugong, who graze among the sea grasses. This is the largest and most stable population of these beautiful, gentle creatures: elsewhere they are threated by human activity encroaching on their underwater world and at risk of collisions with boats. Here, where they are safe, these giant mammals – thought to be the inspiration for mermaids – might take notice of a boat if they feel like it, but are more usually happy to get on with their own lives. Sharing their world for a few minutes is a privilege that not many can boast.

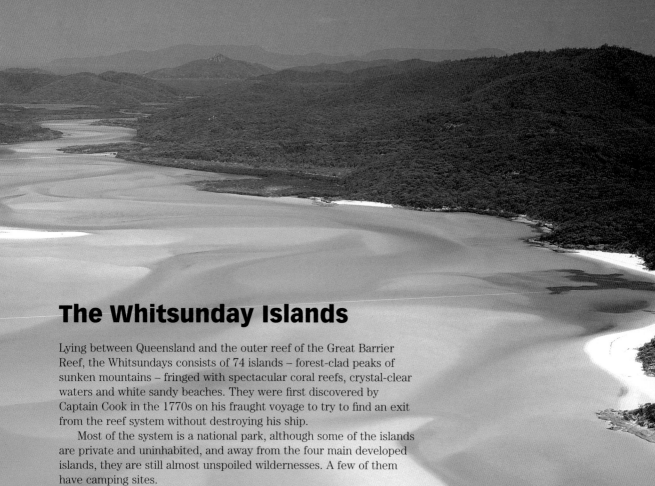

The Whitsunday Islands

Lying between Queensland and the outer reef of the Great Barrier
Reef, the Whitsundays consists of 74 islands – forest-clad peaks of
sunken mountains – fringed with spectacular coral reefs, crystal-clear
waters and white sandy beaches. They were first discovered by
Captain Cook in the 1770s on his fraught voyage to try to find an exit
from the reef system without destroying his ship.

Most of the system is a national park, although some of the islands
are private and uninhabited, and away from the four main developed
islands, they are still almost unspoiled wildernesses. A few of them
have camping sites.

Not only are the Whitsunday's reefs spectacular in their own
right, the islands are ideal stopping-off points for the Great Barrier
Reef itself.

For those who don't want to sail themselves, there is a bewildering
variety of sailing boat, catamaran and cruise trips to the islands and
reefs, many to sites where visitors can scuba or snorkel among the
reefs and watch the fish. Several companies also run trips in glass-
bottomed boats or semi-submersibles. It is also possible to hire sailing
boats and explore where you want, although the waters round the
reefs can be tricky for the inexperienced.

But the islands are not just worth visiting for the marine life: many
have walking trails up to their peaks through lovely rainforest full of
birdsong, and there are so many beaches it is not that difficult to find
yourself a quiet place to look at the beauty surrounding you.

WHAT IS IT?
A group of 74 tropical islands.
HOW TO GET THERE:
Fly to Proserpine and get a boat from
Shutehaven or Airlie Beach or take
the ferry from Brisbane to
Shutehaven, or fly to Hamilton Island.
WHEN TO GO:
Spring to autumn.
NEAREST TOWN:
Proserpine
DON'T MISS:
Whitehaven Beach.
YOU SHOULD KNOW:
It does get busy here in the
peak season.

The fantastic formations of the Rock Islands, a chain of over seventy small islets in the island nation of Palau in Micronesia, 32 km (20 mi) south of the capital city of Koror.

Palau Archipelago

The Palau Archipelago in western Micronesia is renowned for having some of the best dive sites in the world, taking in both wildlife-rich reefs and spectacular underwater caves.

Chandelier Cave is an especially interesting system that is accessed from underwater. The rear caves are above sea level and have coloured crystal growths. Jellyfish Lake has two species of jellyfish that follow the sunlight round the lake.

German Channel is renowned for its 'cleaning station' where sharks and manta rays allow cleaner wrasse to pick parasites and other bits of food off them, and even from inside their mouths. There is also a very good reef and large numbers of small fish here.

Among the more advanced dives sites, the Blue Holes are a vast system of interconnected caves, lit by diffuse sunlight that filters in through fissures. Nearby, the Blue Corner is normally kept until last – it spoils divers for other sites. It is a triangular reef, with sheer drops beside it. Strong currents bring vast quantities of plankton, providing a base for a food chain that culminates in barracuda and grey, black-tip and white-tip sharks. The quality of the fish is matched only by the drama of the site.

Other well-known dive sites in these islands include Turtle Cove, Tombstones, Soft Coral Arch, Ulong Channel, Turtle Cove, Short Drop Off, Siaes Tunnel, Peleliu Wall, Ngerchong Inside and Ngerchong Outside. Each offers a different array of species and a different challenge.

WHAT IS IT?
A group of islands north of New Guinea.
HOW TO GET THERE:
By air from Manila, Guam or Taipei.
WHEN TO GO:
Any time of year.
DON'T MISS:
The Blue Corner.
YOU SHOULD KNOW:
The currents are very strong in places and care is needed.

Christmas Island's Crab Migration

Each November, at the right phase of the moon and once the rains have set in, Christmas Island is host to an amazing sight: millions of crabs emerging and heading for the coast. The island is the top of an old volcano, and its rainforest-central plateau is about 300 m (1,000 ft) above sea level. For most of the year, you would not know that these crabs even existed, but for just a few days they take over the island, compelled by their need to get down to the sea to spawn. Until they are three years old, they live in burrows in the rainforest, but now nothing distracts them from their straight-line dash downhill: they clamber up steps onto people's verandahs and into their houses, cross roads with abandon and (unintentionally) terrorize pets. Christmas Island has more crab species than any other, but the one responsible for the annual havoc is the Christmas Island Red Crab (*Geocarcoidea natalis*). Although they are classed as land crabs, they still breathe through gills that must be kept moist and the larval stage of development must take place in the sea.

The island was first visited in the mid-seventeenth century, but was not colonized until the late nineteenth century. Early residents do not mention the crabs in diaries or correspondence, and it is possible that Maclear's rats (*Rattus maclearr*), which also inhabited the island at this time, ate them and their population exploded only after the rat's extinction in the early twentieth century.

The spectacle is all the more remarkable when you think that as tiny crabs, all of these millions of animals would have had to climb the mountain.

WHAT IS IT?
The spectacle of millions and millions of crabs all heading in the same direction.
HOW TO GET THERE:
From Perth by air.
WHEN TO GO:
November
NEAREST TOWN:
Bandung, Indonesia 550 km (330 mi)
YOU SHOULD KNOW:
The crabs are threatened by yellow crazy ants.

Red crabs spawning

New Guinea's Birds of Paradise

There are more than forty species of birds of paradise, many of which live on New Guinea, from the lowland forests near the coast to the rainforests inland and the high cloudforests. They are renowned both for the males' beautiful plumage and for their

spectacular courtship displays. It can be a challenge to see them, because they live deep in the rainforests, but local guides know the best spots in different areas of the island. Among the best known are the yellow, white, brown and green greater and lesser birds of paradise and the King of Saxony bird of paradise which has two bright blue eyebrow plumes that Archibold's bowerbirds appropriate for their bowers.

There are two main types of display: some species, such as the lesser bird of paradise display in groups in order to try to attract females, while others, like the magnificent bird of paradise display singly. Most of them are polygamous and the females tend the eggs with no help from the males.

Perhaps the most spectacular display is that of the superb bird of paradise: he attracts the female's attention by singing, then hops around in front of her. Then, he extends a cape of velvety black feathers above his head and stretches out his irridescent blue-green bib and dances around.

Whichever species you manage to see, their attempts to attract females as they flap about, flash bright colours, dangle upsidedown, and generally flaunt themselves, you can't help but be impressed.

WHAT IS IT?
A group of beautiful birds.
HOW TO GET THERE:
By air from Australia.
WHEN TO GO:
Late August to early September.
NEAREST TOWN:
Port Moresby.
YOU SHOULD KNOW:
The best way to see them is with local guides.

A lesser bird of paradise displays its wings.

Falealupo Lava Tubes

In the far north-west of Samoa's island of Savai'i, near the Falealupo Forest Preserve, is a rare geological phenomenon – a series of lava tubes. These form when the surface over a fast-moving lava channel cools sufficiently to crust over while lava continues to flow underneath and drain away. Eventually, the outflow from the volcano stops and the tube empties. These tubes can be kilometres in length. The whole of Savai'i is volcanic and there are extensive lava fields in places all over the island, including where villages have been destoyed by lava flows. Here, however, the lava tubes can be of great benefit to people: on occasions in the past when cyclones have threatened, such as during the early 1990s, the tubes provide a safe refuge in an emergency. More ominously, according to local legend one of the caves on the Falealupo Peninsula is one of the gateways to the underworld, through which spirits emerge at night and return before sunrise.

Guides from the village take visitors about 500 m (1,600 feet) into the tubes so they can see the strange texture of the walls and get the eerie feeling of being inside part of a volcano and think what it must have been like when molten rock was flowing through the tube floor and the walls were glowing with the heat.

WHAT IS IT?
A series of tunnels in an old lava flow.
HOW TO GET THERE:
By air or ferry from 'Upolu, then on the coast road.
WHEN TO GO:
Any time of year.
NEAREST TOWN:
Asau 10 km (6 mi)
YOU SHOULD KNOW:
Visitors must be accompanied by a village guide.

Palolo Deep Marine Reserve

WHAT IS IT?
A deep blue hole in a coral reef.
HOW TO GET THERE:
On foot from central Apia to Vaiala Beach, then swim.
WHEN TO GO:
At high tide when the weather is not rough.
NEAREST TOWN:
Apia
DON'T MISS:
The fish and coral.
YOU SHOULD KNOW:
Currents can be strong around the reef.

In this part of northern 'Upolu, the reef is only a few hundred metres offshore, making this spectacular dive site – one of Samoa's best – easily reached from the access point at the secluded and pretty Vaiala Beach just east of the city harbour. Here, you can hire snorkels and goggles. Swimming over the reef and its multitude of fish at high tide, when you are less likely to step on the coral and damage it, you approach a dark circle in the water. When you reach it, you are greeted by a deep blue hole, full of bright, tropical fish and walled with colourful corals. In the hole, and on the reefs around, you will see starfish, sea cucumbers and sea slugs and clown fish. Moray eels hide out in holes among the coral, and while you will see farmed giant clams in cages, you might be lucky enough to spot wild ones as well. The coral-encrusted walls of the hole drop straight down into the depths.

The reserve is also the site of a remarkable phenemonon in October and November of each year, when at the right phase of the moon, the Palolo reef worms release wriggling bundles of spawn that are a local delicacy.

Alofaaga Blowholes

WHAT IS IT?
A group of spectacular blowholes on Savai'i's south coast.
HOW TO GET THERE:
By air or ferry from 'Upalu, then on the coast road.
WHEN TO GO:
Any time of year, at high tide in rough weather.
NEAREST TOWN:
Taga 4 km (2 mi)
YOU SHOULD KNOW:
The rocks can be slippery and dangerous when wet.

Also known as the Taga Blowholes from the village nearby, these are claimed by many to be the most spectacular of their kind on the planet. At the remote south-western corner of Savai'i, these blow holes in the low cliffs are a must at high tide. Tubes in the lava field reach what is now the coast, and the action of waves over the years has led to the collapse of the roofs of several of them so that when rough seas flood into the tubes, pressure forces the water through these holes to an astonishing height, every few seconds. In really wild weather, the fountain of water can reach 60 m (200 ft) into the air before it comes crashing back down onto the shiny black rock.

The locals have a favourite party trick to demonstrate the power of the water: timing it just right, they throw coconuts into the blowholes so that these, too, go soaring into the air.

This wild, dramatic place, where young volcanic rocks meet the Pacific Ocean and white foam surges over the lava and the blowholes create their spectacle, truly is a place forged from the ancients' four elements of earth, air, fire and water.

Blowholes in Samoa

Togitogiga Falls Recreation Reserve

WHAT IS IT?
A lovely set of waterfalls with natural pools to swim in.
HOW TO GET THERE:
On 'Upopu's main South Coast Road.
WHEN TO GO:
Any time.
NEAREST TOWN:
Saleilua 7 km (4 mi)
DON'T MISS:
Swimming in the pools.
YOU SHOULD KNOW:
The waterfalls become a raging torrent after heavy rain.

Surrounded by lush rainforest and overhung by palms, the gentle cascades of Togitogiga are a treat. They are accessed via a 1-km (0.6-mi) track through beautiful greenery. Deep pools sit below each cascade, making wonderful places for a swim in hot weather. Getting into the middle pool requires a scramble on some steep rocks and then a leap of faith. It is possible to get to the lower pool from below, but the jump into it from the middle pool is exilarating. Before jumping into any of the pools, check where the water is deepest and make sure that are no logs just under the surface. The falls are usually quieter during the week.

A couple of hours' hard walk through the jungle leads to the Pe'ape'a Cave (which is in fact within the O le Pupu-Pu'e National Park next door) is an old lava tube that is home to the swiftlets that give it its name. To the south lies more of the national park, through which an extremely rough road and another overgrown trail lead down to the spectacular lava coast, where a rough path leads along the cliffs for amazing views of the ocean and the weird formations in the solidified lava.

The Togitogiga Falls

A banyan tree in the Falealupo Rainforest Preserve, Savai'i

Falealupo Rainforest Preserve

At what could be said to be almost the most westerly point on the planet (the international date line is only a few kilometres away), the Falealupo Rainforest Preserve is an area sacred to the locals. The forest was damaged by severe cyclones in the early 1990s, but is returning to its former beauty. A typical species of the forest is the banyan tree, two of which support one of the highlights of the area, the canopy walkway. Stairways scale 9 m (30 ft) up into the tree tops, leading to a 24-m (80 ft) swing bridge slung between the trees. As you walk across it, you will realize that swing is definitely the correct term for it. Another 20 m (66 ft) higher is a platform in the very top of one of the banyans: from here the views over the forest and up to the island's volcanoes are truly amazing.

The platform doubles as a hotel room, where visitors can sleep under the stars, if they're brave enough.

This is a land rich in legend, and a little to the west is Moso's Footprint, a large indentation in the lava said to have been left by the giant Moso when he stepped here from Fiji (where there is another footprint on Viti Levu).

WHAT IS IT?
A 12-sq-km (4.5-sq-mi) reserve in the far north-west of Samoa.
HOW TO GET THERE:
By air or sea from 'Upolu, then on the coast road.
WHEN TO GO:
Any time.
NEAREST TOWN:
Asau (9 km, 4 mi)
DON'T MISS:
Sleeping on the canopy platform.
YOU SHOULD KNOW:
It was feared in the late 1980s that the forest would have to be sold for logging in order to pay for a local school, but a donation saved it for the villagers.

*Scout Island on South
Tarawa Atoll*

Tarawa

This tiny atoll, perched on an extinct and eroding submarine volcano is one of the most remote spots on earth. Tourist development and infrastructure are minimal, so for people who really want to get away from it all, it is a must. The capital, Bairiki is in the south and there is a small resort on Buariki in the north. The islets are sparsely inhabited and low lying. As the volcano below them erodes, the corals grow to maintain their position at just the right height below the surface, but several of them have already been submerged by rising seas, and others are predicted to be lost the same way within just a few years.

The reefs are topped by sandy beaches and the lagoon is edged by palm trees, making this quiet place, where the only sounds may be the surf crashing against the coral and the calls of seabirds, ideal for relaxing. The island's reefs have a wide variety of different species of coral and pretty shoals of colourful fish. Divers may see rays, snapper, clams or black-tipped shark and bonefish. If lucky, they may catch sight of a wary octopus squeezing itself into a crevice.

This undeveloped and beautiful atoll is a very special place.

WHAT IS IT?
An atoll in the middle of the Pacific Ocean.
HOW TO GET THERE:
By air from Sydney, Brisbane, Auckland or Wellington.
WHEN TO GO:
At any time.
YOU SHOULD KNOW:
Several of the islets have already succumbed to rising sea levels.

426

Franz Josef Glacier

Like the Fox Glacier 20 km (12 mi) to the south, the Franz Josef Glacier is fed by snow and rainfall high in the Southern Alps. Even more dramatically than its neighbour, it exhibits a cycle of retreat and advance caused by the tipping of the balance between how much material is added at the top and how much melts away at the bottom. During the period between 1940s and 1980s, it rapidly retreated several kilometres, but after that, it began advancing again by an average of about 70 cm (27.5 in) a day and is currently 12 km (7.5 mi) long and terminates 19 km (11.5 mi) from the sea at an altitude of 240 m (790 ft) above sea level. At the peak of the last ice age, it probably reached all the way to the Tasman Sea.

There are various ways of getting on to the glacier. From the terminus, visitors can take a guided walk or go by themselves as far as the first ice fall, but from here it is not possible to go any higher up, so a popular way of doing so is to take one of the many helicopter trips on offer to the area between the first and second falls for a guided walk across the glacier and, on some walks, into the ice caves.

WHAT IS IT?
A 12-km (7.5-mi) glacier in New Zealand's Southern Alps.
HOW TO GET THERE:
By road from Greymouth.
WHEN TO GO:
Spring to autumn.
NEAREST TOWN:
Franz Josef township 5 km (3 mi).
DON'T MISS:
The helicopter trip onto the glacier.
YOU SHOULD KNOW:
The Maori name for the glacier is Ka Rolmata o Hinehukatere – the tears of the avalanche girl.

Franz Josef Glacier

Mount Aspiring National Park

Straddling the southern end of the Southern Alps, Mount Aspiring National Park was established in 1964. It is vast, covering 3555 sq km (2210 sq mi).

Like much of the wilderness areas of the south-west of South Island, it is popular with walkers, climbers and hikers because of the beauty and variety of its scenery, which includes high mountains and beautiful river valleys set among a wilderness of lakes, beech forests, alpine and subalpine meadows and tussock grasslands.

The most commonly used route up Mount Aspiring itself, which stands at over 3,000 m (9843 ft), starts from Raspberry Flat, north-west of Wanaka by road, but the park can also be accessed from Queenstown, Haast and Glenorchy.

Among the most popular walking tracks is the Routeburn Track, which partly follows an old Maori route into the area. They came here to find greenstone, a dark form of jade that they used for tools and ornaments.

There is plenty of wildlife to be seen here, from native birds such as the yellow-crowned parakeet, South Island fantail, South Island robin, rifleman, bellbird and New Zealand pigeon in the bushland, while blue ducks and paradise shelducks may be found in the valley. You will also probably see introduced whitetail deer in the lower Routeburn valley and chamois in the mountaintops.

One bird that is difficult to miss in the alpine areas is the kea. These large green mountain parrots are very intelligent, and mischievous, and like nothing better than the challenge of extracting the seals from around car doors, except perhaps unzipping people's bags in order to extract their lunch.

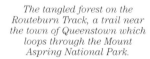

The tangled forest on the Routeburn Track, a trail near the town of Queenstown which loops through the Mount Aspring National Park.

The Bay of Islands

The Bay of Islands Maritime Park's 144 islands are dotted around a bay with clear blue waters and a rich variety of wildlife. It is a paradise for sailors, a mecca for big-sports fishermen and a heaven for wildlife-watchers. Warm equatorial waters mean that it has an equable climate and locals claim that it doesn't have a winter.

The best way to appreciate the coastline of the bay and the islands is from the water, whether from a kayak, yacht, cruiser or amphibious 'duck'. For many visitors, the highlight of a stay here is the opportunity to go dolphin- or whale-watching: sightings are almost guaranteed here. It is even possible to swim with dolphins or, rather, to go on a licensed tour, get into the water and let them decide whether to come to swim with you.

Among the several good dive sites is the wreck of the Greenpeace ship, Rainbow Warrior, which was sunk here by the French secret services in 1985, and is slowly being colonized by marine organisms. Elsewhere, the reefs of volcanic rock are covered in forests of kelp that are teeming with subtropical fish.

Local scenic highlights include Cape Brett, and the Hole in the Rock on Piercy Island, and several operators offer boat trips to them.

This is also a historic area of New Zealand: the treaty between the British and the Maori was signed at Waitangi, overlooking the bay.

WHAT IS IT?
A beautiful bay of the north coast of New Zealand's North Island.
HOW TO GET THERE:
By road or rail from Auckland to Russell or by air to Kerikiri then by road.
WHEN TO GO:
Any time of year.
NEAREST TOWN:
Russell
DON'T MISS:
Swimming with the dolphins.
YOU SHOULD KNOW:
There are strict rules about how closely boats can approach whales and dolphins.

Moturua Island, Bay of Islands

Lake Matheson

Carved out at the peak of the last ice age some 14,000 years ago by the Fox Glacier, when it was much nearer the Tasman Sea, Lake Matheson provides one of the iconic images of New Zealand, as the peaks of Aoraki/Mount Cook and Mount Tasman are reflected in its still waters, framed by the rainforest that surrounds the lake and protects it from breezes that would disturb its perfect surface. Because the lake bed contains large amounts of dissolved sediment left there by the glacier, its waters are dark, increasing its properties as a mirror.

    The forty-minute stroll down to the lake from the Fox Glacier village leads through beautiful temperate rainforest to the jetty, positioned to give the best possible views. You also catch glimpses of the reflection from the lake-shore path.

If you can, the best times of day to come here are sunrise and sunset. As dawn breaks over the mountains in the east, eerie blue light spills over the snow-covered peaks and down into the valley below, highlighting the mist as the reflection gradually becomes clearer and brighter. At the other end of the day, the mountains take on an orange hue as the sun drops, chased up the mountain sides by ever-deepening shades as it finally drops below the horizon.

WHAT IS IT?
A glacial lake that provides some of the most stunning views you will ever see.

HOW TO GET THERE:
By road, then on foot. The lake is 6 km (4 mi) from Fox Glacier township along Cook Flat Road, and the walk around the lake takes about 70 minutes.

WHEN TO GO:
Spring to autumn in good weather.

NEAREST TOWN:
Fox Glacier village/Weheka 5 km (3 mi)

DON'T MISS:
Sunrise and sunset.

Waitomo Caves

WHAT IS IT?
A group of limestone caves known
for their rock formations.
HOW TO GET THERE:
By road from Hamilton,
71 km (44 mi)
WHEN TO GO:
Spring to autumn.
NEAREST TOWN:
Te Kuiti 12 km (7.5 mi)
DON'T MISS:
The glow worms.
YOU SHOULD KNOW:
Gardner's Gut is for experieced
cavers only.

Set in the south of the Waikoto region of North Island, this group of caves is known for its spectacular stalagmites and stalactites. Access ranges from the very easy – Waitomo – to the very difficult – Gardner's Gut. There are about 300 known caves in the area, although many of them are not open.

Waitomo Cave system was first explored in 1887, although the local Maori had known of its existence for years. Chief Tane Tinorau and Englishman Fred Mace discovered the lower entrance and found the underground river, glow worm cave and limestone formations. The chief continued to explore and eventually found the upper entrance, which is the one used today. He opened it to the public in 1889.

From the entrance at the top level, visitors first go to the Catacombs, then down a vertical shaft to the Banquet Chamber. From here, a short detour leads to the Pipe Organ, but this is often shut because carbon dioxide builds up here and cannot escape. The main route from the Banquet Chamber leads down to the Cathedral, a chamber about 18 m (60 ft) high with wonderful accoustics.

Boats depart from the jetty to the Glow Worm Grotto, a cave lit by the ethereal light of these small insects clinging to the roof, and past more spectacular stalactites and stalagmites until the river emerges back out into the open.

Illuminated speleothem including stalactites and stalagmites created by droplets of water depositing calcium carbonate in Aranui Cave, one of the Waitomo Caves.

Whale-watching in Kaikoura Bay

The fluke of an Orca off Kaikoura

Once a whaling town, Kaikoura is now the centre of a year-round whale-watching scene, because of the year-round population of sperm whales. They stay here because the underwater geology provides them with perfect feeding grounds. Two currents of water meet here, a cold nutrient-rich one from the south and a warm one from the north which brings the nutrients up from the deep ocean to form the basis of a food chain that culminates with the whales, seals and dolphins. The other factor here is a series of extremely deep canyons offshore, in which octopus, squid and large fish lurk. The whales dive down into the canyons to feed and then re-emerge to catch their breath, spending about three-quarters of their time underwater. Boat trips out to see them use hydrophones to listen in on their clicks to locate them and estimate when and where they will surface.

Kaikoura Bay is also home to Hector's dolphins, which can be seen from the waterfront. Among the smallest dolphins, they are very rare, so being able to watch them while sipping a cup of coffee in a café is a real treat.

Another, even closer, encounter is the boat trip out to see – and swim with – the dusky dolphins that live a few kilometres offshore in summer. When in the mood, these boisterous animals seem to enjoy showing off for their human visitors and will indulge in synchronized leaps, double somersaults and belly flops just for the sheer fun of it.

WHAT IS IT?
One of the best nature encounters you will ever have.
HOW TO GET THERE:
By road from Christchurch 183 km (113 mi).
WHEN TO GO:
Any time of year.
NEAREST TOWN:
Kaikoura
YOU SHOULD KNOW:
Many of the whales here are 'teenagers', exploiting the relatively easy pickings until they are mature enough to head off to the breeding grounds.

The rocky reef with an underwater forest of kelp (Ecklonia radiata) Mayor Island

Mayor Island/Tuhua

The top half of a dormant shield volcano in the Bay of Plenty, Mayor Island covers an area of 13 sq km (5 sq mi), most of which is occupied by a crater blown out by the last phase of eruption about 7,000 years ago. Two small crater lakes lie within it. The Maori name for the island is their word for obsidian, black volcanic glass, which they prized highly for making cutting tools, arrow heads, etc. The Bay of Plenty still lives up to its name, and the waters near here are a mecca for game-fishermen, although the waters round the island are protected, as is the island itself. The site of the old game-fishing headquarters on Sou'East Bay is on a beautiful beach and the clear waters and rich variety of fish here make the island a popular destination for divers.

There are several tracks on the island, so visitors can explore the native bush and see the birdlife. Because it is protected, the easiest way to get there is with a registered tour operator.

The last eruption breached the north wall of the volcano almost to sea level, so if sea levels do continue to rise as predicted, the centre of this pretty island will one day become inundated with sea water.

WHAT IS IT?
A volcanic island in North Island's Bay of Plenty.
HOW TO GET THERE:
By boat from Whangamata or Tauranga
WHEN TO GO:
Summer
NEAREST TOWN:
Whangamata 36 km (22 mi)
YOU SHOULD KNOW:
The island is a wildlife refuge: permits are needed to land there.

Rakiura National Park

Rakiura National Park covers about 85 per cent of Stewart Island, across the Foveaux Strait from South Island. It is renowned as being the one place where you can almost guarantee to see kiwis in the wild, as there are about 25,000 of them here. Rakiura is one of the Maori names for the island, and means Glowing Skies, which may be a reference to either the glowing sunrises and sunsets that often occur here or to the Aurora Australis – the southern lights: there is a variation in the earth's magnetic field here, which means that this area gets more than its fair share of auroras.

The national park is New Zealand's most recent, having been set up in 2002. Although predators such as cats and rats have wrought havoc on the island's bird populations, and introduced deer have overgrazed parts of the forest, it is in a far better state of conservation than anywhere on the mainland. The Rakiura Track, one of New Zealand's ten great tracks, leads through lush forests with giant tree ferns, ground ferns and epiphytic orchids. The track is a 36-km (22-mi), three-day walk through the bush. As well as kiwis, walkers should be able to see and hear bellbirds, tui, parakeets, fantails, shining cuckoos and, hopefully, kakapo.

WHAT IS IT?
New Zealand's newest national park.
HOW TO GET THERE:
By ferry from Bluff or plane from Invercargill.
WHEN TO GO:
Summer.
NEAREST TOWN:
Oban, located on Half Moon Bay.
DON'T MISS:
The Aurora Australis.
YOU SHOULD KNOW:

Marrow grass growing on sand dunes with native forest in the distance, Stewart Island.

The Southern Alps on South Island

The Southern Alps

Running down almost the entire length South Island is the range that Captain Cook dubbed the Southern Alps, which form the character of the whole island. To the west, they drop sharply almost to the sea along the line of the Alpine Fault, with only a narrow coastal plain, and this land is isolated and sparsely populated, while to the east the plains are dotted with towns, villages and farms, and the major cities cling to the coast.

Seventeen mountains in this 550-km (340-mi) range exceed 3,000 m (10,000 ft) and remain snow-capped for much or all of the year.

The mountains are still actively being formed, as the Pacific Plate is being pushed into the Australian Plate, causing the latter to buckle and crumple. Surprisingly, although they are being pushed up, they are not growing any taller, because they are eroding at the top just as quickly.

The moist winds from the west drop most of their rain and snow on the western side of the range and whereas the glaciers to the east are retreating, several of those on the west side are currently growing.

This beautiful range of mountains is a stunning sight from a distance – Captain Cook described them as 'prodigious high' when he saw them from out at sea – and its mountains and valleys are popular with climbers, hikers and walkers, who enjoy the ever-changing landscape of glaciers and icy tarns, temperate rainforest, alpine meadow, lush woodland and pastures.

WHAT IS IT?
A mountain ridge that forms the spine of New Zealand's South Island.
HOW TO GET THERE:
By road or on the The TranzAlpine train from Christchurch.
WHEN TO GO:
Summer

436

Abel Tasman National Park

The smallest of New Zealand's national parks, the 225 sq km (89 sq mi) Abel Tasman National Park was set up in 1942, the three hundredth anniversary of the Dutch captain's disastrous attempt to land in Golden Bay to the north. However, he lost four of his crew in a skirmish with the local Maori and never returned. The area had been logged since 1855, and part of the park's raison-d'être is to allow the plantlife here to regenerate to its former beauty by removing non-native species and encouraging the local plants to recolonize.

The seventy miles of beaches, which form part of a separate scenic reserve, are beautiful and sea-kayaking and sailing along the bay are popular pastimes here, as is walking. One of New Zealand's famous Great Walks, the Abel Tasman Coastal Track, takes three to five days and features gorgeous views of the beaches, coast and blue-green waters of the bay as it climbs up ridges and then back down to the coast, while the Abel Tasman Inland Track leads through the regenerating forest, where black beech lines the dry ridges and damp gullies are filled with a rich variety of plants. The landscape is beautiful, with occasional granite and limestone outcrops, streams and gorges.

WHAT IS IT?
A national park on the west shore of Tasman Bay, South Island
HOW TO GET THERE:
By road from Nelson, 80 km (50 mi).
WHEN TO GO:
Any time of year.
NEAREST TOWN:
Motekua 20 km (12 mi)

One of the many beautiful beaches in the Abel Tasman National Park

Milford Sound

WHAT IS IT?
A large glacial fiord in the northwest of South Island's fiordland.
HOW TO GET THERE:
By air or sea, or by road from Te Anau.
WHEN TO GO:
Spring to autumn.
NEAREST TOWN:
Te Anau 119 km (74 mi)
DON'T MISS:
The Bowen and Sutherland Falls
YOU SHOULD KNOW:
This was the last refuge in the wild of the kakapo: there may be some still undiscovered in remote areas, but it is doubtful. Birds that could be found here in the 1980s were removed to safe islands away from predators such as cats.

Milford Sound is the best known of the fjords in the isolated area of the southwest coast of South Island, known as Fiordland and the only one accessible all the way by road. Unlike most places on New Zealand's coast, this was not named by Captain Cook, but by John Grono, captain of a seal-hunting ship, who in 1822 named it after his birthplace in Wales.

Glaciers carved out the sounds and lakes of this area between 15,000 and 20,000 years ago, but unlike farther north in the Southern Alps, the glaciers are long gone, leaving a wilderness of mountains, lakes and waterfalls, native bush and temperate rainforest, alpine meadows and the calm, still waters of the sounds

themselves. Even the drive to get here from Te Anau is glorious. An even better way to get here is the Milford Track, a four-day trek that leaves from the northern end of Lake Te Anau and crosses the Mackinnon Pass before meeting up with the road again under the looming 1,412-m (4,633-ft) Mitre Peak. On the way, hikers pass through forests whose giant trees drip moisture-loving lichen, ferns, moss and vines: this area receives a startling 7.6 m (300 in) of rain a year.

Among the activities in the sound itself are wildlife cruises to the mouth of the sound, where you may see seals and dolphins and perhaps penguins in autumn.

Fiordland World Heritage Park

WHAT IS IT?
An amazing land- and seascape in the south-west of South Island.
HOW TO GET THERE:
Across Lake Manapouri by catamaran, then by road to Deep Cove.
WHEN TO GO:
Spring to autumn.
NEAREST TOWN:
Manapouri 80 km (50 mi)
DON'T MISS:
The bottlenose dolphins in Doubtful Sound.
YOU SHOULD KNOW:
Average annual rainfall is 7.6 m (300 in).

Doubtful Sound is the largest sound in the area. It was originally named Doubtful Harbour by Captain Cook because he was not sure whether it was navigable. The glaciers that carved its three arms no longer fling ice into it, and it is a peaceful, if dramatic, place. In good weather, its waters are flat calm, and mirror the cliffs looming above them and the little islands that perch in the middle.

This is a remote area, not as often visited as Milford Sound to the north, and access from the sea is as easy as access from the land. Boat trips explore the length of the sound, while for an even more tranquil experience, sea kayaks can be hired.

The landscape is spectacular, with high cliffs, and several large waterfalls, including Helen Falls, easily visible from Deep Cove and the 600-m (2,000-ft) Browne Falls. After rain, which can be very heavy, the entire side of the sound can seem to be one giant waterfall.

Wildlife in the sound includes friendly bottlenose dolphins, which race to play in the bow wave of the tour boat, fur seals and both blue and Fiordland crested penguins.

Dusky Sound, to the south, is even more inaccessible, reachable only from the sea, on a walking trail from Lake Manapouri or by helicopter from Te Anau.

The Dusky Track, although not classified as one of New Zealand's Great Walks, is varied and challenging. It leads from Supper Cove to the west arm of Lake Manapouri over beautiful, untouched mountain scenery.

Entrance to the Fiords, Fjordland National Park

Lake Taupo

Lurking under the northern half of Lake Taupo is a giant volcano, thought to be a supervolcano. Over the last 330,000 years it has erupted on numerous occasions, although little evidence for many of these eruptions survives as many of the sites are have been destroyed by subsequent events or are under the waters of Lake Taupo. The eruption that is thought to have created the caldera is the Oruanui eruption, which occurred about 26,500 years ago, although it is possible that there was an earlier lake. The most recent eruption was about 1,800 years ago, and spread ash and pumice right across North Island, in some places to a depth of about 5 m (16.5 ft ft).

The volcanic nature of the area can be seen in the numerous thermal features in the area, including hot thermal springs and the geysers and plopping mud puddles at, for example, Wairakei at the northern end of the lake.

However, what this violent past has left is a beautiful landscape, where the largest freshwater lake in New Zealand is surrounded by bush-clad mountains and more distant volcanoes. The lake's crystal clear waters are perfect for yachting and kayaking, while the countryside around is popular for walking, hiking, skiing in winter and wildlife-watching. One day, the volcano may erupt again, devastating the land, but in the meantime, it is a special place to contemplate the forces of nature.

WHAT IS IT?
A lake in a volcanic caldera, surrounded by magnificent landscape.
HOW TO GET THERE:
By road from Auckland 180 km (111 mi).
WHEN TO GO:
Spring to autumn.
NEAREST TOWN:
Taupo 5km (3 mi)
DON'T MISS:
The Craters of the Moon at Wairakei.

Mount Tongariro across Lake Taupo

Mount Tongariro

Mount Tongariro

Mount Tongariro, a complex of peaks and craters, is at the heart of North Island's volcanic landscape. Geologists think that this massif, with a base 15 by 3 km (9 by 5 mi) and a summit 8 by 3 km (5 by 2 mi), used to be higher but lost its top in a series of massive eruptions, and that the craters and peaks seen today are the result of subsequent activity.

The remnants of at least a dozen cones make up the mountain, and the most recent activity in the central part of the massif occurred in Red Crater, in 1926. This feature is still actively venting acrid gases and the ground here is hot to walk on.

The first authenticated ascent of the higher of the two peaks occurred in 1867. Until a year or so earlier the Maori had prevented anyone climbing the mountain because it had been made *tapu* (taboo). The peaks are 1,968 and 1,959 m (6,457 and 6,427 ft) and are not difficult climbs, while the route from Mangatepopo hut in the south to Keleteh Hut in the north, after a steep start up to the saddle, crosses the broad south crater, tops a small ridge by Red Crater, drops to the Emerald Lakes (their colour comes from minerals from Red Crater), skirts the central crater and Blue Lake (in another old crater) and drops down the slope below the north crater.

The views over this harsh volcanic landscape to the forests below, especially from near Red Crater and the Emerald Lakes are panoramic, and absolutely beautiful.

WHAT IS IT?
A volcanic massif on North Island.
HOW TO GET THERE:
By road from Auckland 330 km (205 mi), then on foot.
WHEN TO GO:
Any time of year.
NEAREST TOWN:
Taurewa 16 km (10 mi)

Whakarewarewa's thermal valley and mud pools

One of the most active thermal areas in the strange landscape of Rotorua is the Whakarewarewa Thermal Valley, which hosts an eclectic selection of giant mud puddles, fumaroles, steaming hot pools, as well as the geysers of Geyser Flat.

The appearance and behaviour of mud pools depends on the relative proportions of mud and water. In this valley, the mud is quite thick, and the successive bubble-bursts form concentric rings that disappear only very slowly, leaving a landscape of unearthly ridges.

There are roughly 500 pools in the valley, many of which are alkaline hot springs. Their edges are encrusted with silica and steam rises over their blue waters, adding to the eeriness of the landscape.

To the local Maori, who have lived here since the early fourteenth century, this area is where the fire goddesses Te Pupu and Te Hoata first came to the surface and the geysers hot springs and mud pools are caused by their breath.

Locals say that each of the geothermal features here has its own personality and they can tell their moods from how they sound. The land here is continually changing and careful checks are made daily to see whether hot springs are emerging or new cracks are forming. As you walk, swathed in steam, between areas of bubbling mud, and watch water boiling from under the ground, you will probably feel very glad that they do.

The Prince of Wales Feathers thermal geyser steams and spouts boiling water at Whakarewarewa, near Rotorua.

WHAT IS IT?
The most spectacular part of Rotorua's eerie landscape.
HOW TO GET THERE:
By road or rail to Rotorua city
WHEN TO GO:
Any time of year.
NEAREST TOWN:
Rotorua city.
YOU SHOULD KNOW:
You must keep to the marked paths.

Steam rises from Champagne Pool at Wai-o-Tapu Thermal Wonderland on a summer afternoon.

North Island's Volcanic Plateau

On the southern edge of the lake-filled Rotorua Caldera is a giant volcanic plateau that stretches south from Rotorua for well over 20 km (12 mi). To the west of the city is Kuirau Park, normally the site of mud pools that splat, gloop and plop gently, but sometimes these pools are witness to larger events, such as in 2006 when a mud fountain, as high as 20 m (66 ft) high and 30 m (100 ft) across, gushed into the air for an hour.

In 1886, Mount Tarawera to the south erupted, and a 17-km (10.5-mi) rift opened in the earth's crust, virtually splitting the mountain in half. Within a few years, Lake Rotomahana had become established in the valley, together with the largest hot spring in the country.

In the area known as Hells Gate, you will find boiling lakes, Kakahi Falls – the world's largest hot waterfall – and a bizarre mud volcano. Every six weeks or so, the top of this 1.8-m (6 -ft) cone hardens and once pressure has built up, it explodes, throwing 'bombs' of hot mud flying into the air around it. The mud pool known as the sulphur bath is strongly acidic (ph 1.5) and the air is filled with the rotten-egg smell of sulphur dioxide.

At Wai-o-Tapu, the Lady Knox geyser was discovered by prisoners on work duty in the early twentieth century. It erupts promptly at the same time each morning, and each eruption can last for up to an hour. This area is filled with spectacular coloured pools and terraces.

Set against the beauty of the lake and the green lowland forest that surrounds it, these geothermal areas seem not to belong on this planet at all.

WHAT IS IT?
An amazing geothermal area of geysers, mud puddles and hot pools.
HOW TO GET THERE:
By road from Taupo 80 km (50 mi)
WHEN TO GO:
Any time.
NEAREST TOWN:
Rotorua city.
DON'T MISS:
Kakahi's mud volcano and hot waterfall.

Papaitonga Dune Lake Reserve

Set in the broad coastal Horowhena plain north of Wellington, Papaitonga Dune Lake Reserve holds a rare remnant of the flora that used to be typical of this region: coastal podocarp and broadleaf woodland. On the track that leads down to the lake, visitors will see a variety of tree ferns, tawa – once common here – phormiums and Nikau palms. The lake itself is beautiful and its islands, waters and the surrounding lowland forests and wetland serve as refuges for migrating wildfowl, as well as holding resident species that have been squeezed out of other places through habitat loss. The two islands are called Motukiwi (or Papaitonga) and Motungarara (or Papawhaerangi). The latter is an artificial island, created by the Muaupoko people in the early 1820s. The recreational reserve adjoining the lake has walking trails.

The area around the lake was bought in 1897 by Sir Walter Buller, author of *The History of the Birds of New Zealand*, in order to protect it; the lake was added in 1991 and the total area now covers 1.2 sq km (0.7 sq mi).

The area is important to the Tangata Whenua – the descendents of the people who first inhabited this area – and they still use the lake as a source of food and material for their traditional crafts.

WHAT IS IT?
A rare remnant of this habitat and important for migrant birds.
HOW TO GET THERE:
By road from Wellington.
WHEN TO GO
Apring to autumn.
NEAREST TOWN:
Levin 5 km (3 mi)
YOU SHOULD KNOW:
Access to the islands is forbidden.

Papaitonga

Aoraki/Mount Cook

WHAT IS IT?
The highest mountain in New Zealand.
HOW TO GET THERE:
By road from Dunedin.
WHEN TO GO:
Summer.
NEAREST TOWN:
Mount Cook village 12 km (7 mi)
DON'T MISS:
The view from the bottom of the Tasman Glacier.
YOU SHOULD KNOW:
Mount Cook was 10 m (33 ft) higher until 1991 when 10 million cu m (350 million cu ft) of ice and rock crashed down from the summit.

The highest mountain in New Zealand at 3,754 m (12,316 ft), Aoraki/Mount Cook stands at the heart of a national park that covers 700 sq km (270 sq mi) that contains more than 140 peaks over 2,000 m (6,600 ft) and has seventy-two named glaciers. It was named Mount Cook by Captain Stokes in 1851, and the name was officially changed to Aoraki/Mount Cook in 1998. The Maori name means 'cloud piercer'.

On the approach to Aoraki/Mount Cook village, near the shore of Lake Pukaki and alongside the Tasman river, you gradually realize just how immense this spine of mountains is. The village sits – overwhelmed – at the termination of the Hooker and Mueller glaciers that spill off the southern side of the mountain.

There are walks and climbs for people of every ability in the area, from the gruelling trip to the mountain's peaks (there are three, the northernmost of which is the highest) to tough hikes, which require stamina and experience but are worth it for the views over the glaciers and tarns, and gentle strolls in the lowlands, through temperate rainforest, remnants of beech woods and alpine meadows that are full of wild flowers in summer.

The Tasman Glacier is an immense 27 km (17 mi) long and 3 km (1.9 mi) across at its widest. Unlike some of the glaciers on the other side of the Southern Alps, the glaciers on this side are retreating.

For those who don't want to hike, there are scenic flights from Aoraki/Mount Cook village.

Fox Glacier

WHAT IS IT?
A 13-km (8-mi) glacier in the west of New Zealand's South Island.
HOW TO GET THERE:
By road from Greymouth.
WHEN TO GO:
Spring to autumn.
NEAREST TOWN:
Fox Glacier village/Weheka
5 km (3 mi)
YOU SHOULD KNOW:
There are frequent ice falls and the barriers at the foot of the glacier are for visitors' safety. If you want to go onto the glacier, take a guided walk.

Also known as Te Moeka o Tuawe, Fox Glacier is highly unusual. Not only does it terminate in a rainforest, but – unlike so many glaciers around the world – it is actually advancing, by an average of about 1 m (3 ft) a day.

Fed by four glaciers high in the Southern Alps, Fox Glacier drops 2,600 m (8,530 ft) on its 13-km (8-mi) journey to within 300 m (1,000 ft) of sea level. Unlike glaciers in the European Alps, where winter snowfall is diminishing, the catchment area (névé) of the Fox Glacier (and the Franz Josef Glacier to the north) currently receives up to 30 m (100 ft) of snow a year, as the roaring forties winds bring moist air from the Southern Ocean, which is forced up the sides of the Southern Alps, cools and drops rain and snow in large quantities. This becomes compacted blue glacial ice, which flows under its own weight down the glacier valleys. A layer of water underneath the glacier, and rapid melt lower down its course, allow the glacier to flow anything up to ten times faster than most glaciers.

The valleys through which the Fox Glacier grinds its way down is stepped, forcing the ice to stretch and break up, creating massive crevasses, pinnacles and sheer ice falls. The viewpoint at the bottom of the glacier provides spectacular vistas, but there are also guided walks onto the more stable parts of the glacier for those who dare.

Crevasses cover the surface of Fox Glacier on the west side of Mount Cook on a summer evening.

Boundary Stream Mainland Island

The 'Mainland Island' is not in fact an island but some 8 sq km (3 sq mi) of land on the eastern side of the Maungaharuru Range of North Island, with a variety of habitats from lowland forest at about 300 m (1,000 ft) to montane forest at 1,000 m (3,300 ft). Its importance lies in the highly endangered bird species that are protected here.

Before people arrived here, especially the Europeans, there were very few predators so several bird species, including the iconic kiwis, took to the ground and over the millennia lost the ability to fly and nested on the ground or underground, which made them vulnerable to hunting and to predation from introduced cats, rats, stoats, ferrets, weasels and hedgehogs, while other birds such as the kaka lost out to possums and even wasps in competition for food.

Some of the birds are kept within large enclosures for their own protection and this enables visitors to see them close up, which would normally be impossible, while allowing the birds to live completely naturally. Others, such as the kokako, wander freely.

Scenic walks through the area, which is being restored to provide habitat for the birds, offer panoramic views over this very special area and highlights include the beautiful 58-m (190-ft) Shine Falls. The Tutira Walkway, takes walkers high enough for panoramic views over Hawkes Bay 40 km (25 mi) to the east.

A Kaka parrot

Tongariro National Park

Centred on the three magnificent volcanoes – Tongariro, Ruapehy and Ngauruhoe, the Tongariro National Park is an outstanding area for its landscape and cultural value, and was recognized by UNESCO, who added it to the list of World Heritage Sites in 1990. The core of the land was gifted to the nation in 1887 by Te Heuheu Tukino IV, the paramount chief of the Maori Ngati Tuwharetoa iwi, in order to prevent its exploitation. More land was acquired by the government and the area was established as the first national park in New Zealand and the fourth in the world in 1894. More land has been added since.

The Tongariro Massif is part of North Island's volcanic plateau, which stretches almost all of the way to the Bay of Plenty in the north.

The area in the immediate vicinity of the volcanoes, especially Ngauruhoe, is very sparsely vegetated because of volcanic activity, but lower down podocarp/broadleaf rainforest and beech woodland can be found. Birds that find a refuge here include the North Island brown kiwi, the kakapo, bellbird, southern boobook and silvereye. The only two mammals native to New Zealand – the short- and long-tailed bats – are also present.

Hiking tracks criss-cross the park, including the Tongariro Crossing, which runs from Mount Tongariro to Mount Ngauruhoe, and forms part of one of New Zealand's Great Tracks, the Tongariro Northern Circuit. Walking through this area is certainly the best way to appreciate its beauty.

WHAT IS IT?
The oldest national park in New Zealand.
HOW TO GET THERE:
By road from Auckland 330km (205 mi)
WHEN TO GO:
Any time of year.
NEAREST TOWN:
Taurewa 10 km (6 mi)

Clouds hover over the mountains of Tongariro National Park.

451

Mount Ngaurohoe surrounded by low clouds on a summer evening.

Mount Ngauruhoe

Part of the Tongariro massif, Mt Ngaurohoe first erupted about 2,500 years ago, and since then has grown to 2,291 m (7,516 ft), looming more than 1,000 m (3,300 ft) above its surroundings.

It was one of the most active volcanoes on the planet during the twentieth century. Its last eruption was in 1975, but in June 2006 there was a series of earthquake swarms about 4 km (2.5 mi) below the crater.

The mountain was first climbed in 1839 from the north-west by J.C. Bidwill, and this is still the most popular route today. From the Mangatepopo Hut, the scramble to the crater is supposed to take about two hours, but in practice it can take longer as the volcanic clinker that makes up the mountain is loose and it can be hard to keep your footing.

The climb gets steeper nearer the top, when you suddenly reach the narrow ridge that surrounds the crater. This gaping hole was tailor-made to star as Mount Doom in the Lord of the Rings films: its forbidding dark rim is stained with patches of red reminiscent of dried blood. While the inside of the crater is no longer filled with clouds of steam, hot vents around its edge are still spewing noxious gases, so entry to the crater is not allowed.

If the weather is good, the views from the crater rim across the barren ash and pumice round it to the lush green forests, Mount Tongariro to the north and Mount Ruapehu to the south are stunning.

WHAT IS IT?
A very young active volcano with an almost perfect cone.
HOW TO GET THERE:
By road, then on foot.
WHEN TO GO:
Late spring to early autumn.
NEAREST TOWN:
Taurewa 16 km (10 mi)
DON'T MISS:
The view down into the crater.
YOU SHOULD KNOW:
Mount Ngauruhoe was used as Mount Doom in the *Lord of the Rings* film trilogy.

Westland Tai Poutini National Park

This large national park covers 1,175 sq km (450 sq mi) of spectacular scenery between the peaks of the central Southern Alps and the remote, wild beaches of the west coast of South Island. It contains glaciers, temperate rainforest, scenic lakes, grasslands and wetlands, as well as fantastic beaches. Together with Aoraki/Mount Cook, Mount Aspiring and Fiordland national parks, it potects a vast area of pristine wilderness. The coastal plain is separated from the mountains by the Alpine Fault. The Fox and Franz-Josef glaciers lie within this park. Like Lake Matheson, many of the lakes in the coastal wetlands are dark in colour because of nutrients leached out from the soil and this makes them perfect for waders, such as white heron, and other birds, such as crested grebe. There is also a small population of North Island brown kiwi in the lowland forest.

One of the most popular walking trails, of which there are many, in the area is the Copland Track, which leads up from Highway 6. This 17 km (10.5-mi) hike up the beautiful Copland valley to the pass of the same name takes about seven hours. A diversion is the natural hot pools by the Welcome Flat Hut, although it is important to remember not to submerge your head: the warm water hosts bugs that cause amoebic meningitis.

WHAT IS IT?
A national park with spectacular scenery.
HOW TO GET THERE:
By road from Greymouth.
WHEN TO GO:
Spring to autumn.
NEAREST TOWN:
Fox Glacier village.
DON'T MISS:
The views.
YOU SHOULD KNOW:
It rains a lot here.

The forest canopy in Westland Tai Poutini National Park

Mount Ruapehu

One of the world's most active volcanoes, Mount Ruapehu has suffered sixty eruptions of various sizes since 1945. It first erupted some 250,000 years ago and now has three peaks – Tahurangi, Te Heuheu and Paretetaitonga – which surround the crater. The last major eruption was in 1995, but there were also minor eruptions in 1996 and 2006.

Because Ruapehu is so active, its crater is so hot that snow melts and a warm, acidic lake occupies the crater between major eruptions. Held in only by a thin dam of solidified volcanic ash called tephra, the lake fills year by year until the wall finally breaks and a flash flood – a lahar – bursts down the side of the mountain. In March 2007, a lahar swept 1,400,000 cu m (50,000,000 cu ft) of water, rock and mud down the eastern side of the mountain. The release of pressure at the top of the crater led to concern that a new eruption might occur, but over the following few months activity did not increase markedly.

There are two public ski fields on the volcano's slopes, and hiking and walking trails on the lower slopes. Although the route to the top is classed as a 'tramp' rather than a climb, it can be dangerous because the weather on the mountain can close in suddenly.

Steam rises from the active crater of Mount Ruapehu in between eruptions in 1995 and 1996.

Lake Manapouri

Lake Manapouri

The deepest of South Island's southern glacial lakes, Lake Manapouri is a quite haven. Surrounded on three sides by high mountains, which remain snow-capped for a large part of the year, this beautiful lake and its surroundings are popular with wilderness-lovers from all over the country.

There are several walking and hiking trails that pass by or close to the lake, of which the 67-km (42-mi) Kepler Track and the Circle Track are the best known. These lead through native bush and require a degree of fitness. There is also a longer-distance track to Dusky Sound in the south-west. In winter and spring, the higher parts of the routes will be closed because of snow.

The lake saw the beginning of the early green movement in New Zealand when in the early 1960s conservationists fought, and won against, the proposal to raise the water levels 30 m (100 ft) to enlarge the reservoir for the Manapouri Power Station, which would have drowned most of the thirty-three islands dotted within the lake. The power station was built, but the water levels are maintained as close to natural fluctuation levels as possible.

The bays, islands and beaches are beautiful and there is a rich array of local plants and birds, including the endearing tui, which can often be seen by the lakeshore.

WHAT IS IT?
The deepest of South Island's southern glacial lakes.
HOW TO GET THERE:
By road from Invercargill. It's also possible to take a cruise across the lake from Pearl Harbour which is located on the south eastern corner of the lake.
WHEN TO GO:
Late spring to early autumn.
NEAREST TOWN:
Manipouri.

Bora Bora

One of the Society Islands in French Polynesia, Bora Bora consists of the tip of a submerged volcano almost completely surrounded by a near-rectangular reef. It is simply beautiful. The beaches on the reef have the white sand of ground-up coral, and the lagoon is the exact shade of blue that all lagoons should be. The lagoon and reefs have a bewildering array of fish, crabs, clams and eels, but the best spots to see marine life are in the open ocean beyond, where barracuda, tuna, red snapper, jackfish and several species of ray are to be seen, as well as black-tipped, grey and lemon sharks and turtles. Between August and October, humpback whales may also be seen on migration.

Every sort of water sport ever dreamed of is available in the lagoon or the ocean nearby but for the less active, the reefs, with their huts on stilts and palm trees are the ideal place to relax. Glass-bottomed boats show off the wildlife in the lagoon, while among the most popular excursions are the ray- and shark-feeding trips.

On the main island, the best way to get around is by bicycle. Other activities on offer include horse-riding and tours up to the twin volcanic peaks for lovely views over the idyllic lagoon.

A fringing reef circles the island of Bora-Bora, with Mount Otemanu visible in the centre.

WHAT IS IT?
A volcanic island in the Society Islands.
HOW TO GET THERE:
By air from Tahiti or by boat.
WHEN TO GO:
May to October.
NEAREST TOWN:
Papeete, Tahiti 230 km (140 mi)
DON'T MISS:
The wonderful diving.

ASIA

(INCLUDING EUROPEAN RUSSIAN FEDERATION)

Mountains in Kamchatka

Kamchatka Peninsula

A wilderness peninsula jutting from the mainland of Russia's Far East between the Sea of Okhotsk and the Bering Sea, Kamchatka is a naturalist's paradise, a cultural stronghold of the Itelmen, Koryak, Even and Chukchi peoples, and the most active volcanic region on the planet. A full 27 per cent (3.7 million hectares, 9.1 million acres) of Kamchatka is occupied by six linked nature reserves which provide the most comprehensive view anywhere of volcanic diversity. In the northern Klyuchevskoy Reserve you can see the world being born. It's a world of fire and ice where you can see the lava glowing red on the glaciers, and the lunar landscape is younger than many visitors. As you travel south, there are fewer active volcanoes, but more geysers and geothermal springs bubbling red or translucent turquoise. These landscapes bear witness to the evolution of a volcanic ecosystem over millions of years to the present.

Nalychevo Park is a microcosm of Kamchatka's magnificence and natural abundance, and has the advantage of being relatively close to the region's capital, Petropavlovsk-Kamchatsky. Better still is the Kronotsky Reserve in the peninsula's centre, which will amaze the most experienced traveler. Among the steaming cones and deep blue crater lakes lie the Valley of Geysers, the boiling mud pits of the Burlyaschy Volcano, and the Uzon Caldera where large numbers of Kamchatka Brown Bear (Eurasia's biggest) peacefully gather berries and fish for salmon. At Kronotsky you'll also see warm waterfalls tumbling down basalt rock faces on the Pacific Coast, vast shoals of salmon running the rivers, half the world's Steller Sea Eagles, and a whole ark of other marine and land mammals and birds.

None of the reserves are accessible by road; so there are no easy exits should you encounter one, or probably more, brown bears unexpectedly. There are 10,000 of them, and it's advisable to know how to behave in their territory.

WHAT IS IT?
The world's most active volcanic region.
HOW TO GET THERE:
By air to Petropavlovsk-Kamchatsky, then by road or helicopter.
WHEN TO GO:
June to October.
NEAREST TOWN:
Petropavlovsk-Kamchatsky is the hub for all six Reserves.
DON'T MISS:
The gathering of bears for the autumn salmon run at Kronotsky.
YOU SHOULD KNOW:
Even fat bears can run at 56 kph (35 mph).

The Golden Mountains of Altai

Wild and majestic, the Altai range marks the junction of Central Asia and Siberia, and of Russia with China, Mongolia and Kazakhstan. It's the heartland of Russia's most ancient cultures; but the standing stones and sacred sites of the Altai and Scythian peoples have all but been reclaimed by wilderness. Colossal tracts have now been set aside as Reserves to protect the mosaic of eco-systems that underwrites the region's grandeur and variety. Just one of them, the Altaisky Nature Reserve, has a core area of 881,200 hectares (2.2 million acres), which includes every permutation of steppe, taiga, alpine meadow, highland forest, glacial lake, mountain tundra and snow-capped peak, and at every level, the richest diversity of appropriate fauna and flora, and some of the rarest. The Altaisky also contains the 'Jewel of Western Siberia', Lake Teletskoye. It is 78 km (49 mi) long, a sky-blue ribbon only 5 km (3 mi) wide, snaking between cragged peaks and imperial stands of Siberian cedar forest. Fed by 70 rivers and 150 melt water cascades, its crystal water is among the purest on earth; when wind-shadows refract the huge skies, snowy peaks and swaying forest green reflected on its surface, it is said to re-define beauty.

The Katunsky Reserve holds a cross-section of Altai's natural treasures. 148 separate glaciers within 80 sq km (31 sq mi) feed the mighty Katun River, overlooked by Mt Belukha, Siberia's highest at 4,136 m (13.6 ft). Every step opens a new panorama of crags, forest, lakes and high meadows carpeted with wild flowers; and the nearby Multa lakes, descending the high ridges in a series of 30 – 70 m (98 – 230 ft) waterfalls, are the particular home of bear, ibex and snow leopard. Eventually, the wild Katun gorge opens onto pastures among gentle alps, broadens, and unites with other mountain rivers to become the great Siberian River Ob.

WHAT IS IT?
The high mountain wilderness of southern Siberia.
HOW TO GET THERE:
Bus from Barnaul to Artybash (Altaisky) or Tyungur (Katunsky).
WHEN TO GO:
May to August.
NEAREST TOWN:
Gorno-Altaisk 500 km (312 mi).
DON'T MISS:
Lake Teletskoye.
YOU SHOULD KNOW:
The snow leopard does not roar.

River valley in Altai Mountains

463

Sikhote-Alin mountains

Sikhote-Alin Mountains

The south-central section of the Sikhote-Alin range looks like an ocean of dense forest, set between the Ussuri River and Russia's far eastern coast on the Sea of Japan. Ridge succeeds 1,500 m (4,875 ft) ridge as far as the eye can see, divided only by fissures and canyons carved by torrent streams. It's a vast wilderness, almost completely untouched by humans, and it is a sanctuary for the world's biggest and rarest cat, the Amur (Siberian) tiger.

The World Heritage Reserve that protects this magnificent creature is established where the taiga meets the sub-tropics, so that southern species like the Amur tiger and Himalayan bear live alongside northern species like the brown bear, lynx and ermine. In fact, dual species of every kind abound here – of mammals, insects, plants and birds – and include the rarest of each. The distinctive flora and fauna of each level, be it arctic tundra in the highlands, the conifer and broadleaf forests, the dense valley floors where Tigers stalk their favourite prey of Manchurian deer, or even the thin coastal strip of sheer cliffs and estuarine shallows, is unmatched in Russia or the world for variety and rarity. Just one unusual feature is the Mutta Tract near the village of Arkhipovka in Primorye region's Chuguevsky district. It's a highland marsh alive with the vivid colours and noise of an extraordinary variety of arctic, temperate and sub-tropical birds.

Despite its remoteness, the Sikhote-Alin Reserve is accessible – to poachers and illegal loggers as well as irreproachable eco-tourists. Only the latter can save the Amur Tiger in its last redoubt, by supporting the expansion of the Reserve to double its present core of 401,428 hectares (992, 000 acres).

WHAT IS IT?
The heartland of the Amur tiger.
HOW TO GET THERE:
By truck, plane or boat from Vladivostok to Ternei.
WHEN TO GO:
April to July; September and October (August is the wettest month).
NEAREST TOWN:
Vladivostok 450 km (281 mi)
DON'T MISS:
Lake Blagodantnoe's unique combination of bird habitats.
YOU SHOULD KNOW:
The range of a male Amur tiger is 600-1000 sq km (232-386 sq mi)

Lake Baikal

The coastline of Lake Baikal

The Russian Federation's Lake Baikal lies in an active continental rift at a height of 456 m (1,496 ft). The rift is widening by some 2 cm (¾ in) each year. Its surface area is 31,500 sq km (12,159 sq mi) and it is 1,700 m (5,557 ft) deep, making it the deepest lake in the world. The rift itself is 8–9 km (5–5.5 mi) below the surface, covered in kilometres of silt. Lake Baikal contains 20 per cent of the earth's unfrozen fresh water, more than all of Americas great lakes together.

The lake is renowned for its clear waters and for its wildlife, much of which occurs nowhere else in the world, including the nerpa (Baikal seal). These animals have evolved in isolation, and the lake has been dubbed the 'Galapagos of Russia'. It is also, more poetically, known as the 'Blue Eye of Siberia'.

Baikal's catchment area is vast: no fewer than 336 rivers drain into it, while it has only one outlet, the River Angara, which exits the lake near its western end and flows north.

It is not just its size that makes Lake Baikal a must-see. Much of its coastline and its islands are stunningly beautiful. It is surrounded by forested mountains, with an area of taiga on the north shore. Animals that roam in the national park include deer and bears. Within the lake there are at least 1,550 species and varieties of animals.

Listed as a World Heritage Site by UNESCO in 1996 because of its importance for the study of evolution and climate and for the wildlife in the lake and surrounding areas, Lake Baikal is one of the world's very special places.

WHAT IS IT?
The deepest lake on earth, with spectacular scenery and wildlife.
HOW TO GET THERE:
By air or Trans-Siberian Railway to Irkutsk, then by road or ferry.
WHEN TO GO:
Summer.
NEAREST TOWN:
Listvyanka 1 km (0.6 mi)
YOU SHOULD KNOW:
The rift under the lake is active and earthquakes occur regularly.

Virgin Komi Forests

WHAT IS IT?
The biggest untouched boreal forest in Europe.
HOW TO GET THERE:
By air, rail or bus to Pechora; by road to Troitsko-Pechorsk.
WHEN TO GO:
May to September.
NEAREST TOWN:
Pechora (N) or Troitsko-Pechorsk (S)
DON'T MISS:
The moss swamps of the piedmont.
YOU SHOULD KNOW:
Moose milk is medicinal.

The Virgin Komi Forests cover 3.28 million hectares (8.1 million acres) of tundra and mountain tundra in the northern Urals, the most extensive area of virgin boreal forest remaining in Europe. Almost completely undisturbed by economic activities, the region is a real treasure trove of taiga biodiversity. It accounts for over 40 species of mammals like the brown bear, sable, moose, ermine, arctic fox and wolverine (skunk bear); 204 species of birds including the endangered white sea eagle and fish hawk; and valuable fish like the glacial relic species, the lake char and arctic grayling.

The Virgin Komi Biosphere unites two major sites: the Pechoro-Ilychsky Nature Preserve and the enormous Yugyd-Va National Park. Their combined territory stretches for 300 km (188 mi) along the western slope of the Polar and Northern Urals, marking the transition of mid- and northern taiga to forest and mountain tundra, and the north-western limit of the Siberian cedar's habitat. Their position is important to the entire regional ecosystem: the humid western slopes contribute to the great Pechora River basin where European plant species abruptly replace the Siberian flora of the eastern Urals. Among the Pechora piedmont of spruce, pine and fir forests are both pine and moss swamps, and the Gusinoe Bolota (Goose Swamp) is a 3 sq km (1.2 sq mi) peat bog over 5 m (16 ft) deep, near which a small research establishment is still conducting experiments in domesticating moose.

Current attempts to have the Biosphere's borders moved to legalize the prospecting and mining of gold have failed; only time will tell if the regional Supreme Court can withstand the machinations of the self-same regional government, which seeks the change.

Koip Mountain covered with pristine boreal forest, Pechora-Ilych Reserve.

Mount Elbrus

The Main Range of the Caucasus Mountains marks the border between the Russian Federation and Georgia, and the southern boundary of Europe with Asia. About 10 km (6 mi) north of the Main Range stands Mount Elbrus, the highest point at 5,643 m (18,340 ft), which is wholly in Russia and in Europe. The mountain is surrounded by peaks of over 5,000 m (16,250 ft) in a network of side valleys where a quilt of subsistence farms is scratched among the rocky crags and scree below the permanent snowline. With glaciers protruding through patches of alpine forest the region's nickname 'the Russian Alps' is well deserved.

The outstanding natural beauty of Mount Elbrus attracts as many visitors as does its mountaineering status. Both walkers and serious climbers need to spend time acclimatizing in nearby valleys – but most of these are subject to stringent access rules because of their proximity to national borders. It takes a lot of vital paperwork to get near Elbrus as well as on to or up it, so to avoid problems it's best to approach the mountain only from the Russian side. Near the head of the Baksan Valley is the village of Terskol, just 4 km (2.5 mi) from the end of the road at Azau, where a cable car can take you half way up Elbrus to the Garabashi refuge hut at 3,800 m (12,350 ft). From here, the views are spectacular across the snow and glaciers. The cable car has opened these southern slopes to skiers: you may be lucky enough to share a lift with them on a Ratrak (Snowcat) taking them even higher up to the glaciers as late as April or May.

Standing so tall between north and south, Elbrus suffers temperature extremes that can vary from –30 °C to +30 °C (-22 °F to 86 °F) to + in a day, and weather that often changes dramatically in minutes. High winds can clear a metre of soft powder snow in a moment, leaving unprepared visitors struggling on sheet ice. Elbrus is not benign.

WHAT IS IT?
The highest point in Europe.
HOW TO GET THERE:
By plane to Mineralnye Vody; then bus (4 hours) to Terskol.
WHEN TO GO:
April to October.
NEAREST TOWN:
Nalchik 129 km (81 mi)
DON'T MISS:
The tribal villages of the Baksan Valley.
YOU SHOULD KNOW:
It's usual to share a rented minibus with strangers. Official bus services are erratic.

The distinctive twin peaks of Mount Elbrus in the Caucasus Mountains

Lake Balkhash

WHAT IS IT?
An unusual lake in eastern Kazakhstan
HOW TO GET THERE:
By road from Almaty.
WHEN TO GO:
Spring or autumn.
NEAREST TOWN:
Balkhash

The vast scimitar-shaped Lake Balkhash is the second largest lake in area in Central Asia. Strangely, it is salty in the east and freshwater in the west, and is deeper in the eastern arm although its maximum depth is only about 27 m (90 ft) and its surface is usually frozen solid from November to March. Its surface area is currently 17,580 sq km (7000 sq km) and it is at 14 m (47 ft) below sea level. It is an endorheic lake, that is, it loses water by evaporation as it has no outflow. The two halves of the lake are separated by a sandbar and the main inflow is from the river Ili in west. Lake Balkhash is a vital stopping point for birds during the migrating seasons and the area is becoming increasingly popular with western birdwatchers. The reedbeds of the Ili delta are thought to be among the best places to see various rarities, including Dalmation and white pelicans, several species of terns, spoonbills, night herons, feruginous duck and white-tailed eagle, although there are also other spots on the lake from where many of these can be seen. There has been concern in recent years that water extraction upstream and the damming of the Ili are causing the lake to dry out, but concerted efforts are now being made to prevent this happening as far as is possible and to protect the landscape around at least part of the shore. Away from the populated coastal towns and cities like Balkhash, this beautiful, wild landscape is a peaceful place to visit.

A man fishing in Lake Balkhash

Charyn Canyon

In the east of Kazakhstan, near the border with China is a site that many people say rivals America's Grand Canyon, for spectacle, if not size. The most popular part, the Valley of the Castles (Dolina Zamkov), has fantastic, different-coloured rock formations, showing the history of the landscape. At the bottom are volcanic rocks and above are red gravels and grey rocks formed of ash and stones from later eruptions. Apart from the salt-marsh through which you approach the canyon and the river itself, hidden from view until you are almost upon it, this whole region is an arid desert and the river creates an oasis for plants and a few animals that would otherwise not survive.

It is possible for experienced drivers to get to the base of the canyon in a four-wheel-drive but there is an easy hiking trail from the camp site at the end of the Valley of the Castles. From the trail into the floor of the canyon, the rock formations reach up between 90 and 300 m (300–1,000 ft) and the weird and wonderful shapes really do resemble fortifications. In some places, visitors can see fossils in the canyon walls.

In summer, it is possible to cross the river in a basket, or on a wire, but at this time of year it is very hot. There are excellent hiking trails around the canyon, while the river rapids are popular with experienced white-water rafters.

WHAT IS IT?
An 80-km (50-mi) gorge in eastern Kazakhstan
HOW TO GET THERE:
By road from Almaty.
WHEN TO GO:
Spring or autumn
NEAREST TOWN:
Chilik
DON'T MISS:
The Valley of the Castles
YOU SHOULD KNOW:
It is best to go with a tour group as the gorge is difficult to find if you do not know where you are going.

The canyon of the River Charyn

A pool formed by melting snow in the summer heat on the Inylchek Glacier.

Tien Shan

The Tien Shan mountain range stretches for more than 2,400 km (1,500 mi), here forming the border between north-west China and Kazakhstan and Kyrgyzstan. The highest peak is the Pobeda (7,439 m, 24,406 ft) and also known as the Jengish Chokusu which stands in Kyrgyzstan, while Khan-Tengri (the Lord of the Spirits), the highest peak in Kazakhstan, is a marble-capped pyramid of 7010 m (23,000 ft) and one of the most popular climbs for experts. Because of the dry climate, the snow line is far higher than elsewhere in the world, and is generally above 3,350 m (11,000 ft). The western Tien Shan contain beautiful landscapes, including cedar forests, snow-capped mountain peaks, and deep canyons. Khan Tengri straddles the border between Kazakhstan and Kyrgyzstan, and is a mecca not just for climbers, but for hikers, trekkers, backpackers and riders, too, who make for the lower slopes. Inylchek Glacier lies here, too, and is almost 60 km (37 mi) in length: it holds Merzbacher Lake in its centre. Other beautiful lakes in the region include the three Kolsai Lakes, known as the pearls of the northern Tien Shan, while Lake Marakol is claimed to be as picturesque as Lake Baikal. This stunning landscape is gradually opening up to western tourism so it is probably a good idea to get here as soon as you can.

WHAT IS IT?
A spectacular mountain range.
HOW TO GET THERE:
By road from Almaty.
WHEN TO GO:
Summer.
YOU SHOULD KNOW:
There are 30–40 small earthquakes in the Tien Shan each year and snow-melt in spring can cause mudslides.

Huangshan Mountain

Formed 100 million years ago by movement in the earth's crust, and subsequently carved out by glaciers, this multi-peaked, granite range is known collectively as Huangshan Mountain. Situated in the south of Anhui Province, in eastern China, 77 of Huangshan's peaks reach heights above 1,000 m (3,300 ft), and 72 are poetically named, the three highest, all over 1,800 m (5,940 ft), being called 'Lotus', 'Bright Summit' and 'Celestial'.

Listed by UNESCO in 1990, the peaks have their own, individual beauty – some slender and graceful, others majestic and craggy, and all swathed in a multitude of trees, particularly pines, some of which are over 1,000 years old. Forces of nature have shaped these trees – they grow from crevices in the rock face, cling to the edges of steep cliffs, and overhang deep, dark valleys. Some have roots so twisted that they look like mythical creatures.

Huangshan Mountain in winter

Amongst the trees, streams rush and babble – the area is known for its waterfalls, hot springs and natural pools. Pathways twist and turn around the peaks, which are often shrouded in mist and cloud. Many of the peaks rise above cloud level, and visitors can see fascinating light phenomena as they look down on the clouds from above.

This is a natural work of art, known for centuries, and immortalized by poets and painters from Li Bai (701–762) through the master painters of the Qing Dynasty, to the modern day. There are over 1,500 species of flora here, and every season has a different look. Spring brings a mass of bright wild flowers; summer is voluptuous and verdant; in autumn, the maples and other deciduous species blaze red, yellow and purple before falling in the path of winter, and its frosty world of silver, white and grey.

WHAT IS IT?
A living artwork, known to the Chinese for centuries.
HOW TO GET THERE:
By road from Huangshan.
WHEN TO GO:
Any time of year.
NEAREST TOWN:
Huangshan 72 km (45 mi)
DON'T MISS:
Celestial Peak.
YOU SHOULD KNOW:
The temperature here is always cool: bring warm as well as wet weather clothing.

475

The Three Gorges

WHAT IS IT?
Three beautiful gorges on the Yangtze River. However, the largest hydroelectric project in the world, set in the midst of the Yangtze River is now being constructed here.

HOW TO GET THERE:
Fly to Chongqing, take a cruise.

WHEN TO GO:
October to March

NEAREST TOWN:
Chongqing, at the southern end of the Three Gorges.

YOU SHOULD KNOW:
By 2009, when all the locks, and shiplifts are in place, it will be possible for ocean-going ships to travel the 2,400 km (1,500 mi) inland from the ocean to Chongqing.

Situated in Hubei province, roughly at the halfway point of the Yangtze River, is the famously scenic area of the Three Gorges. The Qutang Gorge is 8 km (5 mi) long, never more than 100 m (330 ft) wide, with almost vertical cliff walls rising up into the clouds. Wu Gorge is 45 km (28 mi) long, and lined with such fantastic cliffs that legend tells of the goddess Yao Ji and her sisters having to turn some wicked river dragons into mountains. Finally, there is Xiling Gorge, at 66 km (41 mi) the longest of the three, and historically considered the most dangerous to navigate.

This area is not only spectacular to look at, but is also bursting with cultural history and many important archaeological sites. For 90 years Chinese governments have been considering putting a dam in these gorges, and the resulting construction, completed in 2006 and fully operational by 2009, is the largest hydroelectric river dam in the world.

The new dam has caused enormous controversy. Proponents point to the clean electricity it will provide, desperately needed by the booming economy, and say that it will help to control the ever more frequent flooding that occurs on the Yangtze River. Opponents point to the 1 million plus displaced people, the loss of hundreds of archaeological sites, 13 cities, 140 towns and 1,352 villages. They say that the ecosystem will be irreparably damaged, that there is a possibility that the reservoir may silt up, causing, rather than preventing, floods, and that the dam has been sited on a seismic fault. It will take some years before we know whether this was a brilliant idea, or a disastrous one.

Wu Gorge, one of the Three Gorges of the Yangtze River

Muztagh Ata

Sheep grazing by Muztagh Ata.

Muztagh Ata is a 7,546 m (24,757 ft) mountain peak on the northern edge of the Tibetan Plateau, in China's Xinjiang province. Although it is only the second highest peak in the Kunlun Mountains, it is enormously popular with mountaineers. It towers over the Karakoram Highway, which runs from Kashi to Pakistan, and is only 24 km (15 mi) from the Chinese border with Tajikistan – thus access to Muztagh Ata is reasonably simple, and it looks deceptively easy to climb.

The first recorded attempt to climb this mountain was by Sven Hedin, in 1894. Hedin, just as so many others after him, was lulled into thinking it would be a relatively simple climb. Further official attempts were made in 1900, 1904 and 1947, all of which failed, due to weather conditions – although it is not too hard technically, any mountain of this elevation is a major climb. The first successful attempt on Muztagh Ata was made by a party of Chinese and Russian climbers, who reached the summit during an expedition in 1956, and since then a great many successful climbs have been made.

Muztagh Ata means 'Father of Ice Mountains', and it is easy to see why it was so named. Not only is it very high, it is also very large in terms of its circumference. Geologically a tilted fault block, the western and southern slopes are gently graduated, though divided into sections by deep, glacial troughs. The east and north faces, however, fall away from the summit ridge in precipitous, 2,100 m (7,000 ft) drops. Over 20 glaciers clothe the slopes, and the mountain has long exposed areas, which are bitterly cold, lashed by freezing winds and covered in deep, treacherous snow.

WHAT IS IT?
A favourite mountain climb for serious mountaineers.
HOW TO GET THERE:
To Kashi by road from Gilgit, Pakistan; Bishkek, Kyrgyzstan; by train from Urumqi, China, or fly to Kashi airport.
WHEN TO GO:
July and August.
NEAREST TOWN:
Kashi 150 km (94 mi)
YOU SHOULD KNOW:
An ascent/descent on skis was made in 1980 by a party lead by Ned Gillette. The south-east ridge was climbed in 2000. In 2002, despite normal weather conditions, only 18 per cent of the climbs were successful.

Prayer flags flutter in the breeze at Nam Co Lake in central Tibet.

Nam Co Lake

Situated in the Nyainqentanglha mountain range in Tibet, Nam Co Lake lies at an altitude of 4,627 m (15,180 ft), and is one of Tibet's three Holy Lakes. Meaning 'Heavenly Lake' in Tibetan, Nam Co is a place of pilgrimage, and Buddhists come here, not only from all over China, but also India, Nepal, Bhutan and Sikkim, to complete a ritual walk around it.

Dorje Gongzhama, the deity of the lake, is also the queen of the deity of Nyainqentanglha. Both were born in the Tibetan Year of the Sheep, and during the summer times of those years, more than any others, pilgrims come here to seek good luck and good harvests.

Measuring some 70 km (44 mi) from east to west, 30 km (19 mi) north to south and with a maximum depth of 33 m (109 ft), the lake can take anywhere from 10 days to one month to circle, depending on how much time the pilgrim spends in contemplation and prayer en route. Four monasteries are situated around the lake, and there are ancient cave hermitages, too.

This is a place of austere beauty – irregular in shape and strongly blue in colour, the water curves around the base of mountain slopes sparsely covered with vegetation. Several small islands dot the lake, and in the past, towards the end of winter, pilgrims would walk across the frozen ice to an island, and stay there in spiritual retreat until the waters froze again at the end of summer. To the north and west stand peak after peak of snow-covered mountains often hidden by mist, and changeable weather brings sudden snowstorms swirling and drifting across the lake.

WHAT IS IT?
One of Tibet's three Holy Lakes.
HOW TO GET THERE:
By road from Lhasa.
WHEN TO GO:
June to September.
NEAREST TOWN:
Lhasa 420 km (260 mi)
DON'T MISS:
The Zhaxi Dorboche Monastery.
YOU SHOULD KNOW:
Even if it is sunny and pleasant during the day, the temperature will plummet at night, so bring very warm clothing.

478

Wulingyiang Scenic and Historic Interest Area

Located in Hunan Province, Wulingyiang's 26,000-hectare (64,250-acre) site is one of the country's 40 most famous scenic spots, and is inhabited by several tribal groups. Some 3 billion years ago, this was an ancient sea, and today's landscape of eroded quartzite sandstone is the exposed and eroded sea floor. The region contains over 3,000 narrow sandstone pillars and peaks, and of these, over 1,000 rise to over 200 m (656 ft). In amongst them are waterfalls, streams and pools, deep valleys, ravines and complex limestone caves. Almost the entire region is forested – 99 per cent is covered with vegetation, including many rare species.

Zhangjiajie National Forest is covered with primitive, sub-tropical forest. It boasts 191 types of tree, and is absolutely draped in flowers – orchids, azaleas and Giant Mountain lotus scent the air. The Lobster flower, unique to the park, can change colour up to five times a day. Suoxiyu is the largest area of the Park, with a creek running from east to west. The valley floor, made of yellow-green and dark green shale, contrasts with the upper slopes of dark red or grey quartzite and shale. Huanglong, or Yellow Dragon Cave, is thought to be one of the largest in China. On four levels, it contains an underground lake, two rivers, three waterfalls, 13 halls and 96 corridors.

The Tianzi Mountain reserve is at a much higher elevation and is rich with strangely shaped peaks and rocks. Famously covered in mist and fog, it is renowned for its beautiful views. There are two spectacular natural bridges here – Tianxia Diyi Qiao, or Bridge across the Sky is 40 m (132 ft) long, 10 m (33 ft) wide and 15 m (50 ft) thick. At 357 m (1,171 ft) above the valley, it may be the world's highest natural bridge.

WHAT IS IT?
A gorgeous, heavily forested national park, dominated by thousands of sandstone peaks and pillars.
HOW TO GET THERE:
Fly to Changsha, then by road to Zhangjiajie.
WHEN TO GO:
September to May.
NEAREST TOWN:
Zhangjiajie (formerly Dayong) is close to the edge of Wulingyiang.
DON'T MISS:
Puguang Temple, the grotto in the Yuhuang Cave.
YOU SHOULD KNOW:
Inscribed on the UNESCO World Heritage list in 1992, Wulingyiang was the first area of China to be thus distinguished.

Sandstone pillars in Wulingyiang Scenic Area

A panda cub eating bamboo shoots.

Sichuan Giant Panda Sanctuaries

Over 30 per cent of the world's Giant pandas live within the Sichuan Sanctuaries in south-western Sichuan Province. Covering seven nature reserves and nine scenic parks in the Qionglai and Jiajin Mountains, the Sanctuaries form the largest contiguous habitat of these charming animals. They also protect the Red panda, and both Snow and Clouded leopards, all of which are globally endangered.

Between 5,000 and 6,000 species of flora grow here, making the region one of the most botanically rich in the world outside tropical rainforests. Giant pandas eat bamboo, supplemented with eggs, honey and fish, if available. A fully-grown male weighs about 115 kg (253 lb) and measures about 1.5 m (4 ft 9 in) long and 75 cm (2 ft 4 in) tall at the shoulder. Their distinctive black and white markings make them instantly recognizable. Genetically, Giant pandas are bears. They do not hibernate and unlike other bears, their eyes have vertical rather than round pupils. They have unusual paws, with five fingers and a 'thumb' to help them hold and skin bamboo.

Despite having a carnivore's digestive tract, bamboo accounts for 99 per cent of their diet, and this is a major factor in their decline. As temperatures increase, pandas moved higher, and only a few of the 25 bamboo species that they eat can thrive at high altitudes. Because it is low in nutrition, pandas need to eat some 13 kg (30 lb) of bamboo shoots and leaves daily. Bamboo is big business and as more is harvested, the pandas' food supply becomes further depleted.

Until recently it was thought that only 1,600 of these much-loved animals still existed in the wild. In 2006, however, thanks to DNA analysis of droppings, scientists believe there could be as many as 3,000. Whatever the exact figure, it seems that the number of wild pandas is on the increase.

WHAT IS IT?
A botanically rich area that is home to several endangered mammals including the Giant panda.
HOW TO GET THERE:
By road from Chengdu.
WHEN TO GO:
October to December.
NEAREST TOWN:
Chengdu.
DON'T MISS:
The Chengdu Research Base of Giant Panda Breeding in town.
YOU SHOULD KNOW:
The Research Base in Chengdu is probably the closest you will be able to get to the pandas. Check if there are any organized trips into the mountain reserves.

Jiuzhaigou Valley

Jiuzhaigou Valley, or the Valley of Nine Villages is a remote nature reserve nestled within the mountains of northern Sichuan. It was not officially recognized by the authorities until 1972, but prior to that it was inhabited for centuries by Tibetan and Qiang peoples. Named after the nine stockaded villages once strung out along the valley, today only six remain, and its permanent inhabitants number fewer than 1,000.

Jiuzhaigou Valley really consists of three Y-shaped gullies, surrounded by fabulous karst mountains from 2,000 – 3,000 m (6,600 – 9,900 ft) high. Covered in virgin forest of mixed broadleaf and conifer, the region looks lovely at any time of year, but is absolutely glorious in the autumn as the leaves turn to gold and crimson.

This is a much-visited area, best known for its network of pristine Alpine lakes. The valley lies on major fault lines, and earthquakes as well as glaciers have shaped its topography over millennia. The naturally formed glacial lakes were produced by a combination of rock falls and extremely high carbonate deposits that make their waters crystal clear.

There are over 100 lakes in Jiuzhaigou Valley, in different shades of jade and turquoise. Five Flower Lake appears multi-coloured, due to its different depths and sediments – it is pale yellow, deep blue and dark green. Lying Dragon Lake has a calcareous dyke beneath the water, which seen from above, resembles a dragon.

Here too are multi-layered waterfalls, splashing droplets like glistening pearls against the rock, the gushing water echoing around the valley. This is home to interesting flora, including endemic species of bamboo and rhododendron. It also shelters tiny populations of endangered Giant Panda and Golden Snub-nosed monkey, but there is concern that increased tourism may be their downfall.

WHAT IS IT?
A magical valley, liberally sprinkled with jewel-like lakes.
HOW TO GET THERE:
From Chengdu by road (10 hours); or by plane to Chuanzhusi Township, then by road, or by helicopter to a helipad near the valley. Transport within the valley is eco-friendly.
WHEN TO GO:
Spring or autumn.
NEAREST TOWN:
Zhangzha, at the exit of the valley.
DON'T MISS:
The Tibetan villages and their traditional culture.
YOU SHOULD KNOW:
This is a UNESCO World Heritage and Biosphere Site. An entry fee is payable.

Waterfalls and trees in autumn in the Jiuzhaigou Valley

Mount Emei Scenic Area

Mount Emei, 3,100 m (10,230 ft) in height, is to be found to the west of the Chengdu Plain, in the province of Sichuan. This is not only a scenically beautiful area, with high plant diversity and many endemic species, but also the site of the first Buddhist temple in China, built in the 1st century AD. As Buddhism spread, more temples were built on the mountain, making it one of the most revered sites in the world. Today more than 100 temples and monasteries can be found here, many of which offer accommodation to visitors.

The three summits of the mountain stand parallel to each other, making Emei recognizable from afar. Here you will find deep gorges, valleys, undulating hills, rivers, springs and waterfalls. Water erosion has formed various karstic features such as an underground river, caverns and the Shisungou karst forest. Five nature reserves are established here, and there are five vegetation belts, from sub-Alpine coniferous forest and shrubs at the highest levels, to sub-tropical evergreen broad-leafed forest at the base.

Altogether, some 3,200 plants have been recorded, including more than 100 that are endemic. 2,300 animal species have been recorded, including a number of internationally threatened mammals such as Red panda, Asiatic black bear, Asiatic golden cat and Tibetan macaque.

Inscribed by UNESCO in 1996, the inscription includes the Leshan Giant Buddha Area, located 40 km (25 mi) from Mount Emei. In 713 AD, a monk named Haitong began carving the largest Buddha in the world from the west cliff of Lingyun Mountain. Located at the confluence of three rivers, the head of this giant Buddha, 71 m (234 ft) reaches the top of the mountain, and its feet rest by the water. If you are interested in Buddhism, there is a wonderfully rich cultural heritage to be found here.

Three Parallel Rivers of Yunnan

This National Park is China's foremost region of biodiversity and superlative natural beauty, as well as being a showcase of the geological history of the area over the past 50 million years. Situated in the mountains of north west Yunnan Province, the Park contains part of the upper reaches of the Yangtze, Mekong and Salween Rivers. These are three of the greatest rivers in Asia, and they pour relentlessly through three deep, parallel gorges, surrounded by spectacular, glaciated peaks.

Every type of landscape in the Northern Hemisphere exists here, apart from desert and ocean, and despite forming only 0.4 per cent of China's landmass, it contains over 20 per cent of the country's most important plants, and 25 per cent of its animal species. The Park contains 118 peaks with altitudes of over 5,000 m (16,500 ft), while many of the Meili Snow Mountains, on the border with Tibet, tower over 6,000 m (19,800 ft). The highest is Mt. Kawegbo at 6,740 m (22,242 ft), from which flows the extraordinary Mingyongqia Glacier, descending to 2,700 m (8,910 ft) – the lowest in the Northern Hemisphere at such a low latitude.

All sorts of plants and animals live here including many that are rare, threatened, and endemic. Asian Black bears hunt in the forests and meadows of the perfect Alpine landscapes of the eastern mountains and valleys, and that rarest of creatures, the Snow leopard, haunts the upper reaches of the mountains in remote splendour.

The river gorges, which run from north to south, lie 18 km (11 mi) and 66 km (41 mi) apart. The Salween is China's longest un-dammed river, and plans to dam the gorge were quashed by the government in 2006. There is now a joint proposal between Thailand and Myanmar for a dam much further downstream that will be even larger than the Three Gorges Dam, currently the largest in the world.

WHAT IS IT?
China's most important national park.
HOW TO GET THERE:
By air to Kunming, then by road to Zhongdian.
WHEN TO GO:
April to September.
NEAREST TOWN:
Zhongdian is within the Park.
DON'T MISS:
The fabulous spring flowers – over 200 species of Rhododendron can be found here.
YOU SHOULD KNOW:
Inscribed as a World Heritage Site in 2003, this is an extremely difficult place to visit, although joining a tour might be possible.

The upper reaches of the Yangtze River in northern Yunnan province

Tianmushan Biosphere Reserve

WHAT IS IT?
A beautiful, forested area, protecting magnificent, ancient trees.
HOW TO GET THERE:
By road from Shanghai or Hangzhou.
WHEN TO GO:
March to September.
NEAREST TOWN:
Hangzhou 100 km (62 mi).
DON'T MISS:
The ancient Ginkgo Biloba trees.
YOU SHOULD KNOW:
The rainfall is highest between June and September, so bring wet weather clothing.

Tianmushan Biosphere Reserve is situated in southeast China, not far from Shanghai and Hangzhou. Covering 4,284 hectares (10,590 acres) of land, it lies on the watershed between the rivers Yangtze and Qiantanjiang. Known as the Kingdom of Big Trees, Tianmushan was inscribed as a UNESCO Biosphere Reserve in 1996 for its extensive and ancient forests and woodlands.

The Biosphere Reserve comprises a number of different 'gardens' that focus on the conservation of rare and threatened species, as well as species of economic importance. Located close to heavily populated urban areas, it is a tourist magnet, and the revenue raised is put back into protecting and managing the area.

The climate here is quite extreme, ranging from -20 °C to 38 °C (-4 °F to 100 °F), with rainfall of up to 1,870 mm (74 in) per year, and the flora is incredibly diverse, including both evergreen and deciduous broad-leafed, bamboo and coniferous forests, as well as marshes and aquatic plants. A little agriculture takes place here, as does managed, commercial forestry of bamboo, mulberry, medicinal plants and tea.

However, Tianmushan is known above all for its fantastic, huge and ancient trees, many of them over 1,000 years old, including wild Ginkgo Biloba. One of these famous 'living fossils' is fondly known as 'the old dragon trying to fly'. Perched on the edge of a cliff, 950 m (3,116) ft high, this tree occupies some 12 sq m (129 sq ft) and consists of 15 trunks, the largest of which is 110 cm (43 in) in diameter.

This area has been inhabited for thousands of years, and all China's major religions have been practised here. Monks were responsible for protecting the forest until 1956, when the government stepped in to help, and banned all tree felling here. Today the permanent population is less than 200.

Mount Wuyi

Mount Wuyi, in Fujian Province, is the most important area for biodiversity conservation, riverine beauty and archaeological significance in south east China. The landscape has been formed by volcanic activity, and eroded by water, and the Nine Bend River, running clear and deep, makes its way through a deep, dramatic gorge flanked by sheer, smooth, rock cliffs. Within this landscape of hills and gorges are a considerable number of ancient temples and monasteries, and although many of them are now completely ruined, the landscape is so perfect one could be looking at a classical Chinese painting.

Mount Wuyi has been protected for 12 centuries, and is the cradle of Neo-Confucianism, a doctrine that was influential in the Far East for hundreds of years. In the 1st century BC, the rulers of the Han dynasty built a large, walled city at nearby Chengcun, and this, as well as many other sites here, is of great archaeological significance.

This is one of the most outstanding sub-tropical forests in the world. The vegetation is divided into 11 categories, the most common being evergreen broad-leafed forest, and there is a wide diversity of fauna too, including endangered species such as the South Chinese tiger, Clouded leopard and Mainland serow. There are 3 species here endemic to these mountains, including the Bamboo snake – indeed, this is definitely snake country, 73 species of reptile can be found, and preserved snakes can commonly be seen as part of the decor of local restaurants and pharmacies.

This is an area of almost otherworldly beauty. Drift through the Wuyi Canyon on a raft, gaze at fold upon fold of lush green mountains. Sit peacefully drinking a seriously delicious cup of tea and meditate upon the marvellous nature of our planet.

WHAT IS IT?
A fabulous landscape of outstanding biodiversity and great archaeological significance

HOW TO GET THERE:
By air from many major Chinese cities, or by train from Fuzhou or Xiamen.

WHEN TO GO:
October to March.

NEAREST TOWN:
Wuyishan City 5 km (3 mi)

DON'T MISS:
The Ancient Xiamei Folk Buildings, where tea merchants, officials and Confucian scholars built impressive houses during the Ming and Qing Dynasties.

YOU SHOULD KNOW:
The Mount Wuyi Scenic Area is classic tea growing country, the origin of Lapsang Souchong and the famous Da Hong Pao.

Mount Wuyi overlooking the Nine Bend River gorge.

Huang Long Valley

Huang Long Valley is one of the most spectacular places in Sichuan Province. Together with the nearby Muni Gorge, it is a World Heritage Site. Sichuan, the 'Land of Abundance', is bordered in the west by the Tibetan Plateau, and it is in the Minshan range at the foot of the plateau that Huang Long lies.

Huang Long means yellow dragon, and according to legend, about 4,000 years ago a great yellow dragon helped the Kia king, Xiayu, to remove floodwater by creating the Minjiang river. The king named the valley in honour of the dragon and had a temple built. More prosaically, the waters of the river have a golden hue because they carry dissolved calcium carbonate, which they deposit as they pass, and the valley could be said to resemble the tail of a dragon because it undulates through its gorge, following the path it has carved through faults in the limestone over the millennia.

The spectacular gorge, about 250 km (155 mi) from the provincial capital, Chengdu, is surrounded by primeval forests and dominated by snow-capped peaks. Its limestone formations are unique, and its massive waterfalls breathtaking. Its emerald-green lakes and thousands of multicoloured, calcium-carbonate encrusted, ponds are fed by melted snow from the mountain above and monsoon rains from May to September. The river has also carved out caves, and several of these contain spectacular stalactites and there are warm springs just above the temples.

The area is also rich in wildlife, with a small population of Giant pandas, lesser pandas, golden snub-nosed monkeys, brown bear and Asiatic black bear, Asiatic wild dog, leopard, lynx, three species of deer and possibly Clouded leopard as well. More than 150 species of birds have been recorded here.

Whether visitors believe the legend of the yellow dragon or not, this beautiful site will stay in their memories.

Snow, mountains and Five Colour Pool in the Huang Long Valley

486

The Gobi Desert

The Gobi Desert is a vast area in southern Mongolia covering 30 per cent of the entire country. It is largely made up of stony desert and gravel plains with rocky outcrops, but it also has mountains, grasslands, desert steppes, sand dunes and oases. This inhospitable landscape contains many rare and threatened species of flora and fauna and has been inhabited for centuries by nomadic herdsmen. For over 50 years the Gobi Desert was off-limits to westerners, only 're-opening' after the break up of the Soviet Union.

The climate here is incredibly harsh – very little rain falls, and the wind blows almost continuously, carrying sand in its wake across hundreds of miles. The temperatures are extreme, reaching 40 °C (104 °F) in summer and -40 °C (-40 °F) in winter - in Eagle Valley, the gorge remains frozen even on the hottest days. It is this very austerity that has helped preserve the Gobi Desert as the last remaining home of the wild Bactrian camel, the Gobi bear (the only desert bear), and many other creatures such as wolves, desert foxes, Snow leopards, gazelles, ibex and Argali sheep.

The Flaming Cliffs were named by the American paleontologist Roy Chapman Andrews when, in 1923, his team discovered the first nest of fossilized dinosaur eggs. These vivid, red sandstone cliffs shelter an astonishing wealth of fossils that are providing the world with ever more evolutionary information. The region is rich with minerals – turquoise, agate, and crystal, as well as large deposits of copper and gold. There is also a sea of sand, stretching 180 km (112.5 mi), with dunes reaching over 76 m (250 ft) high. This is named Hongor Els, or Singing Sands, as the perfectly round, smooth grains create a bizarre musical sound as they are blown across each other by the wind.

WHAT IS IT?
A vast, remote and inhospitable desert in Mongolia, a treasure trove of dinosaur fossils and rare wildlife.
HOW TO GET THERE:
By air to Ulaan Baator, then by road (4 wheel drive).
WHEN TO GO:
June to September.
NEAREST TOWN:
Ulaan Baator is the capital city.
DON'T MISS:
Camel trekking in the desert.
YOU SHOULD KNOW:
Much of the Gobi Desert is difficult to visit. You will probably need to join an organized tour.

The dunes of the Gobi desert loom over herder's yurts.

Shirakami-Sanchi Forest

WHAT IS IT?
A forest ecosystem reserve with a core World Heritage Site of virgin beech forest.
HOW TO GET THERE:
By Shinkansen (Bullet Train) to Akita City, then JR Gono-sen (local train) via Higashinoshiro to Sirakamidake-tozanguchi.
WHEN TO GO:
May to October.
NEAREST TOWN:
Noshiro (S - Akita Pref.); Hirosaki (N – Aomori Pref.)
DON'T MISS:
The thoroughly imaginative presentations of the Shirakami-Sanchi Visitors Centre, close to the station.
YOU SHOULD KNOW:
Strictly limited hunting of black bears outside the core reserve is still practised – with special techniques and ritual ceremonies – by an elite group of local shaman/elders called matagi.

The Shirakami Mountains straddle the border between Aomori and Akita, the two prefectures at the northwestern edge of Honshu, Japan's principal island. Just 15 km (9 mi) from the Inland Sea, they rise sheer into a maze of steep, granite hills with peaks well over 1,000 m (3,280 ft), and there are hundreds of deep, interlaced valleys with slopes of more than 30 degrees. Untouched by glaciation, remote, and above all, protected by their extreme gradients from the threat of agriculture or forestry, the Shirakami are home to the biggest Japanese (Seibold's) beech forest anywhere, and the only one to remain virtually untouched by man since its establishment 8,000 years ago. It stretches across a colossal 130,000 hectares (321,200 acres) of wild gorges cut by a thousand torrents and waterfalls through the broadleaf grandeur of beech, oak and rowan, and the understorey of magnolia, bamboo, and 500 plant species including numerous orchids. But its core of 10,139 hectares (26 acres) has no trails or footpaths at all, and you need special permission to enter it.

This core of virgin forest is home to the black bear, the serow (a kind of goat/antelope), Japanese macaque, golden eagle, and black woodpecker (so rare and valued that the bird has been declared a 'national monument'). Along with many other, equally rare flora and fauna, their success has iconic cultural significance for the Japanese, because they and the Shirakami-Sanchi Forest demonstrate what the majority of Japan used to be like, until the beech forests which covered most of Honshu were destroyed around seventy years ago, for no good reason or benefit. You can see why Shirakami is revered for its natural beauty by visiting the pure crystal Anmon-no-taki falls, the Dairakyo gorge, or the 33 lakes and marshes of Ju-ni-ko, of which the cobalt blue Ao-ike pond, set in particularly dense stands of beech, is the acknowledged jewel.

The virgin forest in the Shirakami

Mount Fuji

Mount Fuji

The perfect cone of Mount Fuji overlooks the town of Fuji-Yoshida about 100 km (60 mi) west of Tokyo, from where it can be seen on very clear days. At its most serene when covered with snow in winter, this is Japan's most sacred peak, in a land where people venerate the beauty of nature. An active stratovolcano that last erupted in 1707, it is instantly recognizable from the paintings of the Japanese master, Hokusai. At 3,776 m (12,388 ft), it is Japan's highest mountain.

It is traditional to make the ascent to the top of the mountain, and perhaps to walk around the crater, too. The full trip from Fuji-Yoshida to the summit takes up to twelve hours so many people take the bus part of the way up and continue on foot from there. The routes are divided into seventeen sections, or stations, and the buses go to the fifth station.

There are four major routes from the fifth station and four from the foot of the mountain. Technically it is illegal to climb the mountain during winter without permission from the police. The peak season is in July and August, when many people make the climb at night so that they can stand at the summit to watch the sunrise over the beautiful landscape that surrounds the mountain. From below, their torches make bright orange trails up the side of the mountain.

For visitors who do not wish to make the climb up the mountain, the best views can be obtained from the shores of the lakes that surround it – Kawaguchi, Sai, Motosu, Shoji, Ashi and Yamanaka – but those who find the energy to do so will not regret it.

WHAT IS IT?
Japan's tallest and most sacred mountain.
HOW TO GET THERE:
By road from Tokyo.
WHEN TO GO:
The peak season in July and August is very busy, but it is the only period when the huts are guaranteed to be open and the buses to operate.
NEAREST TOWN:
Fuji-Yoshida 10 km (6 mi)
DON'T MISS:
Sunrise.
YOU SHOULD KNOW:
It can be very cold at the top.

491

The snow-covered mountains of the Shiretoko Peninsula, in Shiretoko National Park

Shiretoko National Park

The Shiretoko peninsula juts 70 km (44 mi) into the Sea of Okhotsk from the northeastern tip of Hokkaido. Roughly half of it is a complete wilderness, accessible only on foot or by boat. Its spine of volcanic mountains and forest belongs to the largest known population of brown bears in Japan, and to large numbers of wild deer; its extensive wetlands are a sanctuary for huge colonies of cormorants and white-tailed sea eagles, and for countless migratory birds; and its coastal waters host the southernmost ice floes in the northern hemisphere. This unusually southern sea ice has a major impact on the productivity of the local marine ecosystem, and it is the interaction of this environment with the land ecosystem that makes Shiretoko so fascinating.

Mount Rausu on the east coast is the best known of Shiretoko's volcanoes, whose chain continues underwater and out to sea, to resurface as Russia's Kuril Islands. Rausu town attracts visitors to its hot springs, and to Makkausu cave, which wave action has coated with a unique, luminescent moss that glows eerily after nightfall. Rausu is famous for its harvest of edible kelp (a staple of soup stocks), but it's also the start of the 'Shiretoko traverse', the main hiking route to Utoro on the west coast. 10 km (6 mi) north of Utoro brings you to the five lakes of the Shiretoko Go-Ko – quiet ponds surrounded by wild forest, each a perfect mirror for the rugged mountains. Just beyond are the Kamuiwakka-no-taki waterfalls, 32 m (105 ft) high and 2 m (6 ft 8 in) across. Hot spring water mixes with the river as it spills over a precipice into the sea; but the falls descend in a series of hot plunge pools where (with a swimsuit) you can bathe. It's breathtaking, beautiful and dramatic.

You can also travel from Rausu to Utoro by boat. Round the cape, the cliffs rise to a sheer 200 m (656 ft), unbroken for 10 km (6 mi) stretches. The clear black and white striations show where molten lava settled time and again on the sedimentary rock, before the whole lot was lifted out of the sea. It's a wild land and seascape, with screaming birds and an angry ocean: these are virtues of isolation.

WHAT IS IT?
A World Heritage wilderness protecting a unique marine and terrestrial ecosystem.
HOW TO GET THERE:
By air to Memanbetsu; then by car to Utoro.
WHEN TO GO:
May to October.
NEAREST TOWN:
Utoru (W) and Rausu (E); both are within the Park.
DON'T MISS:
The Kamuiwakka waterfalls.
YOU SHOULD KNOW:
Beware bears! Take a bear bell, and talk a lot when you're on the move – especially in spring when bears come out of hibernation.

Shikotsu-Toya National Park

Between Sapporo, Hokkaido's biggest city, and Muroran, to the south on Uchiura ('volcano') bay on the Pacific coast, the Shikotsu-Toya National Park protects a full range of beautiful volcanic landscapes. The bubbling mud pools, crater lakes, steaming fissures, hot springs and sulphurous streams belie the natural peace of the wooded vales and mountain streams, the soaring rock-faces, waterfalls and mossy ravines that inspire visitors' romantic imaginations. Here, the wonders of geology in action are combined with a 360-degree aesthetic of visual beauty.

It's great that such natural loveliness should be easily accessible – but it does mean that the Park can seem crowded. Even so, just an hour by bus from Sapporo, to the east of Yotei and close to the saline springs of Jozankei-onsen, you can bathe in sylvan solitude at the multiple Shiraito-no-taki waterfalls. From there, across the shifting panorama of the Nakayama Pass, you reach Lake Toya itself. Its almost exactly circular disc of crystal blue is in startling contrast to the intense green of the woods that crowd both its shoreline, and Oshima, the miniature island cone set plumb in its centre. Its south shore is dominated by the smoking crater of Mount Uso, one of Japan's most active volcanoes, and parent to neighbouring Showa-Shinzan, which erupted from a flat field in 1944-45 to grow to its present 408 m (1,338 ft). Less crowded than Toya, Lake Shikotsu is an even more beautiful caldera tucked between soaring cliffs – but the relative serenity of both is in marked contrast to the sulphurous frenzy of the hot springs surrounding Noboribetsu, Hokkaido's most popular spa, on the Pacific shore. You can bathe in more than 20 different kinds of hot mineral springs, at hundreds of sites all fed by the vents of Jigoku-dani ('Hell Valley'), a cauldron of steam, fumes and geyser columns which produces 10,000 tons of hot water every day. Sitting in a hot spring at the very edge of the ocean, under a vast sky, you can learn to ignore the crowds as well as the smell of sulphur.

Lake Toya in Shikotsu-Toya National Park

WHAT IS IT?
A showcase for the beautiful landscapes created by continuous volcanic activity.
HOW TO GET THERE:
By air/train/bus to Sapporo; then by bus/car within the Park.
WHEN TO GO:
Year-round.
NEAREST TOWN:
Sapporo (N), Muroran (S)
DON'T MISS:
The spectacular volcanic manifestations of Jigoku-dani.
YOU SHOULD KNOW:
Besides its stunning location, Noboribetsu is famous for its Edo Wonderland, a theme park based on the Edo period, featuring Ninja demonstrations.

*Meakan-dake volcano, Akan
National Park, Hokkaido*

Akan National Park

In eastern Hokkaido, a dense, primeval forest covers a long ridge of volcanic peaks, craters, vents and hot springs; and between them lie three of Japan's loveliest lakes. Especially in autumn, when the red and gold of the sub-arctic forest frames the brilliant blues and greens of the water, Akan National Park adds visual romance to the natural beauty of somnolent vulcanology. Lake Akan itself benefits from the magnificent backdrop of Meakan and Oakan, two volcanoes to its south and east whose reflections are pierced by the many small islands in the lake, which often appears to be a bright green. The colour derives from the marimo, a very rare algae species that forms itself into beautiful, apple-green balls. Left to itself for several centuries, Lake Akan's marimo can reach the size of soccer balls – and at the Marimo Exhibition Centre on Churui-shima Island, across from the little town of Akankohan, there's an underwater viewing room where you can see marimo balls, some hundreds of years old, bobbing up to the surface.

Lake Kussharo, 50 km (31 mi) from Akan, is the biggest of the lakes. The glory of its caldera is best seen from the Bihoro Pass on the north side, and includes the wooded island of Tomoshiri. On the south side are the subterranean hot springs of Wakoto-onsen, which warm the lake and fuel a thriving resort town. Onsen and rotenburo (indoor and outdoor hot spring baths) exist on the shores of all the lakes, and some, with just a few rocks between you and the lake proper, have fabulous views. Better still, most of them are free to use, and you don't even need a swimsuit.

Iozan ('Sulphur Mountain') is the active volcano separating Kussharo from Lake Masshu, considered to be the most beautiful in Japan. Steep rock faces, up to 200 m (656 ft) high and crowded by the intense green of the forest, serve to magnify the extraordinary cobalt blue filling the crater. The water's colour is as famous as the fog that often hides it; but on a clear day, you can see 40 m (131 ft) down into its crystal depths. Honeymooners love the place.

WHAT IS IT?
A national park famous for its beauty, geothermal springs, and volcanoes.
HOW TO GET THERE:
By car from Abashiri (NE), Bihoro (NW) or Kushiro (S)
WHEN TO GO:
April to October
NEAREST TOWN:
Akankohan (SW) and Kawayu (NE), both within the Park.
DON'T MISS:
The free rotenburo and bokke (open-air, hot bubbling mud pools) on Wakoto Peninsula, Lake Kussharo.
YOU SHOULD KNOW:
Japan has designated the marimo a National Special Natural Monument. It takes 200 years for a single ball of weed to grow to the size of a baseball.

Lake Issyk Kul

In northern Kyrgyzstan lies Issyk Kul, 'the Pearl of the Tian Shan Mountains'. With the exception of Lake Titicaca in Bolivia/Peru, it's the biggest mountain lake in the world, with a shoreline nearly 700 km (437 mi) long – big enough to create its own microclimate. It's fed by 118 rivers and streams, plus the melt waters of the snow-capped peaks, which surround it, but it never freezes because of the slightly saline hot springs bubbling up in its centre. Its name even means 'warm lake' in the Kyrgyz language.

The lake's northern shore is a popular holiday resort. At Cholpon-Ata, the Soviet legacy of sanatoria and boarding houses is gradually being refurbished for the new generation of eco-tourists and visitors keen to enjoy the beach life, hydrotherapy and mud baths for which the region is famous. Yet a taxi ride or an hour on horseback from Cholpon-Ata is the Grigorievskoye gorge, on the main hiking route to the lake from Almaty due north in Kazakhstan. Its rugged length and wild beauty is typical of the spectacular landscapes throughout the region, even though it is lined by a series of yurtas offering national Kyrgyz and Kazakh dishes to wanderers.

As good or better as a base is Karakol (formerly Przhevalsk, after the Russian explorer) at the lake's eastern tip. It's the administrative seat of Issyk Kul oblast, or province, but its core is ancient. Its importance as a stopover on the Silk Road is reflected by the 14th century Orthodox church standing in wooden harmony with a mosque built (without using metal nails) by the Uighur people centuries ago. From Karakol you can reach Issyk Kul's southern shore, where development barely touches the pristine wilderness. The savage Kungei Alatau Mountains sweep down close to the water, but folded into the dramatic coves are a few facilities of noticeably high standard – the whole shore was exclusive to Soviet officers and the privilege still shows.

WHAT IS IT?
An mountain lake with no outflow.
HOW TO GET THERE:
Bus or car from Bishkek (Kyrgyzstan) or from Almaty (Kazakhstan)
WHEN TO GO:
May to August.
NEAREST TOWN:
Cholpon-Ata (N central) & Karakol (E)
DON'T MISS:
The Grigorievskoye gorge.
YOU SHOULD KNOW:
Your papers should be in immaculate order, especially if coming from Kazakhstan.

Sunset over Lake Issyk Kul

Pik Imeni Ismail Samani

WHAT IS IT?
The highest mountain in the former Soviet Union.
HOW TO GET THERE:
By plane from Dushanbe to Khorog, then by helicopter or on foot.
WHEN TO GO:
Best climbing months are June, July and August.
NEAREST TOWN:
Khorog 100 km (62 mi); Karaat 80 km (50 mi)
DON'T MISS:
The temples of Kurgan-Tyube.
YOU SHOULD KNOW:
The flight into Khorog from Dushanbe is said to be the most difficult in the world.

Better known as Pik Kommunizma, its name until 1998, or Pik Stalin (until 1962), or Pik Garmo (until 1933), Pik Imeni Ismail Samani is the highest peak in the Pamir Mountains of east Tajikistan. It is a huge, craggy mountain oozing glaciers despite towering over a dry, barren region. Its rock is poor and its approach a crumbling, difficult scramble on snow and ice, but at 7,495 m (24,584 ft), the highest in the region, its summit is a magnet for climbers.

High, cold and remote, the Pamir range is at the hub of Asia, and remains one of the least-explored areas of the world. The bulk of it lies in the east Tajik region of Gorno-Badakhshan. It's often said that these are political as much as geographical 'badlands' – and currently the area is threatened by armed campaigns for even more than its present semi-autonomous status.

But reaching the Pamirs is worth it. From Dushanbe, the Tajik capital, you leave the ancient Silk Road to skirt the mountains and ascend through lush valleys past turquoise lakes. One, Lake Kara-Kul, was formed by a meteor 10 million years ago, and at 3,915 m (12,841 ft) is too high to support aquatic life. A detour south brings you to the remains of the Buddhist temples of Kurgan-Tyube, from which the biggest Buddha in central Asia was removed to storage in Dushanbe, in 60 ignominious pieces. Eventually you come to Khorog, capital of Gorno-Badakhshan. It's a small, one-street town, notable for its museum of stuffed animals and photographs of Lenin. There's little infrastructure for visitors.

Pik Imeni Ismail Samani

K2 and the Karakoram range

The Karakoram range is the greatest consolidation of high mountains in the world. The sinister beauty of hundreds of peaks, spires and fluted ridges makes a spectacular setting for the 60 giants over 7,000 m (22,960 ft) high crammed into an area of 160 sq km (100 sq mi); and even these are just a backdrop to the overlord of the Karakoram, K2. The second highest in the world, 8,611 m (28,252 ft), K2 owes its notoriety as 'the savage mountain' to the extraordinary symmetry of its granite pyramidal summit. Each face drops a sheer 2,800 m (9,184 ft) in under 4 km (2.5 mi). Standing proud from the Qogir Glacier below, it is treacherously steep and exposed to extremes of hailstorms, blizzards and sudden violent winds that frequently pluck climbers off its icy glaze.

Beyond K2 lie Pakistan's borders with India and China, and an ocean of snow, so the best approach is from Skardu, Pakistan's Balti capital. A hair-raising 8-hour drive through dust and grit to the typical Balti village of Askole is a prelude to a trek of several days. Few visitors come to this wilderness of rugged valleys, ice, boulders and towering peaks. Each step reveals a more impressive panorama, until, after crossing the rubble and moraine debris of the huge Baltoro Glacier, you reach Concordia. It's not a village, but a view: from this junction of three major glaciers, framed by four 8,000 m (26,240 ft) peaks and countless others over 7,000 m (22,960 ft) in serried ranks to left and right, K2 rears up in all its solitary, massive grandeur. Concordia is universally and properly known as 'the throne-room of the mountain gods'.

The Karakoram Mountains are more remote and difficult to access than any other range in the neighbouring Pamirs or Himalayas. Not even the engineering triumph of the Karakoram Highway, among many dictates of political modernity in the area, can overshadow its outstanding natural beauty.

Snow on the slopes of K2 in the Karakoram Himalayas

WHAT IS IT?
The second highest mountain in the world.
HOW TO GET THERE:
By plane (45 minutes) or bus (24 hours) from Islamabad to Skardu; then car (8 hours) to Askole; then on foot to Concordia.
WHEN TO GO:
April to September.
NEAREST TOWN:
Askole
DON'T MISS:
The view from Concordia.
YOU SHOULD KNOW:
You can follow a path from K2 to Everest without going lower than 4,594 m (15,068 ft) at Mustang Lo.

497

Lady's Slipper orchids in the beautiful Valley of Flowers

Valley of Flowers

Just 24 km (15 mi) north of Nanda Devi's towering 7,816 m (25,643 ft) peak, the Valley of Flowers in the Paspawati Valley is an outstandingly beautiful high-altitude Himalayan valley cherished by botanists for a century, and by Hindu mythology for much longer. Its meadows of alpine flowers make a gentle contrast with the rugged mountain wilderness characteristic of the Inner Sanctuary of the neighbouring Nanda Devi National Park. The Valley is especially important as a transition zone between the Zaskar and Great Himalaya ranges to the north and south, and between Eastern and Western Himalayan flora.

Almost everything about it is rare. In less than 2,500 hectares (6,178 acres) it contains over 600 specifically sub-, mid- and high-alpine species, including the Himalayan maple and the blue poppy among five unknown elsewhere, 31 officially endangered others, and 45 medicinal plants in daily local use. Several of the latter are collected as religious offerings to Nanda Devi and other deities. The fauna is just as magnificently special. The Valley's 114 species of birds include both the yellow-naped and scaly-bellied woodpecker, the blue-throated barbet and the koklass pheasant which thrives in the thick rhododendron trees and scrub; and all 13 of its native mammals, like the yellow marten, blue sheep, black bear and snow leopard are rare or endangered.

It is no surprise that such a wonderful work of nature should be a place of major pilgrimage. A few kilometres from the Park entrance at the seasonal village of Ghangrea is Lake Lokpal, the site of the Sikh shrine to Hemkund Sahib, and the Hindu temple sacred to Lakshman, brother of Ram. Because the Valley is so easily accessible, thousands visit these and other shrines every year. But no camping is allowed in the Valley, and no other facilities impinge on its pristine natural bounty – visitors are accompanied by a local guide who steers them clear of the most sacred flowers.

WHAT IS IT?
A National Park within a World Heritage Biosphere Reserve. Approx 600 km (373 mi) NE of Delhi
HOW TO GET THERE:
By car to Joshimath then on foot
WHEN TO GO:
June to September
NEAREST TOWN:
Pulna 12 km (7.5 mi) S of Park entrance
DON'T MISS:
Lake Lokpal.
YOU SHOULD KNOW:
Permits are essential to enter the park.

Borra Caves

The Borra Caves spread across 2 sq km (1.25 sq mi) of the Anatigiri Hills, roughly 1,400 m (4,550 ft) high in the Eastern Ghats, and 95 km (59 mi) from the great naval port of Visakhapatnam (Visag, locally) on the Indian Ocean coast of Andhra Pradesh. Their colossal formations have been hewn out of the limestone by the Ghostani River over a million years. In one cave you can hear the torrent rushing above you; in another, you can see it disappear into a hole in the rock at your feet, then peer over a precipice and watch it emerge 90 m (292 ft) below you in an arcing waterfall. Some caverns feel like artfully lit cathedrals or mosques or temples – and the religious association is reinforced by local tribal worship of certain legendary stalactites and stalagmites within them. At festival times, serious crowds flock to the Shivalingam stalagmite, over which hangs Khamdenu, the stalactite idol of a cow whose dripping udder is said to be the source of the Ghostani River.

Around the caves it is wild and rugged. Thick forest tangles in the rocky hollows and ravines. Even the rock glitters with specks of mica. It's an impossibly beautiful landscape at its best in the Araku Valley just 15-20 km (9-12.5 mi) north of the Borra Caves. Araku's lush meadows, streams and waterfalls are home to 19 tribal cultures, distinguished by the dramatic colours of their dress code and spectacular songs and dances. These are not performed just for visitors' entertainment: they are the tribal rituals which give the many religious legends of the Borra Caves their living significance.

Getting there by train is a splendid event in itself. The slow, winding journey from the beaches of Visag – 110 km (69 mi) and over five hours – rises through coffee plantations and the thick vegetation of the Eastern Ghats. This is the highest broad gauge railway in India, and it stops both at the Borra Caves and Araku.

WHAT IS IT?
A limestone cave system.
HOW TO GET THERE:
By train or road from Visag.
WHEN TO GO:
November and December.
NEAREST TOWN:
Araku Hill Station 15 km (9 mi)
DON'T MISS:
The Shivalingam.
YOU SHOULD KNOW:
Rubies have often been mined in the area.

The interior of Borra Cave

Thar Desert

WHAT IS IT?
A desert with a unique ecology.
HOW TO GET THERE:
By rail or road from Delhi to
Jaisalmer (17 hours), then by camel.
WHEN TO GO:
November to March.
NEAREST TOWN:
Jaisalmer 65 km (41 mi) to Desert
Park.
DON'T MISS:
The 3-day Desert Festival in the
dunes at the full moon of Jan-Feb.
YOU SHOULD KNOW:
Take some linament for use after
riding a camel.

The Thar is known as the Great Indian Desert. Approximately 800 km (500 mi) long and 400 km (250 mi) wide, it stretches from the Indus and Sutlej Rivers of east Pakistan to the Aravalli ranges of north-west India. Despite its extreme aridity, it's the most densely populated desert in the world. It harbours thousands of small towns and villages, and Rajasthan boasts some of India's most beautiful and famous cities like Jaipur, Jaisalmer and Jodhpur. They are jewels of Rajput grandeur in a landscape of the living colour of swaying saris and tribal dress, of men's turbans and brightly painted tributes to Hindu mythology.

Jaisalmer sits in the heart of the Thar. Its palaces, forts and temples are typical of the desert cities' magic and brilliance. At sunset, their pink sandstone reflects a glow so intense that Jaisalmer is called the 'golden city'. From here you can ride a camel into the shifting dunes, broken rocks and scrub that characterize the desert's harshness. Swirls of dust shimmer in the midday heat – but when moonlight defines every wind-ridge in the great dunes of the Sam, the starry silence broken only by the shuffle of hoofs in the sand, the desert is a place of eerie romance.

To the south is the Thar Desert National Park, which brings together elements of all the desert's moods. It includes three lakes, the only permanent waterholes, and the Sudashri Forest Post, which is a magnet for rare desert species of antelope, foxes, cats, reptiles and birds like the blue-tailed bee-eater, drongo, quail, demoiselle crane and Indian great bustard. But the concentration of visible wildlife near the only waterfalls or trees in the whole region makes the experience seem artificial. The desert's most intriguing denizens are its shifting tribal nomads and colourful villagers, looming out of the dust and fading back into the enigmatic haze.

Sam Sand Dunes in the Thar Desert, Jaisalmer, Rajasthan

Sunderbans Royal Bengal Tiger Reserve

A Bengal Tiger

A World Heritage Site, the Sunderbans Reserve forms the core 2,585 sq km (1,616 sq mi) of the vast Ganges Delta in West Bengal. Here the silt deposits of a continent form islands connected to the mainland by a series of labyrinthine waterways choked with tangled mangroves. Half the world's species and 80% of all India's mangrove swamps make these the most fecund marshes on the planet, able to support the biggest concentration of tigers along with colonies of rhesus macaques, chitals, boar, otters, salt water crocodiles, monitor lizards, king crabs, Ridley's, green and hawk's bill turtles, innumerable snakes and constellations of the most multi-coloured birds on earth or water.

Twice a day, the mangroves flood with the tide, making access especially difficult. The Sunderbans tigers have long adapted to this amphibious habitat. They are adept swimmers, can survive in and on brackish water, and are known to feed on fish and turtles as well as their usual prey. Their proliferation is a measure of the Reserve's success in limiting poaching and human activities like fishing and the collection of wood and forest produce. It also has its downside: Royal Bengal Tigers are notorious man-eaters, accustomed through generations of proximity to the delights of a human snack treat. The use of electric deterrents, lighting and awareness programmes for villagers and visitors alike has reduced local fatalities from 40 to roughly 10 a year. But any risk seems worth the chance of seeing that glorious black-striped, golden-orange flash between the dense greenery.

Reaching the Sunderbans is an adventure. From the nearest rail station at Canning you must find a way to reach Sonakhali, where you take a 7-hour boat ride to Gosaba, followed by a rickshaw to Pakhirala, and another boat to the Park entrance at Sajnekhali. Your reward is seeing the biggest cat on earth in its swampy paradise.

WHAT IS IT?
A World Heritage Site and Biosphere Reserve.
HOW TO GET THERE:
By boat and rickshaw from Canning.
WHEN TO GO:
September to March
NEAREST TOWN:
Gosaba 50 km (31 mi)
DON'T MISS:
The cruise down many of the creeks.
YOU SHOULD KNOW:
The journey provides the rites of passage to rural Bengal.

501

Kaziranga National Park

On the banks of the Brahmaputra River in the extreme north-east of India in Assam, the 430 sq km (269 sq mi) of the Kaziranga National Park, a maze of forests, swamps and tall thickets of elephant grass, provide the ideal habitat for the Indian One-horned Rhino. There are more here than anywhere else, along with a large population of Indian elephants, Barasingha and hog deer, sloth bears, tigers, leopards, capped langurs, Hoolock gibbons, wild boar, jackal, buffalo, pythons and jungle otters. It is a breathtaking vision of the teeming potential of successful wilderness parks.

In winter, huge numbers of migratory birds descend on the lakes and marshes. Greylag geese, red-crested pochard, gadwall and northern shoveller are among those splashing down to join the oriental honey buzzard, brahminy kite, white-tailed and Pallas's fishing eagles, Himalayan griffon, and more than 100 other species already resident.

The relatively open country makes watching the wildlife easy. You can usually see all the major species within a single day. Early morning is best, when elephants resume their foraging; and the grasslands are a magnet for circling raptors like the serpent eagle, searching for prey among the flashy kaleidoscope of storks, herons, pelicans and teal for whom the marshes are home.

The park changes with the seasons – the major wildlife migrates to different areas within the park during the monsoon, for example, when the Brahmaputra overflows its banks. It is prudent to check in advance which areas are accessible, and whether permits may be necessary.

WHAT IS IT?
A National Wildlife Park and World Heritage site.
HOW TO GET THERE:
By plane to Jorhat, then by road.
WHEN TO GO:
November to April.
NEAREST TOWN:
Jorhat 95 km (59 mi)
DON'T MISS:
The early morning.
YOU SHOULD KNOW:
You can ride elephants (with mahouts) through the park.

Nanda Devi Biosphere Reserve

WHAT IS IT?
A Natural Biosphere Reserve & World Heritage Site.
HOW TO GET THERE:
By train to Haridwar, then by road to Joshimath.
WHEN TO GO:
April to June.
NEAREST TOWN:
Joshimath 23 km (14 mi) to park entrance at Lata Village.
DON'T MISS:
The suspension bridge over the Bharagithi River gorge.
YOU SHOULD KNOW:
Check with your doctor about the implications of high altitude walking.

The Garwhal Himalaya range stretches north from Haridwar past increasingly remote villages, alpine pastures and dense virgin forests until it enters a vast bowl in the hills known as the Outer Sanctuary of Nanda Devi. To the west is Nanda Devi itself, at 7,816 m (25,643 ft) India's second highest mountain, a natural fortress surrounded by an unbroken ridge wall never lower than 6,000 m (19,400 ft). This Inner Sanctuary is breached only by the spectacular Rishi Ganga gorge, a long chasm of tumbled rock along which the dense clumps of fir, juniper and rhododendron trees give way to arid scrub and the Nanda Devi Glacier. Visitors must stop here. The unrivalled magnificence of the panorama is compensation enough – but this wilderness is of far more than ecological significance. The area is revered as one of the holiest places in India, the source of the Mother River, Ganges.

The National Park surrounding Nanda Devi rewards the considerable effort it takes to get there. Against the constantly changing backdrop of multiple snow-capped peaks, you pass 312 floral species among the grasses, alpine mosses and lichens. Warblers, Grosbeaks, Rose Finches and Ruby-Throats are among 80 species of birds, and this is one of few regions where you might actually see the bharal, the himalayan tahr, serow, goral, black and brown bears, leopard, langur, musk deer and fabled Snow Leopard. Global rarity is almost commonplace here.

Most visitors to the Park more or less follow the route taken by Eric Shipton and Bill Tilman, the first outsiders to reach the area in the 1930s. Sadly, their amazing feat of endurance and discovery encouraged too many imitators captivated by Nanda Devi's mystique and unique ecology, and the Inner Sanctuary is closed to allow it to recover.

Nanda Devi East

Kathmandu Valley

The town of Kathmandu is the capital, but it is the Kathmandu Valley, as a whole, which is the political, commercial and cultural hub of Nepal. It's roughly oval, 24 km (15 mi) long and 19 km (12 mi) across, encircled by green terraced hills and dotted by clusters of red-tiled roofs. It luxuriates in its ancient fertility, a natural showcase for an equally rich culture, art and traditional way of life. Until very recently, it was still said that the Valley held as many temples and shrines as it did houses, but the rapid urbanization of the last three decades now threatens its survival as a unique, living, breathing entity developed over more than 2,000 years.

Mist hangs over a settlement in the Kathmandu Valley, Nepal.

The Valley holds three towns of great historic significance: Kathmandu, Lalitpur (aka Patan) and Bhaktapur (aka Bhadgaon). Each is a treasure trove of golden temples, enigmatic Buddhas and fabulous artefacts, which derive their exotic subtlety from the natural beauty of the surrounding fields and gardens. The feeling of place and culture, evolving symbiotically, is reinforced by the smaller villages as well. Pagodas loom out of rural mists, and the sound of creaking might be a prayer wheel or a handcart full of vegetables. The small hilltop town of Kirtipur, 8 km (5 mi) SW of Kathmandu, embodies this faintly surreal time warp.

Happily, the Kathmandu Valley lends itself to walking or riding a bike. Buses are cheap and frequent, but crowded and slow. Best of all for visitors are the eco-friendly 'tempoes', green and white three-wheelers that are cheaper and faster than regular taxis.

WHAT IS IT?
The heart and soul of the Kingdom of Nepal.
HOW TO GET THERE:
By plane to Kathmandu city.
WHEN TO GO:
August to September.
NEAREST TOWN:
Kathmandu city.
DON'T MISS:
The charming glimpse of rural life in Kirtipur.
YOU SHOULD KNOW:
Expect a lot of walking even if you're not planning to trek.

505

Sagarmatha National Park

In Sanskrit it means 'Mother of the Universe', and Sagarmatha is the modern Nepali name for both Mount Everest as a whole, and for the Park in eastern Nepal that covers 1,148 sq km (718 sq mi) of Himalayan ecological zone. The Park's dramatic mountains, glaciers and deep valleys are dominated by the southern half of Everest, which soars up to the border with Tibet and forms the watershed between central Asia and the Indian Ocean. At 8,848 m (29,021 ft) Sagarmatha is the top of the world, its familiar iconic summit guarded by six other peaks over 6,000 m (19,680 ft), and surrounded by gorges and rugged terrain that never drops below 2,845 m (9,331 ft).

Lower down, forests of juniper, birch and silver fir trees provide a spring and monsoon showcase for the brilliant colours of flowering rhododendrons; and a protective habitat for 118 species of birds like the blood pheasant and yellow-billed chough. Large mammals like the Musk deer and Himalayan tahr are common, along with the jackal, weasel, marten, common langur and black bear. It's also occasional home to the Snow leopard and lesser panda. That they exist at all is witness to the still relatively pristine alpine and mountain ecology, now under threat from the tourism it needs for its own protection.

The Park's HQ and Visitor Centre is in the village of Namche Bazaar, a focal point of the Sherpa culture predominant in eastern Nepal. Most visitors enter the park here (there's a southern entrance just north of Mondzo, a hamlet one day's hike from the airstrip at Lukla); and you have only to walk a few paces from Namche's buildings to claim the incredible mountian view as your own: the chain of Lhotse, Nuptse, Cho-Oyu, Thamserku and Amadablam standing homage to the ultimate peak of Everest itself.

Gokyo Lake, Khumbu Valley, Sagamartha National Park

Kangchenjunga

With the tallest of its five peaks at 8,586 m (28,162 ft), Kangchenjunga is the world's third-highest mountain. It straddles the eastern border of Nepal with Sikkim, the autonomous region of India, and is as famous for its dramatic beauty as it is feared for its dangerous power over those who live in its foothills. The mountain is honoured by the Sikkimese as a deity, who is portrayed with a fiery red face and a crown of five skulls representing the five peaks over 8,000 m (26,240 ft) which it incorporates. The religious association is so strong that seasoned mountaineers refuse to desecrate Sikkimese sensibilities, and turn back a few feet short of Kangchenjunga's actual summit.

Despite its fearsome weather – roaring ice avalanches, hailstorms, flash floods and sudden blizzards – the mountain offers the best of any access to the Himalayas' unique flora and fauna. It's only 74 km (46 mi) as the eagle flies, but a whole world from Darjeeling's sub-tropical tea plantations. The contrast between lush lowlands, the band of alpine meadows, and the forbidding majesty of the icy peaks with

Morning sun illuminates the snow-covered peaks of the Kanchenjunga massif which lies on the border of Sikkim and Nepal.

Mount Everest in the background could not be more dramatic. But the best approach to Kangchenjunga and the Himalayas in general is from Nepal. You can trek (with varying degrees of difficulty) from the tiny airstrip at Taplejung to the South Face base camp at Ramche. Besides the magnificent mountain views, you pass rivers cascading down through pristine forests, groaning glaciers and traditional hamlets; and though you may not see many other people you'll enjoy the exotic birds and wildlife unique to the Himalayas.

Actually climbing Kanchenjunga is notoriously difficult, and requires an official permit either from Nepal or Sikkim. Even trekking in the region is subject to strict rules, and it's usually best to join a guided party of some kind.

WHAT IS IT?
The world's third highest mountain.
HOW TO GET THERE:
By plane from Kathmandu to Taplejung.
WHEN TO GO:
April to October.
NEAREST TOWN:
Taplejung.
DON'T MISS:
The glaciers of Ramche.
YOU SHOULD KNOW:
Get your permit to visit Sikkim when you apply for your Indian visa. Specify where in Sikkim you want to go: many areas are completely prohibited to visitors.

Horton Plains National Park

WHAT IS IT?
An unusual, atmospheric, and beautiful national park.
HOW TO GET THERE:
By road from Nuwara Eliya or Talawakale.
WHEN TO GO:
October to March.
NEAREST TOWN:
Nuwara Eliya 48 km (30 mi)
YOU SHOULD KNOW:
For the best views, visit early in the morning, before the inevitable cloud cover descends.

Situated in the central highlands of Sri Lanka, Horton Plains National Park is quite unlike any other national park in the country. Located on a plateau at over 2,000 m (6,600 ft), this is a landscape of undulating hills covered in montane cloud forest and montane savannah grasslands, known as 'patannahs'. Its misty, chilly, windy climate has been compared to that of the moors and highlands of Scotland.

The tree canopy reaches 20 m (66 ft) but there are also many quite distinctive gnarled and stunted trees, draped in tangled creepers and trailing lichens. Giant tree ferns grow here, as do gloriously colourful rhododendrons and many gorgeous species of orchid. Three major rivers originate in the Plains: the Kelani, the Walawe and the Mahawelli, the longest river in Sri Lanka.

Horton Plains is home to a wide variety of creatures: 24 species of mammal, including endemic species such as Slender loris and Purple-faced leaf monkey. There are Rusty, Spotted and Fishing cats as well as leopard, deer, elk, otter, and 87 species of bird, 14 of which are endemic, making it a popular place for birdwatching. This was once prime elephant country, but tragically the elephant population was hunted to extinction during the 19th century, largely by British colonialists.

Within the Park, Sri Lanka's second and third highest mountains can be found, as can the 20 m (66 ft) waterfall, Baker's Fall, which plunges and tumbles over black rock into the gorge below. The most renowned feature of the Park, however, is called World's End. This is an awe-inspiring escarpment at the southern end of the park, a sheer drop of more than 1,000 m (3,300 ft), from which one can see over miles of tea plantations to the distant southern shore.

A view of World's End, over the tea plantations and down to the sea

Yala National Park

Yala National Park, otherwise known as Ruhunu, in south eastern Sri Lanka, is the most visited national park in the country and the best place in which to see large mammals. The landscape is mainly flat, with rocky outcrops of up to 245 m (800 ft) rising suddenly upwards. A seasonal river, the Menik Ganga, and four seasonal streams carry away the monsoon waters, and there are rock pools and natural water holes, essential for wildlife. To the southeast of the park, there are small patches of riverine forest, mangroves, pristine beaches, sand dunes and the sea.

A grey langur monkey in the Yala National Park

Inscriptions found in this region date back to the 2nd century BC, but nothing has been found that is later than 10th century AD. It would seem that the human population departed at that time, leaving the mature secondary forest that we see today to cover their tracks. Much of the area consists of thorny scrub forest, allowing visitors a really good chance of seeing wildlife.

All of Sri Lanka's large mammals are to be found here – leopard, sloth bear, spotted deer, wild boar, jackal, sambar, buffalo and Marsh crocodile. There is also a diversity of smaller mammals such as mongoose, langur and Toque monkey. The park is also known for its birdlife. Over 140 species have been recorded here, including endemic species such as Ceylon junglefowl, woodshrike and swallow, as well as waterbirds, hornbills, storks and eagles. However, it remains best known for both its elephants and its peacocks.

Divided into five blocks, only one of which is open to visitors, the park was badly hit by the tsunami in 2004, which killed both park employees and tourists, including a party of 22 Japanese. Interestingly, there is no evidence of large-scale animal deaths, suggesting that they may have sensed the disaster coming and moved to higher ground.

WHAT IS IT?
The most popular national park in Sri Lanka.
HOW TO GET THERE:
By road from Hambantota.
WHEN TO GO:
February and June to October.
NEAREST TOWN:
Tissamaharama 12 km (7.5 mi)
DON'T MISS:
The wild elephants at Udawalawe National Park.

Sinharaja Forest Reserve

WHAT IS IT?
A small area of primary tropical rainforest.
HOW TO GET THERE:
By air to Colombo, then by road.
WHEN TO GO:
January–April and August-September
NEAREST TOWN:
Ratnapura (44 km, 27 mi)
YOU SHOULD KNOW:
Leeches can be a problem.

One of the jewels of Sri Lanka, the Sinharaja Forest Reserve lies in the southwest of the island and is its last remnant of pristine tropical rainforest. It is 21 km (13 mi) wide and some 5 km (3 mi) long, and provides a last home for such rare animals as wild boar, barking deer, giant squirrels, civets, porcupines, mongoose , purple-faced langurs and extremely elusive leopards. This area is precious because it holds so many species of plants that no longer occur anywhere else in the world as the forests around them have been cut down. Sinharaja has been declared a UNESCO World Heritage Site because of the importance and rarity of its plants.

There are two main habitats within the reserve – tropical lowland rainforest and tropical wet evergreen forest – and more than half of the major plant species here are found nowhere else.

The dense forests are home to many species of birds, among them Sri Lanka blue magpie, greater racket-tailed drongo, white-headed starling, orange-billed babbler, red-faced malkoha and the extremely rare green-billed coucal. Among the other creatures that enjoy the lush green wilderness are hump-nosed and green pit vipers and many amphibians, including tree frogs. There is also a wide variety of insect life, including the common birdwing butterfly, another species that occurs only here.

A Purple-faced langur
(Trachypithecus vetulus
monticola) *or Bear Monkey*

Phong Nha-Ke Bang National Park

A Sun bear, native to forests in South East Asia

Phong Nha-Ke Bang National Park is in central Vietnam, in Quang Binh Province. This is the narrowest part of the country, abutting Laos to the west, with the sea to the east, only 42 km (26 mi) away. It is one of the world's two largest limestone regions, and the oldest in Asia. There is an on-going plan between Vietnam and Laos to jointly manage their adjacent nature reserves, which, if combined, would form the largest karst forest in South-East Asia.

Designated a UNESCO World Heritage Site in 2003, the Park preserves a wonderfully complex system of limestone caves, tunnels, grottos and rock formations, as well as some of the longest underground rivers in the world. The Phong Nha cave, the Park's main visitor attraction, is probably the most spectacular of those explored so far, and contains amazing, giant speleothems with romantic names such as Royal Court and Buddha. Tourboats can venture 1,500 m (4,900 ft) inside. So far, scientists have surveyed 20 caves; however, there are hundreds more to be explored.

The region is covered with tropical forest, much of it primary, which provides habitat for a diverse range of flora and fauna, including 13 species endemic to Vietnam, and one species endemic to this site. Primates thrive here – it contains the largest populations of Hatinh and Black langur, both endangered species, as are Sun bear, serow, Giant muntjac and the recently discovered Striped hare. In 2005, Vietnamese biologists discovered a new gecko. This is a fantastic place for biological research, which, like the exploration of the cave system, is continuous.

WHAT IS IT?
The oldest major karst region in Asia.
HOW TO GET THERE:
By road.
WHEN TO GO:
Spring and early summer.
NEAREST TOWN:
Dong Hoi 50 km (31 mi)
YOU SHOULD KNOW:
The Park has been earmarked as a major tourist attraction, but currently it is very difficult to visit as an independent traveller.

Halong Bay

This utterly beautiful bay is one of Asia's most perfect natural wonders. A heavenly combination of sky, water and stone, it seems almost to be an enormous artwork created by the inhabitants of another world. Halong Bay means 'The Bay of the Descending Dragon' and legend has it that long ago, during an invasion by the Chinese, dragons came to defend the land, spitting out thousands of pearls as they descended, each of which turned into a jade island upon hitting the water. These islands formed a defensive barrier into which the invader's ships crashed and sank.

Halong Bay is situated in the Gulf of Tonkin, close to the border between Vietnam and China, and it contains about 2,000 islands. Dating back millions of years, they are the remnants of a limestone mountain range that was submerged by the sea, leaving the karst

WHAT IS IT?
A glorious bay containing 2,000 islands, with sea arches, caves and floating villages.
HOW TO GET THERE:
By boat or kayak.
WHEN TO GO:
Spring and early summer.
NEAREST TOWN:
Halong City, Hong Gai and Cam Pha are all on Halong Bay.
YOU SHOULD KNOW:
Halong Bay is a UNESCO World Heritage Site.

seascape of today. The islands are mainly topped by impenetrable jungle, and the elements continue to erode them into ever more fanciful shapes, echoed by names such as Elephant, Wallowing Buffalo and Fighting Cock.

Many islands contain caves and grottoes; some are almost hollow. Wooden Stakes Cave is the largest of these, and is accessed by 90 rock hewn steps. It contains three chambers – the first contains spectacular stalagmites and stalactites, some as tall as 20 m (63 ft) and is large enough to hold 3,000 people. Archaeological sites have been found, containing so many artefacts that collectively they have been accorded the term 'Halong Culture' – meaning the Neolithic Age culture of north-eastern, coastal Vietnam. There are fishing communities here, who inhabit floating villages and make a living from some of the 450 species of shellfish and 200 species of fish that swim in these clear, blue waters.

The Marble Mountains

To the west of Da Nang, facing towards the East China Sea, stand five mountains that appear to have risen together from the surrounding plain. These are the Marble Mountains, formed in fact from both marble and limestone, and riven with passages, tunnels and caves. Their Vietnamese name, Ngu Hanh Son, means 'Mountains of the Five Elements', and each peak is named for water, fire, earth, metal and wood.

The mountains are famous for traditional stone carving, and in the nearby village of Dong Hai, 600 families earn their livelihood from carving statues, making jewellery and artefacts such as chess sets. The mountains each have different shades of marble – pinks, whites and browns, but excavating rock directly from them has now been banned. Today the local craftsmen work with material that has been quarried elsewhere, while their children act as guides to the visitors, hoping to be able to sell a souvenir or two for their trouble.

Thuy Son (water) is the highest mountain, and has carved steps to the top that lead to the Tham Thia Pagoda, and the Huyen Khong Cave. During the Vietnam War, many of the caves here were used by Viet Khong soldiers and cave-to-cave fighting took place – as can be seen by the bullet holes in the walls. One of the holes in the roof of the Huyen Khong Cave was caused by a bomb.

Previously the Pagoda was dedicated to both Buddha and Hindu deities, but now it is dedicated to Cham deities. There are several caves in these mountains that are places of worship: high, cathedral-like spaces, redolent with the blue, scented smoke of incense, within which there are some very finely carved Buddha images and temple guardians to be seen.

A statue of Buddha sits in a cave. The Marble Mountains are famous for their cave shrines.

WHAT IS IT?
Five limestone and marble peaks with shrines built into their caves.
HOW TO GET THERE:
By road from Da Nang.
WHEN TO GO:
Spring and early summer.
NEAREST TOWN:
Da Nang 12 km (7.5 mi)
DON'T MISS:
The view from the top of Thuy Son.

The Mekong Delta

With a length of 4,160 km (2,585 mi), the Mekong River is the twelfth longest in the world, rising high on the Tibetan plateau, it descends across south-western China, through Laos and along its border with Thailand, across Cambodia and Vietnam to discharge into the South China Sea. The delta itself is usually regarded as starting in Phnom Penh in Cambodia, where the river divides in two, and then further splits to form the 'Nine Dragons', as the channels are known. The triangle of the plain covers roughly 55,000 sq km (21,230 sq mi) and the distance between Phnom Penh and the sea is some 270 km (170 mi). The delta itself is the result of the deposition of silt washed down by the river and in places the land is reclaiming up to 150 m (500 ft) of land from the sea each year.

The silt makes this a highly fertile region, so it is important to the nation's economy and is densely populated in places, but it is still possible to get away from the crowds and explore the nature reserves and the wildlife that inhabits this flat land of mangrove swamps and melaleuca trees. Twenty-three species of mammals, six amphibians, thirty-five reptiles, 386 species and subspecies of birds and 260 fish have been recorded. The rivers harbour five species of dolphin, including the Chinese white dolphin and Irrawaddy dolphin and other mammals include smooth-coated and clawless otters, the fishing cat and the crab-eating macaque. The wetlands are particularly important for birds, including several large raptors, eight species of kingfisher, large colonies of cormorants, herons, storks, egrets and ibises, cranes, many species of duck and migrant waders. There are also monitor lizards, water snakes, estuarine crocodiles and river terrapins.

The quieter areas of the Mekong Delta are an unexpectedly beautiful find in a crowded land.

WHAT IS IT?
A massive river delta, rich in history and wildlife.
HOW TO GET THERE:
By road from Ho Chi Minh City.
WHEN TO GO:
The monsoon season is from late May to September and is best avoided.
DON'T MISS:
The spectacle of the colonies of birds.

The Mekong Delta

The Bolaven Plateau

WHAT IS IT?
A beautiful, fertile upland plateau, home to many tribal groups and world famous for its coffee plantations.
HOW TO GET THERE:
By road from Pakse.
WHEN TO GO:
November to May.
NEAREST TOWN:
Pakse, 30 km (19 mi).
DON'T MISS:
Elephant treks from Tad Lo.

High above the humid Mekong River valley, in southern Laos, is an area of flat, fertile land known as the Bolaven Plateau. Its average altitude of 600 m (1,980 ft) provides it with a cool, pleasant climate, and rivers cascade and tumble down from it on all sides, producing numerous beautiful waterfalls.

There are several tribal groups living on the plateau, which is named after the largest of them, the Laven. The area has long been cultivated on a small scale, using traditional methods, but in the early 20th century, a Frenchman, Jean Dauplay, realized it was perfect coffee-growing country, and introduced the bean to Laos, bringing it from Vietnam. The region was heavily bombed by the USA during the Vietnam War in the 1960s and '70s, but today it produces some of the finest and most expensive coffee beans in the world, with a distinctive taste reminiscent of smooth, dark chocolate. There are also many tea plantations, vegetables, spices and orchards growing here – even raspberries and strawberries are successful in this climate.

Two of the best-known waterfalls in the area are Tad Lo and Tad Fan. The former, whilst not a particularly high fall, has both upper and lower cascades in a beautiful forest setting, with cool, clear swimming holes, and smooth granite rocks on which to relax. In contrast, Tad Fan is one of the highest falls in Laos – its waters split into two cascades that plunge 120 m (394 ft) from the cliff edge to the pool beneath.

A waterfall on the Bolaven Plateau

Nakai-Nam Theun National Biodiversity Conservation Area

In 1993 the government of Laos created 18 National Biodiversity Conservation Areas, the largest of which is Nakai-Nam Theun. This comprises the region of the Nam Theun River, four other rivers, and the Nakai plateau. This area is now considered to be the world's most significant biodiversity conservation area partly due to its complex range of habitats – including evergreen, montane beech, cloud and riverine forest, the Annamite mountains, which separate Laos from Vietnam, and the plateau. Much of the area is pristine forest, and is home to well over 400 species of bird, about 50 of which are endangered, and 35 per cent of which occur only on the plateau.

Nakai-Nam Theun is best known for its large mammals, many of which are threatened, making the populations here particularly crucial. Three of the last five mammals to be either discovered (or re-discovered, having been thought extinct,) live here. These include the Saola, the Giant-Antlered muntjac and the Black muntjac. There are many rare cats here too: tigers, clouded leopards, Marbled cats, Asiatic Golden cats and many more. It is also home to most of Laos's Asiatic elephants, and gaurs. There are nine species of primate, including the most important population of Red-shanked douc in the world and, in 1999, the Striped rabbit, a new species, was discovered here.

A major hydropower project is planned for this region. The dam itself would be sited on the plateau and would create a 450 sq km (174 sq mi) reservoir, flooding habitats and destroying wildlife. However, the Lao and Vietnamese governments are considering adding other NBCAs to Nakai-Nam Theun, which could result in 7 protected areas straddling the border and forming possibly the most important super-reserve in the world.

Nakai-Nam Theun Conservation Area, Laos

WHAT IS IT?
A National Biodiversity Conservation Area.
HOW TO GET THERE:
By road from Route 8B.
WHEN TO GO:
November, after the monsoon.
NEAREST TOWN:
Nakai, 10 km (6 mi)
YOU SHOULD KNOW:
Because of the proposed dam, you should check accessibility with the tourism authority.

Looking across the Mekong River at the mountainous landscape from the shores of Luang Prabang.

Mekong River Valley

The Mekong River, which rises in Tibet and empties into the South China Sea, runs through very nearly the entire length of Laos, and has an almost spiritual significance for Lao people. About 75 per cent of Laos is made up of remote mountains and plateaux and this, combined with it being a land-locked country, means that the Mekong is deeply important. It is used not only as a source of food and water, but also for travelling upon, although as more roads are built, more people travel upon them.

The river is home to over a thousand species of fish, which provide about 80 per cent of the protein that most Lao people eat. It is home to the largest freshwater fish in the world, the giant catfish, which can weigh over 300 kilograms – as well as the endangered Irrawaddy dolphin, of which less than one hundred live in the widest section of the entire river, just before it reaches Cambodia.

The river swells enormously during the monsoon, and leaves behind it wonderfully rich sediment, ensuring extremely fertile river banks and flood plains. Virtually all of the rice grown in Laos comes from the southern flood plain, and the two largest cities, Vientiane, the capital, and Savannakhet in the south, are situated on the river's edge, in the two broadest sections of river valley. In both these cities, rather charmingly, vegetables are grown on every available inch of river bank.

Inevitably the Mekong is changing: China is building vast dams, and water levels are dropping dramatically. During the dry season in Vientiane the river shrinks to what is virtually a stream. If this trend continues it could prove disastrous to millions of people living in Laos, Vietnam and Cambodia.

WHAT IS IT?
The 12th longest river in the world.
HOW TO GET THERE:
By air or overland to Laos.
WHEN TO GO:
November to April.
NEAREST TOWN:
Luang Prabang, Vientiane, Savannakhet and Pakse are all situated on the Mekong River.
YOU SHOULD KNOW:
The Mekong rises in Tibet and passes through China, Myanmar, Laos, Cambodia and Vietnam. Over 60 million people are dependent upon it and its tributaries.

Kuang Si Falls

The Kuang Si Falls are situated some 30 km (19 mi) south of Luang Prabang, in northern Laos. It is a beautiful, wide and generous waterfall that cascades down over limestone tiers and through a number of calm, shallow pools. The calcite deposits that have covered and rounded the tiers give the water an extraordinary pale, milky-blue cast. At the lower level a pretty park has been landscaped, with seats and picnic tables all arranged to give the best views of both the falls and the surrounding forest.

A forest trail leads upwards to the top of the falls, following the path of the stream, and those who take this come upon a second tier of the falls, where the natural pool is fine for swimming. Venture behind the curtain of water and you will discover a cave that goes back for 10 m (33 ft). Back on the trail, continue scrambling to the top and you will find the stream that feeds the falls surrounded by forest and with a meadow beyond. The view down the 60 m (197 ft) fall is gorgeous, framed with flowering forest shrubs and trees, and swathes of bougainvillea.

Just before you reach the falls you pass by the picturesque village of Ban Ta Baen, with its charming wooden stilt houses, colourful chillies arranged on the roofs to dry, and beautifully situated on the river with its clear bathing pools and mini waterfalls. The sound of water splashing and tinkling is calming, and birdsong and the laughter of children add to the rural charm of this idyllic spot.

HOW TO GET THERE:
By road or river from Luang Prabang.
WHEN TO GO:
November to May.
NEAREST TOWN:
Luang Prabang 30 km (19 mi).
DON'T MISS:
Ban Ta Baen village.
YOU SHOULD KNOW:
A small entry fee is payable.

Kuang Si Falls

Callao Cave

WHAT IS IT?
A fabulous, 7-chambered cave, in a protected area that is riddled with exciting cave systems.
HOW TO GET THERE:
By air to Tuguegarao City and road to the caves.
WHEN TO GO:
November to April.
NEAREST TOWN:
Tuguegarao City 40 km (25 mi).
DON'T MISS:
Mororan; Cagayan Museum.

The Callao Cave complex is located in the Penablanca Protected Landscape and Seascape region, in the province of Cagayan, to the north east of Luzon Island. This is an area of great ecological importance, containing the last of the Philippines' old growth forest, the Cagayan River – the longest river in the country – and a coastline that is home to unique coastal and marine ecosystems.

In recognition of the importance of this region, President Gloria Arroyo expanded the protected area from 4,136 hectares (10,220 acres) to over 118,000 hectares (291,600 acres), connecting it to the northern Sierra Madre National Park, and thus creating a conservation area that is larger than Switzerland. Amongst the animals that are now safeguarded are three critically endangered species, and many that are threatened.

Callao Cave is an amazing, seven-chambered cave, each chamber having natural light that filters through crevices in the rock. During World War II, the Japanese Occupational Forces are thought to have used the cave as a camp. The first chamber is most well-known – a huge, naturally domed 'cathedral', that has been made into a chapel by the local people, and which is much visited by both nationals and tourists. The remaining six chambers have beautiful stalactites and stalagmites to admire.

However, Callao Cave is not alone: this area is cavers' heaven – there are some 300 systems here, only some of which have been explored. The nearby Sierra Cave contains well-preserved, delicate speleothems, and at Odessa, 8 km (5 mi) of narrow tunnels and wide passages have been mapped, but there is much more still to be explored.

A scene shot in Callao Caves in northern Philippines shows an explorer highlighted by a shaft of light from the cave ceiling.

Tubbataha Reef

Tubbataha Reef

The Tubbataha Reef is situated in the middle of the Sula Sea, to the east of the island of Palawan. It is composed of two atolls separated by four nautical miles of water. North Reef is a continuous, oblong reef platform that completely encloses a sandy lagoon. This 4-5 km (2-3 mi) wide, 16 km (10 mi) long reef is shallow and partially uncovered at low tide. South Reef is narrower, triangular in shape, and also encloses a sandy lagoon. On its southern tip, a solar powered lighthouse stands, providing a convenient perch for various seabirds.

The Sula Sea contains over 30 per cent of the world's coral reefs, and Tubbataha are the finest in the Philippines, and a must for serious divers. This remote spot became known for its 'walls' – areas where the shallow reef suddenly plunges sharply down to depths sports divers cannot reach. These walls contain caves and crevices and are rich with coral cover. Large fish such as Dog-tooth tuna and snappers are abundant here, as well as most species of Pacific reef fish in all their glorious shapes and colours. Underwater visibility is often up to 30 m (99 ft) and this protected habitat absolutely teems with life. Other, larger species also found here include manta rays, six or seven species of shark, and endangered sea turtles, which lay their eggs on the coral sand beaches.

During the 1980s and '90s Tubbataha Reef was damaged by illegal fishing practices, including the use of dynamite. However, since 1994 all fishing in the Marine Park has been halted, and the conservation measures put in place have led to a remarkable and entirely natural regeneration.

WHAT IS IT?
The best of the Philippines' coral reefs and a UNESCO World Heritage Site.
HOW TO GET THERE:
By boat.
WHEN TO GO:
Mid-March to mid-June.
NEAREST TOWN:
Puerto Princesa City 12 hours by boat.
YOU SHOULD KNOW:
Dedicated dive boats get booked up long in advance, so book your trip early.

*Puerto-Princesa
Subterranean River*

Puerto-Princesa Subterranean River National Park

The Puerto-Princesa National Park is situated in the St. Paul Mountains, on the north-west coast of Palawan Island. Over 90 per cent of the Park consists of karst topography – sharp limestone ridges and rounded peaks around Mount St. Paul. The hills are largely covered with lush tropical forest, dominated by hardwood species and home to several endemic mammals. At the coast are mangrove swamps, and off-shore there are coral reefs and beds of seagrass, where endangered dugong have been recorded.

The main feature of the Park, however, is the Subterranean River. This rises some 2 km (1.25 mi) south west of Mount St. Paul and then winds its way underground for some 8 km (5 mi) before flowing out into the sea at St. Paul's Bay. The river, which is navigable, is known as St. Paul's Cave. Highly unusual, it passes through huge, domed caverns up to 60 m (198 ft) high and 120 m (396 ft) wide, containing major formations of speleothems. The river is also of particular interest because it empties into the sea – thus having a sweetwater to saltwater ecosystem. The lower portion is brackish and tidal, producing a unique habitat, and the large passages and chambers through which it passes are home to sizeable populations of swiftlets and eight species of bat.

Palawan's flora and fauna are more closely related to that of Borneo than the rest of the Philippines, having once been joined to mainland Asia, and its endemic species include the Palawan stink badger, the Palawan porcupine and the Palawan tree shrew. The lowland forest contains several endangered bird species, and populations of Philippine cockatoo and Palawan Pheasant Peacock can be found here, making it highly attractive to bird watchers.

WHAT IS IT?
A pristine national park containing one of the world's longest, navigable subterranean rivers.
HOW TO GET THERE:
By road and boat.
WHEN TO GO:
November to April.
NEAREST TOWN:
Puerto Princesa 80 km (50 mi)
DON'T MISS:
Calauit Wildlife Sanctuary.
YOU SHOULD KNOW:
The Puerto-Princesa National Park was inscribed as a UNESCO World Heritage Site in 1999.

Khao Sok Ancient Rainforest

Khao Sok National Park is situated in Thailand's southern peninsula, roughly halfway between the two coasts, in Surat Thani province. Its limestone crags are covered by the largest area of pristine rainforest in southern Thailand, and possibly the oldest in the world, dating back 180 million years.

The forest here has more in common with that of Malaysia than that of northern Thailand, being taller, denser, darker and more humid. This is the wettest region in the country, receiving monsoon rains of up to 3.5 m (12 ft) per year from both the Andaman Sea to the west and the Gulf of Thailand to the east. Home to a variety of flora and fauna, it is possibly best known for the rare and bizarre flower, Rafflesia kerrii. This is the second largest bloom in the world, with a diameter of almost 1 m (3.3 ft). The flower itself is a russet brown colour, and rather unattractive, exuding a truly unpleasant smell which attracts its pollinator.

In 1980 the Rachabrapha Dam was built within the park, and the resulting Chao Lam Lake engulfed several entire villages. Although the people were relocated, the wildlife suffered severely. In 2001 the park's boundaries were extended, and wildlife is on the increase. The lake itself is picture-book perfect, with karst islands and towering limestone peaks that surround the emerald waters in which they are reflected. The deep forests are home to tapirs, Clouded leopards, Barking deer, Malaysian sun bears and more. Macaques and gibbons can often be seen and the area is rich with birds, including hornbills, which can be seen flying in their familiar top-heavy fashion in search of food.

WHAT IS IT?
Some of the oldest rainforest on the planet.
HOW TO GET THERE:
By road.
WHEN TO GO:
Late December to early February is the driest time.
NEAREST TOWN:
Khuraburi 65 km (41 mi) and there is a tourist village within the park.
DON'T MISS:
Chao Lam Lake; Ko Chang; Ko Similan.

A view across the rainforest into a valley in Khao Sok National Park

A steamy view of Khao Phra Thaeo National Park, Phuket

Khao Phra Thaeo

Phra Thaeo National Park is situated some 20 km (12.5 mi) north of Phuket town, and is a compact area of well-forested hills and valleys that encompasses a river with two splendid waterfalls, Bang Pae and Ton Sai. However, far and away its most important feature is the Gibbon Rehabilitation Centre.

In years gone by, white-handed, or lar, gibbons were indigenous to Phuket Island, and the forest canopy was busy with these most athletic of tree-dwelling mammals. Lar gibbons are black or brown-bodied creatures, with a white frame around their faces. They are largely fruit eating, but supplement their diet with leaves, insects, invertebrates and the occasional lizard. Gibbons are the only primate, other than man, to live in permanent, monogamous families. They communicate with other groups by whooping and screaming together, and these 'duets' can be heard up to five miles away.

Gibbons are such charming creatures that they make very desirable pets, with the result that they are now an endangered species and protected by law in Thailand. The Rehabilitation Centre is doing an excellent job of rescuing pet gibbons, which even now can be found chained up at guesthouses and bars in Phuket, rehabilitating them and putting them back into the wild. The project makes for a fascinating visit, but don't expect to get up close to a Lar gibbon here – their contact with humans is kept to a minimum while they are re-integrated with their forest home.

WHAT IS IT?
A National Park with a Gibbon Rehabilitation Centre.
HOW TO GET THERE:
By road from Phuket.
WHEN TO GO:
All year round, but best between November and May.
NEAREST TOWN:
Phuket 20 km (12.5 mi)
DON'T MISS:
Sirinath National Park.

Dong Phayayen-Khao Yai Forest Complex

Inscribed as a UNESCO World Heritage Site in 2005, the Dong Phayayen-Khao Yai Forest Complex comprises four National Parks and a Wildlife Sanctuary, spanning 230 km (144 mi) from Khao Yai, 120 km (75 mi) north-east of Bangkok, east to the Cambodian border. Located across a rugged escarpment within the Dongrek mountain range, the elevations in Khao Yai vary from 1,351 m (4,458 ft) to 200 m (600 ft), gradually becoming lower from west to east.

The complex contains seven major types of rainforest, the dominant being tropical, evergreen rainforest, which covers almost 75 per cent of the entire area. There are wild rivers and rushing streams, with scores of waterfalls and gorges on the southern side of the range. This large protected area provides habitats for an enormous amount of flora and fauna that are under pressure elsewhere. At least 2,500 plant species have been recorded here, including 16 that are endemic. There are 200 species of reptiles and amphibians, almost 400 species of bird and 112 species of mammal. These include large mammals such as a population of some 300 Asian elephants, tigers, Asiatic black bears, Malaysian sun bears, Clouded leopards, Marbled cats, Pileated gibbons and two species of macaques

Around 50 km (31 mi) of hiking trails wind through the forest, an extraordinary place of towering trees draped in lianas, mosses and epiphytes. At times, there are huge numbers of flowering trees and shrubs, and wild orchids bloom in profusion. The forest is never quiet: gibbons hoot, cicadas click continuously, apes chatter in the trees and birds constantly trill and whistle. At dusk you can watch over 1 million bats as they leave their cave at the edge of the park to feed.

A White-handed Gibbon (Hylobates lar), *Khao Yai National Park*

WHAT IS IT?
An internationally important area of tropical forest, conserving over 800 species of fauna, including 24 that are vulnerable or endangered.
HOW TO GET THERE:
By train or road to Pak Chong from Bangkok, then by road to the Forest Complex.
WHEN TO GO:
November to May.
NEAREST TOWN:
Pak Chong 23 km (14 mi)
DON'T MISS:
Ayutthaya.
YOU SHOULD KNOW:
An entry fee is payable. During the winter months you will need a jacket in the evenings.

Similan Archipelago Reefs

WHAT IS IT?
A National Marine Park with
marvellous diving and snorkelling.
HOW TO GET THERE:
By boat from Phuket, Thap Lamu or
Hat Khao Lak.
WHEN TO GO:
December to May.
NEAREST TOWN:
Khao Lak 2 hours by speedboat.
YOU SHOULD KNOW:
Entry fee payable. The park office,
visitor's centre and all
accommodation is on Ko Miang. Or
join a 'live aboard' trip.

The Similan Archipelago is truly one of Thailand's most precious treasures, and the reefs around them provide some of the best underwater scenery in the world. A National Marine Park, the nine granite islands themselves are virtually uninhabited, save for park officials and organized dive tour groups. The Thai navy has a presence on one of the islands, where it protects a sea turtle reserve, and the youngest daughter of the present king has a house on another. This has helped the marine park escape some of the worst excesses of damage caused by fishermen, such as dynamiting the reefs for an extra big catch.

The eastern shores are well protected from the monsoon storms, and have white sandy beaches and gently sloping reefs providing wonderful snorkelling territory. The western side catches the full force of the winds and the waves of the Andaman Sea, and the underwater scenery is much more dramatic: granite boulders covered in coral seem to have been hurled into the sea where they have formed arches and passages, cliffs and caves anywhere between 2 m to 30 m (7 ft to 98 ft) deep.

The fantastic, convoluted shapes of the many different corals teem with rich and varied marine life. Shoals of vividly coloured fish such as angel fish, butterfly fish and many more, form and swirl around and through forests of sea anemones and sea fans that sway gently in the currents which, though strong, keep the reefs clear of sand and thus provide crystal clear views of this magical underwater world.

Baitfish and Sea Fans are just a small part of the rich offerings on view in the Similan Reefs.

Tonle Sap at dusk

Tonle Sap

Tonle Sap, which means 'large freshwater river', is a hugely important lake and river system in Cambodia, and the largest freshwater lake in South East Asia. The lake, situated in a depression in the Cambodian plain, formed some 6,000 years ago as the result of a subsidence event, and is drained by the Tonle Sap River into the Mekong, near Phnom Penh.

This is one of the largest inland fisheries in the world, providing the main source of protein for much of the population, and a livelihood for over 1 million people. Moreover, it is a breeding ground and nursery area for fish that subsequently migrate into the Mekong, from which 2 million tons of fish are harvested each year, providing food for people in China, Myanmar, Thailand, Laos, Cambodia and Vietnam.

For much of the year the lake covers an area of 2,700 sq. km, and is only 1 m (3.3 ft) deep. During the monsoon however, a unique phenomenon occurs: the flow of the Tonle Sap river is reversed due to the vast quantities of water pouring into the Mekong. The area of the lake increases fivefold, and the depth increases to almost 10 m (33 ft). During this time, the swamp forest that surrounds the lake, and the eastern shore's grasslands, are inundated, and by the time the waters finally subside, and the flow changes direction again, fish are carried back down to the Mekong and the area is left covered with a rich layer of silt.

Tonle Sap's unique ecosystem provides habitats for a multitude of creatures: over 200 species of fish, 13 species of turtle, crocodile, leopard cat, macaque, and an endemic watersnake. It is also considered to be the most important breeding ground in South East Asia for globally endangered large waterbirds such as Black-headed ibis, Painted stork and Grey-headed fish eagle.

WHAT IS IT?
The largest freshwater lake in southeast Asia.
HOW TO GET THERE:
By road from Siem Reap.
WHEN TO GO:
December to April.
NEAREST TOWN:
Siem Reap 15 km (9 mi)
DON'T MISS:
The floating villages.
YOU SHOULD KNOW:
Tonle Sap was designated a UNESCO Biosphere Reserve in 1997

*Rubber plantation in
Ratanakiri Province*

Ratanakiri

The remote north eastern province of Ratanakiri, in Cambodia, is a world unto itself. Almost untouched by modernity, it is home to 12 separate tribal groups, collectively known as the Khmer Loeu, who make up over 80 per cent of the inhabitants of the region. There is virtually no electricity or running water here, and no paved roads: thus the indigenous population live in very much the same way as their forefathers.

Ratanakiri is rural – much of it is rolling hills and fields, with heavily forested mountains close to its border with Vietnam. Around the provincial capital, Banlung, are large plantations of cashews, coffee, peanuts and rubber trees, but several of the Khmer Loeu tribes still live mainly in the mountains and forests, practising traditional slash and burn agricultural methods, and hunting with crossbows and poison darts. These fascinating people are animists, sacrificing pigs to mark every important event. They wear traditional clothing – for example, Krung women wear waist-tied sarongs and are bare breasted, and Brou women have tattooed faces and adorn themselves with heavy ivory earrings that elongate their earlobes, bead necklaces and brass ankle bracelets.

Banlung makes a good base from which to explore the hill tribe villages, but there are other attractions nearby including numerous waterfalls. Probably the best-known attraction is Yak Loum Lake, which lies in the caldera of an ancient volcano. Almost perfectly circular and surrounded by lush rainforest vegetation and large trees, the lake is perfect for swimming. Its pellucid waters are very deep, about 48 m (157 ft) and it is considered a sacred area by many of the Khmer Loeu. From the pathway that encircles it, parrots and other tropical birds can be seen as they fly from tree to tree.

WHAT IS IT?
A remote and beautiful region where tribal people live according to their ancient traditions.
HOW TO GET THERE:
By air or road and ferry to Banlung.
WHEN TO GO:
November to March.
NEAREST TOWN:
Banlung is the town in which to base yourself.
DON'T MISS:
The semi-precious gem mines.
YOU SHOULD KNOW:
An entry fee is payable to visit Yak Loum Lake.

Coral Reefs including the Eye of the Maldives

The Maldive Islands are located 480 km (300 mi) south west of Cape Cormorin, on the southern tip of India. Consisting of 26 large atolls containing 1,190 islands, they run 648 km (405 mi) from north to south, and 130 km (81 mi) east to west, a double chain lying within the central area. Only 200 of the islands are inhabited and, of these, some 88 are exclusive holiday resorts.

The geomorphology of the Maldivian islands is unusual. An atoll is a coral formation surrounding a circular lagoon, but these lagoons, many of which are very large, are dotted with other, smaller, ring-shaped reefs, each surrounding its own sandy lagoon. These are known locally as 'faros', and this formation is known as the Eye of the Maldives. Natural channels, allowing the free movement of fish and currents between the lagoons and the open sea, cut through each reef.

The islands are formed from coral sand, and are very low lying, averaging no more than 2 m (6 ft 6 in), with vegetation mainly consisting of coconut palms, and mangroves. Just take a look, however, beneath the surface of the turquoise sea and you will find glorious, dazzling coral gardens teeming with multi-coloured fish that are more curious than afraid of humans. The diving and snorkelling here is the main attraction, and the exclusivity of many of its resorts, which appeals to the rich and famous.

Long term, the Maldives are under threat. Climate change is already adversely affecting the coral, which can only thrive at temperatures from 24 to 27 °C (75 to 81 °F), and the natural phenomena of El Niño and La Niña has caused severe bleaching to some of the formations. Sea levels are also rising, and although preventative work is being done, it seems that these fairy tale coral islands will surely slip beneath the surface of the sea in the not too distant future.

WHAT IS IT?
A string of jewel-like coral islands, most of which are entirely devoted to tourism, which provide fabulous diving and snorkelling experiences.

HOW TO GET THERE:
By air to Male and then by boat to the other islands.

WHEN TO GO:
Hot all year round, December to April is the period of least rain.

NEAREST TOWN:
Male, the capital, is on the eponymous island.

DON'T MISS:
Whale and dolphin spotting.

YOU SHOULD KNOW:
This is not a cheap option for a holiday. Tourism is the main source of revenue here, so much so that, whilst happy to sell alcohol to tourists, all luggage is X-rayed on arrival and any alcohol discovered is confiscated and returned only on departure.

Atoll islands of the Maldives

Mount Kinabalu

WHAT IS IT:
The highest mountain in South East Asia.

HOW TO GET THERE:
Travel by bus or hire car from Kota Kinabalu.

WHEN TO GO:
The mountain is driest between February and April, but it is in a tropical climate so expect showers whenever you go.

NEAREST TOWN:
Kota Kinabalu is 88 km/55mi away.

DON'T MISS:
Look out for the pitcher plants, prolific in the area, on your way up the mountain.

YOU SHOULD KNOW:
A climbing permit and Climber's Personal Accident Insurance, payable at park headquarters. , payable at park headquarters, are compulsory

Mount Kinabalu

Mount Kinabalu is the tallest mountain between the Himalayas and New Guinea, towering above the rainforest at 4,095 metres above sea level. It is a relatively young mountain and is still growing at a rate of 5 mm (0.2 in) per year. The local Kadazan tribesmen feared the spirits of the dead that lived on the mountain and it was shrouded in mystery until the first recorded ascent in 1851 by Sir Hugh Low, a British colonial secretary. Now, the mountain is climbed everyday by tourists from around the world who make the climb over two days, completing the last stage in darkness, racing against time to reach the summit in time for sunrise.

You must have a guide if you're climbing to the summit, although you can go without one as far as Laban Rata, three quarters of the way up. The climb starts off steadily as winding stairs cut into the mountainside sweep through rainforest, sheltered by the canopy overhead. Pitcher plants common to the area pepper the side of the footpath, filled with liquid, ready to drown an unsuspecting fly or insect. These and the abundance of other flora in the area earned the park UNESCO World Heritage Site status, and became a Centre of Plant Diversity of South East Asia in 2000. The vegetation and climate change dramatically on the ascent, as lush, wet rainforest becomes short, scrubby trees clinging to the rocky plateau in a bracing wind.

Accommodation on the mountain is varied, with Laban Rata being by far the best with heated rooms and a restaurant. Panar Laban, Waras Hut and Gunting Lagadan are a little higher up the mountainside, but the rooms are unheated and mountain rats are a common sight in the huts.

The second part of the climb begins at around 2 am and the final stage of the mountain is rocky and high enough to cause altitude sickness. The steeper areas of the mountain have ropes to hoist yourself up on. At this point, the famous features of the mountain are shrouded in darkness – Donkey's Ears Peak and Ugly Sister's Peak – so be sure to take in the imposing sight of the jagged granite summit on the way down.

The summit is marked with a pile of rocks and a sign, and emerging at the summit victorious is an adrenalin rush so be sure to wrap up warmly as you wait for the sunrise. As the sky becomes brighter and the clouds begin to burn away at around 6 am, the hard climb and the tiredness are all worth it as you are on top of the world with the best seat in the house. The colours of sunrise are incredible as the cloud and mist around the top of the mountain reflect the sunlight then slowly burn away revealing the world below laid out in a carpet of the most wonderful pattern. On a clear day you can see as far as the coast and the view is absolutely magnificent.

Niah Caves, Sarawak

One of the caves in the Niah Cave system

Niah Caves, one of the largest limestone caves in the world, are part of the Niah National Park which is located near the coast between Miri and Bintulu in northern Sarawak. Excavations in the 1950s and 1960s proved the caves to be of great archaeological significance after the discovery of a human skull revealed that the caves had been home to humans 40,000 years ago. Other relics and important artefacts were discovered, making the caves famous as the oldest human settlement in East Malaysia.

Reaching the caves is not for the fainthearted as you first have to take a boat across the Sungai Niah, then it's a 3km trek along a plank walk which winds through the rainforest and can be very slippery when wet. Add to that the humidity of the rain forest and crocodiles in the river and it can be a little daunting. The route is very easy to follow though and make sure you take some time to admire the rainforest along the way. There's a multitude of insects and animals to see if you're patient and quiet. Macaques and flying lizards swing through the trees and the noise of birds and insects will keep you company as you journey towards to the caves.

The Great Cave is the main attraction as the roof reaches an impressive 75 metres above the floor, and the mouth measures 250 metres across. The sheer scale and also the peppering of stalactites hanging from the ceiling displays an awe-inspiring cave worthy of its name. Green algae covers the rubble and rocks that littler the cave floor, creating an enchanting display that glows green in the jungle sunlight. Make sure you bring a torch as the light soon disappears in the vastness of the cave and your footfalls share the ground with scorpions and poisonous millipedes. Venture further inside and you'll see lengths of rope snaking down from the cave roof and, if you go between August and December, you'll see a guano or birds nest collector at the top of one.

Several species of bat and swiftlet share the cave, living in harmony on different timescales. The best time to see this is at dusk when millions swiftlets return to roost and thousands bats fly out in a mass exodus for a night of feeding. It is a sensory experience with the noise of the birds and the air around you throbbing with the beat of millions of wings.

The other caves are worth a visit, especially Painted Cave where prehistoric human figures adorn the cave walls, watching over burial sites where the dead were laid to rest in boat shaped coffins.

HOW TO GET THERE:
Travel by bus or hire a car. Three hours from the waterfront at Bintulu or two hours from Miri.
WHEN TO GO:
Witness the birds nest collecting season between August and December, and from January to March.
NEAREST TOWN:
Batu Niah is the nearest town, 3.5 km (2 mi)
DON'T MISS:
Wait until dusk and watch the swifts returning to the cave while the bats leave. Keep your head down though!
YOU SHOULD KNOW:
You need to book in advance for accommodation inside the park and you must obtain a permit to enter the park.

The Caves of Gunung Mulu National Park

WHAT IS IT:
Home to the largest underground chamber in the world and magnificent collection of caves.
HOW TO GET THERE:
Fly from Miri, Maurudi and Limbang.
WHEN TO GO:
Gunung enjoys a very high rate of rainfall all year round, but avoid the period from October to March when it is particularly heavy during monsoon.
NEAREST TOWN:
Miri 110 km (70 mi) away, with its good flight connections, is the best place to use as a base.
DON'T MISS:
The daily flight of bats from Deer Cave and the stalactites and stalagmites in Lang Cave.
YOU SHOULD KNOW:
The park and the area around it is very popular among tourists so you should book ahead to avoid disappointment.

Gunung Mulu National Park, Sarawak's largest national park, is home to extensive, world-renowned limestone caves. Set in 530 sq km (205 sq mi) of tropical rainforest comprising the peaks of Gunung Mulu and Gunung Api, the National Park boasts sandstone and limestone formations and a diverse range of flora and fauna. Gunung Mulu was awarded UNESCO World Heritage Site status in 2000 in recognition of its significant geomorphic characteristics and biodiversity. The park is an unspoilt wilderness which can be enjoyed as such or for the more adventurous, there is extensive caving and trekking available.

Underground chambers stretching to 51 km (32 mi) include the largest cave chamber in the world – the spectacular Sarawak Chamber measures a massive 12 million cubic metres (424 million cubic ft). To date, 310 km (193 mi) of passages have been charted but it is believed that there are many more yet to be discovered.

The Deer, Lang, Clearwater and Wind caves are all known as the Show Caves, and each has its own very individual atmosphere. They can all be reached by the 3 km plank walk from park headquarters which winds through primary jungle. Deer Cave, the most famous of the four, is the world's largest cave corridor and home to millions of noisy bats that hang from the ceiling until nightfall, when clouds of bats billow from the cave mouth. Most of the cave is illuminated and the waterfalls that gush from hundreds of feet above after a rain storm are an incredible sight. Lang Cave is entirely different, quieter and smaller, with beautiful stalagmites and stalactites stretching up and down the cave like decorative teeth.

The journey to Clearwater and Wind Caves is a magnificent cliff walk along a river with much flora and fauna to be seen along the way. The river roars through Clearwater Cave and the giant debris scattered throughout illustrates the might of this subterranean force. The water pool which gives the cave its name is a crystal clear swimming pool which is open to the public to cool off in the tropical heat. Wind Cave hosts imposing columns and stalactites that drip from the ceiling like hot wax, in an awesome display of millions of years of geological development.

Deer Cave in Mulu National Park

Deer Cave Bat Roost

Deer Cave, the largest cave passage in the world is part of the cave system of Gunung Mulu National Park. In the past, deer would shelter in the mouth of the cave, and so it became known as Gua Rusa or Gua Payau (Deer Cave) by the local Penan and Berawan people.

The cave is huge: more than a mile long and up to 300 feet high. Scientists have estimated that at least five St Pauls Cathedrals would fit inside the cave and it takes 40 minutes to walk from one end to the other. The cave is a self-contained world with a huge, tall forest growing inside as well as a river, hills and valleys. This terrain sustains a huge population of somewhere between two and five million bats. There are at least twelve species of bat inside the cave, the most prolific being the wrinkle-nosed bat. These chattering and squealing creatures line the walls and ceiling of the cave throughout the day then leave the cave *en masse* in a massive billowing black cloud, streaking across the sky to feed on insects in the jungle. Their guano lines the cave floor in great dunes, 6 m (20ft) deep in some places. The surface is alive, teeming with millions of insects ranging from cockroaches and scorpions to earwigs and giant cave centipedes. This is a necessary nutrition source and over three tonnes of guano is produced everyday.

Once inside the cave, take some time to look back at the entrance as the famous profile of Abraham Lincoln can be seen on the outline of the cave. Be sure to bring a torch as the cave is deep and the floor is teeming with insects that will crunch underfoot if you're not careful. The interior of the cave is colourful despite the dark, as the rusty colour of the guano contrasts with the bright green algae lining the cave walls.

At the end of the cave walk you reach the Garden of Eden. This is a section of collapsed cave which is now a giant sinkhole, a mile wide, full of lush jungle plants and sunshine. Sheer cliffs hundreds of feet tall stretch up into the bright sunshine to meet the rest of the jungle.

WHAT IS IT:
The largest cave passage in the world and most popular attraction of the Gunung Mulu National Park.
HOW TO GET THERE:
There is a 3 km (2 mi) board walk from Gunung Mulu Park headquarters to the cave.
WHEN TO GO:
Make sure you arrive allowing enough time to explore the cave in time for dusk at around 5pm.
NEAREST TOWN:
Miri is the largest town nearby, at 110 km(70 mi) northwest and can be reached by plane.
DON'T MISS:
Wait at the Bat Observatory and safely watch the mass exodus of the bats from the cave at dusk.
YOU SHOULD KNOW:
Be prepared to be showered with guano inside the cave and the smell is so strong it can make your eyes water if it hasn't rained.

Bats leave Deer Cave in Mulu National Park.

Fog hanging over the rainforest.

The Heart of Borneo

Home to six per cent of the world's biodiversity, the Heart of Borneo is 220,000 sq km (85,000 sq mi) of largely unspoilt equatorial rainforest spanning the highlands and foothills of Brunei, Sarawak and Sabah. The diverse land is made up of lush jungle, mangroves, mountains, rapid flowing rivers, swamps and limestone peaks and is an area of immense beauty and uncharted territory.

This is one of only two places in the world where rhinos, elephants and orangutans co-exist, and new species are being found at a rate of three every month – 360 new species have been discovered in the last ten years. It is believed the rainforest still harbours new species and a plethora of plants which could hold the key to curing diseases such as cancer and AIDS. Discovering these botanical secrets is a difficult task as the interior is dense, largely inaccessible, jungle. Several other species are currently under threat, including sun bears, clouded leopards and Borneon gibbons, endemic in the area. This unparalleled biodiversity is now protected under the Heart of Borneo Declaration in recognition of the importance of a forest large enough to sustain successful populations of rare species.

The three governments of the Heart of Borneo – Brunei, Indonesia and Malaysia – have pledged to conserve the rainforest and introduce a network of protected areas. In February 2007 the Heart of Borneo Declaration was signed by all three and they will sustainably manage the area to protect indigenous species and prevent the logging that has been destroying vital habitats. It is hoped that this will protect the 222 species of mammals, 420 bird species, 100 species of amphibians, 394 species of fish and 15,000 plant species in the area. A third of all plants here cannot be found anywhere else.

Indigenous tribes encompassing over thirty ethnic groups still live in the area, sustained by fourteen of Borneo's twenty rivers that flow through this vast space. Living from the land and nurturing ancient traditions these diverse cultures, ranging from Iban and Kayan to Dayak, need the protection of the rainforest to ensure their survival and preservation of a unique way of life.

WHAT IS IT:
The centre of South East Asia's biodiversity and the world's third largest rainforest.

HOW TO GET THERE:
The area is huge so you have a choice of visiting Kalimantan, Sabah, Brunei Darussalam or Sarawak.

WHEN TO GO:
Go from March to October to avoid the monsoon which brings extremely heavy rain, particularly in the interior.

NEAREST TOWN:
Bintulu is an ideal jumping off point for visiting the Sarawak side of the interior, or Kota Kinabalu in Sabah, Tanjung Selor in Kalimantan and Temburong in Brunei.

DON'T MISS:
Trek the dense jungle of the Bario Loop to experience authentic Borneo.

YOU SHOULD KNOW:
Expect leeches and heavy rain whenever you go.

Ujong Kulong National Park

A nature reserve since the early 1920s, Ujong Kulon National Park encompasses some 500 sq km (193 sq mi) of the south western tip of Java, Indonesia's most populous island and home to the country's capital city, Jakarta. The park is situated on a peninsula and it includes several islands, amongst them the notorious volcanoes of Krakatoa and Anak Krakatoa.

Krakatoa blew itself apart in August 1883 in one of the world's greatest eruptions. The sound could be heard in Queensland Australia, which is over 4,000 km (6,400 mi) away, and the resulting tidal waves were traced as far away as France. Anak Krakatoa, literally 'child of Krakatoa' emerged from the sea in 1928. Uniquely interesting to various branches of the world's scientific community, not solely vulcanologists, as it provides the perfect opportunity to study its colonization by the plant and animal species that have found their way across from the mainland.

Some 30 years ago Ujong Kulon was upgraded to National Park status, when it was recognized that its unique ecosystem supports the most concentrated array of species, together with a spectacular combination of habitat – sandy beaches, swamps, mangroves, estuarine shallows, river valleys, hills, grasslands and lowland rainforest – in any Javan reserve. It is home to a wealth of birds, from Asian sea eagles at the shoreline to the rare Green peafowl by the Cigenter River – and also to the estuarine crocodile. There are leopards, civet cats and fishing cats, flying foxes and green turtles, but the rarest animal it shelters is the endangered Javan rhinoceros, a one-horned rhino that may only exist here.

WHAT IS IT?
A national park that encompasses the notorious volcanoes, Krakatoa and Anak Krakatoa.
HOW TO GET THERE:
By road and boat from Jakarta or Labuhan.
WHEN TO GO:
April to August.
NEAREST TOWN:
Labuhan 50 km (31 mi)
DON'T MISS:
Krakatoa, Anak Krakatoa.
YOU SHOULD KNOW:
Indonesia has more active volcanoes than any other country.

120 years after the loudest bang ever heard by mankind Krakatoa continues to smoulder.

Komodo National Park

WHAT IS IT?
A national park, UNESCO World Heritage Site and Marine Biosphere Reserve.
HOW TO GET THERE:
By air to Labuanbajo from Bali, then by boat.
WHEN TO GO:
April to October.
NEAREST TOWN:
Labuanbajo (35 km, 22 mi)
YOU SHOULD KNOW:
Visitors should not wear red.

Komodo National Park was established in 1980 to protect the ancient monitor lizards of the same name, and was inscribed on the World Heritage List in 1991. The three islands are surrounded by one of the world's best marine environments, with coral reefs, seamounts, seagrass beds and mangroves that harbour more than 1,000 species of fish, 70 species of sponges and 14 species of whales, as well as dolphins, sharks, manta rays, dugong and sea turtles. There are at least 260 species of coral in the reefs. The islands are becoming increasingly popular dive sites.

However, it is the dragons that are the lure for most visitors to these barren volcanic islands in Indonesia's Lesser Sundas. Guided tours take tourists to hot spots when the lizards are active during the morning or late afternoon. During the heat of the middle of the day, they burrow in the dry stream bed to keep cool.

These prehistoric predators can grow up to 3 m (10 ft) in length. Despite their stumpy-looking legs they can run as fast as a dog and, given the opportunity, could eat a human-being so when on the beautiful beaches in the sandy bays visitors are advised to keep an eye out for their foot- and tail- prints in the sand. They can also swim and have been spotted swimming from island to island.

A male Komodo dragon walks along the beach on Komodo Island. The reptile uses his tongue to smell.

Lorentz National Park

Lorentz National Park is the largest in South-East Asia. Situated in the Indonesian province of Papua, (western New Guinea), it is the sole area of the world where a continuous, intact transect, from a tropical marine environment, through lowland wetlands, and right up to the snowy mountain peaks, is protected.

New Guinea is in a different bio-geographic realm – Oceania – from the rest of Indonesia. It is also the richest bio-geographical region, with the highest level of endemism. Its main mountain range is on the edge of the Pacific and Australian tectonic plates, and it is one of only three areas in the world where equatorial glaciers still exist. Puncak Jaya, at 4,884 m (16,117 ft) is not only Indonesia's highest mountain, but also the highest between the Himalayas and the Andes.

The entire region is covered in pristine forest, much of which has never been explored or mapped. Over millennia, scores of rivers and streams have gouged deep valleys through the mountains and foothills as they make their way south to the coast, where they form extensive wetlands including mangrove, tidal and freshwater swamps. Around 80 per cent of Papua's mammal species have been recorded here, and 411 bird species, including at least 20 that are endemic. No doubt there are more, but the nature of the terrain does not help the statisticians.

People have lived here for over 25,000 years. Today, some 6,300 people from eight indigenous groups live within the Park boundaries, and there are perhaps 50 small villages, accessible only by foot and the occasional missionary airstrip. These people are mainly traditional hunter/gatherers, who do a little subsistence farming on the steep hillsides. The Park's success depends upon local support for conservation and the tribal people's needs being included in long-term management strategies.

WHAT IS IT?
The only protected area in the world that encompasses the peaks of glaciated mountains right down to the sea, in one continuous sweep.
HOW TO GET THERE:
By plane or boat to Jayapura, then by plane.
WHEN TO GO:
May to October.
NEAREST TOWN:
Most visitors are based in Wamena, in the Baliem Valley, which has an airstrip.
YOU SHOULD KNOW:
Go with a tour – it is very difficult indeed to organize independent travel in Papua.

537

Bukit Barisan Mountains, Sumatra

WHAT IS IT?
A richly forested mountain range, covering the length of western Sumatra.
HOW TO GET THERE:
Plane or ferry to Medan, or plane to Padang, then by road.
WHEN TO GO:
May to September, north of the Equator, March to August, south of the Equator.
NEAREST TOWN:
Towns and villages are scattered throughout the mountains and up and down the coast.
DON'T MISS:
Lake Toba, Bukittinggi.
YOU SHOULD KNOW:
The tsunami of 2004 damaged the north-west coast of Sumatra, as did the earthquake of 2007.

The Bukit Barisan are a range of mountains running almost the entire length of Sumatra's western side, from Aceh in the north to Lampung in the south, forming the spine of this huge island. It comprises three National Parks, collectively known as the Tropical Rainforest Heritage of Sumatra, and was listed by UNESCO in 2004.

Some 70 million years ago, when tectonic plate collision raised the Himalayas, the Barisan Mountains were also forced upwards along the west coast of the island. Here the mountains often meet the shoreline, while east of the range lie low hills, plains and swamps. The terrain consists mainly of densely forested volcanoes, many of which are still active, and includes, at 3,800 m (12,540 ft), the highest volcanic peak in Indonesia, Mt. Kerinci.

This fabulous mountain range is rich in habitat. Several large rivers rise here and many streams; there are extraordinary lakes such as Lake Toba, Kelimutu Crater Lake and Lake Gunung Tujuh, the highest in South-East Asia, stunning waterfalls, hot springs, smoke-belching fumeroles and complex cave systems.

Above all, Bukit Barisan protects over 10,000 plant species, more than 200 mammals, 22 of which are Asian and not found elsewhere in Indonesia and 15 of which are found solely in Indonesia. Here too are almost 600 bird species, including 21 that are endemic. This is home to orangutans and Asian elephants and is almost the last refuge of the critically endangered Sumatran tiger and Sumatran rhino.

Illegal logging, forest clearance for agriculture and poaching are the main threats to wildlife here – over 6.5 million hectares (16 million acres) of forest have been lost during the last few years. Habitat loss equals loss of prey for larger mammals, and loss of vegetation for herbivores such as rhinos. UNESCO's protection is essential to conserve Bukit Barisan for future generations.

Kelimutu Crater Lake

Mount Erebus

Emperor penguins at the foot of Mount Erebus, the southernmost active volcano in the world.

The world's southernmost active volcano, Mount Erebus, looms over the American research station of McMurdo, and New Zealand's Scott Base, both of which are sited at the southern end of Hut Point Peninsula on Ross Island. Discovered by the British explorer James Ross in 1841, it was climbed in 1908 by members of Ernest Shackleton's expedition. Since the early 1970s, the volcano has been under observation – since 1980, continuously so, via a network of six seismic stations. For about six weeks each year, from November to January, scientists ascend the slopes to their camp at 3,476 m (11,400 ft) for active fieldwork.

The summit of Mount Erebus, at 3,794 m (12,444 ft), is almost invariably crowned with clouds of vapour. Unusually, it has an outer crater, 100 m (330 ft) deep and some 650 m (2,132 ft) across, within which lies a smaller crater containing a lake of churning molten lava. Explosions within the lake lob lava bombs that can land up to 1.6 km (1 mi) away. The volcano's sides are dotted with fumaroles or ice chimneys of up to 18 m (60 ft) high. These are formed by heat from within melting the snow to form a cave from which escaping steam freezes the moment it hits the air. Scientists are attempting to discover whether these warm ice caves could ever have supported life.

Glaciers extend from the volcano to the edges of the island. Erebus Glacier Tongue is between 50 and 300 m (164 and 984 ft) thick, and grows every year, stretching several kilometres beyond the island into the bay, where it floats in deep water. In 1979, a group of tourists on an Antarctic sight-seeing flight from New Zealand crashed into Mount Erebus in whiteout conditions, killing all 257 people on board. During the brief Antarctic summer, debris from the crash is still clearly visible.

WHAT IS IT?
The most southerly volcano in the world, covered with glaciers and containing an active lava lake in its summit crater.
HOW TO GET THERE:
Unless you are a scientist you are unlikely to visit Ross Island. However, a limited number of cruise ships visit Antarctica, check out their itineraries.
WHEN TO GO:
During the Antarctic summer.
YOU SHOULD KNOW:
The average temperature here is -20 °C (-4 °F) during summer and -60 °C (-76°F) during winter.

NATURAL WONDERS

FEATURES

animals, birds and marine life 12, 17, 20, 28, 30, 32, 66, 83, 86, 99, 107, 141, 149, 165, 176, 206, 211, 212, 222, 365, 419, 420, 433, 480, 501, 533 (*see also* reserves)
archipelagos, atolls, islands, peninsulas and reefs 47, 48, 80, 92, 96, 97, 100, 105, 110, 112, 118, 120, 125, 155, 189, 190, 203, 216, 221, 225, 273, 288, 359, 393, 394, 407, 410, 412, 415, 416, 418, 422, 426, 429, 434, 458, 466, 467, 521, 526, 529

badlands, *see* deserts and badlands
bays 18, 39, 199, 276, 399, 414, 429, 433, 512
beaches, coastline and sand 94, 101, 154, 206, 259, 274, 300, 326, 348, 354, 471
blowholes 409, 422

canyons 29, 282, 312, 350, 473
capes and headlands 48, 137, 397
caves and underground networks 43, 51, 60, 63, 64, 85, 202, 204, 213, 239, 258, 263, 268, 275, 296, 301, 308, 314, 315, 319, 325, 331, 332, 335, 343, 437, 349, 381, 386, 395, 432, 488, 499, 520, 531, 533
cirques 304
cliffs 255, 277, 284, 300, 375, 486 (*see also* rock and stone formations)
coastline, *see* beaches, coastline and sand
craters and valleys 53, 54, 67, 72, 104, 171, 176, 232, 248, 293, 303, 371, 406, 442, 443, 481, 505, 518

deserts and badlands 44, 75, 138, 144, 154, 194, 195, 210, 382, 386, 396, 417, 487, 500

escarpments 157

fault lines 40
forests and trees 34, 46, 65, 88, 102, 115, 127, 130, 135, 145, 166, 185, 187, 279, 281, 285, 303, 313, 231, 378, 400, 425, 468, 479, 484, 490, 501, 523, 525, 534

geysers 139, 231, 453
glaciers 143, 218, 222, 229, 236, 241, 427, 448 (*see also* ice sheets)
gorges 178, 187, 294, 299, 305, 315, 367, 471, 476
grassland 31

hills, mountains, volcanoes 10, 15, 19, 22, 35, 37, 41, 42, 45, 56, 61, 68, 77, 81, 87, 89, 91, 92, 95, 102, 109, 116, 121, 126, 133, 134, 147, 152, 153, 167, 170, 174, 176, 182, 188, 198, 201, 205, 208, 228, 234, 242, 245, 246, 250, 256, 262, 265, 266, 269, 272, 281, 285, 290, 302, 321, 322, 328, 333, 336, 337, 338, 344, 345, 355, 360, 364, 366, 368, 370, 372, 377, 379, 384, 392, 398, 413, 436, 442, 444,

445, 454, 456, 458, 463, 464, 469, 474, 477, 482, 484, 488, 491, 496, 497, 507, 514, 530, 538, 539

ice sheets 235 (*see also* glaciers)

lakes and lagoons 14, 24, 38, 58, 69, 90, 108, 128, 132, 146, 159, 164, 168, 172, 173, 180, 184, 226, 227, 230, 278, 287, 318, 324, 334, 340, 346, 371, 374, 380, 385, 401, 408, 430, 441, 452, 452, 465, 467, 471, 472, 478, 495, 527 (*see also* lochs)
landscapes 62, 111, 142, 163, 200, 238, 240, 243, 251, 252, 254, 260, 295, 298, 391, 440, 443, 516, 528 (*see also* national parks; reserves)
lava features 421
lochs 264, 267, 271 (*see also* lakes)

marshland and wetlands 131, 197, 306, 316, 328
moorland 257
mountains, *see* hills, mountains, volcanoes

national parks 13, 15, 16, 21, 23, 25, 26, 27, 33, 41, 49, 50, 51, 52, 57, 71, 74, 78, 79, 103, 106, 114, 118, 122, 129, 133, 136, 146, 158, 160, 161, 162, 165, 166, 167, 174, 175, 191, 193, 196, 205, 292, 316, 323, 327, 350, 351, 352, 353, 356, 358, 361, 362, 369, 404, 405, 408, 428, 435, 437, 451, 455, 479, 483, 492, 493, 494, 498, 503, 506, 508, 509, 522, 524, 532, 535, 536, 537 (*see also* landscapes; reserves)

oases 156

rainforests, *see* forests and trees
reserves 82, 84, 112, 124, 136, 140, 169, 179, 185, 189, 192, 207, 212, 289, 391, 425, 440, 445, 460, 470, 484, 501, 504, 510, 517 (*see also* animals; landscapes; national parks)
rivers, estuaries and fjords 85, 123, 217, 220, 261, 280, 307, 438, 483, 515, 518, 522
rock and stone formations 59, 88, 93, 118, 270, 282, 283, 291, 297, 343, 363, 373, 375, 403 (*see also* cliffs)

sand, *see* beaches, coastline and sand
sea stacks 390
sky and clouds 224, 233, 411

trees, *see* forests and trees

volcanoes, *see* hills, mountains, volcanoes

waterfalls 10, 98, 106, 117, 148, 183, 237, 244, 249, 309, 424, 519
whirlpools 342

COUNTRIES AND REGIONS

Front cover: Corbis/Theo Allofs front cover right picture 5, Liu Liqun front cover right picture 6, /Galen Rowell front cover right picture 1, /Paul Souders front cover right picture 3, /Steve Terrill front cover right picture 2, /Ron Watts main picture, /Stuart Westmorland front cover right picture 4

Back cover: Corbis/Theo Allofs back cover main picture, /Angelo Cavalli/zefa back cover left picture 4, /Daniel J Cox back cover left picture 5, /Frans Lanting back cover left picture 1, /Liu Liqun back cover left picture 3, /Kazuyoshi Nomachi back cover left picture 2, /Jose Fuste Raga back cover left picture 6

Aerial Video Australia/Rob Thompson 411; Alabaster Caverns State Park 60; Alamy/Vladimir Alexeev 322, /Arco Images 294, /Atmotu Images 424, /Peter Barritt 168, /Stephen Bloom Images 5 picture 3, 165, /Elly Campbell 504, /CuboImages srl 342, /Roger Day 303, /Matteo Del Grosso 287, /Danita Delimont 101, 112, /dfwalls 304, /Michael Diggin 457, /Diomedia 334, /Mark Eveleigh 535, /Eye Ubiquitous 205, /FLPA 160, /Rob Francis 409, /Robert Fried 82, 93, /Jason Friend 435, /Michael Grant 474, /Nick Haslam 327, /Hemis 111, /Hornbil Images 499, /Chris Howes/Wild Places Photography 239, 395, /Images&Stories 371, /isifa Image Service s.r.o 315, /Israel Images 383, /Piotr & Irena Kolasa 318, /Vincent Lowe 269, /Celia Mannings 508, /John Martin 261, /mediacolor's 244, 293, /Eric Nathan 325, /Nature Picture Library 6 picture 6, 360, /Panorama Media (Beijing) Ltd 482, /A Parada 144, /Edward Parker 377, /Tobias Peciva 425, /Primate-Images 510, /Quincy 520, /Mervyn Rees 7 picture 4, 390, /Ray Roberts 298, /Robert Harding World Imagery 24, 90, 368, /david sanger photography 95, /Kevin Schafer 526, /James Schwabel 69, /Alexander Shuldiner 467, /Jon Sparks 18, /Ulana Switucha 337, /Jan Symank 384, /Katharine Toft 258, /Genevieve Vallee 189, /Kim Westerskov 434, /Worldwide Picture Library 460 centre, 496; Corbis 14, 66, 108, Corbis/Peter Adams 5 picture 5, 170, 230, 491, /Shaen Adey/Gallo Images198, /Aerie Nature Series, Inc 32, /O Alamany & E Vicens 214 right, 351, 353, 356, 358, 361, 362, /Theo Allofs 6 picture 5, 7 picture 3, 141, 193, 196, 388 main picture, 388 right, 393, 400, 404, 416, 460 right, 536, /James L Amos 50, 235, /Roger Antrobus 256, /Adrian Arbib 320, 463, /Arctic-Images 233, /Jon Arnold/JAI 5 picture 4, 255, 382, 506, /Yann Arthus-Bertrand 7 picture 6, 8, 36, 96, 173, 185, 222, 228, 232, 234, 407, 413, /Atmotu Images 517, /David Ball 414, /Tom Bean 40, 44, 115, 335, /Nathan Benn 39, /Hal Beral 151 right, 175, /Walter Bibikow/JAI 366, /Jonathan Blair16, 378, /Tibor Bognar 477, /Christophe Boisvieux 275, 301, 307, 522, /Nic Bothma/epa 200, /Charles Bowman/Robert Harding World Imagery 270, /Bojan Brecelj 350, /Colin Brynn/Robert Harding World Imagery 516, /BSPI 427, /Michael Busselle 245, 257, /John Carnemolla 412, /Demetrio Carrasco/JAI 237, /Angelo Cavalli/zefa 148, /Katia Christodoulou/epa 376, /Ralph A Clevenger 212, /Dean Conger 2 centre, 469, 487, /Diane Cook & Len Jenshel 109, /Anthony Cooper/Ecoscene 432, /Ashley Cooper 345, /Pablo Corral Vega 102, 121, 136, /Daniel J Cox 471, /Joel Creed/Ecoscene 122, /Marco Cristofori 375, /Fridmar Damm/zefa 97, 284, 308, /Barry Davies/Eye Ubiquitous 392, /Nigel J Dennis/Gallo Images 150 centre, 202, /DLILLC 3 right, 501, /Nicole Dupaix 197, /Terry W Eggers 79, /epa 246, 326, /Macduff Everton 8 left, 85, 94, 215 right, 231, /Michele Falzone/JAI 139, 478,

/Malcolm Fife/zefa 265, /D Robert & Lorri Franz 28, /Michael Freeman 23, 538, /Franz-Marc Frei 428, /Paulo Fridman 125, /Roger Garwood & Trish Ainslie 419, /Raymond Gehman 27, /Walter Geiersperger 238, 240, /Robert Gill/Papilio 179, /Shai Ginott 379, /Philippe Giraud/Goodlook 92, /Mike Grandmaison 22, /Farrell Grehan 276, /Darrell Gulin 46, 52, 74, 78, /Klaus Hackenberg/zefa 279, /Rainer Hackenberg/zefa 343, 348, /Karl-Heinz Haenel 436, /Michael Hagedorn/zefa 194, /Derek Hall/Frank Lane Picture Agency 84, /Blaine Harrington III 138, /Martin Harvey 145, 365, /Jason Hawkes 70, /Dallas and John Heaton/Free Agents Limited 398, /Chris Hellier 191, 328, /Gavin Hellier/JAI 494, /John Heseltine 260, 262, /HO/Reuters 344, /Hoberman Collection 201, /Robert Holmes 26, 268, 441, 532, 533, /Jeremy Horner 507, /Dave G Houser 98, 216, /Rob Howard 48, 162, /George H H Huey 72, /José Jácome/epa 119, /Jorma Jämsen/zefa 227, /Ladislav Janicek/zefa 313, /Gavriel Jecan 166, /Mark A Johnson 33, 67, /Peter Johnson 192, /Ray Juno 248, 250, /Wolfgang Kaehler 217, 282, 380, 433, 450, 502, /Milan Kapusta/epa 331, /Catherine Karnow 8 centre, 107, 305, 394, 512, /Mark Karrass 68, /Ed Kashi 330, /Karen Kasmauski 37, /Herbert Kehrer/zefa 286, /Kicking Horse Mountain Resort/handout/epa 9 left, 17, /Karl Kinne/zefa 62, /Richard Klune 2, 252, /Frank Krahmer/zefa 10, 143, /Wildfried Krecichwost/zefa 220, 273, /Bob Krist 104, 110, 207, 418, 423, /Robert Landau 274, /Cory Langley/184, /Frans Lanting 7 picture 5, 20, 86, 129, 151 left, 186, 195, 210, 389 left, 455, 458, /Alain Le Garsmeur 272, /Danny Lehman 81, /Charles & Josette Lenars 54, 296, /Pete Leonard/zefa 288, /Jean-Pierre Lescourret 346, /Michael S Lewis 21, /Liu Liqun 460-461, 476, 479, 481, 485, /Richard List 133, /Eduardo Longoni 146, /Craig Lovell 363, /Frank Lukasseck 71, 285, 290, 310, 475, /Johan Lundberg 221, /James Marshall 117, /Stephanie Maze 131, /Joe McDonald 34, /Mike McQueen 243, /John and Lisa Merrill 152, 339, /Momatiuk-Eastcott 149, 172, /Kevin R Morris 31, 527, 528, /David Muench 41, 43, 45, 49, 51, 56, 58, 61, 64, 65, /NASA 128, 159, 190, 387, /Richard Nebesky/Robert Harding World Imagery 321, /Gregg Newont/SouthernCross Images 123, /Michael Nicholson 6 picture 3, 214 left, 263, /Kay Nietfeld/dpa 214, 242, /Kazuyoshi Nomachi 150 right, 153, 154, 163, 164, /Pat O'Hara 2 left, 470, /Charles O'Rear 534, /Diego Lezama Orezzoli 385, /Douglas Pearson 388 left, 403, /Bryan Pickering/Eye Ubiquitous 6 picture 4, 241, 299, /Sergio Pitamitz 414, /Jose Fuste Raga 6 picture 1, 8-9, 57, 300, 338, 438, /Hans Reinhard/zefa 214 centre, 223, /Reuters 215 left, 347, /Nick Roessler 452, /Bill Ross 53, 59, /Guenter Rossenbach/zefa 277, 364, /Jeffrey L Rotman 112, /Galen Rowell 12, 130, 408, 497, 539, /Thomas Rubbert/zefa 324, /Ron Sanford 15, 35, /Matthias Seitz/zefa 340, /Kevin Schafer135, 150 left, 206, /Schmitz-Söhnigen/zefa 410, /P J Sharpe/zefa 259, /Marco Simoni/Robert Harding World Imagery 355, 373, /Jorge Silva/Reuters 116, /Hugh Sitton/zefa 208, /Skyscan 264, 266, /Paul A Souders 3 centre, 25, 47, 176, 182, 211, 236, 443, 444, 448, 454, /Jon Sparks 352, 442, 456, /Robert Spoenlein/zefa 251, /Hubert Stadler 132, 134, 140, 147, 187, 430, /Hans Strand 229, /Keren Su 461 right, 480, 500, /Torleif Svensson 150-151, 182, /Geray Sweeney 271, /Murat Taner/zefa 369, /Steve Terrill 9 right, 76, /Tim Thompson 336, /Roger Tidman 316, 359, 466, /Joerg Trobitzsch/zefa 224, /Craig Tuttle 38, /Upperhall Ltd/Robert Harding World Imagery 332-333, /Sandro Vannini 157/Steven Vidler/Eurasian Press 127, 446, 451, /Brian A Vikander

518, /Barry Voight/Pennsylvania State University/Reuters 91, /Onne van der Wal 80, 100, 436, 462, /Kennan Ward 180, 511, /Patrick Ward 249, /Ron Watts13, 29, /Christof Wermter/zefa 218, /Stuart Westmorland 99, 105, /Nik Wheeler 75, 89, 106, 225, /Ralph White 465, /Staffan Widstrand 126,178, /Nevada Wier 495, /WildCountry 505, /Peter M Wilson 367, /Adam Woolfitt 292, 374, 529, /Alison Wright 402, /Michael S Yamashita 6 picture 2, 226, 388 centre, 405, 420, 490, 492, 515, /Jim Zuckerman 391; Corbis/Sygma Corbis/Forestier Yves 137, /JIR 7 picture 1, 188, /Micheline Pelletier 370, /Vo Trung Dung 267; Dinodia 498; Ben Edwards, Dickinson College, Carlisle, PA 11; FLPA/Fred Bavendam/Minden Pictures 30, 399, /Jim Brandenburg/Minden Pictures 42, /Peter Davey 171, /Reinhard Dirscher 155, /John Holmes 486, /Mitsuaki Iwago/Minden Pictures 406, /Mike Parry/Minden Pictures 118, /Jurgen & Christine Sohns 199, /Konrad Wothe/Minden Pictures 468, /Norbert Wu/Minden Pictures 526, /Ariadne Van Zandbergen 167; Fotobanka/doktor 7 picture 2, 314; Getty Images/Shaen Adey 204, /AFP 472, /Jerry Alexander 514, /altrendo nature 203, /DEA/C.Sappa 156, /Hauke Dressler 289, /Suzi Eszterhas 169, /Lee Frost 372, /David Hanson 523, /Jean Heguy 19, /Peter Hendrie 440, /Masaaki Horimachi/Sebun Photos 489, /joSon 5 picture 2, 519, /Jonathan Kitchen 254, /Chris Newbert/Minden Pictures 120, Marc Romanelli 453, /Kevin Schafer 114, /Masaaki Tanaka/Sebun Photo 493, /Alfred Wolf 302, /Ariadne Van Zandbergen 174; Hedgehog House/Andy Reisinger 429; Jewel Cave National Monument 63; Jo Archer 531, 530; Lonely Planet Images/Peter Ptschelinzew 417, /Thor Vaz de Leon 426; Masterfile/R Ian Lloyd 397, 401; F McKenzie, Crown Copyright, Department of Conservation, New Zealand, 2005 445; OnAsia/Leisha Tyler 483; Oxford Scientific Films/Michael Fogden 161, /JTB Photo 460 left, /521,/T C Middleton 461 left, 524/ Mary Plage 83, /Röder Röder 396; Scope/J Guillard 297; South American Pictures/Sue Mann 142, /Chris Sharp 87; Still Pictures/Guenter Berthold/transit 281, BIOS Gunther Michel 158, BIOS Popinet S & Friedel C 473, /Brisbois/Andia 312, /Ricardo Funari 124, /H Jungius/Wildlife 464, /McPhoto 283, /A Riedmiller/Das Fotoarchiv 291, /Tack 5 picture 1, 509, /Gunter Ziesler 323; Stockshots.no/Remi M J Eilertsen 219; SuperStock/age fotostock 280, 306, 309, 354, /Steve Vidler 295; Travel Ink/Brian Garrett 88;VisitDenmark/John Sommer 278;